W9-CQO-087

The Joan Palevsky  Imprint in Classical Literature

In honor of beloved Virgil—

"O degli altri poeti onore e lume . . ."

—Dante, *Inferno*

The publisher gratefully acknowledges the
generous contribution to this book provided by
the Classical Literature Endowment Fund of
the University of California Press, which
is supported by a major gift
from Joan Palevsky.

Citizen Bacchae

Citizen Bacchae

Women's Ritual Practice in Ancient Greece

Barbara Goff

UNIVERSITY OF CALIFORNIA PRESS

Berkeley   Los Angeles   London

University of California Press
Berkeley and Los Angeles, California

University of California Press, Ltd.
London, England

© 2004 by
The Regents of the University of California

Library of Congress Cataloging-in-Publication Data

Goff, Barbara E.
Citizen Bacchae : women's ritual practice in ancient Greece /
Barbara Goff.
        p.   cm.
Includes bibliographical references and index.
ISBN 0–520–23998–9 (cloth : alk. paper).
    1. Greek literature—History and criticism.   2. Rites and
ceremonies in literature.   3. Religion and literature—Greece.
4. Women—Religious life—Greece.   5. Women and literature—
Greece.   6. Rites and ceremonies—Greece.   7. Religion in
literature.   8. Women in literature.   9. Women—Greece.   I. Title.
PA3015.W65 G65   2004
880.9'355—dc21   2003011740

Manufactured in Canada.

13   12   11   10   09   08   07   06   05   04
10   9   8   7   6   5   4   3   2   1

To Michael
sine quo non

CONTENTS

ILLUSTRATIONS

ACKNOWLEDGMENTS

It takes a village to raise a book, and my global village comprises at least two continents and at least six institutions. I owe a great debt to all those, in all those places, who have helped this project to fruition. My colleagues at the University of Texas at Austin provided an atmosphere most conducive to interdisciplinary research, as well as to happy and productive teaching; among them, I wish to thank especially Michael Gagarin and Paula Perlman for their friendship, time, and all their efforts on my behalf. I would also like to thank Erwin Cook, Lesley Dean-Jones, Ingrid Edlund-Berry, Karl Galinsky, Lisa Kallet-Marx, and Cynthia Shelmerdine for the various contributions they made to my book and my general well-being. The students in my seminar "Women and Ritual" encouraged me more than they knew. Let me acknowledge too the friends in Texas who enriched my life and whom I miss: Miriam Kuznets, Andrew Cooper, Nancy Seelig, Andy Bullington, Cary Hazlegrove, Robin Bradford, Jim Williams, Jonathan Ayres, and Donna Carter.

A Solmsen Fellowship at the Institute for the Humanities at the University of Wisconsin, Madison, provided the uninterrupted time necessary to immerse myself in vase paintings as well as to draft several chapters. To the members of the Institute at that time, especially Chris Rowe, my thanks. The Department of Classics at Madison provided an encouraging audience and, moreover, the friendship of Laura McClure and her family. Less tangible but still very important support has been offered by colleagues at St. Lawrence University, Colgate University, Syracuse University, and Goldsmiths' College, University of London; at St. Mary's University College the support was indeed tangible, as I had the good fortune to receive a Research Fellowship there. The Department of Classics at the University of Reading is also to be thanked, since they have hired me.

Another kind of debt is owed to those who generously agreed to read parts of the book in draft; for their time and attention, thanks to Cynthia Patterson, Nancy Rabinowitz, Peter Rose, Richard Seaford, and Eva Stehle. Froma Zeitlin has always been an affirming presence, and Helene Foley has provided constant support and friendship, even at a stage in the enterprise that is now long enough ago to be embarrassing. Pat Easterling probably does not remember the early conversation she had with me about the book, but I do, and I thank her for that and for her subsequent interest. Audiences at various meetings of the APA and of CAMWS have also provided encouragement, sometimes in surprising quantities. And the classicists of King's College Cambridge, I fear, watch over me still.

I would also like to thank the officers of the University of California Press. Kate Toll was a very supportive editor in trying times, and at later stages Cindy Fulton and Marian Rogers worked long and hard on the project.

Michael Simpson knows more about women's ritual practice in ancient Greece than he really needs to, but loves me still. To him this book is dedicated. Felix Goff, despite his extensive acquaintance with violent Greek myths, knows nothing of the matters herein; but he does know that *his* college is called Party College, and no grown-ups are allowed.

ABBREVIATIONS

ABV   *Attic Black-Figure Vase-Painters*. Edited by Sir J. D. Beazley. Oxford, 1956.

Anth Pal *Anthologia Palatina* (= *Anthologia Graeca*). Edited by A S. F. Gow and D. L. Page. Cambridge, 1968.

APF   J. K. Davies. *Athenian Propertied Families, 600–300 B.C.* Oxford, 1971.

ARV   *Athenian Red-Figure Vase-Painters*. 2d ed. 3 vols. Edited by Sir J. D. Beazley. Oxford, 1963.

CIG   *Corpus Inscriptionum Graecarum*. 4 vols. 1828–77.

CV   *Corpus Vasorum Antiquorum*.

FGH   *Die Fragmente der griechischen Historiker*. Edited by Felix Jacoby. Leiden, 1999.

GLP   *Greek Literary Papyri*. Edited by D. L. Page. Cambridge, Mass., 1942.

ID   *Inscriptions de Délos*. Paris, 1926–.

IG   *Inscriptiones Graecae*. Berlin, 1873–.

I Mag   *Die Inschriften von Magnesia am Maeander*. Edited by Otto Kern. Berlin, 1900.

LSAM   *Lois sacrées de l'Asie Mineure*. Edited by F. Sokolowski. Paris, 1955.

LSCG   *Lois sacrées des cités grecques*. Edited by F. Sokolowski. Paris, 1969.

LSS   *Lois sacrées des cités grecques: Supplement*. Edited by F. Sokolowski. Paris, 1962.

PMG   *Poetae Melici Graeci*. Edited by D. L. Page. Oxford, 1962.

SEG   *Supplementum Epigraphicum Graecum*. Leiden, 1923–.

WLGR   *Women's Life in Greece and Rome: A Source Book in Translation*. Edited by Mary Lefkowitz and Maureen Fant. Baltimore, 1992.

Introduction

What activities did the women of ancient Greece perform in the sphere of ritual, and what were the meanings of such activities for them and for their culture as a whole? By offering answers to these questions, this book attempts to recover and reconstruct an important dimension of the lived experience of ancient Greek women. Classical scholars have only recently begun sustained investigation of women's ritual practices, but the topic is of increasing interest for the study of women in various disciplines. This book is therefore designed to be of use not only to classical scholars but also to students and specialists in many different disciplines who are interested in the history of women.

The paradigm that informs much writing on ancient Greek women is that of seclusion and exclusion. Often secluded within the private household, or *oikos*, women were also excluded from the public areas of endeavor valued by their culture, such as politics, law, commerce, and art. Sources are unanimous in their approbation of this ideal of seclusion. Andromache in Euripides *Trojan Women* 644–56 claims:

> The behavior that is considered prudent for women,
> That's what I practiced beneath Hektor's roof.
> Firstly, whether or not blame attaches to women,
> If a woman does not remain indoors
> That very choice brings down a bad reputation;
> And so I gave up my desire to go out and stayed within.[1]

---

1. That Andromache is complaining that her virtue brought her no reward only makes her description of the norm more pointed. See Croally 1994 for the irony of this utterance. Since copyright laws continue to be the bane of academic publishing, all translations are my own, except where noted. I have aimed, as will be painfully obvious, for accuracy rather than grace of expression.

Legal minors in most Greek cities, women were often required to act through a "guardian" rather than exercising independent agency, and they were usually restricted in terms of their property rights and rights within marriage. Such material restrictions on women's lives were reinforced by the misogynist tendencies of much Greek discourse, which assigned to women various forms of inadequacy and inferiority, and often represented them as inimical to the projects of the male-dominated culture.

The circumscribed nature of women's lives means that both material and documentary evidence on women are hard to come by. It is the constant lament of scholars writing on women in antiquity that they left no records of themselves; women's literacy levels were never high, and they were never encouraged to gain access to other media such as sculpture or painting through which they might have left traces of themselves. Most public areas of endeavor remained inaccessible to women, and the interior of the house, where most women spent most of their lives, is largely lost to us. The prestigious documents that usually count as evidence for classical culture, such as literary, historical, and philosophical texts, were only rarely produced by women.

Yet there were exceptions both to the rule of women's seclusion and to their silence. Scholars increasingly take note of all the occasions on which many women did go out in public, such as to trade in the marketplace.[2] In the contemporary Mediterranean region, where an ideal of seclusion is still often endorsed, comparative anthropological findings tend to show that women can leave their homes and still claim the respectability afforded by seclusion, provided they engage only in certain kinds of activities while outside and avoid certain locations, such as the taverna, which are frequented by men.[3] In the ancient Greek context, an acceptable exception to seclusion was offered by ritual practice, an activity that not only brought women into the public sphere but also allowed them a public voice. Women took part in organized celebrations and in numerous informal observations over which they exercised a certain amount of control, such as visiting temples to pray and make offerings. The sphere of ritual practice both organized them in formal cult and also enabled them to organize aspects of their lives independently.

A significant proportion of the community's ritual obligations was always discharged by men; by far the majority of ritual practitioners, such as priests, were male,[4] and men were in charge of most major celebrations. Women

---

2. See Gagarin 1998 for the presence of noncitizen women in Athenian courts.

3. See, for example, Cohen 1990.

4. See the figures in Garland 1984. Readers interested in a "normative" account of Athenian religion, which does not foreground female practitioners, may consult Parker 1996, for instance.

were prominent, however, and given their exclusion from other public activities, their extensive participation was anomalous. Women presided over certain public and private celebrations, served the gods in numerous official positions, and were responsible for much of the cult activity that fostered the welfare of household and city. A number of factors may have conditioned this prominence. Since women were often seen as associated with fertility, they, rather than men, appeared to be the appropriate practitioners of many rituals connected to the agricultural year. Women were also considered especially permeable to the influence of the nonhuman, whether as possessed devotees of Dionysos or as the chosen prophetesses of Apollo. Women's activity in the sphere of ritual was thus determined not only by their own decisions but also by the models of female identity available within Greek culture.

Since ritual practice afforded women a public presence and a voice, evidence for women's activities, while still elusive, can be more abundant in this field than elsewhere. The ritual sphere is perhaps the most productive arena in which to actually look for the women of ancient Greece. If we assume not women's invisibility and "mutedness"[5] but instead their presence in history, we can perform a more thorough job of recovery, which in turn will testify more strongly to that presence. The point is made by Mary Lefkowitz and Maureen Fant:

> When we began collecting ancient sources on women's lives, in the late 1970s, we, and our publishers, expected to cover the field in a single medium-sized volume. We now know that an enormous quantity of ancient material on women's lives exists.[6]

Of course, this does not mean that the study of ritual will give us authentic, unmediated access to the subjectivities of ancient women. The obvious objection to such a claim is that only those women's utterances that were acceptable to male-dominated culture would in any case have been allowed publicity.[7] Whatever the determinants of a woman's utterance in the ritual sphere, her independent proclivities were only one of them. The work of recovery must therefore be supplemented by that of reconstruction, for in the absence of almost all testimony from women themselves, we must give them a voice with which to speak before we can begin to listen to them.

While the study of women and ritual in ancient Greece is now under way, general accounts of women's lives can still be written without reference to ritual.[8] Even when ritual is noted as an exception to a general rule of seclu-

---

5. Ardener 1972.

6. Lefkowitz and Fant 1992: xxiv.

7. Kraemer 1992: 10.

8. For instance, Just 1989, an otherwise useful book on women in Athenian law and life, all but ignores women's cult activity.

sion, this observation is infrequently developed into a fully ramified argument. To establish a notion of all that women's ritual activity involved, it would be necessary to develop "thick descriptions" of such activity and to theorize on many levels about its significance for women.[9] Such work is being undertaken throughout the discipline of classics, and the present study is part of this project.

The overall aim of this book is to reconstruct the ritual sphere of women's activity in detail, and to reconstruct the women of ancient Greece in their roles as both subjects and objects of ritual process. My focus, as I discuss later, will be on classical Athens of the fifth and fourth centuries, but I shall deepen and enrich the Athenian analysis with material from other periods and locales. I shall show that ritual activity, far from being a temporary diversion from daily life, constituted a constant element of the texture of lived experience, and that it regularly required women to exercise significant presence and agency in the public realm. Ritual practice recognized women's contributions to culture and foregrounded women as subjects of some of the most important processes by which the community guaranteed its continuing welfare. Despite women's anomalous prominence, however, ritual events and structures often purveyed and confirmed traditional, restrictive notions of female identity. Like any other social practice, ritual is an ideologically charged activity, and as such one of its goals in ancient Greece was to produce women who performed successfully within a male-dominated and often explicitly misogynist community. The ritual sphere thus emerges as an arena of constant renegotiation between women and the ideologies that governed their lives, an arena in which women act out ritual scenarios alternating between cooperation with that governance and resistance to it.

The book is structured as a series of five related investigations, each focusing on a different aspect of women's ritual practice. Chapter 1 establishes the material parameters of such practice in terms of its places, times, and activities, in the context both of private ritual concerned with birth, marriage, and death and also of public cult administered by the city. I show that women's participation in cult allowed them to construct a vivid and complex presence in the life of their community and afforded them the kind of independent agency that was not usually predicated of them. I describe the ritual activity required by major events in the household, such as marriage, birth, and death, and analyze how such crises brought women into the public sphere in order to articulate the changing identity of the house. I examine the various

9. Rose (1993: 225) writes: "Precisely to the extent that an accurate critique of the past is a key component in envisioning a more tolerable future, women have a special stake in the 'thickest' possible description of the situation of women in antiquity."

relationships that can be discerned between ritual practice and women's work. First, ritual in and of itself constitutes work that women are required to do; second, ritual often appropriates from the domestic sphere and dramatizes other female tasks such as weaving and water carrying; and third, ritual offers a compensation and reward for women's otherwise unrecognized domestic work. The chapter proceeds to an account of the responsibilities and privileges of priestesses throughout the Greek world, and following on from my account of the priestess's economic activities, I offer an analysis of the material dimension of women's ritual practice. I conclude that women's ritual activities enabled them to operate as competent economic agents with some control over the distribution of household resources.

An account of ritual would be incomplete, however, without consideration of the ways in which cult practices reciprocally formed the subjectivities of the women who performed them. Chapter 2 therefore investigates the construction of gender conducted by those rituals that addressed women explicitly on the topic of female identity. It steps back from the tropes of "presence" and "agency," in effect placing these terms under interrogation, by its focus on ritual techniques for producing and confirming women as gendered subjects. Drawing on feminist work on the male gaze, I analyze the way in which premarital rituals for young women expose them to that gaze in situations in which they must learn to accept and promote themselves as objects of desire.[10] In choral performances, processions, and races, unmarried girls are displayed to the community, and figurative literature insists that the public festival may consequently form the site of seduction. While the girls thus learn, in the course of the display, to discriminate among sanctioned and unsanctioned gazes, the didactic function of ritual is muted in the case of adult women, and the ritual year offers them instead a number of symbolic positions across a broad spectrum, from chastity to license. Thus in Athens women fast and observe chastity for the Thesmophoria, but utter obscenities and handle pastry models of genitalia in the Haloa. I argue that although all such rituals for adult women can be understood as aiming at the production of a successful wife and mother, their invocation of other versions of female identity entails that their project is always at risk. The chapter proceeds to analyze ritual activity that involves the figures of the virgin, the menopausal woman, the adulteress, and the prostitute, and concludes that these roles are deployed by ritual discourse as foils for the *gyne*, or adult wife and mother, who is in fact the most important focus of ritual activity. Ritual discourse aims at producing women who function well within a male-dominated culture by successfully internalizing a version of themselves useful to that culture.

10. See also on this topic Stehle 1997.

By emphasizing first how women exercise unaccustomed powers of agency within their ritual practice, and second how that practice conversely produces women as gendered subjects, the first two chapters of this book demonstrate the need for a dialectical understanding of the relation between women and their ritual activity. Chapter 3 examines the dialectic as it operates in another context, and considers an area of ritual practice that offers women genuinely alternative versions of themselves. I show that although the ancient city, or polis, may be defined by its exclusion of women, children, and slaves, who cannot be citizens, the ritual sphere provides for women, at least, a parapolitical form of activity and identity that partly remedies their exclusion. Anecdotes attaching to Athenian politicians suggest that they often intervene in women's ritual activities, to divert the women's energies to their own ends, but historical sources also show women in cult office who intervene in the politics of their communities. I investigate the various mechanisms in Greek cities for choosing those women who will participate in ritual service, and for honoring them when that service ends, and show that these mechanisms all figure women as full members of the civic community rather than as dangerous or threatening outsiders.

Despite its prevalence, the discourse of inclusion and parapolitical identity is not the only one elaborated for women by their rituals. Many rituals continue to figure women as the outsiders who reciprocally define the identity of the city. In particular, several claim to perpetuate the memory of a noble or sacrificial gesture performed by a female that ultimately saved the city. I show how this trope of saving the city dramatizes the position of women as the outsiders who can then be mobilized to perform as "unlikely saviors."[11] Similarly, following the lead of scholars who have designated women's ritual collectivities as "cities of women," I demonstrate how such rituals, like the Thesmophoria, the Adonia, and the women's Dionysiac celebrations, both model the political gatherings of men within the polis and simultaneously insist that the women's meetings are "outside" the city and, moreover, antithetical to its interests.

Throughout these first three chapters I stress the dialectical quality of women's ritual practice, which simultaneously governs women and affords them unusual opportunities for self-articulation. The final two chapters involve a shift of focus and offer more speculative analyses. The notion of ritual as parapolitical risks explaining women's activities only on the model of men's; the fourth chapter discusses instead the possibility of a women's subculture focused on ritual forms. I consider first the use of ritual in the poetry of Sappho and other women writers, concluding that the poets develop a speaking position from within the public voice afforded to women

---

11. Kearns 1990.

by their ritual practice. Second, I examine images of women as ritual practitioners on fifth-century Athenian vases and show that these images constitute an important element of the representation of women on ceramics throughout the fifth century. Recent work has suggested that historical women, as consumers, may have had some input into the images on ceramics they used; in line with such arguments I conclude that the ritually inflected images may offer us some Greek women's preferred versions of themselves. My third analysis investigates the phenomenon of maenadic or Dionysiac possession, which in the period under examination was confined to women. Although the significance of this phenomenon for historical women has sometimes been dismissed, feminist critics usually interpret it as a muted form of rebellion against patriarchal constraints. I draw on contemporary work in anthropology to articulate another possible interpretation of possession, which proposes that such experiences are not simply a reaction against deprivation but are intellectually creative episodes, engaged in voluntarily.

Finally, equipped with various contexts for understanding women's ritual activities, the fifth chapter turns instead to representations of women in cult by men, reexamining the familiar dramatic texts of fifth-century Athens with a focus on the changing models of women's ritual practice that can be read in tragedy and comedy. Since Greek dramas were produced within a ritual context, namely the various festivals of Dionysos, the texts they generate are heavily marked by ritual forms of action. Much scholarly effort has been devoted to examining the relations of ritual to the genesis of drama, and in the case of tragedy in particular, critics have been fascinated by the frequency with which ritual motifs are invoked, only to be perverted or overturned. At the same time, there is an extensive literature on the dramatic representation of women, which rarely engages with the ritual dimension of such representation.[12] Coordinating these two perspectives, I investigate the ways in which representation of women as ritual practitioners changes over time, from emphasizing conflict between the sexes to imagining modes of cooperation.

In addition to providing metaphors for the struggle between the sexes, which is so often dramatized in the Athenian theater, women's ritual activity can be mobilized on the tragic stage as part of a quite different political argument. Critics are increasingly disposed to study tragedy in its specific historical context, and to engage seriously with tragic representations of cities other than Athens, such as Delphi or Thebes. Following the work of Froma Zeitlin,[13] I show that women's ritual activity is deployed to represent

---

12. An exception to this rule is the work of Foley: e.g., 1985 and 1993.
13. See Zeitlin 1990c.

Thebes as an anti-city. On the Athenian stage, Theban women are represented as being repeatedly denied the opportunity to complete their ritual actions, and thus prevented from playing one of their most significant roles in the family and the wider community. In the few dramas set in Athens, by contrast, or those explicitly concerned with Athenian identity, women's ritual gestures are highlighted for their contribution to the city's welfare. Modeling their female gatherings on historical rituals for women, the Aristophanic plays *Lysistrata* and *Women in the Assembly* repeat the gesture in the context of comedy. Although the women of comedy seem to threaten the polity, the ritual contours of their action ensure that in the end they will save it.

The choice of structure for this book was determined by several considerations. Since I did not conceive this as a book about particular rituals, but about ritual practice as a whole, I did not want to divide the discussion up among topics such as the Adonia, the Thesmophoria, and so on. Because I envisage the ritual sphere as impinging upon and indeed as shaping several aspects of women's lived experience, I distributed the discussion instead among categories such as gender and political identity. This organization allows the various specific festivals to be examined more than once, under different rubrics, so that their complex relations to one another and to other aspects of female experience may emerge; an extensive index is available for those readers who need to circumvent the book's structure in order to read up on particular celebrations.

Zeitlin noted sometime ago that "for those who would explore the category constituted by the female in ancient Greece, a comprehensive study of women and their cultic roles would be a primary desideratum."[14] Although her appeal has not yet been fully answered, I do not see myself, like Ross Kraemer, working "without significant scholarly precedent."[15] The present project is made possible first, of course, by a different kind of precedent, namely the broad historical force of the women's movement in the second half of the twentieth century, with its renewed attention both to the historical materialities of women's lives and to the representation of women in diverse texts. Secondly, a huge and ever-increasing body of feminist work specifically in classics has conditioned my own thinking and writing even when it cannot be precisely acknowledged by name. Thirdly, the last two decades or so have seen considerable work of varying kinds on ancient women's ritual activity, much of it undertaken by scholars who identify themselves as feminist. While I am more than happy to locate my work in the context of this developing project, there are certain respects in which

---

14. Zeitlin 1982a: 129.
15. Kraemer 1992: 4.

my book differs from earlier studies. Most of the previous work has taken the form of investigations of specific rituals or complexes of rituals, which are examined in their historical and literary aspects; less attention is characteristically paid to how ritual practice is wound into the daily texture of women's lives and identity.[16] Zeitlin offered one paradigm for studying women's ritual activities, stressing the need for a dialectical understanding in her insistence that "ritual is both a contrast to and a parallel of social life,"[17] and the work of Helene Foley has always been attentive to the significance of ritual activities as they emerge into drama.[18] Kraemer's notable book of 1992 attempted a comprehensive study of the part played by cult in the lives of women in the ancient world, but her material was often drawn from the experiences of Jewish and early Christian women. Another significant contribution, that of Sue Blundell and Margaret Williamson in 1998, is as interested in the representation of female deities as much as in their female worshippers. Matthew Dillon's important book of 2002 is close to my own in terms of ambition and scope, but takes a very different approach, seeking to "identify women as individuals"[19] and rejecting explanations that are couched in terms of ideology.[20] My work thus differs from its predecessors in its range and its emphases.

What are the theoretical parameters of this book? An account of women's ritual practice cannot in my view dispense with an account of the workings of gender ideology, which in turn requires an account of ideology generally. Most known societies are structured around an unequal distribution of power and resources, and one consistent inequality is that between men and women.[21] Such a situation inevitably produces conflict, but not necessarily the kind of conflict that takes to the streets. Instead we are concerned with the kind of conflict that informs the daily life of superiors who manage subordinates, and subordinates who have to deal with their superiors. By "ideology" in this context I understand all the social discourses, practices, and institutions that seek to eliminate or disguise the conflict by naturalizing the unequal distribution. What is socially determined, to the advantage of one identifiable group and at the expense of another, is said instead to be nat-

---

16. See, for example, Detienne 1977 on the Thesmophoria and Adonia, and Brulé 1987, Dowden 1989, Sourvinou-Inwood 1988b, and Perlman 1983 and 1989 on rituals for young girls. Cole (1984, 1995) works from a more purely historical perspective.

17. Zeitlin 1982a: 130.

18. See, for example, Foley 1985, 1993.

19. Dillon 2002: 5.

20. See, for example, Dillon 2002: 166.

21. This is the conclusion of Rosaldo 1980, and I have not seen it disproved since.

ural, and moreover to benefit all groups rather than simply the overtly advantaged one. Thus in the ancient Greek context, considerable energy is expended on addressing men and women alike on the topic of women's natural inferiority and the inevitability of patriarchal arrangements. Yet if such inequities *were* natural, little ideological effort would have to be expended in proclaiming them so.

Since this book undertakes to investigate a particular area of culture, rather than, for example, a literary genre already constituted as such, its methodological allegiances are largely with the expanding field of cultural studies. Within this field there is a long-standing debate, which may also be found in the social sciences, over whether the description of human social action can and should begin with the individual subject or with forces that are larger than the subject. The dilemma may be stated with reference to two formulations repeated throughout the works of Marx: men are "engaged in the creation of the conditions of their social life" or "men make their own history, but they do not make it just as they please." To these quotations correspond the "humanist" and "structuralist" positions respectively; the humanist position begins with human agency, whereas the structuralist downplays its significance. An investment in the notion of ideology must to large extent identify with the latter pole; the subject comes to consciousness in the terms of a dominant ideology that has already closed off certain possibilities for him or her and opened only certain others. The category "women," for instance, is ideologically constructed by the alignment of certain sexual characteristics with certain inequalities; the biologically female is made into the socially feminine. Nor is it a question simply of legal or paralegal prohibitions and commands; ideology at its most successful produces the kind of subjectivity that desires only the sanctioned forms of activity and actively rejects others, even when they are clearly more productive or prestigious. As Terry Eagleton puts it, "The study of ideology is among other things an inquiry into the ways in which people may come to invest in their own unhappiness."[22]

A theory of ideology would, however, be incomplete if it stopped here. While it is clear that numerous societies have constructed women by systematically denying them opportunities, and often by deliberately oppressing them, and while it is also clear that the vast majority of women have to a greater or lesser extent acquiesced in these arrangements, it is nonetheless the case that there have always been articulations of dissent.[23] There are

---

22. Eagleton 1991: xiii. Butler (1997) provides a psychoanalytically focused accounts of this "investment."

23. Of course this account of the possibility of dissent is valid for members of other subordinated groups too, such as the working class in Europe and African-Americans in the United States, but my focus here is on the ideology of gender.

even good arguments within feminism and within religious studies that claim that religion in particular is a privileged area of dissent, both for women and for other subordinated groups. Given the pervasive success of ideological discourse, the phenomenon of resistance requires explanation, and one way to approach an explanation is to work with the Gramscian construct of hegemony. The use of the term "hegemony" entails a model in which the ideological discourse may be dominant, and claim supremacy over the other discourses that make up a culture, but cannot be monolithic, and must therefore take some account of alternatives to itself. According to our initial premise, ideology is generated in a situation of real conflict, which it attempts to naturalize, and thus it always faces a potential contradiction of its own blandishments. The work of ideology cannot proceed solely by coercion—although coercion remains a constant possibility—but must strive to win the consent of its targeted subjects, and in order to do so it must to some extent take account of needs and desires generated elsewhere, by aspects of people's lives that come into conflict with the requirements of the dominant ideology. Space is thus opened up within the process of ideological production for the articulation of resistance.

Our working model of ideological production, particularly in relation to gender, may be further modified by closer consideration of the characteristic associations between men and women within patriarchal structures. By "patriarchy" I understand, broadly speaking, a society based on male dominance of all areas of valued activity, where women are seen as subordinate members of society and expressly denied certain desirable opportunities on the basis of their identity as women. Patriarchal societies espouse a thoroughly unequal model of gender relations and thereby ensure that one characteristic of these relations will be conflict. They also, however, characteristically allot to adult women the management of households and the early rearing of the young. Although gender ideology often seeks to deny women active independent agency, it also requires them to be successfully functioning wives and mothers, and thus requires them to exercise an energetic practical agency in their own sphere. There need not, then, be a total contradiction between the two poles of the structuralist and humanist positions with their respective emphases on ideology and agency. Women's agency is part of gender ideology, not in its interstices like bacteria between healthy cells, but like a virus that itself occupies the cell. If women in such societies have been able to retain the possibility of resistance, it is perhaps partly because they have been required to retain the possibility of active agency.

The agency of free adult wives and mothers may, however, be differentiated from the simple material agency required from other subordinates, such as hired workers and slaves of either sex. The institution of marriage, where many women have historically spent a significant proportion of their lives, characteristically legislates various relations of power between the man and the woman, but also often proclaims the desirability of their cheerful cooperation. This move is certainly legible in ancient Greek texts, like Xenophon's *Oikonomikos,* where the young wife's acknowledged inferiority is proved by the text to be totally compatible with an ideal of partnership between herself and her husband. Gender relations are not always characterized only by overt antagonism. While all relations between superiors and subordinates rely to a variable extent on consent and cooperation as well as coercion, women within male-dominated cultures are required to perform the crucial task of producing heirs, and thus far more effort may be devoted to eliciting their cooperation than is expended on hired workers, for example. As scholars such as Gerda Lerner have stressed,[24] the relations between such cultures and the women within them do not consist only of oppression and defeat; male-dominated culture also often addresses women's interests by rewarding them for successful identification with its own projects. Women are offered the tangible goods of security, peace, and respect as well as shown the sanctions that await those women who do not successfully identify. Many historical women have thus been positioned to have a stake in the healthy functioning of their society far greater than that which would be available to slaves, for instance. In ancient Greece, ritual practice often makes this distinction clear by involving free women only and excluding slaves, confirming the logic of its ideological involvement.

The theory of structuration developed by Anthony Giddens, which also foregrounds issues concerning the relationship between ideology and agency, can provide further methodological support for the model that I am elaborating here. For Giddens, the notion of ideology is insufficient to explain social action and social formation, because he takes it to model a situation in which subjects are passive and ignorant, subjected to rather than the subject of a given action. As suggested above, this need not be a complete account of ideology, but even with this caveat Giddens's theory is of interest to us. He goes on to propose that the constraints in social life are actively reproduced by subjects engaging in their own daily routine, and that agency and constraint are thus produced and reproduced in the same gestures. "Constraint . . . is shown to operate through the active involvement of the agents concerned, not as some force of which they are passive recipients," observes Giddens.[25] Giddens's formulation works well with the equivocal version of ideological production that I have been adumbrating, and it is furthermore illuminating for an account of ritual. In performing rituals women of ancient Greece exercise unusual agency and cultural pres-

24. See Lerner 1986.
25. Giddens 1984: 289.

ence and are constituted as active subjects of the ritual process. Yet at the same time and in the same gesture, if the ritual reproduces symbols or narratives that confirm the culture's account of women's inferiority, women may be reproducing the ideological constraints that govern their lives.[26]

A further modification of our model of relations between ideology and agency is made available by the notion of the "subculture," which is often mobilized by studies of contemporary popular culture. Such studies typically investigate the ways in which different groups—often disadvantaged in some way—use and interpret the cultural products offered for their consumption by the institutions of the media. What these studies characteristically find is that people do not relate to such institutions simply as individuals. In other words, the individual subject is not the only site of the agency that may challenge the ideology produced by such institutions. The significant role is taken instead by a third term, that of the group or subculture. So primal is the notion of the group that individual identity, on this hypothesis, arises only from the multiple identifications offered by the different subcultures that contribute to the formation of the subject participating in them. The subject's own identity comes into being as a negotiation among identities offered by groups that validate different and even conflicting aspects of experience. Crucially, identifications furnished by subcultures may conflict with those purveyed by the dominant ideology, and from such conflict can emerge the resistant intuitions and concepts that enable the individual subject to occupy a dissident position.

An obvious objection to working with studies of popular culture, in which the notion of the group or subculture is so prominent, is that they are far removed in historical terms from ancient Greece. Nonetheless, I would suggest that such studies can have relevance for the investigation of women's ritual, because there are formal similarities between the two projects. It is, by contrast, "high" culture that has traditionally attracted the attention of the discipline of classics, which has typically focused on such genres as literature, philosophy, and sculpture. The study of ancient ritual forms, especially perhaps women's ritual forms, often requires instead an investigation of less prestigious types of evidence. The study of women's rit-

26. It will be noted that Giddens's project has some affinities with that of Bourdieu, which describes itself as "opposed to the anthropological presupposition inscribed in the language which social agents . . . use to account for practice. . . . It is also opposed to the more extreme theses of a certain structuralism by refusing to reduce *agents* . . . to simple epiphenomena of structure" (1998: vii–viii). If I do not draw on Bourdieu for my vocabulary, it is because, as Eagleton (1991: 156) puts it, "the term 'ideology' is not particularly central to Bourdieu's work," and also because his theorizing is not characteristically interested in resistance or dissent. This distinction, however, applies primarily to the canonical earlier work; on later work by both figures see Callinicos 1999. Butler (1997: 210 n. 13) notes that "Bourdieu's sense of the *habitus* might well be read as a reformulation of Althusser's notion of ideology."

ual practice is further differentiated from that of "high" culture because women themselves produce their ritual life and are the designated audience of its discourse, whereas they neither produce nor consume the artifacts commonly studied under the rubric of classics.[27] The model of subcultures and their enabling of dissidence may thus illuminate the study of ancient Greek women in ritual process. When gathered together for specific cult celebrations, particularly those that convene only women and exclude men, women may be plausibly seen as invited to think of themselves as a particular subculture per se. Even while ritual may confirm the constraints on women's lives, then, it may also offer the most likely arena for the development of a dissident stance.

This book will propose that for ancient Greek women, ritual practice is the primary arena in which are staged these various negotiations between 'ideology' and 'agency'. Not only is ritual, as part of ideological production, generated out of conflict and contradiction, but it also addresses women, and to some extent men, on the issue of the contradictions that govern women's lives. Enforcing these contradictions on the participating women, who learn female identity from its symbolic practice in cult, ritual simultaneously enables dissidence by its very structure and also by dramatizing the constraints of female identity.[28] It should be emphasized, however, that such dissidence is not to be confused with revolutionary activity; women's ritual actions are all tolerated if not explicitly sanctioned by the male-dominated community and by the individual men who have the final determination over their women's lives. But if ritual forms are sanctioned by men, they are inhabited by women, who remain the subjects of the ritual process and the designated consumers of the rituals' significance. By thus exploring the tensions attendant on female identity, the ritual sphere renders them both more manifest and perhaps more manageable.

Now that some theoretical parameters are in place, I should analyze some of my leading terms. I refer primarily to "ritual" rather than to "religion" because the notion of ritual foregrounds that of practice and agency rather than of disposition, attitude, or belief. Ancient Greek religion was chiefly a matter of behavior and observances rather than of spirituality, personal conscience, and salvation. No ritual practitioners were called upon to be spiri-

27. See, however, Stehle and Day 1996 on possible interpretations by women of public sculptural monuments not obviously designed for their consumption.

28. Seaford (1995: xv) suggests that ritual dramatizes the resolution of social contradictions, but he is addressing the experience of the society as a whole rather than that of its women.

tual guides or counselors. Ancient Greek societies were not theocracies, in the sense of organizing themselves according to acknowledged divine sanction and in fulfillment of an eschatological plan; and in the absence of sacred guiding texts they needed no exegetes of such texts. Ancient Greek religion, while not devoid of spiritual or moral components, was thus largely a matter of structured actions, such as dedication, procession, ceremony, and sacrifice. Ritual practitioners, even those titled "priests" or "priestesses," wielded no spiritual authority, although they might exercise temporal authority over the space of the sanctuary and the performance of ceremonies. This absence of authority may itself have provided one enabling condition for women's prominence in cultic life. A terminology of "ritual" rather than of "religion" thus achieves three goals: it is in keeping with the salient differences of ancient Greek culture from our own, it respects the limitations of the available evidence, which necessarily testifies to actions rather than to attitudes, and it foregrounds the whole issue of material agency, which is my starting point.[29]

That said, it still remains to define ritual and what I am calling the ritual sphere. For the purposes of constructing a database and organizing the field, I have adopted a very broad definition: "women's ritual practice" is whatever women do that constructs for them a relation to the divine. I implicitly ignore the various accounts of "ritual" that would foreground a definition comprising numerous everyday, habitual, and therefore "ritualized" activities; I concentrate instead on the interactions of human females with deities. These include both formal, state-sponsored gatherings like the Thesmophoria and informal actions like visiting a temple. The "ritual sphere" is constituted by the spaces, times, and actions that these various practices occupy and deploy, and it subtends an entire dimension of women's lived experience.

My overall approach is, as outlined above, to stress both how ritual practice constitutes women as its subjects and how it conversely organizes female identity in order to subject it to the requirements of a male-dominated society. Such an approach may, however, be contested. As Kraemer has noted, a dialectical model of ritual, stressing both its "reinforcement" of ideology and its "legitimation of alternatives," is implicitly at odds with "some con-

---

29. There is, of course, a spiritual or salvific or eschatological component to Greek religion, and it is represented by, for example, the Mysteries of Eleusis and, perhaps more challengingly, by the Bacchic "lamellae" (inscribed gold plates found in tombs, which testify to Bacchic initiations). These initiatory practices require a different approach, and I do not address them in detail for this reason as much as for reasons of space. Similarly, I do not mount an investigation into the figure of "the goddess" and what she may mean for female spirituality. I am interested in historical women rather than in transcendent versions of femininity.

temporary theories which contend that religion must do one or the other, but not both, and certainly not both simultaneously."[30] Several such polarizing theories, however, which do in fact claim for religion "one or the other," have been found very useful in the study of women's relations to cult. The work of M. Gluckman and Barbara Babcock has made familiar the notion that ritual events are privileged moments of escape from and inversion of conventional quotidian categories, and that they experiment in a radical way with the idea of "the world turned upside down."[31] If, as A. van Gennep famously proposed,[32] ritual events may be analyzed into the components of separation, liminality, and integration, these theories elaborate chiefly on the moment of liminality in its suspension of the quotidian. In related and highly influential work Victor Turner has argued that social action moves between the two poles of "structure," characterized by social hierarchy and difference, and "communitas," a state in which essential human community is retrieved and celebrated.[33] Ritual events are more likely to conform to the contours of "communitas," but the suspension of "structure" is characteristically succeeded by a return to it that retrospectively validates it. If "social structure" is understood to involve gender as well as status or class, then women are more likely than men to suffer under it and to have a stake in its suspension; consequently this model of ritual as occurring within a time and space apart, where social hierarchies may be dissolved, is important for the study of women in ritual.

Useful though these theories and their conclusions may be for analyzing the relations between women and ritual, they are not matters of consensus. There are several contemporary theories of ritual that insist conversely on the ways in which it upholds the social status quo. Structuralist analysis, which has been particularly influential among classical scholars, relates ritual to the governing categories of its culture and does not usually suggest that ritual challenges or indeed can challenge those categories. The work of Marcel Detienne on women and sacrifice, for instance, concludes that the distribution of sacrificial meat among the Greeks reproduces the hierarchical distinctions between male and female. Similarly, his work on the Thesmophoria and Adonia suggests that these rituals serve to confirm the hierarchical distinctions between respectable wives and licentious prostitutes.[34] Other theories of ritual, such as those associated with the work of René Girard and Walter Burkert, are often concerned with the origins of rit-

30. Kraemer 1992: 12.
31. Gluckman 1954; Babcock 1978.
32. Van Gennep 1960.
33. Turner 1967.
34. Both these analyses by Detienne have been challenged, by Osborne 1993 and Winkler 1990a. See further chapters 1 and 2.

uals and concentrate on cult as a mechanism of social solidarity. In this way they implicitly endorse the view that ritual practice offers no resistance to, dissidence from, or even escape from the status quo.

Throughout the book I shall draw on various models of ritual and its relation to the dominant ideology, but also on a growing body of work that constructs as its object the experiences of women within different ritual or religious systems. Since the late 1970s a number of comparative studies of this topic, informed by a feminist perspective, have appeared at the intersection of feminism, anthropology, history, and religious studies. Including within their purview cultures separated from one another in historical and geographical terms, they characteristically investigate how women operate within different religious cultures, and conversely how religious practice operates within the lives of the women concerned. Since the overall allegiance is feminist, the accounts often focus on how women deploy religious practice to make sense of their circumscribed lives or, better still, to ameliorate them.

Within this body of work, a certain shift is perceptible over time in its governing notions of the relation between religion and gender ideology. Stressing the negative stereotypes of women purveyed by religion, the collection edited by Judith Hoch-Smith and Anita Spring finds that women are excluded from much religious participation and symbolism because of their reproductive work and what the authors call "the myth of feminine evil."[35] The volume edited by Pat Holden explores the position that "religion is invariably male dominated, that it can repress and restrict women, and reinforce accepted female stereotypes," but also widens discussion by considering "how women perceive themselves and their roles within varying religious systems."[36] The collection edited by Clarissa Atkinson and others formulates the whole issue more clearly as a dialectic. Religion is described as part of women's cultural conditioning, but it is also said to make available tools "with which women can create a degree of spiritual, political, and personal autonomy not provided by secular culture." "Religion can provide women with a critical perspective on and alternatives to the conditioning they receive as members of their societies." Religion thus offers to us a critical lens through which to see simultaneously "oppression" and "creativity" in women's lives,[37] and this model of a dialectic, of a practice that can simultaneously accomplish diverse and even opposing tasks, is helpfully compatible with the larger model of ideological production that I have outlined above. It suggests again that a polarized either/or understanding of ritual, as an ideologically charged practice, is insufficient.

35. Hoch-Smith and Spring 1978.
36. Holden 1983: 4.
37. Atkinson, Buchanan, and Miles 1985: 2, 3.

Comparative work like that practiced by such studies of women in religion can help considerably to fill in the gaps left by the absence of Greek women's testimonies, but it brings its own methodological problems. Having insufficient testimony from the historical women of ancient Greece, we are constrained to supplement it with the voices of women who now inhabit preindustrial societies, and this move itself raises at least three serious epistemological issues. Sometimes these women's voices are readily available, but more often they themselves are mediated by a scholarly narrative written from an anthropological or quasi-anthropological perspective. Since the emphasis in studies of women and religion is characteristically on the lived experience of historical women, such studies must assume that women have access to their own experience and can articulate it at least up to the point at which the anthropological narrator can mediate it to the rest of the world. A further important assumption is that the experiences of women removed from each other in time and space are sufficiently similar to render any differences meaningful. This is a claim that grounds comparative work on women but that is increasingly interrogated by feminist scholars in many disciplines.

Not only are there these specific difficulties with comparative work on women, but objections may also be raised to comparative work generally. In classics it has become a common gesture to seek to explain the ancient world by reference to the cultural types of the modern Mediterranean.[38] This procedure may command assent simply by the productive analyses that it makes possible, but some scholars have pointed to weaknesses and limitations in the approach.[39] Some may therefore find the kind of comparative ethnographic evidence customarily marshaled in studies of women's religious experience even less illuminating, since it often ranges across a number of different cultures. The methodological difficulties in comparing women across different societies are related to those that are now occupying the forefront of feminist debate in Anglo-American culture, namely whether it is legitimate to invoke the category "women" or whether the differences among women in terms of race, class, age, and sexual preference are at least as significant as the similarities.

One way to argue for the validity of comparative work, even across differences of history and geography, is to invoke the constant of male-domi-

38. See, for instance, Winkler 1990a and Cohen 1991.

39. See, for example, the strictures in Mook 1996: 35. Sourvinou-Inwood explores the weaknesses of the approach with even more authority, since she is, as she puts it, "a native of one of the cultures that have gone into the making of this construct" (1995: 111) She argues in particular that the "Mediterranean societies" model underplays women's importance in ritual and suggests as an alternative formulation that "in Classical Athens women had an important place in the religious sphere but were excluded from the political and the military, and they were legal minors" (115).

nated culture. If most known societies favor males and are inclined toward misogyny, then even with local variations there will by definition be certain constants linking those variants, and many women may well live out a similar dialectic of cooperation and resistance as they attempt to make sense of a subordinated existence.[40] Here I am borrowing a theoretical paradigm from Marxist criticism, which holds that insofar as all known cultures are characterized by a form of class struggle, they are all susceptible to materialist analysis. Even without this theoretical proviso, comparative work is useful for work on women in ancient societies because without it we are less likely to make the silences of our testimony speak. The unattractive alternative to this admittedly problematic move is to accept the culture entirely on its own terms. An argument from results may also be invoked in further support of comparativism. In the case of studies of women's religious experience, empirical data show women's recurrent prominence in cult activity even in societies where they are kept from other forms of public, valued participation;[41] such results suggest that the ancient Greek model does indeed participate in a pattern characteristic of more than one culture.[42]

The second issue, concerning the legitimacy of the category "women," is potentially more troublesome for my argument. This issue is not only a question of scholarly inquiry but also a major political challenge to the feminist movement in the West, which has increasingly come under the charge of being exclusively white, middle class, and heterosexual, and thereby of inventing a category "Woman" that is just as oppressive as the earlier "Man." The criticisms by women of color, by poor and working class women, and by lesbians and bisexual women are all cogent, and in their similarity to one another doubly so,[43] so that there is now considerable consensus that the feminist movement does need to take some steps toward reinventing and reenergizing itself (see, for example, the observations of Martha Burk and Heidi Hartmann).[44] But the way in which "mainstream" sources have seized on these weaknesses in the women's movement suggests a strategy of divide

40. This is not to argue for the universal application of any one term or model, but to recognize certain persistent facets of human social arrangements. See, for example, Rosaldo 1980: 393, 395: "My reading of the anthropological record leads me to conclude that human cultural and social forms have always been male dominated. . . . Sexual asymmetry . . . seems to exist everywhere, yet not without perpetual challenge or almost infinite variation."

41. Kraemer 1992: 11.

42. One major difference should be noted at the outset, however; in contrast to many, more modern religions, ancient Greek religion offers no equalizing notion of individual salvation and thus could not generate the impulses toward thoroughgoing social reform that have on occasion operated within the parameters of, for instance, the Christian church.

43. The important early statements of these criticisms are found in texts such as Smith, Hull, and Scott 1982 and Moraga and Anzaldua 1983. For attempts to construct a workable feminist politics out of these criticisms see, for instance, hooks 1984 and King 1988.

44. Burk and Hartmann 1996.

and rule; one consequence, in a hostile political climate, of abandoning the notion of work on "women" may be to throw the political baby out with the theoretical bathwater. Is there not a political loss in adopting a politics of identity that abandons all opportunity to speak about, to, and for "women" as some form of commonality, however complex?

A second, theoretical rather than political objection to the term "women" is that it may lead to an ahistorical essentialism. Feminist work of the late 1980s and 1990s, conditioned by varieties of post-structuralism, has instead tended to move away from the binary polarity of "men" and "women" in favor of an emphasis on the construction of gender, which deconstructs that polarity by also analyzing the construction of gay and lesbian identity. Such an emphasis typically demonstrates that neither gender nor identity is a stable given, but that both are instead fluid and conflicted. The very form of binary opposition, however, that such criticism challenged in the model of gender polarity returns to haunt it when it supposes that a simple essentialism is the only alternative to its own radical constructivism.[45] While this body of critical work on gender is extremely compelling (see, for example, Judith Butler's work),[46] it is sometimes in danger of being co-opted by "post-feminism." This recent trend in media and academic circles claims variously that women have achieved equality and can "learn to stop worrying," that feminism itself is responsible for any disadvantages that women might still suffer, or quite simply that political analysis of exploitation and oppression is passé and unsustainable. It is my view that no one can afford to be post-feminist until the historical conditions that generated feminism have been eradicated, and women are no longer disproportionately subject to poverty, illiteracy, and violence. By the same token I do not think that the work of recovery of historical women's experiences is irrelevant until what we know about women is commensurable with what we know about men. The present project, on women's ritual practice, clearly subscribes to a materialist version of feminism that puts the difficult and contested figure of "women," rather than that of "gender," center stage; it does not suppose, on the other hand, that historical women come to subjectivity without being constructed by discourses of gender.[47]

In the context of this study, it is possible to argue that "women" is a relevant category because ancient Greek women are regularly convened by cult practice qua women, to celebrate that which unites rather than divides them, namely their identities as wives and mothers. It is, however, necessary

45. See Fuss 1989 for an account of the mutual complicity of essentialism and constructivism.

46. Butler 1990.

47. For further discussion of these tensions within the discourse of classical studies see, for example, Rabinowitz 1993b: 10–11 and Richlin 1993: 276–77.

to make some distinctions. When dealing with women's ritual practice, we are largely concerned with free women rather than slaves. Although slaves are part of the household, and indeed are critical, like free women, to its domestic working, they are not called upon to perform any of its ritual duties, and their stake in the wider community is not perceived to be such that they can be entrusted with cult activity designed to promote the welfare of the community. Slaves are not to be trusted with ritual, but neither is ritual necessary for the ideological co-optation of slaves; the community does not feel the need to elicit the cooperation of its slaves as it does that of its free women, whose lives are less obviously governed by coercion. A further distinction that must be made is that in each Greek city we are interested chiefly in women who are natives, rather than women who are resident aliens or "metics." In Athens, for instance, metics had some ritual roles to play, but many cult posts and activities were reserved for women who were or who would become the wives of citizens. In other cities that were not organized on democratic lines, not all free adults would qualify as full citizens or citizens' wives, but the criterion for inclusion in organized cult activity was still often that of indigenous birth. There do not, however, seem to have been restrictions in place that prevented nonnative women from engaging in more informal ritual activity; free prostitutes in Athens, for instance, even though often resident aliens, were ritually active in less formal contexts. The question of wealth or class is more complicated. It is prima facie likely that women whose families were wealthier would have been able to engage in more cult activity: they could have offered more dedications, financed more trips to distant shrines, and spent more time on cult, while slaves did more of the domestic work. Some cult posts were in fact reserved for women from certain families, who were likely to be wealthier than others. But very few sources indicate a systematic exclusion of poor women from ritual practices, and certain testimonies suggest their participation. Even if not all women participated in all ritual events, there was a considerable overlap between the categories "women" and "ritual."

Various issues accumulating around two of the terms in my title, "women" and "ritual," have now been ventilated. The term "ancient Greece" remains to be defined. Since the richest single source of textual documentation for ancient Greece is Athens of the fifth and fourth centuries, there is always the problem, in reconstructing any aspect of Greek culture, that the focus of our available evidence on a single city will shape our accounts of the whole. Even though other Greek cities offer us much interesting material on women as subjects of ritual process, in the absence of other detailed evidence about such cities we are not able to contextualize it as well, and so the danger arises of accounting for other cities as if they were classical Athens. Most of my analysis and discussion will in fact concern this city, but I have deployed material from other periods and places to enrich or occasionally to challenge the Athenian account. Although Greeks did characteristically think of themselves as united by a common religion as well as by a common language, there were regional variations in both. In my study I have tried to make clear when the analysis applies only to classical Athens and when it could be profitably extended to other communities; the bulk of the analysis, however, will refer to classical Athens. Non-Athenian material comes from both the Greek mainland and islands, and the Greek cities of Asia Minor and of Italy, and ranges in date from the fifth to the second century B.C.E. Since the moment of the developed polis is the first to offer a wealth of documentary sources, I begin my study there, even though many rituals seem to date from the formation of the polis in the eighth century. I close my study at the juncture when it becomes difficult to discuss "Greek" culture independently of the new formations consequent on the Roman conquest of Greece.

The sources for a study of ancient Greek women's ritual practice include both literary and nonliterary texts, epigraphical and archaeological documents, and vase paintings. Evidence for different kinds of practice extends across several genres, and there is no single unified text that will tell us all we want to know about any one ritual. Information must be pieced together from highly recalcitrant sources, and often the various sources on one practice are widely separated by time and space. One might ask whether we are dealing with a coherent topic at all; should we divide "women's ritual practice" into units by Greek city and historical period?[48] Closely pursued, such methodological rigor would spell the end of the project of classical studies, which largely relies on the assumption that "antiquity must be regarded, first and foremost, as a social, psychological and religious unit in which considerable changes can indeed be perceived, but in which a number of fundamental elements and structures can nevertheless be regarded as constant."[49] When it comes to issues of evidence, we do the best we can with what we have. There are, however, good arguments for supposing that cult institutions and practices will be more insulated from and resistant to change than others. Many historians would agree with Susan Sherwin-White, who observes that "cults were part of the fabric of civic and private life in the ancient Greek city. The old religious rites, regulations and usages persisted through the Hellenistic period."[50] Noting more specific historical continuities, B. Jordan concludes that "whatever their title, the duties and functions of these sacral officials often coincided to a considerable degree; and both

48. Mikalson (1998: 2–4) is in favor of such rigor, where practicable, and in particular warns against retrojecting material from later periods into our accounts of earlier; but his overall emphasis is on historical continuity.

49. Versnel 1981b: 3.

50. Sherwin-White 1978: 290.

the officials and the tasks that they performed appear in the sacred laws throughout the centuries with remarkable consistency."[51] Ritual by its very nature relies on tradition, and even though it may accept modifications, it will rarely admit as much. Religious conservatism is an acknowledged force in many cultures—one has only to witness the struggle over the ordination of women in the Anglican Church of Great Britain to appreciate this—and perhaps still more so in a culture where religious observance is inextricably wound into the texture of daily life.

The Hellenistic period is often adduced as a period when the lives of women were less constrained than they had been under the classical city, so that their ritual practice would acquire different significances. In fact, I shall suggest at various points in this study that the ritual forms in which they participated can still be seen to inculcate the traditional parameters of female behavior and identity. In this I follow Riet van Bremen, for example, who argues for a continuity in the representation of women from the classical to the Hellenistic period.[52] Any material differences in what women actually did, she suggests, are a result of increased wealth throughout the Greek world rather than of changes in fundamental attitudes. Certainly, many scholars who write on women's new opportunities in Hellenistic Greece focus on Macedonian and Ptolemaic queens rather than on the generality of women, and seem to assume without interrogation that such women provided meaningful models for women of lower status. Perhaps they do not give sufficient weight to the traditional gender relations that still conditioned the lives of that generality.[53] Blundell writes more circumspectly of an "erosion of the asymmetry" in relations between the sexes and an ensuing improvement in the status of women, which she attributes largely to greater mobility and migration in the Hellenistic world, with a consequent loosening of traditional ties.[54] Some traditional ties, however, remained strong.

Now that history and geography have added their particular complexities to the mix, we can move on to a final problem in the evidence for women's ritual practice. This is a version, or perhaps a perversion, of the issues raised long ago by Edwin Ardener.[55] Much of what the sources narrate about women and cult simply strains our credulity. When Herodotos tells us that the priestess of Athena at Halikarnassos grows a beard in order to warn her townspeople of impending danger, it is not immediately obvious what to do

51. Jordan 1979: 23.

52. See Bremen 1983.

53. See, for example, Pomeroy 1984: xviii and 1991: xiv and Grant 1982: 194–99. Grant closes his investigation of exceptional women with a brief discussion of female infanticide, which to me indicates that many women were still on the sharp end.

54. Blundell 1995: 199–200.

55. Ardener 1972.

with the information. In consequence, much of what is relayed about women and ritual has at one time or other been dismissed by scholars as unhistorical. I have sought instead to take the contested evidence as registering, if not a trace of historical practice, then at least a trace of the unusual possibilities for women imagined by the ritual sphere. I take the testimonies of many of the ancient sources not so much as precise indications of historical fact as very good indices of cultural attitudes; if we cannot be certain that the priestess of Athena did experience periodic hirsuteness, we can perhaps still say that she operated in a climate where she could be entrusted with the welfare of her people. However distorted, the evidence attests to women's presence in history as ritual practitioners and to their participation in the reproduction of culture; generated chiefly by men, the accounts of women's ritual activity may deform the extent and meaning of that presence, but they do not completely conceal it.

ONE

Working Toward a Material Presence

Most women in most cultures have been discouraged from performing in the arenas of endeavor valued by their societies, and many have been either invited or compelled to confine themselves to domesticity. The women of ancient Greece were no exception; secluded, excluded, largely illiterate, they were never supposed to take a place in history. So what can it mean to invoke the figure of their "material presence"?

There are at least two answers, general and specific, to this question. It is a tenet of women's history that women are in fact present within human history and exert a force upon events, even if that presence and force are subsequently elided in the male-generated representation of events. Practitioners of women's history also subscribe to the methodological assumption that such presence and force can be discerned within male-generated representations by reading them "against the grain," or reading them for other than their ostensible significance, and that the agency and even autonomy of historical women may thus be recovered. Margaret Miles claims, for instance, that "these [i.e., male-authored] texts can be explored for what they *reveal* rather than for what they *intend* to communicate."[1]

A more specific answer would point out that the particular focus of this study, women's activity in the field of ritual, offers better opportunities than many others for reconstructing the material involvement of women of ancient Greece as agents in producing and reproducing their culture. Ritual practice furnished an opportunity for free women to leave the domestic context without abandoning any claims to dignity and personal safety. Since ritual is usually a public activity, women were able to leave more mate-

---

1. Miles 1985: 8.

rial traces of themselves in this sphere; public inscriptions, for instance, record women's ritual activity but have no reason to call attention to other aspects of their lives. Conversely, it is only in the ritual context that we have access to material remains, such as dedicatory inscriptions, that are even remotely female-generated. Finally, given that ancient Greek religion is predominantly a question of practice rather than of belief, it necessarily requires of its women participants action in and on the material world; agency can be predicated of women in the ritual context because it is demanded of them.

The project of this chapter, then, is to reconstruct the contours of women's ritual activity in ancient Greece and to establish the corresponding extent of the material presence within their culture. I shall consider the ritual involvement required of most if not all women at major events such as birth, marriage, and death, and that required of the few selected women who served as priestesses. I shall also consider other material dimensions of women's ritual activity, specifically its relations to domestic work and to economic roles. In attempting a reconstruction of women in ritual, I am trying, in Joan Kelly's useful formulation, "to restore women to history and to restore our history to women."[2] But the recovery of women's cultural agency cannot be the end of the account. More perhaps than for men, Marx's dictum is valid for women; they make their history, but not as they please. I shall contend that while women of ancient Greece do produce their own history and that of the wider culture, and do so especially within ritual activity, they are constrained to make it in ways that reproduce those very constraints. In particular, I shall suggest, women's ritual activity reinscribes on their lived experience the identifications, so useful to patriarchal ideology, with the body, the domestic, and the nonhuman.

CRISES OF THE *OIKOS*

Women's ritual activities were many and varied, but I shall focus first on those that derive in some sense from the household context. The household, or *oikos,* was itself a unit with ritual responsibilities, which were discharged in offerings and libations, and while the men of the house superintended most of this activity, the women of the house regularly took part. In Xenophon *Oikonomikos* 7.8 Ischomachos's wife joins him in sacrifice and prayer as they embark on their joint life together. For my purposes, "the women of the house" include only its free members; slaves might be present at ritual observances but were never responsible for their proper implementation. The household had particular obligations at times when it

2. Kelly 1976: 809.

gained or lost a member from birth, marriage, or death. At these points the altered *oikos* faced outwards in order to negotiate a new relationship with the wider community, and it characteristically drew on the labor of its female members. Both the preparation and the event itself called for the visible participation of women in ritual.

Greek culture, like many others, assigned to women the task of ritual supervision over the processes of birth. While birth is an event readily connected to the domestic environment, it could furnish the occasion for women's mobility and consequent public visibility. Although they might be required to stay away from certain sanctuaries, pregnant women were not completely secluded at home; instead they were often caught up in a complex of ritual activity that encouraged or required them to leave the domestic context.[3] Aristotle *Politics* 7.1335b12–14 recommends that women in the early stages of pregnancy take a daily walk to a temple of childbirth deities.

> Pregnant women should take care of their bodies, neither getting lazy nor skimping on their food. This is easy for the legislator to effect, by requiring them to make some daily excursion for the purpose of worshipping those gods who preside over childbirth.

The prescriptive tone might suggest that in Aristotle's experience women were not in fact taking daily walks to temples, but inscriptional evidence indicates that such visits were required. In Cyrene, a Greek colony on the Mediterranean coast of Africa, a fourth-century inscription shows that pregnant women were obliged to visit the bride-room in the temple of Artemis, and to make a sacrifice *(LSS* 115 B; relevant parts translated as *WLGR* 404). If a woman did not manage to make this trip before she gave birth, she was enjoined to do so afterwards. The restored text runs as follows:

> A bride, when she is pregnant, shall make a ceremonial visit to the bride-room in the precinct of Artemis, and to the Bear priestess she shall give feet and head and skin of the sacrifice. If she does not make a ceremonial visit before giving birth she must make a visit afterwards with a full-grown victim.

If conception or pregnancy proved difficult, women might perform especially energetic ritual interventions. Fourth-century inscriptions from the temple of Asklepios at Epidauros show that the majority of women who visited the site did so in order to seek relief either from childlessness or from difficult pregnancies.[4] Inscriptions from the temple of Artemis at Gonnoi in

3. Censorinus *De Die Natali* 11.7 claims that pregnant women did not visit shrines before the 40th day, but it is unclear exactly when that was. See the discussion in Parker 1983: 48.

4. See especially Edelstein and Edelstein 1945: 1.221–29 = *IG* iv 2121 and *IG* iv 2122. Much of these two inscriptions is translated as *WLGR* 406.

Thessaly indicate that women gave thanks there for successful births.[5] The extent of this mobility and the expense of sacrifices and dedications indicate that this kind of ritual observance was more characteristic of women from prosperous families, who had leisure to visit ritual sites and did not have to support themselves by their own labor. It is not evident, however, that any ritual prescription *excludes* women on the grounds of poverty, and we need not assume that the practices described in this chapter were restricted only to wealthy women.

The act of giving birth required the participation of several women, probably relatives and neighbors. Praxagora in Aristophanes *Women in Assembly* 528–29 excuses her absence, when her husband complains about it, by saying that she had gone to help deliver a friend. It is quite probable that childbirth was surrounded by a complex of ritual activity, the details of which are now lost; for instance, the proliferation of deities who preside over labor and delivery makes it likely that the birthing process was attended with a considerable ritual element.[6] Artemis was the chief such Olympian divinity, and women in tragedy are represented as calling on her in childbirth, as at Euripides *Hippolytos* 166–69. Votive[7] terra-cotta figures of pregnant women have been found on Kos, and in the sanctuary of Artemis Lochia on Delos, a similar votive relief has been uncovered.[8] The goddess Eileithyia was also often invoked to assist women in labor, and was apparently worshipped on Crete in a cave where more figurines were found.[9] On Delos, all the offerings to Eileithyia were from women.[10] Many other minor childbirth deities are also known; a fourth-century votive from Phaleron (*IG* ii² 4547), a few miles southwest of Athens, lists a number of birth-goddesses, and others called Genetyllides were worshipped near Cape Kollias on the east of the bay of Phaleron (Pausanias 1.1.5). These latter divinities were also worshipped in Ionia, according to Pausanias, under the title of Gennaïdes.

The arrival of the baby was greeted with a ritual cry, the *ololuge,* uttered by the attending women.[11] Some sources claim that these attending women also assisted at the ritual called *amphidromia,* a few days after the birth, when the new member was accepted into the *oikos* by being carried round the family hearth and was presented with gifts. According to these accounts, this was

5. Versnel 1981b: 8; Helly 1973: vol. 2, nos. 173, 175. Most of Helly's dedications to Artemis originate with women.

6. Garland 1990: 61–68.

7. See "Sacrifice and dedication" below for a discussion of the process of votive dedication.

8. Van Straten 1981: 99; Bruneau 1970: 191.

9. Van Straten 1981: 99. On the cult of Eileithyia at Amnisos, and its Egyptian connections, see Marinatos 1996.

10. Bruneau 1970: 215.

11. See Garland 1990: 73 and the *Homeric Hymn to Delian Apollo.*

the occasion to purify the hands of the women who had assisted with the birth.[12] Since the *amphidromia* signifies the legal entry of the baby into the *oikos,* however, it seems likely that the male participants were more significant to the ritual (Harpocration and Hesychius s.v. *amphidromia*). The mother, while remaining in a state of ritual pollution for a time, was expected to visit temples soon after the birth to give thanks for a safe delivery.[13] It was usual to dedicate clothes on such occasions; fourth-century inscriptions—for instance, the long list in *IG* ii² 1514 (translated as *WLGR* 402)—show that the temple of Artemis at Brauron received many such dedications, and some of the epigrams collected in the sixth book of the *Palatine Anthology* (e.g., 6.271) play on this practice. The records of dedications at Brauron mostly indicate aristocratic women offering specially festive clothes, patterned and colorful. A passage at the end of Euripides' *Iphigeneia in Tauris* (1462–67) claims that if a woman died in childbirth, similar dedications were to be made on her behalf:

> You, Iphigeneia, must keep the keys of the goddess
> In the holy meadows of Brauron;
> You will be buried there when you die,
> And they will make an offering to you of beautifully woven garments,
> The ones that women leave in their houses
> Who die in the pains of birth.

When the *oikos* turns outwards to negotiate its characteristic crises, its women are released from the domestic into the ritual context. The mother might obtain considerable access to the community beyond the *oikos* when she visited temples before and after the birth, while other women might experience a heightened sociability with each other both in the process of assisting at the birth and in the accompanying ritual activity.

Marriage is the second major household event that offered ritual involvement to many if not most women. Weddings involved men as well as women in ritual activity, but the bulk of ritual obligations seems to have fallen on the bride. Marriage bears a considerable symbolic weight in Greek culture; it signifies humankind's separation from animal life, but it is also one of the signs, along with agriculture and sacrifice, that humankind has fallen from

---

12. See the Suda s.v. *amphidromia,* Apostolius 2.56 in the *Corpus Paroemiographorum Graecorum* 2.278, and the scholion on Plato *Theaitetos* 160E.

13. Three days was common, according to Parker 1983: 50. Parker suggests that pregnant and recently delivered women are polluted only in the sense of our word "delicate," i.e., neither disgusting nor dangerous. Isaios 5.39 mentions a woman sitting in the temple of Eileithyia, and Rouse (1975: 252) takes this to be some kind of purification ceremony after childbirth, but in context it seems more likely that the mother has chosen this place as a respectable, eminently feminine location in which to make her accusations against her son.

an original state of happiness.[14] Its primary purpose is not to join the resources of two households so much as to produce heirs for the husband's line. For this purpose an alien woman, from another family, must be physically brought into the house and prevailed upon to identify her interests with those of her new household. The bride's mobility between two households is what is at stake, and so she is commended a variety of ritual activity to prepare her for this major dislocation.

In Athens the bride must visit the Acropolis with her parents and make offerings known as *proteleia,* "before the ceremony" (Pollux *Onomastikon* 3.38). In the inscription from Cyrene already cited the bride is required to make a ceremonial visit to the bride-room in the temple of Artemis. The restored text *(LSS* 115) runs:

> A bride must make a visit to the bride-room at the temple of Artemis at the festival of Artemis, whenever she wishes, but the sooner the better. If she does not make her ceremonial visit, she must make the necessary sacrifice to Artemis at the festival of Artemis as one who has made no visit, and she must purify the temple and sacrifice a full-grown victim as penalty.

The text adopts the imperative mood, but there is also room for the bride's exercise of initiative in that she may go to the temple "whenever she wishes." Other brides made dedications both before their wedding and on the occasion of it. Girls throughout the Greek world dedicated their toys to Artemis when they reached puberty, which often coincided with the date of their marriage.[15] The bride would almost certainly dedicate her hair, an offering that is a common sign of transition in both Greek and other cultures.[16] Her belt too would be dedicated, as a sign of and preparation for the "loosening" of the belt in the acts of defloration and of childbirth. Pausanias 2.33.1 notes that Troezenian girls offer their belts, before their weddings, to Athena Apatouria.[17] In Sparta, mothers were also involved in dedicatory activity, sacrificing to Aphrodite Hera on the occasion of their daughters' weddings (Pausanias 3.13.9), and at Hermione not only girls but also widows who married again sacrificed to Aphrodite (Pausanias 2.34.12). These acts of sacrifice and dedication took the women involved beyond the immediate domestic context and into a more visible sphere.

The wedding itself took different forms in different places but in Athens at least involved an evening procession from the bride's natal to her marital house. This procession involved women other than the bride herself: in vase paintings the bride's mother often takes part in the procession, carrying

---

14. See especially Hesiod *Theogony* 570–616 and *Works and Days* 42–105.
15. Rouse 1975: 249–50.
16. See the lengthy discussion of Rouse 1975: 240–45.
17. On this rite see Schmitt-Pantel 1977.

torches, and occasionally the mother of the new husband also participates, waiting to welcome the daughter-in-law to her new home.[18] The wedding celebrations also included the bride's attendant, or *numpheutria* (Pausanias 9.3.7), and choruses of young women singing and dancing, all of whom may be said to gain access to a wider context on this ritual occasion. On the day after the wedding itself, called the *epaulia,* presents were delivered to the bride in a procession headed by a *kanephoros,* a young woman bearing a basket.[19] In Athens the husband's kin-group, or phratry, had to be notified of and ratify the marriage, and some hold that the husband introduced his bride to the phratry. It is quite possible, however, that this ratification was accomplished in her absence.[20]

Funerals were probably the most important of the domestic crises in terms of women's ritual involvement, and a consideration of the participation that they offered to women will conclude our survey of the ritual activity entailed by the regular events of domestic life. Like many other cultures, Greek society perceived the processes of birth and death as analogous, and both as particularly suitable for women's management. Women washed and tended the dead body and were responsible for much of the ritual lamentation over the corpse; their physical presence at funerals could be extensive, as is suggested by the scenes on archaic vases used as grave markers, such as the Dipylon Vase. Since women were construed as more prone to emotional expression than men, women played a correspondingly significant role in the articulation of grief or joy on behalf not only of themselves but also of the male population. In Pat Easterling's words, women "articulate and lament the communal sorrows."[21] Plato *Laws* 800E mentions women being hired as professional mourners to increase the effect of a private funeral, although at other times and places this practice was frowned upon, as we shall see.[22] In this allocation of ritual mourning to women, ancient Greece corresponds to many other traditional societies that allot to women responsibility both for the physical care of the dead person and for his or her commemoration in song and lamentation. By their ritual work at funerals, women construct for themselves a highly visible and valuable presence in their communities, but also elaborate on certain terms central to Greek perception of female identity.

Several cities, however, took steps in the early classical period to restrict

18. See Oakley and Sinos 1993 and Sutton 1992 on vase representations of the Attic wedding, and see further chapter 4.

19. See the Suda and the *Etymologicum Magnum* s.v. *epaulia.*

20. See the discussion at Garland 1990: 218.

21. Easterling 1988: 15. Compare Briseis in *Iliad* 19.301–2: "So she spoke weeping, and the women lamented with her, Patroklos their excuse, but each one for the griefs of their own."

22. See also Alexiou 1974: 10.

women's participation in private funerals. In Athens the relevant legislation was held to date from Solon in the sixth century, and a fifth-century inscription from Ioulis on Keos shows that similar legislation was enacted there.[23] The Solonic law limited female mourners, that is, those permitted to enter the chamber of the deceased or to follow the funeral procession to the cemetery, to women within the degree of kinship of second cousin and those over sixty years of age; the law from Ioulis states that only the mother, wife, sisters, and daughters of the deceased, plus no more than five other women, who seem to include the daughters' children and cousins, shall be "polluted" by the death or shall "pollute themselves."[24] A similar law attributed to Solon limited the amount of money that could be spent on Athenian weddings, but not the number of participants (Plutarch *Life of Solon* 20.4).

Various reasons have been cited for this legislation. Robert Parker, citing Plato *Laws* 11:947D, suggests that the corpse might exert a malign influence on a woman's childbearing capacities.[25] In this context women over sixty, who are permitted by the Solonic law to attend, are at little or no risk, but it is hard to account for the immunity to the corpse of, for example, the second cousin. Political rather than eugenic explanations for women's exclusion have found more acceptance; given Solon's role as arbitrator of the conflicting claims of different classes in Athens, it has been held that the legislation for funerals was designed to reduce conspicuous expenditure at upper-class funerals and thus to decrease class tensions.[26] The exclusion of women could also reduce tensions, because of women's alleged special aptitudes for emotional expression. As the privileged emotional conduits and outlets of the culture, women in their lamentations might voice resentments and criticisms of the enemies of the dead and thus exacerbate feuds among the men. Exactly this kind of social disruption is predicated of women's funeral laments in other cultures.[27] Angela Bourke remarks of Irish women singers at funerals that "some women poets gave vent to anger at powerful people, publicly criticized their own relatives and in-laws, and gave graphic accounts of personal violence and miserliness, all in the course of lamenting."[28] Such material also suggests that the disruptive effects of women's lamentation are not confined to women of wealthy or powerful families.

23. See *LSCG* 97 = *IG* xii 593, translated as *WLGR* 77. The "Solonic" law is given at Demosthenes *Against Makartatos* (43) 62. See also Plutarch *Solon* 21.4–5. For legislation in other cities, such as Delphi in the fifth century and Gambreion in Asia Minor in the third, see Alexiou 1974: 18–19.

24. For the explanation of "pollution" as self-defilement, i.e., mourning, see Parker 1983: 41.

25. Parker 1983: 70.

26. See Alexiou 1974: 18–21.

27. See, for example, Alexiou 1974: 21–23 and Bourke 1993: 160–61.

28. Bourke 1993: 160.

Recent feminist work has also stressed a wider political implication of the restrictions on women's lament. Gail Holst-Wahrhaft follows Margaret Alexiou in suggesting that "restrictions on women are another sign of incipient democracy."[29] As the polis, or city-state, developed it found itself in potential conflict with the *oikos* on a number of fronts, and it needed to evolve new forms in order to inculcate new loyalties. One way to undermine the influence of the family was to undermine that of women, particularly on those occasions when they were traditionally prominent and publicly visible. In parallel with restrictions on women, Athens developed the institution of the state funeral for the war dead, which, significantly, all female relatives of the male deceased were allowed to attend. As Nicole Loraux has shown, the democratic discourse of the classical state funeral deliberately failed to acknowledge the possibility of family antagonism or class tension, so that the presence of grieving women could be represented as not dangerous but simply appropriate.[30] One could also argue, of course, that the exclusion of women from private ceremonies is a logical correlate of their co-optation into state funerals.[31]

Solonic legislation for private funerals required that women bring up the rear at funeral processions and that they leave the cemetery separately from men. The corresponding inscription from Ioulis reads: "The women who come to mourn at the funeral are not to leave the tomb before the men" (*LSCG* 97 = *IG* xii 593). But despite this micromanagement of their participation, other evidence indicates that women continued to exert some power of agency in funerary contexts. A fourth-century source, Isaios 8.22, represents a widow who exercises some influence over her husband's funeral arrangements, declaring her wish that the burial take place from her house rather than from her grandson's. Vase paintings continue to dwell on the female participants in funeral ceremonies, although as Christine Havelock points out, the fifth-century representations do not have the huge cast of female characters of the archaic ceramics, and the female characters tend to be confined to certain locations in the geography

29. Holst-Wahrhaft 1992: 117.

30. Loraux 1986.

31. See Seaford (1995: 74–92), who also argues that funerary legislation is about the move from private to public, from kin to polis, but who does not focus on women in the same way as the other critics cited. Stears (1998) takes a different tack and incidentally validates the overall approach to women's ritual practice taken here. Stears argues that "women's lamentations may have fulfilled a number of social functions . . . they enhanced both the women's status and that of their kin-group . . . they may have helped to legitimate claims on an estate, have underpinned a family's ritual health, and have acted as a vehicle for the construction and promotion of family history . . . [but] at the centre of women's lot in lamentation was a display of emotionality which both underpinned and reconstructed ideologies of the illogicality of a woman's nature and her essential lack of self-authority and control" (124–25).

of the funeral.[32] Robert Garland notes that in vase painting, scenes of visits to the tomb feature women rather than men and very often show a group of women rather than a single individual.[33] The village cultures of modern Greece offer a parallel; Lucy Rushton notes that "women take responsibility for visiting the cemetery on the three occasions when those with recent dead are expected to do so."[34] In ancient Greek society too it appears that the association between women and mourning extended beyond the moment of the funeral itself to include regular visits to the tomb; this practice would, of course, afford women movement away from the domestic sphere and an experience of feminine sociability. In the context of funerary rituals, then, women exerted a particular kind of presence within their community: they associated with each other and with related men, left the *oikos* for more public spaces, and could both give vent to emotion and experience themselves as valued for so doing.

As mourners at private funerals, women laid claim not only to a physical presence within public spaces but also to a particular cultural value. The cultural value of women as mourners also afforded them a place in more formal, state-sponsored ritual structures. On the death of a Spartan king women are said to have traversed the city beating on a *lebes*, a vessel used at weddings and funerals, and a free man and a free woman from each household were required to mourn (to "pollute themselves," *katamiainesthai*, Herodotos 6.58.1). Women were often called on to mourn for gods or heroes on festival occasions. At Athens, they took part in the Adonia, a festival of mourning for the god Adonis, while at Kroton (Lycophron 859–65) and Elis (Pausanias 6.23.3) women are said to have held rituals of mourning for Achilles. In addition, fifty young women and men traveled annually from Megara to Corinth to mourn the daughter of the Megarian Klytias, who was said to have married a Bacchiad king of Corinth and subsequently died.[35] These festivals of mourning clearly involved their female participants in contexts much larger than the domestic but also validated their identity as mourners at the private level.

The crises of the *oikos,* then, in their characteristic demands on time and labor, afford women a considerable presence in the community beyond the domestic context. Women enter public spaces, crossing the city in order to reach the temple or the cemetery. But the ritual practices connected with these crises do not necessarily launch the women participants into a fully public environment. While women enter public spaces, they do not operate in the fully public sphere, which is dominated by the masculine practices of

---

32. Havelock 1981: 114–15. See also Shapiro 1991, and the discussion in chapter 4.
33. Garland 1985: 104.
34. Rushton 1983: 59.
35. Bekker 1814: 1.281.

war, politics, law, and commerce. Instead, it seems to me, their ritual actions subtend a ritual sphere, where women are no longer confined to the private, domestic realm but where their actions are still elaborately circumscribed. Funerary ritual, for instance, enabled many women in ancient Greece to operate in an important, visible context, and thus to exert a vivid presence in their community—but it also provides us with the opportunity to register the complex nature of this presence. Given that funerary practice requires women to tend the body of the deceased, the ritual context constructs and enforces a relationship between women and the needs of the body at its most vulnerable and inelegant. The same may be said of the crisis of birth and the ritual activity required of its female participants. The tasks assigned to women, care of the dead and of those giving birth, are "polluting" both in the sense of a perilous transitional experience and in the sense of bodily disorder.

Such a connection between female identity and the materiality of bodily processes is often mobilized by patriarchal ideology to disqualify women from fuller participation in public discourses other than ritual. Ruth Padel has pointed out that in Greek representations, this association with the body is underpinned by a perceived affinity of women for what is "dark"; thus women are assigned "ritual presidency over the transitional experiences, dying and birth, which are perceived as passages into and out of darkness . . . whether the darkness be that of the underworld or of the female body."[36] Nor is ancient Greek culture alone in allotting to women this affinity with the dark and dangerous elements of common human experience and subsequently construing it as sign of their secondary status in human society; Padel points out the similarities in this respect between ancient Greece and early medieval Europe. Women's prominence in ancient Greek funerary ritual, then, not only recognizes their presence, agency, and cultural value but also rehearses the justifications for their marginal status.

A RITUAL YEAR

Events such as births, marriages, and deaths could happen at any time, although in Athens at least marriages may have been concentrated in the winter month of Gamelion (December/January) and many births consequently nine months later. This irregularity means that women could be called on to perform the associated ritual tasks at any time, so that their presence in the ritual sphere, visiting temples and cemeteries, would be a constant in the texture of daily life. If we add to these *oikos*-based events the

36. Padel 1983: 5–6.

organized festivals in which women were required or expected to take part, the visible profile of women involved in ritual processes becomes quite high. In classical Athens, for instance, there are only four months of the year in which there is no recorded ritual activity for some women, although the level and nature of such activity varies considerably from month to month.

Women's ritual activity in classical Athens is concentrated in the fall months, when they celebrate their exclusive festivals of Thesmophoria and Stenia, and are also involved in the Proerosia at Eleusis and the Oschophoria, which includes a procession to Phaleron. On the day before their own Thesmophoria Athenian women may also have had the opportunity to attend a local Thesmophoria at Halimus, eight miles from Athens. Plutarch *Solon* 8.4 (a passage we shall return to in chapter 3) indicates that in the sixth century at least, the "first" among Athenian women as well as others would attend the celebrations and dances there. The Arrhephoria is also an event exclusive to females, but it involves a few young girls rather than a large population of adult women. In early summer the Skira convenes adult women and also seems to involve the priestess of Athena in a procession with the priest of Poseidon and the priest of Helios, walking under a canopy to a place called Skiron, which is on the way to Eleusis.[37] In midsummer the Adonia again convenes adult women, and in the winter the festivals are the Haloa at Eleusis and the rites for Dionysos on Mt. Parnassos near Delphi. We do not know at what season the Arkteia, another festival for young girls, took place, but we do know that it involved a journey beyond Athens to the sanctuary of Artemis at Brauron, in east Attica.[38] Another festival for Artemis, the Mounichia, was held in early spring. Involving the sacrifice of a female goat, held to be a substitute for an original human victim, the ritual seems to have required women to offer special cakes called *amphiphontes* (shining all around).[39]

Women were also involved in major celebrations such as the Mysteries at Eleusis, the Panathenaia, and the City Dionysia, all of which mainly convened men but also offered certain activities to women. The Mysteries, in early fall, were anomalous in the Greek world, and the Athenian calendar, in being open to all without distinction of gender, class, or status as free or slave.[40] Women were involved throughout, in various capacities. They joined

---

37. Lysimachos in *FGH* 366 F3; Conomis 1970: frag. 6.19; Burkert 1985: 230.

38. The exclusive festivals will be discussed in later chapters.

39. Reference in Parke 1977: 138. See also Athenaeus 14.645A and Pollux 6.75 on women's offerings of *amphiphontes*.

40. The cult of Demeter at Eleusis, which probably began as a local and restricted institution, attained Panhellenic status in historical times under the aegis of the Athenian state. See Mylonas 1961: 7. For arguments about the date of Athenian incorporation of Eleusis see Padgug 1972.

in the processions to the sea for purification and to Eleusis for the initiation, they carried the sacred vessels, or *kernoi,* and they figured as dancers and singers in the celebrations at Eleusis.[41] The well Kallichoron was the site "where first the women of the Eleusinians danced and sang in praise of the goddess" (Pausanias 1.38.6). The priestess of Demeter at Eleusis accompanied the sacred objects, or *hiera,* to Athens before the Mysteries began, and may also have taken part in a sacred drama about the abduction and recovery of Persephone, which seems to have been a feature of the events at Eleusis. The priestess of Athena Polias in Athens was also involved, to the extent that she was informed of the arrival of the procession and sacred objects by an Eleusinian official. Other women called *panageis,* or all holy, are recorded among Eleusinian officials, although their specific duties are not known.[42]

The Panathenaia, at the beginning of the Athenian year in summer, mobilized many segments of the population; even the daughters of metics, resident aliens, walked in the procession, carrying water jars and parasols (Demetrius of Phaleron in *FGH* 228 F5). The festival centered on the offering of a new robe, or *peplos,* to the goddess Athena, and this robe was carried in a procession that took a route right through the city from the Kerameikos to the Acropolis. The procession featured women and girls carrying baskets, chairs, sunshades, bowls, jugs, and other sacrificial implements. On the day preceding the Panathenaia, young women as well as men sang and danced in the *pannychis,* or all-night festival, which took place on the Acropolis; comedic sources play with the figure of the country girl come to the big city to see the festival (Menander frag. 558 Kock).

At the City Dionysia in early spring, priestesses seem to have been involved; the theater of Dionysos, where plays were produced in honor of the god, contains seats inscribed with their names. We cannot be sure, however, that these priestesses were in attendance during the classical period, since the surviving seats formed part of the Roman theater.[43] Young women were involved in a procession to the Delphinion, a shrine to Apollo and Artemis on the banks of the Ilissos near the Olympeion, in the spring, and as *hydrophoroi,* or water-carriers, in the Diipoleia of early summer. In late spring two important rites convened the women from the traditional aristocratic or "Eupatrid" family of Praxiergidai. These women were in charge of the Kallynteria and the Plynteria, festivals in honor of Athena. Details of the Kallynteria are obscure, but it seems to have involved beautifying the temple; the Plynteria, which took place a few days before the Kallynteria,

41. References in Mylonas 1961: 231, 241, 245.
42. On all Eleusinian officials see Clinton 1974.
43. See Pickard-Cambridge 1968: 265.

was a cleansing rite that had parallels throughout Greece. The wooden statue of Athena was taken from the Erechtheion to the sea, in a procession that included the ephebes (young men in military training), headed by a *kanephoros* (basket-carrier) who carried a basket of figs. The statue was then bathed by young women called *loutrides* or *pluntrides* (Photios s.v.). This festival did not involve the general female population, but it exerted a felt pressure within the community, because the day on which the goddess left the Acropolis was one of ill omen that also recalled the death of Agraulos, daughter of Kekrops.[44]

Even fewer women participated in the Anthesteria, in winter.[45] It has been customary to describe the festival as divided into three days, the Pithoigia, Choes, and Chytroi (Opening of the New Wine, Jars, and Pots). While the Pithoigia is not elaborated in any primary source and has not attracted much attention in the secondary literature, the scholarly consensus on the day of Choes has produced an account of a very complex observance. On the evening of Choes, it is alleged, drinking contests were held at which the Athenians eschewed their normal symposiastic practices, and each guest ate and drank separately and in silence, from individual jugs, in imitation of the reception of the matricide Orestes. But the same day may have seen an even more exceptional ritual practice, the *hieros gamos,* or sacred wedding, between the *basilinna* (queen) and the god Dionysos.[46] The *basilinna* was wife of the *archon basileus,* an official of the city whose duties included presiding at various ceremonies; the *basileus* (king) element of his title indicates the antiquity of his office. His wife was required to be an Athenian and to have been a virgin at her marriage. A reference in Aristotle (*Constitution of the Athenians* 3.5) indicates that the ceremony of marriage to Dionysos took place not in the shrine "in the marshes" (where incidentally much of the activity of the Anthesteria was concentrated) but in the Boukoleion, beside the Prytaneion, in the center of Athens. Scholars assume that the god was represented by the *basilinna*'s husband, the *archon basileus.* The *basilinna* had other duties, according to "Demosthenes" *Against Neaira* 73, although most of these are couched in terms of such mystery that we cannot reconstruct them in any detail. The *basilinna* "offered the unnameable sacrifices on behalf of the city," "saw what [Phano] should not

44. References in Parke 1977: 152. See also Brulé 1987: 105–14 on the significance of Agraulos to the rite.

45. Hamilton (1992) reassesses the evidence for the festival of the Anthesteria and concludes that many of the events usually predicated of this festival, including those involving women, did not in fact form part of it, although they may have taken place at other times.

46. The chief evidence for this rite is "Demosthenes" *Against Neaira,* and while Hamilton does not suggest that no such rite ever took place, he does point out, following the arguments of S. Peirce (1984), that this text makes no chronological association between *hieros gamos* and Anthesteria. So we may describe the *hieros gamos* as part of women's ritual practice in Athens, but we need not accept a dating to the festival of the Anthesteria.

have seen," "entered where no other Athenian, many as they are, enters," and "conducted on the city's behalf the ancestral rites, many and solemn and not to be named." She was also responsible for swearing in the *Gerarai*, or Revered Women, fourteen women who made sacrifices to Dionysos and celebrated the Theoinia and the Iobaccheia, two otherwise unknown festivals.[47] Whether all or any of these duties occurred in Anthesterion is unknowable, but we may note the prominence of the *basilinna* and of the Gerarai in the ritual life of the Athenian city.

The last day of the festival, Chytriai, or Pots, is generally agreed to have been a day of ill omen on which the spirits of the dead walked abroad. Some scholars have connected it with a ritual called the Aiora, which was marked by the participation of young girls.[48] These girls swung on swings in memory of the mythical Erigone, whose father Ikarios was killed when he introduced his fellow villagers to wine and the worship of Dionysos; since the villagers collapsed intoxicated, their relatives concluded that Ikarios was a poisoner and murdered him. Erigone hung herself in her grief, and the young girls swung in imitation of her death.[49] A priestess of Dionysos officiated at the temple "in the marshes,"[50] receiving from the celebrants of the Anthesteria the wreaths that they placed on their jugs, and *kanephoroi* very likely figured in processions to or from the temple.

Apart from the activities in their exclusive festivals, which we shall discuss later, women can be seen to participate in Athenian ritual chiefly by carrying objects in procession, and often by dancing. Lucian *On Dancing* 15 claims that no sacred mystery *(telete)* was ever celebrated without dancing. Neither of these activities are unknown for men; tasks special to women include the sacred wedding, swinging at the Aiora, and washing the statue of Athena (elsewhere, however, men could be assigned the task of ritual washing).[51] Women's ritual involvement could take them to the heart of the city, to the Pnyx for the Thesmophoria, the Boukoleion for the *hieros gamos*,

47. See as well as Demosthenes 59.78, Hesychius s.vv. *Dionusou gamos* and *gerarai* (= Bekker 1814: 1.231–32), *Etymologicum Magnum* 227.35 s.v. *gerairai*, and Pollux 8.108 s.v. *gerarai*.

48. E.g., Burkert 1983: 240–42.

49. Hamilton has again marshaled the evidence against the identification of Aiora with Chytroi, and concludes that "the most conservative solution is to see this as another ritual taking place at the same time as the Chytroi, perhaps in a different part of Athens or Attica" (1992: 49).

50. *en Limnais;* the location of this temple is now unknown. On the priestess see Athenaeus 10.437D. *LSAM* 48.21–23, from third-century Miletos, cites priests and priestesses of Dionysos in a procession, but as Hamilton points out (1992: 58), there is no incontrovertible argument for assigning such a procession to the Athenian Anthesteria.

51. "The descendants of Pheidias, called Cleansers, have received from the Eleans the privilege of cleaning the statue of Zeus from the dirt that falls on it" (Pausanias 5.14.15). The Phaethyntes at Eleusis cleaned the statue of the twin goddesses and announced to the priestess of Athena in Athens the arrival of the *hiera*.

and to the Acropolis for the Arrhephoria, but it could also take them far outside the city—to the sea, to Phaleron, Halimus, Brauron, Eleusis, and Delphi. (For sites of women's ritual practice in Attica, see map 1.) It could designate a few women by family or priestly profession or convene many women in inclusive groups.

The above account of an Athenian cultic calendar for women can be only a sketch, and there may have been much more activity that was not recorded, or whose record has been lost. An inscription from Piraeus (*IG* ii² 1177) lists among women's festivals the Plerosia and the Kalamaia, festivals obscure to us except for the information from *IG* ii² 949 that the Kalamaia was celebrated by the hierophant and the priestesses.[52] We might also note that the calendar of sacrifices from the Attic deme of Erchia,[53] which is by no means complete, nonetheless includes five different rituals presided over by priestesses, celebrated in four different months, and on occasion involving divinities unknown in the Athenian context, such as the Heroines.[54] These brief notifications can serve as a measure of our ignorance about the extent of women's ritual involvement. At present I wish to stress the quantity and diversity of women's ritual practice, which remain visible despite the limitations of available evidence, and the extent to which such practice provided a real alternative to the customary identification with the private and the domestic. While my sketch cannot delineate the totality of women's ritual engagement, it can suggest how far beyond the domestic environment women might penetrate. Although some ritual activity addressed only a few individuals, much of it invited the participation of a number of women, and afforded them a material, visible presence in the wider community that may have constituted part of the texture of daily lived experience for women and men alike.

We should note, however, that this very presence is also circumscribed by the ritual. Women's exclusive festivals are often held in secrecy or at night, thus perhaps underlining the "dark" side of female identity. Much of women's ritual activity is also in fact related to their primary identification with the domestic context, particularly when that activity figures reproductive work or activities like weaving. We shall examine this phenomenon shortly. What I would like to stress, then, is not only the extent of ritual practice but the way in which such practice constructs a sphere for women that is to be identified neither wholly with the domestic nor wholly with the public, since it brings women only into certain public spaces and allows them only certain actions there. Women's presence in the wider community,

---

52. On the Kalamaia see Deubner 1966: 67–68.

53. A deme is an element of the civic organization of Attica, which operates on the level of locality rather than of birth.

54. See Daux 1963. On Greek heroines see Larson 1995b.

Attica. Some sites of women's ritual practice.

while extensive, is thus somewhat compromised; even while contributing, through ritual practices, to the reproduction of a wider culture, women are also reproducing themselves as domestic operators.

SACRIFICE AND DEDICATION

An Athenian festival calendar can offer only a very partial view of what women did in the ritual sphere, since some of their characteristic actions, like sacrifice and dedication, will not be shown there. Women are often represented in vase painting as pouring libations and making various kinds of bloodless offering, but they also contributed important elements to the process of blood-sacrifice. Blood-sacrifice is of inestimable value to Greek culture as permitting not only the knowledge of divine intent, through inspection of the victim's entrails, but also the opportunity for influencing such intent through the offering of an especially pleasing victim. Although, again, men were the chief actors in these events, women's participation in sacrifice brings them into the heart of their community, to engage in the crucial moment of mediation between mortals and gods.

Young women were allotted the responsibility for bringing water for sharpening the sacrificial tools, and they also carried the basket that contained the grain to sprinkle over the victim's head and concealed the sacrificial knife. A female flute-player might accompany the ceremony. Women's chief task during the sacrifice was to raise the ritual cry, the *ololuge*, when the animal's throat was cut.[55] This was perhaps their most important contribution to the procedure, and it is interesting to us for two contradictory reasons. The *ololuge* requires the active participation of women and allots them a valued place in the ritual process, drawing on women's association with emotional expression and in particular, with mourning. Yet it seems significant too that while the chief defining practice of Greek culture welcomed and indeed needed the presence and agency of women, their principal part in it was to utter a wordless cry. In a culture which fetishized discourse as much as did the Greek, women's sublinguistic performance in sacrifice seems to enact and explain their status as only partial members of the human community.

The same paradox is recognizable in the rules for distributing sacrificial meat. While much productive work on ritual focuses on the ways in which social distinctions are dissolved in ritual gatherings, an equally strong case can be made for the opposing view, namely that such distinctions are reinscribed by the ritual procedures. Helene Foley points out that the distribution of the meat could either "reemphasize the equality of the participants"

---

55. On the details of these procedures see Burkert 1985: 56.

or "reflect the hierarchies of the community."[56] Specific provisions are sometimes made for women's participation in the sacrificial feast, as if it were not
to be taken for granted. On certain occasions, when women were the primary
actors in the sacrifice, they had first claim to the meat. In the Attic deme of
Erchia the goats sacrificed to Semele and Dionysos are consumed by the
women present, and none of the meat is carried away from the sacrifice.[57] At
Tegea, when married women sacrificed to Ares, they consumed all the meat
(Pausanias 8.48.4–5), and the wives of the prytany members, who organized
the annual sacrifice to Artemis at Perge in Pamphylia, apparently shared the
meat with the priestess (*LSAM* 73.21–23). The victors in the girls' races at Elis
were entitled to parts of the sacrificial cow (Pausanias 5.16.2–4). But where
women joined with men in the sacrifice, their share of the meat might depend
on the men and might be unequal. In one of the third-century Athenian religious associations, or *orgeones,* women may partake of the sacrificial feast only
if the victim is an ox, that is, not if it is anything smaller. Wives receive an equal
share in the meat, but their share is entrusted to their husbands, and daughters and female servants receive half-shares.[58] At Thasos, an inscription can be
understood to read that women too share in the distribution of the sacrifice
at the biannual ceremonies for Athena Patroa, indicating that such sharing
might not be a feature of all sacrifices.[59] Women constitute a serious presence
within the community of sacrificers, and their cultural importance is acknowledged as such, but may simultaneously be contained.[60]

An area of ritual activity in which women's participation was more com-
mensurate with that of men was the dedication of votives. A votive could be
any kind of material object, deposited at a sanctuary either in the hope of
assuring the deity's favor or as a sign and remembrance that the deity had
already demonstrated a favorable disposition; because of the contractual
and pragmatic character of Greek religion, the dedication of such objects
was an important part of religious practice. The inscription that sometimes
recorded the reason for the dedication may be recovered from the site, as
may some nonperishable objects, but these represent only a small part of
the whole dedicatory activity that characterized Greek culture.

56. Foley 1985: 33.
57. Daux 1963: 606, 609.
58. *LSS* 20.17–23. See also Ferguson 1944. Other religious associations perhaps indicate
less asymmetry between the sexes. An inscription of 237/36 B.C.E. shows the members of a similar group honoring their leader; the thirty-eight men and twenty-one women members are all
listed together on the stone, although the women come second.
59. This is the reading of Casabona 1966: 349–50, followed by Detienne 1989: 131. But
Rolley (1965: 463), who publishes the inscription, suggests that the verb be translated "obtenir
par le sort une charge ou une fonction," which would be a more radical reading of the possibilities open to Thasian women in the early fifth century.
60. See also Osborne 1993.

The precise process of offering votives, especially where women are concerned, is not easy to reconstruct, but women's dedications seem to testify to the presence and agency of women in a direct and uncomplicated way; time, labor, and resources have been expended on the woman's project, and she has left a material trace of herself in the visible public realm. Dedicatory activity could be intense, even for women; while several items of inscriptional evidence authorize a priest to remove those offerings that obscure the worshippers' view (*LSCG* 43 and notes), Pausanias notes that a statue of Health (Hygeia) at Titane outside Corinth was covered in offerings of women's hair (Pausanias 2.11.6). In Anthony Raubischek and Lilian Jeffrey's collection of votive inscriptions from the Athenian Acropolis fewer than twenty dedicators who can definitely be identified as female appear among nearly four hundred dedications, but M. Lazzarini suggests that nearly one tenth of all private dedications throughout the Greek world from the eighth to the fifth century are from women.[61] Different locations attracted different kinds of dedications, according to the concerns of the presiding deity; dedications concerning personal health were prevalent at Epidauros, for instance. Many dedications made by women are part of the display of the *oikos* at its defining moments of birth, marriage, and death, but such dedications can also be considered to articulate the women's own lives in terms of the gynecological events of conception, pregnancy, and delivery. The material articulation of the relationship between the woman and the deity might supply a special validation and significance, in a context wider than that of the *oikos*, to the woman's particular hopes and fears. The primary communication is between women and the divine, but the act of making the dedication brings women into the partial publicity of the ritual sphere, where that communication is visible to others.

In this connection it may be appropriate to consider more closely the dedications by women to Asklepios, which throughout antiquity outnumber those of men.[62] The cult seems to have offered certain possibilities specifically to women, because within it they are permitted and encouraged to represent themselves publicly, giving sometimes intimate detail of their individual histories. From the fourth-century shrine at Epidauros survives a

61. See the list at Lazzarini 1976: 169.

62. McClees 1920: 17–22. See also Aleshire 1989: 43, 45–46, on the proportion of female to male dedicants in the inventories of the Athenian Asklepieion. Women were responsible for healing within the family. See, for example, Xenophon *Oikonomikos* 7.37, where the wife is charged with tending sick slaves. In *Against Neaira* 55–56, the wronged husband is induced to take back his erring wife when he is sick. The speaker appeals to the jury's shared experience of male vulnerability at the hands of a competent female nurse: "They came to him while he was weak and bereft of anyone who would tend his illness, bringing him what was suited to his disease and looking after him; and you yourselves know how useful a woman is in illness, being there for her sick man."

series of inscriptions describing the cures that have been granted to patients sleeping in the sanctuary, among whom women are extraordinarily prominent.[63] Distressed chiefly by the failure of their reproductive functions, the women concerned have traveled to Epidauros on a mission that combines medical and ritual elements, exerting the measure of control over their own time and movements and over household resources that we have seen as characteristic. The activity of "incubation" requires the patient to sleep in the sanctuary until she or he sees a significant dream, after which she or he is cured. To celebrate their recoveries, the women erect votives, and the accompanying inscriptions describe in dramatic detail the women's sufferings, affording special value to otherwise mundane experiences. As is frequently the case for women in ritual inscriptions, the names of father or husband may be omitted; the woman's domicile is given, showing the length of her journey to the sanctuary, but otherwise the only actors in the medical drama are the woman, the god, and any figures that appear to her in the healing dream.

Many of the healing dreams can be construed as versions of wish fulfillment: water flows out of a woman with dropsy, bodies are cut open painlessly to remove worms. More revealing perhaps are the dreams experienced by women who want children, and who imagine that sacred snakes lie on their stomachs or have intercourse with them, or that handsome men undress them. Various fantasies that might be problematic under other circumstances are sanctioned by the context of the cult, which enables women both to construct a drama out of their experiences and to narrate it themselves. Although most women claim to want sons, at least one, Ithmonike of Pellene, admits to a wish for a daughter; she duly conceives but forgets to ask for a delivery and is back at the shrine still pregnant after three years, requesting successful childbirth. One mother from Sparta practices incubation on behalf of her daughter, who has dropsy and cannot leave home; interceding for the daughter, the mother sees a healing dream and returns to Sparta, where she discovers that the daughter has seen the same dream and is cured. In these instances the cult allows certain women to pursue and celebrate identifications that are not especially valued by the dominant culture. Under the sanction of the healing cult, women can articulate their own needs and represent publicly the particular contours of their lives.[64]

The very act of making a dedication might permit a woman a sense of agency in ordering, or at least articulating, her own life. But it is reasonable

---

63. See Edelstein and Edelstein 1945: 1.221–29 = *IG* iv² 1.121–22. Some of these inscriptions are translated as *WLGR* 406.

64. Herodas *Fourth Mime* (3d cent. B.C.E.) describes women visiting the shrine of Asklepios, probably on Kos (Sherwin-White 1978: 352). They are enjoying the outing, the artwork at the temple, and the chance to discourse on their own misfortunes.

to ask whether women themselves were seriously involved in the offering of votives.[65] Wives and daughters of prosperous men probably enjoyed greater leisure and mobility than women from poor families, and so presumably were materially capable of a journey to the site involved. But one could nonetheless question whether women in fact left their homes to make dedications at all; if dedications were made on behalf of women who died in childbirth, why not on behalf of living women? While this may have happened on occasion, as a general statement of the situation it seems implausible, because of the pervasive and relatively extensive mobility that is otherwise possible for women in the ritual sphere. If Athenian women could travel to Eleusis or to Delphi there seems to be no a fortiori reason why others should not organize excursions to particular dedicatory sites. In the case of dedications at Epidauros, inscriptions indicate that the women concerned had already traveled to the site at least once for the incubation. One woman who is cured when she returns home is ordered by the god to send *(apopempo)* offerings to Epidauros, but other women are said to put up *(anatithemi)* votives. Nor does poverty seem to have been an absolute obstacle to the offering of votives, because we have records of dedications made by women who had to support themselves by their labor. Phrygia the breadseller dedicated a shield to Athena (*IG* i² 444 = *IG* i³ 546); in the sixth century Smikythe, a washerwoman, offered a tithe (*IG* ii² 473 = *IG* i³ 794); in the fourth century Melinna, having brought up her children with the skill of her own hands, offered firstfruits of her work to Athena Ergane (*IG* ii² 4334), and Myrrhine the washerwoman joined with other launderers in an offering to the Nymphs (*IG* ii² 2934).[66] Neither poverty nor general restrictions on mobility, then, seem to have prevented women's activity in this sphere. But we cannot imagine a total autonomy of movement without regard to the rest of the household context, and as we have seen, travel to dedicatory sites could be sanctioned and even required by those crises of the *oikos,* such as pregnancy, that themselves inscribe on the woman's existence her subordination to the projects of the family as a whole. Not only subordination within the *oikos* but marginality within the wider society may also be signaled by women's dedicatory practice. C. Morgan has noted that women's dedications are often found at sites removed from the centers of communities, which suggests that even in moments of ritual agency and mobility women may be constrained to act out their peripheral status.[67]

65. Men might make votive offerings in discharge of vows by female family members; see Kunarbos on behalf of his daughters Aristomache and Archestrate, (Raubitschek and Jeffrey 1949: 79 = *IG* i² 555 = *IG* i³ 745). And as indicated before, the huge majority of Greek dedications of whatever kind is made by men.

66. The last three references are also available in translation as *WLGR* 322, 317, and 323. For women tithing see also Lazzarini 1976: nos. 262, 647, 648, 649, 678.

67. Morgan 1990: 230.

Many dedications by women do in fact consolidate an identification with the domestic sphere, because the dedications are made on behalf of their children. F. van Straten mentions the frequency of such dedications *huper ton paidon* (on behalf of children) in lists of offerings to Asklepios,[68] and we may note among them a statue of her son dedicated by Klearista at Epidauros around 300 (*IG* iv 1101, = *IG* iv² 239) and fourth- or third-century Athenian dedications to Asklepios from Myrrhine and Phanokrite on behalf of themselves and their children, and from Phile, Demostrate, Temene, and three unnamed mothers for their children (*IG* ii² 1534A, 1534B, and 1535).[69] Women made dedications for their families not only because of illness, however; several inscriptions testify to other dedications by mothers "on behalf of children" *(huper ton paidon)*, and joint dedications by family members are often represented as deriving from the mother. Brunhilde Ridgway notes that "such joint dedications of family members headed or largely represented by women are attested through the centuries and from a variety of sites."[70] In the mid-fifth century Mikuthe dedicates a statue on the Athenian acropolis for her children and herself (*IG* i² 523 = *IG* i³ 857),[71] and around 400 Xenokrateia founds a sanctuary of Kephisos at Phaleron on behalf of her son (*IG* ii² 4548 = *IG* i³ 987 = *LSS* 17), raising a votive relief that represents the family members. Fourth-century reliefs show Lysistrate dedicating in Athens to Herakles *huper ton paidon* (*IG* ii² 4613) and Aristonike dedicating to Artemis at Brauron on behalf of her family (Brauron 1151 [5]). In fourth-century Athens Phile dedicates *huper tou paidiou* (*IG* ii² 4588), Archestrate *huper tes thugatros* ("on behalf of her daughter," *IG* ii² 4593), and Hipparche on behalf of her son and herself (*IG* ii² 4883). Two women called Timothea dedicate *huper ton paidon* (*IG* ii² 4671, 4688), in the third and second centuries. It is not, of course, the case that fathers did not dedicate on behalf of their children, or children on behalf of their parents, but neither fathers nor (male) children are usually understood to have been excluded from such publicly visible activity.[72] Interestingly, Ridgway suggests that votive reliefs show female figures with increasing frequency; in the fourth century, she claims, reliefs depicting families show more female than male participants.[73] The *Greek Anthology* also exhibits examples of dedications by women on behalf of children (e.g., 6.148, 150, 356–57), indicating that such a gesture was at least part of the suitable representation of motherhood. These dedications, then, show women as both publicly visible and properly domestic.

---

68. Van Straten 1981: 113.

69. See Aleshire 1989: 201, 202, 287, 290.

70. Ridgway 1987: 401.

71. Raubitschek and Jeffrey 1949: 298.

72. In the dedications at the Athenian Asklepieion that are recorded in the inventories, five fathers are shown dedicating for children, and seven mothers. See Aleshire 1989.

73. Ridgway 1987: 405.

To intercede with the gods on behalf of children can even be seen as part of a definition of the maternal role. In Xenophon *Memorabilia of Socrates* 2.2 Socrates' son, Lamprocles, complains about his mother's ungovernable temper and tongue. Socrates proves Xanthippe's benevolent disposition toward her son by citing not only her care for him when he was ill but also the fact that she "entreats the gods for many blessings on [his] head and pays vows for [him]" (2.2.10). A neo-Pythagorean treatise from the third or second century, attributed to the female philosopher Phintys, enjoins that a woman not go out in public unless she is going to pray for her family. "The manner in which she chooses to leave her house" is said to be an integral part of a woman's virtue (*sophrosune*, also frequently translated as "chastity" or "prudence"), and there is only one valid occasion for leaving the house: "Women of importance in the deme make excursions from the house to sacrifice to the patron deity of the city on behalf of themselves and their husbands and their households."[74] The text, as noted, dates from the Hellenistic period but could just as well have emerged from a fifth-century Athenian context, and it can also be shown that this text and others like it were popular as late as the third and fourth centuries C.E.[75] The contours of the prescription are familiar; seclusion is the desirable norm, but is modified in the ritual context. Here, however, the ritual context is also closely bound up with the domestic, because the woman intercedes with the divine for her family. Ritual is an extension of her domestic nurturing duties in that it involves caring for her family, and one way for a woman to discharge her domestic duties as wife and mother is to perform acts of ritual observance.

These last two examples of women's ritual activity, the vows and prayers of Xanthippe and of the neo-Pythagorean woman, indicate that women could move into the ritual sphere as a matter of their own volition, provided they were engaged on behalf of their families. In neither example is there indication that the women concerned are taking part in a regular festival or managing in ritual a crisis of the *oikos*. Instead, they seem to act on their own initiative, a circumstance that suggests that women could to some extent organize their own time and their own relations to nondomestic, cultic spaces. Other examples bear out this conclusion. A passage in Plato *Laws* 10.909E complains that the ritual observances of some groups, especially women, extend to the founding of sanctuaries and cults, and legislates against the traces of their material presence that they leave in the ritual sphere:

74. The text is Thesleff 1965: 151–54. To "Theano," another Pythagorean woman variously held to be disciple, daughter, or wife of Pythagoras, is attributed the injunction that a woman sacrifice every day when she leaves her husband's bed. See Thesleff 1965: 194.

75. See *WLGR* p. 347 n. 1.

It's the habit of all women especially, the sick everywhere, and people who are in danger or in any kind of distress—and on the other hand whenever people enjoy a stroke of good luck—to dedicate whatever comes to hand at the moment, and to vow sacrifices and promise foundations to gods and daimons and sons of gods, . . . people of this sort fill all their houses with altars and shrines, fill all the villages, and even build in the empty spaces, wherever the fit moves them.

The complaint makes the familiar gesture of aligning women with the irrational and the disadvantaged, but the passage is open to another reading; women exploit the possibilities of the ritual sphere in order to construct for themselves a presence within the community, devoting time and resources to the articulation of their own lives and projecting the representation of those lives beyond the domestic boundaries. The mother of Sostratos in Menander's *Dyskolos,* a fictional character of course but not obviously designed to excite disbelief, travels round the country with a large retinue to make dedications at various shrines (260–63). She indulges her own inclinations and exerts control over some of the household resources, while avoiding any compromise to her respectable domestic identity.

The traditional peasant culture of modern Greece offers a precise equivalent to the mother of Sostratos. The calendar of the Greek Orthodox Church provides its women members the opportunity to perform many religious outings to shrines of different saints. Such excursions involve respite from domestic work, expansion into the world beyond the house, and varied forms of sociability. Lucy Rushton, writing on the visits to neighborhood chapels that attend saints' days and other occasions, concludes: "For those that attend regularly, this means that they go through an annual cycle of outings into the countryside immediately surrounding the village, with coffee and maybe a picnic after the service."[76] These modern Greek women demonstrate a management of patriarchal culture that has more than local relevance. They use the circumscribed forms that are handed to them by a generally repressive ecclesiastical establishment to find a space for self-articulation and for disruption of the daily grind. Their actions do not constitute a reversal of the normal order, such as is often predicated of ritual activity, and cannot be considered subversive of it, because the women remain within the parameters prescribed for female identity and do not fundamentally alter the meaning of those parameters. Nor do they forego those rewards, such as respect from the community, that patriarchal culture makes available to women who successfully implement prescribed roles. But within these quite strict parameters the modern Greek women construct a space for their own gratification rather than that of others. Such seem to me

76. Rushton 1983: 59.

to have been the probable contours of much ritual engagement on the part of women in ancient Greece.

But if women managed their culture through deployment of ritual forms, the converse is also true. Women's relative autonomy within the ritual sphere incidentally reinforces their associations not only with the body, as when they take part in funeral ceremonies, and with domesticity, but also with the nonhuman. We have already encountered elements of this last association: women are charged with the "dark" and dangerous transitions of birth and death, and in sacrificial ritual, women are responsible chiefly for the wordless *ololuge*. In the passage from "Phintys," on the woman who leaves the house to pray for her family, we can read a related notion about the nature of female identity. Out of all the family members, the woman is apparently the best qualified to undertake this ritual task of intercession, and it is her task. Her responsibility in the domestic sphere to nurture her family extends to a responsibility in the ritual sphere to intercede for them with the divine. Theophrastos's Superstitious Man (*Characters* 16.11) takes his wife with him each month to attend his initiation with the Orphic priests. However, if she is not free, he takes the nurse and the children. As Jeffrey Rusten notes in his translation, "Evidently the presence of a woman was required." This privileged position as the intercessor points in two directions. As we have seen, it removes the woman from her usual domestic context, affords her a visible presence in the wider community, and endows her with a measure of autonomous agency. But this presence and agency is bought at the price of an alignment with the nonhuman that can subtract from women's identity as members of a human society; the association with the divine can work in the same way as women's traditional association with the animal.[77] In the same way that women's connections with the materiality of bodily processes are demonstrated and reinforced in the ritual sphere, so women's ability to intercede with the divine on behalf of other mortals can be construed as part of the inadequacy of female identity.

The work of Ruth Padel has clarified how women symbolize for Greek culture what is dark, unknown, and potentially dangerous, and can therefore be assigned the task of making contact, on behalf of men, with the unpredictable aspects of divinity.[78] Related representations construct women as uniquely porous, labile beings whose boundaries of personal identity are susceptible to various kinds of possession.[79] Both notions are, of course, necessary ideological correlates to explain and justify women's real physical and

---

77. On women as aligned with the animal rather than the human see, for example, DuBois 1991.

78. Padel 1983 and 1992: 106–13.

79. See Padel 1983: 12–17 and 1992: 106–13. Sered (1994: 189) amasses cross-cultural evidence for this association between women and susceptibility to possession; several cultures in which women do act as possession specialists figure women as "soft" and "permeable."

political subjection, in which they are possessed not so much by divine influ-
ences as by the projects of a male-dominated polity. But the notion of
women's susceptibility to possession and affinity with the dangerous unknown also enables and ratifies their position as ritual interceders by endowing them with a particularly close relationship with the nonhuman. The
"nonhuman" in this context means the divine, but Greek culture was
equally quick to line the female up with the animal and other beings of low
status; this relationship with the nonhuman, then, while affording women
their unusual prominence in ritual, also validates their exclusion from the
other arenas of human endeavor prized by their communities.

This paradigm, whereby women are perceived as especially fitted for
intercession with the divine and are entrusted with the task in ritual practice
is by no means the only possible way to construct relations between gender
and the divine. In the Orthodox Jewish tradition, for instance, matters spiritual are the responsibility solely of the male, while the woman is confined
to the material sphere. Men are ideally expected to spend their lives in study
of religious texts, while women provide not only the supporting material
labor but also all the activity of mediating between the household and the
outside world.[80] In other, completely unrelated societies, a paradigm similar
to this may be discerned. Among the Borero of South America, for instance,
men are the only members of society who make contact with spirits, and
they claim this particular facility as part of their demonstrable superiority to
women.[81] In the case of ancient Greek culture, the ritual sphere does not
contribute in such a direct and unmediated way to the subordination of
women; instead, it elaborates a dialectical process whereby ritual practice
both governs women and affords them self-articulation.

THE WORKS OF WOMEN

Greek culture ostensibly defined female identity by the notion of the *erga
gynaikon*, or works of women, which comprise weaving and childbirth. We
shall see in the next chapter how ritual events for women often elaborated on
the theme of their reproductive work, but at present I want to examine how
ritual practice deploys women's characteristic domestic tasks, particularly
those of weaving and water carrying.[82] To the extent of this deployment, I suggest, ritual practice too may be considered part of the "works of women."

80. Myerhoff 1978.
81. See, for example, Crocker 1977: 189. Other societies of South America display a similar pattern whereby men exclude women from ritual practices in order to shore up structures
of male dominance; see, for instance, Bamberger 1974. Yet other cultures allot practically all
the religious activity of the community to women; see the examples in Sered 1994: 96.
82. Keuls (1985: 229–66) discusses the erotics of women's work but does not engage with
its ritual dimension.

Women's work, like women's ritual involvement, requires powers of agency and a contribution to the reproduction of culture. Weaving was the chief task of women in ancient Greece,[83] because women were responsible for supplying all members of the household with clothing. Although weaving was a task for all the female members of the *oikos*, it chiefly involved the wife and mother, who taught her daughters to weave and who supervised their work and that of her female slaves, if she had any. Not only a material task but also an index of female respectability, weaving demonstrates that the woman successfully identifies her own interests with those of her family, by remaining secluded rather than exposing herself to a public gaze. So respectable is this occupation that it is possible to represent well-bred women earning their living by their skill. In Xenophon *Memorabilia* 2.7 Aristarchos prevails on his single female relatives, who have been uprooted by the Peloponnesian War and so are living with him as his dependents, to support themselves by their weaving and bread making. Extreme circumstances require extreme remedies, but these forms of labor are, as the Socrates of the dialogue points out, "most honorable and becoming to women" (2.7.10). Aristarchos's relatives do not leave the home to work and do not need to enter the marketplace, because Aristarchos undertakes to trade in their goods for them, but the women are able to abandon a purely domestic role without compromising their status, protected by the virtuous respectability of women's work.

In the ritual context the task of weaving usually involved a group of women in producing a garment that was then presented to a deity. At Amyclae in the Peloponnese, women annually wove a tunic for the huge cult statue of Apollo (Pausanias 3.16.2). At Elis, where Hera had a festival corresponding to that of Zeus at Olympia, a group of sixteen women was responsible for the performance of many important ritual tasks, which included weaving a robe for the goddess every fourth year (Pausanias 5.16.2). They met in a special building in the agora of Elis (Pausanias 6.14.9) and were chosen as "the best" (Pausanias 5.16.5). If we assume that the definition of such excellence might include outstanding performance of female duties, the ritual weaving stands as both a duty and a sign of previous accomplishment. Since selection to the ritual post was an honor, the task of weaving may be considered as a reward for having performed previously in the domestic sphere. As in daily life, so in the ritual context weaving could function as sign and guarantee of female virtue.[84]

---

83. Except, according to, for example, Xenophon *Constitution of the Lacedaemonians* 1.3–4, those of Sparta. In Gortyn on Crete, the law code explicitly recognized the economic worth of women's contribution to the household by allowing the wife, in case of widowhood or divorce, to keep half of what she had woven while in the household.

84. On these women see further chapter 3.

In Athens an important instance of weaving in the ritual context has different contours and involves children rather than adult women. In the fall, during the festival of artisans and craftworkers called the Chalkeia, the looms were set up on the Acropolis for the weaving of the peplos that would be presented to Athena the following year. The priestess of Athena Polias was responsible, assisted by a number of young girls from the old noble families of Athens, the Eupatrid clans, who were chosen to serve the goddess and to live for a period in a special precinct on the Acropolis. The particular girls who assisted in the weaving of the peplos were called *ergastinai*.[85] Selection for this ritual task cannot be seen as a reward for female accomplishments in another sphere because the girls were too young to have proved themselves, but the *ergastinai* did bring honor to their families. The girls involved, about nine years old, probably were not expected to weave the entire huge garment themselves, but they assisted the priestess of Athena in setting up the looms, and presumably in the subsequent work of weaving. Pierre Brulé has suggested that a weaving collectivity was involved, including the mothers of the girls.[86] Whether or not the mothers were present, the priestess of Athena provided supervision by an older woman, and thus reinforced the didactic aspect of the ritual task. This didactic aspect has a double focus; on the one hand, in a purely practical dimension, the little girls learn to weave, but the ritual also teaches the little girls their feminine identity. They learn the *erga gynaikon* that define success and worth for the adult female, and are actively engaged in representing themselves, to themselves and to others, as those who weave and who are charged with the task of weaving.[87]

The *ergastinai* were joined on the Acropolis by other girls employed as *aletrides*. An *aletris* is a corn-grinder, and the scholiast on Aristophanes *Lysistrata* 641ff. claims that they prepared *popana eis ten thusian*, "cakes for offering." Brulé has conjectured that these girls ground the flour for special bread eaten by the *arrhephoroi*.[88] The *aletrides* too were chosen from among Eupatrid families, according to the scholiast quoted above, but in the real domestic context their task was considered inappropriate for free women and was assigned where possible to slaves. It has consequently been conjectured that the *aletrides* ground only a token amount of flour, as otherwise their work

85. References in Parke 1977: 141–43.

86. Brulé 1987: 230–31.

87. Brulé (1987: 227) points out that dedications of textiles are noted in many locations, and suggests that some of these textiles may have been produced by a more or less formally convened ritual collective. While many dedicated textiles may have been woven in the domestic context, of course, they may have been specially woven for a cult purpose rather than being produced and then directed to cult use. That weaving should be a group activity was probably dictated not only by social but also by practical, technological considerations.

88. Brulé 1987: 116. For the special bread see the Suda s.v. *anastatoi*. On the arrhephoroi see further chapter 2.

would have been too hard for them.[89] Their ritual labor would thus have been similar to that of the *ergastinai*. In their future lives as supervisors of households, the girls would not themselves grind corn, but their ritual task provided a general connection to the material work of food preparation that they would be required to perform and that, like that of weaving, was identified with the female and with the interior of the *oikos*. Bread making is recommended as good exercise to Ischomachos's wife in Xenophon *Oikonomikos* 10.11. But even if they did not learn a specific task, the *aletrides* learned that one predicate of female identity is work itself, as opposed to leisure, as is indicated by inscriptions praising them for *philoponia*, or love of work (*IG* ii² 1036). *Philergia*, or industriousness, is an essential component of female worth and success, as Aristotle *Rhetoric* 1.5.6 (= 1361a) makes clear: "For women the excellence of the body is its beauty and stature, the excellence of the soul its *sophrosune* and *philergia* without servility." The ideal woman, as represented in Herodotos's narrative about Darius and the men of Paionia (5.12), is one who can accomplish three tasks at once: she carries a pitcher on her head and works a spindle in her hand while leading a horse to water.

The female work of food preparation is a feature of another Athenian festival, the Oschophoria. This festival was largely interested in the development of young men, but some women served as Deipnophoroi, "dinner-carriers." These women reenacted the roles of the mothers of Theseus and of the young men and women who had gone with him to Crete, who had allegedly brought food to the young people before they embarked and told them stories to encourage them. The Deipnophoroi also walked in the procession from a sanctuary of Dionysos in Athens to the temple of Athena Skiras at Phaleron, where there was a sacrifice and a banquet.[90] Plutarch *Theseus* 23.3 explains as follows:

> And the Deipnophoroi take part in the procession and join in the sacrifice, imitating the mothers of those who were chosen by lot . . . , for they went back and forth carrying bread and meat for their children. And stories are told, because those mothers told stories to their children, so as to assist and encourage them.

The explanation of *deipnophoros* in Harpocration also stresses the maternal care of the "original" mothers, whom the Deipnophoroi imitate and who allegedly sent food every day to the temple where their sons and daughters were waiting.[91] While it is not certain how much of the "original" roles the Deipnophoroi perform, it is clear that they are rehearsing a domestic nur-

---

89. See Parke 1977: 140, for example.
90. References in Parke 1977: 77.
91. On the Deipnophoroi see also Hesychius s.vv. *deipnophoros* and *oschophorion*, Suda s.v. *deipnophoros*, and Bekker 1814: 1.239.

turing identity. The Deipnophoroi seem to have been appointed by an official of the Salaminioi (in collaboration with a priestess),[92] and it may have been their domestic reputation that enabled them to move from the household environment into an honorable public space.

The ritual food preparation is different in the two cases of *aletrides* and Deipnophoroi: the *aletrides* are engaged in learning a future identity, while the Deipnophoroi are mobilized in a reenactment of Athenian history. The *aletrides* perform their ritual task on the Acropolis, while the Deipnophoroi leave the city for Phaleron. The similarity between the two groups is that this female task of food preparation allows the women involved to move from the domestic into the ritual sphere, while still preserving and practicing an unquestionably feminine domestic identity.[93]

Water carrying is a further instance of domestic work in the ritual context. Ritual events often included a procession and a sacrifice, and the water used in the sacrifice was carried there in the procession. The water-carriers, or *hydrophoroi*, were usually young, unmarried women, and in Athens they were commonly selected from Eupatrid families. The task that the *hydrophoroi* performed in the ritual context was also needed in the *oikos*, and was almost invariably the task of women. Fetching water for household use was a daily necessity, and in archaic times at least it was probably performed by free women, chiefly the daughters of households.[94] The *hydrophoroi* who carry water in sacrificial processions are both learning and acting out a crucial component of their identity as females. They might also celebrate their service by dedications, as did women who carried water in the rites at Didyma. The numerous statuettes of young women with water pitchers, found at Tegea in the Peloponnese, may commemorate similar service.[95]

Athens affords a particularly notable example of *hydrophoroi*. In early summer the city celebrated the Diipoleia, a festival for Zeus that included a rite commemorating the mythical first slaughter of the domestic ox (the Bouphonia). While this rite is known from fifth-century B.C.E. sources,[96] the longest account is preserved in a third-century C.E. treatise "On Abstinence" by the Neoplatonist Porphyry (2.30):

---

92. For this detail see Ferguson 1938: 6.

93. Outside Athens the dynamic is not substantially different. The Rule of the Andanian Mysteries (see Meyer 1987) provides in its order of procession for women who preside over the banquet. Their official titles are *thoinarmostria* and *hypothoinarmostriai*.

94. There is controversy over whether or not the task devolved onto slaves in the fifth century. For the arguments from representations of water carrying on vase paintings see Keuls 1985: 236–40.

95. Rouse 1975: 265, 277, 288.

96. References in Parke 1977: 162–67. On Porphyry see Clark 2000.

They chose young women called *hydrophoroi;* these bring water so that they can sharpen the axe and the knife. Once these had been sharpened, one man handed over the axe, another struck the ox, another cut its throat. . . . They set up an inquiry into the murder and called to make their defense all those who had taken part in the deed. The *hydrophoroi* accused the sharpeners, the sharpeners accused the man who handled the axe, he accused the man who struck the blow, and he finally accused the knife; and since the knife could not speak, it was convicted. [Had it been able to speak, it would presumably have blamed the victim.] And from that day to this, at the Diipoleia on the Athenian acropolis they celebrate the sacrifice of the ox in this manner.

In this "comedy of innocence" the young women are at first potentially as important as the men. We might conclude that they are eventually demonstrated to be less significant, since they are first to be accused and thus first to be dismissed from the hierarchy of "guilt"; the main point of interest about these young girls, however, is that they do not just wail in the *ololuge.* Instead they speak articulately in a judicial context, defending their own innocence and incriminating the next in line. Since they thus draw on the legal discourse that so often characterizes Athenian self-perception, their participation in the ritual inserts them right into the heart of valued Athenian practice. Water carrying in processions was a feature of women's ritual activity throughout Greece and was thus probably the domestic work most thoroughly represented in the ritual sphere. But in this Athenian example the women's ritual practice transcends the figuring of domestic work.

Some Athenian women, of the family Praxiergidai, were also involved alongside their men in the annual bathing of the statue of Athena, an event called the Plynteria. While the Praxiergidai in Plutarch's text include males, both Hesychius and Photius mention women as involved with the ritual washing of the statues (s.v. *loutrides).* This ritual task was closely connected to textile work, as the statue often had to be first washed and then dressed in clean clothes. Plutarch *Alkibiades* 34.1 comments:

> The Praxiergidai celebrate these rites on the 25th day of Thargelion, and they are secret. They take off the clothes of the goddess and cover up her image. This is why the Athenians think that among the unlucky days this is most to be avoided for business of any sort.

I have suggested that women are suited for such ritual tasks because in the domestic context they are closely involved with corresponding basic bodily processes. At Elis, the woman who washes the god Sosipolis also prepares his food, barley cakes with honey (Pausanias 2.20.3). But there is a more significant construction of female identity at work in the Athenian scenario, which we have encountered before in the notion of women as privileged intercessors with the divine. The day on which the statue was washed was a day of ill omen, when other business was suspended and all Athenians tried to remain inside.[97] The atmosphere may be registered in Euripides *Iphigeneia in Tauris* 1226–29, when Iphigeneia, as priestess of Artemis, pretends that the goddess's statue has been polluted by the presence of Orestes and announces that she has to take it to the sea for washing and purification. She continues:

> I command all the citizens to stay away from this pollution—
> Anyone who guards the gates and needs his hands pure for the gods,
> Anyone about to be married, anyone heavy with child—
> Escape, get away, don't let this defilement fall on anyone![98]

The historical women who took part in the cleansing ceremonies were presumably exposed to the possible danger directly, yet they suffered no harm. The rite can be seen as exploitative in a quite unmediated sense, since women are induced to perform tasks too dangerous for men. As Padel points out, men "assigned them [women] guardianship and activity by which the women would make contact, on their behalf, with potentially contaminating objects and forces."[99] Women's association with the basic bodily processes disqualifies them from full participation in the civic community but fits them for divine service. Linked to the material body on the one hand and the divine on the other, they buy their ritual agency at the price of partial banishment from the category of human.

The Plynteria displays quite clearly some of the striking features of women's ritual engagement, in that it speaks both to women's domestic tasks and to their particular status within the human community. While the ritual does not involve learning a task, it does involve learning certain predications about female identity. When women act as agents within the ritual context, they are invited to be active, mobile, and relatively autonomous, and all these aspects of ritual engagement may be seen to offer to the female participants identities that are constructed along lines very different from those by which we usually understand women of ancient Greece. But it is important to note that these potential identifications are simultaneously countered by the inscription in women's ritual practice both of their domestic bodily work and of their marginal status within the civic realm. Of course

---

97. Hesychius s.v. *plynteria* and Photius s.v. *kallunteria* explain that the festival also honored Aglauros, the daughter of Kekrops.

98. Possibly these restrictions are exaggerated, both for Iphigeneia's obvious reasons and in order to elicit an Athenian laugh at the dense Taurians.

99. Padel 1983: 6.

we cannot know with any certainty how either men or women responded to these various significations of women's ritual practice, but we can say that these are the figurings of female identity that ritual discourse extended to the perceptions of women and men alike.

These tasks of weaving, water carrying, feeding, and washing are represented in the ritual sphere by activities that are usually open to a small number of chosen women only, even if the rituals themselves are quite prominent. A final domestic task that reappears in the ritual context, at least at Athens, and that involves a larger population of women is that of horticulture. Women were made indirectly responsible for the fertility of fields and crops by their performance of the Thesmophoria, and the cultivation of kitchen gardens is also acknowledged in the Adonia, in high summer.[100] We have most acquaintance with this ritual from fifth- and fourth-century Athenian sources, but we also know, from Theokritos *Idyll* 15, called *The Syracusan Women* or *Women at the Adonis Festival,* of a related event in third-century Alexandria. The Athenian Adonia was structured differently from the ritual tasks that we have been considering so far, because participation in it was neither honor nor family obligation, but a matter of voluntary commitment. The Adonia was a festival of mourning of Aphrodite's young consort Adonis, and its women participants occupied the spaces of the rooftops for the duration of the rite. The main feature of the festival was that the women first planted lettuce and other herbs and spices in broken pots and pieces of crockery; once the plants had germinated they were placed on the roofs of houses and left to shrivel and die in the intense heat. They were then carried down on ladders and thrown into the sea or into springs amid lamentation for Adonis.[101]

In terms of domestic work, the Adonia presents contours very different from other rituals that we have considered. The women's labor is the opposite of productive, and the "gardens of Adonis" were often invoked as a synonym for what is trivial and wasteful.[102] This inversion of the conduct normally prescribed is recognizable as a feature of certain rituals, found in many societies, which suspend normal requirements as a means of making clear the inadequacies of the alternative. As Victor Turner notes, "The ritual [of status reversal], . . . in fact, has the long-term effect of emphasizing all the more trenchantly the social definitions of the group."[103] But "inversion"

---

100. This timing is the conclusion of Weill (1966), who provides a detailed discussion.

101. For references see Detienne 1977.

102. See, for example, the Suda s.v. *Adonidos kepoi* (gardens of Adonis) and *akarpoteros Adonis kepon* (more fruitless than the gardens of Adonis), which is applied "to those unable to give birth to anything worthwhile." The same material is repeated and elaborated in *Corpus Paroemiographorum Graecorum* vol. 1, p. 19, line 6, and vol. 2, p. 140, lines 20–21, and in the scholion on Plato *Phaedrus* 276B.

103. Turner 1967: 172.

is not the only way in which the Adonia signifies its relation to women's domestic work. The perversely unproductive nature of the Adonic horticulture might instead be construed as demonstrating that even within their own proper domestic province, women cannot perform effectively. They begin to grow their gardens correctly—albeit in the wrong containers—but then abandon their work and leave the plants to die in the sun. Their failure in the Adonia can be read to indicate the necessity for all the other inculcation of toil that takes place in the ritual sphere and, of course, in daily life. On this reading of the Adonia, its events induce women to act out and thus confirm their inadequacies, for an audience that implicitly comprises both themselves and their male-dominated polity. This reading does not, of course, exhaust the significance of the Adonia, to which we shall return in subsequent chapters.

Weaving, water carrying, food preparation, cleaning, and gardening all appear more or less prominently in women's ritual activity, at Athens and elsewhere. These are women's tasks within the ritual sphere, just as they are in the domestic, and in this respect the ritual context does not perform any fundamental inversions on the customary gender-based stereotyping of Greek life. These domestic tasks can all be seen as part of the nurturing that is allotted characteristically to women and that is reproduced in the ritual sphere. Some rituals can amount to obligations for specific women, but ritual activity can also on occasion be understood as a reward for successful performance of other female duties. Ritual practice and women's work thus appear in at least four distinct relations to one another. Ritual offers a real alternative to and respite from the daily routine of toil, yet it can comprise work that women are obliged to do. Ritual frequently models women's domestic tasks, but such service can constitute a reward for women's successful domestic labor. While women can be seen to exercise greater control over their own actions within the ritual sphere than is otherwise possible, this is only partly the case if the content of the ritual is domestic work, and since the content of ritual practice is largely dictated to the participants by tradition and precedent, they are never completely in control of their ritual situation.

To pursue the figure of ritual and work further, we can also note that in each instance the ritual itself performs work on the women who participate in it. Women act and are acted upon in the same gesture. Recall the formulation by Anthony Giddens: "Constraint . . . is shown to operate through the active involvement of the agents concerned, not as some force of which they are passive recipients."[104] So in the ritual context, the activity that women perform reflexively produces ideologically determined predications about the agents, which rehearse women in aspects of a conventionally sanc-

104. Giddens 1984: 289.

tioned female identity. Thus the work that women accomplish in the ritual sphere is part of the work of producing women. In the case of younger women, such as the *ergastinai, aletrides,* and *hydrophoroi,* the ritual work helps to position the girls to act effectively as adult women. In the case of older women we cannot identify a simple didactic function, but we can say, for instance, that the involvement of women in the Plynteria reinforces the association of the female with the unpredictable and dangerous aspects of the divine, and facilitates the use of women to perform tasks involving the divine that are considered too perilous for others to undertake. To this extent the ritual sphere models a relation of exploitation that also obtains in the practical arrangements of Greek life, in which women are routinely induced to subordinate their well-being to that of others. In the ritual sphere of ancient Greek society women were constrained to elaborate a female identity that vibrated between the poles of exploitation and reward.

The notion of "reward" can lead us to consideration of one final way in which Greek culture seems to have fashioned a link between women's work and women's ritual practice. Sources on occasion assign to women speakers nothing less than praise of females articulated in these terms. Aristophanes *Women in Assembly* 221–28 represents Praxagora supporting her claim that women are better fitted than men to govern the polity by appealing to women's expertise in housework and ritual, in roasting barley and making honey cakes and in celebrating the Thesmophoria. In a fragment of the Euripidean drama *Melanippe Captive* (13 *GLP*= 499 Nauck) Melanippe asserts:

> Women are better than men. I shall prove it. . . . Women run homes and protect within the house what has been brought across the sea, and without a woman no household is clean or prosperous. And again, look at what concerns the gods, for that, in my opinion, comes first. We have the most important role. . . . All these [rituals] would not be holy if performed by men, but in women's hands, everything prospers. In this way women have a rightful share in the service of the gods.

Women's superiority, on this account, derives from their roles in the domestic context and in the ritual. That a female character articulates this link may at least be construed as evidence that such validation was available within the culture, even if we cannot know that it originated with historical women. Contemporary societies can also feature women's domestic work in a religious context. For branches of the modern Greek Orthodox Church women, who are seen as immersed in the physical and material, rather than having access to the spiritual dimension, can nonetheless so work on the material world as to render it capable of manifesting the divine. As Rushton observes,

> A Velvendos woman belongs to and, more important acts upon the physical, non-human world . . . and is continually involved in processes which trans-

form the material world so that it is capable of manifesting God. These processes include childbirth, and also the preparation of food, the cleaning and display of the house, and particular rituals performed when somebody has died.[105]

Other cultures too subscribe to the notion that women have a special relationship both to the material world and to the sacred, and that there is no contradiction in this.[106]

THE PRIESTESS

I want now to extend my account of presence and agency with an analysis of the specific duties and opportunities accruing to women who served as priestesses. Elements of this analysis will lead us finally to investigate the economic activity and roles available to women in the ritual sphere.

If we assume a free, moderately prosperous, respectable wife and mother, we can predicate of her a quantity of ritual activity that endowed her with some of the functions of an independent agent, gave her access to many nondomestic actions, and required of her mobility that exceeded what was possible in the household context. Women who did not answer to the different elements of such a description would have a correspondingly smaller share in ritual practice, but none would be completely excluded (except for the adulteress, to whom I shall return in the following chapter). Even slaves could enter temples to pray or to seek sanctuary, although they otherwise had hardly any access to ritual activity and consequently are largely excluded from this study. If the woman we describe came from one of a number of certain families—in Athens, for instance, from a Eupatrid house—she was probably qualified for office as a priestess and thereby had access to significantly more ritual practice.

"Priestess" is a misleading translation of the Greek word *hiereia*, because it seems to connote a position of mystic authority, which is not appropriate in the Greek context. Neither priest nor priestess wielded any spiritual or political authority, although each might exercise some cultural authority in

105. Rushton 1983: 58.

106. See for instance Frédérique Marglin's account of the female in Hinduism, in Atkinson, Buchanan, and Miles 1985: 39–59, especially 46. The reappearance of female domestic work in a religious context can be a very charged issue. Many Christian traditions draw on women's labor for innumerable support activities but have historically found it very difficult to accept women in positions of authority. The Christian tradition is able to sanctify domestic work, as in the poetry of George Herbert and the autobiography of St. Catherine of Siena; it can thus extend to the women who work for it the possibility of sanctification, but its oppressive history lays it open to the charge that such a gesture only mystifies and obscures its exploitative attitude to women's work.

certain restricted contexts. Nor was service in any priesthood a matter of religious vocation, because it usually extended over a limited period rather than a lifetime, and because it was usually compatible with other activities, such as politics or trade for men and marriage and motherhood for women.[107]

Priestesses are recorded for most Greek communities, serving one or more male or female deities. Athens provides a great deal of our testimony, but the city is not exceptional in its practice. In late fifth-century Athens there were at least seven priestesses, serving Athena, Artemis, Aglauros, Pandrosos, Kourotrophos, Bendis, and Cybele.[108] A fourth-century inscription from the Athenian deme of Halai Axionides records another seven priestesses and mentions about the same number of male officials (*IG* ii[2] 1356). A priestess might also have assistants; the priestess of Athena in Athens called on the services of two women whose titles were Kosmo and Trapezophoros.[109] The duties of the priestess typically included taking care of the temple and its precincts and making offerings to the deity. Even the priestess's tasks thus reproduce those of the housewife, insofar as she provides physical maintenance and nourishment.[110]

Priestesses might also be called on to perform other quite different duties. The priestess might begin the process of sacrifice, although she would not perform the actual slaughter.[111] If the city demanded that its religious officials curse a certain enemy, priestesses, like priests, complied.[112] Some priestesses, responsible for at least part of the ceremonies held in the deity's honor, had to exert considerable powers of organization and seem to have been accountable for the proceedings under their supervision. Inscriptions commemorate honors granted to Timokrite for having preserved good order during a *pannychis*,[113] and to Chrysis for having con-

---

107. The Mysteries at Eleusis seem to offer a different model, because they do promise life after death and because their priesthood does include exegetes of sacred activity. But the Eleusinian Mysteries are characteristic of Greek religion in the sense that one has to be initiated, not to change one's life, but in order to secure eternal life, and so again one has no need of continuing spiritual guidance. The function of the exegetes was to interpret sacred laws (see Garland 1984: 82–83). Those seers who gained positions of some authority in Athenian politics usually did so as well as, rather than because of, their religious activity, and they were all male.

108. For references see Garland 1984. I should point out that some priestesses served several deities, and correspondingly some deities had more than one priestess.

109. See Harpocration s.v. *trapezophoros*, Conomis 1970: frag. 20, and Bekker 1814: 1.307.

110. See *LSS* 127 = *IG* ii[2] 1346, an Athenian inscription of the imperial period, for a detailed account of a priestess's housekeeping duties.

111. Neither would a priest, by the classical period; see Garland 1984: 76.

112. See Plutarch *Alkibiades* 22.5. The text claims that the priestess in question in fact refused to curse Alkibiades, but see Sourvinou-Inwood 1988a for a convincing refutation of this position.

113. Dontas 1983.

ducted a procession worthily (*IG* ii² 1136, translated as *WLGR* 200). Similarly, priestesses might on occasion be authorized to punish those who infringed cultic regulations (*LSCG* 66, of a second-century B.C.E. priestess of Demeter in Messenia). Their presence or approval was often required for certain acts to be carried out in the sanctuary; for instance, in the fourth century the deme of Piraeus forbids certain actions to be performed in the Thesmophorion without the presence of the priestess (*IG* ii² 1177). Similarly, an inscription regulating the cult of Dionysos in Miletos, which dates from 276/75, forbids private individuals from making certain sacrifices before the priestess has done so (*LSAM* 48). Archias, the hierophant at Eleusis in the mid-fourth century, was accused of performing a sacrifice that should have been the responsibility of the priestess of Demeter and Kore (Demosthenes *Against Neaira* 116), and the priestess of Demeter at Arkesine on Amorgos in the fourth century brings some kind of complaint before the *boule* and *demos* (council and assembly) that Sokolowski conjectures concerns people sacrificing without her presence (*LSCG* 102). At fourth-century Miletos, however, it was the *kyrios,* or guardian, of the priestess of Artemis who was responsible for notifying the authorities if anyone failed to provide the cult with the proper portions from the sacrifices (*LSAM* 45).

Certain offices brought with them particular cultic privileges, such as that of seeing forbidden things or entering forbidden places. At Corinth the priestesses of Demeter, Eileithyia, and Aphrodite were thus privileged (Pausanias 2.35.8, 2.35.11, 2.10.4; and compare *LSCG* 124); at Elis the priestess of Sosipolis, who could approach the god only veiled in white (Pausanias 6.20.2). A first-century B.C.E. decree from Mantinea in Arcadia (*IG* v 2.265) allows the priestess Nikippa to receive the goddess in her house, as her predecessors have done. Among the Pellenians the image of Athena, which was carried by her priestess, was dangerous to laypeople and to trees (Plutarch *Aratus* 32).[114]

Priestesses themselves were subject to various restrictions and sanctions. They were liable to pollution, like priests, from exposure to people dying or giving birth, and Plato *Laws* 947B–D indicates that they could not participate in funerals.[115] The priestess of Athena Polias at Athens was forbidden to eat Attic cheese (Strabo 9.1.11). Since a fragment of a speech by Lykourgos, *peri tes hiereias,* refers to a priestess putting her name to a report,

---

114. We have no way of knowing how individual priestesses reacted to their offices. However, a joke in Plutarch *Moralia* 534C purports to be by Lysimache, priestess of Athena Polias at Athens: "At Athens Lysimache, priestess of Athena Polias, when asked for a drink by the muleteers who had brought the sacred vessels, replied: 'I fear it will get into the ritual.'" The joke indicates at the very least that a priestess could be represented as carrying her authority with ease and grace.

115. See the material collected by Parker 1983: 52.

she seems to have possessed some kind of legal personality.[116] It is, of course, unusual for women to possess a legal personality in the Greek context, but we should note that women were usually considered capable of taking an oath.[117] A priestess could apparently be held responsible for infringements that occurred in areas under her supervision. Aischines *Against Ktesiphon* 18 makes it clear that in Athens priestesses, like priests, were individually subject to annual audit. An inscription from the early fifth century indicates that a priestess was fined more heavily than "laypeople" if she broke the rules pertaining to sites and types of actions to be performed on the Acropolis. The priestess in this circumstance was fined 100 drachmas, other people the much smaller sum of 3 obols (*IG* i^2 4 = *IG* i^3 4, the "Hekatompedon inscription").[118]

Priestesses were also involved in financial transactions to a quite remarkable extent. The economic lives of women throughout ancient Greece were restricted to a greater or lesser degree, especially in classical Athens, where a free native-born woman was particularly disabled. A brief discussion of women's financial competencies makes the priestess stand out in high relief. Our sources are not clear on what power, if any, an Athenian woman retained over her dowry,[119] or on what amounts she was permitted to trade.[120] Women in classical Athens did not own land, although they might do so in other Greek cities, where they might also own other kinds of property. Aristotle's *Politics* (1269b12–32, 1270a23–24) notoriously complains about fourth-century Sparta that its women own nearly half the land. A fifth-century inscription from Gortyn in Crete indicates that women owned property in their own names, could retain it in the event of divorce or widowhood, and could inherit either from women or from men.[121] In the Hellenistic Greek cities of Asia Minor women seem to have disposed of unprecedented wealth, a situation most likely produced not only by a relative increase in the possibilities of self-articulation for women but also by an absolute increase in the amount of wealth circulating.[122]

---

116. See Conomis 1970.

117. See, for instance, the Law Code of Gortyn, col. III.5–9 (= Willetts 1967: 41). This passage is translated as *WLGR* 76.

118. The fine is discussed by Feaver (1957: 142) and Jordan (1979: 103–10).

119. See Schaps 1979: 74–88. His account of the position is generally bleak. See Foxhall 1989: 34–38 for a more complex and positive description, which stresses the power of the wife to remove the dowry from the marital household if the couple divorced. A good general account is that of Just 1989: 98–104.

120. Kuenen-Janssens (1941) suggests that a medimnus represented a week's food for a family, so that a woman could see that her family was fed even if she could achieve little else on her own.

121. See the Law Code of Gortyn, cols. II, III, and IV (= Willetts 1967: 40–42). Relevant passages are translated as *WLGR* 76.

122. Bremen (1983: 233) argues against Pomeroy 1975 for the importance of the absolute

Another possibility for some women was commerce. Even in classical Athens free native-born women appear as small traders, but this may be as a result of particular hardship. For instance, the garland-seller in Aristophanes *Thesmophoriazousai* 443–58 claims that she has to work in the market because her husband is dead.[123] Even in independence a woman's options might be circumscribed. For instance, the popular and successful *hetaira* (companion or courtesan) Theodota in Xenophon *Memorabilia* 3.11 seems to own furnishings and slaves as well as clothes, but she explicitly states that she has no source of regular income, such as a house that she might rent out, other than her reliance on her "friends" (3.11.4).

None of this is to say that Athenian women were totally excluded from the workings of a domestic or larger economy. Edward Cohen has shown that women could be quite prominent in banking businesses when these were owned by their husbands or other male family members, although such women would usually not be free Athenians, but slaves or metics.[124] Women might take an active interest in their families' finances, as is apparent from fifth- and fourth-century legal speeches. In Lysias *Against Diogeiton,* an unnamed widow is represented as having studied her husband's accounts so as to be able to accuse her father, in front of a family gathering, of having cheated her sons of their inheritance. The speaker of Demosthenes *Against Spoudias* (41) claims that his opponent has borrowed money from his mother-in-law (9) and that his opponent's wife conducted some of the family's financial business, with her husband's approval and even in his absence (17). In *Against Euergos* (47) the speaker's wife is represented as protecting his property (which incidentally she claims is hers, mortgaged for her dowry) while he is away (57). Such lawsuits, of course, represent moments of unforeseen family crisis when women might be pressured out of their regular roles, and so perhaps cannot be considered as evidence for normative behavior. Nor should we overlook the rhetorical effect, for the speakers, of the women's presence. The more we conclude that the women's involvement adds pathos or drama to the speech, the less we are compelled to credit the historicity of their interventions.

Despite women's overall lack of agency in the economic sphere the priestess, like her male counterpart, was required to make certain expendi-

---

rather than the relative increase: "What may at first sight appear to have been an improvement in women's status, is in reality not so much a difference in women's status as merely a rather spectacular difference in the size of the fortunes owned by women. But the latter is a consequence of the enormous difference in wealth betw⌐⌐ ⌐ Hellenistic and Roman Asia Minor and mainland Greece in the classical period."

123. See Foxhall 1989: 36 on female heads of household.

124. Cohen 1992: 61–110.

tures as part of her office and received payment for her work in the form of parts of sacrifices and sometimes of a salary. Athenian priesthoods that scholars call "gentile," because they were restricted to certain established and prominent families, were usually remunerated in perquisites from sacrifices.[125] At Athens, several priesthoods were reserved for the members of the Eupatrid Salaminian family, and both male and female officials received bread from the shrine of Athena Skiras. The priestess of Aglauros, who belonged to this family, received a loaf of bread at the Oschophoria, as did the priestess of Athena Skiras.[126] According to the account in Aristotle *Oikonomika* 2.2.4.1347a, the tyrant Hippias legislated for the priestess of Athena Polias, who came from the family of the Eteoboutadai, to receive a gift of food and an obol for every birth and death within the polis. In the deme of Erchia the presiding priestess regularly received the skin of any sacrificial victim.[127] Some women who were not priestesses but who fulfilled analogous roles could receive similar perquisites; the *kanephoroi* at the Panathenaia, for instance, received a portion of the sacrificial meat (*IG* ii² 334).

Outside Athens there were similar arrangements. All the priests and priestesses who served at Eleusis received portions of sacrifices and shared in the proceeds from the sale of the harvest of the Rarian Field (*IG* ii² 1672.255–62). The priestess of Artemis at Cyrene, known as the Bear priestess, received feet, head, and skin of the sacrifice, as we have seen above. In the third century the priestess of Artemis at Perge in Pamphylia (in Asia Minor) received the thigh of the sacrificial animal and other parts as well (*LSAM* 73.11–14).

Some women serving as priestesses handled money rather than payment in kind. In Athens, stipends were usually paid only to those priests and priestesses who did not come from Eupatrid families, and whose offices are therefore entitled "democratic."[128] The priestess of Athena Nike in fifth-century Athens received not only the legs and hides of sacrificial victims but also a salary of 50 drachmas a year (*IG* i² 24 = *IG* i³ 36). Douglas Feaver points out that we can gauge the nature of such emoluments by the fact that 1 drachma was the daily wage of a skilled workman employed in the fifth-century construction on the Acropolis.[129] As we have seen, the priestess of Athena Polias is said to have received an obol for each birth or death in Athens. At Eleusis, the priestess of Demeter, who came from the Eumolpid

125. Feaver 1957: 124.

126. On the perquisites of the Salaminioi see Ferguson 1938: 6.

127. Daux 1963. See Nemeth 1994: 61 on the practice of priests selling hides to local tanneries.

128. Feaver 1957: 124.

129. Ibid., 131.

family, received an obol from every initiate (*IG* i² 6 = *IG* i³ 6); most of these had to be relayed to the goddess, but the priestess was allowed to keep 1,600 drachmas to pay expenses, and 100 drachmas in *apometra,* which seem to have been more like a personal salary.[130] The priestess of Demeter on Delos received money and supplies to enable her to celebrate the Thesmophoria.[131] A mid-fourth century inscription from the Attic deme of Cholargos shows that women officiating at the Thesmophoria were obliged to provide the priestess with various supplies and 400 drachmas of silver (*IG* ii² 1184). In the third century the priestess of Dionysos at Miletos was paid for assisting at private sacrifices and initiations (*LSAM* 48), and the priestess of Artemis at Perge received a drachma from the polis for performing a monthly prayer on its behalf at the time of the new moon (*LSAM* 73.25).[132]

It is of course reasonable to suppose that this money went to the cult rather than to the woman concerned. The case of the priestess at Eleusis, however, with her expenses and her *apometra,* would be an exception to this kind of rule. We have also seen earlier that the Hekatompedon inscription proposes fines for a priestess who infringes the regulations about activities on the Acropolis, and in such a case, it might not make a great deal of sense if the fine were to come from the funds of the cult.

Priestesses might also be involved in more complex economic operations. A second-century inscription, which records the honors granted by the city of Delphi to Chrysis, the Athenian priestess of Athena, includes "the right to own land and a house" (*IG* ii² 1136, translated as *WLGR* 400). We may guess that other postclassical honorific grants would contain similar clauses.[133] The fourth-century Athenian orator Deinarchos claims, in *Against Aristogeiton* 12, that Aristogeiton had filed suit against the priestess of Artemis Brauronia at Athens but had been fined 5 talents for perjury when the Athenians found for his accusers in the countersuit. Some have argued from this that the priestess herself could sue, but the objects of Aristogeiton's vituperation included the priestess's *oikeioi,* perhaps male relatives who might be the principals in the action for redress.

Other transactions definitely included the priestess. Some were required to engage in ritual begging or collecting for their cults. The priestess of Athena Polias visited newly married women to collect money from them, and inscriptions indicate that other priestesses made similar excursions.[134]

---

130. Ibid., 131 and 140.

131. Detienne 1989: 134; Bruneau 1970: 269–74.

132. See also the discussions of priestesses' perquisites in Turner 1983: 384–87.

133. It also appears that at least one priestess, at Pylos, owned a substantial amount of land in the Mycenaean period. See Brulé 1987: 337–38.

134. See Burkert 1985: 101–2, *Corpus Paroemiographorum Graecorum* Suppl. I.65 on the priestess of Athena, and *LSCG* 175 and *LSAM* 73.26–28 on the practice of *agermos,* collection

Women on Delos are said to have lamented for Arge and Opis, two Hyberborean maidens, and to have collected money for their cult (Herodotos 4.35). It is of course possible to argue that such money belonged legally to the women's husbands, but the visits of the priestesses nonetheless construct wives as the primary economic operators on this particular ritual occasion.

In the postclassical period, in Hellenistic Asia Minor, some priesthoods were assigned to their occupants through sale, and women are known to have purchased priesthoods for themselves or for men.[135] In the third century, the priesthood of Artemis at Perge could be purchased by a man, who would then have to provide a priestess, or by a woman who would herself then serve in the office (*LSAM* 73). The inscription *SIG*[3] 1014, from Erythrae and dated circa 250 B.C.E., shows that a priesthood was bought for Astynous, son of Euthynos, by his guardian Nosso, daughter of Simus, and the *kyrios* of Nosso, Theophron, son of Demetrius (119–25).[136] All commentators on the inscription point out that such economic self-articulation would have been impossible for an Athenian woman, and this is of course correct, if only because the opportunity of buying or selling priesthoods was unknown in classical Athens. (We shall return to these commercialized priesthoods in chapter 3.) In classical Attica, however, it looks as if women could make expenditures in the ritual sphere, as when Lysistrate, the priestess of Demeter at Eleusis, dedicates an image in the mid-fifth century and claims, in the inscription, that she does not spare her property but makes abundant gifts according to her means (*SEG* 10.321 = *IG* i[3] 953). In a later period, a third-century priestess also named Lysistrate was honored in Athens for dedications in the cult that she served, and for spending 100 drachmas of her own money on sacrifices (*IG* ii[2] 776). Outside Attica, and especially after the classical period, the economic involvement of the priestess is comparable, but on a far larger scale. For instance, Megakleia, priestess of Aphrodite at Megalopolis in Arcadia in the Peloponnese in the second century, built a guest house and a wall around the temple.[137]

Although the total number of women who served as priestesses cannot be large, at any one time in ancient Greece there would be several such women occupying prominent and visible positions, engaging in complex and

---

of money by priestesses for cult purposes, at Antimacheia on Kos in the fourth century B.C.E. and at Perge in the third century B.C.E. See also Robertson 1983a.

135. See Schaps 1979: 51 and Turner 1983: chap. 5.

136. See on this transaction Turner 1983: 164–65.

137. *IG* v[2] 461.5–8; and see Schaps 1979: 13 and Bremen 1983: 223. Bremen points out correctly (225) that the nature of priesthoods changed between the classical and the Hellenistic periods, so that "many now had public rather than merely religious functions," which included or demanded expenditure on the part of the priest. However, I would argue that women's voluntary spending in the cult that they serve can be discerned within the classical as well as the Hellenistic period.

important tasks that normative Greek gender ideology would have held to be more or less impossible for them.

THE ECONOMICS OF RITUAL PRACTICE

While priestesses might have particular economic responsibilities and powers, the ritual practice of all women might have some economic component, and of all women's ritual practice with an economic aspect, dedication is the most common activity. The study of women's dedications suggests that women could exercise considerable command over the disposal of family resources, providing that those resources were diverted to the ritual sphere. Women's dedicatory activity is the clearest exception to the rule of their economic nonexistence.

As David Schaps points out, the practice of dedication broke down the division of economic labor that otherwise obtained between Greek men and women. Comparative evidence indicates that in other religious cultures such sexual division of labor is reinscribed in the ritual context. For instance, Nancy Tapper describes contemporary Islamic practice as encouraging men to make substantial gifts to the mosque and to gain honor and respect thereby, but continues: "Women, by contrast, cannot alienate household wealth to this extent and I know of no mechanisms for women to convert wealth into prestige in this fashion."[138] In contrast, Schaps notes: "It is abundantly clear that the factors that kept [Greek] women from engaging in other economic activities on a large scale never prevented them from dedicating. . . . There was nothing which might not be dedicated by a woman as well as a man."[139] The most characteristic dedications by women of ancient Greece, however, are "feminine" objects such as mirrors and perfume flasks, to which women may have enjoyed a *de facto* if not a *de iure* title.[140] Women also possessed a *de facto* title to their clothing and jewelry,[141] and they often dedicated precisely these things. At Plataea in the second century B.C.E., Heniocha dedicates *ta ep'autes*, "the things on her," indicating perhaps the very jewels (if not the clothes) that she was wearing.[142] The clothes dedicated by women would usually be their own work or that of their slaves, and wool-working instruments are also frequent dedications.[143] The

138. Tapper 1983: 82.
139. Schaps 1979: 71.
140. Rouse 1975: 74.
141. Schaps 1979: 9.
142. Rouse 1975: 74 and 251, citing Richardson (1891), who suggests, however, that "the things on her" signifies that she gave "what she could," i.e., not much.
143. Rouse 1975: 73. He notes that women might dedicate wool itself: e.g., *Rhode lina epi penois*, "Rhode [dedicates] thread on a spool."

garments dedicated at Brauron on behalf of women who died in childbirth obviously could not be offered by the women themselves but formed part of an observance by survivors; Brulé suggests, however, that some garments, particularly those described as "half-finished," were the work of the dead women.[144]

Women's dedications, then, were often closely bound up with their daily lives and their domestic routine. Not all dedications were small and personal, however, even in classical Athens, and on occasion women made dedications that displayed resources comparable to those available to men. At the beginning of the fourth century Kleostrate of Athens dedicated a silver censer weighing 1,300 drachmas (IG ii^2 1388A.24–26 = IG i^3 342). Impressive dedications are recorded on the part of several women who appear in Davies (1971) as members of Athenian propertied families,[145] and fourth-century lists of dedications to Artemis Brauronia include such items as earrings, a seal with a gold ring, a golden ornament with golden chain weighing 2 drachmas, a silver bowl, and a gold ring.[146] On many occasions, male relatives may have funded women's dedications, but this consideration does not detract from—in fact it emphasizes—the extent of female agency in the ritual sphere.[147] Beyond the confines of classical Athens women are found making expensive dedications. Schaps notes the size of the dedications made by women at a temple in Oropus, on the borders of Attica, in the mid-third century (IG vii 303.55ff.).[148] Arete of Megara, in the third century, bought a garden by the sea for 1,000 drachmas and dedicated half of it to Poseidon (IG vii 43). If a woman had some control over her dowry, she might use substantial amounts of it for ritual purposes; Schaps points this

144. Brulé 1987: 230.

145. The women are as follows: Hippylla, wife or daughter of Onetor, who dedicates a mirror to Artemis at Brauron in 475 (APF 421); Polyhippe, sister of Eurumenes of Acharnai, who dedicates to Athena, along with other women, in the early fourth century (before 398/97; APF 205; IG ii^2 1388.27–28 = IG i^3 342); Kleito, the wife of Kimon, who dedicates an ivory lyre in a carved box to Artemis in the early fourth century (before 398; APF 307; IG ii^2 1388.81–82 = IG i^3 342 (= $WLGR$ 403); Iphidike, daughter of Iphikrates, who makes two dedications to Artemis Brauronia (dated to 352/51 and 350/49; APF 251; IG ii^2 1524.65–68 and 72–73); Diophante, wife of Hieronymus of Acharnai, who dedicates to Artemis at Brauron in the mid-fourth century (before 334/35; APF 243; IG ii^2 1523.8); the wife of Kallistratos of Aphidnae, who dedicates a *thorax* (corselet) to Artemis Brauronia (before 334/33; APF 28; IG ii^2 1523.19–20); Malthake, the daughter of Moschos and wife of Leosthenes, who makes two dedications to Artemis Brauronia (before 334/33; APF 343; IG ii^2 1523.27–29); Meidion, wife of Glaukippos, who dedicates to Asklepios in the last quarter of the fourth century (APF 520; IG ii^2 1534.64); and Timothea, wife of Hagnias, who dedicates to Artemis on behalf of her children in the early second century (APF p. 3; IG ii^2 4688).

146. IG ii^2 1388.78–80, 82–83; IG ii^2 1400.41–42, 46, 47, translated as $WLGR$ 403.

147. See, for instance, Rouse 1975: 155, 167, 209, and Pausanias 5.16.3 on dedications by young girls that presumably were not funded by the dedicators themselves.

148. Schaps 1979: 13.

out in the case of Nikesarete of Amorgos, who around 300 dedicated to Aphrodite houses and gardens that were assessed in her dowry.[149] A large dowry, of course, suggests in itself that both natal and marital families were prosperous and had more surplus to be disposed of at discretion, but Schaps also suggests that women were more likely to exert some control over dowries outside classical Athens.[150]

Women give not only objects, whether personal or luxurious, but also sums of money of varying sizes. The women recorded by the inventories of the Athenian Asklepieion give amounts ranging from 1 to 74 drachmas, although single figures are much more prevalent than double.[151] Some inscriptions show Athenian washerwomen tithing their incomes to make dedications (e.g., Smikythe in *IG* ii² 473 = *IG* i³ 794). If we assume, as is most probable, that women who had to earn their own living could not be wealthy, this tithing on the part of poor women could suggest that women who earned any kind of independent income might dedicate some of it.[152] In the Hellenistic period we have records of the bequests of certain widows who were clearly in a position to dispose of exceptional amounts of money. A Theran widow, Argea, left 500 drachmas (*IG* xii 3.329), and the widow Agasigratis of Calauria (modern-day Poros), at the end of the third century, left 300 drachmas to endow biennial sacrifices (*IG* iv 840). Epikteta of Thera left 3,000 drachmas in the early third century to endow a cult of herself and her family (*IG* xii 3.330). She combined her unusual wealth with the power of agency available to her in the ritual sphere to assert herself in a way more readily available to men.

Epikteta's celebration of herself and her family is remarkable, even in the Hellenistic period with its new possibilities, in its refusal of the self-effacing behavior usually commended to Greek women.[153] We may perhaps understand that it was rendered acceptable to her culture by being contained within the ritual sphere.[154] Anecdotes are recounted that attribute women's

149. See Schaps 1979: 85 and *IG* xii 7.57.

150. Such dedications come close to siting these women in the ranks of civic benefactors, or *euergetes,* who were such a feature of the Hellenistic scene. On female benefactors see Gauthier 1985: 74 and the important study by Bremen 1996.

151. Aleshire 1989: e.g., 136.

152. Rouse (1975: 56) also mentions three other tithes by women. Empedia dedicates a tithe on the Athenian acropolis in the early fifth century (*IG* i² 578 = *IG* i³ 767; Raubitschek and Jeffery 1949: 25), Ergokleia dedicates "firstfruits," presumably of labor or produce (*IG* i² 582; Raubitschek and Jeffery 1949: 232), and Glyke (*IG* i³ 548) dedicates a tithe around 480 B.C.E.

153. Such self-effacement was already flouted in the archaic period, however: for instance, when Nikandre of Naxos dedicated a statue around 650 B.C.E with the description of herself as "excellent among others." See Ridgway 1987: 400; Fantham et al. 1994: 19, 36.

154. See Bremen 1983 and 1996 on the related phenomenon of euergetism in Hellenistic Asia Minor, which permitted women to enter the public realm as "benefactresses," while preserving the contours of a respectable feminine identity.

extravagant dedications solely to the motive of personal display, but such anecdotes characteristically attach to *hetairai*. In Herodotos 2.135 Rhodopis, a famous *hetaira* who allegedly wanted to be even more famous, is said to have dedicated one-tenth of her wealth at Delphi, in a calculatedly bizarre form:

> For Rhodopis desired to leave a memorial of herself in Greece, making an offering such as nobody else had thought of and placed in a temple. . . . With a tenth of her money she had made many iron roasting-spits, as many as the tithe would provide, and sent them to Delphi; and they are still there now, piled up behind the altar that the Chians dedicated.

Both in this case and in that of Phryne, an Athenian *hetaira* who dedicated a gold statue of herself at Delphi,[155] the story turns on the anomalous wealth of the *hetaira* and on the paradox of the "public woman" who wants to be still better known. In the face of such undeniable "pleasures of the text" we may well choose to doubt the stories' historicity.

Some historical women do seem to have given money for ritual purposes without any obvious desire for personal aggrandizement. The list of donors for the rebuilding of the temple at Delphi, in 363, includes six women.[156] They are far outnumbered by male individuals and by cities, but that they are there at all seems significant. Their gifts range from 2 drachmas down to 1.5 obols, which, as the editor of the inscription points out, would barely have paid for the cost of inscribing the names. Three of the women come from Phlius, and one each from Selinus, Larisa, and Sparta. None of these women, then, lived anywhere near Delphi; their gifts could not have been motivated by any local feeling. May we conclude that these women gave what they could, motivated by a genuine desire to honor the god? Their status as dedicators allows them to enter an arena of public recognition, the inscription having been raised on the Sacred Way at Delphi, which is more often reserved for masculine endeavors. In Tanagra in Boeotia, in the third century B.C.E., ninety-eight women contributed money to build a temple of Demeter. Paying about 5 drachmas each, they offered a total of 432 drachmas and were each listed in the inscription.[157] In the second half of the third century five women are found in an inscription listing those who contributed to the restoration of statues at the temple of Asklepios in Orchomenos. Leopold Migeotte comments: "Nowhere does one find traces of the

155. See Athenaios 13.591B, Plutarch *Why Are Delphic Oracles No Longer in Verse?* 401, and Hypereides 60.

156. Tod 1985: 2.140. The women are Eurydike of Larisa, Aischylis of Selinus, Philostratis of Lakedaimon, and Kleino, Echenike, and Kleonika of Phlius. It is interesting that in inscriptional contexts women rarely bear the names of their husbands or fathers. See Schaps 1977.

157. Reinach 1899; Migeotte 1992: 75–81; Cole 1994: 216.

preposition hyper, indicating sums offered by heads of household in the name of their dependents. . . . Like the other contributors, certainly all citizens of Orchomenos, these 'citizenesses' subscribed personally, without the intervention of a guardian."[158] Similarly, each of the few women who are listed as contributors to the restoration of Athena's ornaments on Lindos in the late fourth century "has . . . contributed thanks to her own property and has presented herself to the authorities, with the consent of her guardian but without being necessarily accompanied by him."[159] *IG* ii² 12.5, Paros nos. 185 and 186 shows over sixty women in the second century B.C.E. making contributions to rebuilding a temple.[160]

All this activity suggests that women throughout ancient Greece were able to divert household resources to their own projects of self-articulation in the ritual sphere, and that women with resources of their own to dispose of would divert a considerable proportion to ritual activity. Such economic activity can be seen to increase in the Hellenistic period, when there is both more wealth circulating in parts of Greece and also new opportunities for women; but even in the third and second centuries B.C.E., as we have seen earlier, women are still regulated in terms of their public presence and visibility, so that the economic practice cited here remains quite anomalous. Nor is women's expenditure in general limited to dedications and contributions, for they could also draw on household resources for other projects in the ritual sphere. The speaker of Demosthenes *Against Makartatos* (41), for instance, claims that his wife advanced 1 mina of silver on her father's behalf at the Nemesia (11), an otherwise obscure festival.[161] Aristotle *Oikonomika* 1.7.1 suggests that women exercise explicit control over household finances in the ritual sphere; women spend the money on celebrations that men have authorized: "She [the good and perfect wife] should manage the expenses laid out on such festivals as her husband has agreed with her to keep." An even more intriguing testimony to women's economic agency is offered by the neo-Pythagorean text attributed to Phintys that is cited above. "Phintys" discusses *sophrosune* (virtue) under five headings, one of which, as we have seen, is the conditions under which a woman may leave the house. But another heading is "her readiness and moderation in sacrificing to the gods," and "Phintys" goes on to prescribe for respectable women that "they

158. Migeotte 1992: 74.

159. Ibid., 115.

160. But see Migeotte (1992: 142), who doubts this interpretation of the inscription. Migeotte (371–72) sums up on women contributors to public subscriptions, who appear both independently and as dependents, with or without guardians in religious or secular contexts (but more often, as one would expect, the former).

161. On this festival see Deubner 1966: 230. The wife expected to get at least some of this money back from her male relatives.

make modest sacrifices to the gods also, according to their means." Is the text warning against the fault of diverting too many of the household's resources to female self-articulation? If this is a failing prevalent enough to be recognized as such, it suggests that historical women found a form of resistance to their subjected lives in spending money on their own projects, while protecting their activities with the virtuous respectability of the ritual sphere.

Women's expenditures on ritual activity were not exclusively voluntary, because they were also liable to fines. We have already seen that a priestess could be fined for actions committed under her supervision, and that she was fined more than "laypeople." Women who took part in the Andanian Mysteries in the central Peloponnese had to swear that they had upheld marital chastity or be fined (*LSCG* 65).[162] The wife of the fourth-century Athenian politician Lykourgos, who had forbidden women to ride in wagons on processions to Eleusis, was fined 6,000 drachmas when she violated the regulation.[163] Women could be required to spend money on ritual activities too; the Deipnophoroi, for instance, seem to have provided some of the sacrificial victims for the family of the Salaminioi.[164]

On the other hand, men, who always funded the vast majority of ritual projects overall, were on occasion required to spend money on ritual activities performed by their wives or daughters. Such expenditure could be voluntary, as when Meidias allegedly put his carriage and pair of grays at his wife's disposal for the drive to the Mysteries (Demosthenes 21.158). This anecdote is part of Demosthenes' account of his old enemy's arrogant extravagance and designed at least partly for rhetorical effect, but even if we take it as factual, we can be fairly confident that the outlay was as much for the edification of fellow citizens as for the benefit of the wife. Other such expenditure was compulsory. A speech of Lysias (21.5) indicates that the funding of the Arrhephoria constituted a *leitourgia,* or liturgy, a financial service required by the Athenian polis of its wealthier members as a form of taxation. Other liturgies included outfitting warships and producing plays for the festival of Dionysos, comparisons that throw interesting light on this festival. Funding for the Thesmophoria was obtained in an analogous fash-

162. Meyer 1987: 52.

163. Plutarch *Lykourgos* 842A; Aelian *True History* 13.24. The regulation is like other sumptuary legislation directed toward the activities of women in that it is designed to lessen the gulf between ordinary women and the wealthier. It is of course arguable that husbands and fathers paid such fines, as Lykourgos seems to have done in the case of his wife, but we can imagine that there were consequences for the woman concerned.

164. See Ferguson 1938: 6: "Such victims as the state furnishes from the treasury or as the Salaminioi happen to receive from the oschophoroi or the deipnophoroi, these both parties [of Salaminioi] shall sacrifice in common."

ion. The speaker of Isaios 3, prosecuting in a citizenship case where the status of a wife is in dispute, argues that had the wife been legitimate and not a concubine, the husband would have been required to fund the Thesmophoria and give a dinner for the wives of his demesmen (3.80):

> Again in his deme, since his household was worth 3 talents, if he had been married, he would have been compelled by his wedded wife to feast the women at the Thesmophoria, and perform all the other liturgies that are appropriate in the deme on behalf of a wife when one has a fortune of this sort.

The speaker of Menander *Epitrepontes* 749–50 weighs the disadvantages of keeping two households by pointing out that a man in that position would have to pay for two Thesmophoria and two Skira.

These last few examples can remind us that women rarely exercised total autonomy even in the ritual sphere, and that ultimate control of their ritual expenditure, like other aspects of their lives, usually resided with men. Another important conclusion that we can draw from this compulsory expenditure, by men, on women's ritual practices, is that such practices were not only a site for women's self-articulation or the covert resistance suggested by "Phintys" but were also considered highly conducive to the furtherance of male interests. On the other hand, such expenditure on women's rituals may not have figured for itself a female audience at all but may have been aimed primarily at impressing fellow demesmen. Seen in this light, women's ritual activity would constitute not only independent self-articulation on the part of women but also a component in the agonistic culture of Athenian males. In pre-democratic Athens, and doubtless elsewhere, those families with access to ritual office were likely also to be prominent in secular politics, but women's own expenditure and ritual display may not always have been motivated by analogous desires to improve their standing or that of their families;[165] the drives that led them to dedicate money and artifacts may on occasion have been considerably different from those that impelled their male relatives.

The evidence for the economic implications of women's ritual activity is scanty and scattered, like much of the testimony to women's lives, but it offers the conclusion that even in classical Athens, ritual office opened up different economic experiences for a certain restricted number of women who served as priestesses; while outside Athens, and occasionally inside it, women could employ the resources of the household in the ritual context to articulate their own needs and concerns in a way that was hardly available to them in other

---

165. Davies (1971: 369–70, 454) claims that "the old-established units of Athenian politics such as the Boutadai or Bouzygai or Praxiergidai" relied on "cults and phratries" to exercise "effective power," and suggests that Peisistratos overcame his rival of the 570s, Lykourgos, by exerting influence over regional cult organizations as well as over mining interests.

contexts. The possibility of women disposing of extensive amounts of household resources in the ritual context seems to have been present throughout Greek culture in its historical and geographical extent. If the wealth dedicated is not likely to have been the woman's own in any legal sense, as was the case in classical Athens, then large dedications indicate that women could have some control over household resources and could divert them to certain projects of their own. But women's economic activity in the ritual sphere was thoroughly imbricated with that of men, who appear as voluntary donors, as ultimate arbiters of expenditure, and as participants in a competitive culture who could use women's ritual activity as an occasion for their own display. Women's economic activity may be thought to constitute material presence and agency in their most unqualified form, but to the extent of its reference to male projects, the contours of women's economic practice in the ritual sphere can be seen to follow those of their ritual activity in general.

In this chapter we have been recovering the ritual dimension of women's lives in the most immediate way, by reconstructing types of action in their temporal and geographic extent, and by establishing the relations between ritual and domestic work and between ritual and economic practice. Throughout, our chief focus has been on the ways in which women's ritual practice can be seen to complicate the defining parameters of their lives, seclusion in the private realm and exclusion from their culture's arenas of valued endeavor. At the same time, however, we have had to note how the discourse of ritual reinscribes these parameters of female identity on women's lived experience. The ritual dimension of women's lives offers women agency and autonomy and carves out a space in the public visible realm that women may respectably occupy. But the material presence that women thus elaborate within Greek culture does not only constitute a response to women's own wishes and desires; it also engages in mapping out the proper identities to which women should conform, which are always defined in terms of restrictions rather than of unfettered self-articulation. Thus women's ritual activity elaborates connections to the body, to domesticity, and to the nonhuman that cumulatively reinforce women's subordinate status. This multiply signifying action of ritual, with regard to women, is not anomalous in terms of the production and reproduction of social formations; subjects often engage actively in practices that may have as one of their products the denial or diminution of subjectivity, and ideology often explicitly enlists the assistance of those against whose interests it works. The specificities of these processes are what is important in our inquiry. In subsequent chapters we shall build on the material presence and agency that we have been working to construct in order to examine women's ritual activity in its intersection with discourses of sexuality and of politics.

TWO

Ritual Management of Desire

The Reproduction of Sexuality

Certain theorists of women and religion have held that ritual addresses women exclusively on the topics of their sexual and reproductive work. For instance, Judith Hoch-Smith and Anita Spring observe:

> Women draw sacred attention primarily in connection with their reproductive statuses. . . . In no religious system do women's dominant metaphors derive from characteristics other than their sexual and reproductive status. . . . Women are strikingly one-dimensional characters in mythology and ritual action.[1]

I have tried to show, in chapter 1, that ritual may address women in other aspects of their lives; but if we allow that within the ritual sphere sexuality and reproduction do make particular claims on our attention, it still remains to determine what propositions ritual articulates to its female subjects and to the wider community.

Since the work of Freud, the discourse of sexuality has become a powerful tool for explaining subjectivity. Psychoanalytic theory supposes that a viable subject emerges only as the product of repression, that is, of the organizing and sublimating of biological and instinctual drives. Freud's analyses notoriously fail to explain "woman," or to find out what she wants, but various versions of feminist theory have complicated his male-dominated narrative with accounts of the emergence of the female subject. To acquire a subjectivity at all, according to such feminist analysis, entails acquiring a gendered identity, and gender is not only a biological relation but a relation of political power, which in most known societies subordinates the female to

---

1. Hoch-Smith and Spring 1978: 1–2.

the male. The most significant claim made by such accounts, for my purposes, is that in order to achieve adult female status a woman has to become an object as much as a subject; she has to accept and embrace her objectification by the dominant discourses of her culture and internalize a construction of her identity—including but not limited to her sexual identity—that is elaborated in discourses to which she has only limited access and which are imposed on her subjectivity from without. In this connection I shall be drawing particularly on work (such as that of Laura Mulvey and E. Ann Kaplan) that discusses the role of the male gaze in the construction of female identity.[2]

Since they claim to be able to describe societies far removed from one another in terms of historical, geographical, and cultural difference, psychoanalytic theory and feminist revisions of it have in common an assertion of explanatory power. Much of the project associated with Foucault, on the other hand, including the late work on sexuality, was precisely to historicize the notion of the self and to describe its modern, post-Enlightenment manifestation as the product of historically particular intersecting practices and disciplines. Sexual practice was the third of Foucault's major fields of inquiry and led to his studies of the ancient world, *The Use of Pleasure* and *The Care of the Self.* These interventions in classical studies conversely provoked more or less critical responses such as *Before Sexuality,* edited by David Halperin et al., and *Pornography and Representation,* edited by Amy Richlin. These collections seek to fill the gaps left by Foucault's work, by broadening the range of ancient sources on which the work draws and by addressing the construction of women's sexuality in greater depth and detail. Neither collection, however, includes in its focus the ritual practices designed to produce and regulate a sexual or reproductive identity for women.

One of the major drives within Foucault's work on antiquity is to adjust the notion that Greek and Roman cultures were sexually "free," and to show instead that sexual activity was a site of anxious and restrictive practices. His work analyzes the ways in which discourses of sexual pleasure and discourses of power intersect to ensure that each sexual encounter is an arena for elaborate exercises of mastery, incidentally of the other but crucially of the (male) self. Since the male self in the ancient context is endowed with almost untrammeled power over his prospective sexual partners—women, boys, slaves—any restraint that he applies to his own activity is a striking instance and demonstration of his freedom. Women, whatever their social status, are never as free as their prospective male partners and so cannot

2. Mulvey 1989; Kaplan 1983. Fuss (1992) suggests a way to construct an alternative female gaze, and to attribute it to historical females, but even this gaze has other women as its object. See, for example, Bartky 1990 for a contemporary account of the patriarchal male gaze.

indulge in comparably exquisite exercises. Their "freedom" can be articulated only in careful conformity to rules imposed by others, and only to the extent of this conformity can the female self engage in the self-monitoring activity that, according to Foucault's analyses, defines adult male subjectivity. Ideally, and probably often in practice, a married woman's sexuality was governed by a strict and unequivocal legal discourse; as Foucault's account has it,

> The familial and civic status of a married woman made her subject to the rules of a conduct that was characterized by a strictly conjugal sexual practice. It was not that virtue was of no use to women; far from it; but their *sophrosyne* had the role of ensuring that they would manage, by an exercise of will and reason, to respect the rules that were laid down for them.[3]

In this account of women's sexual practice, the self-monitoring capacity extensively elaborated in the adult male is used up in the attempt to observe prohibitions that derive only from external structures.

Many critics have noted, in response to Foucault's work, that the notions of "will" and "reason" are startlingly at variance with Greek representations of female sexuality. If Foucault's insight was to see contemporary subjectivity as the product of historically specific practices and discourses, of which "sexuality" is one, conversely it is also necessary to recognize that the subject's gender identity is itself the product of different discourses, among which we may cite, for example, the legal and medical as well as the religious. In the cultural milieu of ancient Greece we can read the construction of a sexual and reproductive identity for women in several contexts, which share chiefly an anxiety about the female as an excess, in need of constant regulation. Anne Carson (1990) clarifies the contours of a misogynistic discourse, discernible especially in figurative literature such as the poems of Hesiod and Semonides, which characterizes the female as physically insatiable and untiring. Not only does her body, in its different and inferior organization, threaten the male with desiccating exhaustion, but her speech too menaces the social order because of its propensity for prurient gossip and curiosity. The female is most readily identified with the antisocial potential of untrammeled desire; any sexual initiative undertaken by a woman, any pursuit of her own pleasure, must by definition be at the expense of the male-sustained order and constitute an adulterous transgression. The tragic plots generated by the figures of Helen and Klytaimestra delineate the shattering effects of these women's pursuit of their desire; and even conjugal desire, for instance, in the cases of Hermione in Euripides *Andromache* and Medea in her play, may have no less disastrous repercussions.

3. Foucault 1987: 145–46.

Such representations figure autonomous female desire as necessarily transgressive, and model women as perpetually on the brink of adultery. Within a male-dominated system that distributes access to cultural and civic privileges in accordance with strict criteria of legitimacy, the adulterous woman threatens the entire mechanism of inheriting property and political status, and consequently her desire is the primary site for male anxiety and the primary focus for systems of control and supervision. As the subject of her own desire the woman undermines masculine control, and as the object of others' desire she provides a source of unwanted conflict among men. The disproportionate consequences of the adulterous wife's action justify in advance the minute scrutiny of the actions of all wives. Without such supervision, the Greek sources contend, wives will give in to their natural tendency to adultery; the speaker of Demosthenes *Against Neaira* 86 claims that only "enough fear" ensures that women remain prudent *(sophronein)* and "make no mistakes, but keep house lawfully."

The misogynistic tradition in figurative literature is not the only one that may be understood to have conditioned historical men's perceptions of women, and women's of themselves. Authoritative pronouncements on female sexual identity may also be read, for instance, in the medical corpus, which is not so obviously fueled by misogynist anxieties. Women emerge into this discourse, from the Hippocratics of the fifth century B.C.E. to Soranus and Galen of the first and second centuries C.E., because they suffer from infertility or menstrual problems, and their sexual pleasure appears as part of an account of the mechanics of conception. Recent work has clarified the Greek medical writers' notion of female identity; women are figured predominantly as containers, and the sign of excess that governs their sexuality is shifted to the physiological plane, where femaleness is perceived as a problem in the management of liquids such as blood, milk, and semen. What is crucial is "irrigation, retention, and release at the proper time. Fluids exit from the body of the mature woman in quantity far greater than they do from the body of a man."[4] Women overflow every month if their system is not helpfully regulated by pregnancy. Their very flesh is moister than that of men, a property that incidentally renders them sexually inexhaustible. Their porousness is in addition "advanced as an explanation for certain supposedly female dispositions," all of which have a negative charge.[5]

Women's pleasure in sexual intercourse is acknowledged but is carefully delineated as dependent on men's, and, as Ann Ellis Hanson has described, it is to be harnessed and disciplined in the interests of healthy conception and pregnancy.[6] More central to reproductive functioning than sexual plea-

---

4. Hanson 1990: 317.
5. Dean-Jones 1994: 56–57.
6. Hanson 1990: 316.

sure is the womb, which is portrayed throughout the literature as a self-willed organ in search of its own fulfillment independent of the woman it inhabits. If balked for any reason in pursuing its proper occupations, namely conception, pregnancy, and delivery, it sets off through the woman's body in quest of other recompense, causing suffering to the woman. Her perceived physical vulnerability can be understood as the counterpart of the psychic lability alleged to lead her into the transgression of adultery. Therapy for female pathologies, to stabilize the womb and produce proper balance within the woman herself, therefore consists overwhelmingly in the somatic disciplines of menstruation, intercourse, conception, pregnancy, and delivery. Such therapies are never represented, however, outside the context of marriage.

This discourse on the nature of the womb may be read as an indirect acknowledgment or symbolization of the Greek woman's historical situation.[7] Given the cultural impossibility of reaching adulthood without experience of marriage and repeated pregnancies, the Greek woman was constantly subjected to bodily practices over which she exercised limited physical or social control. By a convenient sophistry, her inability to control her own situation is represented as residing in her physical constitution, a consequence of her female identity rather than of her cultural subordination. As Lesley Dean-Jones shows, the biological construct holds up the cultural characterization.[8] Women's work for the maintenance of viable communities is acknowledged in the term *erga gynaikon*, which primarily denotes their childbearing tasks, but the culture's dependence on women's crucial reproductive activity is not perceived as endowing women with any authority over themselves or others.

These two different discourses, figurative and medical, on female sexuality and reproductive work may be taken together to indicate that the female nature of a woman necessarily renders her problematic to herself and others. The solution to the problems posed by female sexual and reproductive identity is ideally constituted by heterosexual, patriarchal marriage, which fully exercises the female need for conception while simultaneously regulating unruly female desire. But this Greek syllogism on the destiny of the female subtends an obvious contradiction. Removing the woman from her natal home and requiring her to identify fully with the interests of her husband's family, patriarchal marriage can fulfill her perceived needs for reproductive health but fails to fulfill those other perceived needs for antisocial self-expression that result in either virginal resistance or unsanctioned sexual activity. The contradiction powers almost all Greek discussion of the ideology of marriage, which constantly urges that marriage is

7. See Dean-Jones 1994: 76 on how the notion of the wandering womb may occasionally have played out to women's advantage.

8. Dean-Jones 1994: 57–58.

good for women and their only thinkable destiny, and conversely that women have to be tamed into marriage, because it is an institution they are naturally disposed to resist. Such "taming" requires a constantly renewed effort on the part of the whole culture, which includes the rituals that this chapter will discuss. A milder version of this discourse of domestication may be read in Xenophon's *Oikonomikos,* where the husband Ischomachos is represented as responsible for all his child-bride's achievements, even down to her ability to store household items in discernible order.

This figure of the "child-bride" points to further considerations. The arithmetic of Greek marriage is uncompromising; contemporary experts rarely recommend an age at marriage of more than eighteen for the woman or less than thirty for the man and seem to approve the scenario of the ignorant fourteen year old delivered up to a husband twice her age. Total cynicism on our part about this arithmetic may not be appropriate; convenient as it may have been for individual Greek males, it was also construed as a necessary compromise with the perceived difficulty of childbirth for older women and with the alleged short span of the female prime.[9] If we accept the recommended scenario, we may conclude that the Greek husband on his wedding night would have been less likely to confront an untamed, dangerous female than one well-trained in the arts of submission. Produced in part by institutions that included the series of rituals that I shall go on to describe, such a wife would already have been tamed, like the bride of Ischomachos whose mother had taught her nothing but *sophrosune* (Xenophon *Oikonomikos* 7.14), and the figure of the dangerous adulteress would be just that—an imaginary figure to be invoked when necessary as one of the disciplinary procedures directed toward the child-bride's subjectivity.

On the other hand, we are not compelled to credit unreservedly the conventional arithmetic that produces this fantasy scenario. Spartan society favored marriages between partners who were only a few years apart,[10] and even Attic vase paintings, particularly of the late fifth century, frequently show weddings between people who appear to be the same age.[11] Vase painting, of course, cannot be simply construed as realistic representation, but we might also note that second marriages, of men or women, do not seem to be attended by a comparable anxiety about ages. Moreover, one Hippocratic text speaks of a *parthenos,* an unmarried girl, who is twenty years of age (*Epidemics* 5.50).

Faced with the contradiction between the dangerous wife, perpetually on the verge of adultery, and the docile child-bride, we may conclude that both

---

9. See on these topics Garland 1990: 213, Carson 1990: 145–48, and Brulé 1987: 355–67.
10. Cartledge 1981; Garland 1990: 213.
11. Sutton 1992: 26.

were symbolic figures, positive and negative paradigms deployed in a discourse of "taming" directed toward historical women. But to characterize such a contradiction as symbolic is not to absolve historical women from the necessity of living it. We can understand this particular contradiction as a version of the "double bind" inflicted on historical women by familiar arrangements such as require for their proper functioning the various figures of the chaste but fertile wife, the supervisor who is entrusted with the running of the household but characterized as "incompetent" in all other spheres of existence, and the partner held responsible for the couple's infertility or failure to produce a son who is nonetheless without power in other aspects of her sexual or reproductive life. Such contradictions usually operate at the expense of the women who must manage them.[12]

No society, however, can function properly if half its population is in a state of unmanageable contradiction, since under such circumstances women's subjection would be bought at too high a price for the community as a whole. Techniques must be developed to produce women who operate successfully within the prescribed parameters, and such techniques will include forms of positive encouragement as well as of negative control. We might consider the possibility that ritual events constituted one important form of positive encouragement, by providing occasions and symbols for managing the kinds of contradictions that I have identified. An important tradition in ritual studies, associated with the work of Victor Turner, identifies rituals as moments of inversion and liminality that, by suspending normal rules of social interaction and so permitting unlimited experiment in social form, allow their cultures to retrieve a sense of unity and homogeneity, or *communitas*, in the dissolution of strict structural hierarchies. Since a dominant structuring hierarchy, in the ancient Greek context, is that of gender, ritual occasions for women, according to this model, might well afford a genuine release from constricting identities. Such a release would enable women not only to perform the rest of their lives more comfortably, because of the respite from those lives, but also to experience a real difference from themselves that could be a sustaining model in other more mundane contexts. Such possibilities may be read in other cultures; work on African cults of spirit possession, for instance, which commonly attract more women than men, has suggested that such ritual experience "serves to open thought, to free it from limitations of prior associations, to pose challenging problems, and encourage reflection on the everyday. . . . [Possession] 'is a powerful medium for unchaining thought from the fetters of hegemonic cultural constructs.'"[13] In such circumstances ritual practice

12. See, for example, Keuls 1985: 124–28, 204–28.
13. Sered 1994: 184, quoting from Janice Boddy, "Spirits and Selves in Northern Sudan: The Cultural Therapeutics of Possession and Trance," *American Ethnologist* 15 (1988) 23.

may undermine patriarchal constructions of gender difference. Women's ritual practice rarely concerns only women's welfare, however, and other comparative studies can reveal the mutually reinforcing dynamics between the prescriptions of religion and the requirements of patriarchal culture. A recent cross-cultural study of contemporary religious practice suggested that the constructions of gender undertaken in the religious sphere are most effective in the continued subordination of women; "without reinter-pretations of scripture and tradition, most projects attempting to ameliorate woman's status [will] stop short of their objectives."[14]

The figure of "contradiction," which I have brought into play to describe Greek discourses of marriage, raises a third possibility, namely that ritual forms of action will function as mediation, along the lines of the model pro-posed by Lévi-Strauss for myth. While it certainly seems to be the case that few of the rituals I shall describe can be discussed without reference to asso-ciated myths, and that therefore they are available for analysis along these lines, I shall nonetheless offer a possible objection to a theory of mediation at the outset. While myths and rituals may perform mediation of contradic-tion for a culture, understood as a more or less coherent whole, our focus here is women, who are rarely coterminous with the culture they inhabit. Such contradictions as I have isolated are not problems for patriarchal cul-ture, but its necessary concomitants; and while the individual historical woman may experience herself as the recipient and site of conflicting mes-sages, the contradiction itself is in a sense already solved, elsewhere, and at her expense. The rituals that are the focus of this chapter may be under-stood to enforce the contradictions on their female subjects as much as to mediate or manage them.

Ritual representations of women's sexual and reproductive identities cannot be fully accounted for without reference to other discourses such as the figurative and the medical outlined above. On the other hand, the rit-ual sphere does not simply reflect the construction of gender that is under-taken in other spheres, but actively participates in it. The examination of women's ritual activity in this chapter falls broadly into two parts, those rit-uals addressed to unmarried women, or *parthenoi,* and those addressed to adult women, *gynaikes.* In both parts I shall emphasize how ritual works to produce a certain kind of subjectivity within its participants by extending to them certain kinds of identifications. The process is complex because such identifications are often contradictory. For instance, young girls are repre-sented by ritual process as desirable objects of erotic display, but ritual events are also a site of anxiety about the possibility of women's subjective desires. For adult women, this contradiction translates into a series of posi-

14. Becher 1990: ix.

tions on a spectrum of chastity and license that they occupy successively over
the ritual year. Some such identifications implicitly challenge the normative
construction of female adulthood and thus render the rituals for adult
women particularly vulnerable to dissenting or oppositional interpretations
that might be mounted by the women who perform them. I shall also suggest that the very repetitiousness of ritual events might enable historical
women to develop resistant accounts of the activities in which they participated. The chapter will close with a survey of other versions of female sexual identity that are of interest to ritual discourse, such as the adulteress, the
virgin, the postsexual older woman, and the prostitute. The focus of the
majority of the sources is classical Athens, but it will be apparent that
Athenian rituals have parallels in other communities.

THE CHORUS

In order to minimize the possibility of premarital sexual experience, parents who could afford to do so closely guarded and supervised their daughters in nearly all Greek communities. Yet at the same time as the *parthenoi,*
or unmarried girls, were carefully secluded in the domestic environment,
they were also publicly displayed on ritual occasions. The ritual dialectic of
concealment and display may be considered as one of the disciplines for-
mative of the young girl's subjectivity and of her sense of sexual identity. In
many communities, ritual display of *parthenoi* was undertaken by the institution of the chorus. This institution was first subjected to a thorough study
by Claude Calame, whose insights have rightly passed into received wisdom.
While the chorus is most commonly associated with the archaic period and
with Dorian societies, it is attested throughout the historical and geographical span of Greek culture. In the most prominent celebrations of classical
Athens, however, girls' choruses do not appear as often as boys' and men's,
and, moreover, the choral tradition as a whole seems to have been over-
shadowed by the development of the dramatic festivals. Where girls' choruses were active, they convened on public occasions to dance and sing the
community's significant myths, and they also seem to have sung at weddings.
Pollux *Onomastikon* 3.42 has a chorus of girls singing outside the new couple's bedroom door, allegedly in order to drown the bride's cries.

It is arguable, however, that the primary function of the chorus was that
of erotic display, producing readiness for fruitful marriage in both females
who perform and males who watch. In Plutarch *Virtues of Women* 249 this
sexual motive is explicitly attributed to the practices of Keos: "It used to be
the custom of the maidens of Keos to go together to the public temples, and
to pass their days together. Their suitors would watch them playing and
dancing." To Lykourgos, the Spartan lawgiver, is attributed the practice of
having young girls exercise, dance, and sing in athletic nudity or seminudity,

under the gaze of young men (Plutarch *Lykourgos* 14.2). As befits a prescriptive rather than descriptive text, Plato's *Laws* goes the whole way in the eroticization of the chorus. Discussing marriage, the text provides for the arousal of desire in both sexes (6.772):

> To this end we must hold games with boys and girls dancing together, both at the same time looking and looked at, within reason, and when their age offers plausible excuses, both naked, so long as all display modesty and restraint.

Conditioned by admiration for the Spartan system, Plato's proposal is perhaps more revolutionary for its assumption of reciprocity in the gazes of the youthful choristers. Both girls and boys, allegedly, will see and be seen. While male and female choruses may have met, and engaged in mutual inspection, at weddings and at other celebrations, the most common context of the girls' chorus seems to have been the display of young women to men, prospective grooms and fathers-in-law.[15]

Certain choral poems to which we have access seem to arise directly from this situation of female display. In the *Partheneion* of Alkman, from seventh-century Sparta, the young women speakers of the song, who use the first person, single out various women among the chorus who are making the dedication and describe their beauty. Agido and Hagesichora are the most striking, possessed of faces like the sun and hair like precious metal; the other women, such as Nanno, Areta, Sylakis, and Cleesisera, although lovely, are dismissed from comparison. The speakers state explicitly that no one would ask for them in preference to Hagesichora (39–91):

> But I sing of Agido's light. I see her like the sun . . . but the hair of my cousin Hagesichora shines like unmixed gold. And her silver face—why should I say more? Here is Hagesichora. . . . There is not enough store of purple to defend us, nor sparkling snake all of gold, nor Lydian headband, adornment of young girls with soft eyes; nor Nanno's hair, no nor Areta who is like the gods; not Sylakis and Cleesisera. You wouldn't go to Aenesimbrota's house and say: let Astaphis come to me; may Philylla look at me, and lovely Damareta and Ianthemis—but Hagesichora excites me . . . from Hagesichora young girls have come to lovely peace.

---

15. Pindar *Pythian* 9.96–100 offers a rare example of a female gaze, scoping out the athletic victor with an eye to marriage:

> They often saw you win
> In the seasonal contests of Pallas,
> And they prayed silently, each of the girls,
> That you might be their beloved husband
> Or son, Telesikrates.

However, this ode is, as Nisetich (1980: ad loc.) notes, eroticized throughout, so that this moment may be considered overdetermined.

The main problem in interpreting this part of the *Partheneion* has been to determine the relations, institutional or erotic, among the various female figures who are invoked.[16] Calame holds, on the basis of a perceived analogy with Sappho, that Hagesichora is the *choregos,* or chorus-leader, with the speaking name ("chor"), and that Agido is her beloved; D. L. Page had already identified Agido as a "Second-in-Command."[17] For Calame, both are slightly older than the other chorus members, ripe for marriage, and they perform a ritual designed to mark, in the presence of the assembled community, their exit from the process of initiation characterized by participation in the chorus.[18] It is not clear, however, how Hagesichora will leave the chorus and practice as an adult woman if she is in fact the *choregos,* a position that Calame characterizes as requiring the incumbent to be not only of high social status and personal beauty but also the same age as the other chorus-members and hence a lasting part of the chorus.[19] There is some insecurity throughout Calame's account of the *choregos,* depending on whether she or he is seen as primarily a leader of the chorus or primarily a trainer,[20] but at several points in his text Calame writes more productively of the *function* of the *choregos,* which may be divided among a plurality of performers.[21] On this reading a less rigid distinction is in operation than that which would divide the *choregos* from all the other participants in the choral process. Calame points, for instance, to the position of first *choreute,* who occupies the first place in the chorus line and who may assist the *choregos* in the performance of her duties:

> The figure of the *choregos* can be duplicated in her role of leader of the choral group by the young girl who occupies the first place in the line that the chorus forms. It seems then, as the iconographical sources essentially indicate, that the *choregos,* male or female, could receive some assistance in the leadership of the chorus on the part of the first *choreute.*[22]

If in fact the chorus aims, through sexual display, at marriage, the hierarchies within it will have to be fluid, in conformity with the less rigid versions

16. The chief discussions are Page 1951, Calame 1977, Nagy 1990, and Stehle 1997. I reached my conclusions independently of Stehle but am glad to find that where our interests overlap we agree.

17. Calame 1977: 2.94–95; Page 1951: 46.

18. Calame 1977: 2.100–104.

19. E.g., Calame 1977: 1.140–43, 2.142.

20. See, for example, Calame 1977: 1.121 and 396 on Andaesistrota in Pindar's *Daphnephorikon.* At one point Calame says that the *choregos* is a contemporary of the other *choreutes,* but exerts a pedagogic function (1.125); but if she or he is to teach the chorus, then by definition she or he cannot leave it.

21. E.g., Calame 1977: 1.137–39.

22. Calame 1977: 1.143.

of Calame's model, because at some more or less unforeseen point, and in more or less unforeseen order, all its members will start to disappear.

It seems plausible that the designated women in Alkman's *Partheneion*, Agido and Hagesichora, are singled out in the context of a less rigid organization than that indicated by the position of *choregos*, and particularly that they are singled out in the context of the marriage for which the choral exercises provide a propaideutic.[23] While the positions of poet, chorustrainer, and musician will probably have to be filled by the same specialist for a number of years, that of the chorus-leader, who sings and dances most prominently because she is about to leave the chorus, is available for transmission among the various chorus-members in turn so that each girl successively occupies the locus of praise. In the present song Hagesichora and Agido are celebrated as lovely and talented not only because they lead the chorus but also because they are the members of the chorus who will next be wed; and more to the point, the designation "lovely and talented" applies to them because of their impending marriages.

We may cite in this context a possible reading of Athenaeus *Deipnosophists* 6.646. Here, during a discussion of cakes, a *kribanas* is defined as "a cake like a breast, carried round by Spartans at dinners given for women, whenever the girls who follow in the chorus are ready to sing the hymn of praise prepared for the *parthenos*." The *parthenos*, or unmarried girl, may be understood as the virgin goddess, that is, Artemis; but if we understand her as a human girl on the brink of marriage, we have a possible context for the chorus bidding farewell to each of its members in turn.[24]

The speakers of Alkman's *Partheneion*, who are commonly understood to be the remaining members of the chorus (Nanno, Areta, and the rest), complain that they are not nearly as lovely or talented as Agido and Hagesichora. They are young girls—not yet ready for marriage—and they "shriek" like owls instead of singing beautifully.[25] Their self-denigration is combined with the articulation of erotic desire for the chorus-leaders; Hagesichora both excites (*teirei*, 77) and satisfies them (*eirenas*, 91).[26] It is of course possible that the female members of the chorus are here giving voice to their own homoerotic desire, but I would like to stress instead the possible significance of a

23. Stehle (1997: 32) interprets all the chorus members as potential brides.

24. The novel of Xenophon of Ephesos depicts a meeting between choruses of young men and women that results in simultaneous group marriage (1.2), a very different arrangement from that proposed here, but such group marriage is not attested in other Greek sources.

25. On the trope of the chorus's self-denigration see now Stehle 1997: chap. 2 passim.

26. Stehle (1997: 86) suggests another, less erotically charged peace: "By virtue of this lack [of authorization or power], they will enter into peace, that is, be fruitful within the structures of the social system." Following Campbell 1982, some editors have concluded that *teirei* (excites/wears out) should be read as *terei* (guards). "Either or both versions suggest that some erotic affiliation exists between the two leaders of the chorus, or between leaders and choreutes, and/or between members of the chorus" (Wilson 1996: 122).

male poet providing these words to the chorus members. In the context of display of marriageable women to men, the chorus sings of certain women in terms at least as appropriate to the articulation of male desire as to that of their own. Calame suggests that the chorus sings of the desire between Hagesichora and Agido; in this reading the chorus is not singing of heterosexual desire, as I suggest, but it is still singing of desire not its own.[27] I suggest that young women in a historical chorus, singing of desire for the chorus-leaders, would be learning to internalize a male gaze directed first on the most prominent members of the chorus and then by analogy on themselves.[28] John Berger's formulation is perennially useful in this context:

> A woman must continually watch herself. . . . Men look at women. Women watch themselves being looked at. This determines not only most relations between men and women, but also the relation of women to themselves. The surveyor of woman in herself is male, the surveyed female. Thus she turns herself into an object.[29]

By singing the male poet's words that implicitly make them subjects of desire, the chorus members can be seen to learn to accept themselves as objects of desire. This internalized objectification will position each young woman to play her proper role in marriage and reproduction.

The gaze that the girls claim in their song as their own, but that I would understand as an internalized male gaze, will pick out each girl in turn as she leaves the chorus and enters marriage. The *Partheneion* can be understood as a metonymy of this process, which will eventually dissolve the chorus and send the girls each to preside over her own *oikos*. The chorus in fact has only discharged its responsibilities when it is fragmented and no longer convenes a collectivity.[30] By the trope of the *choregos* or first *choreute,* more beautiful and accomplished than the others, each girl can successively occupy a specially favored position and experience herself as addressed with this particular seductive flattery.[31]

27. Calame 1977: 2.138. Without invoking the gaze, Williamson shows how "the love they express . . . , far from being unique to any one of them, is a mark of [the leader's] desirability, and hence her readiness for the destiny that awaits them all. . . . Even apparently personal expressions of desire can, in some context, function as conventional praise of a girl who is readying herself for marriage" (1995: 121, 125).

28. This male gaze, or male point of view, is important also to Stehle 1997 (see particularly 37 and 77). Skinner (1996: 187) writes that the girls "present themselves as unsuspecting objects of heterosexual desire."

29. Berger 1977: 46–47.

30. The chorus as an institution will persist, because replenished with new girls, but the group in which any one girl sang and danced will eventually be no more.

31. There is, then, no need for "Hagesichora" and "Agido" to be the real names of real people; they can instead be titles of positions in the chorus. Nagy (1990: 347) paves the way for this conclusion when he suggests that "Agido and Hagesichora are characters in a sacred mimesis,

Corresponding to the fragmenting function of the chorus is the literary trope of the scene in which the young girl, surrounded by companions or maids, is surprised by sex. While the most compelling version of this scene is that in the *Homeric Hymn to Demeter,* striking instances may also be read in Nausikaa's encounter with Odysseus, Aphrodite's with Anchises in the *Homeric Hymn to Aphrodite,* and Medea's with Jason in book 3 of the *Argonautica.* Although we do not have to conclude that this literary tradition was explicitly addressed to young women, we can say that it intersected with a parallel tradition of ritual teaching that was so addressed. The literary scene singles out one girl from the choric context but does not dwell on the maids or friends, who do not have the chance successively to occupy the favored position of *choregos* or first *choreute.* Instead, their task is to be less attractive, less poised, or simply less aristocratic than the one young woman whose fate is at issue. In its choric contours the literary scene is not necessarily making a concession to the accurate representation of female youth; it seems instead that both the institution of the chorus and the trope of the virgin with her companions point to a social perception of young girls as amorphously collective, differentiated momentarily when they are each at the point of becoming wives.

Apart from the account that centers on Persephone, the various versions of the literary trope attribute to their leading female figures a surprising extent of sexual knowledge and knowingness. Nausikaa has already been brought by Athena into a marrying frame of mind, and her response to Odysseus is plainly conditioned by an interest that is physical. Her discourse is also formed by the countervailing pressure of youthful female modesty, so that it is ultimately rendered incoherent (*Odyssey* 6.240–45):

> It is not against the will of all the gods who hold Olympos
> That this man is made acquainted with the godlike Phaiakians.
> At first he seemed to me of no account.
> Now he resembles one of the gods, who hold high heaven.
> If only the man to be called my husband could be such a one,
> a man living here, if only this one could be pleased to stay here.

The object of Nausikaa's desire is here successively Odysseus, a man like Odysseus, a man like Odysseus who is a Phaiakian, and Odysseus himself happily transformed into a Phaiakian. Aphrodite, of course, simply lies to Anchises about how she comes to manifest herself on his particular stretch of hillside, invoking the full scenario of virginal innocence in order to pros-

---

through the ritual of choral performance, of the cult figures." The names are "ritual" names, denoting roles that different girls take in the performances of the poem, rather than referring to any historical women. Nagy, however, ties the "ritual names" to the particular "cult figures" of the Leukippides, while I offer a less specific reading in terms of preparation for marriage.

ecute her distinctly carnal agenda. Medea's scene, although from a much later work, is not so very different; the heroine carefully composes herself and her companions into the Persephone-drama in order to await the arrival of Jason. Unfortunately for Medea, her control of the encounter does not extend beyond this preliminary staging, so that her discourse, like her characterization, dissolves into incoherence as she veers from authoritative witch to lovesick girl.

The manipulative skills of these prominent young women can be read as a sign of a generalized anxiety over autonomous female desire, but there may be additional significance in the choric context.[32] For historical women, the chorus was often, I have suggested, the first site for ritual display of their youth and beauty and consequently provided the first location for the management of desire, whether of self or others. Here the young women learn to internalize the male gaze that can be seen as central to the development of female subjectivity; but since the gazes attracted by the ritual display of young women may be either sanctioned and preparatory to marriage, like those described by Plutarch and Plato, or unsanctioned, like those that figure at the genesis of many erotic narratives when the heroine is discerned by the lover in a procession or other ritual event, the chorus members must also learn to discriminate among the possible varieties. As Artemidorus *Interpretation of Dreams* 1.26 puts it, "For . . . a woman in the bloom of her youth, to have many eyes is unlucky. For . . . many would-be seducers will be observed around [her]." In the management of the gaze, enforced and dramatized by the ritual occasion, the young women must also learn to guard their own gazes, so as not to unleash the destructive force of female desire into the unsuspecting community. They must avoid the fate of Phaidra, the extent of whose transgression can be gauged by the fact that *she* sees Hippolytos, not the other way round, at the Mysteries (Euripides *Hippolytos* 24–28). Entrusted by the chorus with the management of their own and others' desire, the young women are endowed with a responsibility for erotic discrimination that attributes to them potentially alarming authority over their own position. The dangerously sophisticated conduct of Aphrodite and Medea constitutes one response to this task of sexual discernment.

Figuring young women as subjects of desire, but inculcating the lesson that their proper goal is to be objects, the choral institution elaborates what we might call a double discourse of both pleasure and fear. This is especially the case with songs in the epithalamic genre, which were probably sung by choruses during wedding celebrations. It is a commonplace that the epithalamion represents marriage, for the woman, not only as a misfortune

---

32. This is not to say that other dynamics are not at play in the various scenes analyzed.

entailing physical suffering and separation from family and friends, but also as an honorable reward for her beauty and talents and as a promise of respect and dignity to follow. This contradiction presented itself to each young woman as a problem requiring negotiation, but also as the route to the status of adult womanhood that she must embrace. Marriage is inevitable, but a hardship; marriage is a hardship, but it is also an occasion for praise of the bride's personal qualities and appearance. To put it another way, the inevitable hardship of marriage, for the woman, necessitates that she be reconciled to it by a representation of its pleasures. To the extent that she collaborates in this representation, by her work in the chorus, she can be seen to enact a kind of consent to her own subordination in patriarchal marriage. Consent to a particular partner is not at issue, since women rarely possessed the legal right of disposition of their own persons,[33] and strictly speaking there is no issue of consent to the institution of marriage, since the woman is presented with no alternative. But despite this uncompromising situation, it seems to me, ritual events work to elicit from young women an enacted consent, and thus to manage the underlying contradiction, claimed by Greek gender ideology, between autonomous female desire and patriarchal marriage.

So far I have relied for my description of the chorus on the model that posits a male poet, who himself provides an instance of the male gaze while also furnishing a script for the female articulation of desire. But another model available to us, through certain interpretations of the extant poetry of Sappho, is that of the girls' chorus headed by a female poet who provided the songs and trained the female performers.[34] Sappho's poetry in fact offers no unambiguous clues as to its social context, and in the wake of Holt Parker's critique (1993), commentators have been very cautious as to what social role they assign to the singer of her songs. Lyn Wilson will only go so far as to remark that "whatever the purpose or orientation of the Sapphic

33. Even the heiress at Gortyn, who may dispose of her own person, may do so only if there are no eligible male relatives, or if they choose not to marry her (Law Code of Gortyn cols. VII.50–52, VIII.10–12, 19–20 (= Willetts 1967: 45–46).

34. Calame 1977: 1.396; see also Calame 1996. Lardinois (1994 and 1996) restates, in the context of Parker's 1993 critique, the position that the Sapphic corpus emerges from a choral context. While Parker's reexamination of the sources is timely and provocative, it seems to suffer from assumptions similar to those that it attributes to the other side(s) of the debate. For instance, the assumption that homosexuality among women would not take the form of pederasty, because it would not be structured along lines of unequal power, seems to be in danger of devolving into the proposition that women are nice and lesbians nicer. I also find it anachronistic to suppose that any historical Sappho was a "poet pure and simple" when this construct comes laden with the cultural ideals of the early nineteenth-century Romantic period. It should be possible to retain some notion of a pedagogic context within a choral framework without inflicting on ancient Greece a rash of finishing schools.

community, the co-coordination of its members into some form of collective association that sang, prayed, celebrated, grieved and perhaps loved together, seems indisputable.[35] Eva Stehle suggests that the poetry evokes three separate scenarios for composition and performance, which "choral" or "initiatory" theories try erroneously to synthesize; only one scenario involves *parthenoi,* whom Stehle identifies as performers of Sappho's wedding poetry.[36] Other critics see more emphasis in the corpus on the marriageability of young women. Judith Hallett suggests that Sappho was a "poet with an important social purpose and public function: that of instilling sensual awareness and sexual self-esteem and of facilitating role adjustment in young females coming of age in a sexually segregated society."[37] Margaret Williamson concludes that "there is quite a bit of evidence to support the idea of a link between Sappho's poetry and parthenoi" and continues: "There is good reason to think that religious ritual and the initiation of maidens both figured prominently among the occasions that brought them [Sappho and her female audience] together."[38] If we accept the possibility that some of the Sapphic songs concern the formation of subjectivity in marriageable young females, even if not within the institution of an actual chorus, the homoerotic nature of many of the songs may have to modify our account of the chorus so far.

How might the homoeroticism of the Sapphic songs prepare young women for normative heterosexual alliances? As part of an answer we might point to the Sapphic community's apparent consciousness of its own mortality; many of the songs, while celebrating female companionship, acknowledge its fragility in the face of other forces that separate women from one another. If these songs are understood to refer to the prospect of marriage, the repeated insistence on its inevitability may be construed as a means of reconciling young women to the prospect. Similarly, although the primary play of gazes in the songs seems to be among women, the Sapphic chorus is not oblivious to the male gaze that I have characterized as crucial to the self-definition of female choruses.[39] Usually, however, the male gaze is invoked only to be dismissed. We might cite particularly fragment 31, in which an unnamed man *(keinos)* is represented as sitting opposite the beloved and listening to her, but is quickly replaced in the dynamics of the poem by the (presumably female) speaker, who experiences far more dramatic reactions to the beloved than the apparently stolid *keinos.* Similarly, an implied male

35. Wilson 1996: 121.
36. Stehle 1997: 276.
37. Hallett 1996: 128.
38. Williamson 1995: 80, 84.

39. Stehle (1990: 107–8) argues that the gaze in Sapphic poetry avoids or breaks down the opposition between viewer and viewed, thereby dissolving the customary hierarchies.

gaze in fragment 16 stares at troops of infantry, cavalry, or ships, and has no idea that desire is a far more powerful force. The relationships among the members of the Sapphic community are thrown into greater relief by the "background hum" produced by those male-dominated arrangements that ultimately determine their destinies.[40]

It is conceivable that the Sapphic community, if such there was, prepared for marriage not only by inculcating its inevitability but by training young women in the possibilities of physical pleasure. That the poems of the Sapphic corpus concern pleasure given and received among women seems extremely probable from lines such as 94.21–23, "And on a soft bed . . . you satisfied your desire," despite renewed efforts at bowdlerization such as those by François Lasserre.[41] While not supposing that the exchange of physical pleasure among women would necessarily be preparation for enjoyment of a heterosexual partnership, we might imagine that a knowledge of and acquaintance with their own bodies would in and of itself equip young women to operate within marriage with greater confidence.

We should also consider the possibility that homoerotic pleasure among women provided a paradigm completely independent from marriage and a locus of resistance to, or at least dissent from, institutional heterosexuality. Highly suggestive in this context is John Winkler's work, which argues not only for a complex of clitoral and labial imagery in Sapphic poetry but also for its dynamic function in the exploration of a whole world separate from male-dominated culture.[42] Imagery of female sexual pleasure is part of what Winkler calls Sapphic "double consciousness"; it functions in her poetry as a crucial component of the representation of women within male culture, and for a historical woman, Winkler suggests, remembrance of the imagery of female-centered pleasure could serve to strengthen her subjectivity even if she was separated from her female partners and isolated inside a patriarchal marriage.

In the present understanding of sexual politics, homoerotic desires are commonly construed as exclusive of heterosexual attractions, but this was not the case with Greek representations of male homoeroticism, which was considered as a suitable prelude to heterosexual marriage. Foucault and others have mounted the argument that ancient sexual ideology as a whole addressed itself to practices rather than to persons, and consequently that sexual preference was not considered determinative of the subject's total identity. While ancient Greek culture clearly did construe sexual activity along lines of force different from those familiar to early twenty-first-century Western societies, the converse of the above statement does not hold; the

40. See Skinner 1996: 187.
41. E.g., Lasserre 1989: 137.
42. Winkler 1990a: 180–87.

subject's total identity as a woman, for instance, does dispose her, in Greek representations, to prefer the passive role. In general, however, the loose fit in Greek discourse between gender identity and sexual practice makes it probable that female homoeroticism could be construed as consistent with marriage as the final goal, or *telos,* of women's lives, and to this extent sexual pleasure among women does not necessarily constitute resistance or dissent, because it is not alternative to or exclusive of heterosexual patriarchal marriage. Incapable of producing the illegitimate sons who definitely do undermine the mechanisms of patriarchal inheritance, such pleasure need not be considered as any kind of menace to the system. Modern commentators agree that when ancient sources register a threat from female homosexuality, it is because within such partnerships women are perceived to act like men and thus to contravene the cultural norms that allot to women passivity and subjection.[43] This objection to homosexual intercourse among women is well documented in Greek and also Roman sources.[44]

If the Sapphic poems are generated within a choral context, their homoerotic focus does not necessarily contradict the requirement that young women within such contexts be prepared for heterosexual, patriarchal marriage. Where we can say that the Sapphic community does articulate a form of dissent to patriarchal arrangements is in its consistent valuation of relationships among women. This "chorus" does not look forward to the moment of its own dissolution; instead it looks back, constantly retrieving paradigms of female companionship and projecting them forward as consolations for those women who have had to leave its embrace. The description of the physical beauty of women is not rehearsed for the benefit of a figured male audience, as it may be in Alkman's *Partheneion,* but is evoked as

43. Presumably the logical conclusion is that there could be no objection to the "passive" partner in a homosexual encounter between women. See Winkler 1990a: 39–40 and Brooten 1985.

44. Other grounds for complaint are not so prevalent. For instance, Artemidoros's *Interpretation of Dreams* registers far more distaste for dreams of fellatio and cunnilingus than it does for dreams of (what we would call) lesbian intercourse. This text is very late, dating as it does from the second century c.e., but significantly it exhibits few contradictions with earlier material. The interpretation of such dreams, when dreamed by a woman, runs as follows: "If a woman dreams that she penetrates another woman, she will share her secrets with the woman she has penetrated. But if she does not know the woman whom she penetrates, she will attempt pointless enterprises. But if a woman dreams that she is being penetrated by another woman, she will be divorced from her husband or widowed. She will learn the secrets of the woman with whom she has had sexual intercourse no less" (1.80). "Lesbian" dreams are thus not necessarily interpreted as signs of transgressive desire or hostility to men; they touch instead on women's relations to their husbands or on their nonsexual acquaintance with other women. Relations among women are characterized *(a)* by no obvious difference in age between the women concerned but *(b)* by emphatic inequalities in power, achieved by the learning of secrets.

part of the scenario of remembrance and consolation. A particular kind of premarital experience is valued apparently for itself, and not only for the goal to which it leads. On the other hand, it is perhaps chiefly that externally imposed *telos* that bestows the particular, fragile value on the experience of female companionship.[45]

Choruses of young women, trained by women or by men, prepared their members for marriage in various ways. I have focused on the chorus's representation of marriage as inevitable, charged with the dual weight of pleasure and fear, but the chorus also had other dimensions, which correspond broadly to the contours of women's ritual activities as discussed in the previous chapter. The physical activity of dancing and singing might itself provide a source of pleasure to the female; dancing was a feature of all choral events, and in many Greek communities girls also engaged in other physical activity under the aegis of the chorus. At Elis in the Peloponnese, for instance, the Sixteen Women organized two choruses, named for Hippodameia and Physkoa, and at the festival for Hera they also organized races for the unmarried girls, divided into three age classes (Pausanias 5.16.2–3, 5.16.6). Spartan girls engaged extensively in physical training, as Plutarch and Xenophon variously report (*Lykourgos* 14.2, *Constitution of the Lakedaimonians* 1.4) . Plutarch's account ties such activity directly to the production of healthy children:

> He made the girls work on their bodies . . . in order that their children might take root with a strong beginning in vigorous bodies and might grow better, and that they themselves might go through pregnancy with strength, and struggle well and successfully with the birth pains.

Even very late sources register the health-giving qualities of choral activity; in the second century C.E. Rufus of Ephesus recommends song and dance in a choral context as a means of preparing the young female body for pregnancy and delivery without rendering it masculine and concludes that "choruses were not invented just for the honor of the deity, but also for the purpose of health."[46] That health was not the only result of choral activity, however, is pointed out by the Hippocratic text *Diseases of Women* (2.138), which notes that dancing can figure among the causes of miscarriage. Since here the dance seems to be an activity that could be carried to excess, by married women, even if not by the unmarried who are at present our primary concern, this note may be an indication that the chorus was a source of pleasure and a site for the exercise of female autonomy.

Despite these possible representations of female initiative, the choral

---

45. I shall investigate particular ritual figures in the poetry of Sappho in chapter 4.

46. *peri parthenon diaites* in Oribasius (ed. Raeder) IV pp. 107–8.

institution is primarily concerned with the control of female bodies and with their submission to the project of patriarchal marriage. The young women's sexual identity, as future mothers responsible for the reproduction of the community, necessitates the massive ideological effort that will teach the chorus members the management of desire in the subordination of their own projects to those of others. To this extent we can say that the women's gender identity supplies them with access to ritual activity, which as we have seen may be considered a reward for the proper performance of female identity, as well as a means for ensuring that performance. The relation between women's gender identity and their ritual activity is that of a dialectic, however, because the ritual practice also gives them access to their sexuality by constructing it for them. Not to be overlooked is a further relation into which young women enter by means of their ritual practice in the chorus. Attending as a chorus at the community's important functions and singing its shared myths and legends, the young women are inserted fully into the history and culture of their community, and to the extent of their ritual participation are neither marginalized nor excluded. We can argue that they are fact included and at the center, if we accept that on certain choral occasions the recounting of shared history and the reproduction of cultural identity are entrusted to the voices of young girls. Calame stresses, rightly, the pedagogic aspect of the chorus and notes that "it is by this means that adolescent girls, like ephebes, assimilate the mythic and ethical patrimony of their city."[47] But it is equally important, I would contend, to conceive of the chorus as offering to the community a representation of its traditions and values; the chorus is not only the object of the city's pedagogic efforts but also adopts a subject position whereby it may contribute to the city's discourse.[48]

The chorus, as pointed out above, was characteristic primarily of archaic and Dorian cultures. Little testimony on the chorus derives from Athens, which does, however, afford fragmentary accounts of other rituals for young women. Although our best evidence for these emanates from classical Athens, it is likely that similar rituals were known in other parts of Greece. According to Christiane Sourvinou-Inwood's research into the representation of women's ages,[49] the ritual sphere took an active interest in the female from an early age, and the years approximately seven to fourteen were available for extensive mobilization in ritual practice. Although a famous passage of Aristophanes' *Lysistrata* seems to claim that one woman could and would

47. Calame 1977: 1.410.

48. On this relation between chorus and community see also Stehle 1997. Such a relation would be especially important in the case of, for instance, the standing chorus of women, called Deliades, on Delos. On these see Stehle 1997: 110; Bruneau 1970: 35–38.

49. Sourvinou-Inwood 1988b.

fulfill all the ritual roles allotted to this age group, critics agree that this is likely to be a dramatic exaggeration and that there would not have been such an overlap among roles. What is significant, however, is the proliferation of ritual for this age group, even at Athens where the female career was not as elaborated as in many Dorian societies. This very proliferation suggests that none of these rites was an initiation or a rite of passage—none of them achieved any alteration in the status of the *parthenos* concerned.

Instead of achieving a modification of her status, all the ritual work on the young woman is in preparation for the marriage which *is* able to alter her status and to produce her as an adult wife and mother. Ritual works to obtain from the young woman what Calame calls her full assent, her "pleine acceptation," to the role of wife and mother.[50] The actual modification of the "untamed" young female into wife and mother, the move from virgin *parthenos* to adult *gyne*, is accomplished not by ritual gestures but by the defining somatic events of defloration and delivery, both of which are figured in Greek terms as the "loosening of the belt." Whereas a male achieves majority by being inserted into a legal and political order, the transition to adult female identity is accomplished in the unseen domestic setting of bodily history. Prefiguring that history, rituals of preparation for marriage offer to young women many different signs, among which they must find their way, of the correct female identity that they will eventually inhabit.

The choral model obtains in several of these rites of preparation, in that the young girls are convened to act collectively and in the company of other women rather than with males. Identity is learned and practiced in the context of the "same" rather than the "different"; Greek culture was pervasively homosocial for all ages and at all social levels, although we may imagine that the simple necessities of life enforced more active cooperation among men and women of the less prosperous classes. The importance of this gender exclusivity can hardly be overemphasized in the context of ritual practice; it entails that even when women are being taught, in ritual, the necessity of their own objectification, it is nonetheless women themselves who are entrusted with the actions and discourses that constitute this teaching and who are therefore potentially the subjects as well as the objects of the process.

THE ARRHEPHORIA

The Arrhephoria is one ritual event at Athens that visibly concerns itself with the preparation for female identity and increasingly attracts critical attention. The festival probably occurred in the last month of the year; it is described most fully by Pausanias (1.27.3):

50. Calame 1977: 1.331.

What caused me great amazement is not known to all, and so I shall write
down what happens. Two girls live not far from the temple of Athena Polias,
and the Athenians call them *arrhephoroi*. For a time they live with the goddess,
but when the festival comes round they perform at night the following rites.
They place on their heads what the priestess of Athena gives them to carry—
neither she who gives nor those to whom it is given know what it is. There is a
natural underground passage in the city not far from the precinct of
Aphrodite called "in the Gardens." Down this go the girls. They leave down
below what they carry, and take something else, which they bring back covered
up. At that point they send away these girls and bring to the Acropolis others
in their place.

Pausanias stresses the obscurity of the rite, and perhaps appropriately the
meaning of the word *arrhephoria*, discussed at length by Pierre Brulé,[51]
remains obscure; the suffix *-phoria*, however, clearly indicates the carrying of
something. The Arrhephoria convened a very small chorus, consisting of
four girls aged between seven and eleven; they were selected, by a process
that will concern us in the following chapter, from among the traditional
Eupatrid families of Athens, and it has been suggested that in the
Mycenaean city the Arrhephoria was performed by the daughters of the
king.[52] The ritual does not ever seem to have been open to girls of ordinary
families. Other communities, however, had rituals with similar names that
may have been more inclusive, although how far they resembled the
Athenian model is unknown.[53] To the extent of their families' prominence
we can say that the Athenian *arrhephoroi* were displayed before the city, and
they were also displayed in a more direct material fashion when they occupied the center of the city, the Acropolis, for the period of their ritual service, and when they walked in the Panathenaic procession. At the same
time, however, the *arrhephoroi* are implicated in the dialectic of display and
concealment that characterizes the chorus, because they are secluded on
the Acropolis, away from their customary familial environment. The nocturnal rite that two of them perform is also shrouded in secrecy.

As we have seen, what the little girls on the Acropolis enacted for themselves and for others were the parameters of domestic toil governing the
Greek wife's existence, one component of the *erga gynaikon*, the "works of
women." The missing component is reproductive work, which is represented, according to a current influential interpretation, by the nocturnal
rite. Although the text of Pausanias considers this performance utterly
obscure, modern commentators have found the main contours of the rite

51. Brulé 1987: 80–81.
52. Parke 1977: 142.
53. On other rites that seem to include *arrhephoroi*, at Epidauros and Miletos, for example,
see Burkert 1966: 5 n. 3.

relatively transparent. Walter Burkert did significant work on the ritual event and suggests that it claims to model itself on the myth of the daughters of the Athenian king Kekrops.[54] Entrusted by Athena with the earth-born baby Erichthonios, the Kekropides were charged not to open the casket in which he lay. Needless to say, they disobeyed the order, and were so terrified by what they saw that they leaped off the Acropolis to their deaths. What frightened them in the casket is variously described; either the baby was protected by live or ornamental snakes, or he was himself half a snake, like the girls' father, Kekrops.

The myth of the Kekropides has been understood as an encounter with sex and procreation, attended with a misplaced curiosity and followed by terror and death. The *arrhephoroi* are to follow a similar trajectory, but crucially, of course, they are not to die; the ritual context protects them as much as it terrifies. In other respects, Burkert's work interprets the nocturnal descent of the *arrhephoroi* as miming the fate of the Kekropides. Whatever they carry down—phallic snakes, symbolizing the act of sexual intercourse, in Burkert's account; *phalloi;* or a dewlike liquid that would represent semen in the accounts of others—Burkert urges that the "covered up" thing that they retrieve *(enkekalummenon)* be understood as the representation of a swaddled baby. The *arrhephoroi* thus enact the process of human reproduction. The timing of their ritual, at night, and the descent from the Acropolis by a narrow passage, would ensure that the actions were accomplished in an atmosphere of dread, and the secrecy surrounding the whole event would dramatize for the *arrhephoroi* the necessity of restraining their curiosity, as the Kekropides had failed to do.

But was the rite only about terror and death? As we have seen, the discourse of the chorus offers both fear and pleasure in its representation of marriage. In the Arrhephoria the phallic snakes, whether present only in the myth or also carried in the ritual, can be seen to refer to the erotic physical aspect of marriage, and this aspect may also be seen to be prominent in the journey that the *arrhephoroi* take through the precinct of Aphrodite in the Gardens. The rite of the Arrhephoria seduces as it disciplines, extending to its young practitioners an identity imbricated in the dynamics of desire as well as in those of work. If the rite does prevail upon the girls to perform a representation of human sexuality, it may thus be thought to elicit from them an enacted consent to their destinies as gendered subjects.

Many critics have read the Arrhephoria as a rite of passage or of initiation, while registering the difficulty in applying these terms to a process conducted only in symbols and apparently without the participants' comprehension. Brulé renders the nuanced situation of the *arrhephoros* well:

54. Burkert 1966. See Brulé 1987 for bibliography and discussion.

> The nocturnal gesture has made her move forward a stage in her relationships with sexuality; . . . one cannot consider that the rite constitutes an initiation in a strict sense, but all the context, we have seen, insists on this environment. We could call it initiation by allusion.[55]

What I should like to do here is to place a question mark over the secrecy of the ritual and the consequent ignorance of the *arrhephoroi*, and in the spirit of John Winkler's discussion "The Laughter of the Oppressed" I should like to imagine the *arrhephoroi* "speaking."[56] What leads us to conclude that the *arrhephoroi* and the priestess of Athena were ignorant of the nature of their ritual actions is Pausanias's statement to that effect: "Neither she who gives nor they who carry have any knowledge what it is" (1.27.3). Yet, as I have indicated, contemporary scholars find the rite relatively amenable to explication, and a version of the etiological narrative seems to have been known in the fifth century, because as Nicole Loraux has argued and as we shall discuss later, the contours of the *arrhephoria* are legible in Euripides' drama *Ion*. One way we could explain this apparent discrepancy would be to invoke the passage of time and to say simply that the Athenians' conscious memory regarding this rite had died out by the time of Pausanias's text, in the second century c.e. This would be plausible were it not that this text can almost always supply an explanatory narrative for other rites that it recounts, no matter how bizarre. What enables it to supply these narratives are, on at least some occasions, enquiries made of the ritual practitioners concerned. For instance, at 10.4.3, the narrator explains that he could not understand a certain Homeric phrase until he learned the etiology from some women, the Delphic Thyiades, who were active in cult practice. If we consequently surmise that on some occasions the native informants in Pausanias's text were women, especially women active in cult, we might then invoke the classic article by Edwin Ardener, "Belief and the Problem of Women." This article treats of the absence or even the impossibility of the female native informant and the consequent inadequacy of all current models of other cultures. "Ethnographers report," Ardener famously reports, "that women cannot be reached so easily as men: they giggle when young, snort when old, reject the question, laugh at the topic, and the like. The male members of a society frequently see the ethnographer's difficulties as simply a caricature of their own daily case."[57] In other words, the women refuse to engage—they do not tell.

It seems to me that we could do worse than to plug this refusal into Pausanias's lacunose narrative about the Arrhephoria, to explain not only the

---

55. Brulé 1987: 97.
56. Winkler 1990a: 188–209.
57. Ardener 1972: 137.

narrator's ignorance but also the far less plausible ignorance of the women involved. Priestess and *arrhephoroi* constitute the cultically active women who would likely fulfill the function of native informant. What if the women *were* asked but did not tell? If the priestess concerned experienced herself as entrusted with crucial ritual work undertaken on the subjectivities of young girls, she may well have been reluctant to divulge the secret to the prying ethnographer from Lydia. The little girls themselves may have known perfectly well what they took down and what they brought up, but why inform the anthropologist if he can't work it out for himself? The silence of the *arrhephoroi* need not be that of females alienated from their own actions, from their own history, and from a discourse that would render actions and histories intelligible, but instead a silence of women who exercise a vital function within their community and who preserve the appropriate discretion about it.[58]

If we were to pry loose, in this way, the silence surrounding the *arrhephoroi's* knowledge of their own practice, we would be able to insert a moment of female agency into the account of a rite that seems otherwise driven solely by the ideological imperative of preparing girls for patriarchal marriage. It would, of course, be a moment of agency highly constrained by that patriarchal imperative and would thus conform to the model of agency in the ritual sphere that we elaborated in the preceding chapter. The young girls, by experiencing the possibility of themselves as subjects as well as objects of desire, would have their curiosity aroused at the same time as they were threatened with punishment for that curiosity. As with the chorus, the ritual process does not seem to offer mediation of this contradiction; instead it leads the young girls to act it out.

My interpretation of the Arrhephoria does not differ, in its major contours, from the lines laid down by previous commentators, but we should note that dissent from what Brulé calls the "classic interpretation" is possible and has been articulated by Noel Robertson, who reads the Arrhephoria as designed primarily to ensure the community's prosperity rather than to make any intervention in the lives of women.[59] Corresponding to this is his interpretation of the Arkteia, a rite that we shall consider shortly, as concerned with success in hunting rather than with the preparation of young women for marriage.[60] Robertson rejects the notion that the Arrhephoria or

---

58. For Zeitlin (1982a) the innocence of the *arrhephoroi* is what the ritual turns on; the girls "represent the innocent female element whose connection with the earth is maintained, but whose sexuality is repressed. The Arrhephoroi . . . are not so much preparing themselves in general terms for their future female tasks but serve to guarantee the purity of Athena's robe" (154). This interpretation seems to me to place too much weight on sexual innocence, which I would argue is not the primary concern of Athenian ritual discourse about females.

59. Robertson 1983b.

60. Ibid., 273.

Arkteia follows an initiatory scenario, because, he contends, Greek ritual eschews systematic models in favor of the concerns of "real life." While we have seen in chapter 1 that ritual did indeed address women on the grounds of "real life" and of material labor, it is surely not necessary to sub- scribe to a notion of "real life" that excludes the work of bringing young women to a suitable maturation. It is, instead, highly plausible to argue that women's negotiation of viable adult identities is crucial for the well-being of the society as a whole. There need be, then, no contradiction between a rite striving for the community's prosperity and one that prepares young women for marriage—and they may certainly be one and the same ritual. Robert- son's position seems vulnerable to the charges not only that it cannot deal with the notion of ritual polyvalence but also that it has a very limited model of how women operated in Greek society.

Since the notion of ritual polyvalence will concern us several times in the course of this study, it is appropriate to consider it briefly here. Ritual situa- tions are often characterized as ambiguous or ambivalent because the ritual subjects performing them are withdrawn from normal life and so are with- out clear status markers, capable of being understood as "betwixt and between," "neither here nor there."[61] The polyvalence that interests me, however, is not that of a ritual that can suspend its subjects within social process, but that of a ritual that can effect several processes at once. Since Greek ritual activity is thoroughly imbricated with the texture of lived expe- rience, ritual discourse elaborates varied connections with many of the cul- ture's other governing discourses. Such connections enable any ritual action to resonate within its culture at different levels. In the case of those rituals that primarily address women, it is possible that the same gestures may have one significance for the female participants and another for the wider male-dominated society, which may not be present at the rituals but which obviously maintains some acquaintance with them (otherwise we would know nothing, since the women practitioners could not leave the written documents to tell us). Simon Price makes a similar point about the varied but simultaneously valid constructions of ritual events available for different classes,[62] and if we consider that ritual as an ideologically charged practice is multiply determined by the conflicting needs of its society, then its susceptibility to different interpretations is a logical outcome. The pre- sent chapter, focusing on the construction of sexuality, elaborates an aspect of women's ritual practice that implicitly seeks to restrict their actions and circumscribe their identities in the service of patriarchal arrangements, but as we have seen in the first chapter, ritual practice as a whole is by no means necessarily consistent with this confining agenda.

61. Turner 1967: 95.
62. Price 1984: 116.

We might note in this context that as with the chorus, so the Arrhephoria too displays other dimensions that offer to its female participants identities that are not bounded by the premarital discourse of pleasure and fear. The nocturnal descent is part of a ritual service that includes, as we have seen, living on the Acropolis in the company of the priestess of Athena Polias and helping her set up the looms during the festival of Chalkeia. Honored by their election to this service, the *arrhephoroi* were also distinguished by their special white clothes, their gold ornaments, and a particular bread that was baked for them,[63] but most significantly by their help in weaving the peplos for presentation to the goddess at the Panathenaia. The designs woven into the peplos, showing the founding myths of Athens, insert the girls directly into the symbolic order of the city; not only are they involved in the production of one of the community's most valued material objects, but they are also directly concerned with the reproduction of the city's mythic history and with its self-celebration in its major annual festival. Working to produce a normative, beneficial sexuality that is grounded in the notion of the *erga gynaikon,* the Arrhephoria also connects its participants to a wider cultural sphere. Through their ritual service and its material product, the little girls acquire a place in their city's history, even while the ritual is also preparing them to embrace the routine obscurity of acceptable female conduct. The same gesture may be discerned in the ritual work of the adult women serving as Deipnophoroi, who not only bring food but also recount the heroic myths of their culture.

In this connection it is appropriate to note that a scene in the Parthenon frieze has often been associated with the *arrhephoroi*. A moment on the east frieze shows a child of indeterminate sex helping an older man with a folded cloth.[64] This has become known as the "peplos-scene," in which an *arrhephoros* presents Athena's new garment to the *archon basileus,* the official responsible for most religious ceremonies. Joan Connelly, in an interpretation that has inspired much discussion if not much assent, has identified the whole frieze as a representation of the sacrifice of Erechtheus's daughter, undertaken to assure victory in the war with the Eleusinians.[65] This interpretation puts paid to the representation of the *arrhephoros* on the frieze, although it replaces it with another, perhaps less cheerful, account of how young women may be important to the city. While it is no part of the brief of this study to explain the Parthenon frieze, we might note that essays written in rebuttal of Connelly's thesis typically stress the melding of different versions of Athens,

63. On the clothes and ornaments, see Harpocration s.v. *arrhephorein* and Bekker 1814: 1.202.3. On the bread see Suda s.v. *anastatoi.*

64. No commentator on the sculpture claims that the sex is indeterminate, but I characterize it as such because commentators cannot agree among themselves whether it is male or female.

65. Connelly 1996.

and of Athens's past and present, in a way that could encompass the representation both of historical girls and of their mythical counterparts.[66]

THE ARKTEIA

Tabulating what seemed to him the chief elements of the Arrhephoria and the Arkteia, Brulé concluded that there is a marked morphological similarity between the two.[67] While conceding this, I would like to stress the very different constructions that the two rites seem to offer of female identity. If we accept that it emphasizes the *erga gynaikon* and the restraint of sexual curiosity, then the Arrhephoria can be read as a rite of "taming" or domestication, but it does not seem to work with a representation of female identity as aligned with the wild or the uncivilized, hostile to the projects of male-dominated culture or constitutionally unfit for the performance of its allotted tasks. Instead, the Arkteia is charged with these elements of a representation of the female, and it performs this articulation not only in the ritual gestures but also with the assistance of an extraordinarily punitive set of myths.[68]

For the women of classical Athens, the Arkteia, or Playing the Bear, took place at Brauron, a sanctuary to the east of Athens on the coast of Attika, active at least from the eighth century and until the end of the fourth. From the sixth century there was also a precinct of Artemis Brauronia on the Acropolis at Athens, but the ritual for the young girls took place outside the city. Other sites for the worship of Artemis, throughout Attica, either are connected to similar myths or have revealed archaeological finds similar to those characteristic of Brauron, so there is a plausible case to be made that a version of the Arkteia was performed in many locations, and that many young women would have been exposed to its particular ideological work.

Who precisely constituted the members of the Brauronian ritual collective will concern us in the following chapter, but they numbered more than the *arrhephoroi*. There is some confusion about the age of the *arktoi,* or little bears, because the text of Aristophanes' *Lysistrata* and the scholia to it seem to disagree, but the age range for *arktoi* probably extended beyond that for *arrhephoroi*.[69] Commentators generally agree that the Arkteia was celebrated

66. See, for instance, Neils 1996 and Harrison 1996.

67. Brulé 1987: 249.

68. See Dowden (1989: 24) on the necessity to supplement knowledge of the cult with that of the myth(s). His quest is for the "original cult myth," but a complex of myths seems to me equally effective in discharging the ritual task here.

69. See Demand 1994: 109–12 for discussion of the ancient and modern contributions to this debate. Perlman 1983 and Sourvinou-Inwood 1988b offer the two most polarized interpretations.

every four years, so that all qualifying girls would have a chance to attend. According to the ceramics found at Brauron and corresponding locations, the little girls did not convene alone but were accompanied by older women. In the absence of precise testimony our best guess is that these comprised mothers and other female relatives, and one or more priestesses.[70] Again we see both the choral model of pedagogy by older people, and the necessity of learning gender in the presence of the "same" rather than the "other."

Current understanding of the Arkteia derives from two main sources: the prominent myths connected with the various sites; and the published ceramics and other artifacts from Brauron, a small proportion of the material that has been found.[71] At Mounichion a bear was said to have invaded the sanctuary and to have been killed. Artemis sent a plague and demanded appeasement in the form of the sacrifice of a young girl; one man, Embaros, volunteered his own daughter but substituted for her a goat in woman's clothing. The plague ended, and in some versions the father obtained the priesthood in the cult of Artemis. The myth at Brauron held that the bear, while playing with a young girl, scratched her and was killed by her brothers. Plague ensues; requested for help, the oracle commands the girls to "play the bear" for Artemis before their marriage.[72]

These two accounts display significant elements in common. In each, the death of the bear is atoned for by an averted sacrifice and a ritual foundation. At Mounichion, a daughter is almost sacrificed, and a priesthood is established. At Brauron, daughters are not sacrificed but are sent to serve the goddess, and this obligation is laid upon Athenian families for all time. What each myth stresses is the equation between the daughter and the bear; young girls can play the bear and be offered in exchange for one. The myth at Mounichion also points to an equivalence between girls and other animals, since the latter can be sacrificed in the clothes of the former.[73]

The deer is also present at Brauron, in the person of Iphigeneia. Her

70. Pollux 9.24 mentions a priestess at Brauron, and *IG* i^2 387.36 = *IG* i^3 403, on Artemis at Brauron, mentions priestesses, but priestesses of what is unclear.

71. See Brulé 1987 for discussion and bibliography, to which may be added Sourvinou-Inwood 1988b, Perlman 1989, and Demand 1994.

72. See Harpocration s.v. *arkteusai*, Bekker 1814: 1.206, the scholia on Aristophanes *Lysistrata* 645, the Suda s.vv. *Arktos* and *Embaros,* and Apostolius s.v. *Embaros,* 7.10 (= *Corpus Paroemiographorum Graecorum* 2.397).

73. Scholars have long held that a similar equivalence was also dramatized in ritual. In inscriptions found at Pagasai and Larisa in Thessaly girls are said to *nebeuo* for Artemis *(IG* ix^2 1123). This verb has been translated as "play the deer," and in one case a man, Hippolochos, pays a ransom to Artemis for his fiancée Eubioteia who allegedly "played the deer" (Clement 1934). See now, however, Hatzopoulos (1994), who challenges the interpretation of this word. Hatzopoulos claims that the inscriptions refer to a rite of passage for young girls centering on Demeter rather than on Artemis, and free from overt animal associations.

myth, although it exhibits several variants, offers elements similar to those of Brauron and Mounichion, and in at least one source is said to take place at Brauron. She is sacrificed to Artemis in expiation for a fault committed by her father, who must officiate at the sacrifice; but her death is averted by the substitution of a deer—in some accounts it is the slaughter of a deer that provokes Artemis's anger—and she is subsequently made a priestess of Artemis at Brauron. To her, according to Euripides' *Iphigeneia in Tauris,* are dedicated clothes woven by women who die in childbirth.

A final myth that elaborates connections between young women and bears is that of Kallisto. Erika Simon has argued that this myth is represented on a fragmentary *krateriskos,* a type of vase most commonly found at Brauron, which shows a male and female figure each with a bear's head.[74] Lilly Kahil interprets this scene as concerning a Brauronian priestess and priest,[75] but the myth of Kallisto is so germane to the concerns of the Arkteia that we may prefer Simon's reading. Kallisto, a virgin follower of Artemis, was raped by Zeus; she was subsequently turned into a bear either by a jealous Hera or by an Artemis enraged at her loss of purity. As a bear, Kallisto was hunted by her son Arkas, and matricide would have ensued if Zeus had not intervened and turned them both into constellations.[76]

Directed by this mythic complex, little Athenian girls "played the bear" at Brauron. The series of special ceramics, *krateriskoi,* hordes of which have been found at Brauron and other sites devoted to Artemis, may be read to indicate various stages in this mimetic process. Where the *krateriskoi* show recognizable human activities, they tend to repeat a circumscribed repertoire; young women, ranging from children to near adults, who are either naked or wearing short tunics, run, dance, or process in the vicinity of an altar. The girls often hold torches or wreaths, and sometimes the presence of a palm tree indicates the context of worship of Artemis. Some girls have their hair loose. Although we cannot be sure that these activities alone added up to the notion of "playing the bear," many commentators have drawn conclusions about the rite based not only on the representation of the "bears" but on the significance, at Brauron, of the homology between girl and wild animal. Since the rite of the Arkteia must be performed before marriage, it is an obvious inference that the participants are preparing for marriage, and the symbolism of bear, deer, and goat suggests that the little girls are being purged of their inherent "wildness," their female alignment with savage nature, in order that they may assume the conduct of the tamed and domesticated adult woman. "The ritual therefore condones a type of activity antithetical to that of well behaved Athenian girls and married

74. Simon 1983: 88.
75. Kahil 1977.
76. Ovid *Metamorphoses* 2.409–507, Apollodoros *Library* 3.8.2, and Pausanias 8.3.6–7.

women," observes Susan Guettel Cole.[77] The rite can be seen to teach the girls that they are, inherently, wild and uncivilized, and so must submit to a process of domestication that will fit them for their adult roles, but it can also be seen to be responsible for those very predications of wildness and savagery that it seeks to exorcise. Required to act out their wildness in running and dancing, the girls are induced to perform one identity only in order to replace it with another, approved version.[78]

As many commentators have demonstrated, the bear signifies on several levels within the Arkteia's complex of myths and cult. On one level, the bear at the sanctuary who turns on the girls combines the traits of domesticity and savagery in the same way as the little girls are brought to do.[79] Brulé shows the importance of the bear to many European cultures and indicates that it may symbolize both hyperbolic masculinity and hyperbolic femininity; ascribed a tremendous sexual vigor and lustfulness in both sexes, the bear is also supermaternal, to the extent of being able to form the bodies of her young by licking them.[80] The bear offers the little *arktoi* not only paradigms of gender identity by which to negotiate their own but also, perhaps, the hope that they too may be "licked into shape" and positioned to perform their adult roles successfully.

To what extent can we read in the Arkteia the premarital discourse that I have identified in chorus and Arrhephoria? This discourse, as I have characterized it, plays on several terms; it involves the ritual subjects in a dialectic of concealment and revelation, it requires them to internalize a figured male gaze, and finally it engages them in representations of both pleasure and fear. Unlike those in the chorus, the girls of the Arkteia are "concealed" among women, away from the city, and are not obviously "revealed" by the ritual context. Their condition corresponds instead to the seclusion predicated by A. van Gennep of the first stage of an initiatory scenario. The notion of the internalized male gaze, however, may indicate that the Arkteia retains some of the functions of ritual display. Nudity is very rare in Greek ritual contexts, as Kahil points out, and so it is unlikely that the female nudity of the Arkteia should be understood simply as the "absence of marked sexual polarity" that Turner identifies as part of the "undifferentiated character of liminality."[81] While ritual nudity may be read as contribut-

77. Cole 1984: 242.

78. Cole (1984: 239–40) points out that the adult female activity of weaving is also important, in the many dedications from women at Brauron.

79. Dowden 1989: 34.

80. See Brulé 1987: 214–17, 256–58, and Perlman 1989.

81. Kahil 1983: 238; Turner 1967: 104. See also Lonsdale 1993: 178 on nudity as "unpretentious and egalitarian." Lincoln's survey of contemporary girls' initiation rites suggests that girls are more likely to acquire clothing during the process of initiation than to shed it, thereby perhaps giving additional significance to the Greek girls' nudity (1991: 103).

ing to Turnerian *communitas* by reducing exterior distinctions among the girls, it may equally well be thought to address directly the issue of their developing sexuality, which must be harnessed to their performance of a gendered role as wives and mothers.[82] In the context of a rite preparatory for marriage, the nudity may function as part of the apparatus that enables girls to figure themselves as objects of desire.

If their own nakedness was not enough to figure a male gaze, various legends associated with sexual attack on women's ritual gatherings might have helped the girls to organize their subjectivity around that gaze. An account in Herodotos (6.138), playing on the anomalous vulnerability of women in ritual process, removed not only from their homes but from the men who are their protectors, describes how women were carried off from Brauron by Pelasgians:

> These same Pelasgians, who then settled in Lemnos, desired to be revenged on the Athenians. They were well acquainted with the Athenian festivals, so they took some *pentecontoers* and ambushed the Athenian women *(gynaikes)* who were celebrating the festival of Artemis at Brauron. They seized a large number from there and sailed away, taking them to Lemnos, where they kept them as concubines.[83]

A similar account is found in Pausanias 4.4.2, where it provides the motive for hostilities rather than part of them. Spartan girls celebrating a festival of Artemis Limnatis, in frontier territory between the domains of Lakedaimonians and Messenians, were allegedly raped by Messenians, thus providing the pretext for war. In Plutarch *Life of Solon* 8.4–6, however, the trope is turned on its head as the lawgiver exploits Athenian women's ritual activity in order to defeat the Megarians. The account runs as follows:[84]

> When he sailed to Cape Kolias with Peisistratos, he [Solon] found all the women of the city there, celebrating the ancient sacrifice to Demeter. He sent a trusty man to Salamis, pretending to be a deserter, and urging the Megarians, if they wanted to take the foremost women of Athens, to sail to Kolias. . . . The Megarians were persuaded by him and sent men in his ship. But when Solon saw the ship setting out from the island, he told the women to get out of the way, and those of the younger men who didn't yet have beards, he told to put on the women's clothes and headbands, and sandals.

---

82. Osborne (1985: 165) suggests that "the *arkteia* is a puberty ritual . . . that puts the stress on the emergence of sexual difference."

83. The term *gynaikes*, connoting adult women or wives, may give us pause applied apparently to prepubescent girls, but it is also present in the Suda's account of the Arkteia, and it may be understood as proleptic, looking forward to the maturity anticipated by the rite.

84. See the similar account in Aeneas Tacticus 4.8–4.11 and the discussion in Whitehead 1990.

He told them to carry hidden daggers, and organized them in playing and dancing on the shore until the enemy had disembarked and the ship was in their power. . . . The Megarians were lured on by what they saw . . . and leaped out as if to attack women . . . and not one of them got away.

This narrative bears notable resemblances to the Messenian version of the story cited above; according to Pausanias 4.4.2 the Messenians claim that the Spartans sent beardless men, dressed as women, to the sanctuary in order to attack the Messenians there. These interchangeable narratives of male sexual violence, attempted or achieved, are arguably significant to the notion of their identity that Greek women develop in ritual; these narratives are the counterpart of the erotic narratives in which male desire is excited by a woman at a festival, and the converse, as we shall see later, of the "Thesmophoric" narratives in which women attack men.[85]

The Arkteia also provides for its female participants a more direct encounter with themselves as objects and subjects of desire. The running and dancing that they perform may be understood as emblematic of the exuberant physical activity that females are thought to crave but that they will have to forego in the more disciplined environment of marriage. The bear's hypermasculinity is perhaps relevant in this context of unsanctioned physical activity, and we may find particularly intriguing a *krateriskos* on which the bear is actually depicted, frightening off three girls who are running from it. The girl nearest the bear is apparently turning back to look at the bear even as she flees.[86] Brulé points out that a similar glance can be detected in representations of the Kekropides frightened by the serpents on the Acropolis,[87] and in view of the parallels I would like to suggest that we see here a representation of the combined fear and fascination elicited by these symbolic animals, which, if not actually phallic, at least connote versions of adult sexuality.

The most overtly erotic component of the Arkteia, however, is the garment called the *krokotos*. The *krokotos* appears in *Lysistrata* 644–48, which refers to several rituals for young women:

> At seven I was an *arrhephoros;* then at ten I was an *aletris* for the Mistress Athena; and then wearing the *krokotos* I was a bear at the Brauronia; and then, a lovely young girl with a necklace of figs, I was a *kanephoros.*

A scholion claims that the *krokotos* connotes the skin of the bear whom the little girls imitate, but Brulé also points out that the garment must be con-

85. Such narratives have other significances for the Greek understanding of manhood, of course, but they do not elaborate overt links to any rite of male adolescence.

86. See Brulé 1987: 252; Kahil 1977. The backwards glance is characteristic of ceramic sexual pursuit scenes between humans, or deities and humans.

87. Brulé 1987: 253.

nected to *krokos,* "saffron," which is a basic ingredient in perfumes.[88] The garment is found in a number of contexts that ally it with various erotic scenarios;[89] in particular it seems to signify sexual desire within marriage, as when Lysistrata and her accomplice Kleonike swear to arouse their husbands by wearing it (*Lysistrata* 351, "enticing in our saffron nighties"). When the little girls wore the *krokotos* at the Arkteia, they were inserted into the system of adult sexuality, but the association of the *krokotos* elsewhere with marriage might suggest to them that satisfaction of desire was possible and appropriate only through marriage.

As several scholars have pointed out (e.g., Richard Hamilton), none of the girls represented on the *krateriskoi* seems to be wearing a saffron-colored garment. It is possible, of course, that the name extended to a piece of ritual clothing that had lost its direct connection to the saffron color. Given the lines from *Lysistrata,* however, and the various other notices in the sources, it is almost certain that the arktoi wore the *krokotos* for at least some of the festival. Why does it not appear on the *krateriskoi*—did they perhaps take it off? Shedding ritual garments may, of course, be as significant as putting them on, especially in the context of working to produce a new or modified identity. Sourvinou-Inwood has suggested that we read *kat'echousa,* "then wearing," in *Lysistrata* 645 as *katechousa,* "shedding," a construction that would resonate strikingly with the lines describing Iphigeneia's death in Aeschylus *Agamemnon* 239.[90] Iphigeneia is lifted onto the altar, so that her saffron colored robe falls to the ground, *krokou baphas d'es pedon cheousa.*[91] However we read the lines from *Lysistrata,* we may want to retain the resonances of the scene in *Agamemnon* for our understanding of the Arkteia: Iphigeneia is presented, or presents herself, in the erotic light suitable for the *parthenos* on the verge of marriage, whose sacrifice was itself disguised as marriage; and she expiates a fault with her body, the fate that the ritual of the Arkteia is designed to avert from its little girls.

Wearing and/or shedding the *krokotos,* the *arktoi* mime an adult sexuality and rehearse proleptically the defining female gesture of "loosening the belt" for defloration and for childbirth. The Arkteia obliquely acts out sexual pleasure, and it may also be thought to provide a genuine and untroubled pleasure to its participants, if we may judge from the pride that the Lysistratan chorus takes in its service and from the honorific statues of little

88. Ibid., 241.

89. Ibid.

90. I should point out that her suggestion has found little favor.

91. See Brulé 1987: 242 on interpretations of this line. Armstrong and Ratchford (1985) argue persuasively that the *krokou baphas* are Iphigeneia's veil, rather than all her clothes, which would certainly retain the marital/erotic charge of the *krokotos* that we are here discussing.

girls, presumably *arktoi,* that have been found at the sanctuary.[92] The discourse of pleasure, however, is evoked by the Arkteia only to be disciplined by that of fear. We may read a trace of this discipline even in an apparently ideologically neutral source like the Suda. When this source recounts that a girl teased the bear in the sanctuary at Brauron and upset it by her "lack of restraint" *(aselgainouses),* so that it scratched her, we do not seem to be very far from the terms of the pedagogy usually directed at Greek women and aimed at securing from them absolute restraint, *sophrosune,* in all their dealings with men. Their nudity, too, as Nancy Demand has argued,[93] could contribute to the young women's fearfulness. Since girls at different stages of development were convened together, there would be plenty of opportunity to register one's own inadequacy by comparison with others. Anxiety about her capability to perform as wife and mother might render the young woman eager to learn and to acquiesce in the modes of preparation on offer.

As I have already indicated, the myths of Iphigeneia and Kallisto seem to be the most terrifying elements of the cultic complex. Iphigeneia is offered as a victim to expiate her father's error, and although she is then honored as a priestess at Brauron, her final and defining function at the sanctuary is to receive the garments of women who die in childbirth.[94] As the little girls prepare for the state of adult womanhood they are vividly alerted to the most menacing occupational hazard attending that career.[95] The myth of Kallisto offers no more cheerful an account of femininity. Kallisto is held responsible for the unsanctioned desire of others, and she too expiates a fault in her own body when she is metamorphosed into a bear. But this uncompromising teaching about the loss of virginity is buttressed by another directive from the myth, which can be seen to inculcate both the necessity of abandoning the domain of Artemis and the dangers attendant on an improper or premature move into adult sexuality. A final identification for the bear, in the context of the Arkteia, is that of a woman—Kallisto or any other—punished for sexual precocity.

The various discourses surrounding the Arkteia stress the fragility of the female, pointing up her vulnerability to various kinds of assaults and suggesting that she is liable to dissolve into an animal identity instead of suc-

92. Statues of little boys have also been found, some dating from after the fourth century, which have been explained as dedications from women who want sons or who thank the goddess for having provided sons.

93. Demand 1994: 114.

94. Dowden argues, to my mind correctly, that the "death of the maiden" signifies an initiatory death into a new status rather than an echo of a historical practice of human sacrifice. However, the "death of the maiden" (or the recently ex-maiden) is deployed in another way at Brauron in its insistence on death in childbirth.

95. See Demand 1994: 71–86 on death in childbirth. French 1987: 69 gives useful statistics.

cessfully completing the transition to adult womanhood.[96] Although she is vulnerable, she is held responsible, like Kallisto, for her own sexuality and that of others, and the *krokotos,* which signifies the desire aroused by the married woman, can be read as an index of her responsibility. The Arkteia also takes care to point to one of the most frightening parameters of female identity, namely death in childbirth.

In my account of the Arkteia I have concentrated on the attendant discourse of myth, as much as on material practice, in order to elucidate the possible significance for practitioners of the ritual event. The ritual gestures alone "neither speak nor conceal but sign," as Herakleitos asserts of the oracle at Delphi (frag. 93 Diels-Kranz), and their potential significance is elaborated through the mythical discourse. Even though, conversely, the myths would not signify so much without the bodily gestures of the "bears" in the *krokotos,* the crucial component of the ritual work is to shape not the young girls' physique, but their subjectivities. These must be positioned to internalize an objectification, a version of selfhood deployed for the benefit of others rather than of the self. My method is materialist and deduces a subjectivity from a specific set of actions and narratives, because this is what the ritual attempts to produce. The young Greek girl who identified successfully with the ritual's twofold erotic and punitive aspects would be well positioned to perform as wife and mother.

The discourse of desire that young women needed to learn about themselves in order to function within a male-dominated system elaborated three main propositions. First, they must accept themselves as legitimate objects of desire and learn to discriminate between the sanctioned and the unsanctioned gazes that they may attract. Second, they learn that they may operate as subjects of desire, but that this will be appropriate only in the context of marriage. Finally, however, they must be brought to accept that their identity as females makes them vulnerable to the onslaughts of desire, their own and that of others. These three conditions of their existence require and justify the intense supervision to which their conduct is subject.

THE *KANEPHOROS*

Following the list in the *Lysistrata* chorus, Sourvinou-Inwood suggests that the *kanephoros,* or basket-bearer, is older than the performers of the Arrhephoria and Arkteia, being about thirteen or fourteen and so on the

---

96. I should stress that this period of adolescent transition is of course dangerous for both sexes. The myths of, for instance, Aktaion and Teiresias, metamorphosed after accidentally seeing a goddess naked, suggest that a premature encounter with sexuality is perilous for males as well, but these myths are not, as far as we know, dramatized in young men's ritual practice.

verge of nubility.[97] As we saw in chapter 1, women took part in ritual processions throughout Greece, so that the *kanephoros* was a feature of most ritual activity. She exemplifies in all its complexity the notion of the *parthenos:*
the *kanephoros* is a virgin not because she is simply too young, culturally
speaking, to have engaged in sexual intercourse, like the *arrhephoroi* and the
arktoi, but because her virginity emerges as a focus of interest in its own
right, poised to be abandoned and exchanged for productive sexuality in
the context of legitimate marriage. The *kanephoros* is the epitome of ritual
display, both because there are very few *kanephoroi* in any one procession,
the choral model having ceased to apply, and because she is inspected by
the whole community for marriageability. Her position is like that of the
choregos or first *choreute,* glamorous but exposed and vulnerable. Stephen
Lonsdale offers a highly instructive comparison with the modern Greek
institution of the "first dancer": "As she dances she is expected to display her
beauty, skill, energy, sensuality, and sexuality. But because the Sohoians have
ambivalent attitudes about female sexuality . . . aesthetic expressions of
female sexuality are viewed with suspicion. . . . The limits of acceptable
behavior for a female as revealed through dancing are perilously narrow."[98]

In Athens the *kanephoros* was usually chosen from the aristocratic or
Eupatrid families,[99] and the display of her in the ritual sphere was an element of the system of contracting marriages among these families. When in
the *Histories* of Thucydides (6.54–56) the tyrant Hipparchos prevents
Harmodios's sister from serving as a *kanephoros* in the Panathenaia, his
action threatens more than her honor. By insinuating that she is not fit to
serve the goddess—a charge that in this context perhaps signifies that she
is more sexually experienced than is appropriate[100]—he prevents her from
playing her role in her family's system of alliances and thus implicitly threatens the aristocratic power structure. Aristophanes' *Acharnians,* however,
suggests that the figure of the *kanephoros* was symbolically available, to the
imagination, outside aristocratic contexts. When the protagonist, Dikaiopolis, arranges a private celebration of the Country Dionysia, he installs his
daughter as *kanephoros,* and the fantasized *kanephoros* here serves as a trope
for marriageable youth and beauty rather than for aristocracy (253–56).
The "beauty" *(kallos,* adjective *kale)* predicated of the *kanephoros,* as Brulé has
shown, following Calame, is less an attribute of face and figure than a
description of her age and nubility; beauty, ritual service, and readiness for

97. Sourvinou-Inwood 1988b: 56. For a prosopography of Athenian *kanephoroi* see Turner
1983: 327–42.
98. Lonsdale 1993: 232.
99. See, for example, Hesychios and Photios s.v., and Philochoros in *FGH* 328 F8.
100. Brulé (1987: 303–4) suggests that the insult is to her birth, not her character; but see
Lavelle 1986.

marriage are each a sign and guarantee of the others. Nor is the loveliness of the *kanephoros* at all disturbing: as Brulé demonstrates, it is constituted by a pallor that proves that she spends her time virtuously indoors, even though she is now appearing in public.[101]

We saw above that ritual display is a site for sexual violence. In wartime, as part of the illegitimate exchange of women to which Herodotos at least attributes the status of a founding gesture (*Histories* 1.1–5), groups of men are said to carry off whole "choruses". But there are also peacetime accounts of such aggression; historical sources show the daughter of Peisistratos, performing as a *kanephoros,* insulted by a suitor.[102] Again the glamour of the ritual position is qualified by its vulnerability, and the subjectivity of women on the brink of marriage must be formed by exposure to and embrace of the contradiction. On the comic stage, the dramas of Menander resort to the scene of rape or seduction at a festival to motivate their plot development. The *Arbitrators* features the defloration of a young woman at the *pannychis* held by women celebrating Artemis at the Tauropolia at Halai, while in *The Samian Woman* the daughter of the house is impregnated during the Adonia. In the fragmentary *Kitharistes,* a man falls in love with a woman whom he sees in the procession for Artemis at Ephesus, a festival that incidentally provides the opening scene for Xenophon of Ephesos's second-century C.E. novel, in which the heads of the male and female choruses fall in love. The leader of the girls, Antheia, is fourteen, *kale* like a *kanephoros,* although her scenario also makes of her a *choregos* (1.2).

In a text that claims a less fictional status for itself, Lysias 1, *On the Murder of Eratosthenes,* the allegedly adulterous wife of Euphiletos is first seen by her seducer at Euphiletos's mother's funeral. While she is obviously not operating as a *kanephoros*—although it is intriguing to note that she has given birth to only one child and so perhaps has not been married long— the funeral context works to motivate the seduction not only because, historically, it did provide a material opportunity for men to see non-kin women. Although we have no way of knowing if the speaker of Lysias 1 is telling the truth—given David Cohen's argument about the prevalence of adultery between neighbors, rather than chance acquaintances, we may even be inclined to doubt it[103]—the trope of the woman exposed to unsanctioned gazes during a ritual event would in any case exert a strong pull within Greek culture.

---

101. Brulé 1987: 316.

102. Polyaenus *Strategemata* 5.14 and Plutarch *On Restraining Anger* 457F and *Sayings of Kings and Generals* 189C offer slightly different but related versions of this episode. See also Brulé 1987: 287.

103. Cohen 1990.

THE WEDDING

If a young woman successfully negotiated the preparatory rituals and the somatic events of her early teens, she could marry and fulfill the functions of a properly domesticated *gyne*. *Gyne*, the Greek term for "adult woman," also almost invariably connotes "wife and mother." The wedding may, as at Athens, extend over a few days, modifying from the banquet to the epaulia, but it is more effective at moving the bride from one state to another than are the preparatory rituals. Despite its effectiveness, or perhaps because of it, the ceremony does not mobilize as complex a set of significations as, for instance, the Arrhephoria or Arkteia. Other aspects of the wedding have been discussed in chapter 1; versions of the premarital discourse may, however, be read in the ceremony and its attendant activities. James Redfield and Anne Carson have argued that the *anakalupteria*, the moment when the bride lifts her veil to reveal herself to the new husband, constitutes the pivotal moment of the ceremony.[104] If this is so, the gesture can be understood to demonstrate the bride's acquiescence in her training; she no longer needs the choral context to display her as an object of desire but can undertake that task herself.

Other elements of the Athenian wedding suggested other forms of acquiescence. The procession included a small boy who wore a garland of thistles and acorns, allegedly the sign of the "natural" or "wild" way of life that the bride was presently rejecting (Zenobius 3.98, *Corpus Paroemiographorum Graecorum* pp. 82–83). The bride for her part carried signs of the life of civilized labor *(autourgia)* to which she now consented: a sieve (Pollux 3.38) and a pan for roasting barley (Pollux 1.246). After the wedding, various sources suggest, the priestess of Athena Polias visited new brides and shook an aegis, or at least a goatskin, at them.[105] As we saw in the previous chapter, the priestess also required a monetary contribution from the bride. We cannot tell if the priestess visited every bride, although the sources seem to indicate as much; we may conclude that she confined her clientele to the wives in Eupatrid families, from which social register she herself derived. The visit seems to have aimed at terrifying the new bride, but also at provoking her fertility; this is a combination of motifs that may recall the premarital discourse of pleasure and fear.

THE SPARTANS

At this point we should take note of a wedding ceremony, and some attendant rituals, which may offer a paradigm quite different from the predominantly Athenian model we have explored so far. In the postclassical period

104. Redfield 1982: 192; Carson 1990: 163–64.
105. See Robertson 1988: 213; Burkert 1985: 101–2; *Corpus Paroemiographorum Graecorum* Suppl. 1.65 (s.vv. *aigis, peri polin*). Robertson (1983a: 163) prints the text.

the institutions of Sparta, including the city's sexual practices, were objects of great interest and often admiration. So extensive is the cultural elaboration on things Spartan that one might conclude that the city is a fictional projection of "the other," a discourse of difference by which to measure the shortcomings of Athens. Even if the historicity of classical Sparta's peculiar institutions is granted, however, it is not immediately clear to scholars how Spartan women functioned within them. Two examples of the polarized responses possible are that of Paul Cartledge, who argues that the status of women at Sparta was subordinated to the masculine military machine, and that of Barton Kunstler, who claims that previous accounts of Spartan women have taken their starting point from an assumption of male dominance, and that an account that does not make this assumption will describe a "vital and far from peripheral or powerless female population."[106] Can a study of Spartan women's rituals, particularly those concerned to produce women from girls, assist in reaching some conclusion?

As we saw above, Spartan girls regularly participated in choral activities, a practice attributed to the legislation of Lykourgos.[107] They sang and danced at the most important festival, the Hyakinthia, which was dedicated to Apollo, but were not so prominent at the other Apolline celebrations of Gymnopaidia and Karneia.[108] Like other gatherings for young women, Spartan choruses seem to have been locations of sexual display; Plutarch's account of Spartan pedagogy contends that the girls were exposed to a male gaze that was not necessarily reciprocated (*Lykourgos* 14.2):

> He took away self-indulgent shyness and all effeminacy by accustoming the girls, no less than the boys, to process half naked, and at some festivals to dance and sing, even though the young men were present and were watching.

Heterosexual unions are alleged to result from the choral institution (*Lykourgos* 15.1):

> These were inducements to marriage—I mean such things as the processions of the young girls without much clothing, and the athletic contests in the sight of young men.

But it is also stressed that Spartan women, like men, established homoerotic relationships that spanned the generations (*Lykourgos* 18.4). Development of the girls' physique, however, is represented as more important than for-

---

106. Cartledge 1981; Kunstler 1987: 42.

107. We do not know exactly how such choruses were arranged; Parker (1989: 144–45) points to choruses of Spartan girls organized by village and tribe and suggests that the institutions of Spartan religion may have resisted the weakening of kinship ties that is generally attributed to the legislation of Lykourgos.

108. In the imperial period, at least, there was a hereditary priestess of Apollo Karneios at Sparta, named Damosthenia (*IG* v¹ 1390).

mation of their subjectivity by premarital exercises. The former was to be subjected to an energetic regimen in order to produce healthy babies and make for easier delivery. While it is arguable that such exercise would produce not only physical but also psychic strength,[109] the latter may be only incidental to the primary aim of improving the male population, by providing the state with women well equipped to reproduce.

A similar argument is available concerning another intriguing element of Spartan women's choral activity. Plutarch's account suggests that the female choruses were partly responsible for disciplining the men (*Lykourgos* 14.3):

> And sometimes, telling jokes against each one, they playfully mocked the men who had failed; and again they followed the worthy among them with praises and songs, inspiring the young men with great ambition and zeal.

These lines may be thought to resonate with Hektor's fear of the Trojan women's censure, in *Iliad* 6.440–44 and 22.105, and thus to allot to the Spartan women the important social functions of praise and blame. This is a function that they are said to discharge, for instance, when they are summoned to praise a newly elected senator (*Lykourgos* 26.3). Ephraim David's fascinating article on Spartan laughter, however, has demonstrated that the chorus-women's laughter may be aligned with other instances of pedagogic mockery aimed at securing from the young Spartiate compliance with the various demanding ideals of conduct promulgated by his society.[110] A possible conclusion seems to be that young women were enlisted to work on the fragile subjectivities of Spartan males rather than being an object of concern in themselves.[111] Certainly within the classical Spartan context it seems that all members of society, not only the female, were systematically induced to deny their subjective needs and desires or to subordinate them to the polity as a whole. Although the Spartiate male was said to be more free than any other free man (Plutarch *Lykourgos* 28.5), it was a freedom bought at the cost of severe discipline and intense public scrutiny of his words and deeds. This does not entail, however, that the position and status of Spartan women conversely be idealized as unconstrained and unsupervised. An anecdote holds that when Lykourgos was urged by a Spartan to institute democracy in place of his unyielding system, he taunted his critic with the challenge "First establish democracy in your own household" (Plutarch *Lykourgos* 19.3). The implication may well be that the household is still a

---

109. Some contemporary feminist therapists use sport as one of their techniques for building women's self-esteem.

110. David 1989.

111. Stehle (1997: 34) remarks: "The unusual freedom of Spartan girls was not independence but a license to participate in a system of maintaining social pressure on the members of the society."

hierarchical society in which the husband and father rules over wife, children, and slaves. On the other hand, sources from Aristotle onward insist on the anomalous wealth and consequent freedom of Spartan women.[112]

The marriage ceremony of classical Sparta did not elaborate upon the task of joining two *oikoi*, nor did the ceremony emphasize the bride's virginity on her entry into a new family, since apparently individual paternity, along with patriarchal inheritance, was deemphasized. It is alleged that if they could not obtain satisfactory offspring from their present partners, men were permitted to seek children from women not their wives and women from men not their husbands (Xenophon *Constitution of the Lakedaimonians* 1.8–9, Plutarch *Lykourgos* 15.6). Marriage was supposedly accomplished by capture, or *harpage* (Plutarch *Lykourgos* 15.3–9), and the husband famously was prevented from visiting his wife except in secret. According to Plutarch this arrangement energized the desire of both parties and was thus conducive to eugenics (*Lykourgos* 15.5).[113] Even with these attendant drawbacks, marriage was prescribed for all adult Spartiates. Bachelors were variously dishonored (*Lykourgos* 15.1–2), and in an annual ritual similar to that of the choral insults noted above, married women were apparently encouraged to beat them (Athenaeus 13.555, quoting Klearchos of Soli).

On the wedding night the Spartan bride's attendant cut her hair and dressed her in men's clothes, and in this condition she received her new husband. Although the Greek historians themselves do not elaborate on this transvestite wedding, it has attracted much critical attention in the secondary literature. The bizarre practice can be assimilated to the various known instances of initiatory cross-dressing, as when young men dress as women in the Oschophoria at Athens in order to mark by difference their development of correct masculine identities,[114] but we might note with Froma Zeitlin that female-to-male ritual transvestism is far rarer than male-to-female.[115] This imbalance between the practices of women and men is most readily explained by greater cultural investment in the male, but we may also register a general reluctance to entertain even an imaginary female usurpation of male privileges. Yet the Spartans' apparent conviction that women could, under certain circumstances, play men, may also be explica-

112. The Spartiates were not encouraged to amass wealth, but this imperative was consistently ignored by Spartan families. See, for example, Hodkinson 1989.

113. We might also conclude that the adult Spartiate, like the adolescent, was still being required to steal anything he needed rather than enjoying an untroubled claim to it.

114. On this topic see Vidal-Naquet 1981 and 1986. On Kos, according to Plutarch *Greek Questions* 58, bridegrooms were also transvestite. The bibliography on transvestism in general is of course huge; for a starting place see, for example, Zeitlin 1996: 382–85; Bassi 1998: 105–10, 136–41.

115. Zeitlin 1990b: 66–67.

ble in terms of anxiety about the male, since it induces the bride to "repro-duce" her husband figuratively at the moment when she is also about to do so physically, by bearing male children. The wedding ceremony deliberately eradicates sexual difference, but only by inducing the woman as well as the man to act the masculine part.[116]

A possible footnote to the transvestite wedding is to be found at Athenaeus 13.602D–E (= Hagnon), a passage that refers to a Spartan cus-tom of "consorting with" *(homilein)* girls before their marriage as if they were "beloved boys" *(paidika).* Scholars disagree over whether the phrasing can be read to indicate female pederasty or the anal or intercrural intercourse characteristic of (Athenian) male pederasty. Although some have claimed that Spartan girls were sodomized on their wedding night,[117] the Greek is explicit about "before marriage" *(pro ton gamon),* and if the passage does refer to anal or intercrural intercourse, it may perhaps be construed as a contraceptive practice.[118]

The Spartan denial of sexual difference may be seen to point in the gen-eral direction of Cartledge's conclusions rather than those of Kunstler. Of practical significance as a bearer of male children, the Spartan female acquired symbolic significance only insofar as she dramatized and patrolled the boundaries of male identity, and historical women seem to have con-nived at the role of producing and reproducing men. Certainly the *Sayings of Spartan Women* collected by Plutarch, which Kunstler suggests derive ulti-mately from oral tradition, share this fixation on the male, and the women speakers represent themselves almost exclusively as defining and policing masculine conduct.[119]

THE IDEOLOGY OF ADULT WOMEN

So far in this chapter we have examined women's ritual practice in the cho-rus, in certain premarital rites performed in Athens and Attica, and in the wedding ceremonies about which we are best informed. Once married, the

116. A tacit acknowledgment perhaps by Spartan culture that male identity too is con-structed, fragile, and in need of constant reinforcement. On the wedding ceremony see, for instance, Cartledge (1981), who suggests, following Devereux, that the transvestism allays not the bride's anxiety but that of the husband who left the all-male environment of the barracks for the first time. We might note in this connection that the Argive brides, who were com-manded to wear beards to bed, thus atoned for the error of "despising and neglecting" their husbands, who had not proved as valiant in war as they (Plutarch *Virtues of Women* 245; and see further chapter 3).

117. See the discussion in Parker 1993: 327 n. 38.

118. See Garland 1990: 51.

119. Kunstler 1987: 35. See also Redfield 1978: 149 on Spartan women as "fierce enforcers of the warrior code."

Greek female was not free of those ritual obligations that elaborated on her sexual and reproductive identity. Instead of preparing herself for the position of free adult wife and mother, she was invited repeatedly to demonstrate her qualifications for occupying that position.

Rituals for adult women, who almost by definition were also wives and mothers, seem to have been more inclusive than those for girls. These rituals are usually said to convene simply *gynaikes,* "women" or "wives," and our independent knowledge does not usually allow us to say definitely that only prominent women were concerned. On the other hand, we should remember in what follows first that women with more time and resources to spare would probably be more ritually active than others, and second that we are rarely concerned with slave women or, in the case of Athens, free women from the families of metics (resident aliens).

At Athens we can distinguish a regular cycle of festivals for adult women that can be read to address them as sexual or reproductive subjects. As well as the Thesmophoria, Adonia, Haloa, Skira, and Stenia, we know of the Kalamaia and the Plerosia from an inscription from the Piraeus (*IG* ii² 1177), and the ritual calendar from the deme of Erchia mentions a number of occasions that convene the *gynaikes.*[120] Since none of these rituals affects or alters identity, none of them may be characterized as a rite of passage. Calame suggests that the Spartan series of festivals for young girls, some of which also address older women, be construed as corresponding to the three initiatory stages of withdrawal, seclusion and liminality, and return,[121] but I suspect that this is overly schematic. Instead, I would suggest that the very repetitiousness of festivals for women, their nonlinear construction of time, is what is most significant. Caught up in the sequence of female celebrations, women were presented with a number of contradictory propositions about themselves and offered a number of contradictory subject positions to occupy. While none of the women's rituals can be recuperated as uncomplicated "rebellion," the very repetition of contradiction could allow women to develop resistant readings of their festivals. Moreover, as previously emphasized, the construction of female identity is entrusted to exclusively female rituals, so that women must necessarily operate as active subjects of the process even while producing themselves as objects within a patriarchal system.

That most rituals for adult women address them on the topic of female identity is largely accepted in the literature, but it is worthwhile to point out that the Greek sources usually discuss such rituals in terms of fertility and the propagation of families and fields. Why should we not follow the lead of

120. Daux 1963. At Thorikos (*SEG* 33.147; Daux 1963) there are two occasions that convene *gynaikes.*

121. Calame 1977: 1.355–56.

such descriptions and confine the role of the female practitioners to instrumentality?[122] One answer might be that so many rituals convene adult women, and so many different tropes are employed to figure fertility, that we may suspect that fertility is not all that is at issue. Nor need we find persuasive the notion of a simple, mimetic link between procreativity and female identity, deriving from women's roles as mothers, when we recall that the society that performed the rituals frequently attempted, in medical, philosophical, and dramatic texts, to construct the male as the sole or primary source of generation.[123] That any link between female identity and procreativity might have more complex significance than a simple mimesis is also suggested by comparative studies. As Molly Myerowitz has argued, women's role as mothers often entails that they are identified not only with reproductive activity but also with desiring sexuality. She remarks:

> In a most general way, one should recall that sex, both in the ancient world and in contemporary traditional societies, is understood by both women and men primarily as "women's business" rather than men's. . . . In ancient and traditional societies, a keen, often obsessive, feminine interest in the mechanics of desire is entirely compatible with the strictest social codes of premarital chastity and postmarital fidelity, and not relegated exclusively to professional prostitutes.[124]

I suggest that such a construction again implicitly allots to women, rather than to men, the management of desire, both of the self and of others. Greek rituals for adult women address them not only as signs of a generalized fertility that might extend to land and sea, but also as erotic subjects responsible for producing and reproducing certain parameters of female identity.

The requirement to manage desire, especially female desire, within a system of patriarchal marriage, entails the various contradictions in female identity that we explored in the introductory section of this chapter. In the

---

122. See, for example, Brumfield 1981: 236: "Women generally are thought to be more capable of performing agricultural magic than men, since they are more in touch with the wellsprings of fertility." See also Robertson 1995: 195: "The ritual is not concerned with married life as an institution or a vocation; it does not prepare the girls or reward the women. The stages of female maturity are important only for their effect in promoting the fertility of nature." Foxhall (1995: 105–6) offers a different account again of the relation between women and agriculture, which is more compatible with my arguments; she suggests from the relation between women's festivals of Demeter and the agricultural calendar that "work on the threshing floor and the threshing itself was men's work for which women were ritually responsible. . . . It is as if men's practical activities are ineffectual without the partnership of women's ritual activities."

123. On such attempts see, for instance, Dean-Jones 1994: 148–52.

124. Myerowitz 1992: 151.

case of the rituals for adult women at Athens, I would argue that we can see the contradictions laid out over a period of time, namely the ritual year, in the various ritual positions on the spectrum from chastity to license that women are invited to occupy. The situation is not the same for young women in the ritual sphere; since they are not caught up in the same structures of annual repetition, they are neither subject to such insistent address nor entrusted with such important processes. Adult women's rituals are thus best understood within a model of gender ideology; by this I mean that the rituals aim at producing women who are equipped to perform successfully their roles within a patriarchal order, and who have internalized a version of themselves that is useful to others. The rituals that concern us repeat every year, so that a woman might attend the Thesmophoria, for instance, from her mid-teens until her death, anywhere upwards of ten times. Such repetition, however insistent, need not amount to simple indoctrination; I would claim instead that the repetitiveness of this ritual work, which never issues forth in a new identity or status, as do rites of passage, makes visible its ideological character. The necessity repeatedly to rehearse women in the terms of their proper identity tends to demonstrate that such an identity is not part of the natural biological order but is instead the product of a particular social organization. To the extent that ritual repeats its inculcation of female identity, it also underlines the fragility of that identity and its contradictions.

As I suggested in the introduction, one influential and useful understanding of ideological production, most readily identified with the work of Antonio Gramsci, holds that ideology is never static, but must constantly convince and reconvince people, by repetition, of the validity of the ideologically favored position. Such a process may be particularly crucial if that position can also be seen actively to disadvantage certain groups, who might consequently develop their own alternative positions. The necessity of repetition, however, may also encourage this very development of alternatives; if the ideologically favored position were self-evidently preferable, it would not need to advertise itself so frequently. The repetitiousness of the rituals for adult women may be thought to reveal this element in the process of ideological production, and thus to open the gap which might allow historical women to develop their own resistant readings of their ritual practice. Such a model as that outlined above would also contend, along lines made familiar by the work of Mikhail Bakhtin, that ideology is not monolithic but has to take account of what is not itself, in a "dialogic" relation with other possibilities. Even as the gender ideology of ancient Greece addresses women in order to make them into women in its own image, as it were, it must simultaneously recognize that there may be other accounts of womanhood generated from other needs and wants. Although we may conclude that such other possibilities are explored only provisionally, in order to demonstrate that they are ultimately undesirable, an account of ideological production cannot exclude the significance of these alternatives.

The necessary workings of ideological production are not the only consideration that permits us to develop an account of women's possible resistant construals of their cultic performances. Ritual forms in ancient Greece are ultimately sanctioned by the male-dominated society but are inhabited by historical women, and such forms constitute one of the chief arenas for women's intervention and agency in the production of culture. It is within ritual that the community hands women the means to make and remake culture, and thus, potentially, to articulate their own resistant notions of what that culture is. As John Fiske usefully observes: "People make do with what they have, and if all they have are centrally provided resources, the point at issue becomes what people might do with them, rather than what they might do to people."[125] For women of ancient Greece, "what they have" includes prominently the practices and symbols of ritual events, even if such resources are not exclusive to women and are not generated by them independently of other structures. I do not suggest that women necessarily "rebel" against their subordinate status or "subvert" it with these resources, as do some critics.[126] In view of the rewards that attend conformity and the punishments consequent on rebellion, we cannot simply conclude that a reading that emphasizes female resistance must be the most pertinent to a reconstruction of the ritual's work within lived history. We cannot characterize women's rituals as the sites of simple oppositional self-expression, "relief mechanisms," or "rites of rebellion," which do not elaborate any more complex relations with the male-centered society of which they are a part. But I do not propose either that historical women are "cultural dupes."[127] We need not accept that these polarized options are the only ones on offer; I would contend instead with analysts like Fiske that "women's lives under patriarchy involve a constant variety of tactics with which to cope with the constant forces of subordination,"[128] and that for women of ancient Greece such variety of tactics may be most legible within ritual practice. Such an account of Greek women's ritual practice derives not only from theoretical speculation but from empirical cross-cultural studies into historical women's interactions with ritual forms. As Margaret Miles points out, religion inevitably forms part of women's cultural conditioning but also

> make[s] available tools with which women may create a degree of spiritual, political and personal autonomy. . . . If we look only for oppression we will miss the creativity with which women—never the primary shapers of their cul-

125. Fiske 1990: 135.
126. E.g., Keuls 1985: 349–50.
127. Fiske 1990: 140.
128. Ibid.

tures—have foraged in their cultural environments for the tools with which to make their lives.[129]

Within any one ritual there would be a variety of activities and relationships on offer to participating women, which would make possible correspondingly complex interpretations of their experience.

A final complexity in understanding the repeated rituals for adult women is that any such ritual would have an audience that was divided, at least between women performers and the wider male-dominated community, and possibly in other ways that are no longer so accessible to us. An adequate account of the ritual would have to discuss the possible responses of such different groups. Indeed it has been argued that the significance of rituals concerning reproductive and sexual identity must be sought not among the women who perform them but only among the men who wield the ultimate power in society.[130] In what follows, I shall stress the multiple possible meanings of ritual actions, but I shall try to keep in focus the point that ritual polyvalence is not necessarily generated by "liminality" or by the play of symbols,[131] but also by the gender politics of the society within which rituals take place.

THE THESMOPHORIA

At Athens, the Thesmophoria makes a good claim to be the prime site in which are worked out the contradictory imperatives of female identity. Such a claim may also be valid for Greece as a whole, since the Thesmophoria was the single most widespread festival in the Greek world and even emerges in Hellenistic Egypt.[132] We know that the festival exhibited some regional variations, but it is likely everywhere to have followed similar basic contours. In Athens, where we are as ever best informed, the festival lasted three days. On the first, called Anodos, or Ascent, the women—the free adult population—presumably gathered together and made their way up the Acropolis to the sanctuary of Demeter in order to set up their tents. The second day, Nesteia, or Fast, was apparently a day of mourning when the

129. Miles 1985: 2–3.

130. See Paige and Paige 1981. While their account is highly provocative, it is counterintuitive, and runs counter to much anthropological research, to deny to women an active part in generating the meaning of practices to which they contribute.

131. On these explanations of ritual polyvalence see, for example, Turner 1967: 95; La Fontaine 1972: xv–xviii.

132. Pomeroy 1984: 49. Brumfield (1981: 70) notes thirty different Greek cities in which a Thesmophoria was celebrated. Clinton (1993: 120) has argued that the Panhellenic Eleusinian Mysteries represent the transformation of the Thesmophoria and of other cults open only to women. Earlier (1992: 98), he also suggested that the *Homeric Hymn to Demeter* concerns the Thesmophoria rather than the Mysteries.

women probably imitated Demeter in her grief for her lost daughter. The third day, Kalligeneia, or Beautiful Birth, perhaps celebrated the reunion of mother and daughter, and in any case would seem from its name to have honored the principle of fertility.[133] On either the second or third day women called Bailers, Antletriai, went down into caves in the earth and retrieved the remains of piglets and cakes shaped as snakes or male genitals, which had been thrown there earlier.[134] These women had to observe chastity for three days before the festival. These remains were placed on the altars of the Two Goddesses, and could be subsequently mixed with seed as a fertility charm. The festival thus involves special actions designed to increase the earth's fertility, but in its celebration of Demeter the Thesmophoria also aligns women with the principle of maternal fertility and rehearses them in their proper roles as mothers. The main Greek source for the Thesmophoria represents this ritual as designed to ensure the fertility of both fields and human families (*peri tes ton karpon geneseos kai tes ton anthropon sporas,* scholia to Lucian *Dialogues of the Courtesans* 2.1).[135] But as Detienne and Zeitlin have pointed out,[136] the ritual also explores the contradiction in the term "chaste wife," positing a separation between women's fertility and their sexual desire.

The Thesmophoric women are chaste, because they abandon their husbands for a period that may range from three days in Athens to ten in the Greek colony of Syracuse on Sicily.[137] They sit on mats made out of branches of the *agnus castus,* a plant alleged to suppress desire, and on the second day of the festival at Athens they fast, submitting their appetite for food to a discipline similar to that involved in sexual chastity.[138] If, as is also plausible, the

---

133. Anodos: see the scholia on Aristophanes (Deubner 1966: 508); Nesteia: Athenaios 307F, Alciphron 3.39, and Aristophanes *Women at the Thesmophoria* 78–80; Kalligeneia: *Women at the Thesmophoria* 298.

134. For the Antletriai see the scholia on Lucian *Dialogues of the Courtesans* 2.1 (= Rabe 1906: 276). It is not clear when the piglets and so on were thrown into the caves; Deubner suggests the occasion of the Skira four months earlier, but Simon has gained support for her view that the day was the Stenia, two days earlier. See Simon 1983: 19–20. Clinton (1988) suggests the occasion of the previous year's Thesmophoria, or during the Mysteries twenty days earlier. He has a satisfyingly graphic description of what the Bailers endured on their descent (76).

135. Lowe (1998) offers a very provocative discussion of this text, which he also appends in Greek and translation to his article, and concludes that the source for this description may be an actor in the rites or a priestly official, rather than simply an outside commentator. He does not go so far as to say that the source for this "surprisingly sophisticated model" (156) would then have to be female, although I wish he did.

136. Detienne 1977; Zeitlin 1982a.

137. On the Thesmophoria in Sicily see Diodorus Siculus 5.4.7.

138. *Agnus castus:* Fehrle 1910: 140–41; scholia on Nikander *Theriaca* 71; Dioskorides 1.134. Fasting: e.g., Athenaeus 7.307F; Plutarch *Demosthenes* 30.5; Aristophanes *Women at the Thesmophoria* 984.

Thesmophoric women chewed garlic, it may have had the effect of making them unattractive to men by tainting their breath.[139] In Aristophanes *Women at the Thesmophoria* 493–94 Euripides' In-law claims that women chew garlic in the morning after a night on the town, thus averting the suspicions of their husbands. Such a practice would help to site the Thesmophoric garlic directly on the cusp between chastity and license.

The ritual continence can be understood as a hoarding of sexual energies in preparation for the expenditure required in reproduction and is paralleled by similar practices in other cultures. But within the Greek context, the Thesmophoria can also be seen to demonstrate women's correct management of desire in their refusal to be either its subjects or, significantly, its objects. Characterized as bees *(melissai)*, creatures renowned in Greek sources for their dislike of sexual indulgence,[140] the Thesmophoric women separate themselves physically from men but also, perhaps, use the unpleasant smell of garlic to render themselves unattractive.[141] Their avoidance of attractive clothes and decorative garlands may also constitute part of this refusal of desire, although the latter may also be related to the fact that Persephone was abducted while picking flowers.[142] Simultaneously celebrating their maternity and their chastity, they act out the oxymoron of the "chaste wife" so dear to patriarchal formations. In this way, as Detienne has shown,[143] they demonstrate their primary allegiance to the codes of marriage. Their chastity is not easily construed, as Demand has attempted,[144] as a sign of sex-role inversion and of general disorder, but rather is an index of their ability to withstand the illicit desire of adulterers. Hence the injunc-

139. See Philochoros in *FGH* III.B 328 F89 on garlic at the Skira, and *IG* ii² 1184 on the provision of garlic as part of the Thesmophoric supplies.

140. See Larson 1995a: 353: "The bee represents the ideal wife's industry and sobriety." In Semonides, it is only the woman descended from a bee who makes a bearable wife; she alone "takes no pleasure in sitting with the women where they talk about sex" (90–91). See also on bees' sexuality, or lack of it, Xenophon *Oikonomikos* 7.32–35 and Plutarch *Advice on Marriage* 144D.

141. On the bee-women of the Thesmophoria see Apollodorus of Athens in *FGH* II.B 244 F89. That the sense of smell was registered as important to Greek erotic practices can be deduced not only from the significance of perfumes in seduction scenes like that between Myrrhine and Kinesias in Aristophanes' *Lysistrata,* but also from stories like that of the Lemnian women, who are afflicted with such a horrible smell that their husbands resort to concubines. See also Myrsilos of Lesbos in *FGH* 477 F1a; Burkert 1970.

142. See the scholion on Sophokles *Oedipus at Colonus* 681. For prohibitions on clothing see, for example, *LSS* 32 and 33. Clothes could be a matter of controversy in other ritual contexts too. The Rule of the Andanian Mysteries, in its characteristic micromanagement of women's participation, prohibits transparent clothes and those with stripes more than half a finger wide (*LSCG* 65.16). See also Meyer 1987: 53.

143. Detienne 1977.

144. Demand 1994: 118.

tion attributed to Theano, a woman philosopher, in a neo-Pythagorean text of the Hellenistic period. When asked how soon after sexual intercourse a woman might participate in the Thesmophoria, she allegedly replied that if the man was her husband, the woman might attend straightway; but if her lover, never again. The Thesmophoria demonstrates that women can exercise *sophrosune* to the extent suggested by Foucault's formulation; they can manage to respect the rules laid down for them.[145] As we shall see later in this chapter, in Athens at least convicted adulteresses were in fact prohibited from attending the Thesmophoria and other festivals, and severely punished if they tried to participate.

Detienne's influential account of the women's festivals (1977) suggested that the Thesmophoria and Adonia divided women up between them, the former convening respectable wives in order to celebrate continence and virtuous productivity, the latter assembling prostitutes and women of low repute in a festival of profligate license. Detienne's account has come under some attack, especially in Winkler's 1990 book *Constraints of Desire,* and we may want to suggest instead that the ritual sphere as a whole divides women's sexuality into chastity and license, requiring women to act out different versions of themselves at different times. The Thesmophoria concentrated on chastity but also mobilized figures of license in its elaboration of female identity; the women exchanged insults and "shameful speech" *(aischrologia)* on the day of fasting, and they are also said to have handled models of male and female genitals.[146] The patristic writer Theodoretos claims in *Graecarum Affectionum Curatio* 3.84 that "the female genitals are held worthy of divine honor by the women celebrating at the Thesmophoria." In Sicily, according to Athenaeus 14.647A, "cakes of sesame and honey were fashioned in the shape of the female genitalia, and . . . carried around in honor of the goddesses." The scholia to Lucian *Dialogues of the Courtesans* 2.1, speak of "imitations of snakes and male members." Moreover, the appropriate sacrificial victim for Demeter, the piglet, bears a name that also signifies the female genitals. Despite the chastity of the women at the Thesmophoria, then, we can suggest that they were also able, within the ritual's confines, to represent themselves as erotic subjects.

145. On "Theano" and her various writings see Thesleff 1965: 193–201. Diogenes Laertius 8.43 claims that the saying referred to when a woman was pure rather than when she might attend the Thesmophoria. Plutarch *Advice on Marriage* 142C and Clement of Alexandria *Stromata* 4.19.301.1–3 Stählin give accounts of Theano's legendary modesty. *Stromata* 302.1–3 and Theon *Progymnasmata* 5.98.3–7 Spengel repeat the Thesmophoria quotation.

146. See Apollodoros *Library* 1.5.3 on *aischrologia.* Hesychius and Photius on the Stenia claim that the women make fun of and insult each other *(diaskoptousi, loidorousin).* Kleomedes *De Motu Circulari Corporum Caelestium* 2.1.91 claims that what the women say at the Thesmophoria are words "such as someone would say come from a brothel."

Such a conclusion is even more plausible in light of the fact that the women's *aischrologia,* or shameful speech, was said to derive from Iambe's jesting with Demeter. According to the *Homeric Hymn to Demeter,* the goddess is entertained by Iambe when she is grieving for her absent daughter. Iambe was so ridiculous that the *mater dolorosa* finally laughed and agreed to emerge from her mourning and to eat and drink again (200–204):

> She did not smile, she did not eat or drink.
> She sat, wasting away with desire for her deep-bosomed daughter,
> Until clever Iambe made fun of her
> And with many a joke moved the holy goddess
> To smile and laugh and have a gentle heart.

But other accounts of Demeter's capitulation claim that the entertainer was Baubo, who got to the heart of the matter by lifting her skirts, thus cajoling even the bereaved mother into a cheerful acceptance of female sexuality.[147] In its deployment of erotic figures the Thesmophoria may be read to attribute to its women a healthy interest and pleasure in sex, which will, however, be suspended in the interests of marital chastity. Whatever pleasure the women are to obtain is on offer only inside marriage.

The *aischrologia* that the women use may be understood in a variety of ways. The women are said to engage in *aischrologia* not only at the Thesmophoria but also at the Skira, Stenia, and Haloa, and mutual abuse by women is also known from Aegina, where ten choruses for Damia and ten for Auxesia ritually exchanged insults (Herodotos 5.83, Pausanias 2.32.2). The practice has been understood as provocative of fertility in that "shameful speech" may arouse desire, yet the encouragement of procreation by licentious talk would seem to be more appropriate in the context of a meeting between women and men, not women alone.[148] Turner's discussion of episodes of ritual abuse in African communities indicates as much: "The hilarious contradiction [is] that the more the sexes stress their differences and mutual aggression, the more they desire sexual congress."[149] The practice of abuse exchanged between parties of men and women is attested in the Greek context. At a festival of Demeter at Pellene in Achaia, described

---

147. On Baubo see the introductory essay by Olender 1990. Most of the evidence for Baubo derives from patristic accounts of the Eleusinian Mysteries and hence may be considered suspect. Most commentators agree that the exposure of the female genitals signifies Demeter's acceptance of her daughter's gendered destiny; see, for example, Arthur 1977: 22.

148. There was also an obscure episode when the women beat each other with strips of woven bark. This flagellation may also be understood as a charm for fertility; compare the Lupercalia at Rome when barren women moved into the path of the runners who were equipped with whips.

149. Turner 1967: 78.

by Pausanias (7.27.10), men and women celebrate together for two days, and then

> on the third day . . . the men leave the sanctuary, and the women, left behind, perform in the night whatever is their custom. Not only are men driven away, but even male dogs. On the next day the men come to the sanctuary, and the men and the women take turns to laugh and make jokes at each other's expense.

The festival then continues for another four days, but no further details are given in Pausanias. Since the women's Thesmophoric *aischrologia* is perhaps not to be completely explained by the fertility-charm, we may want to consider other hypotheses. H. W. Parke, for instance, proposes that it be also understood as a discharge of the tensions brought on by a day of fasting,[150] to which formulation one might add the tensions produced when a body of people are forced suddenly to live in close proximity to one another. In an inscription from third-century Mylasa, in Caria, the women celebrating Demeter are instructed not to *othein* (push, shove) each other, which may support this kind of reading (*LSAM* 61.4).[151]

Aischrologia might also be understood as a "carnivalesque" element of the Thesmophoria, in the sense made available by the work of Bakhtin.[152] The women turn the festival over to a celebration of the grotesque and ribald aspects of the body and eradicate distinctions of rank among themselves by the exchange of insults, producing the egalitarian *communitas* described by Turner as characteristic of ritual processes. More dramatically, they challenge all the requirements of the *sophrosune* that defines their role as adult women; by indulging in licentious speech they reject the canonical imperatives of silence and modesty. Belying their cult title of "bees," which is also used in other contexts for priestesses,[153] they refuse to act the part of the Semonidean bee-woman, who "takes no pleasure in sitting with the women where they talk about sex" (Semonides 90–91). Greek sources can be seen to comprehend the women's *aischrologia* in terms of a challenge to patriarchal authority. Aristophanes' comedy *Women at the Thesmophoria,* for instance, represents the assembled women exchanging tales of adultery and domestic theft but ensures that by doing so, they incriminate themselves in the "unseen" presence of the male-dominated audience. Euripides' In-law

150. Parke 1977: 86–87.
151. In the Rule of the Andanian Mysteries the "supervisor of women" is charged with the maintenance of order among women so that they all keep the places in the procession assigned to them by lot (*LSCG* 65.32–33).
152. See, for example, the introduction to Bakhtin 1968.
153. Priestesses of Apollo in Pindar *Pythian* 4.106, and of Demeter and Artemis in the scholia on this line; priestesses of Kybele in Lactantius 1.22.

occupies the position of this audience in that he infiltrates the festival disguised as a woman and shares the women's enjoyment of their naughty narratives, elaborating not a few of his own. The joke is on the women, however, because in the end they find his stories too rude even for them.[154]

Yet the women's *aischrologia* cannot simply be recuperated under the sign of resistance, but may also be read as a technique for confirming historical women in their assigned gender roles. By speaking what should not be heard the women are brought to act out the terms of the common Greek equation between the female and the unspeakable. The Nurse in Euripides' *Hippolytos* makes this equation explicit when she tells Phaidra: "If you are sick with one of the unspeakable *(aporrheton)* diseases, here are women to help with it, but if your disaster may be carried outside toward men, speak, so that this matter may be divulged to doctors' (293–96; I give a literal translation). If we take on board the combined contribution of Iambe and Baubo in the myth of Demeter to the etiology of *aischrologia*, it is hard to avoid the conclusion that what the women at the Thesmophoria do is to speak the body, to speak the female organs. As the women's *ololuge* at the climactic moment of sacrifice offers to reduce their power of articulate discourse to a wordless cry, so the *aischrologia* attributed to them in their exclusive festivals threatens to equate their speech with their genitalia, short-circuiting any other possibilities for subjectivity. They seem to embody the Deep Throat figurines, found at Priene in Asia Minor and dated to the fourth century, which consist of a face superimposed on the female pubic cleft.[155]

Such an image of the Thesmophoric women may seem to correspond to some of the less edifying accounts of the female in ancient Greek culture, but "to speak the body" is also available to women in other, more positive contexts. We know, for instance, that women talked about their reproductive work in ways that claimed knowledge and authority for themselves and that seemed to acquire respect from medical practitioners who recorded the discourse.[156] A dancing girl who worked as a prostitute, owned by a kinswoman of the doctor, monitors the processes of her own body in order not to become pregnant, and she can do this because she has listened to 'the sort of thing the women say to each other' (*On the Nature of the Child* 13). More emphatic is the medical account of women's discourse at *On the Seventh-Month Child* 4.1:[157]

154. On *aischrologia* see also Zeitlin 1982a: 145, 147; McClure 1999: 47–52. McClure points out that there is no "real" *aischrologia* in *Women at the Thesmophoria;* the women do not actually utter any obscenities (230).

155. See the illustrations in Olender 1990.

156. See also Dean-Jones 1994: 26–40.

157. If, as Geoffrey Lloyd has argued, the scientific discourse of the Hippocratics was developed in an agonistic relation with other explanatory discourses such as that of religion, we

You cannot distrust what women say about childbearing. For they say everything and are always talking and always asking questions. And they cannot be
persuaded by word or deed other than that they know what is happening in
their own bodies. If you want to, you can say otherwise, but they are the judges
and give the prizes in this discussion, and they always will inquire about this
subject.

Even without this explicit testimony, it would be difficult to imagine women
of ancient Greece not discussing their reproductive experiences, which constituted the chief significance of their lives; and where better to have the discussion than at the festivals expressly dedicated to their maternal identities?
If we can extend the significance of *aischrologia* in this direction, we can conclude that the Thesmophoria, and possibly other related festivals, provided
an opportunity not only for cheerful obscenities conducive to fertility but
also for useful, practical conversation among women. Such conversation
would not construct women as objects, identical with their physical bodies,
but would construct those bodies as objects of women's knowledge. Lucia
Nixon has suggested that the various herbs associated with myths and rituals of Demeter could contribute to women's control of their fertility;[158] medical discussion along these lines would give women even greater knowledge
of themselves.[159] This discourse, while obviously equipping women to operate as successful wives and mothers, and thus not constituting a resistance to
imposed gender identities, might nonetheless be construed to equip the
women "on their own terms," and thus to represent an element of female
agency and autonomy within the constraints of ritual practice.

Aischrologia may have covered many topics important to women and been
available for different emphases. As well as putting into play representations
of women's sexuality and of their speech, the Thesmophoria stresses, when
it mobilizes the women to rehearse the myth of Demeter and Persephone,
the mother-daughter relationship. The most influential version of this myth
is articulated in the *Homeric Hymn to Demeter,* which memorably represents
Demeter's anger at her daughter's rape and the devastating effects of the
famine that she induces.[160] The Thesmophoria, like the *Hymn* itself, may be

---

might add to the agonistic context the medical discourse of women, who appear here not only
as competitors with the doctors but, in the final sentence, as the judges who award the prize.
On the contests between doctors and others, and among doctors, see Lloyd 1987: e.g., 41–42,
85–90, 100.

158. Nixon 1995.

159. See also, for instance, Scarborough 1991: 145; Riddle 1992: 40–63. The latter passage discusses the herbs known in ancient times to procure contraception or abortion, and
these include several herbs associated with the Thesmophoria. Riddle is, however, shaky on
some of his Greek mythology.

160. It is not within the scope of this study to give a full account of the *Hymn;* see the excellent collection of texts in Foley 1994.

read as an acknowledgment at the cultural level of a female power that cannot be recognized at the overt political level; it compensates women for the denial of their significance in any other sphere. The *Hymn*, however, does not only display female power and anger. While recognizing the cost to historical women of maintaining the system of patriarchal marriage, the *Hymn* pretends that the daughter will return to her mother for part of every year, and consequently provides an imaginary solution to real separations among women. It thus ensures that Demeter is eventually reconciled to the (partial) loss of her daughter, and that she returns the world to fruitfulness. Similarly the Thesmophoria, at least in Athens, moves its participants from a potentially antisocial condition of chastity, fasting, and mutual abuse to the day of welcome for the Beautiful Birth. As Zeitlin puts it, the festival leads "from an original refusal to abrogate feminine power to an acceptance of the limitations placed upon it."[161]

Nancy Demand offers a new reading of the Thesmophoria's representation of the mother-daughter bond and separation. Her brief but provocative analysis suggests that the ritual not only provides a vent for women's negative reactions to their enforced participation in the patriarchal exchange of women, but also offers "a positive view of the problematic separation of mother and daughter."[162] The ritual shows women an endless cycle of female experience in which daughters, separated from their mothers by marriage, become mothers themselves of marrying daughters; the goddesses' endurance is offered to human women as a paradigm of successful strength.

I would like to elaborate further on the possibilities of this reading. The women in the Thesmophoria have left husband, children, and domestic duties behind, they are not sexually active, and they are gathered together in a kind of adult chorus. Do they not resemble to some extent the virgin girls, the daughters, that they once were? If they can be seen to recapture their previous state as virgin daughters, then despite the Thesmophoria's insistence on procreation, its women participants are also celebrating a time before they were entrusted with the responsibility for sexuality and reproduction, and before they became the matrons who are allegedly honored in the ritual. It is, of course, the virgin daughter whose loss is mourned and whose recovery is celebrated in the ritual as a whole. If the women participants may be identified with the virgin daughter as well as with the matron, then the divine reunion between the mother and child will also constitute a reunion between the women and their former, younger selves. The Thesmophoria would thus mediate every woman's personal, gendered history, closing the gap introduced into it by marriage. The "daughter" as such is not addressed by the Thesmophoria, which convenes the *gynaikes* as

161. Zeitlin 1982a: 142.
162. Demand 1994: 119.

opposed to the *parthenoi;* she is instead available symbolically as part of a discourse about the adult woman. If, as Helene Foley has proposed "'the successful maturation of a daughter does involve, and most especially in a traditional society, a symbolic reunity of mother and daughter,"[163] the Thesmophoria would seem to elaborate this unity from the point of view of the woman who is now positioned to be her own mother and to nurture herself.[164] If the Thesmophoria makes available to its participants the model of mother-daughter reunion as a way to understand their own development, as well as a way to recuperate the losses inflicted on them by patriarchal arrangements, then the ritual can be seen to validate a specifically female model of experience without having to mobilize a full-fledged discourse of sex-role rebellion.

Genuine reunions between mothers and daughters would also take place, but probably only when those daughters had themselves becomes mothers. According to Lucian *Dialogues of the Courtesans* 2.1 mothers and unmarried daughters attended the Thesmophoria together, but most commentators doubt the testimony of these lines for the classical period.[165] Menander's *Arbitrators* has been read to indicate that concubines participated; as we saw in chapter 1, one character tries to dissuade another from keeping two households by pointing out that he will have to pay for two Skira and two Thesmophoria. We do not have to take this statement at face value, since it may well be comic exaggeration; but, on the other hand, a free concubine was expected to be as faithful to her "protector" as a wife to her husband, so there would not be any great anomaly in her attendance at the Thesmophoria.[166]

None of our evidence reliably restricts participation to women of Eupatrid birth or recognizable wealth, and the fact that Aristophanes *Women at the Thesmophoria* 446–56 includes the garland-seller who is forced by her husband's death to work for her living clearly points, if we can take it as at all representative, in the opposite direction. Susan Guettel Cole has also argued for the inclusivity of Demeter's festivals from the number and quality of votives left in her shrines throughout Greece.[167] Slave-women did not participate in the Thesmophoria, however, and it is not difficult to see

163. Foley 1994: 134.

164. Rabuzzi (1982: 135) claims that within women's psychohistory this ability to mother oneself is crucial to successful adjustment.

165. E.g., Deubner 1966: 53. Since Lucian is a postclassical source, it may be that the contours of the festival had changed by the second century C.E.

166. Brumfield (1981) argues for a more inclusive festival, open to young women and *hetairai* as well as concubines, but the majority of commentators disagree. Brumfield interprets all the Demeter festivals as primarily aimed at securing good harvests, without regard for the production of useful women.

167. Cole 1994: 203–4.

why.[168] Slave-women are by definition the objects of others' ungoverned desire and so do not have to learn its management. They do not have to be conciliated, compensated, or otherwise induced to identify their interests with those of others, for the simple reason that the primary determinant of their lives is superior force.[169] The difference between the wife and the slave-woman is made explicit by Xenophon *Oikonomikos* 10, in a context where what is at stake is precisely the wife's responsibility for desire within marriage. When the bride appears in makeup and high heels, the husband gently chides her and points out that her natural wifely looks will equip her to contend sexually with the slaves:

> The sight of her, when she is competing with a servant, since she is cleaner and better dressed, as is proper, is arousing in itself, especially when you add the fact that the one gratifies her man willingly while the other is forced to submit.

The naked cynicism of this passage seems to me to guarantee the accuracy of its representation.

The Thesmophoria signifies at many levels, constructing female identity not only out of the various contradictions produced by patriarchal gender ideology but also out of versions of specifically feminine experience. The practices of the women who participate in it are certainly exceptional from the point of view of their difference from women's daily routine but do not offer a construction of female identity that is completely "other" and therefore unacceptable to the male-dominated community. However, there did

168. This is the generally accepted interpretation of Isaios 6.50, although we should perhaps note that this passage concerns not all slaves but a slave-woman who "lives shamefully" *(aischros biousa)*. She "dared to enter the sacred space and see what was not permitted to her."

169. Such compulsion was also available, of course, as a technique in the governance of free women, but the intimate cooperation required from a wife and mother seems to have been perceived as more easily secured by methods that did not also arouse hostility. While an argument from silence is obviously suspect, especially on a charged subject like domestic violence, we might note that physical discipline of wives is not a prominent trope in Greek literature; even the most misogynist text is more liable to lament the ungovernability of women than to advise on how to govern them. Lysistrata canvasses the possibility of domestic violence on two separate occasions, but it doesn't stop her (163, 520). The bitch-woman in Semonides has her teeth "knock[ed] out with a stone," but only as part of a demonstration that even then she will not shut up. In this respect the testimony is very different from that on physical discipline of slaves, which is everywhere celebrated. Violence against free women is most commonly acknowledged in the case of prostitutes and the adulteress. Neaira (who has bought her freedom) leaves Phrynion because she is "treated with wanton outrage" *(aselgos proupelakizeto)*, which may but does not necessarily connote physical ill-treatment. The convicted adulteress, as we shall see, is the target of indiscriminate physical abuse. A curious note in Artemidoros *Interpretation of Dreams* 2.48 claims that it is always auspicious to dream of "strik[ing] those over whom one rules, with the exception of one's wife. For if she is beaten, it means that she is committing adultery." Although this text is late (second century C.E.), it might suggest a psychological resistance to violence against the wife that might be applicable in earlier periods.

circulate various accounts of the Thesmophoria that represented it as menacing the patriarchal order of the state. The speaker of Lysias 1, *On the Murder of Eratosthenes,* plays on the sexual charge of the festival when he makes a point of the fact that his wife went to the Thesmophoria in the company of her seducer's mother (20). Since the young wife had recently given birth to the couple's first child, the husband claims that he saw nothing wrong with her attendance at the festival. Convinced that the birth demonstrated the unproblematic identification of her interests with his, the husband represents himself as subsequently betrayed by the gender-based solidarity of women who gather together without social distinction and refuse to recognize the claims of the individual *oikos*.[170] And who can doubt that the erotic equivocation of the festival, where the women are chaste but talk dirty, assists the fateful loosening of the bonds of their allegiance?

As Detienne has shown, however, the main fear generated among the citizens excluded from the Thesmophoria was not fear of sex but fear of violence.[171] In the Greek imagination, or versions of it, Thesmophoric women attack men physically; in the two narratives examined by Detienne, however, males provoke the celebrating women. In the first, Battos of Cyrene wishes to see what the women do at the Thesmophoria, and will not be dissuaded by them. Even though he does not manage to penetrate to the absolutely private part of the ceremonies, the assembled women turn on him and castrate him with the tools used for sacrifice.[172] That this narrative resonated with the Greek imagination may be judged from its similarity not only to Aristophanes' *Women at the Thesmophoria,* where the In-law is imprisoned by the women, but also to Euripides' *Bakchai,* in which Pentheus is "unmanned," reduced to a child and then to dismembered flesh by the wives and mothers who have convened in honor of Dionysos. Taken together, these accounts indicate a perceived slippage between female gatherings for Demeter and those for Dionysos; both not only raise the specter of "women in charge" and "the world turned upside down" but also suppose that once women have an opportunity to articulate resistance in ritual terms, there will be nothing to prevent them from proceeding to direct action. Despite the ostensible differences between the cults of Demeter and Dionysos, the common factor of exclusive female gathering will entail that the results are the same. Such narratives, implicitly recognizing the possibility of women's anger at their subjected lives, demonstrate a perverse accuracy in representing its outbreak within the ritual scenario. By inculcating the para-

170. Eratosthenes' mother may, of course, have been prosecuting her son's interests, and not acting out of any misguided female solidarity!

171. Detienne 1989. No Greek source, to my knowledge, represents the Thesmophoria in such pornographic terms as does, for instance, Juvenal for the corresponding Roman celebration of the Bona Dea. According to Juvenal *Satire* 6, when the women celebrants cannot have access to men, who are excluded from the festival, they have recourse instead to donkeys (327–34).

172. Aelian frag. 44 Hercher. See the Suda s.vv. *Thesmophoros* and *Sphaktriai.*

meters of proper behavior, ritual provides one of the techniques that will contain female violence, and conversely, the extent of women's anger demonstrates the necessity for the annual repetition of the ritual cycle.

The narratives of female aggression cited above defuse themselves by offering to the women's violence only one, self-incriminating male scapegoat—Battos, Pentheus, and In-law—rather than the entire masculine polity, and the first provocation is again male in Detienne's second narrative of Thesmophoric violence, which is found in Pausanias 4.17.1. During the Second Messenian War, in the seventh century, Aristomenes and his troops attacked the women who were celebrating at the sanctuary of Demeter in Aigila (Lakonia), but the women "were inspired by the goddess to defend themselves, and most of the Messenians were wounded," again by the sacrificial implements. There are some significant differences between the two narratives discussed in Detienne, however, which together suggest that they are not narratives simply of female aggression. The account in Pausanias manages the women's violence far more successfully than does that of Battos; the women do get to tie Aristomenes up, but he is subsequently freed by the priestess Archidameia, who, it is said, had formerly been in love with him. Detienne fails to note that the whole story, moreover, offers a mirror-image to that which immediately precedes it in Pausanias. In 4.16.9–10, a previous episode in the war, Aristomenes attacks the chorus of Spartan girls who are dancing for Artemis at Caryae and carries off the wealthiest and most nobly born. The self-assertion of the Thesmophoric women, then, can be seen to respond to and compensate for the structural vulnerability of the Artemisian chorus. The captured girls are depicted as vulnerable to further sexual assaults from Aristomenes' soldiers, but when the men attempt to rape the girls Aristomenes executes them. Aristomenes' *sophrosune* in this respect, restraining both himself and his troops, is amply repaid by the amorous priestess's lack of it when she betrays her companions and her goddess in the name of desire. Not only sexual violence, but the female management of desire, are at stake in the ritual context.

The pervasive fantasy of Thesmophoric violence may be seen to derive from that account of the festival that claims that it was introduced to Greece from Egypt, by the Danaids (Herodotos 2.171). The Danaids' history, of course, presents the alarming spectacle of wives who kill their husbands individually and at home, without needing to gather together in the ritual context. A persuasive reconstruction of the Aeschylean Danaid trilogy suggests that it closed with the establishment of the Thesmophoria as a compensation and consolation to the Danaids, and by implication to all women, for their enforced acquiescence in patriarchal marriage.[173] A notion of the Thesmophoria as both commemorating ancient violence and guaranteeing

173. Zeitlin 1990a. See further the discussion of Aeschylus's *Suppliants* in chapter 5.

its absence from future marriages by the production of properly successful wives may have proved reassuring to the male community excluded from the ritual; and we can only speculate on what secret satisfaction participating women took from the narratives of their dangerous foremothers.

Not all the narratives of Thesmophoric women, however, represent them as violent. When in Herodotos 6.16 the Chians flee the battle of Lade and attempt to cross the territory of the Ephesians, these latter assume they have come to steal the women who are away from home celebrating the *pannychis* of the Thesmophoria, and accordingly march out against the Chians to leave not one alive. The Ephesians, in this narrative, evidently did not trust their Thesmophoric women to defend themselves. As a footnote to the various religio-military narratives, we may point to one thoroughly obscure element of the Athenian Thesmophoria, the "Chalcidian Pursuit," or *Chalcidikon Diogma.* The only information we have about this observance—which incidentally permits us again to register the extent of our ignorance about women's ritual practice generally, and to underline the provisional quality of much of our analysis—is that the enemy was turned back and pursued to Chalkis on account of a prayer by the women.[174] May we not read here the trace of some heavily repressed account of female violence, conveniently deflected from the citizenry to the generic "enemy"?

THE ADONIA

At Athens, and possibly in many other poleis, the Thesmophoria represents an energetically renewed attempt to align historical women with the favored construction of female sexual and reproductive identity. What of the other rituals that convened adult women? The Dionysiac rituals construct female identity out of a different ritual vocabulary from that deployed within the discourse of reproduction and sexuality, and I shall consider them in the next two chapters. About the Skira and the Stenia little can be said in the present state of our knowledge, so the final festivals for adult women that I shall discuss will be the Adonia and Haloa. The Adonia in particular has been a focus for critical attention in recent years, especially that of Detienne (1977) and Winkler (1990). Recent studies have established a relatively firm framework within which we may attempt to understand the Adonia, at least as it emerges in classical Athens. The festival convened chiefly adult women, who planted seeds of lettuce and herbs in broken pots and bits of crockery, and took these, once they had sprouted, up onto the rooftops where they quickly withered and died. The women seem to have spent at least one night of the festivities on the rooftops lamenting the death of

174. See the Suda and Hesychios s.vv. *chalcidikon diogma* and *diogma* .

Adonis, and then they cast the desiccated gardens into springs or into the sea, amid more lamentation (see fig. 1).

The fifth and fourth centuries yield most testimony for the Adonia, but celebration of Adonis was apparently popular, especially among women, at other periods. Adonis appears twice in the poetry of Sappho (fragments 140 and 168), inviting the interpretation that the poems are choral laments to be sung by a group of women, which may also be the case for the fragment of Praxilla said to derive from a speech allotted to Adonis (747 PMG). In Theokritos *Idyll* 15 two Syracusan women in third-century Alexandria visit Arsinoe's palace to see the special festival of Adonis that she has produced. The female musician who sings the lament describes how Adonis will die and be cast into the sea, and how the women will mourn for him. Some of the contours of the observance thus seem to remain recognizable between the fifth and the third centuries B.C.E. Pausanias, writing in the second century C.E., refers to a special building in which women of Argos mourn for Adonis (2.20.6).

Detienne's work opened up the Adonia by putting it into a dynamic relationship with the Thesmophoria. The Adonia was seen to draw its significance from its elaboration on promiscuous, indulgent sexuality, construed as inferior to the laborious productivity signaled by the Thesmophoria. Detienne's analysis shows how the antithesis informs several elements of the two rituals: in the Thesmophoria women smell of garlic or of fasting, whereas the Adonia is characterized by the use of perfumes; the Thesmophoric women are chaste, but the Adonia is scene of licentious encounters; the Thesmophoria convenes respectable, married women, but prostitutes dominate at the Adonia.

Detienne's achievement was to shift the focus of the Adonia away from the "dying vegetation god" beloved of previous criticism and onto the construction of female identity, but his analysis also displayed the weaknesses of its strengths, particularly in its very rigid separation of the Adonia and Thesmophoria. Recently Winkler has demonstrated that the issue of participants, at least, is not at all clear. We have seen that concubines may have attended the Thesmophoria, although this does not necessarily entail that the festival was also open to those prostitutes who had a plurality of clients rather than being supported by one man at a time. Conversely, it is apparent that married women attended the Adonia. Aristophanes *Lysistrata* 390–96 seems to confirm as much:

I heard it once in the assembly;
Demostratos, damn him, was saying
we should sail to Sicily, and his wife, capering about,
goes: "Woe for Adonis!"—and Demostratos
says to get the hoplites from Zakynthos,
and the wife, a bit the worse for wear, up on the roof,
goes: "Beat your breast for Adonis!"

Figure 1. Aphrodite performing the Adonia. Lekythos, ca. 380 B.C.E. Badisches Landesmuseum B39. Reproduced with permission.

While the orator argues for the expedition, his wife howls from the rooftops. The scholia to this passage claim that the *gyne* is *tis gyne*, "some woman or other," rather than "his wife," but there is no lexical indication to this effect, and the syntax would seem rather to indicate a *gyne* in a specific relation to the orator. Equally relevant is the observation that the passage loses much of its punch if we construe *gyne* as *tis gyne*. The point, after all, is that Athenian men cannot control even their own wives, let alone all the rest of the "monstrous regiment."

Other sources on the Adonia, which have been read to indicate the attendance of prostitutes, can show that the festival also convened married women. In Menander's fourth-century *The Samian Woman*, a wife attends the Adonia along with her next-door neighbor's concubine, with whom she has become friendly. The epistolary fictions of Alkiphron, written in the second century C.E., include letters purportedly written by *hetairai* inviting other *hetairai* to come to the Adonia, but even they point out that a newly married bride is among the celebrants.[175] Whatever polarity was elaborated between the Adonia and the Thesmophoria, it does not seem to have conformed unequivocally to a distinction between the chastity of the married woman and the license of the prostitute.

This is not to say, however, that we should eradicate all trace of sexual indulgence from our account of the festival. The *Samian Woman* claims that the seduction of an unmarried girl took place under cover of the nocturnal rooftop celebrations, and while we need not suppose that such disorderly conduct was ever condoned, we should not ignore the other erotic signs attaching to the festival, such as the use of exotic perfumes and the identification with Aphrodite in the lament for Adonis. Eva Keuls interprets the Adonia as a fully developed expression of a sexuality alternative to that available within patriarchal marriage; in mourning for Adonis, the women of Athens lament their own subjected and sexually unfulfilling lives, and in the figure of Aphrodite's young consort they fantasize a lover far more satisfying than their stern, grizzled husbands. The Adonia, according to this reconstruction, is a site for women's autonomous articulation of their own sexual needs, and Keuls explicitly labels the festival "counter-cultural" and "rebellious."[176]

There is obviously a difficulty in predicating rebellion of a festival that was, if not sanctioned, at least tolerated by the male-dominated community. Winkler offers a reading of the ritual which tries to construct a gynocentric perspective without relying on too polarized a notion of gender politics.[177] Aligning the Adonia with other adult women's rituals, like the Thesmo-

175. See Winkler 1990a for a more detailed account of all this testimony.
176. Keuls 1985: 24–25.
177. Winkler 1990a.

phoria and the Haloa, he concentrates on their similarities rather than their differences and asks: "Why are the women laughing?" He proposes that the women's ritual gatherings offer a space in which women can recognize and articulate their own worth, particularly by drawing an ironic contrast between their own labor and bodily investment in the task of human reproduction, and the unpredictable, fallible, short-lived male contribution. The helpless plants of the Adonic gardens represent male sexuality in all its brief glory and swift collapse, whereas the Thesmophoria signals the enduring patient work of conception, gestation, delivery, and lactation. Frederick Griffiths' analysis of the Adonia in Hellenistic Alexandria, as represented by Theokritos's *Idyll* 15, suggests that the emphasis on female significance may be read in this context too; Griffiths proposes that Arsinoe has chosen the festival of Adonis as a subtle symbol of her anomalous political power.[178]

I would like to build on these productive analyses in at least two ways. It is not necessary to choose between the Adonia as sign of a negative male sexuality (Winkler) and the Adonia as sign of a negative female sexuality (Detienne), particularly since both these readings rely on construing the Thesmophoria *only* as sign of a positive female sexuality and not, for instance, as sign of female anger. Instead of making such choices, we can retain the principle of ritual polyvalence, and especially the possibility of conflicting readings generated on the one hand by the female participants and on the other by the male "audience." [179] This "audience" does not necessarily spectate, of course, but they do have opinions about women's ritual activities, and, crucially, they have considerable impact on how women perceive themselves and their own actions. It does not seem to me sufficient to elaborate a gynocentric perspective on the Adonia, for instance, without taking account of the references to the "gardens of Adonis" that associate them with trivial, meaningless activities (see chapter 1). Within the model of Adonia-as-trivia the women in the festival would simply be acting out their own inadequacy and peripheral status in the community, as I suggested in chapter 1. Even though it may conflict with other valuable readings, I do not see how we can eradicate this particular significance from our reconstruction of the ritual.

The first observation I would like to make outside the terms of the polarity set up by Detienne and Winkler is as follows. If we inspect the gestures of the Adonia themselves, without reference to other festivals, we may want to develop yet another reading, which represents women's generative capaci-

---

178. Griffiths 1981: 254–59.

179. Reed (1995) suggests that the vase paintings of the late fifth century show the appropriation of the figure of Adonis for a male gaze. Reed points out that we cannot ever ascertain a female understanding of the Adonia, but suggests, with others, that we construe it within a female "culture of lamentation" that refers back to women's work as mourners.

ties in a different light. To start small growing things and then deliberately to deprive them of sustenance might be, among other things, a parody of maternal nurturance. The Adonia speaks to the contradiction inherent in patriarchal organization, whereby women, entrusted with the responsibility for life, are necessarily also equipped with the power to bring death. Within a system where women's dissatisfactions are not publicly articulated and where women have access to no valued outlets for their energies, such power can be recognized within the culture as a whole only as an unmediated threat of destruction hanging over the head of every woman's son. We can see this fantasy played out repeatedly in the most valued literary and artistic productions of the ancient Greek world, where women are routinely attributed homicidal proclivities.[180] The ritual sphere can be seen to speak to the same anxieties, but it finds a more satisfactory solution; the only public articulation available to women is provided within this sphere, where they can deflect their destructive energies by dramatizing them. The ritual process can thus be seen to guard men from women's deadly impulses and simultaneously to protect women from themselves. Women are taught the ever-present danger of their antisocial tendencies but are shown a symbolic form with which to satisfy them; men have confirmed their distrust of women but see that the all-powerful mother has already been reduced to the status of an incompetent gardener.

If we can accept that the Adonia explores the destructive potential attributed to wives and mothers, can we still say that the ritual's task is to produce successfully functioning adult women? We may need to construct a more complex notion of this process of production than would be indicated by an account of a "safety valve" or of a circumscribed "rebellion." I would like to retain the insight that a system of ideological production necessarily canvasses alternatives to itself in a ceaseless process of renewing consent to itself. The structure of production will consequently be a dialectic, dynamic and unstable, and the attempt by the ideological formation to confirm its own desirability will not necessarily be unequivocally successful.

One other way in which the Adonia may be seen to renew its participants' consent to their positions within patriarchal culture is by elaborating a kind of marital erotics, a notion that I offer as my second departure from the polarity outlined by the debate between Detienne and Winkler. Perhaps it is no coincidence that Aristophanes' *Lysistrata*, the drama that shows us the wife screeching on the rooftops for Adonis, also offers the sexiest representations of respectable Athenian marriages. The encounter between Kinesias and Myrrhine, for instance, suggests that the use of perfumes might not be confined to illicit unions (938–48). If we agree that properly married

180. See Johnston's work (1995, 1997) on female child-killing demons for a specific instance of such proclivities.

women attended the Adonia, along with women living in less stable circumstances, then any figures of eroticism or "license" are on offer to wives as well, available both to modify the role of respectable matron and to renew women's allegiance to it.

The various festivals for adult women can be seen to equip them to perform their roles and duties in a variety of ways. At an elementary level, such festivals allow them a respite from domestic life in which to recreate, and so to return refreshed. There are also strong arguments that hold that the women's festivals may be a more or less pure expression of female autonomy and thus constitute an opportunity for historical women to subvert, or at least ironize, the prescriptions of the patriarchy. The argument sustained here, which may function as a supplement to rather than a replacement of others, is that the festivals position women to function successfully by dramatizing the contradictory identifications required of them, both within the confines of a particular festival and over time as the ritual year unfolds. Such dramatization both explores the terms of the contradictions and, ultimately, enforces them.

THE HALOA

The Haloa is only attested for Eleusis and thus addresses itself only to women from Attica; in practice it was probably available only to local women and those from Athens. Since it seems to combine elements of the Thesmophoria and Adonia, the Haloa is a difficult festival to interpret. The Eleusinian site may be seen to connote a chaste, sober fertility, such as that of the Thesmophoria, and Eleusinian metaphors of female power seem to be deployed when the archons provide a feast for the women participants and leave them to enjoy it alone, in a striking modification of the normal codes of food preparation. According to the main item of testimony, the scholia to Lucian *Dialogues of Courtesans* 6.1, the women feast on many different kinds of food, except for those prohibited in the Mysteries, and drink a lot of wine. Most scandalizing to the scholiast, however, and most at odds with any notion of Eleusinian chastity, is the fact that "all the women shout rude and disrespectful things to each other, and they wave about models of body parts—improper ones, both male and female. . . . There lie on the tables pastry models of the genitalia of both sexes." It is also claimed that "the priestesses stealthily approach the women and whisper in their ears of *klepsigamia* (stolen, or illicit, love)."

The precise identity of the Haloa's participants has sometimes proved a problem. The notion that the Haloa was a gathering only for prostitutes has been discredited, and indeed there would be no point in proposing *klepsigamia* to women who practiced it for a living. That prostitutes attended is indicated by a reference in Demosthenes *Against Neaira* 116–17. The speaker Apollodoros claims that the hierophant Archias was charged with impiety *(asebeia)* for, among other things, sacrificing a victim brought to him by the *hetaira* Sinope on the occasion of the Haloa, when the priestess (presumably of Demeter) should have been the only official offering sacrifice.

Prostitutes and married women are apparently convened by the Haloa without regard to status, in what appears to be a celebration of activities sexual and gastronomic. We might note that in this festival, more than in others of the Athenian ritual year, the women are represented as consumers rather than as producers. Their contribution to the fertility of the land is to devour its fruits—all of the produce of the earth and sea, according to the scholia—as well as presumably eating up the pastry models of sexual organs. Perhaps the women are to be contrasted with the archons, who leave the temple, according to Lucian's scholiast, after having provided the women's feast, and remain outside, explaining to the community (presumably its male members) how civilized nourishment was discovered and disseminated throughout the world ("showing to all the locals that civilized food was discovered by them and shared with all humankind"). The archons' part in the festival brings into play the Eleusinian myth, but they may seem to appropriate the sober productivity characteristic of Eleusis to a version of male identity.

On the other hand, the scholia to Lucian also describe other male participants who carry phallic symbols in memory of a punishment from Dionysos.[181] The mythical narrative for this observance holds that after Ikarios, who introduced the use of wine to a group of shepherds, was assassinated by them for apparently "poisoning" them, they were driven mad and remained "in the state of shame" *(tou tes aischunes schematos)*. Presumably this means that they had permanent erections. Deliverance from this affliction was achieved by making and dedicating clay models of genitals. Both men and women participants in the Haloa, then, are involved with sexual toys, and both are irreverently figured in almost comic roles.

The parallel actions of women and men on the occasion of the Haloa tend to decrease its emphasis on the exclusive female collectivity and thus to drain the event of sexual hostility. To this extent it offers an alternative to the Adonia or Thesmophoria, though the figure of *klepsigamia* may be thought to reintroduce an element of antagonism. As A. C. Brumfield notes the term may refer to the rape of Persephone, who was herself "stolen" in marriage, and so concern the women's relation to the Eleusinian version of female maturity rather than any of their more mundane relationships.[182]

181. Brumfield (1981: 109 and n. 20) claims that this description is not connected to the Haloa, but the Greek syntax, particularly adverbial *kai,* seems to suggest otherwise. See also Winkler 1990a: 195 for connections between the male and female roles in the Haloa.

182. Brumfield 1981: 113.

The term is usually understood, however, as a reference to adultery, and certainly to air the possibility of adultery can be seen as the logical conclusion of the different occasions, throughout the ritual year, for the women's "shameful speech" *(aischrologia)*. What we can say is that any discourse of female sexual autonomy would have to remain only a symbolic alternative to their normal acquiescence.

Apart from the role of the archons, the Haloa seems dominated by a cheerful sense of the ridiculous. The setting at Eleusis seems to promise a gravity that is never quite delivered. The participating women are perhaps brought to represent themselves as gluttonous libertines, but they do not present the same kind of menace that can be read within accounts of the Adonia and Thesmophoria. The ritual draws on Eleusinian metaphors to figure its women participants but simultaneously predicates of them the interest in adultery that, as we saw toward the beginning of this chapter, Greek gender ideology conveniently attributes to all women. These various different positions for the women participants again explore the contradictions and incoherences in the Greek construction of female identity.

THE OTHER WOMEN

A considerable proportion of the community's ritual energies is soaked up in the cultural effort to produce and maintain free women who can identify successfully with the role of wife and mother. Other versions of female sexual identity also attract some ritual elaboration, and the rest of this chapter will consider the figures of the virgin, the older, postsexual woman, the adulteress and the prostitute as they emerge within ritual discourse. What is significant about all these figures, however, is that they do not attract as much ritual attention as does that of the wife and mother, who is responsible for the reproduction of the community and for the management of desire.

The Virgin

If construed as a sign of moral superiority, or of the ability to engage in further ascetic practices aiming to produce a readiness for divine revelation or spiritual experience, physical virginity may be heavily emphasized in religious culture. The pragmatic disposition of Greek religious culture, however, rarely made such an issue of virginity for either sex. Since their rituals are explicitly preparatory for marriage, the girls who participate in the chorus or in versions of the Arrhephoria and Arkteia are presumed to be virgins, but their sexual inexperience appears to be a function of their age rather than an object of ritual interest in itself or a qualification for ritual service. As Giulia Sissa points out, Greek culture was acquainted with very few tests of female virginity, and Greek sources represent such ordeals of virginity as part of the culture of "others."[183]

Some recorded priesthoods required the incumbents to be virgins, but these were almost invariably filled by young men or women before marriage, and did not require an artificially prolonged virginity. At Sikyon, Aphrodite demanded the services of a young female *loutrophoros* (carrier of the bridal bathing vessel), who worked in the temple for a year (Pausanias 2.10.4). We do not know anything more about the office, but it presents a contrast with most virgin priesthoods, in which the occupant usually served until she was married. Such priestesses were most commonly found in the service of Artemis, and their sexual status can easily be explained as appropriate for the virgin goddess who presided over the move into adulthood. Virgin priestesses of Artemis, who serve until marriage, are attested for various locations throughout the Greek world; they were known in Crete, Pagasai in Thessaly, Aigeira and Patrai in Achaia, and Orchomenos in Arcadia, and in Sparta young virgin girls also served the Leukippides, mythical daughters of Leukippos.[184] Another young woman was assigned to the temple of Poseidon at Kalauria, opposite Troizen (Pausanias 2.33.2)— surely a risky job for a virgin.

Since the terms of service for these unmarried girls probably did not extend beyond their early teens, some scholars have concluded that they did not perform all the duties of an adult priestess.[185] This conclusion seems too sweeping, especially when we recall that some of a priestess's responsibilities simply mimed those of the household. Moreover, even young women working in a temple might be endowed with special ritual privileges; for instance, the unmarried *loutrophoros* in the sanctuary of Aphrodite at Sikyon is one of only two people who are permitted to enter the temple. Such privileges might also entail corresponding responsibilities. More persuasive, as part of an account of the virgin priestess, is the notion that she can be understood by analogy with the first *choreute* or even with the *kanephoros;*[186] she is singled out by the ritual institution for especially visible service. While her priestly service need not be interpreted as a preparation for marriage—except perhaps insofar as it inculcates the necessity of service itself—arrangements for her marriage were evidently in train while she occupied the position, and her virginity did not prevent her from being perceived as potentially a sexually active adult.

183. Sissa 1990: 83–86.
184. See Pausanias 3.18.4 (Crete), 7.19.1–2 (Patrai), 7.26.5 (Aigeira), 8.5.11–12 (Orchomenos), and 3.16.1 (Sparta).
185. Dowden 1989: 31.
186. Ibid., 131.

Like the chorus member and the *kanephoros,* the *parthenos* priestess is
often figured as vulnerable to the onslaught of sexual desire. Her vulnerability, however, may well take the form of her own desire rather than exposing her to the violence of others, and her autonomy in this scenario may
perhaps be understood as a function of her actual prominence as a priestess. The priestess of Artemis Knagia on Crete is said to be seduced by a pris-
oner of war (Pausanias 3.18.4) and runs away with him, incidentally taking,
like Iphigeneia, the image of the goddess. At Patrai in Achaia the priesthood of Artemis Triklaria was allegedly once held by the lovely Komaitho,
who, prevented from marrying the man she loved, had sex with him in the
temple. Since to have sex in a sanctuary or to enter a sanctuary immediately
after sex was prohibited throughout Greek culture,[187] Komaitho brought
down on her community various forms of disaster (Pausanias 7.19.1–3).
These narratives of the amorous virgin suggest that the status of *parthenos*
immediately and inevitably attracts its own dissolution, and thus emphasize
the necessity of protecting virginity, or *partheneia.* The figure of the sexually
autonomous priestess indicates by negative example not only the work that
all girls must perform to develop correctly into sexually mature women but
also the work entailed for the wider community in transforming dangerously desiring or desirable females into marriageable, domesticated daughters. That much of this work takes place in the ritual sphere underlines the
threat offered by the sexual initiative of the *parthenos* priestess.[188]

Another set of narratives indicates a provisional solution to the problem
posed by the virgin's sexuality. Pausanias's account of Arcadia claims that
the priesthood of Artemis Hymnia was always held by a young girl, until the
incumbent was pursued and raped in the sanctuary by Aristocrates (8.5.11–
12):

> When the daring deed became known to all, the Arcadians stoned him, and
> from then on the law was changed too; instead of a girl they give to Artemis as
> priestess a woman who has had enough of intercourse with men.

This narrative presents a structural parallel to that of the Pythia, as told in
Diodorus Siculus 16.26:

> It is said that in ancient times virgins gave the oracles . . . but in more recent
> times [the late third century B.C.E.?] people say that Echecrates . . . saw the vir-
> gin who uttered the oracle, desired her because of her beauty, snatched her

187. Parker 1983: 74.
188. In Plutarch *Oracles at Delphi* 404F–G a young man, appointed to a priesthood that
requires chastity and that for that reason is usually reserved for old men, succumbs to his desire
for a young woman. The young of both sexes are similarly vulnerable to desire; but the multi-
plication of narratives about women rather than men indicates perhaps a greater cultural anxiety on their account.

away with him, and forced her; and that the Delphians because of this terrible event made a law for the future that no virgin should prophesy but that an old woman of fifty should declare the oracles.

The Pythia will concern us further in the following chapter, but at present we shall note the equivalence between young girl and old woman that is suggested by the fact of their being substituted for one another.[189] This equivalence derives, of course, from the status of the adult wife and mother, which defines the equation by remaining outside it. While the sanctioned sexual activity of the *gyne* contrasts with the prescribed abstinence of both *parthenos* and old woman, the homology between the latter two terms is not absolute, because the girl is never substituted as priestess for the old woman. What is at stake is not only the presence or absence of sexual activity but also that of desire. The older woman is presumed not to arouse desire in others, while the young girl almost inevitably does. Significant too is the anxiety registered, even in accounts of rape, about the virgin as subject rather than object of desire. The older woman in Pausanias is carefully delineated as "having had enough of intercourse with men"; can we restrict the meaning of this phrase to an indication that she has passed her childbearing years, or should we take it more literally and conclude that she suits the priesthood because, unlike the young girl, she has learned the effective management of desire?

If the drive behind much ritual activity for Greek women is the production and practice of successful female identity, within a patriarchal construction of that identity, then we would not expect an intense cultic elaboration on the anomalous status of permanent virginity. Priestesses who practiced perpetual chastity instead of the bodily compromises usual for Greek women have been discerned in the sources, but they are often arguably the constructions of a post-Christian scholarly tradition. As Parker notes, even some references to the Pythia, the most celebrated "virgin priestess," show her as sexually active, at least in her pre-oracular career.[190] One unequivocal case of a lifelong virgin priestess is that of Herakles at Thespiae (Pausanias on Boeotia, 9.27.6), an intriguing instance given the frequent exclusion of other women from the shrines and cult of Herakles. The prophetess of Apollo at Larisa (Pausanias 2.24.1) is a woman "debarred from intercourse with a man," but we do not know if the prophetess started functioning as such when she was a young girl or after she had raised a fam-

189. On the cultural significance of the "old woman" see especially Brulé 1987: 351–78, and also Bremmer 1987. On Echecrates' date see Parke 1939: 257.

190. Parker 1983: 93. See Parke and Wormell 1956: 1.44 n. 90 on a Pythia from the third century C.E. who was a grandmother. Parker (1983: 90) effectively demolishes other cases of the "virgin priestess."

ily. Comparative material may be thought to point to the latter possibility; in many African cultures, where women notably practice as possession specialists, they are commonly called to this vocation after they have had children.[191] It is possible that the priestess of the Arcadian shrine mentioned in Pausanias 8.13.1 was a lifelong virgin. Both priest and priestess here are said to "live their whole lives in purity, not only sexual but in all matters, and they do not wash, nor spend their lives as ordinary people do, nor do they enter the house of a private person." Again, we cannot be sure that the span of "their whole lives" extends from birth or simply from the date of appointment. Ken Dowden claims that the priestess of Hera at Argos is a lifelong virgin, but he admits that he cannot prove the claim.[192] Chryseis, the priestess who served during the Peloponnesian War, occupied the post for fifty-six years (Thucydides 2.2 and 4.133), but there is no explicit indication that she was prevented from having a family. We might compare Lysimache, the Athenian priestess of Athena Polias, who was eighty-eight when she died circa 360 B.C.E., having served for sixty-four years and raised four children (*IG* ii² 3453).

On the other hand, some priestesses and other women who worked in sanctuaries could be required to observe various specific kinds of abstinence. At the temple of Aphrodite in Sikyon there was not only the virgin *loutrophoros* but also a woman serving as *neokoros* (a type of custodian), who was forbidden to have intercourse with a man after she took up her appointment (Pausanias 2.10.4). The priestess of Earth in Achaia remained chaste after her appointment, and had to certify before taking up the post that she had not had intercourse with more than one man (Pausanias 7.25.13). More significant perhaps is the fact that she had to drink bull's blood to test the veracity of her testimony; the ordeal of marital chastity seems in this context more important to Greek culture than ordeals of virginity, which as we have noted are rarely attested. Other restrictions were temporary, like the chastity demanded of the Gerarai at Athens or the Bailers participating in the Thesmophoria, who had to abstain from intercourse for three days before they performed their ritual task. These temporary injunctions indicate that most ritual practice for women was compatible with the status of sexually active wife and mother, and there are several references in the inscriptional record to priestesses and other ritual practitioners who maintained families while in office. Several priestesses are honored in dedications made by their husbands or children, such as Lysimache herself, the third-century priestess of Athena Lysistrate, honored with her husband in *IG* ii² 776, and the second-century priestess of Helios in *IG* ii² 3578. The priestess of Nemesis at Rhamnus in the third century could be wife and mother

191. Keirn 1978.
192. Dowden 1989: 133.

(*IG* ii² 3462), as could the priestess of Artemis Brauronia (Hypereides frag. 199 Blass), and Satyra, the priestess of the Thesmophoroi at Athens in the second century, is a wife.[193] The commentary on a fragmentary inscription from Sparta (*LSS* 28) suggests that the priestess of Demeter there was required to be a married woman. Although the Eleusinian priestess of Demeter and Kore, and the Eleusinian hierophantides, lived in special houses, Parker notes that this does not necessarily entail that they were completely separated from their husbands.[194]

The Postsexual Woman

Sacerdotal office for women does not appear to have consistently required sexual abstinence, and physical chastity is not so important to Greek ritual practice that cult functions are reserved for sexually inactive populations such as virgins and old women. Although both Plato (*Laws* 759D) and Aristotle (*Politics* 1329a) discuss priesthood as an occupation suitable for people over sixty, their concerns are as much prescriptive as descriptive, and in fact references to older women in cult office are rare. As we have seen, they appear in certain narratives as the structural equivalent of unmarried girls, distinguished primarily by their inability to arouse desire, and in other contexts too they are assumed to be chaste. Plutarch *Numa* 9.11 claims that perpetual fires in Athens and Delphi are tended by women who have "ceased from sex," a phrase reminiscent of the woman in Pausanias who has "had enough of intercourse with men." At Elis, the deity Sosipolis is tended by a *presbutis,* an old woman, who remains chaste. Unmarried and married women are also involved in the cult of Sosipolis, but they may not approach the inner part of the sanctuary as may the *presbutis* (Pausanias 6.20.2–3). Strabo 7.7.12 mentions old women who prophesy at Dodona, and one priestess of Athena Polias at Athens, Lysimache, apparently drew on the services of a *presbutis* who was commemorated by a statue (Pausanias 1.27.4). No information is given, however, about her sexual status. Similarly, the four old women (*graes*) who slaughter the sacrificial cows at the festival of Demeter Chthonia, at Hermione in the Argolid, are not distinguished by their sexual practice or lack of it (Pausanias 2.35.4–8).[195] Outside cultic office as such, we have seen that the ritual sphere sometimes distinguishes older women for particular kinds of participation, as in the various instances of legislation for private funerals that restrict attendance to kin and to women over sixty. No issue of sexual practice is raised within such legislation.

Even in her potential to symbolize the end of sexual activity, the *presbutis* or *graus* is not of overwhelming interest to Greek ritual practice. Rather

---

193. Broneer 1942.
194. Parker 1983: 89. On married priestesses see Turner 1983: chap. 6, esp. 215–28.
195. On this bizarre rite see Detienne 1989: 140–42.

than displaying a chastity defined only by the activity of the body, her importance sometimes seems to consist in the ability to offer much younger
women a paradigm for resistance to unsanctioned desire. In the offices
filled by mature, sexually active women, specific forms of abstinence might
occasionally be required, but just as frequently no conflict is constructed
between sexual activity and ritual service. Observance of marital chastity is
of more interest to Greek culture than is indiscriminate asceticism, and similarly premarital chastity is a guarantee of the ability to resist unsanctioned
desire rather than sign of an otherworldly purity that would be contaminated by the somatic involvements consequent on female adulthood.

The Adulteress

If marital chastity is of interest to the ritual sphere, then the converse also
holds; at Athens, and probably elsewhere, adultery disqualifies. No woman
was ever excluded from ritual participation so completely as the convicted
adulteress. If the adulterous wife was not protected by a cooperative husband, who might be reluctant, for instance, to expose to question the legitimacy of his children—not to mention his own inadequacy—then she was
prohibited from attending any ritual gathering. This is made clear by
Demosthenes *Against Neaira* 85–87:

> No woman convicted of adultery is permitted to go to any of the public
> sacrifices, even though the laws allowed both the foreign woman and the slave
> to attend these, whether as spectator or as suppliant. . . . If they [the adulter-
> esses] do break the law and attend them, they must suffer whatever they suf-
> fer at the hands of anyone who wants to [punish them], except death, and
> that with impunity. . . . It is for this reason that the law brought it about that
> she may suffer anything except death . . . that there may be no pollution and
> profanation in our sanctuaries. The law presents our women with enough fear
> that they behave prudently and make no mistakes but keep house lawfully. For
> it teaches them that if a woman makes such a mistake, she will be cast out both
> from her husband's home and from the sanctuaries of the city.

The practical prohibition described in Demosthenes' speech is reproduced
figuratively in the Hellenistic text allegedly written by "Phintys," a woman
Pythagorean, and addressed to women, which claims that for the adulteress
"there is no means of atoning for this sin; no way she can approach the
shrines or the altars of the gods."[196]

Such strict exclusion clearly serves to indicate to married women where
their primary responsibilities lie. If the city, in P. Vidal-Naquet's terms, is
defined by the exclusion of women,[197] then women's ritual practice may be

196. Thesleff 1965: 153; see also Stobaios 4.23.61a.
197. Vidal-Naquet 1981: 178.

said to be defined, correspondingly, by the exclusion of the adulteress. The adulterous wife and mother betrays her husband's trust and disinherits her children; she has obviously disqualified herself from interceding with the divine on their behalf, which I proposed in chapter 1 is an activity properly predicated of the successful wife and mother. Conversely, the exclusion from ritual of the adulteress allows us to see that the woman most insistently addressed by ritual is the free, adult wife and mother, whose sexual and reproductive activities are so crucial to the welfare of the community.

The Prostitute

The adulteress who abandons her identity as wife and mother is excluded from ritual practice, but the sexual promiscuity of the prostitute, who is only doing her job, does not present the cult context with a problem. As we have seen, the female prostitute might be active in ritual, and her professional conduct rarely disqualifies her from any but the most prominent forms of cult participation. Anecdotal and other evidence often constructs a relation between the semipublic ritual sphere and the anomalous "public woman." Greek sources themselves can be seen to be aware of the play between these categories; Artemidoros *Interpretation of Dreams* 1.57 makes the equation explicit when it claims that if a woman dreams of riding publicly through the open streets, she will become, depending on her current social status, a priestess or a prostitute:

> It is good for women and girls who are both free and rich to drive a chariot through a city; it means good priestesshoods for them. But for poor women, riding on horseback through the city announces prostitution.

The designation "prostitute," as one whose body is commercialized for the sexual gratification of others, covers a range of identities in Greek as in contemporary culture. Slave prostitutes could not dispose of their own bodies, of course, and pornographic vases of the early and mid-fifth century in Attica show women who are apparently slaves, with shaven heads, being subjected to a variety of abuses (see fig. 2).[198] On the other hand, free women who operated as companions, or *hetairai*, like Theodota in Xenophon *Memorabilia* 3, are represented as not only wealthy but also independent and assertive. The latter version of the *hetaira* is unlikely to be completely accurate, since it is vividly contradicted by accounts such as that in Menander's *Samian Woman*, where the previously favored concubine Chrysis is threatened with return to the status of *hetaira:* "Whores like you, Chrysis, make ten drachmas running round to dinner-parties, and drink neat alcohol until they die; and if they don't look sharp and jump to it, they starve" (392–96

198. Keuls 1985: 180–86.

Sandbach). If she leaves the relative security of the concubine, attached to one man only, she will be forced instead to operate as a *hetaira*, with a multiplicity of customers and all the attendant risks to health.

Greek testimony to the involvement of prostitutes in the ritual sphere concerns mainly, but not exclusively, the women who worked in more secure conditions as the "companions" of prominent men. The anecdotes that accrue around them advertise not so much their historical veracity as the pleasure involved in scandalous discourse about scandalous women. While some religious cultures prize prostitutes as women who are permanently and hyperbolically "married" and thus conform to prescribed female roles, Greek sources do not claim any particular symbolic value for prostitutes as such within the ritual context.[199] Ritual discourse on prostitutes tends to direct attention back to the respectable matrons with whom they are implicitly contrasted.

Accounts of prominent *hetairai* are also often motivated not by interest in the women themselves but by political attacks on their male protectors, who were obviously playing for higher stakes in the economy of power and notoriety. It is Demetrios of Phaleron (the grandson of the tyrant) who transgresses by seating his *hetaira* Aristagora next to him at the Mysteries, rather than the *hetaira* herself (she also has a special viewing platform at the Panathenaia; see Athenaeus 4.167). On the other hand, the orator Lysias's initiation of the *hetaira* Metaneira is represented as a special favor that cannot be contaminated by external considerations. The speaker of Demosthenes *Against Neaira* (21) contends that the orator, considering that all his other gifts eventually found their way to Metaneira's owner, desired to initiate her in order to secure advantage for her and her gratitude toward him. Since Metaneira and Lysias appear in this speech as foils to the dreadful Neaira and her protector, however, we can draw from this account no very secure conclusions about the actual ritual practices of historical prostitutes.

The whole speech *Against Neaira,* of course, deploys the alarming figure of the rapacious prostitute in order to obtain the conviction of the man who supports her, Stephanos. Similarly the case of Sinope is mobilized in the prosecution of Archias the hierophant, a man, according to his defenders, of noble ancestry and civic virtue (*Against Neaira* 117). Sinope, as we have seen above, is said to have prevailed upon Archias to sacrifice a victim that she had brought to Eleusis, on the occasion of the Haloa, when only the priestess should have been officiating. Sinope may be understood to have acted out of ignorance or out of malice, but she is not condemned as was Archias; she was not at fault either in her attendance at the Haloa or in her

199. See, for example, Narayanan 1990. According to Artemidoros 1.78 it is very auspicious to dream of prostitutes, because they signify "profit."

Figure 2. Men and prostitutes. Exterior of a cup by the Brygos Painter. *ARV* 372/31, Florence 3921. Reproduced with permission from the Soprintendenza archeologica di Firenze.

desire to provide a sacrifice. What is dangerous, however, is how the action of the unruly woman can ultimately prove the downfall of the well-regulated man, particularly when it is seconded by the legal action of the priestess.

The famous *hetaira* Phryne, on the other hand, allegedly was herself prosecuted for impiety *(asebeia)* and defended by the orator Hypereides. While the object of the prosecution may have been her lover Praxiteles, the representation of Phryne herself in the different versions of the story is consistent in foregrounding her anomalous wealth and predilection for public display, terms that are also prominent in the Herodotean account of the *hetaira* Rhodopis. Phryne is said to have dedicated a gold statue of herself at Delphi (see chapter 1), and the account in Athenaeus also claims that she publicly took off her cloak and let down her hair at the Eleusinian celebration and at the festival of Poseidon (13.590). While such display would have been reasonable business practice for one in Phryne's business, we can discern within these anecdotes about the outrageous *hetaira* the familiar anxiety over the publicity of the ritual sphere, which can undo, as well as affirm, the virtue of wife or daughter.

Stories about the involvement of *hetairai* in ritual practice can be seen to be driven by the same concerns as generate much of the ritual discourse on female sexuality. The narratives concerning *hetairai* also demonstrate in uncomplicated ways the prescribed behavior for respectable Greek women, which consists conversely of a self-effacing avoidance of autonomy. This distinction between prostitute and respectable woman might seem to be potentially undermined on those ritual occasions where Greek practice allowed different orders of women to mingle, but there are no secure Greek instances of prostitution forming part of a cult observance for otherwise respectable women. Klearchos in Athenaeus 12.516a claims that the families of Italian Locri vowed to prostitute their daughters if they were victorious in war, but then, as Justin 21.3 shows, they declined to carry out the vow. The *Histories* of Herodotos predicate "ritual prostitution" of Babylonian culture; according to the account in 1.199, each Babylonian woman must at some point hire herself out sexually to a stranger. She is required to wait in the precincts of the temple of Aphrodite until someone offers her a silver coin, which then becomes sacred and presumably converts into part of the temple revenues. While the custom is condemned in the text as "shameful," the Babylonian women return to lives of virtue subsequent to their temple service and suffer no stigma. Herodotos claims a similar practice for Cyprus, but it is not otherwise known to us, and in general "ritual prostitution" seems to constitute part of a representation of the "other," particularly the Eastern "other." Lucian *De Dea Syria* 6 threatens any woman who does not shave her head for Adonis with the prospect of having to work as a prostitute for a day in support of the temple. In this context "ritual prostitution" is obviously unpleasant and to be avoided, but we may note that historical women seem to have been able to recuperate positively other versions of the experience. An inscription from second-century c.e. Anatolia commemorates a woman who had served the temple as a prostitute, as had her mother and other female ancestors.[200] This testimony does not fall within the historical parameters of this study, but we may note it as an extreme example of the ways in which cult activity may both require women's work, as we saw repeatedly in chapter 1, and simultaneously constitute a recognizable reward for it.

In mainland Greece the city that most nearly approaches the practice of "ritual prostitution" is Corinth.[201] Corinth's commercially significant position at the crossroads of ancient Greece obviously promoted the trade in flesh—Apollodoros's nemesis Neaira lived there in her youth—and some sources claim that the prostitutes of the city acquired a role within it that extended beyond their contribution to the exchequer. Athenaeus 13.573 reports the Corinthian practice of convening the prostitutes to join in

---

200. See Robert 1937: 406 and Ramsay 1895: 115, no. 18.
201. On the prostitutes of Corinth see Salmon 1984: 398–400.

prayers and sacrifices to Aphrodite for the city's welfare and goes on to describe the dedicatory tablet, which is known also from Plutarch *Moralia* 871A, raised by the city in honor of the prostitutes who had prayed en masse for deliverance from the Persian invasion.[202] The prostitutes of Corinth are thus represented as particularly active in the ritual sphere, and indeed as miming the familial roles of respectable women when they undertake the task of intercession. Once the text has offered to collapse the categories of "prostitute" and "respectable," however, it quickly moves to reinstate the distinction. Athenaeus's discourse goes on to claim that prostitutes could be dedicated to the temple as *hierodouloi*, "sacred slaves," in the same way as other objects, a practice that is also attested by Pindar *Olympian* 13 of 464 B.C.E. in honor of Xenophon of Corinth.[203] Athenaeus's text finally asserts that prostitutes and respectable women celebrate separate festivals of Aphrodite (13.573). This practical distinction is absent from the principal gatherings of Athenian women, as we have seen, and we might suggest that it compensates for the prostitutes' anomalous intrusion into the category of "respectable" in their other ritual activities. Temples erected to Aphrodite in Abydos and Samos honored other prostitutes; in Abydos they were credited with helping to save the city from oppressors, and in Samos the prostitutes themselves, who were accompanying Perikles' besieging army of Athenians, raised the money to fund the temple (Athenaeus 13.572).

A plausibly historical instance of a prostitute's self-assertion within the ritual sphere is afforded by the early fourth-century Ninion tablet, which depicts a woman, usually identified as the *hetaira* Ninion herself, being initiated into the Eleusinian Mysteries.[204] Since Ninion by definition did not form part of an acceptable family, it is unlikely that a male relative financed her dedication, although the example of Lysias and Metaneira cited above suggests that a lover or lovers might contribute. While it is also possible that a friend or client made the dedication in honor of Ninion and her cultic experience, it is equally likely that Ninion causes herself to be thus commemorated. The tablet would thus be one of the few artistic productions originating in women that also represent the woman patron.[205]

If we construe the Ninion tablet in this way, we may wish to account for it in terms of Ninion's profession. Working outside the normally sanctioned

---

202. See also the scholia on Pindar *Olympian* 13.32 and Simonides 2.104 Diehl.

203. Strabo 6.2.6. claims a similar practice "in early times" for Eryx in Sicily. Inscriptions show the term used for men elsewhere, such as in Greek Egypt.

204. For a general account of the tablet see Clinton 1992: 74–75 and Mylonas 1962: 213–21.

205. Ridgway (1987) offers an account of women as patrons of art in the archaic, classical, and Hellenistic periods but does not include the Ninion tablet. She does note (405 n. 35) that women initiates in the Eleusinian Mysteries might raise statues of themselves, at least in Athens.

structures, she may have been well positioned to articulate a sense of self in ways different from those available to women operating under more securely defined conditions. This is not to say, of course, that the *hetaira* was "more free" than the respectable woman, only that she may have availed herself of different avenues of behavior.[206] But we may also want to explain the Ninion tablet not only in terms of Ninion's profession but also as a function of the ritual context. This we have already identified, throughout chapter 1, as a sphere that offers to women the possibility of greater self-articulation than is available to them in other dimensions of their lives.

Our focus on the activity of prostitutes has returned us to the terms prominent in chapter 1, where we discussed women's presence, agency, and autonomy in the ritual sphere. To some extent this is because the *hetairai*, operating outside familial structures, can "write large" the alternatives to domesticity that are offered to all women by ritual practice. But it would be extremely naive to suppose that *hetairai* inhabited an unstructured environment determined only by their own whims; the examples from Corinth indicate how even a large population of prostitutes could be governed and required, as in the separate festival of Aphrodite, to enact its difference from that of "respectable women." As we have previously noted, many of the anecdotes about the cult actions of *hetairai* play on the same anxieties that fuel the ritual discourse about nonprostitute women. This latter group, those who are called to perform as successful wives and mothers, are the target of most ritual attention, because they must repeatedly be encouraged to subordinate their projects to those of others, in the interests of patriarchal marriage and the reproduction of a male-dominated culture.

In the first chapter of this study, our concern was to challenge the definition of ancient Greek women as "secluded" and "excluded" by mobilizing the versions of female presence, agency, and autonomy made available in the ritual sphere. The versions of women's sexual and reproductive identity

---

206. Work on reclaiming the prostitute subject position has directed attention to the autonomy and power possible for a given prostitute, and has also argued for a more detailed understanding of different versions of prostitution that do not fall into the dichotomy of helpless victim or evil temptress. Even contemporary prostitutes themselves, however, as represented by such groups as Prostitutes Anonymous, do not claim that power and autonomy are the defining characteristics of prostitution, and in general "[Prostitutes'] rights activists are careful to hold the tension between the positive and negative aspects of prostitution" (Bell 1994: 116). I have been unable to find any history of prostitution that did not advertise itself, albeit unwittingly, as fantasy, but it is interesting to note, in the absence of an authoritative history, that contemporary prostitution activists and "prostitute performers" like Annie Sprinkle are deliberately reconstructing and reclaiming for their own a history of sacred prostitution. See, for example, Bell 1994: 19–39, 150.

offered by ritual discourse, however, do not present clear alternatives to those elaborated within, for instance, legal and medical institutions, or within the misogynistic tradition of much figurative literature. Indeed I have proposed that the ritual discourse on female sexual and reproductive identity cannot be understood without reference to these other institutions. All this cultic activity, I contend, is geared to producing women who have internalized a version of femaleness more useful to others than it is to them. Such cultic activity is not, then, an uncomplicated assertion of women's independence, or of their dissent from and resistance to the versions of themselves with which they are usually presented. Yet for a number of reasons this process of ideological production of women is necessarily troubled and incomplete. As we have often noted, ritual activity entrusts historical women themselves with their own production, so that they are automatically subjects as well as objects of the process. Moreover, in order to enforce on women the contradictions necessary to the operation of patriarchal society, ritual activity must rehearse them in all their terms. Hence the constant doubling of ritual discourse, which is anxious about concealment *and* display, fear *and* pleasure, chastity *and* license.

There is another dimension to the contradictory nature of ideological production, which we have explored earlier and can now recap. Ritual discourse on the preferred identity for women constantly registers the pressure of alternatives to that identity, if only in order to prove their inadequacy. Furthermore, the repetition of propositions about women's identity, in the course of the ritual year, can work to expose instead of to consolidate the socially constructed nature of femaleness. These potential incoherences in the ritual process could allow historical women to develop their own dissenting or resistant readings of the cult activities in which they participated. To this extent we can reinscribe women's own agency into a scenario that is chiefly concerned with their subjection to patriarchal ideology, and we can see that even within the ritual activity that aims at the management of desire, women may have been able to negotiate a productive relationship to the constraints under which they lived. What is crucial is that women themselves are enlisted in ritual to reproduce these very constraints. Even in its discourse on sexuality, the ritual sphere can make visible the complexities of this process of reproduction.

THREE

In and Out of the City

Imaginary Citizens

Although the models of ritual action elaborated in the first and second chapters of this study subtend an obvious tension, I shall not attempt to resolve it here but rather re-stage it, on different terrain. Emphasizing a model of female presence, agency, and autonomy as exercised in the ritual sphere, I have also stressed that sizable tracts of that ritual elaborate versions of female identity that can only operate at the expense of those women themselves. To understand the ritual sphere comprehensively seems to require that we elaborate a dialectical model, in which both possibilities are seen to be simultaneously at work. In this chapter I shall consider, in the light of such a model, the intersections of women's ritual practice with the political culture of the Greek cities. I shall seek to show that in such intersections, women's ritual practice dramatizes their marginality in or exclusion from the determining structures of the city yet conversely fantasizes that they are fully qualified citizens.

The political experiments among the Greek cities of the classical period produced a highly developed self-consciousness about systems of governance and decision making. Aristotle's *Politics* compares not only the functioning constitutions of Athens, Sparta, Carthage, and Crete but also the ideal cities planned by Plato, Hippodamos of Miletos, and Phaleas of Chalkedon. While the field of practice and theory embraced by the term "politics" *(ta politika)* is necessarily different from what is implied by the modern understanding of the word, we can nonetheless identify a relatively consistent and coherent discourse about the distribution and transfer of authority and about the regulation of internal strife. The object of this discourse is the independent, self-governing city (and to some extent its surrounding rural territory), and the agents targeted by this discourse are the "citizens," who comprise either all or a selected part of the population of free adult males. The significance of the city as primary unit of organization and identification did not disappear even under the changed conditions of Hellenistic and imperial times. Jon Mikalson points out that "the political and social institutions with which traditional religion was affiliated—the Ekklesia, Boule, tribe, deme, phratry, family and so forth—all continued to operate in the fourth century and would do so, in one form or another, for centuries under a wide variety of democracies, oligarchies and monarchies."[1] Similarly, Simon Price observes that "possession of local citizenship was still an important source of pride and security,"[2] even though specifically political activity might be variously circumscribed by the rule of Hellenistic monarch or Roman emperor.

One of the significant characteristics of "citizenship" was its restriction to certain groups of inhabitants. Whatever the permutations of governance envisaged by Greek constitutions, none of them proposed a wholesale enfranchisement; governance was usually conducted without reference to groups such as the poor, the low-born, and resident aliens (metics), but almost always without reference to slaves or to women. In the Hellenistic period, grants of citizenship might occasionally be made, or even sold, to individual slaves, foreigners, or women,[3] but apart from these exceptional grants the privilege of citizenship was still carefully guarded and restricted to free, native-born adult men.

There is, however, a range of testimony that suggests that the Greek city could also conceive of itself as an inclusive rather than exclusive entity, and specifically that it could elaborate a discourse of participation or "belonging" that extended civic identification to free, native-born women. We may cite in this context Aristotle's *Politics,* which defines a citizen quite strictly as one who shares in the offices of *dikastes* (juror) and *ekklesiastes* (assembly member) (3.1, 1275a20–32), but which in discussion of the Spartan con-

---

1. Mikalson 1998: 71.

2. Price 1984: 28.

3. See, for example, Aristodama of Smyrna, an epic poet who was made a citizen of Lamia in the late third century for her impressive performances there (Walbank 1992: 73). Because the Hellenistic or imperial city had a more restricted field of action, it could perhaps afford to be occasionally less jealous of its privileges. Even in the classical period such exceptional grants were not unknown; in Athens, at the end of the Peloponnesian War, slaves who fought in defense of the city were freed and made citizens. See also a fourth-century inscription granting citizenship to two women of Epirus and their children (*SEG* 15.384; commentary at *SEG* 18.264, 19.425, and 23.470).

In the light of this chapter's concerns it is perhaps significant that Smyrna, the city that in the third century produced the poet and citizen Aristodama, in the second and first centuries is site of a number of grave monuments that repeatedly represent women in traditional terms, emphasizing their modesty and personal charm (Zanker 1993: 222–27). The only exceptions to this rule are a subseries of grave monuments to priestesses of Demeter, who are represented as more active and imposing (Zanker 1993: 226).

stitution explicitly acknowledges women as comprising half the city: "Just as husband and wife are alike essential parts of the family, so a state should also be considered as almost equally composed of men and women members" (2.9, 1269b5). The *Politics* does not proceed to its logical conclusion, however; women's participation in the city does not entitle them to a share in governance and decision making, but means instead that the legislator should devote half his regulatory effort to controlling and inhibiting their potentially antisocial energies.

In its assumption that women cannot be securely identified with the project of culture the *Politics* resonates with more straightforwardly misogynistic texts like those of Hesiod or Semonides. For ancient Greek culture the founding myth of sexual difference, and of its social consequences, was that of Hesiod's Pandora, which explains the existence of women as the product of a separate act of creation. The consequences of this unfortunate invention may with effort be imagined away in order to restore the notion of a "world without women."[4] The work of some scholars, such as P. Vidal-Naquet and Nicole Loraux, has proposed that the classical city achieved this feat of imagination and that the polis as such should consequently be understood as "founded on the exclusion of women, just as . . . upon the exclusion of foreigners (metics) and slaves."[5] Forced to remain "outside" the community of citizens, women instead rehearse the terms of Hesiod's or Semonides' discourse in which women are each undifferentiedly "own daughter of her mother," all descended from Pandora and members of "the race of female women."[6]

In this chapter, however, I shall try to tease out the implications of the Aristotelian admission that women constitute half the city, and in particular I shall suggest that the kind of equivocation about women's participation legible in Aristotle also characterizes much of ritual discourse. Significant for an account of women's participation in the city is the proposition, increasingly articulated in the secondary literature, that an explicit discourse of political governance offered only one set of terms by which the ancient city understood itself. When Pausanias describes the various communities of Greece, for instance, his text confines itself almost entirely to each city's religious monuments and practices, and the working definition of a city given at 10.4.1 comprises, as well as "government offices," the gymnasium, theater, marketplace, and fountain. While we might explain this emphasis as a product of a politically less articulate culture, conditioned only by Roman hegemony, it is clear that the identity of the classical city too

4. Arthur 1983.

5. Vidal-Naquet 1981: 178.

6. See Semonides *Female of the Species* 12 and Hesiod *Theogony* 590–91 for these phrases, with Loraux 1978.

was thoroughly imbricated with its ritual activities, many of which were dependent on women's participation.

Recent work on Greek discourses of participation in the city has moved away from a legalistic or institutional definition of "citizenship" and relies increasingly on the notion of "civic ideology," which involves a "holistic" view of the city as a set of interrelated practices in the fields of politics, law, economics, religion, art, and domestic life.[7] Much of this work has concentrated on classical Athens, which appeals not only because of the wealth of documentary evidence that it affords but also because it developed an unprecedentedly inclusive political practice. Since a correspondingly insistent discourse on the exclusion of women from the city can also be read in the sources, the Athenian model provides the two extremes of "legalistic" and "holistic" accounts of itself. Some studies have suggested, however, that our contemporary criticism tends to undervalue women's participation in classical Athens because we understand the city's operations only in terms of our own categories of narrowly political activity. Cynthia Patterson emphasizes the inclusive model not of "citizenship" but of "being an Athenian," noting:

> The relevant Athenian notion is rather that of "sharing in" *(metechein)* the city or being a member of the Athenian family. Whether or not *we* call the women of Athens "citizens" may indeed reveal more of our ideas about what is essential to membership in a community or state than it reveals about Athenian attitudes toward "being an Athenian."[8]

Roger Just concurs, in terms that could probably be extended to include the ideology of other cities: "As a 'citizens club' whose members all shared in the governance of the state, the Athenian polis excluded women. But as a closed community bound together by ties of kinship and religion it most certainly included women."[9] Such work on "civic ideology" and its possible targeting of women has not yet addressed, however, the varied testimony about women's participation in the city that may be read within the ritual sphere. When Patterson writes, for instance, that "however difficult it may be to define the woman's share . . . it is not a mere token and not limited to the payment of a child-bearing 'tax,'"[10] she does not proceed to adduce women's ritual activity as definitive of this "share."

Some scholars who write on women's cult practice, conversely, have begun to construct political or quasi-political models to explain aspects of

---

7. See Scafuro 1994a and also the essays by Manville, Connor, and Frost in Boegehold and Scafuro 1994.

8. Patterson 1987: 49.

9. Just 1989: 23.

10. Patterson 1994: 202.

that practice.[11] C. Sourvinou-Inwood concludes that Greek women could exercise a merely "passive" citizenship that was available to them only in cult activity.[12] While I am not in fundamental disagreement with this position, I would like to modify the emphasis and to suggest that women may be understood instead as possessed of a "latent" citizenship that could be rendered visible, in its various contours, by ritual participation. The notion of "latent citizenship" has been deployed by R. Sealey to characterize women in classical Athens, but only in the context of their ability to bear "children who would be citizens" and thus to transmit what they do not themselves possess.[13] In this chapter I follow and expand upon the ideas of Marcel Detienne in proposing an alternative interpretation of "latent citizenship" as a way to indicate not only the possibility of transmission but also a persistent potential that may be called into existence under certain circumstances, particularly within ritual practice. Between the operations of politics as narrowly defined and those of ritual, various intersections may be traced, such as methods of selection for sacerdotal officials, or the practice of subjecting ritual events to scrutiny by the deliberative bodies of the state,[14] and such intersections can apply to women's ritual practice as well as to that of men. The homology thus constructed between ritual and politics might be understood to extend to cultically active women the contours of a political identity. If we pursue this homology, I suggest, we are in a position to argue that ritual dramatization of women's citizenship offers a genuine, if qualified, alternative to the customary figuring of women's exclusion from the city. We can consequently argue that the ideological work undertaken by the ritual sphere on women as political subjects is very different from that involved in the reproduction of their sexuality. We may even conclude that the "civic ideology" of the ritual sphere actively offers to remedy the exclusion of women from other accounts of the city.

This chapter will explore the significance of various testimonies that can be seen to represent ritually active women as participants in the civic community, and will also reconstruct some explicitly political models for selecting women for cult office and for honoring their service. Women's ritual interventions in the city may be paradoxically enabled by their position outside the city; the male-dominated polity can at times be seen to call on the female "outside" to identify with the city in the specific cultic role of its

11. See Detienne 1989, for example.

12. Sourvinou-Inwood 1988b: 112.

13. Sealey 1990: 14. In an inscription cited by Scafuro (1994b: 162) a son establishes legitimacy and citizenship by producing his "patronymic and demotic, together with his mother's name with patronym and *father's demotic*" (emphasis added). The mother's name alone is not sufficient to establish anything; her father's citizen identity must be added to the equation.

14. See also Davies 1971: 369–70 and Garland 1984: 77 for varying assessments of the possibility that ritual activity or office overtly served the political careers of male individuals.

"unlikely savior."[15] Exemplifying the dialectic of "inside" and "outside" in detail are the ritual "cities of women" known to us chiefly from Athenian evidence but probably convened throughout Greek culture. These "cities" incidentally suggest that the women who constitute the chief targets of ritual discourse on sexuality, namely the wives and mothers of citizens, are also most insistently addressed on the subject of their political identity. The ritual activity of these women might then be said to mediate between their sexual and their political, or quasi-political, identities. Not to be overlooked, however, is the equally insistent demand that many women who participate as imaginary citizens be qualified by wealth or birth. One woman who occupied a site of politically discursive authority apparently without such qualification was the Pythia, an investigation of whose position on the cusp of ritual and politics closes the chapter.

Any discourse to be discerned within ritual activity that does construct elements of a political identity for women, however, is much less prominent than that which concentrates on female sexuality or on women's work. It is clear from the material already assembled that women primarily serve the *oikos* and the gods. Exemplifying this paradigm with remarkable clarity, the figure of Hekabe in *Iliad* 6 emerges into the text in order to tend Hektor and to supplicate Athena. In both their characteristic capacities women are implicitly disqualified from participating as full members of the civic community; since one form of service is below the civic organization and the other above, domestic and ritual work can be read alike to bypass the city. Inasmuch as the relation between "women" and "the city" is a real contradiction, in Lévi-Strauss's terms, it is amenable only to imaginary solutions.[16]

The issue of evidence for the articulation between women's ritual practice and the city's political practice is more problematic than for the investigations mounted in the preceding chapters. We are more than usually hampered by the Athenian focus in the majority of available documents, which has ensured that we can construct a much more detailed representation of classical Athens as a political entity than we can of other states. This means that although we may have access to highly relevant material about women's ritual practice in other cities and at other periods, we are not in a position to contextualize it so effectively. In this chapter I have drawn on testimony from other communities and from the imperial era (first and second centuries C.E.), but I have tried to do so only in order to amplify similar evidence from classical Athens. It is classical Athens that provides the most detailed examples of a ritual negotiation between the two poles of inclusion

15. Kearns 1990.

16. The full formulation follows: "The purpose of myth is to provide a logical model capable of overcoming a contradiction (an impossible achievement if, as it happens, the contradiction is real)" (Lévi-Strauss 1967: 226).

and exclusion, but versions of such negotiation can also be read in other contexts and other cities. Of course, our inquiries are chiefly hampered by the lack of testimony from women practitioners themselves. Comparative accounts of contemporary women can occasionally permit speculation on historical women's reactions to their own experience, and can also remind us that the dialectical quality of much of women's ritual practice may enable them to elaborate a productive relationship to the ideologies that otherwise govern their lives.

IMAGINARY INTERVENTIONS?

A number of items of testimony, more or less anecdotal, can be read to construct relationships between women's ritual practice and the political activity of men. Not all the passages I shall discuss here readily lend themselves to a "historical" reading; some declare themselves as part of the Greek or Athenian imagination. But together they bring female ritual practitioners into the political sphere and demonstrate their paradoxical importance there.

Among such practitioners the most publicly visible and politically engaged were likely to be priestesses, especially if they were conspicuous officials such as the priestess of Athena Polias in Athens. Such prominent operators are often explicitly said to perform cult activities on behalf of the civic body. The fourth-century priestess of Athena acts "on behalf of the people" (*huper tou demou, LSCG* 35), and the third-century priestesses of Artemis at Perge in Asia Minor and Dionysos at Miletos "on behalf of the city" (*huper tes poleos, LSAM* 48 and 73). Specifically Athenian narratives sometimes construct more complex intersections between politics and the activity of prominent priestesses. As we have seen in chapter 1, the late sixth-century Athenian tyrant Hippias ruled that the Athenians "offer to the priestess of Athena on the Acropolis, on behalf of every one who died, one choenix of barley and another of wheat, and an obol besides; and that the same offering should be made by every one to whom a child should be born' (Aristotle *Oikonomika* 2.5). This bizarre regulation is found alongside other economic innovations by Hippias, "skillful contrivances" (2.2) that the text claims were designed to enrich the state, such as changing the coinage and the sale of exemptions from liturgies. Hippias's father, the tyrant Peisistratos, had earlier, in the 550s, ensured his return to Athens by employing a woman disguised as Athena to lead him in procession to the city (Herodotos 1.60).[17] Qualified for this task by her height and looks, Phye

17. Sinos (1993) provides a useful and detailed discussion of this episode but does not relate it closely to women's ritual activities or to Peisistratid interference in them. Bassi (1998: 174–180) offers a very good analysis, but one that serves an argument unrelated to mine.

was dressed in full armor and placed in a chariot that was preceded into the city by heralds, and although the Herodotean narrator is much displeased by this trick, it seems to have succeeded. While it might be stretching any definition to include this woman's activity under the rubric of "ritual participation," we have already noted that the priestess of Athena Polias was required to impersonate the goddess as part of her sacerdotal duties, when she visited newly wed women and shook the aegis at them, and we shall consider other related impersonations later in this chapter. Peisistratos's tactic, then, can be seen as suggestive of the activity of the priestess.

The sons of Peisistratos can be detected in other significant manipulations of female ritual activity. Hippias's brother Hipparchos famously avenged himself on Harmodios, when Harmodios refused his sexual advances, by denying his sister a place in a procession as *kanephoros* (Thucydides 6.56). As we have seen, the sister's participation as a *kanephoros* would be public indication and celebration of her aristocratic birth and marriageable status; Hipparchos's gesture, by excluding her, undermines her family's ability to form profitable alliances through her marriage. Aristotle *Constitution of the Athenians* 18 claims that the festival in question was the Panathenaia, to which the Peisistratid family devoted considerable energy in their project of consolidating a newly self-conscious Athenian identity. The tyrants' concern with this identity is perhaps articulated partly in their manipulation of the ritual activity of these women: priestess, Phye, and *kanephoros*.

It may easily be objected, of course, that all such accounts are fictional, and one sign of fictionality might be that they participate in the traditional construction of the tyrant as a ruler who appropriates the citizens' women to his own purposes. Such an objection does not disable the inquiry, however, since if these accounts *are* fictional, it is nonetheless the case that democratic Athens, as represented by the histories of Herodotos and Thucydides, elaborated stories about the tyrants that showed them pursuing political advantage by means of intervention in the domain of women's ritual practices. This in turn entails that Athenian society could conceive of women and their ritual tasks as having significance among men in power.

Such significance might on occasion be predicated of women not only as objects of men's political maneuvers but also as subjects of autonomous political interventions. Herodotos 5.72, for instance, recounts how Kleomenes, the Spartan invader of 506 B.C.E., seizes the Athenian acropolis and enters the temple. Dramatically, the priestess of Athena Polias rises from her seat and says: "Spartan stranger, go back. Do not enter the shrine. For it is not right for Dorians to enter here"; Kleomenes' equivocating answer is that he is no Dorian, but an Achaean. This brief encounter offers to construct the Acropolis as an enclosed and feminine space, vulnerable to violation by the armed male, but the priestess's confrontation of the intruder dismantles this representation and can be seen to draw instead on the sexually ambiguous figure of the patron goddess Athena. Warrior-goddess and defiant priestess together defend the integrity of Athenian space. The priestess's characterization of Kleomenes as an outsider is described as an omen that is fulfilled by his eventual flight, and the implication perhaps is that she was not responsible for her speech but was uttering the goddess's words even at the moment when she inserts herself into history. But if we accept that the priestess spoke on her own account, we can conclude that her assertive gesture was made possible by the authority of her cult position. Again the precise historical status of her speech is not at issue; what counts is the fact that even classical Athens could imagine political intervention on the part of a cultically active female.

Installed by her city in probably the highest cultic office attainable by a woman, and momentarily, perhaps, incarnating the goddess, the priestess speaks for and about the city at a critical moment in its history. We can, of course, understand her identification with the city as a mystification of the real exclusion of women from the city's most important practices: as Eva Keuls puts it, certain women are allowed prominence in order that all women may take the city's priorities as their own.[18] But we can simultaneously read the priestess's gesture as a resistance to that exclusion, affirming instead her commitment to the city. Another priestess of Athena makes an equally significant gesture at the time of Salamis in 480 B.C.E. According to the Herodotean account (7.140–43), the Pythia's injunction to rely on the "wooden walls" gave rise to intense debate at Athens, which resolved into two main lines of interpretation. The "old men" (*presbuteroi*, 7.142) and the professional interpreters maintained that the Acropolis was indicated by the term, while another party, of which Themistokles emerged as spokesman, identified the navy as the means of salvation, thus aligning itself with what eventually became the radical naval democracy. When the time came to evacuate Athens in accordance with the Themistoklean plan, the priestess of Athena announced that the holy snake on the Acropolis had ceased to eat the regular offering of a honey cake, indicating that the goddess had abandoned the site (Herodotos 8.41). The priestess's utterance thus indirectly supported the Themistoklean party against that which may have included her natural allies, such as the professional interpreters and the treasurers of Athena who remained on the Acropolis to await the Persians.

While it is unlikely that the priestess consciously espoused a radical political agenda, it is equally improbable that she had no idea of the potential of her statement.[19] If we dismiss the whole episode as part of the intense mythol-

18. Keuls 1985: 306.

19. Plutarch *Themistokles* 10 asserts that Themistokles suggested the interpretation of the snake's disappearance, but it is still unlikely that the priestess imagined, for instance, that she was supporting the conservative party by announcing that the snake had left. That it is

ogizing generated by this critical period in Athenian history, then we should note that our choice removes from history a woman who uses her cult position to intervene in political process. To make this choice is thus to silence the priestess even more effectively than has the male-dominated culture of classical Athens, since that culture at least imagined and sanctioned her intervention. It is also possible to trace the significance of the priestess's utterance in terms of the construction of the Herodotean text. The Pythia's speech, which opens the narrative, is shown to be inadequate as a vehicle of revelation because it invites, and in fact requires, the work of interpretation carried out by political debate in the democracy. The political struggles among men are then finally assisted, and closed, by a further speech from a female cult practitioner that ratifies the human decision by showing that it is in accordance with divine dispensation. However we decide to interpret the narrative, it represents the priestess's timely utterance as promoting the city's welfare in a way that I suggest is characteristic of historical cult practices among women.

In contrast to the two narratives last cited, Plutarch *Alkibiades* 22.5 places the woman concerned in a position of antagonism to her city. This frequently cited passage claims that the priestess Theano refused to curse Alkibiades when required to do so by the Athenian polis. The account is usually cited without comment, such as by Robert Garland in his account of religious authority,[20] but Sourvinou-Inwood's reexamination argues that the narrative is essentially a fantasy of female disaffection that has been squeezed into the inappropriate context of cult practices in fifth-century Athens, when no priest or priestess could have operated independently in any matter of such urgency as the punishment of enemies of the community.[21] The political initiative that Theano[22] is alleged to have taken would indeed have put her in conflict with her city in a way that has not characterized the previous anecdotes about priestesses. It is perhaps significant that this narrative is the only account of a ritually prominent woman's active intervention in the politics of the later fifth century; whereas the developed democratic discourse readily imagined the earlier tyrants as manipulating women in order to carry out their political agenda, such discourse may have worked to exclude women from even the symbolic order of

---

Herodotos's text that foregrounds the independent action of the priestess may resonate with the *Histories'* emphasis on women as upholding and demonstrating the boundaries of mortal existence; see Dewald 1981, especially on the Pythia. Jordan (1979: 64–76) usefully points out that to stay on the Acropolis and entrust oneself to Athena might be the first inclination of cult officials, which again sheds an interesting light on the priestess's utterance.

20. Garland 1984: 77.

21. Sourvinou-Inwood 1988a: 29–30.

22. The priestess here is named, but, as Sourvinou-Inwood points out, her name is identical to that of the priestess of Troy in *Iliad* 6.297–300, which tends to undermine the account's claim to historicity.

its own politics. Perhaps Theano's gesture should be understood as part of the attribution to Alkibiades of a tyrannical identity that orchestrates erotic and aristocratic loyalties in pursuit of its selfish ends.

In the fourth century, too, Athenian women's ritual activities can be represented as vehicles for male political ambitions, as when the fourth-century orator and politician Lykourgos, of the Eupatrid family the Eteoboutadai, included in his measures for the renewal of Athens the provision of gold crowns for one hundred *kanephoroi*, as well as golden figures of Victory for the procession in honor of Athena.[23] This is part of a large-scale programme for the remaking of Athenian institutions after the defeat at the battle of Chaeroneia, which, as Mikalson remarks, happily combines Lykourgos's personal interest in the cult of Athena Polias with his statesmanlike promotion of the polis as a whole: "in enhancing his and his family's cult he was also enhancing the major state cult of Athens."[24] Lykourgos's favor to the daughters of prominent families may be considered as an attempt to consolidate support from the male heads of such families, as well as simply to advertise himself, but it eschews an overtly political gesture in favor of mediation by the sphere of women's ritual practices.

Women figure frequently as the conduits for transmission of wealth and legitimacy in the legal discourse of the fourth century, which discourse shares with political activity the work of redistributing power and resources among men. Women can also become prominent in legal struggles over cult prerogatives or accusations of *asebeia* (impiety); one of Lykourgos's speeches is even titled *On the Priestess (peri tes hiereias),* although we cannot be sure of all its content. We have already encountered the priestess of Artemis who sued Aristogeiton, and have surmised that this may have been a conflict primarily among men. In a case argued by Deinarchos, the priestess of Demeter at Eleusis brings suit against the hierophant in defense of her particular ritual privileges;[25] a similar struggle between priestess and hierophant is reported in Demosthenes *Against Neaira* 116–17. Although we should probably see the male relatives at work here too, it is possible that the priestess acted on her own initiative, since the different families who supplied the cult offices at Eleusis do not otherwise seem to have had a history of antagonism that might predispose them to seek legal redress.[26] The

23. Ps.-Plutarch *Lives of the Ten Orators* 852C; *IG* ii² 333, 2.10–11; Pausanias 1.29.16. This gesture might be considered analogous to that of Herodes Atticus, in the second century C.E., who altered the color of the ephebes' processional cloaks from black to white. See Vidal-Naquet 1981: 153.

24. Mikalson 1998: 290.

25. *Dinarchi Orationes* (ed. Conomis) 35, *diadikasia tes hiereias tes Demetros pros ton hierophanten.*

26. Feaver (1957: 140) claims that the families *were* antagonistic, but only on the basis of these references.

postclassical inscriptions from various cities, cited in chapter 1, which actively require priestesses to report or to discipline those who infringe cult regulations, also make it likely that we may reconstruct the priestess in Demosthenes as the subject of the legal and political process.

The fourth-century speech most often cited in discussions of ancient Greek women, and most blatant in its exploitation of women as a means to conduct men's political struggles, is Demosthenes' *Against Neaira*. It is probably not a coincidence that this speech also offers a quantity of information about women's ritual practice. Neaira herself, although accused of being a freed slave, prostitute, and concubine, does not constitute the main issue; tales of her exploits are mobilized by the prosecution in order to discredit and impoverish the citizen who protects her, Stephanos. One of the scandalous allegations against the couple is that Neaira's alleged daughter Phano is herself a prostitute yet had been passed off as the legitimate daughter of an Athenian citizen and married to Theogenes, "a man of good birth, but poor and without experience in affairs" (72). This marriage constituted the cement of an alliance Stephanos had formed with Theogenes, whom he assisted when the latter was elected by lot to the position of *archon basileus*. As wife of the *archon basileus*, Phano was called upon to perform as *basilinna* (queen) in the ceremony of the *hieros gamos*, or sacred wedding, and to officiate at other ritual events. Apollodoros, the speaker of *Against Neaira*, is loud in his outrage that such a woman should have performed such critical ritual tasks (73):

> And this woman offered for us the unnameable sacrifices on behalf of the city and saw what she should not have seen, since she was foreign; and even though she was what she was, she entered where no other Athenian, many as they are, enters, except the wife of the king; and she swore in the venerable priestesses who preside over the sacrifices and was given as wife to Dionysos; and she conducted on the city's behalf the ancestral rites, many and solemn and not to be named. If it is not proper that anyone hear of them, how is it properly reverent for her, who just happens along, to perform them, especially when she is what she is and has done what she has done?

While the profession of prostitute did not disqualify women from all cult participation, as we have seen, certain roles *were* restricted to other categories of women. Although Apollodoros goes into exquisite detail about Phano's and Neaira's life, Phano would in fact have been disqualified from performing as *basilinna* simply by failing to be Athenian or a virgin when married, neither of which conditions requires a lengthy career of depravity.

The *hieros gamos* with Dionysos, performed by the wife of the *archon basileus*, links Athenian practice to the various examples of intercourse between gods and human women described at Herodotos 1.181–82, with one significant difference; the women in the latter accounts are usually forbidden any intercourse with men, whereas at Athens the *basilinna* is a functioning wife and possibly a mother. In the early period of the city's history the position of *archon basileus* was reserved for members of the ancient Eupatrid families, so that the *basilinna* herself would most likely also derive from such a family. As a Eupatrid, claiming autochthonous birth and symbolic origin in the soil of Attica, the *basilinna* might find particular significance in the sacred wedding, designed to ensure that soil's fertility. By the date of Apollodoros's speech, however, the position of *archon basileus* had been democratically reformed, so that it was decided by the lot among all the citizens, entailing a similar random allotment among citizens' wives for the position of *basilinna*. When the city implicitly claims that any man may discharge the office of the *basileus,* it also concedes, by offering the position of *basilinna* as a kind of prize available to all women, that *any* legitimate wife of an Athenian citizen may be trusted with the important task of symbolizing the soil. A democratization of men's political functions generates a similar adjustment in the sphere of women's ritual practices.

What is interesting for my purposes is that in his prosecution Apollodoros can be seen to draw upon exactly this construction of the role of the *basilinna*. In the closing section of his speech (110), Apollodorus calls on the jury to imagine the scene of their return, after the trial:

> What will each of you say, when he goes home to his wife or daughter or mother, if he has acquitted this woman? When they ask you: "Where were you?" and you answer: "We sat in judgment," "On whom?" they will ask immediately. "Neaira," you will say, of course, will you not? "because although she is foreign, she is cohabiting with an Athenian contrary to law, and because she gave her daughter, who had lived as a prostitute, in marriage to Theogenes, the *archon basileus,* and this daughter performed on the city's behalf the unnameable sacrifices and was given as wife to Dionysos." . . . And the women, when they have heard, will say: "Well, what did you do?" And you will say: "We acquitted her."

This lengthy dialogue, which incidentally provokes comparison with Lysistrata's account of how her husband gruffly dismisses her questions about political decisions (*Lysistrata* 512–20), ends with the wrath of the women at the man's confession that the jury acquitted (111):[27]

> Surely then the most prudent *(hai sophronestatai)* of the women will be angry at you *(orgisthesontai)* because you judged that this woman should share *(metechein)* in the affairs of the city and of religion just like they do; and to those who are not women of good sense, you show clearly that they may do whatever they like, for you and the laws have freed them from fear.

27. Lysistrata, unlike the wives in *Against Neaira,* goes on to repudiate completely the male position on the issues.

Unable, of course, to resist the temptation to insist on women's proclivity for temptation, the speech nonetheless makes another, more significant contribution to the Athenian representation of women. As Patterson stresses in her analysis of the speech,[28] Apollodoros continually conflates Neaira with Phano, so that by the end of the speech the jurors are confronted with a two-headed monster of sexual *and* ritual depravity, and against this monster the jurors' womenfolk are mobilized in their capacity not only as chaste wives but also as ritual practitioners. They are depicted as having a stake in the exclusivity of the city and in the claims of citizens against the incursions of noncitizens, which they articulate on the grounds of "public ceremonials and religious rites"—the very rites that they would have been entitled to perform if they had been democratically selected as wife of the *archon basileus,* but for which the supposedly foreign-born Phano and Neaira could never qualify. What is at issue is not only Phano's or Neaira's sexual virtue, although that is clearly important, but also their ability to participate in the rituals that constitute the female "share" (metechein)[29] of the city, and that consequently parallel the assembly and the courts for the jurors. If the jurors acquit, they will confound the terms on which participation in the city is possible not only for themselves but also for their womenfolk, who claim the quasi-political cultic qualifications of Athenian birth and sexual conformity. As Patterson puts it, "The *timai* [honors] of Athenian women are epitomized in the responsibilities of the Basilinna."[30] We might even go further and say that Apollodoros's scene of return envisages the possibility that the juror's failure to respect the women's share will transform his chaste wife—a real *basilinna*—into the adulteress, a *basilinna* of Phano's type.

The domestic vignette of the juror's return repays further study. Addressed as a collectivity, taking action in the public sphere, the male jurors are also reminded that they must each leave that sphere and return to the private domain where they meet those excluded from public decision making. If they do not listen to the prosecutor, they will have to listen to their wives. It is of course open to us to argue that the women who make their appearance in the ensuing dialogue are a mere function of Apollodoros's rhetoric and the objects of an exploitation not very different from that which is directed toward Neaira, both in her (alleged) life and in the almost literally pornographic speech. The women do not speak; Apollodoros speaks for them and ensures that they say what he wants to hear. A

28. See Patterson 1994.

29. This is, of course, the term isolated by Patterson's analysis quoted above (1987: 49). Throughout her more recent study of this speech (1994), however, she stresses marriage rather than ritual service as the fulcrum on which Apollodoros's scenarios turn.

30. Patterson 1994: 209.

more positively inclined reading might stress instead the remarkable fact that the speaker experiences a need for the women's voice so great that he actually imitates it. To deliver the final clinching argument in a case that has previously investigated all the possible ways in which Athenian citizenship can be gained or lost, he must bring into the courtroom the ambivalently franchised women of Athens. That it is the women's identity as ritual practitioners, rather than simply as chaste wives, that positions them to enter legal and political discourse may also emerge from a reading that gives weight to the details of the scene of return, which in retrospect seems to have convened the women in an identifiable ritual. Although the text begins by describing a wife or daughter or mother, one woman for each juror, by the end of the passage the feminine substantives are plural, as if the women too have gathered in a collectivity to confront the erring men. Or better still, as if each man alone is faced with a monstrous regiment. This collectivity is united in virtue (hai sophronestatai) and anger (orgisthestontai)—who else can these women be if not the celebrants of the Thesmophoria, gathered to insist on not only their chastity but also their cultic privileges, and prepared to offer violence to any man who disrupts their ritual?

CHOOSING WOMEN

So far I have been considering certain items of Athenian testimony that can be read to construct an intersection between women's ritual activity and men's political practices. More systematic articulations are also discernible between masculine politics and women's rituals, emerging from structures rather than from particular moments, and these structural similarities suggest that women's ritual activity could elaborate for them elements of a political identity.

The various attributes that qualified a woman for participation in ritual activity were often similar to those for men in the political context. Although we have seen that much ritual activity could be open to many categories of women, nonetheless named roles and offices usually required the incumbent to satisfy certain conditions. Poor women could offer dedications, and slaves and metic women could enter temples, but most forms of ritual practice were more or less exclusive; as we have seen, festivals that convened wives and prostitutes might exclude slaves, and young women would participate in events separate from those of older women. To qualify for named cult offices women in Greek cities would usually have to be of free, native birth, not slaves or foreigners, and in many contexts they were also required to be members of a certain select group of families. Ritual practice addressed women at different stages of their lives, in the same way as different levels of political participation were available to men of different ages.[31] As we saw in the previous chapter, however, the ritual articulation of women's lives followed and confirmed their sexual and reproductive practice, while men characteristically qualified for different political offices according to age and military service, without reference to other aspects of a nonpolitical identity.[32]

Significant differences between male and female may be observed in the area of sexual conformity. Several cult positions for women in different communities required that the incumbent be married, whereas this was not a common regulation for men either in ritual or in political practice. Adultery in the male, namely the act of intercourse with a woman other than his wife, incurred no political penalty, although if a man seduced another man's wife, he was liable, at least in Athens, to loss of money and perhaps of life. The convicted adulteress, as we have seen, was prohibited in Athens from sharing in either her husband's *oikos* or women's ritual events. Conversely, while the female prostitute was not usually debarred from ritual activity as such, the male who sold his body for penetration by other men was liable, in Athens, to lose his political rights; he could not speak in the Assembly, and if he did, he was liable to prosecution (Aischines 1, *Against Timarchos*). Since a male prostitute who took the active role in intercourse was, apparently, inconceivable, the difference between female and male prostitutes as regards their ritual and political participation is most readily understood as deriving from the general cultural construction of male and female identity; while women are represented as enjoying and desiring sexual submission, any male who consentingly submits to sexual penetration is not likely to protect his city from political submission to others (Aischines 1.29).[33]

Qualification for ritual office by aristocratic birth or property ownership was common for male and female alike. Within the chief cults of a city, the leading official was often likely to serve for life and often also to be a member of an old and prominent family. The priestess of Athena Polias at Athens was drawn from the Eteoboutadai, the Salaminioi provided the priestesses of Aglauros and Athena Skiras, and the priestess of Demeter and Kore at Eleusis derived from the Philleidai. At Athens and Eleusis the chief priestesses held their offices for life, as did the priestess of Hera at Argos. Within the traditionally important families various arrangements might obtain for producing the sacerdotal official; the Eumolpidai and Kerykes of

31. E.g., only men over thirty could serve on juries; supervisors of ephebes had to be over forty; and "arbitrators" over sixty (Aristotle *Constitution of the Athenians* 63, 42, and 53).

32. Deinarchos 1.71 claims that *strategoi* and *rhetores* at Athens must "father children according to the laws," but this is likely to be a desirable attribute rather than a regulatory requirement. Children qualify a man to take decisions regarding the city's future, because they are his "hostages to fortune" (Thucydides 2.44.3–4).

33. On this topic see, for instance, Winkler 1990b: 186–97. Aischines 1.13.8f. also indicates that male prostitutes could not hold priesthoods.

Eleusis seem to have decided succession by family members' votes, but the use of the lot, with or without a selected panel from which the lot would finally choose, is attested even among such families and was employed among the Salaminioi to choose the priestesses of Aglauros and of Athena Skiras.[34] A defining characteristic of democratic practice, like accountability and public deliberation (Herodotos 3.80.6), the lot also fulfilled a religious function by providing a space for divine intervention in the selection process. Among aristocratic families, the lot may also have operated as a way of reducing antagonisms.

Not only priestesses but other ritual participants like the *kanephoroi* and, in Athens, the women involved in the Plynteria might be drawn from prominent families. Other levels of political organization, such as demes and tribes, might also provide cult officials chosen in various ways. As we have seen, the ritual calendar from Halai mentions seven priestesses who serve the deme,[35] and an inscription from the deme of the Piraeus enumerates the responsibilities of the priestess attached to the Thesmophorion there (*IG* ii² 1177). Arguments that we shall discuss later suggest that within Athens specifically, both the pre-Kleisthenic and the post-Kleisthenic tribes performed certain roles in selecting women for cult office, and the example of democratic Kos also indicates that tribal organizations could continue to supply cult officials even when they exerted no discernible influence on political structures.[36]

The most significantly "democratic" method of selection, the lot applying to the generality of the population, is attested both for Athens and for other cities, although it may be modified by some form of preselection. At Antimacheia on Kos, at the end of the fourth century, priestesses of Demeter were chosen by lot, and women who could not be present to participate in the lot itself could be represented instead by their husbands (*LSCG* 175). The selection procedure thus presumably reached the largest possible number of women and can be characterized, in conformity with the island's contemporary political organization, as democratic.[37] At some time prior to the appearance of the inscription concerned, however, the priesthood had been modified so that it was transferable by purchase (*LSCG* 175.6, *prin poletan genesthai*), thus implicitly disqualifying from the lot those women who could not command the necessary resources. Since the inscrip-

34. Thus Ferguson 1938: 6. On family members' votes see Mylonas 1962: 233. On preselected panels, see Feaver 1957: 148. Aleshire (1994) argues for restricted allotment for gentilician priesthoods, including those of the Salaminioi.

35. Daux 1963.

36. See *LSCG* 154 A.ii.34–35 on the election of a priestess from among tribal kinship groups; Sherwin-White 1978: 169–70.

37. On the fourth-century and Hellenistic democracy of Kos see Sherwin-White 1978: 65–66, 85.

tion seems to emerge from a change in the selection procedures, rather than existing to codify them, J.A. Turner plausibly concludes that this introduction of "qualified allotment" constitutes a direct response to contemporary democratic discourse.[38] An even more democratic procedure, implying an element of self-selection, is attested for Achaia; Pausanias claims that women compete for the priesthood of Earth and that if several women present themselves as applicants for the office, it is bestowed by lot among them (7.25.13). This arrangement suggests that certain women actively desired to serve as priestess and may also imply that the position was open to all women without further qualification. Although we do not know the political history of all the Achaean cities, the "democratic" contours of this selection process may be thought to conform to what is known of the Achaean League's practice.[39] At Elis, Pausanias states, the priestess of Eileithyia, the birth goddess, was chosen every year (6.20.2). Since it is unlikely that one family or group could supply so many women, this arrangement may imply a more democratic practice that opened the priesthood to a number of families or to the whole population. Such a practice would probably have been at variance with the traditionally oligarchic politics of Elis (Aristotle *Politics* 5.6, 1306a). In this case it may be that women are identified simply with their reproductive tasks rather than with their city's organization.

These several methods of selecting women for ritual office may be understood to elaborate various relationships between those women and the communities that they serve. Women in ritual may be organized by their cities along "democratic" lines or selected by "aristocratic" criteria of birth, and their cult office may also follow the contours of deme or tribal organization. It is important to note that none of these arrangements seem to construct "women" as a separate entity outside the structures of the city. When the Hellenistic practice of selling priesthoods becomes widespread, so that officials choose themselves rather than being produced by their relations with the city, cities can be seen to take steps in order to ensure that the incumbents continue to identify with the community in particular ways. Very specific types of relationship with the city could be required of women in cult office. In the third century B.C.E. the priestess of Artemis at Perge had to be an *aste,* or resident of the city, descendant of city residents on both sides, through three generations (*LSAM* 73.6–8).[40] She was assisted in her duties by the wives of the prytany members and shared in the proceeds of the sacrifice to Artemis equally with them. While the priestess does not share power within her city, she must be recognizably attached to and

38. Turner 1983: 97, 104–6.
39. Tarn and Griffith 1952: 74–75.
40. On this inscription and its regulations see Turner 1983: 155–56.

identified with its structures of political governance, and the women who help her, wives of the prytanists, can also be seen to model an equivalence between male political activity and female ritual participation. Although we cannot tell to what extent the requirement of three generations of resident ancestors was anomalous within the ritual practice of Pamphylia, we do know that it parallels the declaration of ancestry demanded of Koan men who wished to be enrolled on citizen lists.[41] Since the priesthood was acquired by purchase but nonetheless held for life, J. A. Turner, who discusses this inscription in detail, suggests that the requirement may be explained as a means to ensure that the incumbent of this anomalous office would identify unproblematically with the city.[42] The bonds of the polis may have been loosened in the Hellenistic period, but we may see here that they could also be reasserted.

Opposite Halikarnassos on Kos, in the second or first century B.C.E, the priestess of Dionysos Thyllophoros, who also purchased the position, was permitted to choose an assistant priestess, or *hyphiereia*, from each deme, who had to be a *politis*, a female "citizen" (*LSCG* 166.23–26). Similar *hyphiereiai politidai* are also attested for fourth-century Kos, serving Demeter at Antimacheia (*LSCG* 175). While it is not the case that these women were "citizens" in the sense of exercising any authority outside the ritual sphere, it is the case that their "citizenship"—their legitimate and valued participation in the city—emerges into view insofar as they are targeted by the processes of selection for ritual office. Kos is also the provenance for two inscriptions that state that the priestess concerned will be installed by the polis, even though she may have purchased her office (*LSCG* 154.A.35. [third century B.C.E.] and 166.21 [second or first century B.C.E.], *tan hiereian telezei/telesei ha polis*). While the practice of buying and selling priesthoods is often cited as a sign of the increasing individualism of Hellenistic culture and of the accompanying dissolution of those civic bonds that formerly supplied paradigms of "belonging," the insistence on the priestesses' civic role legible in these inscriptions from Kos and Perge may be thought to modify this conclusion.[43]

ATHENIAN INTERSECTIONS

The fifth and fourth centuries in Athens allow us to examine changes in practices of selection that seem to elaborate precise relationships to the

41. Sherwin-White 1978: 153–54.

42. Turner 1983: 156.

43. Interestingly, Kos also displays a series of statuettes dedicated by women in the temple of Demeter and Kore. These date from the mid-fourth to the mid-third century. See Ridgway 1987: 406.

political history of the city. It was, of course, this city that in its classical period most insistently theorized the exclusion of women from all its political processes, and Meiksins Wood has formulated an explanation for this phenomenon in terms precisely of the city's otherwise radical political inclusivity:

> The privileged political status of the male widened the gap between men and women; and perhaps pressures for the cultural devaluation of women were reinforced as the extension of citizenship carried with it a concomitant ideological impulse to harden the remaining principles of exclusion.[44]

Despite the force of this argument, we have repeatedly stressed that women were in fact culturally valued, even at Athens, in the sphere of ritual, which also offered forms of quasi-political participation. In the early period of the city's history it is highly probable that the Eupatrid families that provided female ritual officials were also those prominent in secular maneuvers, so that the preeminence of women family members would reproduce and confirm in another sphere the men's role in governance. Theorists of women's history often claim that some women can play unusually significant roles in aristocratic political structures because women symbolize and indeed perform the lineages of birth on which such structures depend,[45] and this aspect of Athenian ritual practice would seem to bear out this conclusion.

When Kleisthenes, the politician credited with the initial architecture of what became the radical democracy, reorganized the Athenian polity in 508/7 B.C.E., he left most cultic procedures and regulations outside his new structures (Aristotle *Constitution of the Athenians* 21.6). This move has been interpreted as an attempt to ensure that the Eupatrid families would exert no influence within his new state except that deriving from religious office, which in the Greek context was negligible.[46] Certain of the ritual roles that were reserved for the Eupatrid women, however, seem to have undergone a measure of "democratization." For instance, the *arrhephoroi* are said by various sources to derive from "good" families, which in this context probably implies Eupatrid. But in the democratic period a panel of young girls is chosen each year in a process of preliminary selection and final ratification that seems to involve both the *demos* (the people in assembly) and the *archon*

44. Meiksins Wood 1988: 118.

45. See, however, Rose 1992: 359 n. 64 , citing Plato and Aristotle on the "freedom and equality" available to women under democracies. It seems to me that such representations are at least as likely to be part of these writers' antidemocratic discourse as they are to be accounts of a historical situation.

46. See Feaver 1957: 133–34. Kearns (1985), however, argues that the primary effect of the Kleisthenic reforms was to introduce new layers of cult commitment for Athenians rather than to dilute former allegiances.

basileus.[47] This latter official, as we have seen, had formerly possessed considerable power and significance within the state, and the position had been reserved for a member of the Eupatrid families. The reforms of Solon in 594 opened the position to wealthy Athenians who did not belong to such families, and after further reforms in 487 the selection process involved sortition among candidates chosen by the demes. At a later date sortition was introduced at the deme level, and in the second half of the century the office was opened to all but the very poorest citizens.[48] By the time of the developed democracy the aristocratically born *arrhephoroi* were consequently subject to a number of democratic procedures at the hands of the *demos* and the reformed office of the *basileus.* Aristotle *Constitution of the Athenians* 49 even claims that whereas the *boule* used to decide on the patterns for Athena's peplos, which some of the *arrhephoroi* helped to weave, the decision is now taken by a jury selected by lot in order to avoid partisanship. Pierre Brulé suggests that the four *arrhephoroi* derived from the four pre-Kleisthenic tribes, and points out that on Kos the nine young female attendants of Athena, called *agretai,* seem to have been drawn from the three ancient Dorian tribes.[49] If the *arrhephoroi* did derive from the pre-Kleisthenic tribes, the selection process for them would display elements of both pre-democratic and democratic procedures in a way that could identify the girls involved both with their traditional families and with the newer political structures.

In the previous two chapters, we elaborated an interpretation of the Arrhephoria that concentrates on the female participants as weavers and potential mothers, but noted too that the rite mobilizes those participants in a direct rehearsal of founding Athenian myths. Not only do the *arrhephoroi* actively represent the city's mythical identity when they help to weave the designs into Athena's peplos, but the "swaddled thing" that they bring back from their nocturnal journey can be understood as the baby Erichthonios, the earth-born ancestor of all Athenians. Since the *arrhephoroi* are Eupatrids and thus claim to be directly descended from the ancient Athenian monarchy, they might readily identify with these myths of the Attic soil. What is interesting is that the increasingly democratic elements in their selection process could also allow them to function as representatives of

47. See Burkert 1966. Harpocration s.v. *arrhephorein* claims that "four were chosen by a show of hands, according to their *eugeneia,* but two were picked to begin the weaving," but the Suda s.v. *epiopsato* gives the technical term for the *basileus's* ratification of the *arrhephoroi.* See also the Suda and the *Etymologicum Magnum* s.v. *arrhephorein,* and the scholia on Aristophanes *Lysistrata* 642.

48. Stockton 1990: 108–9.

49. Brulé 1987: 207. See Feaver 1957: 131 for the continuing importance of the pre-Kleisthenic tribes within the developed Athenian democracy. On the Koan *agretai* see Hesychius s.v. and Brulé 1987: 207.

Athens as a whole rather than of one traditional group within the city. Situated in a nexus of different political ideologies, both inside and outside the city's governing structures, the *arrhephoroi* would be well placed to address instead its transcendent mythical identity, annually renewing the peplos of its goddess and retrieving the Erichthonian baby from its soil.

The Arkteia in classical Athens offers another example of possible articulations between women's ritual practice and political process. The Brauronia, during which the girls' ritual took place, was one of the penteteric, or four-yearly, festivals supervised by the Athenian religious officials called *hieropoioi* (Aristotle *Constitution of the Athenians* 54). There is considerable scholarly disagreement over which young women actually participated at Brauron. *Lysistrata* 644–48 and the accompanying scholia fuel the controversy:

> At seven I was an *arrhephoros;* then at ten I was an *aletris* for the Mistress Athena; and then wearing the *krokotos* I was a bear at the Brauronia; and then, a lovely young girl with a necklace of figs, I was a *kanephoros.*

This passage, supporting the chorus women's claim to advise the city from their position as well-bred women, places the Arkteia among other women's ritual activities, namely serving as *arrhephoros, aletris,* and *kanephoros,* which we know are reserved for girls from aristocratic families. The priestesshood of Artemis Mounichia, a deity who seems to be involved in a cult similar to that at Brauron, is also known to be restricted to a particular family.[50] Contradicting these indications of "aristocratic" identity are the scholion to the *Lysistrata* passage and the lexical authorities, which insist that "all" girls participated before marriage. From these latter testimonies there seems to emerge some indication of an element of democratic practice in the selection of the *arktoi,* or bears.

Despite these testimonies, many scholars, in line with the implications of the *Lysistrata* passage, have interpreted the rite as restricted to a few girls of good family. Ken Dowden argues this conclusion on the basis of the numbers that would otherwise be involved, Robert Garland from the small size of the sanctuary and the relative paucity of the finds.[51] Such arguments also invoke the widely available model of a once-inclusive rite, an "initiation" for all the members of an age group, which becomes restricted over time to a few. Any argument for aristocratic participation only, however, has to confront the poor quality of the dedicated pottery, which Erika Simon cites as evidence for the festival's democratic inclusivity.[52]

---

50. Garland 1987: 113.

51. Dowden 1989: 27–28; Garland 1990: 190. There are, however, large numbers of *krateriskoi* as yet unpublished.

52. Simon 1983: 86.

There are a number of possible exits from this impasse. Nancy Demand has suggested that only girls from the Athenian elite fulfilled their obligations to Artemis at Brauron (which would explain the Lysistratan chorus's inclusion of the service in a list of their notable achievements), while other girls performed the rite in other locations.[53] This model incidentally accounts neatly for *krateriskoi* found in other locations but is open to the objection, already formulated by Dowden,[54] that those found at Brauron are less elegant and expensive than one would then expect. Dowden proposes instead that the inclusivity of the festival, insisted on so strongly by the lexical authorities, was a feature of the Arkteia as performed at Brauron *before* that community's incorporation into the Athenian polis, when the numbers of local girls would not have exceeded the sanctuary's capacity. In the historical period, aristocratic families were the chief supporters of the rite, and the substandard *krateriskoi* were dedications sent to Brauron in place of those Attic girls who did not participate themselves.

Another way to reconcile the poor quality of the pottery with a notion of selection is to invoke the tithe. Several of the lexical sources offer *dekateuein* as a synonym for *arkteuein*, "to perform the Arkteia," and claim either that it refers to the age of the participants (a usage otherwise unknown) or that it refers to a tithing method of selection.[55] If the participants are selected by means of a tithe or similar allotment, the rite might be said to address "all girls" even if not every single one makes the journey to Brauron. While it is quite possible that the scholia and lexica use the term "all girls" in order to denote only the daughters of aristocrats, it is also the case that they have the vocabulary to distinguish girls of good birth if they desire to do so, as with the descriptions of *arrhephoroi*, and in their accounts of the Arkteia they do not. It therefore seems that the available evidence should encourage us to retain elements of democratic practice in our model of the ritual. We might conclude that the rite was indeed open to all, which would explain the pottery, but that families with more time and resources would characteristically participate to a greater extent than others. On the other hand, random selection by the lot of a "tithe" of all eligible girls, or of an unknown proportion, would conform to democratic practice and would explain the *krateriskoi* as the gifts of girls who might come from any class, and who therefore would chiefly come from poorer classes. Moreover, Brulé and Sourvinou-Inwood independently suggest that the "tithe" could refer to the ten post-Kleisthenic tribes.[56] Such an arrangement would align the girls' ritual practice with the

53. Demand 1994: 112.
54. Dowden 1989: 27–28.
55. *Deka* is Greek for "ten." See Harpocration, Hesychius, and *Etymologicum Magnum* s.v.; Bekker 1814: 1.234; Perlman 1983: 123 n. 44 and 128 n. 75.
56. Brulé 1987: 207; Sourvinou-Inwood 1988b: 113.

new proto-democratic organization of the Athenian state undertaken in 508/7 B.C.E. and might also suggest that the political leaders had deliberately interfered with a preexisting ritual—perhaps even an aristocratic one—in order to make it conform to a new, more inclusive ideology.[57]

In this context it is perhaps significant that the *krateriskoi* so far discovered date from the classical period, even though archaeology shows some cultic activity at Brauron from the eighth century until the sanctuary was destroyed by a natural disaster at the end of the fourth.[58] Simon points out that the goddess Artemis emerged into new prominence during the wars and speculates that "in those troubled years the Athenians . . . vowed all their unmarried daughters to Artemis."[59] We might perhaps invoke as well the newly found confidence in their democratic institutions that the Athenians experienced after their defeat of the Persian autocracy, and that might encourage them to participate more fully in a rite that was already organized on democratic lines.[60]

A final Athenian example of intersection between male political structures and the female ritual sphere concerns the selection process for the priestess of Athena Nike, known to us only from epigraphical evidence. The important inscription is most recently available as *IG* i³ 35 and dates, it is agreed, from the mid-fifth century.[61] Commentators concur that the decree seems not to establish the office but to modify it, so that we may posit a historical change in the method of selection. It is hard to avoid the conclusion that the office became, precisely, more democratic. Some have restored the decree to read that the priestess served for life, which was not a "democratic" feature, but the decree appears to rule too that the priestess be selected "from all the Athenians" (line 4). The phrase, as restored, is open to different interpretations. While most scholars restore the feminine genitive plural,[62] "from all Athenians" could also refer to male citizens who might choose a woman from within an unspecified pool or category of candidates, so that the "democratic" element in the selection process would then refer to men rather than to women. If, however, we assume with the majority of

---

57. Osborne finds that lists of dedicators of clothes at Brauron, who of course are not identical with *arktoi,* show few women who can be definitely identified as members of wealthy or prominent families (1985: 158–160, 173).

58. See the discussion of the sanctuary's history at Perlman 1983: 127; also Osborne 1994.

59. Simon 1983: 86.

60. On this question see also Cole 1998: 40–42. Mikalson (1998: 53) suggests that Artemis Brauronia declined in the Hellenistic period by analogy with Artemis Mounichia, who became inaccessible to Athenians because of a Macedonian garrison. On Artemis Mounichia see Palaiokrassa 1989.

61. For commentaries see especially Turner 1983: 70–95; also Garland 1984: 90–91 and 1992: 102–3.

62. See, for example, Patterson 1987: 53.

interpreters that the phrase refers to all Athenian women, then we are faced with two further possibilities. Either the women may vote or they may be the subject of an allotment. In fact the phrase that comes before "from all the Athenians" in the text of the inscription has been restored to read that the priestess will be chosen by lot, and it is in any case unlikely that the women of Athens would be called upon to elect one of their number by vote. Even if we challenge the restoration of the reference to the lot, the reference to all the Athenians marks this priesthood as a serious democratic alternative to the preexisting restricted offices. The salient feature of this selection process seems to be that it is arranged with an unprecedented extension of democratic practice to women.

Two other Athenian priesthoods, those of Bendis and Asklepios, which are known to have been established subsequent to this, in the mid- to late fifth century, are also characterized by their relation to democratic practice. Asklepios was served by a priest whose office seems to have been annual and bestowed by lot.[63] Since the crucial lines of the inscription are not well preserved, the evidence for the official or officials serving Bendis is more refractory, but a *gynaika* (woman or wife) is involved, and so are "all the Athenians" (*LSS* 6.15–16 = *IG* i³ 136). It is possible, however, that the *gynaika* is the wife of a priest rather than a woman who will be chosen to serve as priestess.

The cult of Bendis was a state foundation that subsequently ran parallel with private organizations already established by displaced Thracians in Athens;[64] that of Asklepios was a state foundation for a god previously without cult in the city. The cult of Athena Nike, on the other hand, seems to have existed in some form prior to the inscription that regulates the selection for its priestesshood, and the nature of the divinity served might have indicated as appropriate a priestess from a traditional Eupatrid family. Several scholars have in fact suggested that the priestess of Athena Polias previously discharged the duties accruing to the new priestess.[65] In this context the democratization of the office may imply a felt need to bring ritual practice into line with development in the sphere of politics, as Douglas Feaver argued for Athenian religion as a whole.[66] What seems to me utterly crucial, however, and yet is largely overlooked in the secondary literature, is that this reorganization of ritual practice also aligns women, specifically, with the democratic procedures of their city. The politically self-conscious city rearranges an element of women's ritual practice so that it deliberately models the political practice available to male citizens. Whether such rearrangement constituted a response to articulate pressure from historical

---

63. Feaver 1957: 138–39.
64. Garland 1987: 118–22.
65. E.g., Garland 1992: 102.
66. See Feaver 1957.

women or men for the greater inclusion of women in the city's procedures cannot be known, but it is arguable from the texts of tragedy that the contradictions in the Athenian discourse on the city's women were visible by midcentury. What is also arguable, I suggest, is that any partial remedy for women's contradictory situation would be enacted in the ritual sphere.

HONORING WOMEN

Opposite selection, in the ritual process, is the award of public honors to those women who have discharged their cult responsibilities satisfactorily, and here too we can discern a homology between women's sphere of ritual service and men's sphere of political participation. Throughout the geographical expanse of Greek culture, women were rewarded for their ritual activity with the same kinds of public honors, statues, and decrees that rewarded men for all their forms of public participation, including the political. Although women in general were more frequently honored in the Hellenistic and imperial periods than earlier, the majority of such honors continued to be assigned to priestesses and other cultically active women.[67] Moreover, the statues and inscriptions often occupied precisely those civic spaces of the city that women themselves were usually discouraged from entering. If these honorific representations cannot simply be thought of as addressing historical women, exhorting them to further identification with the city in a positive feedback loop, they can nonetheless be understood to address men on the subject of women's participation in the community. For either male or female audiences, I suggest, public honors for women's ritual activities perform an acknowledgment of women's stake in the city.

While some monuments to women's achievements were sponsored by male family members, the majority of honorific inscriptions known to us are the product of decisions taken by politically authoritative bodies, characteristically the *boule* (council) and *demos* (people in assembly).[68] Even if the authoritative institution did not generate the decision to honor a woman, its permission might nonetheless be required to ratify a private initiative. Such activity on the part of the institutions means that in the political process

---

67. Pomeroy 1975: 125. Men too, were more often honored in this period than earlier on, for all their different activities. Mikalson sums up the mutual admiration society of Hellenistic Greece thus: "This is just part of the broader trend of Hellenistic Greeks to honor one another with crowns, statues, decrees, and titles for an increasing variety of reasons" (1998: 310).

68. Despite this language, of course, Greek cities in the Hellenistic period were usually ruled by more or less distant monarchs. It is therefore not the classical polis, with its careful exclusions, that honors these women, and indeed one might argue that honors for women are one of the signs that the classical polis has disintegrated. My point is that although the Hellenistic period did see various modifications in the public pursuits available to women, women continued to enter the civic realm largely under the sign of ritual.

men had to devote some of their energies to observing and acknowledging women's cult service. Although women are excluded from those parts of the political process that concern deliberation and decision, they exert enough pressure on the process to achieve recognition and reward in the sphere of cult activity.

Several commentators note the prevalence of honors and awards for women who have discharged cult responsibilities,[69] but do not remark that such honors represent an anomaly in our characteristic accounts of women in the ancient Greek world. Burkert claims that priests, priestesses, and children of both sexes who had served as cult officials regularly erected commemorative statues in order to extend their association with the deity they had served, but does not speculate that such commemorations might construct particular relationships with the civic contexts in which they were placed. Some examples indicate the types of honorific monuments that might commemorate women's ritual practice (see also chapter 1). The fourth-century priestess of Athena Polias in Athens, Lysimache, was painted by Demetrius (Pliny *Natural History* 34.76), and on her death her statue was erected by her family (*IG* i² 3453). Another fourth-century priestess receives an honorary decree on a relief panel.[70] In the third century B.C.E. Timokrite, priestess of Aglauros, is congratulated by the Athenian state on maintaining good order *(eutaxia)* at an all-night festival *(pannychis)*,[71] and the priestess Lysistrate was crowned by the *demos* for her *eusebeia*, her prayers on behalf of the community, and the expense of 100 drachmas of her own money *(ton idion)* on sacrifices (*IG* ii² 776). An unnamed third-century priestess was honored, and the inscription erected in the precinct of the temple of Demeter (*IG* ii² 863). In the second century B.C.E. the Delphians bestowed extensive honors and privileges on Chrysis, an Athenian priestess of Athena, after a procession to Pythian Apollo (*IG* ii² 1136), while Satyra, a second-century priestess of the Thesmophoroi at Athens, receives a myrtle crown and the right to put up a picture of herself in the temple.[72] At the end of the second century Onaso, priestess of Kybele in the Piraeus, is similarly honored by a portrait in the sanctuary at the close of her period of office (*IG* ii² 1334), and in the third century previous priestesses had been honored with inscriptions and statues (Zeuxion, Glaukon, and Krateia; see *IG* ii² 1314–16). At Larisa in Thessaly Eubioteia was honored by the *demos* as priestess of Artemis (the inscription dates from the second century).[73]

In the majority of such instances the women probably belonged to the

---

69. E.g., Rouse 1975: 271; Burkert 1985: 93.
70. Ridgway 1987: 405.
71. Dontas 1983.
72. Broneer 1942.
73. See Clement 1934.

aristocratic families who customarily supplied the restricted priesthoods, and in that case the honors they received might be counted as a familial possession rather than as the achievement of the particular women concerned. Certainly in the Hellenistic and imperial periods it is common in inscriptions to praise a prominent woman because, among her other achievements, she has upheld the reputation of her family.[74] As we saw in chapter 1, the decision of Megakleia, second-century priestess of Aphrodite, to improve the temple at Megalopolis is attributed in a commemorative inscription to her noble heredity as the descendant of Philopoemen. Operating against the assumption that women are understood chiefly as representatives of their families, however, is the fact that in honorific inscriptions the women are always individually named.[75]

At Cyzicus in Asia Minor, in the Hellenistic or imperial period, certain women, who themselves served the Mother, appealed to the council to be allowed to set up the statue of the benefactress and priestess of the Mother and Artemis Mounichia, Kleidike, in the men's agora (*en te andron agora, CIG* 3657).[76] Although scholars disagree, as we have seen, about whether the position of women in Greek culture of the Hellenistic and imperial periods should be explained chiefly by legal and social changes or by economic shifts,[77] it is accepted that certain wealthy women attained a much more public life than was possible earlier, and operated in the civic dimension by supplying their cities with, for instance, loans, buildings, and charitable foundations. Any activity that could be construed as obviously political, however, remained alien to the newly public version of female identity, which is why it seems significant that at Cyzicus the women concerned represent themselves as entitled to address the chief political institution of the city. While they also seem to understand themselves as defined by gender, as indicated by the fact that they want to erect the statue of Kleidike in the men's agora, it is open to us to conclude that their incipient political identity is mediated by their common ritual service.

There are also indications that certain cult offices were regularly rewarded with public honors. The inscription honoring Satyra points out that the privilege of putting up her portrait in the temple is consistently awarded to other priestesses;[78] the privilege also extended to the girl victors in the races at Elis (Pausanias 5.16.3). A series of votive statues of girls at the

74. See, for example, Mikalson 1998: 310–11 on the importance of family rather than wider community in Hellenistic ritual practice.

75. Schaps (1977) remarkably fails to emphasize that women in cult contexts are consistently identified by personal name.

76. See also Bremen 1996: 171.

77. On legal and social changes, see, for example, Grant 1982 and Blundell 1995; on economic shifts, Bremen 1983.

78. Broneer 1942.

sanctuary of Artemis Orthia in Messene may commemorate ritual service.[79] Several sanctuaries exhibited statues of past priestesses, such as that of Demeter at Corinth (Pausanias 2.35.8), of Hera in Argos (Pausanias 2.17.3), and of the Eumenides in Achaia (Pausanias 7.25.7). Even though Chrysis, the contemporary priestess of Hera, was responsible for the temple burning down in the fifth century, the Argives did not remove her statue (Thucydides 4.133). At Eleusis the *hierophantides* had the right to erect their own statues in the sanctuary.[80] As far as other civic spaces are concerned, by the imperial period priestesses at Mytilene, Didyma, Aphrodisias, and Termessos, as well as Athens, were honored with special seats at the theater.[81] Certain priestesses laid a greater claim on their cities' history than that articulated in a physical artifact. The lifelong priestesses of Hera at Argos and of Demeter at Eleusis were eponymous, so that the calendars of those communities took as their reference points the years of service of the priestess (Hellanikos in *FGH* 4 F74–84)[82] In many cities the calendar used the office of a male political incumbent, such as the annual archons at Athens. Yet a mid-fourth-century inscription from the Athenian deme of Melite (*SEG* 22.116.5), which refers to the refurbishment of the temple of Artemis and which is set up in the temple, dates itself not only by the names of men presiding in the council and assembly but also by the priestesshood of Chairylle.

Public honors were not only assigned to adult women. The function of the *pais aph'hestias,* "child from the hearth," who was annually initiated at the Eleusinian Mysteries, was usually discharged by a male in the classical period, but later on girls often officiated, and both boys and girls might be commemorated by statues.[83] K. Clinton notes that the statues for the *pais* are the most abundant form of dedication at Eleusis.[84] In third-century Chios girls performed in contests for Leto and could be publicly honored with dedications.[85] A series of inscriptions from second-century Athens indicates that girls who took part in the Arrhephoria were regularly honored by the Assembly. Since the girls themselves cannot approach the Assembly, their

79. Van Straten 1981: 96.

80. Mylonas 1961: 231.

81. Bremen 1983: 241 n. 63.

82. See Mylonas 1961: 231. O'Brien (1993: 133) suggests that each priestess of Hera memorized the names of previous incumbents and that the list thus represented a continuity between the Mycenaean past and the Dorian present.

83. Mylonas 1961: 236. See, for instance, *IG* ii² 3475, 3476, 3477, 3478, and 3480. Clinton (1974: 100) cites a fourth-century inscription that purports to show that any Athenian could enroll his child for selection (by the *basileus* by lot) as *pais.* The first inscriptional references to girls as *pais* date to the second century B.C.E. On the *pais* see Clinton 1974: 98–114.

84. Clinton 1974: 113.

85. Graf 1985: 60–62.

fathers represent them, mediating between the female sphere of ritual and the male sphere of political decision *(IG* ii² 1034 and 1036, *prosodon poiesamenoi pros ten boulen hoi pateres).*[86] Both the familial and the political structures thus recognize the girls' cultic service, and the girls are finally commemorated by inscriptions on the Acropolis.[87]

Other forms of honorific acknowledgment constructed other relations between the women concerned and their city. As we have seen, the city of Corinth is said to have convened the prostitutes to assist in its prayers on occasions of importance, and to have honored them for their intercession during the Persian invasion of Greece (Athenaeus 13.573). The prostitutes are thus periodically summoned to enact their identification with the city. We have already suggested that women's ritual practice in the city of Sparta could work to maintain the paradigms of male identity, helping to govern the self-identifications of the *homoioi,* or equals. In this context it may be significant that the priestess of Artemis was present at the festival of Artemis Orthia, a characteristically gruesome celebration in which boys attempted to steal cheeses from the altar and were whipped in the process. Pausanias (3.16.10) claims that Lykourgos instituted the ritual bloodshed in order to avert other forms of civil strife, and while scholars agree that this ritual displays the contours of initiation, Plutarch's text notes that it occasionally resulted in real deaths *(Lykourgos* 18.1).[88] What is interesting for my purpose is the role of the priestess; during the proceedings she holds a wooden statue of the goddess, and, according to Pausanias 3.16.11,

> if ever the floggers spare a boy because of his beauty or prestige, the idol becomes heavy and hard to carry for the woman; she puts the blame on the floggers, and says she is being weighed down by them.

If we assume that the scourgers then increase their efforts, we can see that the priestess is charged with the task of ensuring that the *homoioi* really are *homoioi*—they all receive an equal whipping. Her ritual office thus partici-

---

86. See, for example, *IG* ii² 1034 and 1036, 1942 and 1943 (late second or early first century B.C.E.).

87. Such inscriptions, dating from the second century B.C.E. to the second century C.E., include *IG* ii² 3461, 3465 (restored), 3466, 3470–73, 3482 (restored), 3488, 3496–97, 3515–16, 3528, 3554–56, 3566 (restored), and 3634. Mikalson speculates that the institution of *ergastinai* may have been created in the second century in order to *(a)* provide more opportunities for honoring prominent families and *(b)* provide a parallel for females to the male *ephebeia.* But the institution could equally well have proceeded in earlier centuries (as most scholars presume) without its young participants coming in for honorifics. In the second century, fathers who serve as magistrates or priests frequently appoint their daughters as *kanephoroi* and subsequently honor them in inscriptions: see, for instance, *IG* ii² 896 for Timothea at Athens and *ID* 1867–73 for Delos.

88. See also David 1988: 10.

pates directly in the maintenance of Spartan ideology regarding both heroic endurance and the egalitarianism of the citizen body.[89]

A disputed passage of Plutarch's life of Lykourgos points to another form of honor for ritually active Spartan women that constructs further homologies between their practices and those of men in other public spheres. *Lykourgos* 27.2 claims that no Spartans were allowed to have their names engraved on their tombs except for men who had died in war and women who had died in cult office *(andros en polemo kai gunaikos ton hieron apothanonton)*. Latte's emendation from *ton hieron* to *en lecho* (women who die in childbirth) has been largely accepted, despite the fact that *ton hieron* is the *lectio difficilior* in the text of Plutarch.[90] Although Latte cites epigraphical support for his emendation, inscriptional evidence can also be read to show the existence of inscribed grave markers for *hieroi* and *hierai*, "sacred men and women," from Lakonia and Messenia.[91] As D. M. MacDowell, quoted in Demand, argues, the parallelism of death in battle and in childbirth confirms the Spartan requirements of military prowess from men and motherhood from women, but we might also note the importance of religious observance within Spartan culture as a whole, as detailed by Robert Parker.[92] Xenophon, for instance, claims a precise equivalence between the Spartans' technique as sacrificers and their military success (*Constitution of the Lacedaemonians* 13.2–5), an attitude that, if shared by the community as a whole, could perhaps lead to the institution of exceptional honors for women who die in ritual service. The case against honors for such women is not closed; nor should we be too ready, perhaps, to erase these women from the historical record and replace them with their all-too-familiar sisters, women who die in childbirth.

At Elis in the western Peloponnese the institution of the "Sixteen Women" suggests a still more striking identification between the women's sphere of ritual and the men's sphere of politics. Pausanias offers two accounts of the institution's genesis, the first relying on a timeless mythical paradigm and the second describing an alleged event in political history (5.16.4–6):

> They say that in gratitude to Hera for her marriage with Pelops Hippodameia brought together the Sixteen Women and with them first established the Heraea. . . . Concerning the Sixteen Women they tell another story as well,

89. According to Pausanias 6.10.8–9 the Olympic Games are watched by the Elean priestess of Demeter Chamyne, and also by *parthenoi*, who may perhaps be thought of as discharging similar functions to that of the priestess of Artemis and the choruses who mock young Spartan men.

90. See the discussions at Parker 1989: 163 and Demand 1994: 220 n. 2.

91. Parker 1989: 163.

92. Parker 1989.

which goes as follows. Damophon . . . , ruling as tyrant of Pisa, did much harm to the Eleans. But when he died, the people of Pisa did not want to participate as a people in crimes of the tyrant, and the Eleans too became quite happy to dismiss their grievances against them. Thus, since there were sixteen cities in Elis inhabited at that time, they chose a woman from each to settle their differences . . . the women from these cities organized treaties between Pisa and Elis. Later on the Eleans turned over to them the festival, for them to arrange the Heraean games and weave the peplos for Hera.

While the first account needs very little comment here, the second is extremely relevant for our purposes. Even if an "original" sixteen were convened at some early pre-polis period solely in order to celebrate Hippodameia's marriage and to prepare young girls for theirs, the explanation of the women's origin is modified by events of the early sixth century, so that they are seen quite clearly to be representatives of the cities. They are chosen for qualities of age, worth, and reputation; each woman *proiesen,* "stood out," for *helikia, axioma,* and *doxe* (5.16.6). While there is obviously a potential conflict between being the oldest and being the worthiest and most respected, we can conclude that to be selected, a woman would have to fulfill certain requirements of age, esteem, and, plausibly, good birth, so that the selection of the Sixteen Women would conform to the oligarchic contours of Elean politics (Aristotle *Politics* 5.6, 1306a). Although we can be fairly certain that the final arbiters of the women's qualifications would be men, especially in their role as husbands, it seems likely that some of the women chosen to serve would either be well known to the community already or would become so during the period of their office. A possible parallel is offered by an Achaian rite described by Pausanias that convenes nine men chosen by the *demos* from the entire population. These men are distinguished by their "worth" *(axioma),* a term that in Greek as in English spans the semantic fields of "intrinsic merit" and "noble birth," and they are accompanied by nine women described as "equal" (Pausanias 7.20.1.) Whether "equal" refers to number only or to reputation as well is unclear. Unless these women are the wives of the men, which is not obvious from the text, they are also probably known, in some sense, to the *demos.* Such public lives would constitute part of the material presence of cultically active women in the community for which I argued in chapter 1.

Given the overwhelming identification in Greek culture of the female as the source of strife among men, the Sixteen Women's alleged peacemaking mission at Elis seems significant. There are a few literary references to women as peacemakers: Arete in the *Odyssey* (7.74) is distinguished by her ability to settle even the quarrels of men; Jokasta tries to make peace between her sons Polyneikes and Eteokles in the Euripidean *Phoenician Women* (452–68); Jokasta's daughters Antigone and Ismene leave Colonus in order to attempt to pacify their warring brothers in Thebes at the end of

Oedipus at Colonus (1769–72); and Lysistrata calls the sex strike in order to end the Peloponnesian War.[93] These peacemaking acts primarily address familial relations and so do not constitute a very close parallel to the work of the Sixteen Women. Perhaps we can best understand the designation of the Elean Sixteen as peacemakers if we suppose another tradition in the representation of women that identifies them with the welfare of the community, a tradition that may be discerned chiefly in reference to women's ritual work.

The Sixteen Women's "original" task is clearly political, and they function as representatives of the sixteen Elean cities. By Pausanias's time, the second century C.E., some of the cities involved had been destroyed, but "the Eleans still adhere to the other ancient customs. . . . For they are now divided into eight tribes, and they choose two women from each" (5.26.8), so that the principle of representation is retained. The institution of the Sixteen Women seems to provide a good occasion for examining the notion of women's "passive citizenship." Since it consists in an active intervention in political affairs, I would contend that we cannot designate the Elean women's citizenship as "passive" at all; instead, I would again propose a notion of latent citizenship. If some of the women of Elis can be called into being as political operators by a decision on the part of Elean men, then they must have been understood as always having the potential to exercise political skills for the benefit of the community. Like the women of Athens who are symbolically called upon in *Against Neaira* to define and defend the parameters of civic identification, so the women of Elis may be summoned by the men to perform temporarily as qualified citizens in the political realm. While we cannot know the reactions of women selected to the post, it is conceivable that historical women, weaving the peplos for Hera and organizing the young girls' races, were also conscious of themselves as part of a tradition that acknowledged and valued women's contributions to the community.

A Plutarchan narrative in *Virtues of Women* 251 suggests a possible self-identification along these lines on the part of a historical group of Sixteen Women. In the third century B.C.E. the tyrant Aristotimos of Elis imprisoned a large number of respectable wives who had tried to join their refugee husbands in exile. The current group of Sixteen Women, described in Plutarch's text as "holy" and dedicated to Dionysos, went to supplicate the tyrant in the agora for the women's release. The tyrant's guards let them through to his presence, respecting their position and intent, but Aristotimos himself drives them away and in addition fines each woman two talents, a sum that either indicates the great wealth of the Sixteen Women's

93. See also Plutarch *Virtues of Women* 246, on the Celts, and of course Roman stories such as that of the Sabine Women.

families or suggests the extent of the tyrant's savagery. That the narrative appears in the *Virtues of Women* suggests that the Sixteen's action is unusual and requires explanation; it is hard to account for it without supposing forms of solidarity for the Sixteen with their gender and class, and an incipient self-awareness as a political entity. Conscious of a historical mission as preservers of the polity, the women represent themselves as entitled to approach the ruler, whose guards admit their authority even if he himself does not.

By Pausanias's time, sixteen women are still selected, but they continue to preserve the polity only by the perennial female gesture of weaving a peplos for Hera (Pausanias 5.16.2). While the narrative structure suggests that the women's "original" political contribution has disappeared into a ritual gesture, we may perhaps construe the ritual weaving as itself an active commemoration of their political intervention. Lysistrata, after all, deploys the weaving metaphor to demonstrate women's aptitude for civic organization (*Lysistrata* 567–86: e.g., "In the same way, we'll see to the city./We'll lay it out on the carding-frame,/Comb out the riff-raff, pick off the yes-men"). Even if we suppose that the ritual was generated in an early period of the community's history and directed its energies primarily toward the marriages of young girls, the attachment to the ritual institution of an explicitly political narrative allows the ritual itself to imagine a female identity characterized not only by domestic toil but also by productive political intervention. The historicity of the Elean narratives is perhaps not as significant as the possibilities that they imagine for women.

SAVING THE CITY

If we were to ask what conditions qualified the Elean women for their limited political intervention, we might suggest that free women in Greek cities can be called on as peacemakers precisely because they are not characteristically identified with politics; they are not contenders in the competitive systems that award power and resources. When the Sixteen Women of Elis exercise the limited political function of preserving the city by bringing peace, we might conclude that their political role is enabled by their cultural location outside politics. They may be seen to qualify for this role in the same way that women within the domestic setting qualify to intercede with the divine for their families because of their nearness to the nonhuman; the equivocal location of the female, part and not part of the community, positions her to intervene on that community's behalf.

While the methods of selecting women for ritual office, and of honoring them subsequent to it, can be seen to generate connections to the political dimensions of the cities that these women inhabit, some of women's most spectacular ritual interventions in the city can also be seen to depend on their position at the margins of their communities. Women's ritual practice often commemorates or otherwise figures instances of women "saving the city"; frequently what is rehearsed is the death of a young woman whose sacrifice protected or rescued her community, thereby supplying the most dramatic instance of what Emily Kearns calls the "unlikely savior."[94] Such mythical deaths, and the ritual practices within which the trope can be identified, have generated considerable critical interest, and several explanations have been proposed for the prevalence of the motif in Greek culture. Walter Burkert links the virgin sacrifice to a renunciation of sexuality and reproduction on the eve of hunting or war, while Dowden focuses on the "death of the maiden" as a figure for "the end of maidenhood" in an initiatory scenario.[95] Such accounts persuade to a point, but the work of Brulé, in its emphasis on the expiating and mediating function of such deaths, more compellingly situates the motif of maiden sacrifice firmly within the ideology of a patriarchal culture; the "daughters" die in order to ensure the survival of "fathers" who cannot themselves so effectively approach the divine. Although the living *parthenos* does not attract ritual attention to the same extent as the *gyne* nor participates as fully in cult activities, her death is an extraordinarily potent element in accounts of ritual foundations. As Brulé notes, it is good to build on the blood of daughters.[96]

The daughters may be potent, but this factor alone need not qualify them as the victims most auspicious for the city's preservation. It is hard to account for the trope of virgin sacrifice without reference to an apparently structural hostility, fostered by patriarchal imperatives, to the female on the part of the male. On the other hand, that such hostility also obtains between old and young is suggested by the fact that young victims of both sexes are often represented in the etiological narratives of ritual. Very few accounts of the sacrifice of young men alone are recorded, however, and a plausible conclusion is that the young female may be offered up by the city because she is viewed as one of its more expendable members. Her chief task, after all, is to marry and produce children, itself a life-threatening occupation. The figure of Iphigeneia presents the alternatives: sacrifice in the service of the wider political project, or death at home in childbirth.

94. See Kearns 1990. Other "unlikely saviors" in her account include foreigners, children, and slaves. One child-savior, Sosipolis at Elis, is celebrated historically by women rather than by the community as a whole. It is important to note, as Kearns does (1990: 335), that slaves appear in this role only rarely; not only is it historically less plausible that slaves would rescue their masters than that free women would their families or cities, but the absence of such narratives also suggests less need to conciliate or co-opt slaves, whose lives seem to be determined by a more present and active threat of force.

95. Burkert 1983: 64–66; Dowden 1989. See also Rabinowitz 1993a: 31–38 for an overview of scholarship on this issue.

96. Brulé 1987: 206.

Despite the various ideological imperatives that position the young female as the most acceptable offering, we should note that no utterly marginal figure is ever contemplated, in Greek representations, as a plausible candidate for sacrifice. At the moment of her death the *parthenos* is thus paradoxically acknowledged as a necessary and integral component of the city's identity.[97] If, as Kearns has cogently argued, the paradox of the "unlikely savior" represents precisely the city's attempt to negotiate between the exclusive and the inclusive versions of itself, then it is no coincidence that the salvific action of the *parthenos* is commemorated in the ritual sphere.

Whether or not all accounts of human sacrifice in Greek culture are legendary, without basis in historical events, versions of such sacrifice were enacted in women's ritual practice. The most striking such analogy is provided by the ritual involving the Locrian maidens.[98] Each year two young women from Locri were sent to Troy as a human tribute in expiation for Ajax's rape of Kassandra. Required to enter Troy unseen, the girls were allegedly executed if caught. Once in Troy they served in the temple of Athena, although they were denied access to the goddess except at night; they shaved their heads, wore only one garment, and went barefoot.

The combination of terror, danger, physical discomfort, and spiritual isolation that seems to characterize this experience has marked it for many scholars as a rite of passage or initiation.[99] The girls are suspended in a liminal state—although to describe the temple of Athena at Troy as a liminal location may be stretching a point—far from home, and they endure the characteristic nonfatal ordeals. Pointing out that on safe arrival in Troy the girls became "priestesses," Dowden suggests that they were engaged in a one-year passage rite devoid of real threat.[100] As we have seen, however, the office of "priestess" does not necessarily connote special authority or privileges and may prescribe menial domestic duties as well as others, so that the title alone by no means indicates that the girls enjoyed an easy life. Moreover, we cannot be sure that their servitude lasted only one year; even if two new girls arrived in Troy every year, there may nonetheless have been more than two in service at any one time.

97. Eva Stehle has suggested to me in a private communication that the notion of "virgin sacrifice" may also construct the virgin daughter as the city's "best thing," its most precious possession. But I would contend that the rest of the ritual/ideological discourse surrounding the *parthenos* makes the situation overall more negative.

98. See Hughes 1991: 166–84 for a thorough account with bibliography. The chief source is Lycophron *Alexandra* 1141–73 and scholia. See also Plutarch *The Divine Vengeance* 557D and Apollodorus *Epitome* 6.20.

99. Graf (1978) provides the locus classicus for this interpretation. See also Hughes 1991:180–81.

100. Dowden 1989: 130.

Despite the vigilance of the Trojans, alleged by Aeneas Tacticus (31.24), writing in the mid-fourth century B.C.E., commentators agree that the Locrian maidens regularly survived the trip to Troy, so that they could successfully enter on their duties, and that the threat of death was a purely mythical component of the initiatory scenario. That the ordeal was not devoid of all danger is, however, suggested by a possible parallel in the Agrionia at Orchomenos in Thessaly. Women who claim descent from the mythical Minyads, the daughters of King Minyas, are ritually pursued every other year by the priest of Dionysos, in order to rehearse the fate of the "original" Minyads, who, maddened by Dionysos, killed their children and were pursued by their bereaved husbands. According to Plutarch (*Greek Questions* 299), the priest of Dionysos bore a sword and was entitled to execute any woman whom he caught. During Plutarch's lifetime the priest Zoilos did apparently kill a participating woman and subsequently died himself of a lingering disease; the citizens took the unusual step of removing the hereditary priesthood from his family. While Burkert proposes that the second-century C.E. priest mistakes the requirements of his role and breaks, as it were, the dramatic illusion, Dennis Hughes finds it more probable that priest and Minyad were involved in a simple accident.[101] In any case, despite the threatening terms of the ritual, the consequences of the woman's death prove that women did not usually die. If we apply the paradigm to the case of the Locrian girls, however, we can perhaps conclude that their ordeal need not always have been entirely free of real menace.

Even though Polybios (12.5.7) claims that the "hundred houses" that provided girls were honored, the ways in which the ritual emerges into the historical record indicate that it may also have occasioned some distress. Both a fragment of Aelian (frag. 47 Hercher) and a scholion on Lycophron *Alexandra* 1159 claim that the tribute was discontinued in the fourth century and only reinstated after an injunction from Delphi. At some point a certain Antigonos, perhaps Monophthalmos, emerges to mediate among the Locrian cities involved and arranges that selection of the city delegated to send the girls will proceed in future by lot (Aelian frag. 47 Hercher). Other sources, however, claim that selection was always managed by lot among the families responsible for the tribute (Polybios 12.5.7). Finally, a third-century B.C.E. inscription[102] seems to indicate that the citizens of Naryx, birthplace of Ajax, take over the entire charge of the tribute in return for various privileges among the rest of the Locrians. The tribute seems to have ceased completely in the second century B.C.E.[103] While no completely coherent history of the ritual can be reconstructed in the pre-

101. Burkert 1983: 175; Hughes 1991: 13–33.
102. *IG* ix² (Inscriptiones Locridis Occidentalis) pt. 1, fasc. 3, no. 706, dated to 280 B.C.E.
103. Hughes 1991: 177.

sent state of our knowledge, a recurrent feature seems to be conflict over whether there should be a tribute at all, and who should bear the brunt of providing it. The apparent reluctance or hesitation of the Locrian cities to furnish Trojan Athena with their daughters seems to indicate that even though the ritual did not necessarily encompass the death of the girls, it may nonetheless have occasioned distress among the families concerned. Such distress would suggest that the ritual might collapse under its own contradictions, since it would figure the supposedly marginal and expendable members of the community as objects of concern.

While the literary sources for the rite that emphasize its terror and suffering, such as Lykophron's *Alexandra,* may be judged to exaggerate and to offer myth rather than history, it is perhaps significant that a historical ritual, with which living witnesses may have been acquainted, could be so readily represented in sacrificial contours. The literary texts are not offering an inaccurate, mistaken account; instead they are responding to Greek culture's implicit assertion that the city's crimes can be expiated by representatives drawn from its vulnerable female population. These qualities in the Locrian tribute of expiation and representation radically distinguish it from those rituals of passage, initiation, and preparation for marriage that are known for other Greek communities. While some, such as the Arkteia, commemorate the death of a young woman, the participants are said to perform the cult service precisely in order to avoid the necessity of any such sacrificial destiny themselves. The same paradigm is discernible elsewhere; at Patrai in Achaia, for instance, children of both sexes perform cult services for Artemis in memory of an alleged tradition of human sacrifice, which itself was instituted as expiation for a crime (Pausanias 7.20.1). Expiation is a recurrent motif in ceremonies for young people, but it is characteristically commemorated rather than performed; the Locrian girls, on the other hand, expiate in their own persons the original crime by Ajax. While most initiatory scenarios thus qualify their gestures of expiation more than does the Locrian tribute, they also fail to exhibit such a clear element of representativeness; in no other comparable rite are participants delegated to travel from one country to another, whereas the Locrian maidens explicitly represent their cities to the goddess at Troy.

In the representative and expiatory contours of their cult service, the young women from Locri offer a historical analogy to the mythical accounts of daughters sacrificed to preserve the polity. If we assume that the most appropriate way to interpret such a ritual overall is as an address by mortals to the divine, then the message may readily be understood as one of renunciation, as Burkert argues, because the young women can be seen to signify the future that the community voluntarily risks in an act of devotion to the gods. If, however, we suppose that the ritual also addresses its participants, the propositions that it articulates to them seem contradictory. The city

identifies the young women as "belonging" to the extent that they can perform an expiation for it, but in this expiation they are constructed as more
expendable than its other members; on the other hand, since the community is troubled by its ritual obligations, the girls cannot be endlessly expendable. Since young women must be transformed into the adults who will
reproduce the community, they are crucial to its future, but a male-dominated culture must persuade its young female members that their needed
contribution does not conversely qualify them as full participants in the city.

Like the contradictions in gender ideology that we explored in the previous chapter, these political contradictions provide a motor rather than an
obstacle to the reproduction of culture. Given that the contradiction
between the exclusive and the inclusive versions of the city is real, it is
amenable only to symbolic solutions, such as those supplied by ritual, and
thus insists on repeated staging. Unlike the ritual gestures studied in the
previous chapter, however, the ritual practices at issue here, by aligning
women participants with the political dimensions of their cities, construct
for those participants an identity considerably at variance with the other
possibilities on offer to them. While the ideology of gender enacted in ritual practice canvasses alternatives to itself in order finally to dismiss them,
the alternatives supplied by the ritual discourse of women's civic participation are offered as a positive version of female identity.

In this context it may be useful to consider the Leokorion in Athens, the
shrine to the daughters of Leos who allegedly sacrificed themselves to save
the city. When this site was excavated, a number of items were found in its
vicinity, such as perfume bottles, jewelry, infant feeding-bottles, and loom
weights, which have been construed as women's dedications.[104] A second-
century C.E. source (Alciphron 3.2) maintains that this shrine was a gathering place for prostitutes,[105] who may of course have identified themselves
by loom weights as readily as may other women. What can we make of this
apparent devotion of at least some women to the tomb of the dead daughters? Keuls claims that the dedications suggest that "the women of Athens
gloried in the notion of self-sacrifice,"[106] but we need not construe such an
attitude only as proof of the damage inflicted by the city's patriarchal ideology. That Greek gender ideology damaged women is highly likely, but we
too may sell those women short if we deny the possibility of their identification with the city's welfare. The sacrificial deaths of courageous virgins may
even have provided a focus for heroic aspirations otherwise denied in
women's daily lives. While the Leokorion seems to enlist for the city an

104. See Thompson 1978: 101–2.
105. The speaker of *Against Konon* is beaten up in the vicinity of the Leokorion too
(Demosthenes 54.7–8).
106. Keuls 1985: 138.

audience that might otherwise be potentially hostile, and thus seems to perform the ideological work of eliciting women's consent to their own objectification, the dedications at the shrine can also be read to show that audience transforming a given cultural resource to its own ends. That some Athenian women honored the Leokorion need not mean only that they failed to recognize their own conditions of exploitation; it could also signify that they asserted an identification with the city that could reappropriate and recharge its misogynist symbols. While the trope of "saving the city" can be deconstructed so that it demonstrates the Greek city's exploitation of its women, historical women might mobilize different accounts of the trope to emphasize their participation in the city rather than their exclusion from it.

As well as the daughters of Leos, the city of Athens offers other examples of the "unlikely savior," the *parthenos* who sacrifices herself to preserve the city. The paradox of this *parthenos,* necessary because expendable, or in Kearns's terms central because marginal, is particularly visible in the ritual discourse generated by the figure of Aglauros. We have encountered Aglauros as one of the daughters of Kekrops who jumped from the Acropolis and incidentally provided an etiology for the Arrhephoria, but another account claims that she leaped voluntarily in order to save the city from defeat in battle. She thus became a heroine honored not only with cult but also with the oath of the ephebes, young warriors on the verge of adult manhood, who swore in her name to defend the city.[107] Present at the origin of the city and involved in the work of reproducing it, the sacrificial *parthenos* renounces the possibility of giving the city children but acquires numerous paradoxical "sons" in the young ephebes, whom the city identifies with itself in her name.[108]

A doublet of Aglauros's myth is legible in the fragmentary Euripidean *Erechtheus,* in which Praxithea, the wife of Erechtheus, willingly yields her daughter as a sacrifice to ensure victory over the Eleusinians. Since the drama goes on to claim that she was subsequently installed by Athena as her first priestess, we can discern the converse of the civic identity elaborated in the honors bestowed for ritual service; ritual service constitutes a reward and recognition of a woman's ability to identify with her city. The text of Plutarch claims a historical analogy to Praxithea's reward when it describes how Xenokrite of Cumae helped to overthrow the tyrant Aristodemos, in the late sixth century, and was subsequently elected priestess of Demeter by the citizens, who considered that "the honor would be as pleasing to the

107. The Greek text is given in Daux 1971: 370–71.

108. If "marriage is for the girl what war is for the boy," as in the well-known formulation of Vernant (1980: 23), then the death of virgins for the city seems actually to combine the two otherwise mutually exclusive terms.

goddess as it was appropriate to the woman" (*Virtues of Women* 262).[109] A similar construction is available for a narrative in Strabo (4.1.4). When the Phocaeans founded their colony of Massilia, in the early seventh century, they were advised by an oracle to take with them a guide from Ephesos; simultaneously, Artemis appeared to an Ephesian woman called Aristarcha and told her to leave with the strangers. On arrival Aristarcha was made priestess of Ephesian Artemis for the new settlement.[110]

Most ritual activity that can be understood under the rubric of "saving the city" commemorates the death or sacrifice of a young woman, but there are variations on the theme. Children of both sexes are enlisted to supplicate potentially hostile divinities, who have previously sent plague or other afflictions, for instance, at Patrai (Pausanias 7.20.1–2). At Corinth, the scholia on *Medea* 264 explain, seven boys and seven girls of good families were annually required to serve in the temple of Hera for a year in order to expiate the deaths of Medea's children and prevent the plague from returning (see also Pausanias 2.7.7). Plutarch's life of Theseus 18.2 describes how even into the second century c.e. on the 6th of Munichion the young women of Athens walked in procession to the Delphinion, a temple on the bank of the river Ilissos, to supplicate Apollo and Artemis. Although this procession does not explicitly recall a death or plague, it was understood to commemorate the voyage of Theseus to Crete with the Minotaur's tribute of youths and maidens and may thus be seen to align the female participants with the trope of salvation. The festival of the Hybristika at Argos and that of Ares at Tegea in Arcadia allegedly honor active female interventions with equally dynamic ritual forms. In 494 b.c.e. the women of Argos, under the leadership of the woman poet Telesilla, are said to have defended the city against the Spartans, and their prowess is commemorated in a ritual that involves cross-dressing for both sexes (Plutarch *Virtues of Women* 245). The festival at Tegea is marked by a similar disruption of normal categories, in that the women appropriate all the sacrificial meat as a reward to themselves for their military valor under Marpessa against Sparta (Pausanias 8.48.4–5).

Comparing these various narratives of salvation, we may conclude that in order to "save the city" women may assert their identification with it either in the gesture of sacrifice or in anomalous military action. In both cases the women's intervention is commemorated in the ritual sphere. Despite the

109. This unamiable tyrant made boys dress as girls and girls as boys, a practice offering not only an example of his perversity but also perhaps a paradoxical warning of how his downfall would be encompassed by women.

110. Plutarch *Oracles at Delphi* 403B and *Life of Nikias* 532A both narrate that the Athenians, seeking advice from Delphi about their invasion of Sicily, were told to get the priestess of Athena from Erythrai, as if she would provide the kind of assistance and leadership offered by Aristarcha and Xenokrite; but her name, Hesychia (Peace and Quiet), turned out instead to be a joke at the expense, ultimately, of the Athenians.

parallelism thus asserted between sacrifice and military action, however, the rituals consequent on the latter insist strongly on its abnormality. The Hybristika requires women to wear men's tunics, and men women's dresses and veils; the festival of Ares deprives men of sacrificial meat. What is signified by these ritual anomalies is not simply an inversion of roles, but rather the zero-sum structure of Greek patriarchal culture; according to this uncompromising arithmetic, if women participate in the city's preservation, men will inevitably begin to lose the signs of their participation and experience instead the feminine contours of exclusion. This equation is particularly clear at Tegea where the customary organization of sacrificial meat between the genders is not inverted, which would still provide both sexes with meat, but completely altered, so that men receive none. At Argos the narrative develops along similar lines; the relatively simple ritual inversion of cross-dressing is followed in the Plutarchan account by the information that owing to the wartime shortage of men, the Argive women married either slaves or *perioikoi*, "neighboring peoples," whom they then treated with contempt; hence "the law that orders married women to wear beards when they go to bed with their husbands" (Plutarch *Virtues of Women* 245). The narrative follows its own ruthless logic to furnish the women with the beards that their act of saving the city has, as it were, prevented their menfolk from wearing. But the law is said to "order" the women to wear beards, indicating that they are to experience the custom as a punishment rather than a tribute, and in this way the law redresses the balance of power between men and women.[111]

The "bearded ladies" of Argos perhaps strain credulity, but if we were to excise from the historical record everything that the Greek sources retail about women that seems bizarre or unlikely, we would eventually reconstruct a history in which no women appeared at all—a history, that is, with no virtue other than that of conforming to some of Greek culture's cherished notions of itself. The historicity of all the narratives discussed here, however, is considerably less important than the particular cultural constraints that both generate them and condition their telling. Such constraints also produce and are reproduced in material practices such as ritual, where these ideologically charged narratives are retold. In this connection we may note that the bearded brides of Argos find a complement in ritual practice, or a version of it, at Pedasos near Halikarnassos, where, according to Herodotos 1.175, "these people used to get warning of any impending disaster to themselves and their neighbors by the priestess of Athene growing a long beard." The priestess is enabled to "save the city," or at least to render it forewarned and forearmed, not by any sacrificial or mil-

111. On transvestitism see also the discussion of the Spartans in chapter 2.

itary gesture but by the anomalous masculinization of her own person. However the priestess's remarkable gesture may have been motivated, or indeed facilitated, we may speculate that its interpretation was made possible not only by the equivocal gender affiliation of her patron goddess but also by the ready identification performed in the ritual sphere between women and the city. Perhaps, like the priestesses of Athena in Athens, whose interventions we examined earlier, the priestess at Halikarnassos may be thought momentarily to incarnate the goddess.

An impersonation of Athena is represented as responsible for "saving the city" in two related accounts by Plutarch and Polyaenus, first- and second-century C.E. writers recounting the history of third-century B.C.E. Argos. According to this history, in 241 B.C.E. the Aetolian invaders at Pellene were routed by an apparition of Athena, but how this apparition was produced is explained in different and opposite ways by the two texts. For Polyaenus (*Strategemata* 8.59), the priestess of Athena, who is the "most beautiful and tallest of the maidens," deliberately dons the goddess's helmet and panoply in order to perform the day's ceremony and so terrifies the enemy. For Plutarch (*Aratus* 31–32), however, the woman concerned is a war captive— also distinguished for beauty and height—who is forced to wear her captor's helmet as a sign that she belongs to him. When she emerges from the temple where she is being kept she terrifies the enemy with her resemblance to Athena. The difference between these two female figures seems to be situated within the familiar anxiety about whether women are or are not part of the city; while the war captive signifies the necessarily mobile allegiances of women whose role is to be exchanged among men, the priestess is installed at the heart of the city. Her operation in the ritual sphere allows her to take an initiative in order to "save the city," whereas the hapless captive performs the rescue only by accident. Significantly perhaps, the Pellenians themselves espouse the version that relies on the priestess's initiative (Plutarch *Aratus* 32).

In the course of this study we have seen repeatedly that the ritual sphere imagines solutions for the contradictions produced by patriarchal culture, but also restages those contradictions in its own terms. While ritual activity constructs for women a civic identity and affiliation and can thus be seen to remedy their exclusion from the city's dominant discourses, nonetheless the important trope of "saving the city," legible in many ritual forms and gestures, reproduces the equivocation about whether or not women participate in the city by deploying that participation within an economy of sacrifice and loss.

One trope not yet addressed in this chapter is constituted by the "cities of women," the festivals for women only, which are often said to reproduce men's political gatherings more or less explicitly, and which are therefore important for my argument. Brulé, for instance, remarks that "the female community restores, in these organisations from which men are excluded, the image of the total society, which is to say the society of men and of their organisations."[112] Although all the festivals that I shall go on to discuss have known analogues in other cities, the city of Athens in particular seems to represent itself either as able periodically to convene, or as periodically invaded by, a parallel "city of women," constituted only within the ritual sphere. This "city of women" both models the city of men and also presents the possibility of an anticity offering a threat, or at least an alternative, to civic stability.

CITIES OF WOMEN

Arrhephoria and Arkteia

The Athenian ritual collectivities that I intend to examine comprise the Arrhephoria, the Arkteia, the Thesmophoria, the Adonia, and the women's celebrations for Dionysos. We have already noted how between them the Arrhephoria and Arkteia can be seen to map out very different possibilities for the sexual maturation of young women, but these rites can also be seen to coordinate with those gendered destinies the available varieties of engagement with the city. The Arrhephoria occupies the heart of the city, the Acropolis, and concerns itself with the reproduction of founding Athenian myths, but brings together young women who may be classified chiefly in terms of their Eupatrid families. The Arkteia, in contrast, occupies a coastal site, a remote and peripheral location characteristic of young women's rites of preparation for marriage,[113] but if the rite convenes a considerable number of girls, it probably models the democratic city more effectively than the Arrhephoria.

An alternative interpretation of the Arkteia's remote location is nonetheless available. Historians of the archaic period, in the wake of F. de Polignac's important work, increasingly note that polis formation is carried out partly by the location of temples, so that major sanctuaries mark out both the center of the city and its territorial borders. While this development is characteristic of the eighth century in most poleis, it is generally agreed that not until Peisistratid rule in the sixth century was Athenian territory thus consolidated.[114] As C. Morgan observes,

112. Brulé 1987: 104.

113. Brulé (1987: 187–92) and Dowden (1989: 39) discuss the siting of the Arkteia and comparable events.

114. See, for example, Morris 1993: 32–37. Osborne (1994) takes issue with this position and constructs a narrative whereby cult and politics are linked from an early date, with no reference to Peisistratos. The question, according to Osborne, is not "of rival centres but of cultic activity in which the claims of a single community to possession of the whole of the territory of Attica were increasingly clearly and strongly marked" (1994: 159).

> In the case of Athens, Peisistratid attempts to consolidate an exceptionally
> extensive territory included the development of cult sites close to state bor-
> ders (such as Brauron, Eleusis and Eleutherai) and their systematic relation to
> cults and festivals in central Athens. . . . In the cases of Eleusis and Brauron,
> the link was further cemented by the physical movement of people.[115]

Although the cult of Artemis at Brauron was ostensibly coordinated with
that of Artemis Brauronia on the Acropolis, we can perhaps also discern a
similar balancing act between the gathering of girls in the Arkteia and that
in the Arrhephoria. In any case, such an understanding of the relations of
sanctuaries to borders allows us to develop another reading of the Arkteia;
the young women at Brauron are not only dramatizing their marginal status
in relation to the city but are also actively engaged in mapping out the
extent of Athenian territory and dominance.[116] Such a relationship between
the women's rites and the city's identity is clarified in the narratives concerning the shrine of Artemis Limnatis, in territory on the frontier of
Messenia and shared by Messenia and Sparta (Pausanias 4.4.2). As discussed
in chapter 2, one of these narratives describes the rape of Spartan girls who
are celebrating at the sanctuary. While in the previous chapter our focus was
on the heightened desirability of women in the ritual context, we can also
see that the girls are tempting because their very presence in the sanctuary
constitutes an assertion of Spartan territorial claims. At Brauron a related
narrative recounts not only the rape but also the kidnap by Pelasgians of
Athenian women, who are taken away to serve as concubines. Such narratives vividly represent the remoteness and isolation of young women's cultic
spaces, but the continuation of the Herodotean account (6.138) allows us
to offer another interpretation. The Athenian concubines on Lemnos produce sons whom they teach to speak Attic Greek, to observe Athenian ways,
and, crucially, to despise Pelasgians:

> If one of the Greek boys was hit by one of them [the Pelasgian boys], they all
> came to help and took vengeance for each other. And indeed the sons [of the
> Greek women] decided to be the chiefs among the children and became the
> stronger by far.

The adult Pelasgians come to the conclusion that they had better do away
with both sons and mothers, and this murder, according to Herodotos, as
well as the earlier slaughter of husbands by Lemnian women, is responsible
for the notion of "Lemnian deed." Despite their exposure at the marginal
site of Brauron, and despite that forced mobility between groups of men
that marks all females as only temporary and provisional members of any

---

115. Morgan 1993: 31–32.
116. I reached this conclusion independently of Susan Cole (1998) but am glad to note
our agreement.

collectivity in which they may participate, the women who celebrated the Arkteia were able to uphold the parameters of Athenian identity on Lemnos. In fact, by transmitting that identity to their sons, they were also able to constitute themselves as a whole alternative culture inside Lemnian society.

The Athenian concubines on Lemnos thus present their Pelasgian captors with the paradigmatic nightmare of a parallel "city of women," a community of disaffected dissidents inside the city proper. Let us imagine that they learned this strategy from the rituals for adult women in Athens itself, which repeatedly, in the course of the ritual year, organized groups of women into various quasi-political alignments that offered to the participants an understanding of themselves both as members of the polity and as the outsiders who conversely define the polity.

Thesmophoria

The metaphor of the "city of women" is mobilized quite explicitly in Aristophanes' *Women at the Thesmophoria,* where the women meet in assembly complete with herald, opening prayers, president, secretary, speakers (372–74), and disputes over precedence (832–39). The women's assumption of the decision-making apparatus could well be an Aristophanic joke at Athenian women's expense, or better still at the expense of those Athenian men who had, depending on the dating, perhaps recently voted to suspend the workings of democracy, in the oligarchic coup of 411 B.C.E. It is equally probable, however, that the comedy draws on a trope already available within its culture and that the Thesmophoria already figured, at least for the democracy, as a quasi-political event. As we have seen, the festival is imbricated in many ways with men's political practice. A prytany sacrifice to the twin goddesses on behalf of the *boule* and *demos* took place during the festival of the Stenia, on the day before the Thesmophoria itself (*IG* ii^2 674). Husbands worth 3 talents, as we saw in chapter 1, were required not only to finance their wives' attendance at the Thesmophoria but also to feast the neighborhood wives. In Isaios 3.80 the absence of such Thesmophoric feasting demonstrates that since the wife in question is merely a concubine, the child of the union is not a citizen and cannot inherit the estate that is the cause of the dispute. Again, in Isaios 8.19–20, the legitimate marriage of the woman in question is demonstrated not only by her wedding feast but also by her being chosen to preside, along with another legitimate wife, at the Thesmophoria. In the absence of registers to establish births, deaths, and marriages, the testimony of relatives and neighbors to public events such as ritual gatherings is essential,[117] and a woman's demonstrable attendance at the Thesmophoria permits her to perform her proper role in

117. Scafuro 1994b.

transmitting to her children legitimacy and its concomitant rights and privileges.[118]

The passage in Isaios 8 also indicates a further instance of political identification for the participants in the Thesmophoria. The wives of the demesmen are said to "choose" *(prokrino)* two women who "rule" *(archein)* at the Thesmophoria and who "perform the customary/required actions" *(poiein ta nomizomena)*. Since the deme wives are represented as choosing actively, and since their choice reflects favorably on the women concerned, there seems to be some element of conscious, knowledgeable election rather than a simple allotment among women not acquainted with one another. Similar women leaders, or *archousai*—the feminine counterpart of the Athenian magistrates, the archons—are also found in the Athenian deme of Cholargos in a fourth-century inscription that shows them providing the priestess of Demeter with supplies for the celebration *(IG* ii² 1184). This raises the possibility that numerous women outside the category of named priestesses might engage in organizing or supervisory activities. In chapter 1 we pointed out the existence of some subsidiary offices for women, like that of *neokoros,* or custodian, alongside the office of *hiereia* itself, and we have also seen in this chapter that the priestesses of Dionysos and of Demeter on Kos could appoint assistants. In the cult of Demeter, particularly in the postclassical period, we meet with a female ritual official called the *thoinarmostria,* who is especially prominent in the Peloponnese; she is known in second-century B.C.E. Messenia, where she seems to be assisted by other women officials called *prostatinai (LSCG* 64 and 66), in the Mysteries at Andania *(LSCG* 65), and in Sparta in the second century C.E. *(LSS* 29). In her charge are not only the banqueting arrangements but also the exaction of fines for wrongdoing *(LSCG* 66).[119] Second-century C.E. inscriptional evidence from Sparta shows a woman *archeis* and *theoros* chosen to preside over the Hyakinthia on account of her "self-restraint" *(sophrosune),* her "religiosity" *(semnotes),* and "all the other virtues pertaining to women" *(IG* v¹ 586, 587). In third-century B.C.E. Athens a woman, Nikippe, emerges as leader *(proeranistria)* of a group worshipping Isis *(IG* ii² 1292).[120] The existence of varied authoritative roles for women in ritual service not only points to the quasi-political contours of such service but also suggests the extent of the alternatives to domestic subjection that historical women might experience in the ritual sphere.

---

118. *LSCG* 96.20–22 shows that in third-century B.C.E. Mykonos the festival of Demeter was similarly connected to civic legitimacy; any native woman who wanted to could attend, but attendance among nonnative women was limited to those who had undergone an initiation.

119. See also Bookidis 1993: 51.

120. Mora 1990: 2.274. Perlman (1995) shows that at least five women between the fourth and second century B.C.E. served in the traditionally male role of *theodokos.* The *theodokoi* assisted the *theoroi,* or sacred ambassadors, when they arrived in the various Greek communities in order to announce Panhellenic festivals. See Perlman 1995: 123–24 for detailed discussion.

The beginning of the Thesmophoric process, in the selection of officials, bears signs of a relation to political practice. What of the subsequent operations? In Athens, the timing and site of the festival seem especially significant. Although Homer Thompson's excavation of the Pnyx and discovery of the alleged site of the Thesmophorion was challenged a few years later by Broneer, who locates the Thesmophorion on the northwest slope of the Acropolis, scholars have generally concurred in placing the festival near the Pnyx, the location of regular meetings of the Athenian Assembly.[121] Such a location agrees not only with the overall theme of Aristophanes' play *Women at the Thesmophoria* but also with some of its more specific references (e.g., 658). We know from the Aristophanic text that the daily business of the democracy was suspended at least on the Nesteia, or Fast, the second day of the Thesmophoria (78–80), and this may have been a practical accommodation as much as it was an acknowledgment of the women's temporary usurpation.[122]

The site of the temple of Demeter in other cities can be seen to follow the zero-sum logic of Greek gender politics, whereby men and women cannot simultaneously occupy the same civic spaces, but does not always instantiate its tropes quite so vividly.[123] In Thebes and on Sicily the Thesmophoria seems again to have occupied the acropolis and consequently to have interrupted civic space (Xenophon *Hellenika* 5.2.29 and Plato *Letters* 349D). Outside the city walls of Plataia in Boeotia, the temple of Demeter seems conversely to stress the women's detachment from the city (Pausanias 9.4.2), and the same significance is legible at Smyrna (*CIG* 3194, on "the great goddess Demeter Thesmophoros in front of the city"). At Hermione in the Argolid the bizarre festival when four old women sacrifice four cows (Pausanias 2.35.4) is celebrated at the temple on Mt. Pron, some ways outside the city. Four other temples of Demeter are found in outlying areas around Hermione, and one is located inside the city. At Pellene in Achaia a seven-day festival is celebrated at the sanctuary of Mysian Demeter a few miles (sixty Greek stades) from the city. This festival, as we saw in chapter 2, includes periods when men and women are together, when women alone occupy the sanctuary, and when the two sexes exchange insults (Pausanias 7.27.9–10). Archaeological evidence suggests a similar location outside the city walls for the Thesmophorion on

121. Thompson 1936; Broneer 1942.

122. Clinton (1996) restates Broneer's conclusions and claims that only individual demes celebrated the Thesmophoria, without the "national" celebration that Aristophanes' play envisages. He further suggests, however, that the celebration by the deme of Melite, held in the center of Athens, would have convened women who did not live in their demes, and so would have provided a certain "national" flavor.

123. Cole (1994: 205) notes, with de Polignac, that many sanctuaries of Demeter are located between the walls of the city and the city's agricultural territory.

Thasos;[124] the temple at Corinth, however, according to Nancy Bookidis, is "within the bounds of the city but removed from the center," a position she finds characteristic of shrines to the twin goddesses.[125] Pausanias (1.43.2) claims that even in his day (the second century C.E.) the women of Megara perform a version of the story of Demeter's search for Persephone, occupying a site at a rock, named "Recall," which is near the prytany building. If the phrase "near the Prytaneion" has any significance, it would seem that at Megara too the women's ritual performance occupied a nominally civic space. At Paros we know of the Thesmophorion and of its attendant ritual through Herodotos 6.134, which describes how Miltiades was inspired to leap the fence of the precinct, situated on the hill in front of the city, in order to enter the temple and there perform some unknown symbolic act that would lead to his capture of the island. What is interesting for my purposes is the fact that the sanctuary was betrayed to him by Timo, the assistant priestess of the goddesses, who thus exemplifies the potential mobility of women's allegiances, and the dangers of the autonomy at their disposal in the ritual sphere. The anxieties are thrown into stronger relief by the affinities exhibited by this narrative with that of the priestess Archidameia, who betrays the Thesmophoric women at Aigila and rescues the invader Aristomenes (Pausanias 4.17).

Whether they are outside the walls or vying with masculine establishments for the center of the city, the locations of Thesmophoric sites can be seen to elaborate an uneasy relation to civic space.[126] In Athens, as we have seen, the Thesmophoria interrupts civic time as well as space, in that the business of law courts and of the *boule* was suspended. The month during which the Thesmophoria takes place can also be seen to have significance in this context. As we saw in chapter 1, the month of Pyanepsion (September/October) is crowded with ritual activity for women, but it also sees a number of festivals that are concerned to site men within political structures.[127] The Theseia and Oschophoria, which take place before the Thesmophoria, claim to rehearse

124. Rolley 1965.

125. Bookidis 1993: 45. Cole (1994: 207) notes that it is "some distance from the agora and densely inhabited areas of the city."

126. In Thebes, Cole (1994: 210) remarks, Demeter is acknowledged as a civic divinity as well as a patron of agriculture and of women. Her shrine is in the center of town, and the Thesmophoria is held, according to Xenophon *Hellenika* 5.2.29, in midsummer, thereby loosening its connection with the rhythms of the agricultural year. Thebes was exceptional: "In most other cities sanctuaries of Demeter were either within the wall but removed from the central area or outside the wall altogether" (Cole 1994: 211). Cole further notes that even when within the walls the precincts were characteristically remote and isolated (213).

127. On these festivals see Parke 1977: 77–92 for references and Zeitlin 1982a: 139–41 for accounts of their relation to the Thesmophoria. Women were not excluded from these festivals of masculinity; the Deipnophoroi, for instance, were involved in the Oschophoria.

episodes from the career of Theseus and mobilize the city's young men to enact the roles of the hero and his companions. Founded in 475 B.C.E., when Kimon brought Theseus's bones from Skyros to Athens, the Theseia is attested in the second century B.C.E. to have included races for young men of different age classes and competitions in manly excellence, while the Oschophoria featured two young men dressed as women, ostensibly in commemoration of Theseus's ruse of taking men instead of women with him to Crete. Vidal-Naquet has persuasively argued that the Oschophoria thus draws on an initiatory scenario.[128] More explicit about this scenario was the Apatouria, which occurred after the Thesmophoria and sought to integrate young boys into their fathers' phratries, or kinship groups; registration in the phratries would later serve to guarantee the young man's legitimacy and place in political society. Taken together, these various rites can be seen to prepare and position men for their adult roles in the political life of the city.

The contiguity of the paradigmatic women's and men's festivals may be variously construed. Thrown into relief by the surrounding efforts to identify men with political roles, the Thesmophoria emerges as an institution for elaborating parallel female versions of citizenship. Yet at the same time the festival's relation to its surroundings replays an important distinction between male and female identity: while the males move through explicit, ritually delineated stages in order to attain a politically authoritative adulthood, no amount of ritual work on the part of women will produce them as fully equipped citizens.

If the Athenian women appropriated both time and space to practice a form of politics, in certain locales women seem also to have appropriated political vocabulary for their ritual performance. In the third century B.C.E., the Carian women's activities at Mylasa in Asia Minor were recorded in the phrase *hos edoxe tais gunaixin,* "as the women decided" (*LSAM* 61.5).[129] This phrase can be seen to offer an exact parallel to the other formulations used by the various Greek cities for male political decision making, which characteristically begin: "As the *boule/ demos*/assembly decided," even if political authority is in practice restricted to a few. There is, however, a potentially significant difference; "the women" in Mylasa seem to constitute an authoritative body without any internal divisions analogous to those of the *boule* or assembly. Apparently defining itself solely by gender, the women's collectivity represents itself as politically constituted, yet the lack of differentiation in its terms—no "women's *boule*" or "women's *ecclesia*"—can also be seen to detract from its claimed political identity.[130]

128. Vidal-Naquet 1986: 114–17.
129. On this phrase see Detienne 1989.
130. At Aristophanes *Women at the Thesmophoria* 302–9 the assembled women pray for the "*demos* of the Athenians" and then for that "of the women." See Patterson 1987: 53.

If the Thesmophoria, of all the women's festivals, claims most explicitly to organize female noncitizens in relation to the polity, it is enabled to do so because it also works to produce those women as responsible wives and mothers. In their personal chastity, and in their contribution to the productivity of crops and herds, the Thesmophoric women work at preserving the polity, and for this salvific gesture they are rewarded with the acknowledged emergence of their citizenship. Yet however explicitly the Thesmophoria inscribes its women participants into the city's political arrangements, it also offers signs of their reexclusion; complexly imbricated with Greek gender ideology, rather than acting as a simple alternative to it, the Thesmophoria takes with one hand what it gives with the other.

Several elements of the Thesmophoria may be understood within this generative paradox whereby the rite both identifies women with their city and detaches them from it.[131] According to one source, prisoners in Athens were freed during the festival, as they were, on the provision of securities, during the Dionysia and Panathenaia.[132] Associated by this practice with the festivals possibly most definitive for the city's identity, the Thesmophoria can also be seen to follow the contours of a rite of inversion, whereby the "women in charge" disrupt the judicial processes of the state. Some of the festival's components were construed as representations of a prehistoric, rather than civic, way of life. Diodoros Siculus 5.4.7 claims that the celebrants of Demeter and Kore in Sicily are said to "imitate the ancient way of life" in their conduct of the festival, and, as we have seen, the Athenian women at the Thesmophoria dispense with furniture and even with food. In *Greek Questions* 298B–C Plutarch asks about the Eretrian women's practice: "Why is it that at the Thesmophoria the Eretrian women cook their meat not by fire, but by the rays of the sun?" Although he goes on to offer a pragmatic explanation, we can see that this custom too could be construed within the rubric of prehistory. While the women meet, as I have suggested, in part to celebrate their own prehistory as virgin daughters, they also reenact an imaginary era before the constitution of the city, marked by deprivation and the absence of the civilized arts. Joan Bamberger has cogently argued that patriarchal cultures characteristically produce myths about their own origins that associate rule by women with a primitive or brutal organization that men have to overthrow in order to establish the viable order of male dominance.[133] If the Thesmophoric "city" of women, which

131. See also Zeitlin 1982a: esp. 142.

132. See Markellinos in Walz 1833: 4.462. The scholia on Demosthenes 22, 68, 170b (Dilts 1983) are the source for the information that prisoners were freed on security during the Dionysia and Panathenaia. Deubner argues for the element of sympathetic magic in the metaphor of "unbinding" (1966: 58–59).

133. Bamberger 1974; Zeitlin 1982a: 142.

seems to give weight and validity to specifically female versions of experience, is also construed within its own culture as the remnant of a prehistoric matriarchy, then its participants can be seen to enact their own disqualification from the flourishing city of the present. They are like the anticity of Amazons in Aischylos's *Eumenides,* perpetually encamped in rivalry and perpetually liable to defeat by the forces of Theseus.[134]

Adonis and Dionysos

In Athens at least, and possibly in other cities, the Thesmophoria can be read simultaneously to establish and deny the citizenship of its participants. Traversing the "city of men" in a variety of ways, the ritual collectivities convened for Adonis and Dionysos also produce versions of a city of women. The Adonia elaborates no specific relation to any male festival but may be seen to challenge patriarchal arrangements generally in its collocation of women of varied sexual status; as we saw in chapter 2, it convenes not only respectable wives and mothers, but also unmarried daughters, concubines, and *hetairai.* It thus implicitly confuses the distinctions drawn, notoriously, by Apollodoros in *Against Neaira* 122: "*Hetairai* we maintain for pleasure, concubines for the daily care of our bodies, but wives to give us legitimate children and to be loyal guardians of our households." Obnoxious as it is, this passage seems less neatly analytic and more synthetic when read in the context of Apollodoros's whole argument. Apollodoros points out to his opponent Stephanos that "this is what is meant by living in marriage with a woman—to have children by her and introduce the sons to the members of the phratry and of the deme, and to engage the daughters to husbands as being one's own," so that the three categories of women emerge not as oppositions but as increasingly inclusive, with the wife as the sole category equipped not only to provide pleasure and personal care but also to furnish the *oikos* with children and possessions. Although the Adonia refuses to respect these possible divisions among women, by convening them to perform collectively, its refusal does not necessarily entail a threat to patriarchal arrangements but may even be seen to conform to the hierarchy outlined in *Against Neaira.*

Generally speaking, the Adonia does not seem to generate as much anxiety in the male-authored sources as does the Thesmophoria. A notable exception to this rule is provided by the scene in Aristophanes' *Lysistrata* when the Magistrate enters, determined to put a stop to the women's excesses.[135] Threatened with the women's occupation of the Acropolis,

134. Zeitlin 1982a: 146.

135. The Magistrate *(proboulos)* is a member of the recently formed "Committee of Public Safety," an oligarchic modification to the democratic Athenian constitution that was established toward the end of the Peloponnesian War.

which many commentators have likened to the historical ritual of the Thesmophoria, the Magistrate concludes that he is facing the kind of disorder that he associates with the Adonia: "So it's broken out again—women's shamelessness and their drum-beating and their incessant cries of 'Sabazios,' and those Adonis rites on the roofs" (387–89). As we noted in chapter 2, the Magistrate goes on to describe the women wailing for Adonis on the rooftops during the Assembly's debate on the Sicilian expedition, contrasting the purportedly rational discourse of the politician with the excited cries of his wife (390–96). If we can take this momentary conjunction of the men's political debate and the women's ritual lamentation not necessarily as a historical meeting but instead as a figure that articulates contemporary perceptions, we might conclude that it sketches a "city of women," which does not replace that of men, as does the Thesmophoria's temporary occupation of the Pnyx, but which pursues a parallel yet disruptive existence. The women do not share political space, because they are on the rooftops; but they can be seen to menace it, by being almost literally "imminent." The orator's proposals and his wife's laments set up an antiphonal chant, so that the Adonis festival repeatedly interrupts political time as well as space, and the language of ritual mourning clearly offers to overthrow political discourse by telling the unpalatable truth about the fate of the Sicilian expedition. Plutarch *Life of Alkibiades* 18 claims that the Adonia took place as the expedition was about to sail, rather than during the debate, but whatever the precise historical relationship between the expedition and the Adonia, the treatment in Aristophanes suggests that Athenians registered some sort of conjunction and construed the women's festival as an uncomfortable commentary on the men's doomed politics.[136] As in the *Lysistrata* as a whole, so in this momentary representation of the Adonia the women of Athens emerge as the more clear-sighted citizens. Perhaps they may be understood to prefigure the state-sponsored mourning that they will perform at the funerals of the war dead.[137]

The vantage point from which the women are enabled to launch their

136. See the discussion in Sommerstein 1990: 173. Plutarch attributes the citizens' anxiety to a fear that the fleet would wither away and die like the gardens of Adonis. Keuls (1985) has suggested that the *Lysistrata* hints at a genuine act of rebellion on the part of the women: the mutilation of the Herms (phallic statues placed outside each house), which so alarmed the city on the eve of the Sicilian expedition.

137. Such mourning might even be considered culpable in the sense of bringing about the event that it laments. We might compare Andromache's mourning for Hektor in *Iliad* 6, where she laments him as if dead before she is aware of his fate. Ronda Simms argues that the Adonia is attractive to women because it offers them an expansion of their traditional role in collective lamentation; she suggests that this would be especially meaningful for Athenian women in the wake of the Solonic legislation restricting their participation in private funerals (see Simms 1998: 130).

constructive interruptions is the rooftop, the anomalous location of the festival. That the festival was not always so sited is suggested by Pausanias's mention of a special building, in a sacred precinct, in which the Argive women mourn Adonis (2.20.6). The Adonic city of women at Athens, however, is potentially coextensive with the city of men, occupying a parallel terrain that is just one or two storeys above. Up there in a no-man's-land, the women are removed from the down-to-earth practices of the political city, yet they are no longer operating in a confined domestic context but have arrogated to themselves a highly visible public role.[138] Suspended on the roof between two spheres, they may be thought to dramatize in the ritual the uncomfortable dialectic of their simultaneous presence in, and exclusion from, the city they inhabit. If we explore further the significant terrain of the roof, we may note a historical context in which it was used to articulate exactly this anomaly. According to the work of Martha Vicinus, the British suffragettes of the early twentieth century included among their tactics the occupation of roofs and analogous sites, from which they could both harangue their male audiences and vividly demonstrate their exclusion from the masculine arena of political discourse.[139] Can we be sure the Adonic roof elaborates no such significance?

Positioning its participants on the roof, the Adonia can be seen to occupy a middle ground between the Thesmophoria, which characteristically collects women in the center of political space, and the Dionysiac festivals, which take women outside the city to the dangerous open spaces of the *eschata,* the mountainous edge territories "where the wild things are." In the secondary literature, the Thesmophoria has been contrasted with both the Adonia and the Bacchic rites,[140] but we can also elaborate a more complex ritual experience than is indicated by a model of binary polarity. Dionysiac celebrations continue to present scholarly commentary with acute problems of analysis; despite access to a mass of varied material, the combined efforts of many critics have constructed no very stable model. The ancient Greek city celebrated a number of ritual events in honor of the god. Aristocratic symposia were convened under the sign of Dionysos, as were the dramatic festivals of Athens and other cities. Recent discoveries of inscribed metal plates, or *lamellae,* from graves throughout the Greek world, indicate that initiatory practices associated with Dionysos, which were open to women as well as men, were known in Greece in the fifth century B.C.E.[141] In this con-

---

138. Keuls (1985: 25) claims that the Adonis is the most public of the women's festivals. The roof need not always exercise this particular significance, of course; in Aristophanes *Acharnians* 261 Dikaiopolis's wife watches his private celebration of the Rural Dionysia from the roof.

139. Vicinus 1986: esp. 213.

140. Detienne 1977; Zeitlin 1982.

141. For discussion see Graf 1993 and Johnston and McNiven 1996.

nection we may note that the *Lysistrata* opens with the eponymous heroine's complaint that the women have not arrived at her meeting, although they would have been prompt participants in a Bacchic celebration. Private, informal or initiatory events were not the only Dionysiac experiences available to women, however, because they also seem to have participated in collective rites of ecstatic possession, or "maenadism," which can be read to convene a "city of women" in opposition to that of men.

Our notions of women's maenadic, Dionysiac experiences have been conditioned to a considerable extent by fifth-century representations on vases and by Euripides' *Bakchai,* both of which bodies of evidence will concern us again in the following chapters.[142] The "hard" evidence for these practices, archaeological and epigraphical, is not available until the Hellenistic period. I shall leave certain necessary discussions about all this evidence to subsequent chapters, concentrating here on the testimony that seems to construct the maenads or *bakchai* (the bacchantes, the possessed women worshippers) into a city of women. While the vases variously show single women or small groups of women, usually identified as maenads, in the grip of Dionysiac possession, or celebrating among themselves in intimate scenes characterized by the presence of a mask of the god set on a pillar, the *Bakchai* elaborates a far more totalizing scenario. All the women of Thebes have left the confines of the *oikos,* and even of the polis, to convene on the mountain and engage in the trance-inducing worship of the god. This "city of women" is constituted in resistance to that of the men, because the women refuse their assigned feminine roles, attack men who come near them, and celebrate their own superiority in the masculine acts of hunting and warfare. The "city" is organized along aristocratic lines, in that it is arranged in three bands, or *thiasoi,* led by the Theban princesses, Agave, Ion, and Autonoe. But in some ways it is a far more "democratic" city than even that of the Athenians, who supply the audience for the drama, for it deliberately convenes both old and young, married and unmarried, and women of varying social status (694). The only category of women excluded from this Bacchic collectivity are slaves, whom not even the theatrical imagination could emancipate; in other respects, the Bacchic collectivity offers a parody of Athenian political inclusivity combined with the common Greek nightmare of women's refusal to accept their subordination.

The notion of the female as characteristically maenadic is immensely appealing within Greek culture, even though no historical Greek woman may have participated in rites like those of the *Bakchai*. Varied material in postclassical Greek sources does indicate the historical reality of certain maenadic practices. Diodorus Siculus, who writes as a contemporary of

---

142. I hasten to point out that neither here nor in subsequent chapters am I attempting a full account of the *Bakchai* or its criticism. That way madness lies.

Caesar and Augustus, claims that many Greek cities host Bacchic collectivities in which the *parthenoi* bear the *thyrsus,* or cult staff, while the *gynaikes* sacrifice and praise the god (4.3.2–3). Both groups are said to be "possessed," to *enthousiazein* or *bakcheuein.* This Dionysiac inclusion of different age groups, which are often kept separate by other ritual institutions, goes some way to validate the totalizing representation in the *Bakchai.* Such testimony to historical maenadic practices, however, almost invariably shows women exercising leadership roles and organizational skills, constructing the Dionysiac "city of women" out of civic identifications rather than aligning it with the wildness of the mountains or *eschata.* When Pausanias, for instance, mentions what is sometimes called the Lenaia, the biennial expedition of the Thyiads of Athens who journey to Mt. Parnassos with the women of Delphi (10.4.3), it is hard to reconstruct the event without concluding that the women drew on techniques of large-scale organization and management, probably forming temporary alliances and networks of acquaintance that extended well beyond the family and neighborhood.

Inscriptional evidence from the Hellenistic period goes even further in placing Bacchic women in positions of authority. Although, as we have seen, women in general had more access to the public sphere in postclassical times, the examples of the "Bacchic women" are still remarkable. Advised by the oracle at Delphi, in the first half of the third century B.C.E., the city of Magnesia in Asia Minor obtained women leaders for their three Dionysiac *thiasoi* from Thebes, where they could draw on the services of the female descendants of Ino.[143] According to Stephanos of Byzantium on Semachidai, a deme of Attica (Meineke vol. 1, p. 562, 12–16), the priestesses of Dionysos there claimed descent from the daughters of the man alleged to have first entertained the god. We might accordingly conclude that the matrilineal transmission of authority among women is a powerful figure in the Dionysiac context.[144] That the three Theban maenads were possessed of particular personal resources might be suggested by the fact that they were able to uproot themselves from Thebes and flourished in Magnesia, where they eventually died and were buried with honors.

Other Hellenistic inscriptions testify to similar authoritative roles for women in Dionysiac ritual. On Miletos in the third century B.C.E. the priestess of Dionysos, who performs cult activity "on behalf of the city," is to be consulted and remunerated by any man or woman who wishes to make a sacrifice to the god (*LSAM* 48). An epitaph for a Dionysiac priestess, also from Miletos and dating to the third or second century B.C.E., honors the woman Alkmeonis and exhorts the "Bakchai of the city" or "citizen Bakchai"

143. Details are given in *I Mag* 215. See also Parke 1939: 340 and Henrichs 1978.

144. See also Strabo 7.7.12 on the claim of contemporary prophetesses at Dodona to descend from the original prophetesses in the maternal line.

(polités bakchai), whom she led to the mountain, to greet her. Not only is Alkmeonis associated with "citizen women," *polités*, but she is said to have led the Dionysiac processions "in front of the whole city" *(erchomene pases pro poleos)*.[145] The priestess of Dionysos on Kos, as we have seen, was authorized to appoint an assistant citizen priestess from each deme of the city (*LSCG* 166). Dionysiac roles, at least for Hellenistic women, could thus provide specific structures within which women were identified with their cities, even while sending them, as with Alkmeonis, to the mountain outside the civilized territory.

That the Dionysiac context also allowed some women to develop a sense of personal authority may be suggested not only by the careers of the Theban maenads in Magnesia but also by a narrative in Plutarch *Virtues of Women* 13.[146] In the mid-fourth century B.C.E., according to this account, the Thyiades from Delphi lost their way in their nocturnal mountain wanderings and arrived in Amphissa. Allegedly still in a state of trance and unable properly to perceive their surroundings, they fell asleep in the agora. What they did not realize was that they had strayed into enemy territory; the Phocians, who had occupied Delphi, were in alliance with Amphissa, so that the town was full of soldiers. The celebrating women were thus, as usual, extremely vulnerable to sexual attack. The women of Amphissa came to the rescue: they

> all ran out into the agora and stood silently in a circle around the sleeping women, and did not approach them. When the Thyiades at last got up, one by one the Amphissian women took care of them and fed them, and finally . . . accompanied and escorted them safely to the frontier.

Even though the women of Amphissa are not themselves practicing maenads at the moment of the story, the gender solidarity that they exhibit and the bold initiative that they apparently feel capable of taking may perhaps be referred back to the notion of the ritual sphere as providing models of female agency and autonomy. We might note, however, that in this case the solidarity among women denies precisely those allegiances to specific cities and identifications with civic structures that this chapter has been concerned to demonstrate, since the women of Amphissa apparently identify with the Thyiades simply as vulnerable females.

The ritual collectivities of the Thesmophoria, Adonia, and Dionysia are all to some degree represented in Athenian sources as "cities of women," organized in parallel or in opposition to the normative civic collectivity of men. Each festival for women can also be seen to address and to reproduce

145. See Henrichs (1978), who prints the text of this epitaph.
146. See also the Sixteen Women of Elis, examined earlier in this chapter, who approach the tyrant in their capacity as dedicated to Dionysos (Plutarch *Virtues of Women* 251).

the cultural ambivalence whereby women are constructed both as participants in the city and as the outsiders who conversely define the possibility of such participation for others. Taken together, the three festivals have a claim to construct the defining experience of ritual collectivity for the free adult woman in Athens, and the predications that they articulate and enact about the female are correspondingly complex. Moving the participants from the Pnyx to the rooftops to the mountain, the ritual events trace a trajectory from the center through an equivocal parallel site to the outside of the city. Although each festival offers a number of ways for its female participants to represent their relation to the governing political entity, through structures that model those of the city to a greater or lesser degree, it seems that the Thesmophoria makes women's "citizenship" most visible, the Adonia less so, and the Bacchic festivals least of all. Since many Athenian women could have participated in all three rites for adult females, each woman would repeatedly experience her identity constructed in ritual on a spectrum of positions aligned with the polity and opposed to it. This ritual process is perhaps more complex than is suggested by positing only a binary opposition between the Thesmophoria and Adonia or the Thesmophoria and Dionysia.

We may note in passing that there are very few ritual "cities of men." Cults of Herakles were often restricted to male participation, as was the cult of Mithras in the imperial period, but the Thesmophoria, Adonia, and maenadic festivals have no precise counterparts in Athens or, as far as we can tell, anywhere else. Young boys were usually involved in a series of public events designed to articulate their transition to manhood, but once they had achieved this transition, the cult context seems to have lost interest in them.[147] Why is this? One answer must be that men can graduate to the collective actions of war, law, and politics, while women must remain outside history and consequently inside ritual. At Athens, the various activities undertaken in Pyanepsion delineate this difference very clearly; while the events for men are designed to signify and accomplish their move into adulthood and are therefore to be performed by each man a limited number of times only, the concurrent festivals for adult women invite those women to perform them repeatedly, marking each year of their adulthood with the sequence of Stenia, Anodos, Nesteia, and Kalligeneia.

We noted this discrepancy between cult events for men and women in the previoius chapter and suggested there that it is produced by the focus in women's rituals on women's sexual and reproductive identities; since male

147. Although Keuls (1985: 302) holds that there were more rituals for women than for men, some critics maintain the opposite; Dowden (1989: 194) argues that Athenian rituals for women lost "sense and centrality" because of the rapid development of democracy. Dowden, however, does not accept that the Arkteia, for instance, convened a large number of girls.

sexuality is not the site of such extensive cultural anxiety, it does not provide the occasion for similar cultic elaboration. While the ritual collectivities of the Thesmophoria, Adonia, and Dionysiac celebrations are at stake in this chapter because of their political discourse rather than their sexual,[148] their task remains the same; they continue to elaborate the parameters of femininity in its various transformations not only from legitimate wife to adulteress but also from citizen to outsider. Only for women, it seems, was this task of definition and redefinition perceived as necessary; once Athenians had become men and citizens, they apparently needed little help from ritual in continuing to be so.[149] Any contradictions in male relations to the city were presumably not such as to require constant symbolization, or else they were negotiated in those men's collectivities that claimed to have a goal or *telos* other than their own performance. Since the perception of women as both part of the city and part of its outside was a real contradiction within Greek culture, however, it required repeated solving; ritual provides the sphere in which this solution, which is also a restatement of the terms of the problem, is undertaken.

If the figure of the "city of women" represents the most dramatic solution to the problem of women and the city, it is nonetheless a solution that should be investigated further. The Athenian example of a plurality of festivals indicates that the city of women is always changing, elaborating different relations to the political city that at times conform to its governing principles and at times refuse to do so. While the city of women is always circumscribed, moreover, in space and duration, the city of men may be seen by contrast to endure, and to remain the same. We might even conclude that the permanent establishment of the city of men in the political sphere is what conversely makes possible and necessary the city of women. The per-

148. Women in the Dionysiac context are rarely represented as sexually licentious or aggressive. In the *Bakchai* this representation of them is frequently proffered by Pentheus, only to be dismissed by other characters. In vase painting, maenads usually fend off the advances of Dionysiac satyrs. In Rome, Bacchic sects were prosecuted for sexual license, but interestingly the Roman sources also testify to a political fear of people meeting in groups per se. Consider Livy 39.15, where the consul addresses an assembly after the Bacchic groups have been broken up: "Unless the standard had been raised in the citadel and the army had been led out for an election or the tribunes had announced a meeting for the people or one of the magistrates had called you to a gathering—other than this your ancestors did not want even you to come together casually and without a reason; and wherever there was a crowd, there they thought that there should also be a legitimate leader of the crowd."

149. Leitao (1995) has suggested, however, that Greek initiation ceremonies for young men often register the anxieties experienced by older men, who organize initiations, about the maintenance of masculinity. Gleason (1990) examines the physiognomic texts of the imperial period to show that Greek masculinity is an achieved and perilous condition. The earlier text of Aristotle that she cites regarding the "great-souled man," however, is remarkable for its *lack* of anxiety.

sistent Greek fantasy of a "world without women," which can be discerned especially in the Hesiodic ontology and in the Athenian tragic speeches, such as those of Jason, Hippolytos, and Apollo, that imagine a society reproduced physically by men alone, is dramatized in the context of a political city exclusive of women. Women are relegated to the temporary cities of ritual collectives, where they act out modified versions of citizenship. Although a good case can be made for ritual as a sphere in which redress may be offered for the exclusion of women from governance of the city, which is maintained in part by their work, such redress is never more than partial.

A final observation may be made about ritual "cities of women" in the light of comparative work on women's gatherings in contemporary communities. In her study of Muslim women's gatherings in a Turkish town, Nancy Tapper concludes that two such formal gatherings in particular constitute a paired set, and that they

> so condition the women's perception of relations among themselves, particularly by focusing on the areas of equality and inequalities between them, that they discourage women from examining the underlying issue—the position of women vis-à-vis men—which determines relationships among women.[150]

One gathering, the explicitly secular "reception day," groups women in accordance with the status of their husbands, so that the periodic meetings of the women have the effect of demonstrating and consolidating that status. The second gathering, however, the *mevlud,* which celebrates the birth of the prophet Mohammed, convenes women of varying social statuses in a sacred context and may even have a redistributive effect, because the wealthier hostess entertains poorer women. Moreover, the *mevlud* addresses women in their role as mothers, a role highly valued by Turkish Islam, and posits an equality among all women insofar as they perform this role. According to Tapper's analysis, the paired gatherings sort women first by social status and then by an uncomplicated biological notion of gender, consequently mystifying and rendering invisible the male domination that both potentially unites women and also actually divides them from each other. Tapper suggests an analogy with other paired gatherings for women in South Africa studied by Susan Keirn, who herself concludes that such secular/sacred pairs may be understood as an alternation between the states of "structure' and "communitas."[151] Keirn is concerned, however, more to recover the significant spiritual experiences in women's lives than to analyze their possible relations to the formation of gender ideology.

These models drawn from contemporary lived experience are potentially very illuminating, but that may be because of their differences from the

150. Tapper 1983: 72.
151. Keirn 1978.

ancient Greek scenario rather than as a result of an uncomplicated correspondence. The women's gatherings featured in this chapter are all "sacred" rather than secular, and I have at times identified a group of three rather than a pair. It seems to me, moreover, that the architecture of the related gatherings does not conform precisely to an alternating rhythm of being "in" the city and being "out" of it, since each ritual collectivity can be seen to elaborate more and less explicit versions of each condition. It does seem important, however, to note, in line with the analyses of Tapper and Keirn, that the Greek ritual year can extend to participant women a variety of experiences of fantasized citizenship, which in the end, perhaps, occlude and mystify their exclusion from the real thing.

THE PYTHIA

Turning from the ritual collectivities, I wish finally to examine the figure of the Delphic Pythia, a woman operating in the cult context alone, yet producing a series of pronouncements on the welfare of the various Greek poleis. That this specific conjunction of the female, the cultic, and the political is particularly intractable may be deduced from the secondary sources' refusal to treat it; critics are characteristically interested either in the oracle as a institution that played an important role in Greek history or in the Pythia as a female medium. Giulia Sissa's study, for instance, is a timely discussion of the representations of femininity attributed to the figure of the Pythia but does not engage with the political activity of the oracle, whereas Morgan's work on the role of the institution barely mentions the gender of the speaking subject at Delphi.[152] Parker, who delivers an impressive account of various responses, points to the paradoxical authority of the "entranced, uneducated woman" but does not explain how such a woman can also "pick her way with care" as an "expounder" of political subjects.[153] For an earlier generation of commentators it was possible to evade the paradox of the politically adept prophetess by claiming that the oracle was a fraud, that the Pythia raved under the influence of trance or intoxication, and that the male priests who interpreted and translated her rantings for the inquirers simply pursued a specific Delphic agenda. The century-long excavations at Delphi have failed to produce testimony to any aspect of this representation, however, and commentators now propose a Pythia who "by modern standards, appeared to act rationally, giving straightforward answers to simple alternative proposals, or to a suggestively worded question dealing with past or present circumstances."[154] Although it remains notoriously difficult

152. Sissa 1990; Morgan 1990.
153. Parker 1985: 300, 315.
154. Morgan 1990: 156.

to reconstruct a Delphic consultation, modern commentators agree that the process devolved onto the figure of a Pythia both calm and articulate.[155] But such a figure may present criticism with more problems than did the previous fantasy of the maddened priestess.

The disappearance of the intoxicated woman and of the mediating male priests presumably entails that the Pythia would contribute to consultor states' political arrangements directly, by her prophetic utterances, and thus can plausibly be said to occupy a political as well as a cult position. Since a series of astute women offering independent political commentary from the tripod would constitute a phenomenon unparalleled in ancient Greek culture, we might consider the ways in which any historical Pythia might acquire her expertise. According to Plutarch (*Why Are Delphic Oracles No Longer in Verse?* 405C), the current Pythia cannot be described as gifted or indeed as an exception in any way, and this is part of an explanation for why she does not deliver her oracles in hexameter verse.

> . . . like the woman who now serves the god, who if anyone was born here lawfully and properly, and has lived a well-ordered life *(nomimos, kalos, eutaktos);* but brought up in the house of poor peasants *(georgon peneton),* she goes down to the shrine equipped with nothing in the way of technical skill or any other experience or ability *(technes, empeirias, dunameos).*

While this passage is the most detailed account that we have of the Pythia's possible origins, it is not in fact very informative. Although most commentators assume that a cultic conservatism would ensure continuity, despite fluctuations in the popularity and influence of the oracle, we cannot be sure if conditions at Delphi in the first century C.E. reproduced those of earlier periods. Crucially, we cannot know if the Pythia in Plutarch's text was brought up lawfully and honorably *in order that* she might serve as Pythia, or if her upbringing had incidentally qualified her to be selected as Pythia. Since the current Pythia seems to be unsophisticated in comparison with

---

155. This notion of the consultation is compatible with the only explicit graphic representation of a Delphic consultation to which we have access, the painting on the Vulci cup (*ARV* 1269.5, 440 B.C.E.) of Aegeus consulting an oracle variously identified as Themis or Ge. The prophetess is seated on a tripod, holding a phiale (libation vessel) and a twig of laurel, Apollo's tree. There is, of course, no need to conclude that this painting is an accurate representation of a historical process any more than are the textual accounts. Two references in Plutarch to the "normal" practice of the Pythia testify to heightened emotion, if not to ravings: in *Moralia* 759B and 753A the Pythia is said to experience excitement when she "lays hold of" the tripod, and an ensuing tranquility when she leaves it.

Maurizio (1995) begins from the premise that the oracular responses were delivered by the Pythia herself without priestly interference, and subsequently investigates the cross-cultural phenomenon of spirit possession to account for the scenarios thus engendered. I examine this aspect of the Pythia's experience in chapter 4.

earlier incumbents, we could conclude that birth "in the house of poor peasants" was not a requirement but an accident. On the other hand, the upbringing of the Plutarchan Pythia does constitute evidence that the position was not always confined to the daughters of the wealthy or of special families. That the peasants were destitute or struggling is not conclusively shown by the vocabulary of the text, given Greek culture's tendency to denote as "poor" all those who need to work for a living. If there were no general rule as to the families from which the Pythia might be drawn, we could conclude that an element of self-selection operated within the process.

The question of the Pythia's upbringing is, of course, allied to that of her sexual experience. Certain texts seem to presuppose that the Pythia is a virgin, and the speaker of Plutarch's *Oracles in Decline* 435 claims that the institution "employ[s] one women for the oracle and give[s] her a hard life by insisting on lifelong chastity and purity" *(hagnen dia biou kai kathareuousan)*. None of the Plutarchan vocabulary, however, claims explicitly that the Pythia is a physical virgin.[156] While the study by Sissa is predicated on the virginity of the historical Pythia, such a reconstruction is hampered by accounts in other texts. As we saw in the previous chapter, the version espoused by Diodorus Siculus has the Pythia's position filled first by a virgin and subsequently, after the virgin's abduction and rape, by an older woman. This woman was required to wear the costume of a *parthenos*, "as a sort of reminder of the prophetess of olden times" (16.26). Such an older woman would be unlikely to be a physical virgin, unmarried, unless she had been designated as a future Pythia at a very early age. Origen *Contra Celsus* 7.4 claims explicitly that the Pythia is not a virgin, which would perhaps coincide with Diodorus's account, but Origen's Christian text is driven by the need to attribute base motives to the Olympic pantheon, which it can do by eliminating virginity from the Delphic scenario. On the other hand, we have seen that H. W. Parke and D. E. W. Wormell also doubt the absolute requirement of physical virginity for the Pythia, at least in the imperial period.[157]

The issue of virginity is significant for our inquiry only because it throws into relief the question of how, if at all, the Pythia was prepared for her office, and therefore of how she was positioned to deliver her contributions to consultor states' politics. If the Pythia was to be a virgin, and yet not serve until she was over fifty or at some comparable stage, then she would have to

---

156. Given that *hagnos* may be qualified by phrases such as "from the bed," "from marriage," "from a man," it does not necessarily connote physical virginity; *kathareuo* also has a range of connotations that are not restricted to the physical plane. At *Why Are Delphi Oracles No Longer in Verse?* 405 however, the Pythia is compared to the bride in Xenophon's *Oikonomikos* 7.5, who is completely ignorant and inexperienced, and a virgin.

157. Parke and Wormell 1956: 35.

be selected at an early age, when she might not have had the opportunity to exhibit special aptitudes for the post. Self-selection would thus not play a large part in the process of producing a Pythia, and this aspect of the process would, in fact, set it apart from institutions in other cultures that produce women who prophesy or perform related roles.[158]

If the Pythia did contribute in some way to her selection, then it would be more likely that she was chosen when older, and probably married, with or without children. Either way, virgin or married woman, if she did not practice until age fifty she would probably have to serve a long apprenticeship after she was identified as Pythia-elect. It is in fact very difficult to see how the institution would function without such an apprenticeship. On the morning that followed the unexpected death of the Pythia described in Plutarch *Oracles in Declines* 438, for instance, the Delphic authorities would immediately have had to pick an appropriate fifty year old from the city's available women. An apprenticeship was identified by Parke and Wormell as the process that would induce the Pythia-elect to internalize the requirements of her office and become adept at receiving and transmitting the prophecy of the god. They emphasize the several references to the collegiality of the Delphic institution, which all work to modify any representation of the Pythia as isolated, either physically or spiritually. While women could not enter the sanctuary as questioners, *Oracles in Decline* 414 points out that there used to be a college of three Pythiai, two serving in rotation and one in reserve, and Parke and Wormell note also the older women who are charged with the task of keeping the fire on the temple hearth lit (Plutarch *The E at Delphi* 385C).[159] To these we might add the Delphic Thyiades, who in the first or second century C.E. were headed by Klea, the addressee of some of Plutarch's dialogues, and who performed various rituals for Apollo as well as those for Dionysos (*Greek Questions* 293C). The fact that Plutarch is a priest at Delphi and Klea a Thyiad may itself be an argument for close cooperation between these two branches of the cult establishment. Even if we do not cite these collectivities as contexts from which a potential Pythia might emerge, they might be instrumental in forming her disposition as a prophetess once she was identified as a Pythia-elect. These female collectivities would, of course, be supplemented for the Pythia by that of the two Delphic priests and the five *hosioi*, or sacred men (*Oracles in Decline* 438). Since all these collectivities considerably modify the notion of

158. An element of self-selection operates in the careers of all the possession specialists and similar practitioners studied by Paul, Dougherty, Spring, and Keirn in Hoch-Smith and Spring 1978, and by Sered 1994. I shall return to the issue of possession specialists in the following chapter.

159. *Greek Questions* 292A notes a priestess of Athena at Soli on Cyprus who is similarly charged with keeping the fire.

the Pythia's splendid isolation, any Pythia operating within such a context might internalize not only the contours of a possession process but also those of Delphic politics.

This reconstruction of the political practitioner on the tripod becomes more plausible when we consider the parameters of Delphic discourse. After the seventh century, "poleis . . . almost never consulted oracles about internal political issues or non-religious legislation,"[160] and within this relatively specific field of inquiry the question was commonly "either a simple statement for confirmation or refutation, or alternatives requiring the expression of a preference. By contrast, open-ended questions or predictions of the future were rare."[161] On many occasions, the form of the question can be seen to indicate the appropriate answer, as in the example from the mid-fourth-century inscription *IG* ii² 333.25–26: "Is it better for the *demos* of the Athenians to make the holy dress and adornments larger and finer for Artemis or to leave it as it now is?"[162] We can conclude, then, that any individual Pythia would have had opportunities to imbibe a general level of cultic and political expertise that would allow her to continue the Delphic line. Such a conclusion allows us to dispense with the mediation by the male priestly establishment at the sanctuary, and to restore a measure of autonomy not only to the Pythia's speech but even to her political pronouncements.

Where the ancient sources explicitly attribute independent political tactics to the Pythia, and where incidentally they often identify her by name, is in cases where she is accused of corruption.[163] Given the long history of the oracle, there are in fact remarkably few such allegations; the two most famous are described in Herodotos. In 6.66, when the Spartans decide to inquire of the oracle whether Demaratos is King Ariston's legitimate son, Demaratos's enemy Kleomenes befriends one of the most powerful Delphians, Kobon, who subsequently prevails *(anapeithei)* upon the Pythia Perialla to answer in the negative. That this was understood as a clear case of corruption of the Pythia may be seen from the fact that Kobon had to flee the city and Perialla was sacked; but we may note that the text does not speak explicitly of bribery, that is, of the Pythia consciously and cynically *selling* her services. Since Kobon was already influential at Delphi, it may have been possible for him to make his wishes known without any overt contractual arrangement with the Pythia.

160. Morgan 1990: 160.

161. Ibid., 155.

162. See Fontenrose 1978: 221 and the catalogue of "historical responses" H33. See also Parker 1985: 314 on the "conservative," "emollient," and "conciliatory" tone of the Pythia's responses.

163. See Dewald 1981: 123 and Parker 1985: 324–26. Pausanias 4.6 states that there are no other tales of corruption except that attached to Kleomenes. Aristonike is named not for corruption but for her struggle with the Athenian envoys (Herodotos 7.140).

A similar reading is available at Herodotos 5.62–63. The Alkmaionids, exiled from Athens, rebuild the temple at Delphi and subsequently bribe the Pythia to instruct any and all Spartan inquirers that they must free the Athenians. In Aristotle *Constitution of the Athenians* 19 a slightly less damaging story relates that the Alkmaionids rebuild the temple and then win support generally, so that the Pythia almost inevitably gives answers favorable to them. What the Alkmaionids did in this instance was to cultivate the whole institution, rather than the individual Pythia, but the latter's allegiances presumably accorded with those of the Delphic establishment. Even when suborned the Pythia may not have been acting in total cynicism about her role and position; and in any case we should note that to claim her corruption would always be an easy consolation for the loser from her decision.[164]

If we reconstruct a Pythia prophesying calmly and in good Greek, the product of lengthy training, and so imbued in Delphic traditions and priorities that she articulates them effortlessly, we may perhaps be able to account for the political dimensions of this cultic role. In this connection we may note too that the origins of the oracle insert the first Pythia into a narrative with political dimensions, in that it is a narrative about "saving the city." Diodorus Siculus's account of the institution's origin (16.26) records that the oracle first manifested itself as a chasm, the sight of which inspired goats to leap about and utter strange sounds. The goatherd, curious, approached the chasm and promptly became possessed *(enthousiazein)*, with the ability to foretell the future. The same thing happened to everyone else who heard the story and visited the chasm, with the interesting variation that many of them, in their excitement, fell in. Consequently, "it seemed best to the dwellers in that region, in order to eliminate the risk, to station one woman there as a single prophetess for all and to have the oracles told through her." Qualified by her gender, her precarious position in the city, and her uncomfortable affinity with the unknown divine to mediate the risk for her community, the Pythia is promoted to a role that exploits her, with the ambivalence characteristic of the ritual sphere. Excluded from her city yet representing it, and at Delphi, as Morgan has shown,[165] outside the boundaries of consultor cities yet at the center of the known world, the Pythia's political pronouncements emerge from the familiar equivocal contours of women's ritual practice.

The lived experience of most women in ancient Greece may be understood in terms of two categories, the domestic and the divine; women serve the *oikos* and the gods. In this chapter I have tried to qualify this model by exam-

---

164. See, for example, the response to the Knidians discussed at Parker 1985: 316.
165. Morgan 1990: 183–84.

ining the extent to which the ritual sphere can be seen to construct a quasi-political identity for women and to articulate their otherwise latent citizen-ship. While practical aspects of ritual activity such as mechanisms of selec-tion and of award, sites, and times can be seen to construct this civic identity for women, I have also argued that such a construction is legible in domi-nant figures within ritual discourse, such as "saving the city." Since such figures can be read to question women's civic identification at the same time as they propose it, however, the complexities of the ritual sphere require the elaboration of a dynamic, dialectical model. The ritual sphere provides the solution to the problem of women and the city in its fantasies of female cit-izenship, but the solution remains imaginary.

FOUR

Representing Women

Ritual as a Cultural Resource

Our concern in this study has been first to establish the material dimensions of women's ritual work, and subsequently to relate that work to Greek discourses of gender identity and of civic participation. We have often found it useful to construct dialectical models in order to understand how women might negotiate the constraints of patriarchal culture by means of their ritual practice. A possible objection to the analyses developed in the previous two chapters, however, is that men and male-dominated practices occupy the center, so that the focus is less on women's historical agency and more on the construction of their identity that is undertaken by the dominant culture. While not denying the importance of such constructions for historical women's perception of themselves, in this chapter I shall seek to redress the balance by examining three different areas of cultural production in which women may have deployed their ritual practice in a less mediated way as a resource for representing themselves and their needs. I shall examine the use of ritual figures in women's poetry, representations of women as ritual practitioners on Attic vases, and the phenomenon of maenadism in its various manifestations. This is not to suggest that rituals like the Thesmophoria, for instance, did not offer positive resources for women; but, as we have seen, the Thesmophoria takes away with one hand what it gives with the other. The practices investigated in this chapter may instead have been those in which the familiar dialectic was less visible.

One theoretical construct that may prove useful in this investigation is that of "women's culture." This term is mobilized in many contexts to analyze both women's history and their specific cultural productions, and requires some definition if it is not to lose in clarity what it gains in semantic reach. The notion has been extensively criticized as being "essentialist," and it is certainly necessary to avoid implying "that women share a universal set of experiences or [an] essentially 'female' understanding or world-view."[1] Similarly, the notion that a women's culture might unproblematically link people of different races or classes has been rigorously questioned. Like most interpretative tools, the concept of "women's culture" is most power-ful when it is put to work within a model of the entire society in question to account for the specificities of different women's lives within that society. Determining the possibility of a "women's culture" in a given community is a degree of physical, spatial division of labor that separates women and men of the same class, and that may consequently generate practices and "struc-tures of feeling," to use Raymond Williams's term, common among women of that class as distinct from their men. As Joan Radner puts it, "In many, if not most, societies there is a realm of practice that is primarily or exclusively women's domain, through which women may develop a set of common sig-nifying practices (beliefs, understandings, behaviors, rituals—hence a cul-ture)."[2] Since most societies that insist on a gendered division of labor also prescribe relations of hierarchy between men and women, consistently to women's disadvantage, a more or less separate "women's culture" may also provide the best means for historical women to reclaim for their lives and products the significance that is often denied by the dominant culture.

The impulse among feminist scholars to construct models of "women's culture" derives from a number of sources. One of these was the collective practice of feminists in the 1970s and 1980s, which, according to M. E. Brown, developed

> an ideological stance which bound women together in positions for which cur-rent social myths about women had no set position, i.e. loyalty to other women could replace jealousy over men or aggressiveness in women could exist alongside tenderness. These women developed the idea of a woman's culture based on theory and practice which cut across existing constructions of the feminine.[3]

Influential critiques of this phase of the feminist movement have pointed out that this "women's culture" was in practice largely restricted to white middle-class women, and that in any case the notion of such a culture sup-presses real divisions among women along lines of class or race. The general construct of a "women's culture" has, however, been mobilized by feminist historians and anthropologists to explicate the roles of women in numerous societies. Writing on the nineteenth-century American doctrine of "separate spheres," for instance, which allotted to white middle-class women an unprecedented confinement to domesticity, Nancy Cott views the "women's

1. Radner 1993: 2.
2. Ibid.
3. Brown 1990: 14.

sphere as the basis for a subculture among women that formed a source of strength and identity."[4] Such "strength and identity" derived from a positive evaluation, within the women's subculture, of female sociability and activities characterized as female, which were likely to be dismissed or trivialized by the dominant culture. By elaborating on these elements of their assigned identity women could articulate for themselves and for their own ends "the gender identification . . . so thickly sown and vigorously cultivated in contemporary social structure and orthodoxy."[5] Within anthropology, disagreements are possible, but the notion of "women's culture" can work as a productive heuristic. Juliet du Boulay, writing on contemporary women in rural Greece, cautions that women rarely speak with "a single voice" because "the indivisible nature of the family," on the one hand, and "the custom of virilocal marriage," on the other, "set up considerable barriers to the development of any crosscutting affiliation between women as members of a common sex."[6] Yet Anna Caraveli finds

> a universe of female activity outside the realm of men. Although based on the village's larger system of values and interpretations, this universe had its own variants of these, while many of the tasks, social roles, and expressive genres were gender-specific, limited to women only.[7]

Study of this "muted" culture, to use Edwin Ardener's term, can ensure that women are "accorded full status with men as culture producers and social actors."[8]

While noting with du Boulay that women are likely to observe other allegiances in addition to those conditioned by gender, we can pursue the idea of "women's culture" further with help from theories of popular culture, which is itself often typed as "female" in its alleged meretricious triviality. Although the analysis of popular culture does not characteristically include religious practice, it can nonetheless be relevant to the present project because of its commitment to describing how people without access to economic or discursive power make sense of, and even find pleasure and significance in, a cultural context that may be hostile or oppressive. An example in the field of women's studies is that of romance novels or soap

---

4. Cott 1977: 197.

5. Ibid., 194. Cott refers only to the "women's culture" of the late eighteenth and early nineteenth century in North America, which she points out was in any case the product of a very specific set of historical and economic circumstances. She also suggests that historical women could embrace the parameters of this culture and of the new "women's sphere" more readily because it represented an alternative to, and an advance upon, the previous ideology of women's God-given inferiority.

6. Du Boulay 1986: 145.

7. Caraveli 1986: 169–70.

8. Ardener 1972; Boddy 1989: 5.

operas, which often supply only one-dimensional representations of women conforming to patriarchal imperatives, but which have been shown in various studies to render the world intelligible and manageable for the women who use them.[9] To mount these kinds of descriptions, popular-culture analysis typically questions the power of the text or image in question to determine fully the identifications of its audience. Such analysis posits instead

> actual social subjects who by virtue of their complex histories and multiple cultural affiliations (educational, religious, vocational, political, etc.) always . . . exceed the subject implied by the text.[10]

Such an account does not assume, however, that these "excessive" subjects are autonomous agents sprung fully formed from their own heads and not already produced by the very educational, religious, vocational, and political affiliations that offer them more or less determined identities. Instead of the argument proceeding on an assumption about the subjects' autonomy, the notion of "subculture" is deployed to suggest that individuals are simultaneously members of several groups. As Tania Modleski expresses it, subjects are "caught up in a network of discourses inharmoniously clamoring for [their] allegiance" and so are positioned to use one, as it were, to play off against the other.[11] Within this model a female culture or subculture can offer a structure whereby the sociability of a group can enable women to reappropriate hostile images of themselves projected by other discourses, or perhaps even to articulate resistance by women to those images. It is the social dimension of the subculture, according to this model, that positions the individual to negotiate the demands of the dominant culture successfully. Thus in a study of women's consumption of soap operas (which, as I have noted, could often be seen as derogatory to women), it was found that these programs could be enjoyed because of the part they played in membership of a group:

> These popular texts form an important part of their friendship and association in their [the women's] everyday lives and give a focus to an almost separate female culture which they can share together within the constraints of their positions as wives and mothers.[12]

The notion of "subculture" is thus a useful modification of the model of ideology that I elaborated in chapter 2, because it opens a space for the theo-

---

9. See, for example, the essays in Brown 1990. The seminal work is Radway 1984. A criticism of her work may be read in Modleski 1991.

10. Modleski 1991: 36.

11. Ibid., 37.

12. A. Gray, "Behind closed doors: Video recorders in the home," in *Boxed in: Women and television*, ed. H. Baehr and G. Dyer (London: Pandora 1986), 49; quoted in Brown 1990: 207.

rization of alternatives to dominant discourses without supposing a free, autonomous individual as the source of those alternatives.[13]

In the search for helpful theoretical models we have come a long way from women's ritual practice in ancient Greece, and it is time to return. Since the gendered division of labor characteristic of Greek culture was sustained not only by spatial differentiations but also by ideologies of women's inferiority, women who did convene socially might have a significant interest in reclaiming for themselves the value of their own lives and occupations, and as we have seen, ritual tasks provided the most prominent occasions not only for leaving the domestic context but also for engaging in collective, social activity. Women's sociability is frequently mediated by their ritual practice; even in representations from the Hellenistic period, when women are generally understood to have had increased access to the public realm, a ritual context is often supplied to account for their voluntary association. Women meet in an organized festival for Adonis (Theokritos *Idyll* 15) or in a less formal excursion to the temple of Asklepios (Herodas *Fourth Mime*). When the women in Menander's *Epitrepontes* hire the flute-girl Habrotonon to play for them, they do so as part of their arrangements for the Tauropolia festival. Episodes of female solidarity may also be represented as mediated by a ritual context, as we have seen when the Sixteen Women of Elis intervene on behalf of imprisoned wives or when the women of Amphissa protect the sleeping Thyiads. To pursue the ritual articulations of Greek women's culture any further, testimony from historical women themselves would be desirable, which as ever is in short supply. What we do have access to, however, are the slender remains of Greek women's poetry, much of which have recently been very convincingly read in terms of their representation of a female subculture.[14] The first topic of concern for this chapter, then, will be the role of ritual as a resource for the production of women's poetry in ancient Greek culture. I shall show that although we cannot simply read back from the texts to a historical female subculture that conversely generated the texts, we can say that the poets represent themselves as finding a voice within ritual contexts, and that the poems use figures of ritual to construct images both of female sociability and of poetic authority.

WOMEN WRITING

The historical context for the Sapphic poems is, as we saw in chapter 2, a matter of debate, and it is consequently difficult simply to posit a historical

---

13. Cf Homans's suggestion (1987: 173) that "collective female discourses" offer an escape route from the impasse over whether individual subjectivity is to be understood as determined or free. Skinner (1996: 183), who argues for a female subculture as the generative matrix for Sappho's poetry, cites this suggestion.

14. Winkler 1990a; Skinner 1991 and 1996.

women's culture as the productive matrix for the poems on the basis only of the texts themselves. Questions have also been raised about the objective status of women on archaic Lesbos. If it was as high as some commentators suggest,[15] would there have been strict separation of the sexes and the consequent devaluing of women? Given that some of the women represented in the Sapphic corpus bear aristocratic names (see, for example, fragment 155),[16] they probably cannot be taken as representative of the generality of women on Lesbos in any case, and since we know little about seventh- or sixth-century Lesbian society except what we can make the poems of Sappho and Alkaios tell us, many arguments are bound to be somewhat circular. We can note, however, that Sapphic wedding songs (epithalamia) indicate that the bride is given to the groom in an unequal partnership and that the bride's loss of virginity is a lamentable event. The broader social context for the poetry, as represented by the epithalamia, is thus marked by a familiar gender inequality.

Whatever may have been the social realities of Lesbian culture, it is clear that the poetic project of the Sapphic corpus is to represent an aristocratic female subculture. Women and the relations among them are its chief concern, and women comprise almost the entire population of the extant texts. Nor do these women function simply as figures in a narration undertaken by the poet; despite the elaboration on the biography of Sappho in the secondary literature, the first person is only one of the ways in which the poetry is voiced. Comprising at least three addresses to "Sappho" herself (fragments 1, 65, 133), several poems that presuppose a number of speakers (fragments 94, 114, 140), and others that identify other women who are themselves musicians and perhaps poets (fragments 96, 153), the corpus enacts a female subculture by deploying this plurality of voices in which many different women speak.[17] Other versions of society are eschewed in favor of this gynocentric vision; while the epithalamia gesture toward another social reality, there are in the extant texts very few overt references to, for instance, Lesbian politics, even though the island was the scene of repeated factional conflict, which by some accounts involved Sappho herself.[18] In this

15. E.g., Pomeroy 1975: 56.
16. All references to the Sapphic corpus are to the edition of Voigt (1971).
17. On fragment 1 see, for example, Winkler 1990a: 166–78.
18. The Parian Marble (= Voigt 1971: no. 251) claims that Sappho was exiled. In this context we might even argue that the Sapphic poems do engage with factional conflict on Lesbos, representing exile, for instance, with the image of the colorful headband that is no longer available to the speaker of fragment 98. Given that some of the poems feature the names of aristocratic families involved in factional conflict (the Penthilidai in frag. 71, the Polyanaktidai in frags. 155 and 213b, the Kleanaktidai in frag. 98b; see also Campbell 1982: frags. 99 and 214B), it is even possible that what disperses the Sapphic subculture of women is not marriage but exile. The first speaker of fragment 94, for instance, laments: "We have suffered dreadful

silence the extant poetry of Sappho offers a contrast to that of Alkaios, which claims to convene male companions around political ends as Sappho's does female around the tropes of a highly idealized, aesthetic version of female identity.

The particular choices made by the corpus, however, are not produced by an unwillingness or inability to engage with the traditional "masculine" topics of war and politics. John Winkler suggests that the poetry reworks the Homeric epics, resisting the values associated with "masculine" topics and with the epic genre in favor of an alternative set of gynocentric themes.[19] To divisive politics the poetry opposes a shared culture of aesthetic femininity that can span geographical distance and overcome the passage of time with memory. Women who have left are present in the poetry, although far away, and women about to leave are consoled with memories of shared experiences. These female versions of exile are not products of a female subculture in the sense of deriving from a narrow, partial vision, but instead can be read to oppose their microunderstandings to those masculine macrohistories that rashly claim to be the only possible or relevant versions of reality. This resistance is facilitated, according to Winkler, by the existence of a separate subculture that makes possible a "double consciousness" in women; as subordinates they must know both their own meanings and those dear to members of dominant groups. In a similar vein Marilyn Skinner argues for both a historical "women's culture" that provided the context within which the poet Sappho could flourish, and a transhistorical dimension to such a culture that ensured the preservation of the poems.[20]

Whatever the precise historical context of the Sapphic corpus, the work of ritual figures within the poetry remains to be considered. Although we have seen that the Sapphic poems may have been produced within a ritual context of choral activity, this does not require that the ritual practice represented in the poetry be understood as a historical event.[21] While study of archaic poetry has stressed its performative dimension as a useful correction to older notions of lyric as the outpourings of a naive heart,[22] to fetishize performance is as reductive as to ignore it. Too great an insistence on performance has led to unconvincing conclusions, such as those of François

---

things" *(deina peponthamen);* the phrase might refer to conflicts preceding the separation from "Sappho" equally as well as to the separation itself. Since aristocratic marriage often removes women from their familiar environment and sends them to foreign lands in order to consolidate family alliances, there is no necessary contradiction between exile and marriage. In this context it is perhaps significant that Helen, who combines the tropes of desire and distance, should be an important figure in Sapphic poetry (see, for example, DuBois 1984).

19. Winkler 1990a.
20. Skinner 1996.
21. Winkler 1990a: 165.
22. See, for example, Gentili 1988.

Lasserre, who posits an actual historical ritual as the genesis for each and every poem.[23] Whatever the significance of ritual practice for any women who associated with the historical Sappho, ritual enters the poetry not as itself but as a specific figure in the work of representing both the poet and her female culture.

The speaker of Alkaios 130B, exiled from Lesbos and dreaming of return, represents the island with, among other tropes, that of the Lesbian women in their ritual roles:

> where the Lesbian women in their long gowns walk back and forth as their beauty is judged, and all around rings the holy echo of the women's sacred annual shout . . .

The ritual practice represented in the Sapphic poems, by contrast, is almost always private, performed for and among women rather than offered as a spectacle to others. Fragment 94 opens with an unnamed woman lamenting her enforced departure;[24] the speaking part is then taken up by "Sappho," who consoles the departing woman with the remembrance of various pleasures they have shared, mentioning in particular garlands, perfumes, and a soft bed. Concluding (for us) the list of shared pleasures are the words *hieron* (shrine) and *alsos* (grove), which appear in these fragmentary lines that might be translated "Nor any . . . / nor any holy . . . / was there from which we kept away, / nor grove." If we understand the poem to say that there was no shrine or holy grove from which the women stayed away, then ritual practice is being represented as a significant part of a shared life and as one of the activities that bring pleasure in themselves. Given the overt sensuality of the pleasures previously said to be common to the two speakers of the poem, we might even suggest that ritual practice is represented as somehow partaking of this eroticism.[25] "The intimate pleasures and satisfactions of these women are of a piece with worship at shrines, groves, choral performances."[26] Although the poem is too fragmentary to pursue this reading much further, Winkler has previously proposed an erotic reading for another fragment usually attributed to Sappho, fragment 16 (Incerti Auctoris), which also claims to represent ritual practice:

23. See also Snyder 1989: 12 on unhelpful attempts to make Sappho into a priestess of Aphrodite.

24. Anne Pippin Burnett's argument (1979) that the first lines are spoken by the unnamed woman, not by "Sappho" the narrator, has been accepted by many commentators but not, for instance, by Stehle 1997. See also DuBois 1995: 140.

25. Williamson (1995: 90–132) has an excellent discussion of the relations between ritual and sexuality in the poetry of Sappho and is particularly helpful both on the polyvalence of ritual for the women who participated (102–3) and on the importance of ritual as a hermeneutic with which we may think about women's experience.

26. DuBois 1995: 144.

The Cretan women now
How rhythmically, with their soft feet,
They dance around the lovely altar,
Treading the smooth soft flower of the grass.

If, as Winkler suggests, the scene at the Cretan altar, with its lush grass, is an oblique evocation of female sexuality and of the erotic female body,[27] it is nonetheless also a scene of women's ritual practice; the conjunction indicates that women's pleasure could be portrayed in their poetry by their shared rituals, and may offer the possibility that ritual activity was historically experienced as a source of particularly female pleasure.

Equally important in these two fragments on ritual, and in others, is the sign of shared, collective action. This quality of ritual, which is characteristically part of a "realistic" description of its successful completion, may also be read as a figure for the idealized female community that the Sapphic corpus undertakes to construct. Two Sapphic fragments (140 and 168), referring to Adonis, dramatize women's mourning for him in a way that suggests a version of the Adonia. While one reads simply: "Alas for Adonis," the other is a call and response between "Cytherea" (= Aphrodite) and the *korai,* or girls or young women, who are bidden to mourn for Adonis. In its amoebic structure the poem can be seen to enact not only the women's mourning but also an orderly reciprocity among them. A further scrap (fragment 154) runs:

The moon appeared in its fullness,
And the women stood around the altar . . .

Like the poem on the Cretan women, these lines can be seen to offer ritual action as a paradigm of shared action. Convening women in an orderly aesthetic, it represents the shared life of the female culture that the poems both celebrate and work to recreate. Even more extensive claims are also legible here; if the women group round the altar in a circle, then they mimic the shape of the full moon even as they synchronize their collective action with its moment of rising. Figuring thus completion and plenitude, and moving in harmony with the moon, the women in the fragment can be read to represent themselves as somehow achieving, through their ritual gestures, a union with nature and among themselves. Ritual practice may or may not have provided the actual ground for a historical performance of the poem; what we can say is that ritual practice works as a figure for the female community that performance and poem project.

In the fragmentary poems, figures of ritual action can be read as

27. Winkler 1990a: 185.

metaphors for women's pleasure and for the shared life of the subculture that the corpus desires to image forth. Some of the longer poems allow the development of a further argument, for they deploy figures of ritual as part of an investigation into the poetic process. Adopting the traditional form of a "cletic" hymn, invoking the gods, these poems claim a performative context in which they may even represent themselves as part of a ritual event. "The form is relatively conventional. . . . Even though we may not want to go so far as to say that these songs were meant to be performed at some specific occasion, they nevertheless seem in some way connected with familiar rituals of a public character."[28] To posit an occasion for the poems is not to explain or interpret them, however, since their status as texts means that they exceed the material constraints of any single performance, even though they may fantasize such a performance for themselves. Two of the poems are addressed to Aphrodite; one, about the speaker's brother, to Aphrodite and the Nymphs; and one to Hera. Of these, the two songs to Aphrodite are most interesting for my purposes.

Although we cannot know exactly what preceded the first line in the text as we have it, fragment 2, which begins with the words "Hither to me from Crete," does not reveal until the final stanza that its addressee is Aphrodite. While the place-name "Crete" may supply a sign of Aphrodite at the beginning of the poem, the body of the text is occupied with an evocation not of the deity but of a sacred grove:

> Hither to me from Crete, to this holy
> temple, where your lovely grove
> of apple trees is, and the altars
> smoke with frankincense.
>
> Herein cold water rushes through
> apple boughs, and the whole place is shaded
> with roses, and sleep comes down
> from rustling leaves.
>
> Herein a meadow where horses graze
> blooms with spring flowers, and the winds
> blow gently . . .
>
> Here, O Cyprian, taking [garlands],
> in golden cups gently pour forth
> nectar mingled together with our
> festivities . . . [29]

While a Sapphic collectivity may have celebrated in a grove, it was not this one, and it is simplistic to claim, as Richard Jenkyns does, that there is "no

28. Snyder 1991: 3.
29. This translation is taken from Snyder 1989.

reason to doubt that Sappho is describing a real place. . . . Sappho's Fragment 2 is a vivid and perceptive recreation of real experience."[30] The grove is described not in realistic terms but as a site for the play of the senses, in which altars steam, cool water burbles, roses provide shade, and flowers bloom, and in which the apples and horses of the poem can be read, as often in Greek poetry, as signs of desire.[31] So heavily eroticized is the evocation of the grove that the drowsiness *(koma)* that descends *(katairion)*, perhaps from the rustling leaves, seems nothing short of postcoital. It is hard to avoid the conclusion that the poem enacts a seduction, in which the goddess of desire furnishes the target for the same kind of erotic magic that she customarily practices herself.[32] Since the goddess then arrives, in what is our final stanza, the seduction can be described as successful; the poem enacts that fulfillment of its own desire that can be seen to be characteristic of erotic poetry. The speaker's task in this poem is to make the absent present, an abiding concern not only of love poetry but also of the poetry of memory and loss that constitutes (for us at least) so significant a part of the Sapphic corpus.[33] At the same time, however, the power to make absence presence is attributed here to the ritual gesture of cletic invocation, and by figuring Aphrodite in the final stanza the poem ensures that it successfully enacts not only the seduction but also the cletic function. Yet the power in the poem is not all the speaker's; the very eroticism of the earlier lines can suggest retrospectively that Aphrodite was already present and inspiring the speaker. The last stanza enacts this reciprocity when Aphrodite presides over the "mingling" in golden cups of her divine nectar with the celebrations. The deity is brought down into the shared life of the Sapphic collectivity, and in the last line of the text as we have it she is asked to pour nectar for the collectivity in a gesture that makes her part of it and thus seals the success of the speaker's evocative authority.

The ritual dimension of this poem seems to relate not so much to a context of performance as to a claim about performance, in which the text asserts its authoritative power to make the absent present in a work of successful seduction. The ritual context is pressed into service in order to represent the poet's authority and power. Fragment 1, the one poem of the Sapphic corpus that is still available to us in its (probable) entirety, can be read to dramatize similar assertions. Opening the poem by representing

30. Jenkyns 1982: 31–32.

31. "The piece is delightfully sensual" (Snyder 1989: 16). Apples are frequently represented as a love token, as in the myth of Akontios and Kydippe, and horses may also signify desire, as they do in Anakreon (see *PMG* 417).

32. See Winkler 1990a: 186.

33. On presence and absence in this poem see, for example, DuBois 1995: 52 and McEvilley 1972.

herself as erotically powerless and vulnerable, the first-person-singular speaker proceeds instead to a virtuoso demonstration of the cletic authority that transforms the potentially dangerous, maddening Aphrodite of the first stanza into the almost maternally helpful figure of the poem's second half:

> O immortal Aphrodite of the many-colored throne,
> child of Zeus, weaver of wiles, I beseech you,
> do not overwhelm me in my heart
> with anguish and pain, O Mistress,
>
> But come hither, if ever at another time
> hearing my cries from afar
> you heeded them, and leaving the home of your father
> came, yoking your golden
>
> Chariot: beautiful, swift sparrows
> drew you above the black earth
> whirling their wings thick and fast
> from heaven's ether through mid-air.
>
> Suddenly they had arrived; but you, O Blessed Lady,
> with a smile on your immortal face,
> asked what I had suffered again and
> why I was calling again
>
> And what I was most wanting to happen for me
> in my frenzied heart: "Whom again shall I persuade
> to come back into friendship with you? Who,
> O Sappho, does you injustice?
>
> "For if indeed she flees, soon will she pursue,
> and though she receives not our gifts, she will give them,
> and if she loves not now, soon she will love,
> even against her will."
>
> Come to me now also, release me from
> harsh cares; accomplish as many things as my heart desires
> to accomplish; and you yourself
> be my fellow soldier.[34]

Unlike the formula prevalent in the cletic hymn, this poem ignores completely what the speaker may have done for the deity but concentrates instead on the goddess's previous acts of compliance; since the speaker has in the past proved as irresistible as the divinity herself, she will prove so

---

34. Again, the translation is from Snyder 1989.

again both to Aphrodite and to the reluctant beloved. As commentators have noted,[35] the poem plays havoc with chronology; both the description of Aphrodite's arrival and the direct quotation of her speech refer to events that the speaker claims took place in the past, and are being recounted as an encouragement to Aphrodite to rehearse them again in the future. Aphrodite, in the past tense of her previous epiphanies, indicates that she had helped the speaker in an even more distant past, but even as she does so, the shift into direct quotation in the fifth stanza—"Whom again shall I persuade to come back into friendship with you?"—moves her compliance into a dramatic present. Collapsing past and future into one immediate present, the poem ensures that Aphrodite appears and speaks, so that the success of its cletic function is dramatized in the epiphany of the goddess, as it was in fragment 2.

Especially teasing in this poem is the complex interplay of voices. Although modern texts are divided between speeches attributed to Aphrodite and to the human speaker "Sappho," a monodic performance or an unpunctuated ancient text would not make such precise discriminations. The poem uses the goddess's epiphany and direct speech to elide distinctions between the human speaker and the divinity, implicitly augmenting the status of the speaker both as lover and as accomplished rhetorician.

When in the fourth stanza Aphrodite arrives (or arrived), her speech is first represented indirectly, so that we may conclude that the human speaker is, as it were, speaking for her, even though Aphrodite seems to be simply repeating what the speaker said on a previous occasion: "asked what I had suffered again and/why I was calling again/And what I was most wanting to happen for me/in my frenzied heart." The sudden shift into direct speech highlights the paradox; although Aphrodite now speaks, we know that the human speaker ventriloquizes her words, and that the terms the goddess uses, particularly *adikeei*, "does you injustice," are those that the human speaker would approve. If Aphrodite is to be prosecutor *and* judge, and if she is so patently on "Sappho's" side, then the beloved doesn't stand a chance. The incantatory sixth stanza identifies the human and divine speakers more closely; since it bears a strong resemblance to charms and spells historically recorded in Greek culture, and since it is then echoed in the repetitions of the final stanza ("accomplish . . . accomplish"), it would be as appropriately allotted to the human speaker as to the goddess.[36] The incantation can also be read as a minicommentary on the poem itself; both

---

35. See, for example, Snyder 1991: 5 and 1989: 15. On time in other poems see, for instance, DuBois 1995: 104.

36. See Winkler 1990a: 173–74.

cletic hymn and love magic promise erotic success to the speaker who can effectively deploy powerful language. That this poem is an instance of that power is made clear by its ability to draw on other discursive forms in its pursuit of the unwilling beloved.

The last stanza of the poem, usually attributed to the human singer, begins with the general address "Come to me now," which might even be read to target the beloved rather than the goddess. Since the stanza then proceeds to the closing request that "you yourself be my fellow soldier *(symmachos)*," however, the whole speech seems in the end to address only the goddess. What is interesting is how far the speaker has come from her initial posture of helpless supplication; whereas at first she was in danger of being "overwhelmed with anguish and pain" through the designs of the goddess, it now appears that Aphrodite will act in a supplementary capacity alongside the speaker's own efforts. The poem has worked; the epiphany of Aphrodite has already occurred in the course of the song, and this ritual invocation operates as sign and guarantee not only of a poetic authority that can fulfill its own desire, by making the absent present and by identifying the dangerous goddess of love with itself, but also of an erotic mastery that can only serve to tame the recalcitrant beloved "even against her will." If she is listening, she had better watch out.[37]

In these two cletic hymns, the contours of ritual performance serve not to ground and anchor the language in a historical action but to stage a claim about the authority of the poem itself. In other parts of the corpus, as we have seen, representations of ritual can signify the pleasures of the shared life of an aristocratic female subculture that the poetry desires to project. It is plausible to suggest that Sapphic poetry was produced and nurtured within the context of a subculture with ritual dimensions, for instance, within a choral model, but what is significant here is that ritual forms offer important resources for imaging a version of the poetic process. The voice of the woman poet claims to emerge within a context of women's ritual.

Later women poets can also be read to mobilize ritual figures, and some of the fifth-century poets, in particular, seem to represent their work as conditioned by a choral context.[38] The poetry of Korinna, who wrote at Tanagra in Boeotia, consists for us largely of mythical narrative yet also includes some lines on her poetic practice:

---

37. DuBois (1995: 9) usefully writes of this poem: "This scenario of pursuit and flight, of subject and control, seems to me to give the lie to an essentialized, ahistorical version of passive or even reciprocal feminine sexuality: Sappho participates more in the aristocratic drive for domination, in the agonistic arena of Greek social relations, than in some projected vision of non-violent eros."

38. See also Snyder 1989: 40.

Terpsichore [called] me
To sing the lovely old stories *(geroia)*
To the women of Tanagra in their white robes.
And the city rejoiced greatly
At my clear, beguiling voice.

These lines can be read to convene a choral group of Tanagrean females, but this audience immediately gives way to "the city'—a significant collocation in view of the issues raised in the previous chapter. Some lines from one of Korinna's contemporaries, Praxilla of Sikyon near Corinth, derive from a lament by Adonis that seems to have presupposed a ritual performance by a chorus. These lines were famous in antiquity for their representation of Adonis as a confused youth who in death misses not only the light of the sun, moon, and stars but also ripe apples, pears, and cucumbers. Pausanias 2.20.8 calls Telesilla of Argos "famous among women," which could indicate either that she was unusually prominent in comparison with other women or, as Jane Snyder takes it, that she was famous among women as opposed to men.[39] This interpretation allows for a relatively independent female culture that could prize women's achievements and public roles. That it might have a ritual or choral dimension could be suggested by a fragment of Telesilla that is addressed to "maidens" and takes as its subject the goddess Artemis. Since Telesilla's alleged generalship of the Argive women made possible the defeat of Sparta and gave rise to the festival of the Hybristika, we can even read the possibility that it was her skills as *choregos,* or chorus-leader, that seemed appropriate for transfer to the military sphere.

The exiguous remains of archaic and classical women poets indicate that such poets may well have been produced and sustained by a female subculture articulated in a ritual institution such as the chorus, even though the invocation of ritual forms in the poetry need not refer simply to its material context. Although the choral institution persists, it is not foregrounded in extant poetry by Hellenistic women; this poetry finds form in genres such as the funerary or dedicatory epigram, and the relations among women that can be represented in such genres are restricted in scope. Although these genres gesture toward derivation from ritual practice, they are equally indebted to poetic convention; again what we see is not so much women's poetry springing from women's ritual but women's ritual being deployed by women poets as a figure for their own creativity. Almost all the surviving work of Erinna, who wrote at Telos in the fourth century, is comprised of laments for her dead friend Baukis; two poems are funerary epigrams[40] that might be inscribed on a tomb, and the third is a description, in three hun-

---

39. Snyder 1989: 60.
40. These are often considered pseudonymous.

dred hexameter lines of which fifty-four are extant, of the shared childhood of the two women. In each text the traditional role of women as mourners is foregrounded, but the lamenting first-person voice (as with Sappho) shifts among different speakers. Of the two epigrams, one is spoken by the tomb, who addresses the passerby and instructs him or her on how to mourn for Baukis. The second is spoken by Baukis herself, who claims to repeat the inscription on the tomb: "This tomb holds a bride, my father called me Baukis, I came from Tenos"; and concludes by remembering: "My friend Erinna inscribed this epigram on my tomb." In contrast to these epitaphs, the hexameter poem, the *Distaff,* closely identifies poet and speaker in a compelling evocation of the domestic world of women before marriage, in which childhood games and monsters, relations with mothers, and the onset of Aphrodite are all dramatized as part of an emotional lament for Baukis.

The contrasts between the poems invite an interpretation that centers on the division between public and private; whereas the epitaphs advertise themselves as for consumption by a wide public, the *Distaff* seems to insist on the interiority of its domestic world. As Snyder remarks, however, the existence of two separate epigrams suggests that neither was designed for actual use on the tomb.[41] If neither poem is making a bid for its public material embodiment, they may perhaps be considered instead as more private experiments in the articulation of grief. Conversely, the *Distaff* claims that its first-person speaker is not allowed to lament properly or in public: "So crying for you I leave aside . . . my feet do not . . . from my house permitted, nor to see . . . or to lament with my head uncovered." Even though the poem clearly is performing a lament for Baukis, it presents itself as the private response that substitutes and compensates for the prohibited public mourning. Although, as we have seen, women's mourning practices could and did attract legislative and other interference, the text as we have it in fact succeeds in addressing a public more extensive than the dead Baukis alone, and its effectiveness as a protest against restrictions on women's traditional role is facilitated by its public dimension.[42] The poetry of Erinna as it has been preserved for us seems to constitute an exploration of the possible speaking positions available to women as mourners, in which both private and public voices are mediated by the traditional, sanctioned yet disturbing genre of lament.

Although not all Hellenistic women poets wrote about women's lives, those who did, particularly Anyte of Tegea and Nossis of Locri, who both

41. Snyder 1989: 91.

42. See Snyder 1989: 95 and notes for various explanations for why the speaker cannot participate in mourning. See Caraveli 1986: 189 for the persistence of informal restrictions on lamenting women in modern rural Greece.

wrote in the third century, deployed the funerary or dedicatory epigram. Of the twenty-four poems attributed to Anyte in the *Palatine Anthology,* four are for women who died before marriage, and one, which also commemorates an early death, is for three women from Miletos who died rather than face the invasion of the Gauls in 277 B.C.E. While the latter poem can readily be understood as a pointed variation on the others, which lament death before marriage under "normal" circumstances, it can also be seen to resonate with the myths and ritual practices examined in chapter 3, which correlate versions of female heroism with self-sacrifice. In the other four poems there is little public dimension to the women's deaths, but they seem to be mourned especially by women. In *Palatine Anthology* 7.490, a first-person speaker weeps for the dead girl Antibia and describes her beauty and talents in terms of the many suitors who are now disappointed. Poem 7.486 describes the grief of the mother, Kleina, for her daughter Philaenis, and a mother also appears in 7.649, as responsible for erecting on the tomb a marble image like her daughter Thersis. In its address to the dead girl Thersis this poem concludes: "So now we can speak to you, although you are dead." Focusing on the mourning mothers and suggesting the possibility of continued relationships with the dead, these poems of Anyte may gesture toward a subculture that values versions of female experience and their poetic articulation in forms that register women's ritual work of mourning.

The poetry of Nossis of Locri (in Greek Italy) may well have included erotic verses to and about women,[43] but she is represented for us by a series of epigrams, many of which claim to accompany dedications by women. Since most of these alleged dedications are portraits of the women concerned, the poems engage with the women not only as ritual practitioners but also as individuals with personal qualities and attractions. Skinner has argued that "we receive the distinct impression of writing directed exclusively toward a relatively small, self-contained female community," which is further defined as "a relatively autonomous women's subculture at Locri."[44] While any such subculture, like Sappho's, would be restricted to members

43. See Skinner 1989 and 1991: 34–35. Nossis worked in a culture distinguished by the descent of honors in the female line, according to Polybios 12.5.7, but also, according to the historian Klearchos (in Athenaeus 12.516A), a practice of ritual prostitution. The rite of the Locrian maidens belonged to the mainland Locrians, but Sourvinou-Inwood (1974) has suggested a connection between that rite and the Italian Locrians' vow of 477/76 that they would dedicate their daughters to prostitution if they were allowed the victory in war. The first of the two distinguishing features just cited might seem to undermine the assumption of a patriarchal order that conditions the possibility of a female subculture. The second, however, might seem equally to confirm it, and in the absence of any more precise information about Locrian society we may not need to differentiate it radically from other parts of Greece in terms of its gender ideology.

44. Skinner 1991: 21, 37.

of the elite and not available to "women" generally,[45] we might also note that the poetry figures and represents such a subculture rather than claiming directly to derive from it. Like that of the Sapphic texts, to which one epigram explicitly refers (poem 1 = *Palatine Anthology* 5.170), it is an idealized and aestheticized vision. Whatever the ontological status of the Locrian women's subculture, however, it is arguably significant for our investigation that the ritually inflected forms of dedicatory epigrams are used to represent that subculture.

Since the epigrams describe a series of portraits, they collectively represent a tiny gathering of women, which may be thought of as evoked only in the texts of Nossis or as materially present on the walls of a temple. The poems lavish appropriately "feminine" adjectives on their subjects but also take care to differentiate among them, so that Kallo (poem 6 = *Palatine Anthology* 9.605) is charming, Thaumareta (poem 7 = 9.604) proud and ripe, Melinna (poem 8 = 6.353) benign, and Sabaithis (poem 9 = 6.354) wise.[46] While judging the portraits' verisimilitude, the speaker claims an acquaintance with the women dedicators that goes beyond a knowledge of their physical appearance; she remarks on the resemblance between mother and daughter in one case (poem 8), and in another she knows about the little watchdog kept by the woman (poem 7). The speaker thus represents herself as part of the community that she evokes in the poems. What is at stake in the insistence on verisimilitude, moreover, is not simply the normative criteria of Greek art criticism. The likeness of the portraits is asserted in order to gain the assent of the reader/viewer; it is rhetorically underlined by repetition of the exclamatory "how," as in "how truly" (poem 8), and of the imperative "see!" (poems 6, 8, and 9). Since the reader is expected to perform this assent and recognize the likenesses, she or he too is drawn into the collectivity projected by the poems, which may thus be understood to have the potential of indefinite expansion. Poem 4 (= *Palatine Anthology* 9.332) makes the gesture of inclusion explicit when it opens with the feminine plural participle *elthoisai:* "Let us [women] go to Aphrodite's temple to see her statue." The claim that this collectivity operates within the ritual sphere grounds it in the material possibilities of historical women's lives, who would often be able precisely to "go to the temple," in company with other women and, as we have seen, at times of their own choosing.

The female culture evoked by the poems, and implicitly offered to subsequent readers, is one in which the women's personal charms are advertised with, as Skinner puts it, a "delicate sensuality."[47] The ostensible ritual

---

45. For Nossis's aristocratic affiliations see Skinner 1991: 23, 34, and n. 42.
46. Skinner (1991) argues further for differences in age among the women represented.
47. Skinner 1991: 35.

context of the dedicatory epigrams may be relevant here, for, as we have seen, the ritual sphere is frequently eroticized by its display of women. Some of the poems may be understood to engage with this eroticism deliberately, by depicting dedications from *hetairai*. Poem 4, which convenes the collective audience in the feminine plural participle discussed above, celebrates Polyarchis, who dedicated a statue to Aphrodite, "having made great fortune/out of the splendor of her own body." Despite the fact that Nossis herself seems to have been an aristocrat and therefore probably far removed in status from women who had to earn a living with their bodies, the text offers no censure of the woman but only praise. Other women who dedicate portraits or, in one case, a headband to Aphrodite have also been construed as *hetairai*, and this possibility suggests that association among women in Locri, particularly when mediated by the ritual context, may in fact have crossed class lines. If, on the other hand, as Skinner plausibly suggests,[48] these poems were commissioned and paid for rather than being spontaneous tributes, then the material class distinctions may have persisted, even though the poetry seeks to elide them in its undifferentiated celebration of female personal beauty. Skinner suggests further that the absence of censure in poems 4, 5, and 6 (see especially poem 6: "her way of life is blameless") is a pointed correction of a misogynistic literary tradition.[49] Since we cannot be certain about the women's status, we cannot securely define the poems as resisting gender ideology,[50] but we can, for instance, claim a resistance to patriarchal imperatives in poem 8, which praises a likeness between mother and daughter in defiance of the Hesiodic tenet that children should resemble their fathers.

The ritual context evoked by the poems can be seen to facilitate the representation of a female subculture and also of its eroticization. We may also conclude that in some sense it facilitates the writing itself, for it is ritual practice that most readily positions women to speak and act in the public sphere. As Skinner perceptively notes, Nossis's texts combine a private voice of intimate acquaintance with public utterance,[51] but it may be significant that the poems that can achieve this mediation claim to derive from women's ritual practice, which itself moves between private and public spheres. Poem 3 (= *Palatine Anthology* 6.265) insists still more strongly on the connection between women's ritual practice and their poetry:

48. Ibid., 27.

49. Ibid., 24.

50. If we suppose ritual prostitution at Locri, then we may be able to reconstruct a female tradition of celebrating commercial sexuality that is indeed at variance with mainstream views. Robert (1937: 406–7) cites two inscriptions in which ritual prostitutes celebrate their métier, but they date from the imperial period.

51. Skinner 1991: 20–21.

Honored Hera, you who often come down from heaven
and look upon your fragrant Lacinian temple,
Accept a linen cloak that noble Theophilis, daughter of Cleocha,
wove for you, together with her daughter Nossis.

While the dedication of the linen wrap, woven by mother and daughter, resonates with the historical occasions on which weaving was performed by a collectivity of women and the product used as part of a cult festival, Skinner has also shown that the metaphor of weaving as poetic work is in play in this text.[52] Nossis thus puts herself in the figurative temple, not with a portrait but with a sign of the poetic practice that will then put all the other women there, weaving them together into the elegant sodality that the poems project.

Whether or not we posit historical dedications as the occasion for Nossis's poetry, we can draw some conclusions about the possible relations among women's writing, women's culture, and women's ritual practice. If we suppose historical dedications, we can conclude that on such occasions women dedicators might appropriately request the poetic labor of other women. If we suppose instead that the poetry determined its own objects, we might conclude that for a poet who is "woman-tongued"[53] and writing about women, a series of fictional dedications provided a possible context. Insofar as ritual practice supplied historical women with experiences of collective action and of a valued role within the culture, it might offer a suitable context for their representation of themselves; but more crucially, we have seen that the poetry represents ritual practice as providing women with a voice, nurtured in a gynocentric subculture and then deployed in the construction of a poetic persona and poetic authority. Sappho's hymns, Erinna's laments, and Nossis's epigrams mediate their claims to a poetic voice by means of the speaking positions offered by ritual practice.

Figures of ritual within Greek women's poetry encourage the conclusion both that ritual collectivities may have facilitated the historical production of women poets and that these poets conversely deployed ritual tropes to claim a public voice and to represent their own poetic authority. Although it would be a mistake to conclude an identity of attitude among women as far removed chronologically from one another as Sappho and Nossis, Nossis's texts do nonetheless invoke Sappho as poetic model (poems 1 and 11 = *Palatine Anthology* 5.170 and 7.718) and thereby raise the possibility that the female subculture, in which ritual played an important part, had some transhistorical significance. A similar conclusion may be suggested by

52. Skinner 1989 and 1991: 22–23.
53. *Theluglossos*, an epithet applied to Nossis by Antipater of Thessalonica in *Anth Pal* 9.26. See Skinner 1989 and 1991: 22.

the fact that Sappho is one of the two poets most frequently represented on the ceramics of fifth-century Attica.[54] Since there are significant arguments, which will be discussed below, that some of these ceramics deliberately seek a female audience, it is possible that representations of a female subculture held relevance for women of Attica in the fifth century. In the second of this chapter's investigations, we shall consider to what extent representations of women in vase painting register historical women's own needs and concerns, and in what ways these representations figure women's ritual practice.

WOMEN READING

In recent years feminist scholars have increasingly turned to evidence from painted pottery in order to refine current notions both of Greek women's lived realities and of the ways in which the male-dominated culture of fifth-century Athens might have represented women. From this work have emerged at least two distinct arguments: one claims that images of women on pots "can offer a needed corrective to the negative picture often presented by literary and legal sources,"[55] and the other that these images are consonant with other products of the Athenian "reign of the phallus."[56] Both schools of thought, however, and points on the spectrum between the two, acknowledge the importance of this body of graphic testimony. More than 30,000 attributed Attic vases survive, dating from the seventh century through the fourth; and that number, by T. B. L. Webster's calculations,[57] represents about 1 percent of the total manufactured. As Robert Sutton suggests, "this quantity indicates that we are considering a popular art that is comparable in relative scale to contemporary mass-market media."[58] Although other areas produced their own pots, Attic manufacturers exported their wares to various parts of the Greek world, and that trade indicates if not the cultural hegemony of Athens, then at least the relevance of Attic images to other communities. A striking characteristic of these Attic images is that the vases are decorated with scenes not only from mythology but increasingly, from the second quarter of the fifth century onwards, with scenes of domestic life or what are termed "genre" scenes. In these, women figure more prominently than in any other contemporary art form.

Such a large repository of images of women in apparently domestic settings might be thought to offer a comprehensible version of these women's lives, including their ritual practice, but in fact the vases often prove

54. Sutton 1992: 28; Snyder 1989: 6–7.
55. Havelock 1981: 117–18.
56. Keuls 1985.
57. Webster 1972: 3–4.
58. Sutton 1992: 4. Beard (1991: 15) suggests 50,000, but concurs on the 1 percent.

extremely difficult to interpret. In what follows I shall first canvass some problems of interpretation before moving on to the kinds of predications that I think can be made about representation on these vases, first of female culture and second of women's ritual practice. Although many scenes seem to illustrate the domesticity of "real life," scholars point out that we cannot always draw a firm distinction between human mortals and the heroes and divinities of mythology.[59] A further problem is presented by the frequent nudity of the women depicted; since female nudity was rare in fifth-century sculpture, some scholars assume that all naked women on vases are to be understood as *hetairai*.[60] That this approach is inadequate may be demonstrated by the example that Sutton cites, of a pot that shows a woman bathing, naked, in a scene otherwise occupied by similarly conventional preparations for the wedding ceremony.[61] The difficulty of determining the role of women on vases is dramatically illustrated by the mutually exclusive conclusions reached by two scholars who nonetheless share the same assumptions about the overall ideology of the Attic vases. For Dyfri Williams a red-figured hydria (water pot) of ca. 480 B.C.E. *(ARV 276/60)* shows

> a hetaira seated in the porch of what is surely a brothel. . . . [She] is warmly dressed and is preening herself with the aid of a mirror as a boy leads forward her customers. . . . Before the porch of the brothel is a man leaning on his stick as he holds out a heavy purse; behind him stands a young customer waiting his turn.[62]

Eva Keuls, writing of the same vase, claims:

> the woman is characterized as the "disagreeable matron" and the colonnade suggests the inner part of a private residence, not an entrance from the street, and hence we probably have a vignette of family life here, perhaps a henpecked husband trying to appease his wife with money.[63]

While there is considerable consensus in the secondary literature about the import of various vases, disagreement like this between Williams and Keuls can serve to alert us to the difficulties of making predications about "women" in relation to vase images.[64]

---

59. Beard 1991: 20–21; Webster 1972: 243.

60. Williams 1983: 99; Williams also assumes (100) that all females shown reading are in fact Muses.

61. Sutton 1992: 24, fig. 1.9.

62. Williams 1983: 97–98.

63. Keuls 1985: 260.

64. It is not part of this study's brief to attempt a grammar of images of women such as Lissarrague (1990a) constructs for warriors. But I note with Osborne in a related context (1997: 193) that "the hermeneutic control which other images exercise over any particular image is inevitably much looser" (than in the case of texts) and that the project of a grammar is therefore somewhat troubled at the outset.

The work of interpretation might be facilitated if there were a scholarly consensus about the audience for these ceramics, but this issue too is vexed. While many vases have been discovered in tombs and may have been specially produced as offerings, all vases have shapes determined by practical uses, and even dedications may have been in circulation before being offered. Some vases show signs of having been mended in antiquity, which also might indicate regular use.[65] If the pots were thus used, in the home, it becomes increasingly likely that they were seen and handled by women; this is particularly plausible for those pots, such as alabastra (perfume jars) and pyxides (trinket boxes), that seem designed for female use and that often display corresponding images of women. Even assuming women's use of vases, however, we cannot proceed directly to the conclusion that vases deliberately target a female audience as opposed to one composed of the men who might buy or commission the pots. Any inquiry into the sociological context of the Athenian vases, moreover, is hampered by the history of scholarship, which for years has been dominated by the practices of a "connoisseurship" that concentrates on formal and technical aspects of the ceramics and on attribution to various "authors." Although iconographical analysis in now being undertaken, a great deal of such analysis is still conducted along the lines of an unreflective empiricism.

The issue of a female audience for images of women is closely involved with the question of the extent to which historical women participated in the production of images. Few women, if any, seem to have been painters,[66] and given the familiar restrictions on women's movement, that women themselves went out to buy vases does not seem probable in every case. Webster concludes that the demand for images of women "came from men rather than from the women themselves. The vases were more often presents from men to women (or offerings at women's tombs) than purchases by women."[67] Yet do all these considerations mean that the vase images were to no degree determined by the preferences of women who might use them? Again the divergences in critical opinion on this question are striking. For Keuls, "even those vessels specifically designed for use by women . . . reflect essentially a male conceptual framework,"[68] and the phallocratic masculine eye is responsible for all images. Domestic tasks, for instance, are illustrated not for verisimilitude or from a desire to record women's contributions to culture, but because of the erotic charge of female virtue.[69] Williams concurs: "Athenian vase-painting was essentially a man's view of a man's point of view"; and Françoise Frontisi-Ducroux agrees,

65. Burn 1991: 126.
66. Sutton 1992: 4.
67. Webster 1972: 242.
68. Keuls 1985: 118.
69. Ibid., 229–66.

arguing that women are deployed on vases as part of Athenian men's investigation of their own identity.[70] Opposing such positions, Claude Bérard
robustly asserts: "It is to them [women] that the painters address themselves
directly, and it is they who express their preferences."[71] Arguing that the
Greek housewife would not have surrounded herself with images of *hetairai*
or of any domestic labor that was simply "painful and boring", Bérard
claims that the images visible on vases "present an extremely positive view of
female society and of the dignity of women."[72]

Since few of these arguments are particularly nuanced, the lines laid
down in Sutton's study of wedding imagery on fifth-century vases seem more
productive. Sutton offers a sophisticated account of how historical women
may have influenced vase imagery even within the obvious constraints
placed on them by their society. Sutton's first, historical argument derives
from the date when the domestic, or "genre," scenes of women begin to
appear; other changes in vase painting also make this date significant. After
480 B.C.E., and the end of the Persian Wars, commentators agree that vase
painting underwent a transformation that resulted in fewer scenes drawn
from mythology and more that seemed to offer a version of "real life."
Although, as we have seen, there is not always a clear distinction between
the two, a plausible explanation for any change is the groundswell of pride
and confidence in their democracy that the Athenians experienced following the defeat of the Persian invasion, which might well have enabled the
vase-painters' "fanfare to the common man." As Lucilla Burn points out,[73]
this iconographical modification is matched by a decline in the number of
vases in shapes associated with the symposium, the male drinking party that
had aristocratic connotations and often involved some form of sexual enter-
tainment. The place of these symposium shapes, with their frequent images
of violence or sexual aggression, is taken by the "female" shapes of perfume
and oil containers, which offer correspondingly "female" images. The
female nude, Sutton claims, ceases to appear in an overtly pornographic
context, for consumption by a male gaze, and is found instead bathing, on
pots apparently designed for women. Following Webster's analysis of wedding vases and wedding scenes,[74] Sutton further notes that before 480
B.C.E., wedding scenes are found chiefly on amphorai (general containers,
especially for wine) and on hydriai (water pots), which would probably be
used in those parts of the wedding preparations that involved men, especially the symposium and banquet. Subsequent to this date the scenes

70. Williams 1983: 105; Frontisi-Ducroux 1995.
71. Bérard 1989: 89.
72. Ibid., 89, 90, 93.
73. Burn 1991: 120.
74. Webster 1972: 105–6.

migrate to vessels used by women to prepare the bride's bath, namely the nuptial water jars called loutrophoros and lebes gamikos. Shifting their emphasis, moreover, from proceedings involving men to those centering on women, the scenes abandon the earlier images of huge processions escorting the nuptial chariot in favor of images of the bride's bath or of her arrival at her new home, on foot, and accompanied only by the groom and a few women attendants.

Given these various iconographical changes and their specific historical juncture, Sutton concludes that "during the course of the fifth century, vase painters discovered and cultivated a feminine market"[75] and that the images produced for this market

> help one understand how . . . women and other disenfranchised members living in conditions that seem extremely restrictive to contemporary eyes, might have generated in themselves the allegiance to the values of their culture that allowed them to carry out the various roles society had decreed for them.[76]

Sutton's conclusion is informed, however, not only by a version of historical narrative but also by his second, theoretical argument. Drawing on a model of cultural production that dismantles the rigid dichotomy between "producer" and "consumer," in this case male painter and female spectator, he proposes that "the evidence . . . should not be used to suggest that women played only a minor role in selecting vases for their own use," positing instead a "feedback loop' in which women's preferred versions of themselves could emerge into the representations on pots. In an explicit comparison between the ideological work of vase images and that of modern romance novels, Sutton suggests that the images helped fifth-century Athenian gender ideology gain "popular acceptance even from those who would seem to have had little to gain from . . . [such] adherence."[77] How it achieved this acceptance, according to the argument, was by offering versions of that ideology palatable to a subordinate group that, despite its subordination, had its own desires and goals. Arguments such as these represent women of Athens as capable of constructing viable relations with their visual environment and avoid attributing to them the position of passive, helpless consumers of hostile images that are beamed at them from the domestic interior.[78]

The modification in emphasis from Williams's essay of 1983 to Sutton's

75. Sutton 1992: 28.
76. Ibid., 32.
77. Ibid., 6–7.
78. Oakley and Sinos (1993: 46–47) come to a similar conclusion about wedding vases, but without the theoretical underpinning. They emphasize that the bride is represented as "seductive" and suggest that she "has possession of a power that men find irresistible."

of 1992 can be read to reproduce a shift in the field of women's studies generally, whereby the attention that was first directed to establishing the extent of women's exploitation has subsequently been drawn to how women actively manage the constraints of a subjected life. Seconding the comparison between Attic vases of the fifth century and contemporary mass-produced commodities, Mary Beard has recently claimed, in contrast to Sutton, that the repetitiveness of the images, particularly those emerging from what she calls the fifth century's "cultural fixation" on the female, means that the vases offer only the images favored by patriarchal ideology and are not determined in any way by women's own needs or preferences: "Athenian pots constantly presented to the women of the city images of how they could and should behave. . . . By their constant repetition, their constant presence, they served to establish that behaviour . . . as the norm."[79] As we saw in chapter 2, however, the very repetition of an image may expose its ideological character and open a space for the formulation of an alternative reading. Highly relevant in this context is the work of Eva Stehle, who compares narrative myths about a goddess's love for a mortal man with vase paintings on the same subject. While narrative myths organize closure so as to maintain a male/female hierarchy, the suspended narrative of visual images may be seen to keep open a space for fantasies of alternative endings and for identifications not sanctioned by the dominant culture:

> The meeting of these two figures is not pre-scripted: it must be played out according to the dictates of individual fantasy. It can be staged in the imagination according to the script of male dominance, but also from the position of a woman's desire. . . . In each case the painting is sexually suggestive and permits more than one response—that is, the processes of gaze and identification may be variously deployed.[80]

Stehle proceeds to analyze the different positions of desire that men and women could occupy with relation to the same image, and the different ideological charges that that image could thereby convey.

If we conclude, on the basis of these various arguments, that the sign of women's input into fifth-century vase images cannot be suppressed, whether it takes the form of a feedback loop or of women's rereading of the images, we may want to go further and suggest that even though they were not materially produced by women, the vases can be read as part of an expression of a fifth-century women's culture. This is the conclusion drawn by Sutton, who

---

79. Beard 1991: 27. Beard (1991: 30) goes on to point out that some vases "undermine" or "question" the stereotypes set up by other pots, so that "visual images can subvert as much as establish and uphold the norms," but the vast majority of ceramics must still, on her argument, be assigned to the "stereotype" rather than to the "subversion."

80. Stehle 1990: 100–101.

explicitly compares the "atmosphere" of many gynocentric vases to that of Sapphic poetry:

> Characteristic of her [Sappho's] poetry is a delicate yet intense romantic sensibility focused on clothing, flowers, birds, Aphrodite, and feminine companionship, which finds close reflection in the vase paintings showing feminine life.[81]

While the sheer physical quantity of female images on vases might facilitate this conclusion, we might also note that many vases themselves display a plurality of women, which may be thought both to substantiate the notion of a historical subculture that convened women in sociable domesticity and to extend to the female viewer a form of symbolic participation in such a culture. In either case, the model of a subculture can strengthen the suggestions previously made about women's reappropriation of images.

We may be able to pursue the notion of symbolic participation further, by means of the image of the mirror. Objects that look like ancient mirrors are common in domestic, or "genre," scenes of women,[82] and although some of these are sometimes identified by commentators as distaffs instead, enough appear without other signs of wool working to suggest that the mirror itself is a prominent trope. As Keuls points out, the indeterminacy is overdetermined, by the fact that both mirror and distaff can signify "female identity," even though they have very different practical applications.[83] On a late archaic cup by the Brygos Painter (*ARV* 378/40) the solitary woman holds a small sash or circlet and what is generally accepted as a mirror; a wool basket *(kalathos)* is on the floor, and she is standing near a bed, so that she seems primed for almost all aspects of female existence. The scene of a woman alone, holding a mirror, is very common and figures prominently on the "female" shapes of lekythoi, pelikai, and alabastra (all small containers for oil or perfume).

If the mirror is a dominant trope in gynocentric scenes, does it signify anything beyond femininity itself? I suggest that when the woman holds or gazes into a mirror, she may be understood to enact the cultural imperative, which we noted in chapter 2, to monitor herself by internalizing the gaze of others.[84] If, as often, she is alone in the scene, her own gaze must perform the work of the other's gaze, and must additionally be seen to do so by the

---

81. Sutton 1992: 28.

82. Webster 1972: 228–41.

83. Keuls 1985: 243–45. While a woman is frequently shown holding a mirror/distaff among women who hold other impractical objects, like flowers or sashes, the presence of other wool-working implements in a scene that includes the mirror/distaff does not necessarily stress the distaff side of the equation, since the scene could be juxtaposing opposed rather than convergent notions of femininity. See, for instance, the cup *ARV* 815/1, the alabastron *ARV* 726/16, and the hydria *ARV²* 1103/7.

84. See now on the mirror in art Frontisi-Ducroux 1996 and Stewart 1996. This chapter took its final form before the appearance of these essays.

woman viewer of the pot, who herself must be reminded of the cultural imperative. The woman-with-mirror on the pot thus offers to the woman viewer of the pot a figure of herself and thereby substitutes for the mirror that the woman viewer might otherwise look into. For the woman viewer, the pot seems to claim, looking in the mirror and looking at the pot with the woman-with-mirror are the same act, both equally constitutive of female identity.[85] If we may say that she is encouraged to identify with the women on the pots, then perhaps we may say that she sees herself as part of the scenes on them. The woman viewer is thus perhaps offered a position that simultaneously constructs her as object of the internalized male gaze and subject of her own gaze. The gaze that is invited by the vase images seems to be not only the gaze of the male-dominated culture, but also that of the woman herself. The figure of the woman-with-mirror on the vase suggests that a culture can be imagined that is characterized by the exchange of gazes among women; it both shows such a culture and invites women in.[86]

It is perhaps no coincidence, then, that some of the very few female figures who look frontally out of the pot, toward the viewer, are women with mirrors.[87] On a late archaic cup by Douris ($ARV 432/60$) the woman stands between a bed and a washbasin, holding a mirror and staring outwards (see fig. 3).[88] On a classical pyxis (box) by the Painter of the Louvre Centauromachy ($ARV 1094/104$), the woman with the mirror is seated to the right of a bedroom door, while round the rest of the pyxis are other women holding a hand loom or a box, playing knucklebones and folding clothes (see fig. 4). Although Keuls identifies this mirror as a distaff,[89] presumably on the evidence of the hand loom, the other implements held by the women in the scene make it equally probable that the series of female accoutrements could include a mirror. Looking up from the distaff/mirror, where she sees herself, the woman looks out of the pot and "sees" another version of herself in the female viewer. The female viewer, both subject and object of this play of gazes, is constructed by it as a participant in the figured culture of women. The distaff in this scene, if it is a distaff, is a mirror as well.[90]

85. Plutarch's *Advice on Marriage* imagines a scene when "the housewife has her mirror in her hand" and soliloquizes about the relation between virtue and beauty (25).

86. See Frontisi-Ducroux 1995: 99 on an analogous male society constructed from the exchange of gazes on symposium vessels.

87. Frontisi-Ducroux (1995: 114, 120) notes that the frontality of the female face is rare on vases, and understands such frontality in terms solely of the male gaze and of gender inequality.

88. On this cup see Frontisi-Ducroux 1995: 125 and 1996: 88–89. She claims the image is "conceived by and for the masculine gaze."

89. Keuls 1985: 118.

90. Wasowicz (1988) claims to be able to distinguish between mirror and distaff on each occasion. Frontisi-Ducroux (1995: 122) types this image as a distaff and interprets it as having to do with seduction. Later, however, she mounts a much longer and more detailed investiga-

Figure 3. A woman holding a mirror, between a basin and a bed. Interior of a red-figure cup by Douris. *ARV* 432/60, Musée du Louvre S 1350. Photo RMN-Hervé Lewandowski. Reproduced with permission.

Figure 4. A woman holding a mirror, facing the viewer. Red-figure pyxis, ca. 430 B.C.E., by the Painter of the Centauromachy. *ARV* 1094/104, Louvre CA 587. Photo RMN-Chuzeville. Reproduced with permission.

While the self-aware trope of the mirror is a sign that what is represented on vases is not simply a faithful reproduction of the historical, material life of women, this does not mean that vase images are extraneous to our project of reconstructing the ritual dimension of those lives and recovering the contribution made by ritual to women's cultural resources. Like Sapphic poetry, the vase paintings project for their female audience a particular version of a female culture that may be motivated into representation by desires articulated by historical women rather than by the fantasies of historical men. It remains to be seen, however, what part is played by the representation of ritual practice in the vases' projection of what may well be historical women's preferred versions of themselves and of their culture.

My analysis is indebted to Webster's useful study of iconographical topics and the vase shapes on which they appear. Of the scenes he identifies that are of interest to the present project, the most significant are first the various cult scenes, second the scenes of libation between women and men, and third the scenes of women alone dancing or with torches. I shall consider mourning scenes and scenes of maenadism later in this chapter. Representations that can be unequivocally tied to specific festivals such as the Thesmophoria or Adonia are relatively rare.[91] In the first category—cult scenes—identifiable scenes of sacrifice to identifiable divinities do not convene many women.[92] Where women *are* prominent is in cult scenes depicting one person or a few people at an altar;[93] twice as many fifth-century vases (seventy-two in Webster's list) show a single woman in this scene as show a single man, and scenes that show more than one person are likely to include women. When one woman alone is shown, the pot is very likely to be a lekythos and thus designed for a woman's use, and although such pots with such scenes appear throughout the fifth century, they are most common in the early classical period (475–450 B.C.E.). This is the period when scenes involving women first begin to emerge on vases. Prior to this period such cult scenes predom-

---

tion of the figure of the mirror on the boundary between masculine and feminine and devotes an entire section to the ambivalence of images of mirror and distaff (1997: 92–111).

91. Signs of the Thesmophoria, for instance, are absent, except perhaps for a lekythos that shows a woman bending down with a piglet in one hand and an offering tray in the other (*ARV* 1204/2; Keuls 1985: pl. 295). (See also *ARV* 658/31, in which a woman at an altar holds a sucking-pig and a sacrificial basket.) Several scenes show women tending phalli that seem to be planted in the ground, and these have been associated with women's festivals generally (Winkler 1990a: 206). Representations of the Adonia on lekythoi show participants climbing ladders to the roof (*ARV* 1482/5–6) or watering the Adonic gardens (*ARV* 1175/11; on other vases women approach plants, and these may also be evocations of the Adonia; see, for example, *ARV* 1202/11–13, 1203/2–3, 707/9, 721/1). Late fifth-century hydriai (*ARV* 1312/1, 1313/3) evoke the festival when they group human women around Aphrodite and Adonis.

92. Webster 1972: 128–41.

93. Ibid., 145–48.

Figure 5. Women working wool; on the
exterior of this cup, which is damaged, is
visible a woman at an altar. Cup by the
Steiglitz Painter. *ARV* 827/7, Florence 3918.
Reproduced with permission from the
Soprintendenza archeologica di Firenze.

inate on cups, and subsequently they show some migration to the small
pelike and squat lekythos, which are also "female" perfume vases. While
scenes with more than one figure at the altar, male or female, appear on
many types of vase, some of these too seem designed for women. The pelikai
in particular always show women as well as men and sometimes show only a
group of women. *ARV* 267/1, for instance, shows on one side two women at
an altar, and on the other two women who approach with a phiale, a shallow
cup from which libations were poured. A cup by the Steiglitz Painter (*ARV*
827/7) shows on its damaged exterior several women and an altar, while the
interior is occupied by an image of two women, one of whom cards wool on
her knee while the other holds—according to your preference—a mirror or
a distaff (see fig. 5).[94] This vessel as a whole can be read, like others that feature a plurality of women with different attributes, as mobilizing various versions of femininity, among which it is possible to see here ritual activity at the
altar emphasized to the same extent as wool working.

One cult scene that convenes only women, never men, is that of the

94. Mirror: Webster 1972: 146; distaff: Keuls 1985: 255.

group bearing torches, which Webster relates to the *pannychis,* or all-night festival, that is featured in several ritual events. According to Webster's chart, torch scenes emerge only in the early classical period, after 480 B.C.E., and occur most often on the lekythos and amphora.[95] Although after 450 B.C.E., as noted earlier, such scenes migrate to the small pelike, they are not common in the latter half of the fifth century and fade out completely after 425 B.C.E. Lekythoi and amphorai featuring these scenes consistently show on the other side men leaving home or women presenting them with arms, a scene that is usually interpreted as "departure for war."[96] Connecting the scheme of such vases to the trope of "war and peace," Webster suggests that the women's torchlight celebration is a metonymy for peaceful pursuits.[97] While this interpretation attributes considerable symbolic power to the women's ritual, we may also want to consider the possibility that the vases are working with a model whereby the women's cult practice, situated on the cusp between public and domestic, helps to ensure or to celebrate victory. Another reading of the vases might stress their representation of gendered destinies, their claim, in a modification of J-P. Vernant's phrase,[98] that "war is to men what ritual is to women." However we decide to construe the paired scenes, it is plausible to conclude that they were understood as complementary in some way.

On the "female" vases, such as small pelikai, scenes of women with torches are often paired with scenes in which women perform other cult acts, such as pouring a libation (*ARV* 655), bringing a phiale (1220/5), bringing a basket for offerings (1219/2), or praying (727/2, an alabastron). Sometimes the woman with the torch also holds a phiale herself (as in *ARV* 211/203 and 838/12). Since the total number of torch scenes comes to sixty-four, the scene seems to have a significance comparable to that of "woman alone at altar," and, taken together, the motifs indicate that a sizeable component of the fifth century's "cultural fixation" on women was the ceramic representation of them as ritual practitioners.

Fifth-century scenes involving men and women together, without overt cultic reference, are many, but the fifth-century libation scenes always make up a respectable proportion of the total "men and women" scenes: in the late archaic period (500–475 B.C.E.) 3 out of Webster's 65 identifiable vases (4 percent); in the early classical (475–450 B.C.E.) 15 out of 140 (10 percent); in the classical (450–425 B.C.E.) 10 out of 72 (13 percent); and in the late fifth century (425–400 B.C.E.) 6 out of 21 (28 percent).[99] Unlike the female-

---

95. Webster 1972: 141, 127 (chart).
96. See, for example, *ARV* 525/40, 568/28, 853/2, and 1194/2.
97. Webster 1972: 144.
98. Vernant 1980: 23.
99. Given that in the later period elaborate and elegant scenes exclusively of women

only "torch" scenes, then, libation scenes involving both men and women do not decline in comparative popularity as the century wears on. Although few of the libation scenes suggest a context for themselves, several can be read to mark the departure of the male, such as the two early classical column-kraters by the Florence Painter, and a calyx-krater of the Group of the Villa Giulia Painter.[100] In the classical period such departure scenes, and in fact most of the libation scenes, move to pelikai and other smaller vases[101] and thereby suggest again an audience increasingly understood to be female. The division of labor in a libation scene follows strict gender lines but seems complementary; the woman, who usually stands, holds the oinochoe (wine-pourer) into order to pour wine into the phiale held by the man, who may be seated, and whose task it is to pour the libation onto the ground or the altar. The harmonious reciprocity of the scene may be registered in the inscription on an early classical neck-amphora (*ARV*655) that shows the woman with oinochoe, the man with phiale, and the Greek words KALOS and KALE, "beautiful" (masculine) and "beautiful" (feminine), in a rare play on the custom of inscribing vases KALOS for a favored youth.

The cult scenes that involve women without men, but that do not include altars or torches, make up a small proportion of the whole: in the late archaic period there are 7 women-only cult scenes listed out of Webster's total of 143 vases (nearly 5 percent); in the early classical 26 out of 749 (3 percent); in the classical 6 out of 410 (1.5 percent); and in the late fifth century 2 out of 260 (0.7 percent). By themselves, then, these scenes do not constitute a notable presence among the ceramics, and, like the "torch" scenes, they decline in popularity over the century. If, however, we add the scenes already discussed of women alone at an altar or with torches, we get a total figure of 177 for fifth-century women-only cult scenes, out of Webster's total for women-only scenes of 1,603 (11 percent). If, moreover, we proceed as Webster proposes and add to the total of cult scenes those of women bearing sprigs, which could indicate ritual activity, or running, which is a possible representation of dancing, then the cultic reference of the vases is noticeably increased.[102] Even some of the baskets and vessels that the women hold, Webster suggests, may be offerings and thus may sign further cult activity.

That the gynocentric scenes on vases apparently designed for women targeted a female audience is agreed by most scholars, but whether that audi-

---

predominate, we might conclude that of scenes featuring men *and* women, the libation scene found particular favor, which allowed it to persist.

100. *ARV*541/15 (*CV*Copenhagen pl. 145, 2) and 541/16, *ARV*633/7 (*CV*Louvre pl. 14, 1–2 and pl. 15, 2).

101. See, for example, *ARV* 1176/31, 32, and 33; *ARV* 1206/6.

102. Webster 1972: 243.

ence was provided with images deriving from historical women's own needs and desires, or with those of conformity to patriarchal imperatives, is still at issue. We have seen that there are good, if not conclusive, arguments for a feedback loop whereby historical women's preferred versions of themselves may be registered in the images offered to them, and we have also noted the constant possibility of a female reappropriation of ideologically conditioned images. That the vase images are unequivocally "patriarchal" is also not clear; of those scenes that Webster counts as involving only women, no more than a dozen for the entire fifth century are described as definitely including children, and no more than a hundred scenes of wool working (as opposed to scenes including a wool basket) are recorded for the century.[103] Even taking into account the vagaries of preservation, these numbers do not immediately speak of a univocally didactic project. Instead, as Sutton notes, gynocentric scenes are likely to concentrate on elements of a female culture also legible in the texts of Sappho and Nossis, where women are distinguished by their aesthetic and delicately eroticized pursuits. Although no one suggests that this was the reality of most Athenian women's lives, or even that of most women viewers of vases, it may be that the scenes are conditioned at least as much by women's projections of themselves as they are by the patriarchal yearnings of their men.

If we accept the possibility that the fifth-century vase painters provided their female audience with a version of a female culture, we may want to reassess the significance of ritual activity within the representation of that culture. Given the arguments advanced in this study about the ritual sphere's importance for women in ancient Greece as a site of negotiation with patriarchal constraints, it seems plausible that their identity as ritual practitioners would have been prized by historical women. It is hard, too, to avoid the subjective impression, when studying these images, that the women are represented in dignified and benign terms that, while not offering women images of themselves powerful and subversive enough to undermine traditional gender ideology, seem nonetheless to bypass entirely the trope of the female as unstable, marginal, and alien (see fig. 6). We should not conclude, however, that the vases offer us an otherwise elusive "authentic" image of women, articulated in women's own voices; even the scenes of cult activity are limited to a very few types and determined at least in part by the size of the ceramic concerned. Nor do these cult scenes continue to be popular throughout the century; instead they give way increasingly to the very general scenes of women together, without obvious occupation and surrounded by the Erotes, which are characteristic of the late fifth-century "Meidian" style.[104] It is chiefly between the Persian and the Peloponnesian

103. See also Sutton 1992: 28.
104. Sutton 1992: 28–30.

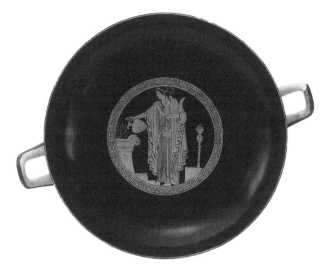

Figure 6. Woman pouring offerings. Makron, red-figure
kylix (tondo), ca. 480 B.C. Wheel-thrown, slip-decorated
earthenware. H. 4⁷/₁₆ in., diam. at lip 11⁵/₁₆ in., diam. with
handles 14¼ in. Toledo Museum of Art, Toledo, Ohio.
Purchased with funds from the Libbey Endowment, Gift
of Edward Drummond Libbey, acc. no. 1972.55.

wars, then, that women emerge into ceramic representation as ritual practitioners, and, as we have seen, the scenes of their cult activity are often
paired with those of men's military preparations. We might conclude that
part of the vases' project is to negotiate a productive place for women in the
newly democratic state, which can be effectively achieved by stressing not
only women's contributions to child rearing and textile manufacture but
also their important role in ritual practice.

Although women are not provided with images of their specific rituals,
one area of their cult practice that is heavily registered in ceramic images is
their role as mourners. As H. Shapiro points out, the scene of lamentation
for the dead persists throughout the changes in ceramic fashion from the
eighth to the fifth century;[105] women are always prominent in these scenes
and often have particular roles to play. During the course of this period,
however, the representation of mourners, and especially of women, under-
goes several modifications. On the huge Geometric vases of the eighth century, which served as tomb markers, massed ranks of mourners of both sexes

105. Shapiro 1991: 629.

Figure 7. Scene of *prothesis.* Funerary plaque, black-figure, ca. 500 B.C.E., attributed to the Painter of Sappho. Louvre MNB 905. Photo RMN-Hervé Lewandowski. Reproduced with permission.

gather, among whom women sometimes seem to lament more expressively than men, raising two hands to their heads instead of one.[106] Black- and red-figure funerary vessels of the sixth and fifth centuries generally convene fewer people and concentrate on the more private components of the burial process. Since the vase paintings seem to eschew the procession to the tomb and the public scenes of lamentation, especially by women, in favor of a concentration on the *prothesis,* the laying out of the body at home, many scholars have suggested that the new style of scene registers the pressure from Solon's funerary laws (discussed in chapter 1). One ceramic plaque even identifies the mourners not by name but by relationship to the deceased, as if to show that they are family members and thus in conformity with the legislation restricting mourning to close relatives (see fig. 7).[107] In the context of this legislation, however, it is significant that the scenes of mourning that do appear on vases continue to award a special prominence to women, placing them nearer to the corpse and allotting to them the more dramatic expressions of grief. Even though funerary laws deliberately tried to deemphasize the role of women as mourners, the ceramics with which families actually discharged their responsibilities toward the dead can be seen to reassert the importance of women in the mourning process.

The same mechanism of redress can be read in the second half of the

106. Havelock 1981: 109–10.
107. See Shapiro 1991: 631 and fig. 1.

fifth century, when the white-ground lekythos emerges as the funerary vase of choice. Since the paint applied to this type of vessel is fragile and flaky, it seems unlikely that the vases were ever used in the domestic context. Another sign that they were manufactured specifically as offerings for the tomb is that many have a false bottom; they hold not a complete measure of oil or perfume but just a token amount. Since they are found chiefly in graves that have three or more pots placed in them as offerings, Ian Morris suggests that "although white-ground lekythoi were not extremely common, neither were they restricted to a narrow elite group."[108] The most notable feature of the white-ground lekythoi for most commentators, however, is their almost exclusive focus on the role in the mourning process of women, who are usually represented as dignified and restrained in their grief. The characteristic scene is even more restricted than in black- and red-figure vases, consisting of a group of two or three mourners that almost invariably includes women, and the focus of the representation shifts once again to a different moment in the mourning process. While there are a few scenes of the *prothesis* and of the mythology of death, featuring Charon and Hermes, the most important scenes are that of the visit to the grave—sometimes including a vision of the dead person at his or her tomb—and a scene of women at home, which is usually interpreted as a preparation for a tomb visit, and which never includes men.[109]

Why these scenes can be described in terms of "redress" is because they emerge as a significant cultural form in the second quarter of the fifth century, at a point marked not only by the increasing popularity of "genre" scenes of women on women's vases but also by the institution of the Athenian state funeral for the war dead.[110] As is documented most prominently by Nicole Loraux,[111] this institution removed the task of mourning from the private to the public realm and replaced the lamentations by women of the family with the oration over the war dead delivered by the leading public man. In this context it comes as no surprise that the Funeral Oration attributed to Perikles in Thucydides' *Histories* should have included the injunction to women to play no part in the discourses of the city: "The greatest glory of a woman is to be least talked about by men, whether they

108. Morris 1994: 79.

109. Reilly (1989) has argued that these scenes show a bride and her companions preparing for a wedding, and that these vases were placed at the graves of those who died unmarried. While this is a plausible reconstruction in many ways, I do not think it accounts for those scenes that show not one woman being attended by another but two women engaged equally in the task of preparation. Reilly's suggestion that these are women attendants shown without the bride does not convince me.

110. Shapiro 1991: 646–48. There were no private grave stelae erected between about 480 and 440 B.C.E.

111. Loraux 1986.

are praising you or criticizing you" (2.46). Despite this state-sponsored denial of their role as mourners, on funeral vases women are represented at the center of the mourning process; erased from one of the city's discourses, they emerge more insistently into another.[112]

Given the possibility, explored here and elsewhere, that vase painting may register historical women's preferred versions of themselves, we may want to consider the likelihood that the compensatory representation of women on white-ground lekythoi may also be driven to some extent by women's own claims. Since the vases were not used by women but were produced only for the grave, this particular argument can be advanced only so ·far; but what we can say is that despite Solonic legislation and the state funeral, images for domestic consumption continued to allot the chief roles in mourning to women.[113] As the polis moved to displace women in the task of mourning, so the ceramics more insistently registered their traditional role. It is hard to avoid the conclusion that the ceramics in some way represent if not the independent, resistant voice of historical women, then at least a "private" or domestic voice not identical with that of official ideology, and are able instead to value women's contributions to culture and to preserve some aspects of their important role as mourners. Either way, the ceramic evidence encourages the conclusion that their identity as ritual practitioners represented to historical women a significant cultural resource of their own.

One example of their ritual practice that is not offered to women on ceramics for their own use is maenadism. Although a number of vases, the so-called Lenaia vases, show women celebrating in front of a mask of Dionysos, it is not clear that the women are to be understood as maenads, that is, human women entranced and maddened by the worship of Dionysos (see fig. 8).[114] Maenadism as a form of Dionysiac worship is almost invariably confined to women in the period under investigation here, but representa-

112. Holst-Wahrhaft (1992) has a fine account of the move from private lamentation, dominated by women, to public orations, delivered by men, but does not make use of ceramic evidence.

113. It should be noted, however, that the white-ground lekythoi rarely represent women in the throes of emotion; when they do, as in some vases by the late fifth-century Woman Painter, the woman is alone at the grave and so can be read to observe the requirement that she not make her lamentation public. Similarly, the two new scenes favored by the lekythoi, the visit to the tomb and preparations for it, assume that the funeral with its lamentations has taken place, so that the women in these scenes need not be shown grieving extravagantly. Although they implicitly entrust the women with the upkeep of the tomb and the remembrance of the dead, these scenes sidestep the iconographical legacy of earlier ceramics that centered on the women's emotional gestures of lamentation.

114. Discussions of this vexed group of vases include Hamilton 1992: 135–38 and (more briefly) Osborne 1997. Hamilton is inclined to doubt that they constitute a group. There is, as he notes, no consensus as to what if any festival is represented on these ceramics. Frontisi-Ducroux (1991), declining to identify any festival represented on the vases, concentrates instead on the unusual frontality of the god-mask and on the exchange of gazes thus facilitated between god and worshipper.

Figure 8. "Lenaia" vase, Dionysian scene showing women celebrating at an image of Dionysos. Exterior of Attic red-figure stamnos, mid-5th century B.C., attributed to the Chicago Painter. Terracotta. Gift of Gilbert M. Denman, Jr. 86.134.64. Courtesy of the San Antonio Museum of Art.

tions of it on Attic ceramics are equally confined to the "male" shapes of symposium vases.[115] So close is the connection that Cornelia Isler-Kerényi claims the Dionysos of the vases is identified with men rather than with women.[116] Robin Osborne shows that maenad scenes peaked in the late sixth century and in the fourth, while during the "drop-off" period of the fifth they were confined to large (= symposium?) vases.[117] Since the scene of maenadism is not so prominent on fifth-century ceramics and is not unequivocally offered to women, it will not form a large part of my discus-

115. Henrichs (1984) argues cogently against male maenads, at least for the classical period. He claims that by the Hellenistic period there was participation in maenadic rites by both sexes, but he bases this claim largely on his translation of the word *kataibaton* in an inscription from Magnesia on the Maeander (*I Mag* 215). If this word denotes a group of people in a *thiasos*, then as a masculine plural it does indicate male participation in maenadic celebrations. However, in his more recent translation of the inscription for the second edition of *WLGR*, Henrichs translates the relevant passage as "the *thiasos* named after Cataebates," which does not commit us to a *thiasos* comprised of men and women jointly.

116. Isler-Kerényi 1991.

117. Osborne 1997.

sion here, but two observations may be in order on the possible symbolic value of the painted maenads on symposium vases. (The next section of this chapter will deal in more detail with the nature of historical maenadism.)

Scholars agree that the troupe or train accompanying Dionysos, as represented on early black-figure vases, consisted largely of satyrs, quasi-human creatures with animal ears and tail and usually in a state of advanced sexual excitement. While they may be accompanied by women, the latter are not clearly distinguished by maenadic attributes such as the thyrsus (a special long wand) or the fawnskin. The maenad proper only starts to differentiate herself around the beginning of the fifth century, which is also when the popular scenes of sexual hostility between maenad and satyr begin to appear.[118] Prior to this period, nonmaenadic women and satyrs dance amicably in pairs or large groups.[119] F. Lissarrague has convincingly identified the new antithesis between satyr and maenad with a famous amphora in Munich by the Kleophrades Painter and dated a few years after 500 B.C.E. (*ARV* 182/6; see fig. 9). Since the painting takes the form of a frieze that runs all the way around the amphora, instead of being confined to two panels, it is perhaps not correct to describe it as two scenes or sides; but in one group the figure of Dionysos seems to occupy the central space, holding a wine jug *(kantharos)* and flanked by two satyr-maenad pairs in which the maenad repulses a sexual advance from the satyr. On the other side, a satyr plays the double flute *(aulos)*, facing frontally out of the vase and thereby displaying his characteristically enormous erection. Flanking him are two maenads, for whom he presumably plays. "Each maenad is lost in a private experience, one, snake-wreathed, in gentle reverie; the other in wild abandon, with flung back head."[120] As Lissarrague points out, the vase divides up the "gifts" of Dionysos, namely wine, sex, music, and trance, and distributes them between maenads and satyrs with strict discrimination.[121] In what follows I shall briefly pursue the themes of "sex" and "trance," identified with satyr and maenad respectively, and consider the possible significance of the maenad figure for the predominantly male audience of the symposium vases.

The first twenty to thirty years of the fifth century are marked by a series of cups and other vessels, particularly by the Kleophrades Painter, the Brygos Painter, Makron, and Douris, which play on the dramatic possibili-

118. See Lissarrague 1991: 267. Many commentators argue that the newly defined iconography of these maenads registers real changes in Bacchic practices among historical women. See, for example, Henrichs 1978: 144.

119. Macnally 1978: 116–19.

120. Ibid., 127.

121. Lissarrague 1991: 259. Lissarrague (1993: 215) similarly points out that satyrs do not engage in trance or sacrificial violence.

Figure 9. Dionysos and maenads. Pointed amphora by the Kleophrades Painter. *ARV* 182/6, Munich 2344. Reproduced with permission from the Staatliche Antikensammlungen und Glyptothek München.

ties of sexually hostile encounters between maenad and satyr. Two scenes seem to have caught the early fifth-century imagination: that of the satyrs who creep up on or more actively molest a sleeping maenad, and that of the maenad who defends herself with a strategically aimed thyrsus. A significant characteristic of these scenes is their momentary quality; given that they cannot tell a complete narrative, and that "the issue is in doubt,"[122] the viewer is emphatically drawn into supplying the discursive content of the scene. A cup by Makron from about 480 B.C.E. (*ARV* 461/36) shows on one side a sleeping maenad accosted by satyrs, but on the other side a maenad who starts to get up and brandish her thyrsus. There is no way to decide whether or not the satyrs succeed in their harassing mission.[123] An earlier amphora by Oltos (*ARV* 53/2) entrusts the narrative even more teasingly to the

122. Macnally 1978: 129.

123. That is, unless we conclude that the "sleeping" scene is second and that the maenad's eyes are closed in sexual ecstasy . . .

Figure 10. Naked woman tying sandal. Attic red-
figure amphora, 525–515 B.C.E., by Oltos. *ARV*
53/2, Louvre G2. Photo RMN-Hervé Lewandowski.
Reproduced with permission.

viewer. On each side a hopeful satyr grabs at a brawny maenad well
equipped to resist his advances; neither image is conclusive about his success or failure. On the neck of the amphora, the question of the direction
of the narrative is re-posed: a naked woman, presumably a *hetaira*, is tying
her sandal (see fig. 10). Or is she untying it? Pornography here may well be
in the eye of the beholder.

The erotic equivocation of the vases can also constitute a joke at the
expense of the viewer. A hydria by the Kleophrades Painter (*ARV* 188/61)
bears on its shoulder a scene of a sleeping maenad (identified as such by her
thyrsus) whose garment is being lifted by an ithyphallic satyr, who also
gropes for her thigh. Another satyr kneels behind the first and seems to
stare down in surprise at his own erection (see fig. 11). What is intriguing
about this picture is that the maenad is arranged to be exposed to viewer as
well as to satyr. If the viewer is implicitly identified with the scopophilic satyr,
then the vase can be read as a joke against him; scanning the symposium

Figure 11. Sleeping maenad and satyrs. Detail of red-figure hydria, ca. 500 B.C., by the Kleophrades Painter. Terracotta. *ARV* 188/68. Reproduced with permission from the Musée des Antiquités, Rouen.

vases for lewd images, he is rewarded with the exposure of the maenad but simultaneously sees himself reduced to a hairy satyr.[124]

An equation between the satyr and the male human viewer can be pursued further. As Lissarrague has shown, satyrs on vases engage in a variety of human activities, and some vases offer two similar scenes, one a "straight" version occupied by human men and the second a cartoon involving satyrs.[125] More likely than any other single figure to stare frontally out of the vase,[126] the satyr engages the human viewer closely despite his various bestial characteristics. Chief among these is his ludicrously exaggerated sexual drive, which as many commentators point out, is never satisfied; he strives but can never attain. In this context we may note that Keuls has related the

124. Carpenter (1986: 85) describes a vase that displays a picture of a "satyr-molesting-sleeping-maenad" vase. See now on the sleeping maenad Osborne 1996 and Frontisi-Ducroux 1996. This chapter took its final form before the appearance of these essays.

125. Lissarrague 1990b and 1993; 1990b: 232–33.

126. See Lissarrague 1993: 219 on the satyr's curious gaze.

iconographical scheme of the sleeping maenad to the mythical paradigm of
Dionysos discovering the sleeping Ariadne.[127] Since the molesting satyrs are
rarely shown consummating their desires, their relation to the paradigm
can perhaps be seen to represent them as constantly striving after a divine
bliss that they are unable to achieve. In this inability they contrast strongly
with maenads, who are shown entranced and possessed by the god but who
perform few other human actions; satyrs never enter a trance, and instead
they are often represented as literally instrumental to the maenadic possession, playing the music that allows the maenads to experience the god.[128]
One consequence of this distinction is that maenads, unlike satyrs and even
Dionysos himself, rarely engage the viewer by turning to the outside of the
vase;[129] since they achieve trance by means other than that of wine, they do
not need to become even a symbolic part of the human symposium in order
to experience the ecstasy of the god.

This division of labor corresponds to that obtaining in archaic, classical,
and probably Hellenistic culture, whereby women were subject to Bacchic
mania and men in general were not. Although the symposium vases do not
attempt to offer a realistic depiction of Dionysiac worship, their allotment of
trance only to maenads may be significant in relation to the presumably male
viewer who scans the vase. If he is to be identified, however unstably, with the
satyr, then he is presented with a caricature of his own reaction to the gift of
Dionysos—drunkenness and lust—in contrast to that of another figure, the
maenad, whose intoxication is of quite another order. Given that both figures
are presented for his consumption, it may be productive to read the maenad
as mediating between the viewer who is present at the symposium and the
god whom he worships; representing a more radical response to the god
than is predicated of either the male human viewer or the satyr whom he
more nearly resembles, she makes it symbolically available to him. The
painted maenads can thus be seen to conform to the model that we have outlined before, insofar as the particular characteristics of their female identity
position them to mediate between men and divinity.[130]

A brief examination of the maenads represented on Attic vases, particularly in their relation to both satyrs and the posited male viewer, has led to

127. Keuls 1985: 366.

128. Examples include a kalpis of the early fifth century by the same painter (*ARV* 189,
73), a cup by the Brygos Painter of the 480s–470s (*ARV* 371, 15), a cup by the Briseis Painter
(follower of the Brygos Painter) (*ARV* 406, 2), and a cup by the Telephos Painter of the 460s
(*ARV* 819, 44) (all of these are illustrated in Boardman 1975). There is a similar division of
labor in some modern possession cults; Giles (1987: 243) notes that in some African cults, men
may be involved chiefly as musicians.

129. Korshak (1987: 65) notes four who do. Frontisi-Ducroux (1991) stresses the significance of the god's constant outward turn from the vase to the human viewer.

130. See Schlesier 1993: 98 and 101 for a related argument on the maenad as female
model for male activity.

a familiar conclusion about the advantages of women's ritual activity for the male-centered culture of classical Athens. In the practice of maenadism, however, many commentators have discerned a striking instance of historical women's ability to develop ritual forms that answered their own needs and that positioned them to challenge effectively the varieties of subjection characterizing their lives. Other scholars, however, insist that the experience of maenadism was only "a half-hearted rebellion,"[131] or that its allotment to women, rather than to men, ultimately served the interests of patriarchal culture by enabling men to refuse their own raw meat while letting the women eat it for them.[132] In the third investigation undertaken by this chapter I shall examine the significance of maenadism and other "ecstatic" forms of ritual practice as resources for historical women.

THE AUTHORITY OF POSSESSION

The figure of the maenad, which Froma Zeitlin has read as a dominant Greek metaphor for the feminine,[133] is complex not only in her iconography but also in what we can reconstruct of her historical practice. Although maenadic experience may have been available to women throughout the historical and geographical span of Greek culture, the most compelling representations of it emerge in the vase painting and drama of fifth-century Athens. Euripides' *Bakchai* is for us the lone survivor of a number of plays that seem to have featured maenadic women,[134] but has attained paradigmatic status in its representation of maenadism. Possessed and maddened by Dionysos, the women of Thebes, led by the princesses Agave, Ino, and Autonoe, leave the city for the mountains, where they suckle the young of animals instead of their own babies, handle snakes, wear fawnskins, live on milk and honey that they strike from the bare ground with the thyrsus, and spend their time singing and dancing in praise of the god. When attacked by the Thebans, the maenads not only defeat the men but go on to terrorize the nearby villages by tearing apart their cattle in an act of *sparagmos* (dismembering). They are invulnerable to weapons and can carry fire on their heads without burning. Finally they deal with the Theban ruler Pentheus, who is Agave's son, by subjecting him to the *sparagmos* while under the delusion that he is a mountain lion. In the final moments of the play, before she has emerged from her trance, Agave is made to glorify in her new role of lion-hunter precisely by contrasting it to the reserved domestic existence

131. Bremmer 1984: 285.
132. Zeitlin 1982a: 138.
133. Ibid., 135.
134. For example, Aeschylus *Bakchai, Pentheus, Semele*. See also Osborne 1997: 192 and Dodds 1960: xxviii–xxxiii. We should note that Euripides *Bakchai* was composed in Macedon, not in Athens.

usually prescribed for women. When she invites the chorus to join her in feasting there is an unmistakable threat of cannibalism and *omophagia* (eating of raw meat, in defiance of all Greek alimentary codes), but she is eventually returned to sanity by the persuasive speech of her father, Kadmos.

Despite this compelling fifth-century representation of maenadic practices and of their possible significance for women participants, several commentators have doubted whether the experiences of historical women ever remotely corresponded to that of the Euripidean maenads. Some scholars argue that there were in fact no historical human maenads, no real women who underwent Dionysiac possession, but most commentators espouse "weaker" versions of the argument to question various aspects of maenadism. While few would argue that historical women regularly killed their children or suckled animals, as Agave and her sisters do in the *Bakchai,* questions have been raised as to whether they handled fire and ate raw meat,[135] convened in maenadic groups *(thiasoi)* that were as undifferentiated socially as the drama claims, or underwent a trance of possession by the god. A further objection leveled against the Euripidean paradigm of maenadism is that no corroborating testimony survives from archaic or classical culture; the "hard" evidence, such as that from inscriptions, emerges only in the Hellenistic period. Since such testimony exhibits continuities with the Euripidean representation, however, some of the skepticism may be misplaced. The epitaph of Alkmeonis, the third-century priestess of Dionysos at Miletos, claims that she led the "Bakchai of the city" *eis oros,* "to the mountain," thus replicating the scene of the Theban maenads' worship in the *Bakchai.* A further cultic regulation from Miletos makes a cryptic reference to the practice of eating raw meat. When the priestess sacrifices on behalf of the city, no one is to *omophagion emballein* before she has done so (*LSAM* 48.2–3). While *emballein* should connote "to throw in" or "put down," *omophagion,* object of the verb, is more obscure; the morphology of the word connects it to the eating of raw meat celebrated in *Bakchai* 138, but at Miletos it is not clear who if anyone ate what. Although Albert Henrichs concludes that "the alleged omophagy at Miletus was nothing but a peculiar type of Dionysiac sacrifice,"[136] the issue is not so clear-cut, and we should in any case register the possibility that participants experienced the ritual as something other than just another sacrifice. Given the potency of "raw meat" as a metaphor for everything opposed to and outside the ideology of the civilized polis, the significance of even a decorous ritual gesture may have resided in its implied offer to jettison a fundamental tenet of Greek identity, the eating of cooked as opposed to raw meat.

The dismissal of the omophagy is not the only strategy by which contemporary scholars seek to downplay the significance of maenadism for

135. Bremmer 1984.
136. Henrichs 1978: 151.

historical women. Some suggest that historical maenadism was restricted to an elite and therefore could not represent (what otherwise seems historically plausible) a response by women to deprived lives. J. N. Bremmer claims that "wherever we have more detailed information about them, maenads appear to belong to the elite," and Keuls also suggests that historical maenads, at least in the fifth century, were "ladies of a certain class."[137] These critics suggest, then, that since "maenads" seem to have been drawn from the upper strata of society, maenadism could not be a result of any kind of oppression. While this conclusion is itself arguable (upper-class women could be oppressed by upper-class men, for instance), I would also point out that the epigraphical prominence of "elite" maenads does not rule out the historical possibility of maenads of lower status. Although we should not read the *Bakchai* as a historical account of women's maenadic practices, the arguments canvassed so far do not, to my mind, disprove maenadic participation by women of varying social status, and certainly do not offer reasons to dismiss the possible significance to such women of that participation.

Scholars also express skepticism about other aspects of the ritual pratice. Henrichs questions the nature of Dionysiac possession and concludes that "it cannot be demonstrated that 'madness' understood as an abnormal psychological state was an authentic quality of the historical maenad. . . . The peculiar religious identity of the maenads had more to do with sweat and physical exhaustion than with an abnormal state of mind."[138] Henrichs's argument is directed against the tradition associated with the work of E. R. Dodds and has been challenged by a study by Bremmer, which deploys the discourse of neurophysiology in order to reinstate "madness" without having to accept Dodds's theories of "collective hysteria."[139] What disables Henrichs's argument against maenadic "madness" or trance from the outset, however, is the opposition he constructs between "Greek ritual in general," on the one hand, which is "repetitive and stereotyped, externalizing and unreflecting . . . a studious re-enactment of an inherited response," and "personal expression of inner feelings or religious sentiment," on the other.[140] If maenadic possession lines up with the second, the argument

137. Bremmer 1984: 284; Keuls 1985: 360.Keuls bases her statement on the clothing assigned to maenads in vase paintings, but such clothing is not necessarily a realistic representation. Graf (1993: 255) similarly stresses the apparent elite status of known female followers of Dionysos. He refers especially to the burials of women found with gold "lamellae," or plates, on their bosoms, which show them to have been initiated into the "mysteries" (*telete*) of Dionysos. Whether these were maenadic in the fashion of the *Bakchai* is not yet clear. On such plates see Johnston and McNiven 1996.

138. Henrichs 1982: 146–47.

139. Bremmer 1984: 267.

140. Henrichs 1982: 144, 145.

assumes, it can have no part in the first, and vice versa. Modern anthropological work, however, posits no such disjunction between the trance of possession and behaviors that are organized, socialized, even ritualized. In this
debate the findings of E. Bourguignon are important;[141] out of 488 societies
studied, 90 percent were analyzed as displaying altered states of consciousness that took a more or less institutionalized form. "The West of the present day is quite unusual by world standards in radically devaluing the
trance state," observes Michael Lambek.Although forms of possession vary
from society to society, within one culture possession takes a more or less
standardized form; Lambek suggests that insofar as the contours of any
individual possession trance conform to a culture's available models, it
constitutes a learned behavior rather than an ungoverned "personal
expression."[142]

A more fundamental argument on the topic questions not simply
whether human women, maenads, experienced anything like the maenadism of the *Bakchai,* but whether there were fifth-century maenads at all:
in other words, do the images on the vases and in the *Bakchai* actually show
human women, or are these "maenads" beings of a purely imaginary order?
T. H. Carpenter, for instance, writing on the archaic vases of Attica,
describes a move in iconography from nymphs to maenads proper, with
fawnskin and thyrsus.[143] Later, however, writing on the vases of the fifth century, he concludes that such vases show no maenads, that is, no entranced
human worshippers of Dionysos. Instead, all apparently maenadic representations must be held to show nymphs, nonhuman beings.[144] (The Lydian
women of the *Bakchai*'s chorus are similarly redefined.)[145] While Carpenter
does not proceed to query the reports of maenadism in other kinds of
sources (e.g., epigraphical), his work does seem to situate itself in the skeptical tradition that we are discussing. Carpenter types attempts by other
scholars to discern human, maenadic women on vases as "troubling in the
way they require the merging of mythic and cultic traditions."[146] As with
Henrichs, we see an effort to separate out categories, of myth and of lived
cultic experience, which Webster and Beard, for example, have already concluded are on vases thoroughly intertwined. Against Carpenter's overall
position I would invoke the work of Robin Osborne, who shows that "the
artist's frame of reference includes both life and myth, life imitating myth

141. Bourguignon 1973.
142. Lambek 1981: 6.
143. Carpenter 1986. On this shift see also Edwards 1960. The "nymphs" are most familiar from the François Vase (*ABV* 76.1).
144. Carpenter 1997. Hedreen (1994) independently came to a similar conclusion, which
is effectively countered by Osborne (1997: 197).
145. Carpenter 1997: 109.
146. Ibid., 67.

and myth imitating life." [147] He deploys a complex argument concerning the Lenaia vases mentioned above that points to "the reality of ecstatic cult in both archaic and classical Athens," but he also, and perhaps for my purposes more significantly, invokes the comparative context: it is the maenads' experience of oneness with divinity that is imaged on pots and in the *Bakchai*, and it is this that "invites comparison between maenads and ecstatic cults elsewhere."[148] Given the historicity of ecstatic possession in other cultures, that is, there is a strong presumption that maenadism was a historic condition. If we adopt the nonskeptical position, and if we accept the import of the comparative evidence, what will such comparison enable us to say about the maenads of ancient Greece?

One theory of possession that has conditioned much feminist work on maenadism is that associated with the anthropological work of I. M. Lewis. Drawing on studies of several cultures, Lewis concluded that possession constitutes an oblique strategy of aggression that disadvantaged, marginalized members of a given society deploy to exert an anomalous and illegitimate, if only temporary, power over dominant members.[149] The strategy is successful because it is never pursued too far, but remains the object of a constant negotiation; dominant members of the society indulge the victim of possession with the special attention and cooperation necessary to manage the episode, but the social hierarchies persist and prevent the peripheral member from being elevated, by possession, to a position where possession would be no longer necessary. Given that possession is most prevalent in hierarchical societies, and that women are always and everywhere more prone to it than men, Lewis's model has obvious explanatory power, and it has been deployed by both Ross Kraemer and Froma Zeitlin to account for Greek maenadism.[150] In this context it may be significant that some of the Greek narratives about allegedly historical maenads represent them precisely as powerless. In Plutarch *De Primo Frigido* 953D maenadic women from Athens and Delphi, celebrating in the mountains, are cut off by a snowstorm and have to be rescued by a male search party, while in *Virtues of Women* 13 (249), as we have seen, the maenads from Delphi are exposed to attack in Amphissa. These narratives can, moreover, be read to work a systematic reversal on the dominant tropes of the *Bakchai* (whether consciously or not is irrelevant for this particular analysis): instead of being impervious to fire, these maenads are overcome by cold; instead of being self-sufficient, as

---

147. Osborne 1997: 194. Osborne also takes to task on this issue Versnel 1990, a book that is itself more sympathetic to maenads as historical and maenadism as a genuine possession experience.

148. Osborne 1997: 208.

149. Lewis 1971: 32.

150. Kraemer 1979; Zeitlin 1982a.

Agave boasts, they rely on male help; and instead of being alert to the possibility of male intrusions, like the Theban maenads on the mountain, they fall asleep in an enemy town.

While feminist analyses of maenadism that explicitly derive from Lewis have been criticized within the field of classics, the theory of marginality and disadvantage, or "deprivation theory," has itself come under fire within the discipline of anthropology.[151] Alice Kehoe and Dody Giletti, for instance, stress that women are not always construed as peripheral, and question the notions of both "aggression" and "stratagem."[152] Another analytic position, which may be discerned in the work of Lambek, Linda Giles, and Janice Boddy, questions the "deprivation theory" more closely by identifying it as "a classic but unhappily androcentric portrayal of women, who are forever seen as *re*acting to men rather than acting for themselves within a specific cultural context."[153] Anita Spring suggested earlier that possession rituals might "constitute the basis for membership in a female community of specialists, with models of society separate from men."[154] Elaborating a more explicitly gynocentric theory of possession, Giles proposes that "women perceive the [Swahili possession] cult as a means of establishing contact with powerful forces which are crucial to society. . . . The cult is not a protest against male domination but a positive assertion of female value."[155] Of particular importance to this contemporary work on possession is the conclusion that a possession trance is a demanding, laborious experience that not only must be learned but also cannot be negotiated by subjects who are already disturbed or otherwise in a weakened state. Lambek, writing of the Mayotte (who inhabit an island off southern Africa, claimed by France), concludes: "Successful participation requires the engagement of a self-control that may be greater than severely disturbed individuals can manage"; and Boddy, on the zar cult of Northern Sudan, concurs: "Successful negotiation of the possession context requires the patient to have or develop considerable cultural awareness. It is thus inapplicable to those who suffer

151. Kraemer (1979) builds on Lewis's analysis to suggest further that those attracted to maenadism were not only female, and therefore marginalized and disadvantaged by definition, but also were often at a critical and vulnerable period in their lives, such as the onset of motherhood or old age. Her findings have been criticized by Bremmer (1984: 284) and Graf (1993: 255), among others, who reiterate the charge that maenads were of elite status and so could not have been "marginal" or "disadvantaged."

152. Kehoe and Giletti 1981. Kehoe and Giletti (1981) propose that possession commonly results from calcium deficiency, which is characteristic of women's diets in societies that strictly regulate dietary distinctions between men and women.

153. Boddy 1989: 140. See, in general, Lambek 1981 and Giles 1987 as well as Boddy 1989.

154. Spring 1978: 167.

155. Giles 1987: 235–36.

severe psychological disturbance."[156] If the Greek maenads who emerge into historical records do often seem to derive from elite backgrounds, it may be that their social status equipped them with the poise and control necessary for productive maenadic participation.

What is stressed by recent work on possession is not only the poise of the women concerned but also the intellectual and creative possibilities of the experience. Lambek remarks that "in Mayotte the juxtaposition of human culture and spirit culture . . . is essentially constructive, providing a fertile field for the generation of novel intellectual and emotional experience."[157] Combating the view, which she attributes to "Western scholars," that possession is "a consequence of women's deprivation rather than their privilege, or perhaps their inclination," Boddy's work concentrates on possession as a "subtle restructuring of women's perceptions."[158] As Boddy stresses, the possession ritual "hints, and hints ambiguously," offering itself as a text that may be read differently by different participants, so that it is always possible for an individual participant to gain a new perspective on her own experience and a new "consciousness of her own position in society."[159] In particular, the ritual of zar possession functions as "a powerful medium for unchaining thought from the fetters of hegemonic cultural constructs," because it plays on the antitheses of the norms that usually govern Sudanese village women's life.[160] Instead of respecting the orientation of the Sudanese woman toward "enclosure"—the interior of her body, house, family, and village—zar possession requires her to become open to other versions of reality, encouraging her to become aware of the constructed nature of those conventions that organize her existence. Since Dionysiac maenadism similarly offers to invert the Greek tropes of female identity, by disassociating the woman from her domestic environment and from her customary approved behaviors, it may have served Greek women in the ways that Boddy outlines for her Sudanese subjects. If possession is understood along these lines, as an intellectually productive experience that requires for its successful performance women with poise and intact subjectivity, then it may be possible to modify accounts of maenadism that identify it with "rebellion," or even "half-hearted rebellion,"[161] on the part of women rendered abject by their lives and maddened by a departure from them. Instead, we could see maenadic possession as a cultural resource for women

---

156. Lambek 1981: 52; Boddy 1989: 147.
157. Lambek 1981: 10.
158. Boddy 1989: 140, 339.
159. Ibid., 338, 340.
160. Ibid., 356.
161. Bremmer 1984: 285.

that could afford them an intellectual or creative experience as well as "respite"[162] or "release"[163] from a subordinate existence.

A further gynocentric hypothesis about the significance of possession is offered by the cross-cultural work of Susan Sered on religions dominated by women. Sered notes first that men's experience of possession is often that of the shamanic type, whereby the subject seems to himself to leave the body, whereas women seem to themselves (and to observers) to incarnate another being. Second, Sered draws on the analyses of Nancy Chodorow and Carol Gilligan, who posit that women's development in cultures characterized by gender inequality often leads them to value connection more than separation, and consequently to develop more permeable ego boundaries than those deemed appropriate for men. Sered can thus suggest that a disposition to possession may be as much a product of women's socialization as is a disposition toward motherhood: "The same process that constructs adult women who seek to share their bodies with their babies, also sometimes constructs adult women who willingly share their bodies with spirits, ancestors or gods."[164] Relevant to this hypothesis is the observation, valid also for Dionysiac maenads, that most possession cults target adult married women rather than unmarried girls. It has been convincingly argued that for Greek culture the maenad is not only a powerful antithetical representation of the feminine itself but also, specifically, of the married woman.[165] While this cross-cultural constant of the association between marriage and possession could be explained by deprivation theory, on the grounds that marriage and motherhood introduce the woman to new levels of stress and hardship, Boddy interprets marriage as a necessary precursor to the intellectual labor of possession: "It is only in the context of full feminine consciousness—sexually active, reproductive—that the allegorical messages of the zar can have their sharpest impact."[166] If the work of possession is to "place an alternative construction on lived experience without denying the validity of culturally salient categories,"[167] then the woman must be fully positioned within those categories in order to be able to engage productively with the experience of possession.

Despite the force of these recent gynocentric analyses of possession, the prevalence of possession in cultures that are hierarchical rather than egalitarian still indicates that sexual hierarchy, and its concomitant disad-

162. Kraemer 1979: 78.

163. Zeitlin 1982a: 113.

164. Sered 1994: 190.

165. See, for example, Seaford 1995: 301–11. As we have seen in chapter 3, Diodorus Siculus 4.3.2–3 notes that in many Greek cities maenadic *gynaikes,* or adult women, sacrifice and praise the god, while *parthenoi* carry the thyrsus.

166. Boddy 1989: 341.

167. Ibid., 340.

vantaging of women, may be understood as a necessary condition for women's possession.[168] Lambek suggests that Mayotte women are predisposed to possession by experience of the cultural contradiction that requires them to work hard but represents them nonetheless as fundamentally irresponsible, [169] and Boddy similarly suggests that possession emerges from women's "double consciousness," whereby they become aware that the social system, which they are committed to uphold, also exploits them.[170] Several recent studies conclude, moreover, that in many contemporary Muslim societies the possession cults dominated by women help to define reciprocally the male role in Islam, which allots to men responsible self-control, deliberation, and the maintenance of strict ego boundaries.[171] For men to be possessed would be dangerous and detrimental to the society as a whole; to women, then, is assigned the "symbolic expression of all the 'others,' . . . the unarticulated aspects of the whole society,"[172] which may take precedence over the specific complaints and grievances of the disadvantaged, marginalized group. In the same way, Greek maenadism has been understood as a projection onto women of the categories of the wild and irrational that Greek gender ideology rejected for men.[173] As in the case of other rituals studied here, however, the role of participant women as subjects of the ritual process, as well as its objects, suggests that men are not the only determinants of the meaning women might find in their cultic practices. We have already seen, for instance, the enthusiasm of Lysistrata's friends for Dionysiac celebrations (Aristophanes *Lysistrata* 1–3l; see also chapter 3), and even in the discourse of the "hard" epigraphical testimony, women can be found who are willing to pay for the privilege of sacrificing to Dionysos, or of initiating worshippers "in the city, in the country, or in the islands" (*LSAM* 48.18–19, an early third-century inscription from Miletos on the responsibilities of the priestess). In these testimonies women act with spontaneity and relative autonomy and presumably find in the Dionysiac celebrations a valued resource.

Since the figure of the maenad is overdetermined by various anxieties in Greek culture, and since modern anthropological work does not allow us to retrieve the subjective experiences of women participants in maenadism, it may be appropriate to examine briefly another form of possession familiar

---

168. See Bourguignon 1973.

169. Lambek 1981: 68. Lambek also draws on the work of Chodorow to explicate women's possession (see Lambek 1981: 68 n. 14).

170. Boddy 1989: 346. This is not the same "double consciousness" as that in Winkler 1990a, although the two doubles are certainly related.

171. Lambek 1981: 661–62.

172. Giles 1987: 249.

173. Zeitlin 1982a: 138, paraphrased above.

to Greek culture, namely that of the Delphic Pythia.[174] The only system-atized account of the Pythia's possession is provided by Plutarch *Why Are Delphic Oracles No Longer in Verse?* and *Oracles in Decline* (henceforth *Verse* and *Decline*), which date from the second century C.E., and which subtend the polemical design of defending the oracle from charges that it has fallen into decline. Nonetheless, we can probably assume that the relevant passages have some significance for a general understanding of the Pythia's posses-sion, even for the period under discussion in this study. Dramatically differ-ent from the experience of the maenad, the Pythia's role in the oracular possession was modeled, Giulia Sissa has argued,[175] on an idealized Greek marriage whereby the prophetic woman was always pregnant with the god's words, yet simultaneously always a virgin, available to the god and forbidden to all other males. If the maenad is an antiwife, the Pythia is a wife writ large. According to Plutarch, however, more is involved in the scene of oracular possession than a posture of wifely submission.

At several points in the two dialogues the possession of the Pythia is differ-entiated from models that might support a simple hierarchy; the relationship between Pythia and god is expressly distinguished from that of an actor and prompt who is "speaking out of masks" (*Verse* 404B) and from that of a ven-triloquist (*Decline* 414E). Instead of submitting to a hierarchical relationship, the woman is said to supply voice, utterance, diction, and meter for the prophecies, while the deity is credited with providing *fantasiai*, which we might translate as images, and a "light in the soul oriented toward the future" (*Verse* 397C). Inspiration, or *enthousiasmos,* is said to consist in precisely this, the *fantasiai* and the light in the soul, but later in this dialogue the account is modified so that the experience of *enthousiasmos* is seen to be the product of two elements, the external force at work upon the Pythia and the nature of the Pythia herself (*Verse* 404F). Without the Pythia's disposition toward inspi-ration, the prophetic process could not take place, any more than the unmu-sical could be moved musically or the illiterate by literature (*Verse* 405A). This argument is seconded in *Decline* by the observation that were the prophetic "breath" or "exhalation" *(pneuma)* to produce inspiration in everyone indis-criminately, as allegedly happened in the very early history of the oracle, then it would be foolish to employ one woman alone for the task of prophecy and to harass her *(pragmata parechein)* with the necessary restrictions on her life.[176]

---

174. Maurizio (1995) also argues for the relevance of a cross-cultural understanding of "spirit possession" for our accounts of the Pythia's prophetic practice. Against the skeptical view often articulated in the secondary literature, she notes that "the Pythia at Delphi produced utterances that are a genuine expression of a cultural system which believed in and codified behaviours and speech that it understood as indicating the presence of the divine" (1995: 79).

175. Sissa 1990.

176. In line with these aspects of Plutarch's text, Maurizio (1995: 86) comments that "to

Within the scenario of prophetic possession, then, the Pythia appears as an active component necessary for and complementary to the activity of the god. Toward the end of *Decline* (437D) the final speaker offers a further account of the Pythia's contribution to the experience of prophecy:

> For many annoyances and disturbances that she perceives, and many more that are obscure, lay hold upon her body and seep into her soul; and whenever she is full of these, it is better that she should not go there and should not give herself over to the god.

Since the Pythia is ascribed here a self-monitoring faculty that makes her aware of some, if not all, of the psychic disturbances that might interfere with her proper functioning as oracle, it is possible to read the Pythia in Plutarch's texts as endowed with a blend of innate aptitudes and subsequent training that together equip her to perform successfully. Although the sacrificial goat must be employed in order to ascertain, from its responses, whether the occasion is properly auspicious for prophecy, the Pythia is made responsible for at least part of her state of mind as she "descends" (*katelthein,* the technical term) and prepares for the oracular session. In *Verse* 408, the Pythia is further attributed a self-conscious, self-monitoring attitude toward her task when she is said to be "noble in character" and to care more for the proper discharge of her duties than for "men's praise or blame." She thus transcends Perikles' notorious dictum in the Thucydidean Funeral Oration (book 2), which adjures women to avoid being spoken of by men, whether in praise or blame.

Two episodes in the history of the Delphic institution may serve to corroborate this representation of the active, engaged, and self-monitoring Pythia. *Decline* 438 famously recounts the death of a Pythia who was required to "descend" and prophesy even though the omens given by the sacrificial goat were desperately unfavorable. Since the abnormal session that resulted became the paradigm for later literary versions of normal prophetic possession, such as the account of the Sibyl in Virgil *Aeneid* 6, most interest in this passage has concentrated on the representation of the Pythia under duress, rasping and shrieking. What may also be of interest, however, is that the Pythia is described as going down "unwillingly and reluctantly" (438B), so that it seems as if she either knew from her own subjective experience that the time was not auspicious, or else respected the signs given by the goat and resented the priests' insistence. Either way, the Pythia may be read as actively engaged with and committed to the techniques of her oracular task, collapsing only when others disrupt the proper management of the prophetic scenario. On another occasion, narrated in Plutarch *Alexander*

---

remove the Pythia from the centre of this religious drama and deny her agency is to render the spectacle of consulting Apollo incomprehensible."

14.4, the Pythia declined to "descend" for Alexander because it was not the right time.[177] Refusing to compromise the requirements of her office, the Pythia emerges even more clearly from this episode as responsible, in part at least, for the success of the session, and self-consciously aware of her responsibility.

Various accounts of possession, both in Greek sources and in modern anthropological literature, indicate that far from offering a simple primal "release," the experience of possession is usually structured and learned; and rather than diminishing or negating the subjectivity of the woman concerned, the experience can provide a demanding intellectual engagement that requires poise and self-control from the participant. These aspects of possession notwithstanding, however, its characteristic association with hierarchies of gender suggests that it may be best understood as a resource with which women negotiate and resist their subordination, not only by engaging in alternative behaviors but also by cultivating alternative perceptions of themselves and their role within society. One alternative perception might be of the female as authoritative speaker, and this version is clearly available in the persona of the Pythia. In the last part of this discussion of maenadism and possession, I want to examine some ways in which Dionysiac cult offers authority to women. The exercise of authority need not, of course, take place at the exact same moment as the trance (and the classical period, when maenadism is most strikingly attested, offers only one account of "authority"), but I want to stress how Dionysiac practice makes available these two very different versions of female identity, both of which may have been particularly significant to historical women. We have already noted in chapter 3 the Theban women who leave home and travel to Asia Minor to lead the *thiasoi* there, the Elean women said to confront a tyrant, and the women of Amphissa recorded as protecting the Delphic maenads. A similar commitment to their Dionysiac practice can be read in Pausanias's account of his encounter with the Thyiades. We have encountered these women in our account in chapter 2 of the Arrhephoria, where they represented for us the possibility of female "native informants." Supplying the historian with information that elucidates details of the text of Homer as well as of their cult, the Thyiades suggest that their practice positions them not only to negotiate the constraints of their lives but also to develop a consciousness of a specifically female tradition (10.4.3):

> The former passage, in which Homer speaks of Panopeus with the beautiful dancing-floors, I could not explain until I learned from the women whom the Athenians call Thyiades. The Thyiades are Attic women, who go to

---

177. Fontenrose (1978: 227) doubts that this event is historical, but its occurrence in Plutarch's narrative may still constitute evidence for the Greek perception of the Pythia.

Parnassos every other year, and they and the Delphic women hold the celebrations in honor of Dionysos. It is the custom for these Thyiades, along the road from Athens, to hold dances in various places, including Panopeus. The epithet Homer applies to Panopeus is thought to signify the dance of the Thyiades.

What is striking about this passage is not only that the contemporary Thyiades represent themselves as competent informants, but also that they claim the text of Homer as conditioned by the ritual performance of their female predecessors in the office. The dancing Thyiades bridge the gap between ecstatic cult and authoritative speech.

There are in fifth-century Athens at least two other cults that have connections with Dionysiac ritual[178] and that offered women access both to "ecstasy" and to "authority." In early fourth-century Athens, according to Demosthenes *On the Crown,* a cult of the Asian deity Sabazios was organized and led by Glaukothea, the mother of Demosthenes' opponent Aischines. That this cult bore some affinities with that of Dionysos is suggested by some of the terms in Demosthenes' address to Aischines,[179] which also indicates the prominence of women within it (258–59):

> When you became a grown man you read the books when your mother was performing initiations, and you helped her with the other preparations. At night, you mixed the libations, purified the initiates, put on the fawnskins, and cleansed them off with clay and cornhusks. Raising them up from the purification, you bade them say "I have fled the evil, I have found the good." . . . In the daytime, you led your bands through the streets, garlanded with fennel and white poplar. You rubbed the snakes' cheeks and swung them above your head, shouting: "Euoi Saboi" and dancing to the tune of "hues attes, attes hues." Old women called you Leader, Guide, Bearer of the Ivy, Carrier of the *Liknon,* and the like.

Since the speech and its account of the cult are motivated by the desire to damage Aischines, the detailed description of bizarre activities, and in particular the foregrounding of women participants, may be construed as hostile fantasy rather than an accurate rendering of historical practice. On the other hand, that women were in fact dominant within the cult is made probable by its association with that of Dionysos. Although "old women" are given prominence by this text only to the extent that they acclaim Aischines, a form of praise that will presumably incur blame from Demosthenes' audience, it is not implausible that older women, relatively free from familial commitments and supervision alike, should have maintained a high profile in the cult. Aischines' mother, Glaukothea, is attributed a leadership role, and Walter Burkert notes

178. For these connections see Burkert 1985: 178–79.
179. See also the discussion of these similarities at Kraemer 1979: 61–63.

that she was descended from a line of seers.[180] If, as Burkert suggests, Glaukothea was developing her following in order to support herself and her family in the aftermath of Athens's defeat in the Peloponnesian War, then it is plausible to consider participation and leadership in ecstatic cults as a material resource that some women could use to construct a productive position for themselves in times of economic difficulty. That not all Athenians might approve of Glaukothea's enterprise is made clear by the hostile tone of Demosthenes' speech; on the other hand, Glaukothea did develop a constituency, and we may speculate that she was supported in her project by the similarly disposed members of her family. According to Demosthenes' speech, she seems to be training her son to take her place as leader. [181]

In addition to the cult's ecstatic profile and consequent alignment with female identity, another factor that may be relevant in the development of Glaukothea's leadership role is the fact that Sabazios was understood by Greek culture to be non-Greek, to be imported, in a way that did not characterize the Olympian gods. Although Dionysiac cult itself is known to the Homeric texts and is probably of even greater antiquity, the founding myths of Dionysos represent him as a foreign god, an intruder who forces acceptance on a resisting community. In the late classical and early Hellenistic periods a number of cults were established in mainland Greece that were similarly represented as "foreign," deriving from the many non-Greek cultures of Asia Minor, and we can argue that women like Glaukothea would find it easier to establish a leadership position in such a "new" cult than in a cult whose formal structures were already in place.[182]

Another cult whose ecstatic dimension and non-Greek origin may have facilitated the participation of women was that of Kybele, the Anatolian Great Mother or Mother of the Gods. Although Kybele had occupied a shrine in Athens since the early fifth century,[183] didactic texts addressed to women represent her cult as both alien and explicitly subversive of the patri-

180. Burkert 1987: 33.

181. Given the resemblances between worship of Sabazios and Bacchic worship, and the ambiguous importance of the mother-son dyad in the latter, this is ironic at least.

182. The cult at least of Kybele was not "foreign," in that the deity had had a presence in Athens since the fifth century. The Egyptian cult of Isis did not reach Greece until the Hellenistic period (Burkert 1985: 179) and so does not form part of this study, even though it was of considerable importance for women, as may be seen from, for example, Mora 1990, Walter 1988, and Heyob 1975.

183. Themistokles, while in Persia, made his daughter a priestess of Kybele in response to a dream. See Plutarch *Life of Themistokles* 30.

184. Photios s.v. *Metragyrtes* gives the narrative of Kybele's arrival in Athens, which includes the Dionysiac contours of special attraction for women and initial rejection by the community. On this narrative and on the cult generally see Versnel 1990: 105–11.

archal household.[184] A Hellenistic text purportedly by Phintys, the female Pythagorean, reminds women that one component of a woman's *sophrosune,* or "chastity," is "her refusal to join in secret cults or Cybeline ritual," which are alleged to "lead to drunkenness and ecstasy."[185] Contrasted throughout the text with a woman's proper ritual responsibilities, which include sacrifices for husbands and households, these Cybeline rites are also said to be prohibited by law. Whatever the situation for Greek Italy, where this text probably emerged, Cybeline practices are not legally prohibited in other periods or other areas of Greece. Nevertheless, a few centuries later Plutarch's didactic *Advice on Marriage* reiterates the injunction to wives. *Advice* 19 reads:

> It is fitting for a married woman to worship the gods whom her husband hon-ors and to recognize these alone. She should shut the door on strange cults and outlandish superstitions. For with none of the gods do rites performed by women secretly and furtively find favor.

At *Advice* 45 Plutarch's speaker elaborates, gesturing more precisely toward the cult of Kybele, which was distinguished by its use of the *tympanon,* or cymbal:

> Now some men, if they see scarlet or purple clothes, are terribly pained, and others hate drums and cymbals. What is so terrible, then, if women keep away from these things and do not upset or irritate their husbands but live with them gently and peaceably?

In these passages "strange cults and outlandish superstitions" are opposed to "the gods whom her husband honors," and so may be understood as those that are independently attractive to women. Against these cults are ranged not only the gods, who do not look upon them with favor, but also the husbands, whose fine-tuned constitutions cannot stand the lurid col-ors and harsh noises associated with, for instance, the worship of Kybele.[186] If the woman aligns herself with husband and gods, by "shutting the door" and remaining inside, she will be happy and successful; if she succumbs to the temptations outside the door, she will disrupt not only the household but also the proper ritual order whereby she mediates with the divine for family members and is positioned, by her correct cult prac-tice, to participate acceptably rather than "furtively" in the civic life beyond the door.

What these injunctions presuppose is women's use of the cult of Kybele

185. Thesleff 1965: 154.
186. The delicate irritability of men is still at issue in relations between men and women of modern rural Greece; see, for instance, du Boulay 1986: 150 and Kennedy 1986: 123–34.

to articulate domestic resistance, and it seems unlikely that such statements refer only to a rhetorical trope without connection to women's experience. The attraction of Kybele for women need not, however, have been confined to vivid celebrations and domestic dissent, because women might also occupy positions of authority within the cult. Even though the most dramatic expression of commitment to the goddess, self-castration under the influence of *mania,* or possession, was by definition reserved for male adherents,[187] women played important roles that on occasion they modified to suit their own needs.

As well as dancing and participating in processions, women in the cult of Kybele could serve as priestesses. A Hellenistic relief shows a woman with a key, which has been interpreted to indicate that she has the authority to initiate others into the cult.[188] On first-century Amorgos an inscription shows a priestess of the Mother, who may serve for up to ten years if she wishes (*LSCG* 103.17), charged with the task of performing *telete,* or initiations (*LSCG* 103.11), and recompensed with a portion of the sacrifice. What is particularly intriguing about the cult on Amorgos is that it was reorganized after the intervention of a woman: Hegestrate, daughter of Ainesikratos and wife of Hermokrates, who is honored in the inscription. Although her intervention dates to the first century B.C.E., we can discern similar initiatives on the part of women in the Piraeus nearly a century earlier. A series of inscriptions informs us about the cult society of citizens, called *orgeones* or *thiasotai,* who worshipped Kybele there and who were led by priestesses chosen by lot for short terms of one or two years. Responsible for the quotidian activities of the cult, in which she might be helped by her husband, the incumbent priestess was also required to make a financial contribution, even though her appointment was by sortition and did not depend on her wealth. In 183/82 B.C.E. the current and former priestesses, acting collectively, complain that these contributions are excessive, and request a reorganization of the group's finances in order to reduce the level of the priestess's expenditure (*LSCG* 48A). Although the priestesses are subject to the authority of the male *orgeones,* who make the final decisions on cult procedure and have the right to punish a priestess who ignores regulations (*LSCG* 48A.9–10), the priestesses have evidently developed working relations among themselves and a sense of a collective identity that positions them to intervene in the cult's procedures. Some of the relations among these women were actively constructed by the cult; for instance, each incoming priestess had to select an assistant, or *zakoros,* from among the former priestesses. A further

187. These *metragyrtai* or *galloi* are unequivocally condemned by our surviving sources. Ferguson (1944: 110) claims that these male practitioners had no role in the Piraeus cult of Kybele.

188. Gasparo 1985: 22. Vermaseren (1977: 80) identifies this figure as Persephone.

rule enjoins that no woman serve as *zakoros* twice until all have had the chance to fill the position; formulated in *LSCG* 48A.13–15, this rule is broken eight years later, again by the collective action of present and former priestesses. Since Metrodora has served so well as *zakoros* to the previous priestess, Aristonike, the present incumbent, Simale, requests that she be confirmed by the priestesses as *zakoros* for life, a decision that is duly ratified by the *orgeones* (*LSCG* 48B, 175/74 B.C.E.).

Such independent initiatives are, as J. A. Turner notes,[189] "exceptional," even within the context of the relative autonomy exercised by women in their ritual activity. It is intriguing that the *orgeones*, while ostensibly retaining final authority over the priestesses, nonetheless capitulate to their demands so readily; and one wonders whether the pressure exerted by the united women of the cult was not even greater than the inscriptions will admit. Although mainstream didactic literature like that of "Phintys" or, later on, Plutarch, condemns women's association with the cult of Kybele because of its threats to marital harmony, the male *orgeones* of the Piraeus seem to have acquiesced in the anomalous authority of the women cult members. One factor that may have facilitated their acquiescence in the case of Metrodora's new lifelong appointment is family tradition; Metrodora will serve properly and reverently as her mother Euaxis did before (*LSCG* 48A.22–23). Metrodora herself, "gift of the Mother," is quite likely named for her mother's devotion to the cult. If this reference to matrilineal inheritance is seen to recall the similar claims by Bacchic women noted in chapter 3,[190] we may conclude that women's personal authority within the cult of Kybele was conditioned not only by simple weight of numbers but also by the cult's ecstatic dimension, which linked it to those of Dionysos and Sabazios. Foregrounding an experience culturally typed as female, and therefore even under the best circumstances suspect, the ecstatic cults provided historical women with a resource that could, paradoxically, position them as authoritative leaders.

In this chapter we have examined three different discourses in which women may be seen to deploy ritual forms in order to delineate their own needs and articulate their own culture, more or less independently of men. Women's poetry adopts the public voice afforded women by ritual practice or advertises its performative claims by means of ritual forms; vases designed for women's consumption offer them idealized images of themselves as rit-

189. Turner 1983: 135.

190. Instances are the Theban maenads descended from Ino and the Bacchic priestesses of the Semachidai in Stephanos of Byzantium, already encountered in chapter 3. See also Strabo 7.7.12.

ual practitioners; Dionysiac ritual supplies the complex experience of possession yet positions certain women to act with authority. Throughout this study I have stressed the dialectical relationship between women and their ritual practice, which is neither simply a result of their autonomous self-expression nor only a technique for their continued exploitation, but which must constantly labor at the production of their consent to a system that is not geared to their interests. As part of that labor, the discourse of ritual must register those needs and desires of women that are not otherwise addressed, and must indeed afford them a space for creative engagement with itself. It is this space, or versions of it, that we have been exploring in this chapter. In the next and final chapter, we shall examine a particular instance of creative engagement with women's ritual practice on the part of men, when we consider the representation of ritually active women in Athenian drama.

FIVE

Women Represented

Ritual in Drama

Thus far we have examined women's ritual practice in ancient Greece from a variety of perspectives, exploring its connections to discourses of work, sexuality, and civic identity, and its possible role in a women's subculture. Throughout, numerous different kinds of testimony have been marshaled, and attempts have been made to circumvent the fact that our evidence is almost entirely generated by men, rather than by the women who were both the subjects and the objects of the ritual process. This chapter, then, marks a departure as well as providing a conclusion, for it concentrates on a single, well-defined body of texts and abandons all attempt to investigate women's experience of women's ritual in favor of a focus on a particular genre of representation by men: drama.[1] What are the justifications for such a proceeding?

One answer is the simple prestige of the dramatic texts; along with Homeric epic, they are the ancient Greek literary productions most accessible to nonspecialists and most frequently offered to them in the form of new translations and new productions for the stage. If these dramas have anything at all to say about women and ritual, the dominance that they exert in the field of Greek studies would probably assure them a place in an investigation such as this. A more cogent reason for their inclusion is that they actually have a great deal to say, about both ritual and women, and have therefore generated an extensive secondary literature on these topics. The

---

1. Chapter 5 incorporates in revised form material previously published in the following articles: "Aithra at Eleusis," *Helios* 22.1 (1995) 65–78; "The Women of Thebes," *Classical Journal* 90.4 (April–May 1995) 353–65; "The Violence of Community: Ritual in the *Iphigeneia in Tauris*," *Bucknell Review* 43.1 (1999) 109–25. I am grateful for permission to use that material here.

specific intersection of drama with women's rituals, however, has not been exhaustively studied.[2] The third justification for this chapter is that having worked extensively to reconstruct women's rituals, and having explored the possible models of subjectivity offered to historical women by their rituals, we are now in a position to see how women's cult practice was deployed by a specific male-authored genre in the short but intense period of the second half of the fifth century. I do not claim that the analyses below will provide an exhaustive account of the topic of women and ritual in drama, for there is undoubtedly much more that could be said; similarly, I do not suppose that in any one case I have given an account of the play as a whole.[3] My aim is to offer a preliminary account of dramatic discourse on women's cult practice, which, as we have seen, was crucial not only for the welfare of oikos and polis, but also for the formation of women's subjectivity.

The dramatic festivals were themselves cult occasions celebrated in honor of Dionysos, and, in the case of the tragic festival at least, the plays were preceded by a series of other ritual events.[4] Yet the reciprocal movement whereby drama, a product in some sense of ritual, draws on ritual forms for its own plots and gestures, was not explicitly studied until the period of the Cambridge Ritualists at the beginning of the twentieth century. The excessive zeal with which these scholars uncovered the same Year-God within numerous and otherwise varied tragedies scared off any possible *epigonoi*.[5] Although by now discredited, the Cambridge School made a major contribution in its exploration of ways of accounting for Greek culture and drama, especially tragedy, as "other," rather than assimilating them to some presumedly universal paradigm of liberal humanism. Rather than confining ancient Greece discursively to the contours of a Europe presumed to be understood, the Cambridge School similarly experimented with accounting for it in terms of non-Western paradigms. These directions taken by the Cambridge Ritualists have been important for contemporary work on tragedy and ritual.

Such contemporary work is conditioned largely by two perspectives on ritual, and on ritual and tragedy, namely the structuralist and the evolutionist.[6] Identified primarily with the "Paris school," comprising principally J-P. Vernant, P. Vidal-Naquet, Marcel Detienne, and Nicole Loraux, the

2. The exception to this rule is the work of Foley, e.g., 1985 and 1993. See also Zeitlin 1981.

3. Because of my very specific aims in this chapter, I have chosen not to refer to all the relevant secondary literature in each case. I would like this note to stand as an acknowledgment of the various works on which I draw.

4. On these other rituals see Goldhill 1990.

5. For a brief history of the Cambridge Ritualists and of theories of ritual within classics generally, see Morris 1993.

6. See Foley 1985: 30–56.

structuralist project within classics has for nearly three decades performed virtuoso unravelings of the connections among ritual, tragedy, and myth. Committed to explaining tragedy by its references to the larger drives within Greek culture, structuralist analysis characteristically privileges the practices of sacrifice, marriage, and agriculture, and the homologies among them, showing how the proper performance of these actions is held by Greek culture to guarantee a healthy community and the maintenance of productive relationships among gods, mortals, and animals. If proper ritual practice thus produces the healthy community, then tragedy is drawn instead to its opposite, the ceaseless investigation of its breakdown— signified particularly by human sacrifice and perverted marriage ritual— and the accompanying devastation of oikos and polis.

The second strand in contemporary work on ritual and tragedy, the evolutionist, which is associated with the work of René Girard, does not generally confine its claim to Greek culture but works with larger hypotheses about the place of violence in human nature and human culture. On the evolutionist hypothesis, ritual, especially sacrificial ritual, is designed to articulate and control the violence inherent in human society while mystifying its origins. Tragedy is like ritual in its interest in violent action, but it serves less to conceal the origins of culture in violence than to reveal them, in the plots that repeatedly end by generating new rituals out of the death and disaster that overtake the characters.

Despite R. Seaford's complaint of a "general failure to investigate ritual on the part of literary and textual critics," many such critics have learned a great deal from these approaches to ritual in tragedy and have conversely produced several studies that investigate not so much how ritual informs tragedy but how tragedy uses ritual metaphors for its own ends.[7] Seaford's own work is an important contribution to the developing discourse on tragedy and ritual. He places tragedy's use and misuse of ritual firmly within the context of state formation, emphasizing its role in the historical moment of the fifth-century Athenian polis. Although it is not possible here to summarize his impressively complex argument, the salient parts that concern tragedy suggest that while the polis arrogates to itself many of the functions of the oikos and makes corresponding claims on the loyalty of the citizens, so tragedy repeatedly stages the downfall of the oikos—especially of the royal oikos—and erects the polis on its ruins. Those rituals that might be seen as conducive to the welfare of the oikos, such as sacrifice, wedding, and funeral, are thus systematically perverted and undermined by tragedy in order to promote instead the good of the polis.

Although they approach an explanation from very different levels of his-

---

7. Seaford 1995: xiv. One could cite, as well as the work of Foley previously noted, Zeitlin 1970 and Easterling 1993, for instance.

torical generalization, all these theories take as the thing to be explained the prevalence in tragedy of perverted ritual. A further way of accounting for this prevalence would be to say that ritual is one of the important discourses in fifth-century Athens, like those of the assembly and the law court, which tragedy can mobilize for its own ends and with which it perhaps sees itself as vying for cultural prestige. With its idealizing version of the relations between gods and mortals and among mortals, ritual offers a normative discourse that tragedy can most effectively upset. Aware of the productive tension between itself and ritual discourse, tragedy offers numerous moments of meditation on the similarities and differences between the two forms. The ritual etiologies that close several plays, and that often restate the concerns of the drama in a new form, make this self-consciousness about the relation between tragedy and ritual especially visible.[8]

The study of the representation of women in Greek drama, like that of the representation of ritual, has expanded exponentially in the last two or three decades, so that drama's concern with gender is now widely acknowledged to be one of its most important components. In the earlier part of this century Athenian plays were simply quarried for what they could be made to say about a generalized "status" or "position" of women. The most notoriously positive conclusion is that of A. W. Gomme in 1925, who sums up: "There is, in fact, no literature, no art of any country, in which women are more prominent, more carefully studied and with more interest, than in the tragedy, sculpture, and painting of fifth-century Athens."[9] The inconclusive debates between the proponents of this view and those who held that Athenian women were instead confined in "Oriental" seclusion quickly ran into the sand, but interest in the female figures of drama was rekindled by the external political impetus of the women's movement. In the absence of classical texts authored by women, feminist scholars were drawn to texts that displayed striking female characters, so that tragedy, and to a lesser extent comedy, became privileged within feminist inquiry. The question of why dramatic women seemed so blatantly to flout the familiar Greek requirements of silence and submissiveness was posed with a new urgency.

Numerous explanations might be adduced for why Greek drama displays so many memorable females. One possible answer would be that drama in fifth-century Athens is a radical genre that challenges social norms and exposes the constructed nature of gender identity, and in particular of female inferiority, by mobilizing female characters who actively resist the identifications offered by their culture. In this vein, R. Rehm remarks that "tragic characters frequently posed radical challenges to traditional ways of

8. On such an ending see Goff 1990: chap. 5.
9. Quoted in Foley 1981a: 128.

thinking and dealing with the world."[10] Tragedy would thus expose the limitations of Greek gender ideology by virtue of its position as a privileged cultural artifact. This notion of tragedy as a radical genre is, however, very much at odds with the central role of the dramatic festival in the Athenian ritual calendar and with its multiple connections to normative democratic discourse. A more favored explanation of women's prominence in tragedy has been sought instead in the explicitly ideological character of the festival and in the acknowledged role of poets as teachers of the community. This view, recently exemplified in the work of Nancy Rabinowitz,[11] holds that tragedy inculcates normative gender ideology in both men and women by its deployment of female characters. Despite the appeal of their strong natures, female characters who do not conform to expectations are punished and destroyed; the only way for a female character to win the play's— and the audience's—approval is by a gesture of self-sacrifice. Female characters thus offer only a temporary challenge to gender ideology that ultimately reinforces it. Rabinowitz writes that tragedy "recuperates the female figures for patriarchy. . . . Female characters [are endowed] with great understanding and . . . give voice to important ideas; nonetheless, their experience is shaped to the end of supporting male power."[12]

A third way to look at the issue is to concentrate not on tragedy's more or less deliberate manipulations of female characters but to consider instead the role of the female in the historical forces that produce tragedy as a genre. What pressures are there in the historical context that induce tragedy to foreground the sign of the feminine? The fifth century as a whole is a time of considerable upheaval, compounded in its second half by the added stresses of the Peloponnesian War and the consequent disintegration of the Athenian empire, and the figure of the female is often deployed in drama in ways that signify and track these changes. But this figure is prominent specifically because many of the stresses accumulated around the issue of gender relations. The developing democratic polis had found it necessary to loosen the ties that bound citizens to older forms of association, most notably the oikos. As we have seen in the case of funeral lamentation, in thus redefining the oikos, the city sharply reduced the public profile of women. In the fifth century, as opposed to what can be deduced about earlier periods, women's role was formally acknowledged as confined only to the management of the household and the production of legitimate heirs. Helene Foley writes of Athenian "consciousness of these historical shifts in women's role and an uneasiness concerning this aspect

10. Rehm 1994: 137.
11. Rabinowitz 1993a.
12. Rabinowitz 1993a: 14. Rabinowitz writes with explicit reference only to Euripides, but it seems to me that much of what she says is also applicable to the other tragedians.

of the new democratic society," observing that "the radical separation of the domestic sphere from the political sphere, and the relatively greater subordination of household to state and of female to male undoubtedly posed more problems in reality than it did in the ideal."[13] As Ellen Meiksins Wood argues, the ideology of equality among men required a devaluing of that which could disunite them, namely women. Drama, then, as an arena where the city works through the various tensions accumulating around its new identity, cannot help but foreground the issue of the construction of gender and pose repeatedly the question of how the polis is to deal with that which both is and is not the polis.[14]

We might go further and say that the plurality of voices that constitutes drama makes the theater a contested arena, where the otherwise muted protests of historical women may find a voice, however distorted. Several scholars have found it plausible to suppose that historical women did articulate resistance to the new encroachments of the polis, especially because the radical equality among men may well have thrown into relief the subordination of their women.[15] The male-authored protests by women characters on the Athenian stage may have had female-authored counterparts offstage; the statements supportive of gender ideology made so frequently on stage by both male and female characters perhaps presuppose articulations of dissent elsewhere. Related to the issue of multiple voices is that of the extent to which women were present as members of the audience. Repeatedly rehashed, the discrete pieces of "evidence" for and against have as yet led to no single compelling conclusion, but it is interesting for our purposes to note that feminist scholars often hold that women were present at dramatic festivals precisely in their role as participants in ritual events. J. Henderson has set out other reasons for claiming women's attendance at the festivals; Goldhill takes issue with much of his argumentation but does not deal very fully with the issue of women's general cultic participation.[16] Even if women were present as spectators, however, it is unlikely that they were considered the primary audience for the dramas' discourse; the dramas' account of women's cultic activity, for instance, which I shall develop below, often presents it as a problem for the male citizens to solve or as an

---

13. Foley 1981a: 150–51. See also the introduction to Foley 2001.

14. See Meiksins Wood 1988. The claim that tragedy is concerned primarily with the polis, rather than with, for example, enduring humanistic values has gained increasing attention. Christian Meier's work (e.g., 1993) is predicated on the notion that "the Athenians need tragedy" to allow them to negotiate the new demands of living in the polis; Hall (1989) argues that tragedy is the arena in which Greeks, and particularly perhaps Athenians, negotiate a relationship with what is not the polis, i.e., the barbarian.

15. See, for example, Rose 1992: 357–58. Few scholars suggest that such resistance ever took an organized political form, but see Keuls 1985: 387–92.

16. See Henderson 1991 and Goldhill 1994.

issue for them to address, rather than as a representation of women's independent contributions to their various communities.

Discourses on ritual, and on women, are highly significant for an overall account of tragedy. In contrast, the discourse on women and ritual or on women as ritual practitioners is relatively muted, but aspects of it are of increasing interest to scholars.[17] Within this discourse, women are represented as involved with the polis as well as with the oikos. The public activity of ritual is useful to drama in that it can motivate women's emergence onto the outdoor space of the stage; once in the public eye, however, women may need to be controlled and contained even in their roles as ritual practitioners. One reason for this need is that the trope of women's ritual practice offers a limit case by which the city may judge its potential for success or failure. If women as ritual practitioners are upholding the claims of the city, then the city has successfully embraced even its most marginal members; if, on the other hand, women's ritual practice is positioning them to resist the claims of the city, then it is rendered unbearably vulnerable. To this extent, the concerns of this chapter can be seen to relate to those of chapter 3. The dramas do not, however, simply enact an oscillation between the possibilities of fruitful and pernicious ritual action on the part of their female characters. I shall try to suggest that there is instead a distinct historical movement, whereby tragedy first shows a conflict between women and the city, which gives way to a model of cooperation in the 420s and 410s. This new model is itself then replaced by renewed conflict in the difficult closing years of the century. The model of conflict and resolution (of a sort) is not the only narrative that can be discerned within plays that take an interest in women's ritual. I shall also show that drama differentiates between the women of Athens and those of Thebes, and I shall investigate the figure of the priestess/prophetess to show how she contributes both to the overall discourse on ritually active women and to the dynamics of the individual play(s) that take an interest in women's rituals.

CONFLICT STUDIES

Seven Against Thebes

Produced in 467, Aeschylus's *Seven Against Thebes* opposes women's ritual autonomy to the masculine-identified values of the ordered polis, without, however, offering to judge conclusively between the two. Thebes is under siege by Polyneikes, who invades his homeland at the head of an Argive army. Eteokles, brother of Polyneikes and ruler of Thebes, opens the play with an address to the citizens, who are invoked as males of different gen-

---

17. On women's mourning in tragedy, for example, see Foley 1993 and Holst-Wahrhaft 1992.

erations (10–11), responsible for their city, its gods, and its soil (13–16). Equipped with both a prophet (24) and scouts (36) to find out what the enemy is up to, Eteokles here exemplifies the rational planning and decision making that he later deploys to virtuoso effect in the scene where he chooses the seven Theban warriors best suited to face the Argive champions. In this he is implicitly contrasted with the Argive leaders, who are reported to be making their dispositions by lot (55).

Between Eteokles' final prayer (69–77) and the scene of his choice of warriors intervenes the lengthy exchange with the chorus of Theban women. Not addressed among the "citizens," and identifying themselves as *parthenoi* (110), they enter and take over the theatrical space by clinging to the images of gods on stage. Their cries take up over 100 lines, during which they not only perform the present supplication for the besieged city but also remind the gods of previous observances (175–80). These female entreaties, however, Eteokles finds objectionable and detrimental to the city's salvation. According to him the lamentation makes cowards of the soldiers; the women abet the enemy outside the walls and cause destruction to those inside the city (191–94). Far from upholding the female virtue of *sophrosune* (186), they illustrate instead the tendency of women to do things by extremes; either women are "in power," *kratousa,* and so unbearable (189), or else they are fearful *(deisasa)* and then cause more trouble to both oikos and polis (190). At the end of his speech Eteokles modifies the taxonomy of inside and outside, so that Thebes, which was "inside" while the Argives were outside, now has both an outside and an inside; the women are to stay inside *(endon),* since what is "outside" *(exothen)* concerns the men (201). He insists throughout that the women belong indoors, in silence, and thereby refuses to acknowledge the access to a public sphere and a public voice that is typically offered to women by ritual practice. The cult practice that provides them a place "inside" the city and an identity as part of it, Eteokles reads here as rendering them "outside" and hostile to the city.

Although Eteokles sees the situation in terms of a simple gender opposition, it is not clear that we should follow him.[18] He claims (230–32) that cult in time of war is men's concern, but *Iliad* 6 shows us Hekabe and the women of Troy offering a robe to Athena on behalf of the besieged city. In Troy, however, the women are instructed by Hektor to perform the supplication, whereas in Thebes they act independently; Eteokles reacts to what he sees as overly autonomous action on the part of females and responds accordingly. His language in this scene, however, is as intemperate as the women's cries. Although he claims that the women are uttering ill-omened words and should be more guarded in their language (250, 258), it is he who suggests

18. For different views of gender within the play see, for instance, Zeitlin 1982b and Jackson 1988: 289–90.

that gods depart when a town is taken (217–18), and goes on to speak of men dying and wounded (242). On occasion he tropes the women's language as he will do that of the Argive champions throughout the scene of appointing warriors (253–54):

> *Chorus:* Gods of our city, do not let me fall into slavery.
>
> *Eteokles:* It is you who enslave yourself and me and the whole city.

Just as in the later scene his verbal skill will not avert the fated meeting with his brother, however, so here he cannot overcome the women's language but instead is caught up in their paradigm.

Eteokles and the women reach a modus vivendi when he asks them, and they agree, to continue their prayers in a more moderate vein (260–63). After a more restrained song by the chorus the following scene is that in which Eteokles pits Theban warriors against Argive, finding himself to be the inevitable seventh who will meet his brother at the final gate. His reservation of sacrifice and other cult activity for men turns out to be correct when it transpires that he and his brother are the sacrificial offerings that the gods desire (702–3):

> The gods, I am sure, have already abandoned us.
> The favor that is desired is our deaths.

Addressing him now as "child" (*teknon*, 686), the chorus women adopt the voice of civic responsibility and urge him to avoid the pollution of fratricide at all costs.[19] They recommend proper sacrifices to the gods (700–701), but he, like them earlier, can speak only ill-omened words about his father's curse and the enmity of the gods. Unable to sustain the posture of calm, rational leader, Eteokles, rather than the women, is displayed as the internal threat to the city's peace and security.[20] His notion of how the polis is constituted and what it means is found to be inadequate; he understands neither the women's membership of the community that he leads nor the relation between that community and his doomed family.

The ending of the play as we have it is agreed not to be Aeschylean but is commonly thought to be fifth century.[21] The chorus women are joined by the sisters Antigone and Ismene, who mourn for their brothers slain in a mutual act of fratricide. A herald announces that Eteokles, the defender, will be buried but that Polyneikes, the aggressor, will be left for the dogs. While Ismene and half the chorus agree to obey the edict and bury Eteokles, Antigone, defying the order, leads the other half off to bury

---

19. On the chorus's later speeches and songs see Jackson 1988: 300–303.

20. See in this vein Sommerstein 1996: 121.

21. For a discussion of the arguments see Foley 1993.

Polyneikes. The women's ritual work of mourning here reproduces the previous division in the fratricidal city, prolonging its agony and denying the possibility of healing closure. Some critics propose, however, that the Aeschylean play ended with the institution of a hero cult for both brothers. If so, the ritual autonomy of the women in the earlier scene, which so provoked Eteokles, would end by being organized into a form more acceptable to the city. The movement from women's autonomy in the sphere of ritual, and its challenge to male authority, to a more contained version of female cult practice that allows for closure has also been discerned in other Aeschylean tragedies, such as the *Suppliants* and the Oresteia trilogy. We should note, however, that in most cases the gesture of ritual closure is a critical reconstruction based to a greater or lesser extent on a reading of the *Eumenides*, the final play in the Oresteia trilogy; what our extant texts, including the *Seven*, actually give us is a representation only of the disorder provoked by women's ritual autonomy.

Suppliants

In Aeschylus's *Suppliants* of 463 women's ritual action poses another problem for the male ruler and tends again to expose the limitations of the masculine polis-based order. Fleeing a forced marriage with their cousins, the suppliant women from Egypt take refuge in Argos. There they claim kinship through the legend of Io, the Argive princess loved by Zeus and persecuted by Hera, who in the shape of a cow wandered around the known world until she came to rest in Egypt. As in all suppliant drama, the Danaids present their "hosts" with a critical situation: to disregard the plea of the suppliant is to invite the wrath of the gods, but to honor it is almost inevitably to be plunged into war or some other danger to the polis. After the Danaids have established their claim to Argive identity by recounting the history of Io, Pelasgos, the Argive ruler, accepts their supplication in principle but begins to point out the difficulties attendant on it. Fearing war with the suitors, Aigyptos's sons, the king asserts that he will not make any decision until he has shared the problem with the whole polis; since all the polis will be involved in the coming danger, all must have a part in deliberation (365–69). To which the Danaids reply, usurping the speaking role that among Greeks would normally go to their father (370–75):

> You are the city, you are the people.
> Ruler[22] without judge, you control
> The altar, the hearth of the land;

22. The Greek term translated as "ruler" is *prytanis,* the name for a specific official within the Athenian democracy, so that the misnomer gives more point to the Danaids' weird notion of Argive politics.

Commanding with your single vote,
Enthroned with your single sceptre,
You accomplish all that is needed; guard against
Pollution.

That Pelasgos reiterates his dilemma, without taking the Danaids to task for their misconception of democratic practice, indicates that this theatrical version of Argos combines the proceedings of monarchy with those of democracy, but it may still be relevant for the representation of the Danaids that they do not understand Argive political procedure and thus are ready to turn to other forms of action. For the rest of the dialogue the Danaids continue to urge the justice of their cause, while Pelasgos returns to the need to involve Argos in the decision-making process or risk the city's censure (398–401). The Danaids then dramatically force the issue by pointing out that if their supplication is denied, they will use their sashes to hang themselves on the holy images, and so inflict intolerable pollution on the city. Having already referred to their wool-decked branches, the proper suppliant equipment, as "weapons" (21), they show themselves ready to bring violence to the city of Argos unaided and without the need for war. Pelasgos, who thought he had the luxury of debate and deliberation, capitulates immediately, and devises an interesting political remedy for his impossible situation (480–85):

You then, aged father of these girls,
Quickly take these suppliant branches in your arms
And lay them on the other altars of our native divinities
So that all the citizens may see the sign of this appeal,
But no word may be let fall of me;
For the people love to blame their leaders.

The king and Argos are now represented as separate, and the king takes active steps, if not to deceive his people, at least to be economical with the truth. Later he is said to have obtained the unanimous decision of the Argives, in favor of the suppliants, not only by the content of his speech but also by employing *demegorous . . . strophas* (623), "rhetorical tricks" or "crowd-pleasing twists and turns." These words bear an almost inescapably pejorative charge.

A theme that will be rehearsed many times in Greek tragedy thus finds an early articulation in this play; the Danaids dramatically illustrate the danger for the polis of incorporating that which is not the polis. Their excessive ritual action, which has emphatically moved them from a position of powerlessness to one of power, has begun to corrupt the Argives. Although their ignorance of democratic practice may perhaps be forgiven in women and foreigners, it is matched by their lack of restraint in those ritual actions that women may legitimately perform in the public realm. The major act of the lost part of the trilogy is their subversion of marriage ritual when they kill their husbands on their wedding night. According to a reconstruction of the trilogy favored by many scholars, this deed is ordered by their father, Danaus, who also becomes the ruler of Argos. In this context his acquisition of a bodyguard (492, 985) has been found ominous, since historically such an act was often the precursor of a tyrannical coup d'état.[23] The Danaids' threat to the polis on the ritual level is thus perhaps matched by the political danger presented by their father.

As we saw in chapter 2, Herodotos (2.171) claims that the daughters of Danaus brought the Thesmophoria to Greece from Egypt. Following this lead, several scholars have suggested that the trilogy ended with the foundation of the Thesmophoria.[24] If this is so, we can see with Froma Zeitlin that "ritual compensation therefore is a way of acknowledging female power but also of limiting it to the ritual sphere. . . . The ritual power [the woman] exercised as a suppliant at the beginning of the trilogy was necessarily a political strategy; . . . ritual power now would be transferred to another rite that in her changed status of wife and mother is now the symbolic token of her incorporation into the community."[25] To develop a ritual that provides an honorable position for women repeats symbolically the gesture of incorporating the suppliants, while addressing in addition the larger question of women's role in the city that the *Seven* also canvassed. Governing and defining married women, the Thesmophoria would repair the breach in the ideology of marriage that the Danaids dramatically created, and could further be seen to compensate the Danaids for their eventual acquiescence in patriarchal arrangements. Another interpretation, however, might explain the Thesmophoria as a means of controlling the autonomous ritual energies that the Danaids exercised to devastating effect in the first play of the trilogy. Instead of women performing ritually as they please, and devising dreadful innovations, they will be regularly convened by the Thesmophoria and permitted a temporary, circumscribed version of that independence of action that the Danaids briefly enjoyed. Women's ritual energies, we might suggest, are released by tragedy partly in order to be brought under a new kind of control. Without that control, those energies are liable to prove destructive to the patriarchal system of the polis. With it, they serve as the demonstration that the polis can manage what is exterior and sometimes inimical to itself.[26]

23. Garvie 1969: 199.

24. Ibid., 227.

25. Zeitlin 1992: 237.

26. See also Zeitlin 1988 on women in the *Suppliants* as essentially exterior to the city; this article does not develop a focus on ritual.

The Oresteia

Produced in 458, Aeschylus's Oresteia makes clear, in its management of women's ritual energies, what has been suggested in or deduced from the earlier plays.[27] Since the city emerges as a term only in the last play of the trilogy, women's cult activities do not present a threat specifically to the polis-based order, but female ritual autonomy does menace the oikos and even the ordered cosmos itself. Female autonomy in the ritual sphere, as in so many others, is exemplified by Klytaimestra, who not only organizes ritual actions but reorders their whole significance. Her activity thus exemplifies the drive in the play, identified by Zeitlin and others,[28] to highlight the sacrificial metaphor by disrupting and perverting it. Although Agamemnon is arguably responsible for the first corrupt sacrifice, that of his daughter Iphigeneia before the expedition to Troy, it is Klytaimestra's dangerous ritual practice that is foregrounded in the drama. Her first action is to administer burnt offerings throughout the city for the homecoming of Agamemnon (85–91), behavior perfectly consonant with what is prescribed for women in times of crisis, but here perhaps also resonating uncomfortably with her power over fire demonstrated in the "beacon-speech" (281–316). Despite this foreshadowing, the propriety of her actions throws into relief the horror of the human sacrifice of Iphigeneia that is the subject of the chorus's first song. Even though they have previously stated, in their account of the fall of Troy, that neither burnt nor liquid offerings can charm away anger (69–71), the chorus take Klytaimestra's sacrifices to be a sign of hope (102). Yet their description of her offerings is equivocal; the flame leaps up "drugged" with the "soft guileless persuasions" of oil (94–95). The language of persuasion and enchantment, which is to be highly destructive in this play, is thus used early on for Klytaimestra's rituals.

Before she emerges as murderer of her husband and usurper of his power, Klytaimestra proleptically takes over the ritual initiative. She fulfills the proper female role of ritual practitioner but also exercises a sinister autonomy. When Agamemnon returns from Troy, she meets him at the entrance to the palace and prevails upon him to enter it by walking over expensive tapestries, the wealth of the house, that are dyed red. This requirement that Agamemnon enter his palace only on her terms is presented as a rite extemporized as part of the ceremonies surrounding his

---

27. My discussion of women's ritual in the Oresteia is indebted for its overall approach to Zeitlin 1978. See also the useful discussion of Sommerstein 1996: 255–73. Bowie (1993b) discusses references to Athenian rituals and their attendant myths, "which carry the message that Athens has met and coped satisfactorily" with events similar to those of the trilogy, but does not develop a specific focus on women.

28. See Zeitlin 1965.

homecoming; Klytaimestra compares the action to a vow that Agamemnon might have taken (933), and he obligingly responds by calling it a *telos*, or rite (934). Klytaimestra's ritual innovation turns the sacrificial metaphor back on Agamemnon; as he devised a new and strange sacrifice of Iphigeneia, so she devises a ritual whereby he consents again to trample the possessions of the house and to enter it by a blood-red path.

The murders of Agamemnon and his concubine Kassandra are referred to proleptically as sacrifices when Klytaimestra says (1056–58):

> For by the hearth, the navelstone,
> The victims already stand for knife and fire,
> For those who never hoped to have this joy.

When she returns on stage after the death of Agamemnon, she compares the three blows she struck to the customary three libations (1384–87), and the murder itself is a twisted libation in which the corpse of Agamemnon is forced to drink the cup of sorrows that he had filled for his household (1394–98). Describing the dying man's last convulsions, Klytaimestra famously compares her body, drenched in his blood, to the earth when fertilized by rain (1388–92):

> Thus in his fall he pushes forth his life
> And gasping out a sharp burst of blood
> He strikes me with black drops of bloody rain,
> Me, rejoicing no less than does the corn
> In the god-given moisture, when the bud gives birth.

With her corruption of sacrifice into murder, Klytaimestra introduces a cosmic disorder that also undermines the meaning of marriage, figured by the wife's fertilized body, and of agriculture, figured by the productive earth. Linked here are what are often analyzed as the three defining parameters of Greek culture: agriculture, which regulates relations between humans and the natural world; marriage, which regulates relations between men and women; and sacrifice, which positions humans in relation to gods. The murder of Agamemnon, described in terms of the rituals that help to preserve culture, thus destabilizes all the practices that make culture possible. Klytaimestra's ritual initiative in the *Agamemnon* unhinges cult practice, as it does other important practices, and the work undertaken by the next two plays of the trilogy has consequently to continue to address women's relation to ritual.

In the *Libation-Bearers,* the sacrificial metaphor itself temporarily drops out of sight, but the actions of women in the ritual sphere provide much of the motivating force for the play. Klytaimestra initiates the action by sending libations to her dead husband's tomb, in response to a terrifying and ultimately prophetic dream in which she gives birth to and suckles a dangerous snake

(523–32). As we have seen, the offering of libations and the tending of the tomb are appropriate actions for females, but in Klytaimestra's vicinity these gestures are hopelessly compromised. That the murderer should try thus to appease the victim produces a situation so distorted that neither ritual forms nor even language itself can manage it, and the drama is effectively prevented from proceeding while Elektra and the chorus engage in debate about what prayer to say over the libations (106–23).[29] Since the chorus eventually prevail on Elektra to accompany the offerings with a prayer for the destruction of her enemies, Klytaimestra's ritual gesture is undermined, and this symbolic defeat in the sphere of cult may be understood to prepare for her eventual downfall. Instead of repeating the gesture of the corrupt sacrifice, Elektra and the women of the chorus take up the mourning energies generated by the visit to the tomb and convert them into the drive of the *kommos,* the lament for Agamemnon that helps motivate his son Orestes toward vengeance. Klytaimestra's dangerous ritual innovations in the first play give way here to more acceptable forms in which a collectivity of women transfer their energy to the man who must save the house. Unable to act decisively except in the ritual sphere, the women of the *Libation-Bearers* turn that ritual activity to their own account. Their action differs from Klytaimestra's initiatives in the crucial respect that they use ritual practice to promote not their own ends but the intervention of Orestes, who will restore the patriarchal power that Klytaimestra has so devastatingly challenged.

It may be significant, however, that readers' opinions vary as to how much influence the *kommos* has over Orestes; was he already set on vengeance for his father and the consequent matricide, or must his reluctance be overcome by the women's insistence?[30] The play certainly leaves room for the latter interpretation, which has the women urge Orestes on to a deed, the matricide, that provides no solution to the troubles of the Atreid house and that instead drives him insane. Foley has argued that the *Libation-Bearers'* version of revenge is inadequate and is shown to be so by being associated with women who wield the emotional power of the mourning lament that was regarded with such suspicion in fifth-century Athens.[31] Although the choruswomen's ritual initiatives represent an advance on those of Klytaimestra, because they are used in the interests of male authority in the house rather than against it, they remain problematic.

The task of the *Eumenides,* final play of the trilogy, is to contain the mayhem that the previous plays have unleashed, by building a new Athens on the ruin of the fallen Atreid house. To take the place of those that have been demol-

---

29. Goldhill (1992: 441) notes that "the effective performance of religious rites in this play is co-extensive with Elektra's speaking role."

30. Garvie (1986: 123f.) gives an overview of different interpretations.

31. Foley 1993.

ished in the course of violent action, the *Eumenides* generates new ritual forms. In this gesture it sets a precedent for several subsequent tragedies, but it builds on a bigger scale and out of materials that it portrays as more recalcitrant. The vengeful Furies of Klytaimestra, who desire a living sacrifice from the body of Orestes to crown the series of perverted offerings, are prevailed upon to accept instead a new home beneath the Acropolis and offerings from the people for marriage and children (903–15). Retaining some of their fearful aspect, they will ensure prosperity for the city by securing a place in it for the wholesome fear that keeps people virtuous (927–37). These new roles and honors may be considered as a recompense for the devaluing of the female that is enacted by Apollo's argument, which persuades about half the jury, that the father is the only true parent of the child (657–66).

The cult of the Furies seems to be entrusted primarily to the women of Athens, whom Athena expressly summons to worship the new divinities. At 1024 the Furies will be accompanied by the attendants, *prospoloi,* who guard Athena's statue; plausible historical candidates for this category include the priestess of Athena and her attendants Kosmo and Trapezo, but Athena goes on to speak in addition of "a glorious company of *paides* and *gynaikes*" (where *pais* can mean either "child" or "young woman, maiden") and also of "a band of older women" (1026–27). Despite a lacuna in the text, it seems that large numbers of women are the principal participants in the cult of the Furies; and in the later Euripidean *Melanippe Captive,* a woman speaker claims for her sex exactly this task of worship: "And as for the sacred rituals for the Fates and the Nameless Goddesses [i.e., the Furies], all these would not be holy if performed by men, but in women's hands, everything prospers."[32] Responding to the tripartite structure of the trilogy and to the cross-generational anxieties that have fueled it, the women of Athens are convened in a community of maidens, wives, and older women that offers to solve those anxieties and to guarantee the safety of both oikos and polis.

The Propompoi, or Escorts, who close the play and trilogy with a final song exhort their listeners to give the *ololuge* (1047). Since this is a traditionally female cry, it may be that they are addressing themselves, rather than the audience, and if so, then some of the last figures prominent on the stage are women. As A. Sommerstein notes in his edition, if the cultic servants of Athena join in the procession with the Areopagites, we can understand this as a final reconciliation between the sexes, whose conflict has determined much of the course of the trilogy. A less positive reading might stress instead the differences between the Areopagites and the ritually involved women; excluded from public, political, or juridical speech, the women of Athens share in the city only to the extent of their ritual service and their cry of

32. Frag. 13 *GLP* = frag. 499 Nauck.

ololuge. Moreover, that ritual activity is here denuded of the dangerous autonomy or challenging energy predicated earlier of Klytaimestra or the chorus
in the *Libation-Bearers.* The women are summoned to work for the polis, and
they are an anonymous mass, without the specificity that animated other
female characters. The fate of the Furies suggests that ritual action may compensate the female for a loss of authority in other contexts, but the deployment of the massed women of Athens indicates that ritual action itself must
be controlled in case it becomes a further source of power.[33]

The Aeschylean plays here considered stage conflicts that the polis can
try to heal, in part by redeploying women's ritual energies. Two other plays
from the 440s and 430s posit conflicts that the polis is unable to resolve, in
one case because the polis has little purchase on the events and in the other
because the polis is all but rendered irrelevant by the challenge presented
by the ritually active woman. The former play is *Medea,* the latter *Antigone.*
The latter play does make attempts to contain the authority and power of its
female figure, but the former declines to do so—and it stands alone in this
as in other respects.

Antigone

The mourning woman, as we have seen, can be a powerful figure; controlled and contained by Athenian funeral practice, she emerges ever more
insistently on grave ceramics. At some point probably earlier than 441
B.C.E. Sophocles produced the *Antigone,* which emphatically stages the
mourning woman and the incipient questioning of or reservation about
polis ideology that she can represent. The play is set in Thebes, in the aftermath of the attack enacted in the *Seven Against Thebes.* Eteokles and
Polyneikes are both dead; Kreon, their uncle and the new ruler, decrees that
Eteokles shall be buried and Polyneikes left to rot. Antigone defies the
injunction and determines to give her brother Polyneikes proper burial.
The ensuing events lead to her death and Kreon's downfall.

Throughout her appearances in the play, Antigone identifies with her
responsibility to the familial cult undertaken by women, and in her final
speech, before she is led away to death, she describes her whole life as one
of mourning rituals. She hopes that her arrival in the underworld will be
cherished by all her dead relatives, because of the services she performed
for them on their deaths (900–902):

> When you died I washed you with my own hands,
> I laid you out, I poured the libations
> for your graves.

---

33. For a positive discussion of this ending, which exonerates it from the charge of misogyny, see Rehm 1994: 56–58.

Antigone never makes the argument, popular with modern commentators, that she is called upon to bury her brother because funeral rites are particularly women's responsibility. She does claim, however, in her opening scene with Ismene, the right as a family member to bury Polyneikes, and she sees Kreon's edict as expressly directed against Ismene and herself as the last remaining relatives.[34]

While the demands of polis and of family did not necessarily collide under all circumstances, the democratic polis of the Athenians was renegotiating their relationship to the extent that they might indeed conflict. The polis arrogated certain familial functions to itself, such as the education of boys left fatherless by war, and, as we have seen, the oversight of family funerals. As well as the family, however, Antigone sees herself as defending the rights of the divine sphere. In her speech before Kreon, she claims sanction for her deed from the unwritten laws; exactly what these are is left conveniently unclear, but it is plausible to conclude that they are natural or divine laws mandating burial for all (453–57):

> Nor did I think that your pronouncements were strong enough
> To overcome the unwritten, unshakable laws of the gods—
> And you a mere mortal.
> For these do not live today and yesterday, but forever,
> And nobody knows when they appeared.

Antigone's gesture challenges the polis from two directions at once, from the subpolitical level of the family and from the suprapolitical level of the divine. Whereas family, polis, and gods should rightly be in harmony with one another, the play stages their confrontation. From these two directions Antigone's ritual gesture can expose weaknesses in the ideology of the polis, or at least in Kreon's conception of it. Because Kreon identifies the polis, as the play unfolds, so unequivocally with himself, nobody is left by the end of the drama who can plausibly speak for it, and no healing gesture is offered.

The speech with which Kreon begins is a rousing articulation of civic principles and as such found a hearing in Athens a century later when

---

34. Commentators dispute the extent to which an Athenian audience would see Antigone as justified in her defiance of the polis and pursuit of the familial imperative. See Foley 1995 for an account of two diametrically opposed views, those of Sourvinou-Inwood and of Blake and Tyrrell. We might note that even Ismene never questions Antigone's right and duty to bury her brother—in fact she feels the necessity to ask forgiveness herself from the dead for not assisting in the burial—but she calculates that the risk of a shameful death outweighs the familial responsibility. Since Ismene, the character who articulates various other forms of opposition to Antigone, does not point out that she is not required to bury her brother, I conclude that there probably is an obligation.

Demosthenes (19.247) quoted it with approval. Since the speech is set up as a test for Kreon himself, however, he necessarily fails (175–77):

> It's impossible to know a man completely,
> His soul, his thoughts, his judgment,
> Until he stands before you
> Proved in the arts of command.

The first stress of office, when the guard comes to report the corpse's burial, finds Kreon inadequate to the task of ruling. Threatening torture and death, Kreon amply justifies the guard's initial fear of him, and then turns on the chorus when they wonder aloud if the burial is the work of the gods. Instead of the gods, Kreon suspects a cell of dissidents—men described as having been long dissatisfied with his rule, even though its inception was at the beginning of the play (289–92)—who have articulated their political threat through this ritual gesture. In fact, of course, the converse has happened; Antigone's ritual gesture has *become* politicized because of the division that Kreon has introduced into Thebes. Kreon's second explanation for the defiance of the unknown traitor is money; it is greed that allegedly motivates the guard, the putative conspirators, and, later on, the prophet Teiresias (221–22, 294–303, 322, 325–26, 1037–39, 1046–47). Kreon pits his version of the city not against another version, but against mere venality, and such a model of politics cannot cope with the real alternative that Antigone incipiently represents. The corruption that Kreon sees everywhere is already part of himself.

Against Haimon, who questions the decision to execute Antigone, Kreon cannot wield the accusation of venality, but he attributes to him other base motives instead. Accusing him of being a "woman's slave" (746, 756), Kreon not only arrogates for himself the right to autocratic rule but also claims that he alone has a viable conception of civic order and civic discourse. He resists Haimon's urging to listen to other voices in the city and insists that Thebes is his to rule alone. "Is Thebes about to tell me how to rule? . . . Am I to rule this land for others or myself?" (734–36). This utterance completes his descent from the opening statement of principles, which is also compromised in his earlier speech to Haimon (666–67):[35]

> . . . but the man whom the city puts in charge,
> That man must be obeyed even in small things,
> And whether he's right or wrong.

He explains that to rule a city is the same thing as to rule a household, with its implication of hierarchical subordination among members. Since

---

35. The edition of Lloyd-Jones and Wilson restores these lines.

Antigone's rebellion threatens not only the structures of the city but those of the household as well, it is doubly disturbing—is anarchy, in fact, as Kreon claims (672). Kreon presents a paradigm in which oikos and polis are on a continuum of authority, both excluding the female, at least implicitly, from positions of importance. Armed with her ritual obligations and her determination to fulfill them, Antigone challenges this version of rule and exclusion in all its manifestations. Unable to conceive of a modification to his model, Kreon resorts to the traditional misogynist discourse that accuses women of wanting to rule:

> Now indeed I am not the man, but she is,
> If she wins this victory and gets away with it. (484–85)

> For it's better, if we must, to fall to a man,
> And never be called weaker than a woman. (679–80)

He decrees for her the peculiarly female death of being walled up and starved—the ultimate form of seclusion—rather than the politicized death of stoning by the united community that he had previously planned for the traitor who buried Polyneikes (36). His preferred punishment descends from the political to the familial level in the same way as his discourse descends from political sense to misogynist censure.

Why Kreon cannot have Antigone stoned is at least partly because the city is no longer united; Antigone's gesture does not stem from an avowedly political dissidence, but it has created one. Both she and Haimon claim that the Thebans are on her side in the matter of burying her brother; Antigone says that the citizens would praise her if they were not silenced by fear of Kreon (504–5, 509), and Haimon asserts that the city mourns for her (693–95). Antigone's loyalty to family and gods has apparently brought about what is indeed a new version of the city, and one that challenges Kreon's vision. The chorus, however, who comprise the only citizens of Thebes to appear onstage, do not fully bear out the claims of Antigone and Haimon. When Antigone is brought out to die, the chorus say: "But now, even I would break all bounds when I see this" (801–2), but after she begins to speak, they seem less sympathetic: "You went to the limit of daring, / you struck the high seat of justice, child, with your foot" (853–55); "Your self-willed passion has destroyed you" (875); "Still the same storms, the same tossing of her soul has her in its grip" (929–30). Antigone in fact accuses them of mocking and abusing her (838).[36] The events of the play obscure the locus of authority that should be the polis and do not in the end replace it with anything more viable.

---

36. Tyrrell and Bennett (1998: 103) have the very interesting argument that the chorus censors its discourse because it is within hearing of Kreon.

The mourning woman here represents a kind of crowbar with which the play uproots the polis, at least as represented by Kreon; Antigone is largely vindicated by Teiresias, and her opponent is utterly destroyed. Some gestures toward containing the power thus unleashed are made, however, so that some of Antigone's achievements are undermined in her final appearance. She retreats from her former position on the city, regretting that she acted *bia politon* (907), "against the will of the citizens," using a phrase that Ismene used against her in the opening scene (79). Rather than being united in her defense, as was her previous claim, the city is now represented as united against her. She begins to term herself a *metoikos*, a "resident alien," (852, 868), and the word is repeated by Kreon at 890. The term could refer to her change of abode between life and death, but it can also be understood as marking her excluded and marginal position within her own city. Although Antigone begins this scene by calling upon the chorus, as "men of my fatherland" (806), to witness her end, she quickly turns instead to the "springs of Dirce" and "holy grove of Thebe where the chariots gather" (844–45), abandoning the civic for the natural dimension.

This depoliticizing or "privatizing' of the play is underlined by the long lament for the marriage and children, the family, that she will not have. Foley has read this scene as Antigone's political challenge to Kreon, who is depriving her offspring of their rights as rulers of Thebes,[37] but it also signifies the positive rituals that she has given up in favor of the death ritual for Polyneikes. So impoverished has her ritual life subsequently become that she even has to sing the funeral lament for herself.[38] At the same time, marriage and childbirth, as well as measuring the extent of the sacrifice that she has made, represent socially sanctioned activity that contrasts with the autonomy that Antigone has previously shown in the burial of her brother.[39] The ritual authority that she then exercised has been subsumed within the more acceptable ritual figure of marriage, and the play thus ensures that some measure of containment takes place.[40]

Even her notional marriage and children are quickly taken from her. Expanding on the theme of the will of the citizens, Antigone says (905–11):

> For never, if I had been the mother of children
> Or if my husband was dead and rotting,
> I'd never have taken this trouble upon myself,

---

37. See Foley 1993.

38. Tyrell and Bennett (1998: 101) point out how Antigone "improvises rituals."

39. On marriage and death in this play see especially Seaford 1987 and Rehm 1994: 59–71.

40. The perceptive argument of Ormand 1999 is that Antigone is enabled by the use of wedding imagery to develop for herself a subject position, which is then lost in that same imagery.

Against the will of the citizens.
What law, you ask, do I satisfy when I say this?
If my husband died, I might have had another,
And a child from another man, if I lost the first,
But with mother and father lying in Hades
There is no brother who can ever spring to life.

These lines are so extraordinary, and so unpalatable, that many have wished to excise them, but editors now increasingly leave them in on the authority of Aristotle *Rhetoric* 1417a28–32. Antigone apparently abandons the "laws" that she had previously revered—even using the same loaded term, *nomos* (908)—in favor of temporizing with public opinion. At the same time, her newly articulated commitment to marriage and family is made highly problematic by the information that she would not have buried husband or child. Her reason for the bizarre calculus may be traced to a passage in Herodotos,[41] but it becomes no more acceptable in that context. It is hard not to conclude that Antigone's stature as ritual practitioner and advocate of a different version of politics is diminished in her final scene, the potential power unleashed by her gesture of burial contained.

Antigone leaves the stage for good at 943, with over 400 lines of the drama still to come. She abandons the stage to Kreon, whose tragedy then works itself out in the scene with Teiresias and in the king's frantic attempts to undo what he has done. In this silence about Antigone the play imitates the gods, who despite her need (925–26) give her no final sign as to whether she is justified or not.

The Sophoclean *Elektra* (date unknown) also stages the mourning woman and also allows her power and initiative, although the play does not seem to interrogate the ideology of the polis as closely as does the *Antigone*. The dramatic moment is the same as that of the *Libation-Bearers*. Constantly lamenting the murder of her father by Klytaimestra and Aigisthos, Elektra uses her mourning as a political tool against those now in power, but Mycenae is presented simply as a royal palace without a civic dimension; the chorus is comprised of local women rather than of male citizens. Aigisthos and Klytaimestra are relatively uncomplicated tyrants who do not start out, as Kreon does, by defending a viable version of the polis.

Elektra has made a source of power out of the passivity of mourning and the static quality of a life prohibited from developing in the directions of

---

41. See Herodotos 3.11.9, the encounter between Darius and the wife of Intaphrenes, where a woman chooses what male relative shall live, rather than who shall be buried. Both Murnaghan (1986) and Neuburg (1990) seek coherence and relevance in the *Antigone* passage rather than seeing it as a diminishment of Antigone. Ormand (1999: 97) offers an impressively complex account.

marriage and children.[42] For Elektra, as for Antigone, mourning is an alternative to these: "I have no child, no man to love, / I carry my never-ending burden, / Washed in my tears" (164–67).[43] On the stage Elektra's mourning garners no support, and both the chorus and her sister Chrysothemis try repeatedly to dissuade her from her posture. Yet certain moments in the play indicate that the mourning is politically effective: Klytaimestra claims: "And yet in front of many you say / That I am arrogant and rule outside the bounds of justice / Doing violence to you and yours" and that Elektra may "with envy and garrulous cries / Spread pointless rumors through all the city" (520–22, 641–42). Elektra's mourning is so effective, in fact, that Aigisthos and Klytaimestra are determined to hide it and to shut Elektra away in a dungeon (378–82). Her mourning rituals are contrasted to the choral dance and sacrifice that Klytaimestra has established to celebrate the anniversary of Agamemnon's death (278–81), and later, in her fantasy of revenge, to the feting of the sisters that will ensue once they have murdered Aigisthos (982–83). Klytaimestra tries to initiate another ritual movement, in sending offerings to Agamemnon's tomb, but Elektra trumps it, as in the *Libation-Bearers,* when she persuades Chrysothemis to take instead gifts from the sisters. Similarly, her presence makes it impossible for Klytaimestra to complete her prayers (638–40). Elektra's measure of efficacy, however, is bought at the price of a social isolation that seems even greater after Orestes enters the scene.

With the false report of Orestes' death, which is to gain him access to the palace, the focus of Elektra's mourning shifts from Agamemnon to Orestes. Foley has argued that Elektra's mourning is shown to be an incorrect method of generating vengeance that must give way to the masculine plans of Orestes and the Pedagogue,[44] and certainly in the latter part of the play the potentially effective mourning for Agamemnon is replaced by the misplaced—albeit immensely moving—mourning for Orestes. Once Orestes is recognized, both he and the Pedagogue try to impress upon Elektra the need for silence, in a grotesque parody of other characters' efforts to muzzle her.[45] She does not leave the stage but remains to pray to Apollo (1376–83) and then to urge on the two killers in a way that many commentators have found disturbing (1411–12, 1415, 1416). Neither her mourning nor her new aggression offers a paradigm that the play embraces unequivocally.

---

42. On her lack of action see Ormand 1999: 60–61, 67.

43. Both women also compare themselves to Niobe.

44. See Foley 1993.

45. Ormand 1999: 77 is good on this scene, and on the earlier wrestling over the empty urn; Ormand suggests that Elektra can be seen briefly to have occupied the position of the *epikleros,* the anomalous female heir, and that she now has that position wrested from her.

Medea

In the *Antigone,* and to a lesser extent the *Elektra,* the mourning woman is a hermeneutic with which to expose the corruptions of vested authority, but she cannot finally offer an alternative, and no obvious healing process is undertaken. The *Antigone* thus differs from the Aeschylean plays, at least as their endings are reconstructed. Euripides' *Medea* of 431, while generally as bleak as the *Antigone,* offers a very different version of the conflict over ritual and shows the road emphatically not taken in the dramatic representation of women's ritual activity. Repudiated by her husband, Jason, and threatened with exile by Kreon, the king of Corinth, Medea nonetheless turns every aspect of her weakness to strength. She defies the established authorities, concludes an alliance with the king of Athens, murders Kreon and his daughter, Jason's new bride, and finally kills her own two sons in order to put an end to Jason's lineage. On two occasions she deploys the ritual act of supplication, and at the end of the play, when she escapes with the bodies of her sons in a chariot drawn by dragons, she founds a commemorative rite. Medea wins all the conflicts over ritual because the men who are her opponents do not even know that they are fighting. The structures of the polis are largely absent from this play (just as is Medea's family), and Medea expands to fill the vacuum with the structures that she puts in place.

Supplicating first Kreon, to be allowed to stay in Corinth, and then Aigeus, king of Athens, to be provided asylum in his city, Medea adopts what Rehm identifies as the quintessential position of a helpless woman kneeling in front of an authoritative man.[46] That supplication may be understood within a gendered paradigm is indicated by Aristotle *Oikonomika* A.4.1 (= 1334a), in which the husband is instructed not to harm his wife, but to treat her with the respect due to a suppliant from the hearth: "and the first of these [rules of marriage] forbids him to do her wrong . . . as stringently as though she were a suppliant whom one has raised from the hearthstone." Partly at least because she plays on the trope of her vulnerable femininity, Medea's supplication is in each case successful. As soon as Kreon has left the stage, however, Medea reveals that her scene of supplication was exactly that, a stage performance that enabled her to prevail over her enemies.[47] The ritual gestures are manipulated for her own destructive ends, corrupted even before the deployment of the sacrificial metaphor for the murder of her sons. This metaphor, which first surfaces clearly at the midpoint of her great speech (*thuma,* "sacrifice," 1054), is transformed into a historical reality when at the end of the play Medea invokes a version of a rite performed annually at Corinth.

46. Rehm 1994: 98.
47. According to Medea at 496–98, Jason was the first to corrupt the gesture of supplication.

According to nondramatic sources, seven boys and seven girls annually served in the temple of Hera Akraia, wearing black and with their heads shorn, in remembrance of and atonement for the death of Medea's children.[48] Most non-Euripidean accounts of the children's end make Medea indirectly responsible at best, laying most of the blame at the Corinthians' door, and the narrative of the ritual seems to have conformed to a pattern whereby the Corinthians, guilty of the deed, suffer various plagues and hardships until they make recompense by sending their own children to perform cult. The historical ritual seems to have combined elements of marriage and funeral; the children are dressed as if for mourning, but their youth, the participation of both sexes, and the service to Hera lead most commentators to interpret the ritual as prenuptial. The *Medea* thus ends, like many Euripidean plays, with a ritual etiology that claims a connection between the play and the realities of Greek culture while also rehearsing in a new form the concerns of the play itself.

Much critical work has addressed the relation between Medea's ritual and what seems to be Corinthian historical reality. A useful contribution is that of Francis Dunn, who shows that where cult and history do not seem to match, the discrepancies point up the innovation of Medea's infanticide.[49] The issue of the children's burial, for instance, which is important in the drama to both Medea and Jason but which plays no part either in Corinthian cult or in the non-Euripidean myth of Medea, instead draws attention to the playwright's departure in assigning the murder to the children's mother. When Medea claims that she will bury the children in the temple precinct in order to protect them from the violence of her Corinthian enemies (1380–81), Dunn points out that this anxiety is more applicable to the other version of their death in which the Corinthians were responsible.[50] Similarly, when Medea says she will found the rite "in place of" *(anti)* this "impious murder" (1383), Dunn suggests that she is using a term more appropriate for a deed perpetrated by others.[51] He concludes that the lines on the cult foundation "emphasize the shocking novelty of Euripides' passionate and vengeful Medea" and "point to the originality of a playwright who not only rewrites the persona of Medea, but rewrites the institutions associated with her."[52]

While Dunn's metatheatrical point is well taken, I would like to direct attention instead to the unprecedented nature of Medea's ritual gesture. In

48. See Pausanias 2.3.6–7 and 11, the scholia on Pindar *Olympian* 13.74g, and the scholia on *Medea* 264.

49. Dunn 1994. See also Johnston 1997.

50. Dunn 1994: 113.

51. Ibid.

52. Ibid., 115.

the *Medea* the typical Euripidean ending in ritual etiology is made to stand on its head; whereas the founders of cult are usually divinities or prophets, Medea here takes on those roles for herself as the only mortal in the corpus to found cult. The effrontery of commemorating a murder is familiar from the history of Klytaimestra, but Medea seems, in the language with which she founds the cult, to convert the murder into something else—not only into a sacrifice, but into one made by the Corinthians. Already transformed in the dragon chariot, she further transforms her bloody deed and makes it into the sacrifice she claimed by aligning it with historical Corinthian cult. The rite focuses not so much on the creativity of the playwright as on the anomalous authority thus assumed by the female character. Although she has brought only disorder and mayhem to Corinth,[53] she claims the authority to make the healing gestures associated with the closure of etiological cult; with none of the distance from the violent action that usually characterizes the figures who proclaim etiological rituals, she nonetheless arrogates to herself that speaking position. The contours of the historical rite show, moreover, that she succeeded in her attempt to rewrite her action and ascribe the deed to the Corinthians. Herself the murderer, she nonetheless legislates for how the murders will be perceived, and commemorated, for the time to come right down until the moment of the play's production.[54]

Medea's assumption of the authoritative position of the *dea ex machina* undermines the movement of healing closure typically attributed to ritual. The female is here far from contained, because the ritual gesture is instead a further sign of her frightening power. No other extant Greek play follows this pattern, although ritual authority is attributed to and taken from female characters in varying proportions. How extraordinary the *Medea* is in this respect can be seen from the fact that Euripides' *Hippolytos* of 428 B.C.E. reverts to the Aeschylean dynamic, whereby the female's suspect ritual initiative is converted into sanctioned ritual activity for a plurality of women. Aphrodite's prologue describes how, before the beginning of this drama, Hippolytos had left Troizen for Athens, where he was due to visit the Mysteries. His stepmother Phaidra saw him in Athens and fell in love. According to Aphrodite, she founded a temple to the goddess to commemorate her love, which, in gazing constantly (*katopsion,* 30) across from Athens to Troizen, where Hippolytos is based, replicates the gaze that first fell on Hippolytos. Phaidra's transgressive desire is thus articulated in a ritual initiative. At the end of the play, another new ritual form is generated that convenes a number of females instead of one dangerously autonomous woman. To commemorate the death of Hippolytos and to compensate him

---

53. See McDermott 1989 on Medea as the "incarnation of disorder."

54. Boedeker (1991: 109) makes the point about Medea as "author" of her own new myth but does not mention her ritual innovation.

for his death with the honor of cult, young women of Troizen before their marriages will cut their hair for him and sing of Phaidra's love (1423–30):

> Unmarried girls before their weddings
> Will cut their hair for you,
> And through long ages you will reap
> A rich reward of tears.
> Girls forever will have a care
> To make music in your honor,
> And Phaidra's love for you
> Will not fall silent or be nameless.

As numerous scholars have shown, this ritual has a complex relationship to the play it closes. Rabinowitz argues that "Euripides inscribes [Phaidra's] story within Hippolytos' apotheosis" and sees the marriage ritual as "ideological" because it binds the virgins to a patriarchal institution and makes them worship the woman-hating Hippolytos.[55] I have argued instead that the ritual affords women a voice, to compensate for the silencing of Phaidra, and installs them in the privileged position of reproducing their culture, after Hippolytos has represented women as having no part in culture at all.[56] Equipped with the Aeschylean paradigms, however, we can see that another task this ritual discharges is to correct Phaidra's earlier cult initiative by providing institutionalized ritual activity for a collective of women. Although women's ritual practice does not here afford the grounds of conflict between male and female, as it does to a greater or lesser extent in the other plays we have considered, the move from autonomy to containment may still be read in the Euripidean play.

WOMEN OF THEBES AND OF ATHENS

Several Aeschylean plays, and in later years the *Antigone* and *Medea,* represent women ritual practitioners as oppositional subjects, at odds with the polis or with males of their family. This dimension of tragedy's representation of women as cult practitioners is perhaps particularly visible in those plays set in Thebes, a city that has been seen to serve the Athenian tragic stage as an image of the anti-polis.[57] While the clash between the Theban city and the ritually active woman is especially clear in the *Antigone,* we have already seen a similar conflict in the *Seven,* and the *Bakchai* at the end of the century, which we shall examine later in this chapter, offers another version of it when the maenads oppose Pentheus. By contrast, some plays from the

55. Rabinowitz 1987: 135, 136–37.
56. Goff 1990: 116–17 and 128.
57. See, for example, Zeitlin 1990c.

late twenties and teens of the fifth century, focusing on Athens, sketch a different and more productive relationship between ritually active women and the city.

Theban Women

In the *Antigone* not only the central character but other women too are caught up in the dynamic of rituals prohibited or opposed. The song sung by the chorus subsequent to Antigone's departure recounts how Dionysos imprisoned Lykourgos, the young king of Edonia who had resisted his worship. Like Kreon with Antigone, Lykourgos had tried to stop the women from performing their cult but came to recognize the power of the god as he was destroyed by him.[58] As Lykourgos and Kreon block women's ritual commitment, so the play itself blocks the action of Eurydike. After the hymn to Dionysos, the queen comes onstage in response to the outcry she hears at the Messenger's entrance. She explains that she was just drawing back the bolts on her way to pray to Pallas Athena for help in the city's and Kreon's crisis, when she heard the cries and fainted (1185–89). The Messenger's news about Haimon's death is then delivered to her. Endeavoring to participate in civic healing to the extent appropriate, namely by her ritual activity, the queen is instead interrupted by the narrative of her son's death. What happens then is intriguing. Eurydike leaves in silence (1245), like her counterparts in other Sophoclean plays, Jokasta (*Oedipus Tyrannos* 1075) and Deianeira (*Women of Trachis* 814), and the Messenger concludes that she may have gone inside to set her maids to mourn rather than showing her grief to the city. Her mourning, then, is significant and potentially problematic in a way similar to Antigone's, but unlike Antigone she is thought to be conforming to the Solonic norms, keeping her participation in the mourning process wholly within the private sphere.[59] A few lines later Eurydike too is dead. Instead of performing prayers, she has killed herself at the altar (if the text is sound), and her silence has turned into curses that she calls down on Kreon. Her mourning for Haimon is compressed into the few moments between her exit and the entrance of the second messenger

58. The last choral song, sung while Kreon and his attendants are burying Polyneikes and supposedly freeing Antigone, is throughout an invocation of Dionysos, who is called upon to come and heal his people of Thebes (1142). Since Dionysos is here represented as a healer and a bringer of civic peace (Oudemans and Lardinois 1987: 154, quoting Rohdich), no tension is allowed to emerge between the needs of the city and those of the maenads. Thebes is even called the mother city of the Bakchai (1122). The ode thus seems to imagine a way in which the city could coexist peacefully with the women's ritual work, but it makes its own project problematic by invoking Dionysos, already responsible for the downfall of another resistant king, and always potentially opposed to the values of culture.

59. See Rehm 1994: 67 on the similarities and differences between Antigone and Eurydike.

with the news of her death. Meanwhile, however, Kreon enters, and we see then that it is he who has gathered in all the mourning energies of the play and who now gives vent to the lengthy lament denied to the two women.[60] The play's attention comes to rest on Kreon, as he and the play appropriate for their own ends the voices of the women who have died.

The similarity of the situations of Antigone and Eurydike may suggest not simply their affinity but a wider implication for Theban women in general. If theatrical Thebes is mobilized as an anti-city ceaselessly struggling with the problems that Athens represents itself as having solved, the women of theatrical Thebes contribute to this representation when their ritual performances are denied or otherwise made problematic. On occasion their ritual activity is crucial for the welfare chiefly of the private sphere, as in the case of Antigone, but in several narratives prohibition of ritual activity also prevents the Theban women from playing the only civic role permitted them by the ideology of the polis. In other plays the movement to block women's ritual actions is not the mainspring of the drama but is nonetheless a persistent part of the representation of theatrical Thebes. Antigone, in other plays that feature her, such as the *Phoenician Women* and the *Oedipus at Colonus,* is repeatedly denied the satisfactions of ritual. In the *Phoenician Women,* she exits into exile with her father at the close of the play, lamenting that she can no longer keep company with her contemporaries, nor the gods, nor dance in a "Kadmeian fawnskin" as she used to (1747–57). Like the other characteristics of youth, the veil and the virginal modesty that she casts aside to mourn her brothers (1485–91), the cult dances to Dionysos are henceforth denied her. Even in the *Oedipus at Colonus,* a play that in other respects offers to correct the negative paradigm of Thebes by bringing it into a closer relationship with Athens, Antigone and Ismene too are denied the opportunity to bury the body of Oedipus or even to know where it is. The Athenian hero Theseus is the only one permitted to know the end of Oedipus. As we shall see, he performs a similar role in the Euripidean *Suppliant Women,* where Thebes once again denies the right of burial, this time preventing the mothers of the Seven from reclaiming the corpses of their sons. Theseus leads an attack on Thebes, regains the bodies, and himself performs the rites due to the dead.

In other plays women are differently afflicted. Jokasta in Sophocles' *Oedipus Tyrannos* is placed in a situation similar to that of Eurydike; she comes on stage in order to visit the temples and dedicate garlands, giving as her reason for this ritual intervention Oedipus, who is beginning to suspect himself of killing his father, and whose anguish is reducing the citizenry to "passengers who shudder, / seeing him, the pilot of the ship, struck with ter-

60. See Segal 1995: 126–27.

ror" (922–93). Like Eurydike she endeavors to heal both public and private distress by her ritual gestures but is prevented by the movement of the drama; her action is interrupted by the Messenger, who will eventually reveal the whole terrifying story of Oedipus's Theban origin. In both plays the scene that begins with the woman's prayers ends with her suicide. The Phoenician women who leave their name to another Theban play also exemplify that city's inability to allow women to perform ritual properly. Although Phoenician, the women are on their way to Delphi, where they will take up a ritual post singing and dancing in honor of the god. In a curious variation of this movement to block women's ritual action, they are trapped in Thebes by the outbreak of civil war; they do perform as a chorus but point out that they still long to be one in their proper destination, Delphi (236).

Suppliant Women

In theatrical Athens, I suggest, the dynamic is different. The Euripidean *Suppliant Women,* dated to around 424 B.C.E., shows women's loyalty to Athens to be mediated and indeed enabled by ritual service. The play concerns the bodies of the seven Argives who had fallen in the attack on Thebes, to which the Thebans refuse to give burial. The mothers of the Seven, who comprise the chorus of the drama, intercept Aithra, mother of Theseus, at Eleusis, where she has gone to perform a ritual, and persuade her to intervene for them with Theseus. Theseus resists the pleas of Adrastos, who accompanies the mothers, but yields to his own mother. The Thebans are defeated in battle, and the bodies retrieved; Theseus prepares them for burial, and Adrastos delivers over them a potted funeral speech. Evadne, the wife of Kapaneus, throws herself onto his funeral pyre. The Epigonoi, sons of the Seven, enter, promising to avenge their parents, and Athena finally enters to close the play by exacting an oath of allegiance to Athens from the Argives.

What is relevant to my investigation is the ritual that Aithra has come to Eleusis to perform, and its relation to her ability to persuade Theseus to undertake the burial of the Argive bodies. The play as a whole is structured round a denial of ritual by Thebes, in that it prevents the Argive mothers from properly lamenting their fallen sons, and thereby opens the way for Athens to correct the denial. In the opening moments of the play the Theban disease threatens to affect Athenian women too, because the mothers interrupt the ritual space of the Eleusinian sanctuary of Demeter and Persephone, and the ritual time of Aithra's performance of the Proerosia. We may conclude, however, that Aithra is in some sense able to complete her ritual performance, because it is the tropes of the Proerosia that she later mobilizes in her definitive speech to Theseus.

The play's evocation of the Proerosia has often been dismissed as a simple device to get Aithra to Eleusis. D. Conacher remarks that the presence of the ritual opens the possibility that the whole play be understood as a fertility rite, and Foley gestures toward the Proerosia's coordination of Demetrian motifs with politics, but the majority of criticism on the play is not interested in the ritual.[61] Our documentary evidence for the historical rite is scanty and contested, but it seems to have centered on a ritual plowing of the Rarian Field at Eleusis. We may reasonably conclude, then, that the festival was concerned with agricultural fertility; some references also mention an offering of firstfruits.[62] Agricultural fertility is a dominant note at Eleusis, where Demeter and Persephone were said to have first taught humankind agriculture, but Eleusis is also significant in other ways that relate to the concerns of the play. Primarily, Eleusis can connote the separation and subsequent reunion between parent and child, as when Demeter loses and then regains Persephone. This reunion, or a version of it, is what the Argive mothers of the chorus desire, and so they appear on stage, weeping, as a multiplicity of Demeters. Their grief affects Aithra, so that she too weeps, and it is as a mourning mother that she intercedes with Theseus. Theseus, and to some extent Adrastos, contrasts the chorus women's mission with the kind of sanctioned ritual activity that should be taking place at Eleusis, and Theseus even admonishes his mother not to cry in the goddesses' precinct (289–90; see also contrasts drawn between the mothers and Demeter at 97 and 173).[63] But in their mourning and their desire to see their children again, the Argive mothers rehearse the primary Eleusinian trope in a way that is completely appropriate.

When Aithra urges Theseus to retrieve the bodies from Thebes and return them to the mothers, she can be seen to speak with the authority of the Eleusinian imperative that requires the reunion of parent and child. By the late fifth century, Eleusis also played an important part in Athenian self-definition, so that Aithra's deployment of Eleusinian tropes here is a condensed version of the city's own ideologically charged notion of its identity. Eleusis had become part of the Athenian polis; it was a deme of Athens, and its people part of the Hippothoontis tribe. Athens thus appears as the chief provider of the two Eleusinian gifts to humankind, namely agriculture and the Mysteries. Sources persistently link the two institutions and, moreover, link them to Athens. Isokrates *Panegyrikos* 28 claims that Athens gave the world "the two gifts that happen to be the greatest, the harvest . . . and the rite." Xenophon *Hellenika* 6.3.4–6 represents Kallias, an important official

---

61. Conacher 1967: 98 n. 11; Foley 1993: 124 n. 57.

62. See Parke 1977: 73–75; Parke and Wormell 1956: vol. 2, no. 164; and Foucart 1914: 56–59.

63. In a similar vein, Zeitlin (1970) shows how the Argive festival of Hera offers a normative measure by which to gauge the perversions of the Euripidean *Elektra*.

at Eleusis, promoting the unity of Athens and Sparta by recalling that the ancestors of the Spartans were the first to be taught agriculture at Eleusis. Cicero *De Legibus* 2.14.36 comments: "For your Athens seems to me to have provided many excellent and divine benefits for the life of humankind, and nothing better than those mysteries." Athens can thus be seen to appropriate not only the territory but also the symbolic significance of Eleusis,[64] and hence to claim its status as the major provider of both physical and spiritual nurture to the entire Greek world. This trope of Panhellenic provision will figure prominently in my argument about Aithra's speech to Theseus.

Aithra speaks to her son with the authority of the Eleusinian mourning mother, but Eleusis also has wider resonances in an Athenian context. One of these, the stance of Panhellenic provision, also has relevance for an account of the Proerosia. As I indicated before, some accounts of this ritual mention an offering of firstfruits, and the history of this offering is of particular interest to us. These accounts all appear in sources later than the *Suppliant Women,* but this does not mean, of course, that they could not have been current in the fifth century as well.[65] The narrative behind the offering, as given in H. W. Parke and D. E. W. Wormell, is from a passage in Lykourgos (fragment 86):[66]

> They say that there was a famine throughout the world, and when the Greeks and barbarians consulted him, Apollo ordained that the Athenian people should offer prayers on behalf of all. Many peoples sent ambassadors to them.

A passage from the Suda reads:[67]

> For some say, that famine took hold of all the land, and the god said that the Athenians should perform a sacrifice, the Proerosia, to Demeter on behalf of all; on account of which they send firstfruits to Athens from all parts, as thankofferings.

According to this narrative, Athens holds a position that can indeed be described as Panhellenic, in that the city rescues all Greece from a famine and thereby establishes itself as the focal point for all Greece. The new relationship between Athens and the rest of Greece is then dramatized in the

---

64. Primarily of course we are concerned with the Mysteries themselves as an index of the "symbolic significance" of Eleusis; but in a related gesture, the Athenian mythology of Theseus involved the defeat of various figures who had been heroes in or near Eleusis but who for Athenian purposes were recast as monsters. See Mylonas 1962: 28 and Spaeth 1991: 352.

65. F. Jacoby (*FGH* III.B [Suppl.] 1.84), who supplies further bibliography, claims that in the Euripidean Proerosia we have an archaically simple ceremony or only part of a ceremony. This does not exclude the possibility, of course, that the drama may register a more complex late fifth-century ceremony.

66. See also Lykourgos (ed. Conomis) frag. 87.

67. S.v. *eiresione;* see also the Suda P 2420.

sending of firstfruits.[68] The details of the Proerosia correspond to the over-all notion of Athens as Panhellenic provider through the city's appropria-tion of Eleusis. I suggest, then, that the Proerosia not only functions as a convenient way of getting Aithra to Eleusis. The festival's ideological con-tours, and the version of Athenian identity that it helps to promulgate, also lay the groundwork for what Aithra will do in her speech to Theseus.

The most important intervention that Aithra makes in the course of the drama is to exhort Theseus to yield to the suppliant women and to return the bodies of the Seven to their mothers (297–331). The appeal is all the more central because both Adrastos and the Argive mothers (at 277–85) have already appealed to Theseus and have failed. Theseus's discourse has been eminently rational and pragmatic, and as such completely inadequate to deal with the situation of supplication.[69] His refusal to aid the suppliants produces a situation in which the mothers might threaten to hang themselves and thus pollute the city, like their Aeschylean namesakes. Instead, Aithra saves both the mothers and Athens. In many ways, then, this speech is crucial.

The success of Aithra's discourse can be seen to depend on a combina-tion of appeals to the ideology of Demeter, the mother exalted in her loss, and appeals to the ideology of Athenian identity. The figure of Aithra can thus be seen to combine two categories that, at Eleusis, can be particularly potent: the maternal and the Athenian. Before she speaks, Theseus tries to separate her from the Argive mothers and points out to her the ritual oblig-ation not to cry in Demeter's precincts (289–90, 292). But the mothers too invoke the twin goddesses (271), and, armed with these influential symbols, Aithra can inculcate the necessity of reuniting parent with child, even when the child is dead. But the crucial appeal is made not so much by a mother as by an Athenian. Aithra invokes the Athenian identity and mission, and the Athens she is concerned with is the same kind of city as that which claims to have promulgated the benefits of Eleusis, a city that labors on behalf of others: "For by struggles [the city] will increase" (323). Athens is linked in the appeal with the gods (301) and with the "laws of all Greece" (311). The Panhellenic law that allegedly guarantees the right of burial to the fallen is offered here as a moral imperative that ideally outweighs the specific hostilities of war; it has not been invoked before, despite the various appeals that have been made to Theseus. It is only here that Athens is charged with the defense of a Panhellenic institution, as well as of divine prerogatives and of its own standing.

68. Mikalson (1975: 67–69) argues that the Proerosia was primarily for the Eleusinians; Athenians were invited to it but were not its focal point. He argues from the fact that a possi-ble meeting of the Athenian council, or *boule,* can be attributed to the day when the Proerosia was celebrated.

69. On his speech see Michelini 1991.

Aithra's speech is also concerned with Theseus's own character and reputation, which he makes much use of in his reply to her (338). Later on in the play, however, the element of her speech most reworked is precisely its Panhellenic dimension. At 526 Theseus, replying to the Herald from Thebes, claims that to bury the Argive dead is to save "the law of all Greeks," and he insists on this point again at 538: "This is common to all of Greece." The Messenger reports that Theseus had addressed the Theban army in similar terms, announcing that the Athenians came "to save the law of all the Greeks" (671–72). The Panhellenic imperative that Aithra first articulates is thus made particularly important by its subsequent career in the play. This Panhellenic orientation is, as I have said, unmentioned in the play until Aithra speaks. If we ask what equips her to broach this political issue with her son, rather than confining herself to the motives that she first mentions, we may decide that her performance of the Proerosia is the facilitating factor. Even if we did not accept all the possible ramifications of the festival, we could still argue that Aithra's speech is facilitated by her ritual performance, in that she can be seen to espouse the cause of parent-child reunion invested both with the authority of Demeter and with the sign of fertility provided by the Proerosia. But if we accept the link with the firstfruits and with the mythic narrative of Athens's crucial intervention on behalf of Greece, then we can also suggest that the Proerosia enables Aithra to move beyond maternal imperatives and equips her with a powerful discourse of Athenian identity and mission. The appeal to Panhellenic law in Aithra's speech is not unprecedented, because the narrative of the Proerosia already awards Athens a position of Panhellenic significance. The myth of the Proerosia displays the contours to which Aithra wants Theseus's action to conform; the Proerosia already announces what the play sets out to prove, namely that Athens is the city that makes a salvific and ritually sanctioned intervention on behalf of all the Greeks, and that is consequently rewarded with undying loyalty and gratitude.[70]

Erechtheus

Two other plays make firm identifications between women's ritual practice and their access to Athenian identity. In Euripides' fragmentary *Erechtheus* of 423/22, Praxithea, wife of the Athenian king, consents gladly to sacrifice her daughter in order that Athens may be victorious over Eleusis.[71] Her

---

70. My reading here differs from that of Foley 1993 and from the broad argument of Holst-Wahrhaft 1992. Whereas Foley stresses the appropriation of women's mourning ritual by men, I stress here Aithra's appropriation, through ritual, of politics. I should point out that many scholars subscribe to a pessimistic overall interpretation of the play; Rehm (1994: 120–21) stresses in this context the perversion of mourning ritual by Evadne.

71. For the fragments of this play see the edition of Carrara (1977). The speech is

enthusiastic speech on the topic, which is the longest single fragment of the play remaining, collects and recycles all the possible tropes in Greek discourse that contrast the worth of daughters versus sons, girls versus boys, and the family versus the state. Its wholesale approval of the kind of human sacrifice that in other Euripidean plays is rendered highly problematic has meant that is often read as ironic.[72] In the absence of most of the play it is difficult to measure the impact of the speech, but a "straight" reading of such tropes must always be available along with its ironic antithesis, and Praxithea's identification with the city is unequivocally rewarded by the *dea ex machina,* Athena, who makes the queen her own first priestess. Having proved her suprafamilial loyalty to the polis, thereby reversing the characteristic error of other tragic females, Praxithea is offered a position within the polis, not in its political structure, which remains closed to her, but in the ritual articulations where women's latent "citizenship" may be expressed. The positive possibilities for Praxithea seem, however, to be undermined by another fragment, in which she seems to lament that not only her daughter but her husband and remaining children have also all been lost in the war.

Ion

Euripides' *Ion,* third of the plays to offer to women an Athenian identity that is mediated through ritual, is currently dated to the teens of the fifth century. Informed by the contours of the Arrhephoria, the *Ion* never mentions that ritual's name, but its metaphors condition the representation of several characters, especially that of Kreousa.[73]

As we have seen, the historical Arrhephoria implicitly claims to derive from the history of the daughters of Kekrops. Athena was pursued by Hephaistos but repelled him, so that his semen fell to the ground. A child was born from the earth, Erichthonios, whom Athena received from the goddess Earth (Ge) and gave to the Kekropides in a casket. Commanded not to open it, they did so and were terrified by the snakes or snakes inside. They then leaped from the Acropolis to their deaths. The ritual service of the *arrhephoroi,* who recall the mythical daughters, foregrounds two activities: the nocturnal descent and the weaving of Athena's peplos.

For the play, the Kekropides are the first generation of doomed Athenian daughters. A later generation, comprising the daughters of Erechtheus, was sacrificed by their father for the sake of the land, and only the baby Kreousa

---

preserved in a speech by Lykourgos, himself a member of the Eteoboutad family, which supplied the historical priestesses of Athena.

72. See Vellacott 1975, for instance.

73. Loraux (1990: 199) mentions the connection between Kreousa and the Arrhephoria but does not pursue it.

was spared. The *Ion* takes up her story at a later date. Raped by Apollo in a cave near the Acropolis, Kreousa leaves her baby there; he is transported by Hermes to Delphi, where he grows up in the service of the temple. Meanwhile Kreousa has married Xouthos from Boeotia, but their marriage is childless. When they visit Delphi for help and advice from the oracle, events are set in motion that will deliver Ion to his rightful place on the Athenian throne, but not before mother and son in ignorance of their true identities have each tried to kill the other.

Kreousa's story reworks that of the Kekropides and of their descendants the *arrhephoroi* in complex ways. Unlike the Kekropides, Kreousa is not terrified by the snake symbols of the royal Erechtheid house, but instead, like Athena, she places golden snakes in her baby's cradle (21–26). She does not jump from the Acropolis, like the daughters of Kekrops, but she is threatened with being thrown from Parnassos at Delphi when her attempt on Ion's life is made known (274, 1222, 1266–67).[74] Unlike the historical *arrhephoroi*, she endures an encounter with sexuality not mediated by ritual, but real and brutal. Instead of retrieving a swaddled baby from the ground, like the *arrhephoroi*, she places one there. Like the *arrhephoroi*, however, she satisfies in her own person the competing imperatives of autochthony (birth from the earth) and maternity. The *arrhephoroi*, daughters of the ancient and "autochthonous" Eupatrid families, rehearse the paradigm of autochthony when they retrieve the baby from the ground, and Kreousa, of the autochthonous Erechtheid house herself, guarantees Ion's right to succession. Yet at the same time, she is clearly a physical mother, and the text of the *Ion* insists repeatedly on the womblike nature of the enclosures that punctuate it (e.g., the cradle, the tent, the circular bracelets that Kreousa wears, the shrine itself). The *arrhephoroi* prepare for sexuality and maternity when they perform the nocturnal descent that both frightens and seduces.

Kreousa and the *arrhephoroi* are connected especially through the figure of weaving. Mythmaking of every kind is foregrounded in the *Ion,* and the contribution of women specifically is implicitly claimed as weaving. Even the Amazons, paradigms of antiwomanhood as they usually are, are here pressed into service as weavers. Although they display a series of signs of Athenian and Greek identity, the tapestries of the tent in which Xouthos celebrates Ion's "birthday" are said to be woven by the Amazons (1145). For once the Amazons are subsumed peacefully into Athenian discourse, foreshadowing perhaps the "happy ending" of the play, when Kreousa and Ion are reconciled and can forget the violence of their mutual assassination attempts. Weaving is also a sign of solidarity among women; Kreousa addresses her chorus of slave-women as "companions of my loom" (747–

74. See Loraux 1981: 243 n. 194.

48), and they do indeed prove completely loyal to her, braving Xouthos's wrath and threats of death in order to tell her that he has discovered a "son" whereas she is still without a child.

Rejecting the paradigm of Philomela, an Athenian woman who, when raped and unable to speak to name her attacker, wove an image instead, the chorus and Kreousa deploy the practice of weaving in order to facilitate their speech. When they hear that Kreousa was raped by Apollo, the chorus claim that "never in words or in webs" (507) have they heard that marriage with a god was good for a mortal woman, giving their own productions the same cultural authority as other retellings of myth. When they first enter the stage, admiring the sculptures at Delphi, they say that they have woven similar narratives (196–97; they could also be understood to say that they have told similar stories while at their looms). They refer explicitly to Herakles and Iolaos, but the other major narrative on the sculptures that they go on to describe is that of the Gigantomachy, the battle where the Olympian gods defeated the earth-born monstrous Giants. If the chorus have also woven this scene, as is plausible, then they have woven the scenes that were prominently represented on the peplos annually presented to Athena. The weaving of this peplos, as we have seen, was begun by the *arrhephoroi*. Kreousa too has woven a tiny part of the Gigantomachy; the unfinished work of her youth, her "virgin's work," swaddled Ion in his cradle, and on the cloth was woven the Gorgon. The Gorgon was defeated by Athena at the Gigantomachy, but since the goddess wears her head as the aegis, the Gorgon can also work as a sign of the royal Erechtheid house. This unfinished cloth and other tokens left in his cradle are what enable Kreousa finally to identify Ion as her son.

Despite her weaving, Kreousa, who has been forcibly inserted into the system of adult sexuality, could never be a proper virgin *arrhephoros*. Yet as the tokens are found and described, the play magically makes her a *parthenos* again; with the wicker cradle that does not decay (1391–92) and the olive sprig placed in it that is still flourishing (1435–36), her virginity returns. The words that cluster around her start to feature variations on the term *parthenos* (1418, 1425, 1473, 1489, 1523), and when time comes round full circle, and Ion is born again in the cradle, Kreousa returns to the state of *arrhephoros* that she could not properly occupy before. Now she takes up the autochthonous child—and it is hard to resist the conclusion that she will complete her unfinished weaving.

The Arrhephoria offers a combination of weaving and sexual initiation that together prepare the young practitioner for her adult female identity. The play takes Kreousa, who is suspended in time as a childless wife, unable to move forward in the accepted female trajectory, and makes her into an adult woman and mother of a son—incidentally, in Athena's closing speech, promising her many more sons. As an adult woman she is also able to take up her position as an Athenian, capable of perpetuating the Erechtheid house, in the same way as the *arrhephoroi* annually retrieve the symbolically autochthonous baby. Kreousa's initiation into sexuality, of course, is very different from the ritual of pleasure and fear prescribed for historical *arrhephoroi*. Her motherhood begins in violence, and if the lines she speaks describing Apollo also seem to indicate his beauty and a reciprocity of attraction, they modify that violence only a little if at all (887–90):

> You came to me with hair flashing gold
> As I was gathering into the folds of my dress
> The yellow petals that shone in response.

But the violence in Kreousa's story, as in that of Ion, is not only directed against her, but also directed *by* her against others. The task of becoming a woman and an Athenian, fostered by the metaphors of the Arrhephoria, involves negotiating the violence, the monstrosity, that is part of the inheritance of autochthony. Linked by their shared birth from the earth, the monstrous Giants and Gorgon contest the ideological space of the play with the legitimate Erechtheids.[75]

For Kreousa, at first, the violence of her narrative seems to come from elsewhere, from her father who sacrifices his other daughters and from Apollo who rapes her. In response to this she initiates her own sequence of violence, beginning with the exposure of Ion. Although it is hard to see what else she could have done in the circumstances, her attitude to the exposure is telling. Hermes claims that she put the baby out to die, using the participial form, which can act as an expression of purpose as well as meaning simply "as one about to die." In her own proliferating narratives she exposes the baby unwillingly, in the hopes that he may be saved, and Apollo is the only villain (386, 897–904, 949–65). When she is finally reunited with Ion, however, she can freely admit her part in his "death." She has also of course tried to kill him a second time, by having him poisoned in the tent. When the Old Man encourages her to take revenge for what he sees as a plot by Apollo, Xouthos, and Ion to foist Ion off as heir to the Athenian throne, she demurs at attacking either the god or her husband but is perfectly ready to murder the innocent stranger who has done her no deliberate harm. Again, when mother and son are reunited, Kreousa can admit "I killed you"; in fact she says it twice, and Ion also admits his attempt to kill his mother (1500, 1544, 1515). Both, then, begin to come to terms with the monstrosity that is their autochthonous birthright.

Unlike the Kekropides, Kreousa is subject as well as object of violence, and has to negotiate both these positions in order to become an Athenian and an

---

75. The Gorgon is, exceptionally, described as earth-born in this play. On the relations between monsters and Athenians see Goff 1988.

adult woman. The Arrhephoria offers a paradigm for achieving this twofold identity, but proposes a transition that is peaceful rather than marked by violence. Its promise of a secure achieved identity as female and Athenian is eventually fulfilled for Kreousa by the play, but it remains unclear whether the play subscribes fully to the Arrhephoria's point of view. The notion that there can be a stable Athenian identity is rendered problematic by the play's insistence on the ambivalence of autochthony, and its closing reference to Athenian imperialism, when Athena prophesies for Ion's descendants the colonization of the Mediterranean, may suggest that the monstrosity of the Athenians has for the moment gained the upper hand.[76] As we have seen, the *Erechtheus* is probably equally equivocal about Athenian success, and the *Suppliant Women* articulates as many doubts about Athens's mission and identity as it does hopes for the city that is celebrated in the Proerosia. Despite these ambivalences, however, it seems that certain of the plays of the 420s and 410s offer a version of the city in which women are full and valued participants, their Athenian identity mediated by the forms of ritual.

PRIESTESS AND PROPHETESS

So far we have traced a shift in the representations of ritual from conflict between women and the polis to the possibility of peaceful coexistence. Before moving on to the final tragedies of the fifth century and to comedy, I want to examine a very different strand in the dramatic treatment of women ritual practitioners, and look at the figure of the prophetess and priestess. This figure is important in the *Agamemnon* and *Eumenides* and in the *Ion, Helen, Trojan Women,* and *Iphigeneia among the Taurians.* Like the male prophet, she can challenge or correct the perceptions of the secular authority; unlike him, she often suffers a diminution of her own authority when she appears on stage. She also contributes to the overall dramatic discourse on women's relation to sexuality and to language and may sometimes, in a metatheatrical move, be identified with the organizing energies of the play itself. At the close of this section, with discussion of the *Iphigeneia among the Taurians,* we shall return to the issue of Athenian identity.

Oresteia

Two Delphic women appear in the Oresteia trilogy: Kassandra, the prophetess of Apollo, and the Pythia. Kassandra dominates the scene in *Agamemnon* 1035–1330, first by her stubborn silence and then by her inspired prophetic speech, while the Pythia opens the *Eumenides* and is on stage for sixty-three

---

76. That Athenians could feel disquiet about their empire is suggested, I think, by the speeches of the Mytilenian Debate in Thucydides 3.36–50. See also, on Aeschylus and Athenian empire, Rosenbloom 1995.

lines. Kassandra's relationship with her prophetic task is important. Pursued by Apollo, she agreed to gratify his desire and was rewarded with the gift of prophecy; refusing him at the last minute, she was punished by never being believed. Throughout her scene, Kassandra's relationship with Apollo is one of pain and suffering; she begins by reproaching him for bringing her to the Atreid house (1072–92) and proceeds to shed her ritual insignia, the wreath and rod, before entering the house to take part in Klytaimestra's "sacrifices" for Agamemnon's homecoming (1264–68). Despite this resistance, Kassandra remains a prophetess and the mouthpiece of Apollo throughout the scene, speaking a truth that is guaranteed by Zeus. That the chorus repeatedly fail to comprehend her seems to be a result of her sexual compromise with Apollo;[77] when she recounts the past history of the Atreids, describing Thyestes' feast on his dead children, the chorus claim that they do believe her, but they cannot follow her in her visions of the coming death of Agamemnon. Language itself is found to be inadequate to the monstrosity of Klytaimestra's crime; despite Kassandra's warnings to beware of the female, the chorus ask: "What man prepares this horror?" (1251).

Kassandra's sexual status is compromised in the same way as her language; a virgin devoted to Athena, she has been raped and abducted by the Greeks, so that she has become an anomalous *parthenos* like other female figures in the trilogy, such as Iphigeneia, Elektra, the Furies, and Athena, and a perverted bride, like Helen and Klytaimestra herself.[78] Klytaimestra and Kassandra are further opposed with respect to their language; whereas Klytaimestra's accumulates ever more sinister connotations, that of Kassandra tries to shed its layers of prophetic metaphor and appear naked (1178–83):

> No more will the oracle peep
> From veils like a newly wedded bride.
> It will come bright like the wind to the east
> . . . .
> I shall not speak any more in riddles.

The opposition that Kassandra and Klytaimestra offer between ritual service, virginity, and truth, on the one hand, and deceitful sexuality, on the other, will reemerge in Euripidean plays and may be approached along the lines laid down by A. L. Bergren.[79] Working with the paradigm of the

77. Goldhill's discussion (1984: 81–88) of this scene concentrates on its linguistic rather than its sexual dimensions. Neither Lebeck (1971) nor Conacher (1987) discusses the figure of the prophetess in great detail.

78. On marriage and death throughout the Oresteia see Rehm 1994: chap. 3.

79. Bergren 1983. See McClure 1999: 92–97 for a discussion of the ways in which Klytaimestra and Kassandra relate and contrast. McClure does not bring the Pythia into this discussion.

Hesiodic encounter with the Muses in the *Theogony,* she proposes that female figures deployed by male poets tend to be polarized, figured as offering a threatening deception or a divinely inspired truth, both of which forms of language may then be appropriated by the male poet in order to facilitate his own practice. Although the *Agamemnon* can be seen to stage this polarization, it complicates it in a number of ways. In the corrupt atmosphere of the play, even a truth guaranteed by Delphi cannot be heard, so that Kassandra's language is as opaque and disturbing for the chorus as is that of Klytaimestra. But Kassandra is also the only character who can see through Klytaimestra, understanding her sacrificial references and revealing, albeit to an uncomprehending audience, her plots. She is even able to reduce Klytaimestra's usually complex, highly wrought language almost to nonsense. Preserving a stubborn silence in the face of the queen's commands to come inside, Kassandra forces Klytaimestra finally to say: "But if being incapable of understanding you do not receive my word, / you, instead of a voice, speak with a foreign hand" (1060–61: my literal translation). The second "you" could easily be understood as an attendant or member of the chorus, as translators such as Philip Vellacott and Robert Fagles have taken it, but in that case it is hard to see why a Greek character, rather than a Trojan, should be speaking with a foreign hand. It seems possible that Klytaimestra, with Housman's "Fragment of a Greek Tragedy," is indeed reduced to saying: "But if you happen to be deaf and dumb, / And do not understand a word I say, / Then wave your hand, to signify as much."[80]

What happens to the contours of the Kassandra figure when it is translated, in the *Eumenides,* to the Pythia? At least on one level, we move from a cult office that is of mythic dimensions to one that is governed by the procedures of an institution. Identifying completely with her ritual task, in which she operates as the representative of the city whose founding she describes in her prologue (1–19), the Pythia throughout her scene preserves the calm of iambic trimeters and resorts neither to lyrics nor to extrametrical exclamations. She has no special identifying features beyond those of her institutional position; her relationship with Apollo is not as personal as that of Kassandra, but neither is it so antagonistic. She may be thought of as opening the possibility of a productive relationship between humans and gods such as that which is finally sealed between Athena and the Athenians. In this context, her reaction to the Furies is also of interest. Kassandra is the first in the trilogy to "see" the Furies, in the prophetic vision that so disturbs

80. Quoted from A. E. Housman, "Fragment of a Greek Tragedy," in *Collected Poetry and Selected Prose,* ed., with introduction and notes, Christopher Ricks (Harmondsworth, 1988) 236. Quoted with permission from the Society of Authors as Literary Representative of the Estate of A. E. Housman.

her (1186–93), and her state of distraction can be understood to provide the model for Orestes' madness at the end of the *Libation-Bearers,* when he too "sees" them. In neither of these cases is it probable that the Furies are on stage for the audience itself to see. At the beginning of the *Eumenides* the Pythia enters, then leaves the stage to go inside the temple (33), where she sees the Furies. Reentering terrified (34–38), she is nonetheless not maddened, and when she leaves the stage again the Furies enter and are visible to the audience. The Pythia may thus be understood as marking a stage toward a manageable relationship between Furies and humans, which is an important component of the *Eumenides'* final settlement.

Since it constitutes a history of the mantic shrine, the Pythia's prologue is the opposite of a prophecy. She describes how ownership of the oracle at Delphi descended in a series of peaceful transfers from Earth to Apollo, from the ancient chthonic goddess to the young Olympian god. It has long been recognized, however, that the oppositions that the Pythia's speech puts into play—old and young, female and male, father and mother, chthonic and Olympian, force and consent—are exactly those that inform the volatile action of the *Eumenides,* so that despite its historical content the speech may indeed be read as prophecy.[81] If it is a prophecy, however, it is a dubious one; the untroubled narrative of a peaceful transfer of power gives way, in the development of the drama, to a conflict where nothing is as yet resolved and everything is still to play for. The "prophecy" is flawed in another way as well; recounting her narrative, the Pythia qualifies it with *hos logos tis,* "as an account has it" (4), thereby acknowledging the possibility of competing accounts. Since most such competing accounts, such as those rehearsed in the *Homeric Hymn to Apollo* and the *Iphigeneia among the Taurians,* describe the transfer of power at Delphi as dominated by Olympian male violence against chthonic females, the veracity of the Pythia's prophetic history is open to question. The equivocations of the Pythia's prologue may suggest that, when away from the tripod, she possesses no discursive authority such as accrued, albeit with difficulty, to Kassandra. The inspired truth of Delphi, as partly personified by the Pythia, must in any case give way in the *Eumenides* not only to the persuasive discourse of Athena but also to the plurality of male voices, in law court and assembly, that characterizes democracy.

A similar loss of authority may be read in the second part of the Pythia's scene, when she returns from the shrine in terror at having seen the Furies. Despite her role as mouthpiece of the god, she cannot describe the Furies and is reduced to comparative inarticulacy; in her fright she describes herself as an old woman crawling on all fours like a child. As well as recalling the similar utterance of the chorus at *Agamemnon* 72–75, the description

---

81. See, for example, Lebeck 1971: 142: "The resolution of the play is contained within its prologue"; also Conacher 1987: 139. For a different emphasis see Goldhill 1984: 208–11.

may be thought to refer to the historical appearance of the Pythia, who, as we have seen in chapter 3, was an older woman who dressed as a *parthenos*, according to Diodorus Siculus 16.26. The sexual paradox of the Pythia foreshadows that of the Furies, who are referred to as "ancient children" throughout the play (e.g., 69, 1034), and perhaps even that of Athena, the anomalous *parthenos* who solves the problems generated by the other anomalous *parthenoi* of the trilogy. On all fours, however, the Pythia is a far more ridiculous figure than any of these, and her authority may be thought to be correspondingly diminished.

The Pythia's peaceful, institutionalized relationship with her ritual task foreshadows the eventual settlement for the women of Athens, as well as offering a paradigm for Athens as a whole of productive relations between mortal and immortal. What is lost is the ritual autonomy characteristic of Klytaimestra and the paradoxical authority that had accrued to Kassandra; what is gained is a culture within which women's collective ritual practice unproblematically serves the interests of the wider community and no longer functions as a counter in a gendered conflict.

Ion

The *Ion* further deploys the sign of women's ritual practice not only in the Arrhephoria but also in the figure of the Delphic prophetess. The pairing of Pythia and Kreousa in the *Ion* offers some similarities to that of Kassandra and Klytaimestra in the Oresteia: the Pythia is chaste and identified with the sanctuary's voice of truth, whereas Kreousa's sexual and maternal identity subtends a language that is mired in falsehood and fictions. By deliberately withholding the truth from its characters and obstructing access to the oracle, however, the play takes care not to unleash the Pythia's truthful voice into the arena of its competing discourses. The chorus, Kreousa, Xouthos, and Ion all in turn desire the voice of the oracle (219–21, 346, 420–21, 1546–48), but all are denied, except Xouthos, who is deceived. Throughout the play the stress is on the difficulty of gaining access, and on the significant differences between the forbidden inside and the outside. Despite being covered with alluring and diverting images, the outside of the temple is ultimately satisfying to nobody but the chorus, who say: "The outside charms us enough" (232). The final emergence of the Pythia from the inside of the shrine to the outside of the theatrical space, then, signals the beginning of the end for the play and the closure of its many narratives.

The Pythia enters the stage with a certain amount of authority, although it is noticeable that she retains no special knowledge from her sojourn on the tripod; she has no idea about the provenance of the tokens that were abandoned with the baby Ion. On entering, she deploys her authority to dissuade Ion from attacking Kreousa while she is in the sanctuary, and thus incurring the guilt of her death. She proceeds to admonish him for his attempt against Kreousa, and when he claims that "all men are pure *(katharos)* who kill their enemies," (1334) she endeavors to redefine the force of the term for him. By this gesture of saving him from his violent "earth-born" self, the Pythia initiates the movement of rescue that will take Ion from Delphi to Athens in safety as an autochthon. She interprets Apollo's will to him and provides him with the cradle that will facilitate the search for his identity. Penultimate in the play's series of substitutes for Apollo, who include the red-footed bird in the tent and of whom the last is Athena, the Pythia is also the first in the series of three female figures who combine to usher in the end of the play and the rescue of Ion.

These three figures, Pythia, Kreousa, and Athena, exemplify the struggles that inform the play between virginity, maternity, and autochthony. Athena is the virgin goddess, the Pythia's office requires chastity, and Kreousa, while not literally a virgin, is still a *parthenos* inasmuch as she is unable to make the full transition to the status of *gyne*, or adult woman. Yet despite their virginity, all three are mothers: Kreousa has given birth to Ion, but Athena and the Pythia also have a stake in a symbolic motherhood. Athena is the "mother" of Erichthonios because of the attempted rape by Hephaistos, and through Erichthonios mother of all Athenians; Ion tells Kreousa that he thinks of the Pythia as mother, and she greets Ion by saying how pleased she is with the name (1325). At the same time, all three female figures are caught up in the discourse of autochthony. Athena founds the autochthonous royal house of Athens when she raises Erichthonios, and Kreousa is the latest representative of that house; but the autochthonous myth of Athens is so powerful that even the Delphic Pythia is co-opted into it. Hermes deposits the baby Ion in a half-closed cradle on the temple steps; the Pythia, although loath at first, takes him up and rears him. In this gesture of taking a baby from the ground she not only rehearses Athena's initial action toward Erichthonios but also repairs Kreousa's less successful enactment when she abandoned her baby on the ground. The discourse of autochthony binds Kreousa and Pythia in at least one other way. In the prologue, when describing Kreousa's placing of snakes in the cradle to guard the baby, Hermes says she was "preserving a law *(nomos)* of the ancestors and of earth-born / Erichthonios. For him the daughter of Zeus / provided guards for his body, placing on either side of him / twin snakes" (20–23). When at the other end of the play the Pythia leaves the temple and comes up on the stage—her first and only appearance and the beginning of the unfolding of Ion's history—she describes herself as preserving the ancient law *(nomos)* of the tripod. The "law" turns out to be the same in both cases, the preservation that of Ion.[82]

---

82. Loraux (1990) does not elaborate on the Pythia's contribution to the play's discourse on virginity, maternity, and autochthony; see, however, Zeitlin 1989: 151–52.

Giving Athenian motherhood a Delphic flavor, as this play does, produces not only positive consequences. The uneasy relationship among the different possibilities of autochthony, virginity, and maternity has as one of its chief effects to undermine the final term. Despite her chastity, the Pythia operates as a satisfactory "mother" for Ion right up until the dramatic moment of the play. Both she and Ion seem to be happy with their present relationship until Ion meets Kreousa and hears her story, which is the converse of his; he then is "given" a father by the oracle and begins to feel more acutely the lack of a mother. A form of "cultural" rather than physical motherhood has up to now sufficed. Later, when Ion has received from the Pythia the tokens that will enable him to find his real mother, he expresses the desire for a mother who is a free Athenian and who will thus enable him to inherit *parrhesia* (669–72). *Parrhesia* is the right of free speech that characterizes the citizen, and that Kreousa can transmit to her son, even though she herself has conspicuously lacked it throughout the play. It is Ion's luck, and Kreousa's, that she turns out to be the mother who will satisfy this particular cultural need as well as biological needs; the mother who can satisfy only the latter is not sufficient in herself to launch Ion into the adult world of Athens.

Maternity loses even more resoundingly to autochthony, if not to virginity, at the very end of the play. Athena delivers the triumph when she announces that Ion's descendants will constitute the four Ionian tribes that will colonize the Mediterranean; the autochthonous Athenians' immemorial claim to their own land will translate effortlessly into a claim on that of others. Since the oracle was always consulted on the founding of historical colonies, Athena's speech is appropriate for delivery at Delphi, but its significance is not exhausted there. Its deployment, or rather the nondeployment, of the trope of maternity is crucial. Whereas the play has proved that even Ion needed a mother to get off the ground, Ion produces sons, and the sons tribes, without any female intervention. This male-dominated succession obliterates even the women of the autochthonous house, and the females who usher in the play's triumphant close are abandoned by the history it projects.

In the *Ion,* the Pythia is an integral part of the play's discourse on language and on the uneasily coexisting metaphors of virginity, maternity, and autochthony. Although she is instrumental in twice rescuing Ion, her authority is somewhat compromised once she leaves the tripod and enters the play, and her maternity, like that of Kreousa and even of Athena, is subsumed in the imperial Athenian metaphors that close the play. Like the Pythia in the *Eumenides,* she can be read to indicate the overcoming of the Delphic project by that of Athens; in the *Ion* the truthful voice from the univocal tripod is abandoned in favor of a city characterized by proliferation and exchange of voices not only in political debate but in drama.

Helen

Theonoe in Euripides' *Helen* also represents a voice around which the desires of different characters are organized; like the Pythia, she has just one entrance and exit and yet is quite central to the unfolding of the drama.[83] Both prophetesses are mobilized in an effort to save a man, and both are paired with women who present a maternal and sexual identity rather than being concerned exclusively with chaste ritual service. Theonoe, the virgin prophetess, is contrasted with Helen, who for the purposes of this play is a loyal wife who has been spirited away from home and deposited in Egypt; a phantom double, made by the gods, has gone to Troy, so that "Helen" is falsely thought to be an adulteress. Meanwhile she is fending off the advances of the king of Egypt, Theoklymenos, the brother of Theonoe, who has sworn to kill all Greeks—and especially Helen's husband, Menelaos—who land on his shore.

Although Theonoe's part is not extensive, she is important to the drama as being in possession of the truth, accessible to her through her cult service. Such access contrasts with the welter of appearances that surround Helen, who is caught in the disjunction between her conduct and her reputation. The possibility of absolute knowledge such as that of Theonoe is destabilizing for drama, since it might put an end to the competing claims of other voices and thus to drama itself. The *Ion,* as we have seen, restricts access to the Pythia's voice; in the *Helen,* all the characters in turn need speech from Theonoe, but it is not always forthcoming. Early in the play the chorus suggest to Helen that she ask Theonoe what has happened to her husband (317–20), which she does, but if she were constantly to depend on Theonoe's knowledge, there would be no suspense to the play and very little plot. But in the *Helen* there is plot, because Theonoe's allegiance to truth can finally be compromised. Offstage, Theonoe sets Helen's mind at rest about her husband, and Menelaos duly appears onstage. Once the recognition has been effected, and the Helen-phantom has left, pointing out to the Greeks on her exit that they wasted ten years in front of Troy, Menelaos's servant, joined by the chorus, berates prophets and prophecy in general (748–54). No Greek prophet was able to tell the troops that they were chasing a phantom; if the gods did not want the Greeks to know, what is the use of prophets at all? But he is mistaken in his wholesale dismissal of prophets; Theonoe is still a danger to Menelaos and Helen because she can tell her brother that Menelaos has arrived. For Menelaos and Helen to be saved, Theonoe must be prevailed upon not to tell what she knows.

Theonoe finally emerges onstage, to the dismay of the newly reunited

83. On this prophetess see especially Sansone 1985 and Rehm 1994: 121–22. Bushnell (1988) concentrates on the figure of the prophet in Sophoclean drama, but her remarks on pp. 4–7 are of interest here too.

couple. She explains that there is a second contest among the gods that repeats the quarrel responsible for the Trojan War, of which she (rather than Paris) must be the judge. Hera is determined that Menelaos shall get home with his wife and that the Greeks shall discover that Aphrodite's gift to Paris was a phantom; Aphrodite conversely wants Helen to stay in Egypt as the bride of Theoklymenos. Theonoe intends to follow the path of truth, tell her brother about Menelaos's arrival, and thus secure the Greek's death and Aphrodite's victory. Helen and Menelaos then separately supplicate her to change her mind. While Helen's supplication combines appeals to Theonoe's honor with reference to her own comfort (934–35), Menelaos addresses himself chiefly to the prophetess's dead father and threatens— like the Aeschylean suppliants—that he and Helen will kill themselves on the tomb if betrayed to Theoklymenos (980–87). Compromised by a situation, like that exemplified by Helen's predicament between reality and appearance, in which a simple knowledge of absolute truth is insufficient, Theonoe agrees to help the married couple and to risk the homicidal wrath of her brother. Her salvific action comparable with the intervention of the Pythia in the *Ion,* Theonoe functions to some extent as a *dea ex machina* within the action.

After Theonoe leaves, the ritual initiative passes to Helen, who devises a fake funeral for Menelaos that facilitates their getaway. Such a move, like Theonoe's compromise, is not entirely devoid of a negative charge— Menelaos is initially suspicious of a plan that involves announcing his own death (1051–52)—but the destructiveness often predicated of the female in general, and of Helen in particular, is here turned away from her own family and city and toward those who, like the Egyptians, can be called "barbarians." When the "funeral" ship is at sea, and the Greeks in it turn on the Egyptian sailors, Helen is there urging them on with remembrance of their prowess at Troy (1602–4):

> There was Helen cheering
> From the stern: "Where is that Trojan renown? Come on,
> Show these barbarians."

Helen here completely identifies with the Greeks' projects, present and past.

The *Helen,* like the *Ion, Erechtheus,* and *Suppliant Women,* empties ritual practice of any residual gender antagonism. Helen and Theonoe together, like Kreousa and the Pythia, combine their talents for ritual action in order to rescue, rather than threaten, the male. Even though the exotic virgin priestess and the famed adulteress ought to be poles apart, they are joined not only by their salvific project but also by their shared immersion in a world where things are not as they immediately appear. One sign of this is the way in which the figures of Theonoe and Helen are occasionally conflated.[84] Both have extensive reputations: Helen is notorious, and that Theonoe is widely known is suggested by the fact that Teukros, a Greek sailor, comes to Egypt expressly to ask for her help. Helen actually substitutes for Theonoe, answering Teukros's questions so that the prophetess does not have to appear. More telling than this is the question of their names. When she was young, Theonoe was called Eido (11), a name that seems to invoke the *eidolon,* or phantom, that went to Troy in place of Helen. Whereas Theonoe has two names, the single name of "Helen" denotes both the phantom adulteress in Troy and the genuine chaste wife.

That Theonoe is thus assimilated to Helen, and that she, like Helen, practices a deception, may indicate the price that a prophetess has to pay for being allowed onstage. Even though the prophetess is not a figure around which gender hostility accumulates, she finds her authority somewhat diminished when she appears in the theater. We have seen how Kassandra and the Pythia in the Oresteia mark the move from women's ritual autonomy to their containment; the Pythia in the *Ion* and Theonoe in the *Helen* do not participate in this movement, but both find their particular kinds of authority inadequate to the situations they are in, and both are assimilated to the myths belonging to other female characters. Caught up in the play of different discourses, both the Pythia and Theonoe are forced to abandon simple models of truth and are finally superseded by women who are more closely identified with the ambiguous energies of drama itself.

Trojan Women

Like the Pythia and Theonoe, Kassandra in Euripides' *Trojan Women* of 415 makes only a brief appearance, but brings with her a disproportionate significance. The play is concerned with the end of the city, which it enacts partly by the series of impoverished rituals that the captive Trojan women perform. Kassandra celebrates her "wedding" with Agamemnon, who is taking her away as his concubine, and Hekabe has to perform a hastily devised funeral rite for Astyanax, son of Hektor and Andromache, who has been thrown from the walls of Troy on the Greeks' orders.[85] As a prophetess Kassandra, like the gods Poseidon and Athena who open the action, allows the play to look beyond that end and offers another perspective. But within the play Kassandra has little real power; the unpalatable truth that she represents is drowned out by the mourning of Hekabe and the political rhetoric of expediency offered by Helen and the Greeks.

What Kassandra can and does do, however, is to set a paradigm for the

84. Segal (1971) gives detailed analyses of the various and shifting relations between Helen and Theonoe.

85. Rehm (1994: 138) points out that the herald Talthybios has to play a woman's part in helping to lay out the corpse. See Croally 1994: 70–84 on the "ritual disorder" of the play.

other daughters and daughters-in-law of Hekabe. She is the first to leave, and she goes with Agamemnon as a perverted bride, as Andromache will with Neoptolemos, Polyxena with the ghost of Achilles, and Helen with Menelaos.[86] Kassandra's discourse also offers a pattern that the other women will follow. Pointing especially to the fact that the Greeks will lie in a foreign land, unwept and unburied by their female relatives, while the Trojans have died fighting for their fatherland and are buried in it, mourned by their women, she argues at length that the Trojans have in fact won the war and the Greeks have lost. Her prophetic knowledge extends to the deaths and suffering not only of Agamemnon but also of several of the other returning Greek captains, strengthening her argument for their defeat and the Trojans' victory. But the important point about her discourse is that it elaborates an impossible paradox, exactly what one would expect from a prophetess cursed never to be believed. What then happens is that other female figures also present Hekabe with compelling paradoxes. Andromache sets out to prove to her that the dead Polyxena, sacrificed to the shade of Achilles, is better off than her living sisters. Since the order is then given for Andromache's son to be executed, it is hard to resist her conclusion. Subsequently Helen debates with Hekabe in front of Menelaos and argues that not she but Hekabe, as mother of Paris, bears ultimate responsibility for the Trojan War. Since Hekabe's rebuttal involves denying the myth of the Judgment of Paris, and thus throwing into doubt most of Greek myth, along with the Trojan War itself, it is small wonder that Menelaos is dissuaded from his object of killing Helen immediately and decides to take her back to Greece. He says he intends to execute her there, but all those familiar with the *Odyssey* know that the pair will fetch up together in Sparta, ending their days in a more or less hostile truce. At least one listener, then, is persuaded by Helen's most outrageous paradox of all.

That Kassandra sets the pattern for other characters makes her a stronger figure than other Euripidean prophetesses, who, as we have seen, are more likely to get caught up themselves in other characters' paradigms. Most critics agree that the play was produced in 415, just after the sack of Melos, itself "dramatized" in the Melian Dialogue in book 5 of Thucydides, and the play's scenes of postwar devastation are usually understood as an indictment of Athenian policy. If this interpretation is correct, then perhaps we can see the prophetess as identified even more closely with the organizing principles of the drama. If the play itself is trying to show the unshowable, speak the unspeakable, and warn the apparent victors of their imminent failure, then it could choose no more appropriate figure to carry out the task than the prophetess who cannot be believed.

86. Seaford (1987: 128) points out that, anomalously, she organizes her own wedding.

Each of the five tragic prophetesses possesses a knowledge or an access to the truth that aligns her with the driving energies of the drama. At the same time, however, the price of each prophetess's appearance on the polysemic tragic stage is a compromise of her authority. The prophetess, like the male prophet, is a powerful figure for drama to deploy, but not even she is permitted to transcend entirely the containing gestures that tragedy regularly makes in respect to its female characters.

Iphigeneia among the Taurians

Although there are five prophetesses featured in the extant plays, there is only one priestess, and Iphigeneia among the Taurians is no ordinary official; she has survived one sacrifice only to preside over an endless series of others. Offered at the altar by her father, Agamemnon, in order to appease Artemis and secure a fair wind for Troy, she was rescued by the goddess and transported to the barbarian polis of the Taurians on the Black Sea. Like Io, whom the chorus commemorate (394), Iphigeneia is a Greek outside Europe, in a land beyond the Symplegades, or Clashing Rocks, which are repeatedly invoked as the boundaries of the civilized world through which the characters of Euripides' play have passed (241, 260, 355, 421, 1389). As Iphigeneia is displaced, so is her ritual service distorted; her task is to prepare for sacrifice all strangers, and especially Greeks, who fall into the hands of the Taurian king, Thoas. The strangers are sacrificed to Artemis as Iphigeneia herself nearly was. To this land come Orestes and Pylades, obedient to the command of Apollo, which requires the theft of the image of Artemis and its transportation to Athens. Captured by the Taurians, the men are nearly sacrificed, but a letter effects a recognition, and the Greeks escape under cover of a mock purification of the statue.

Iphigeneia's ritual practice, and the practice that was inflicted on her, form dominant motifs in the play. The materiality of ritual is stressed: the altar stone is soaked in blood (72–73), the temple walls hung with trophies from the dead victims (74–75), and the theft of the wooden statue that Orestes must steal, in order to be freed from the pursuing Furies, is described in all its logistic detail (96–101). Regrets for the Greek homeland are also cast in the discourse of ritual. The chorus of captive Greek women long for wedding celebrations such as they used to join (1143–51), and with her supporting chorus Iphigeneia laments that she is (221–24)

> Not hymning Hera in Argos
> Nor standing at the singing loom
> To embroider with my shuttle
> The image of Attic Pallas, and Titans.

If the Argive hymns can plausibly be imagined as uttered in a ritual context, the weaving for Athena may well recall that of the *arrhephoroi* in Athens, so that her song combines the rituals of different communities. Away from Greece, Iphigeneia imagines it not riven as it was contemporarily by the Peloponnesian War but united Panhellenically by the figure of women's ritual.

Where Iphigeneia has a surfeit rather than a shortfall of ritual is in the practice of sacrifice, which in Tauri is no longer a metaphor for intrafamilial murders such as dominated the Oresteia but is translated literally. The object of sacrifice now extends out from the Atreid family to encompass all strangers to the Taurian shore, and the metaphor is almost swallowed by the violent reality when Iphigeneia comes within an inch of sacrificing her brother. The "death" of her brother is accomplished instead by the mourning that she performs for him earlier, immediately after she has dreamed, as she thinks, of his death (152–77). At the end of the play, in the closing speech of Athena, both sacrificial metaphor and rite are transformed into other, perhaps more manageable, Athenian forms.

Violent as Iphigeneia's unwelcome service is, it gives her considerable authority among the Taurians. To an extent she can identify with her service, especially when she feels called upon to defend the sacredness of the temple context; at 468–69 she orders the soldiers guarding the prisoners to unbind them, since "they are dedicated and should not be bound." Her authority is most clearly seen when she exploits it to deceive Thoas, the king. Thoas delights in a vision of reciprocal respect, whereby the city *thaumazei*, "admires," Iphigeneia (1214), and she in return cares for it (1212). Instead, the contours of her barbarian service allow Iphigeneia to act as a "wise Greek" (1180) and to deceive him with her authoritative pronouncements as to Artemis's desires. Earlier on, Iphigeneia had berated the Taurians for disguising their own murderous tendencies beneath the veneer of ritual observation (389–91) and reproached Artemis herself with the equivocation of demanding human sacrifice while shunning the pollution associated with death or childbirth (380–84). The duplicity she had thus earlier assigned to barbarians, and to an extent to Artemis as well, she now deploys herself.

In the scene of deception Iphigeneia is no longer constrained by her enforced ritual practice but is enabled by it; when she stages the mock purification ritual that will conceal the getaway, it is the conditions of her life among the Taurians that allow her to escape from it. She herself is deceived only as to the fictional dimension of the ritual. As Christian Wolff notes,[87] this fake ritual will turn out to be the real purification of Orestes and will recover the ground lost in Athens when the trial for matricide failed, in this play's version, to deliver a definitive judgment. The theme of

---

87. Wolff 1992: 317.

purification has already been broached when the herdsman informs Iphigeneia that he has been washing his cattle in the sea (255). When she in turn tells the king that her rite must take place in the sea, as opposed to fresh water, because "the sea washes away all human evils" (1193), her discourse transforms the earlier characterization of the sea in the *Oresteia*, where Klytaimestra's words represent it as a boundless source of corrupt wealth (958–60). Even the sacrificial metaphor begins to recover a peaceful profile when Iphigeneia takes lambs to the sea with the captives: "I already see the strangers coming from the house, / The adornments of the goddess, and the newborn lambs, so that blood for blood / I can wash out the stain" (1222–25). Deploying it as the pretext for the purification, Iphigeneia manages, as Orestes had suggested, to turn the matricide itself to good account (1034). Thoas's incredulity at the matricide—"Apollo! No barbarian would have dared this deed!" (1174)—is as inadequate a response as his credulity in the face of Iphigeneia's detailed arrangements for her ritual. She meanwhile, in an inevitable polarity, shows how "Greece has raised [her] to be wise" (1180).[88]

Ritual practice in *Iphigeneia among the Taurians* thus appears as a double sign, subjecting Iphigeneia to an abhorrent life, but also affording her dramatic means of agency and authority. The significance of ritual within the play is not exhausted, however, by an account of Iphigeneia, since the play deliberately introduces three different ritual etiologies that look beyond its temporal and spatial boundaries in barbarian Tauri toward the ultimate goal of the drama, Greece, and within Greece, to Athens. For the Taurians, ritual in the form of their idiosyncratic sacrifice delimits a clear boundary between inside and outside. While violence, in the form of sacrifice, is directed entirely toward the exterior, it seems to be absent from the Taurian community; that community operates a very simple scheme whereby strangers instantly die. For the Greeks, by contrast, violence is always internecine, as it is for the Greece riven by the Peloponnesian War at the time of the play's production, and the matricide, although largely muted in the play, can be seen to be paradigmatic of this situation. After Iphigeneia dreams, as she thinks, of the death of Orestes, she becomes hostile to all Greeks, and particularly so to Helen and Menelaos, whom she longs to be able to sacrifice (354–60). Her father is not so severely blamed, although his sacrifice of her is another example of internecine Greek violence. Her own inheritance as an Atreid is one of violence, as is made clear when Orestes enumerates the tokens of family history that enable her to recog-

88. Hall's analysis of this play (1989), and of this moment, is disappointingly straightforward; she rarely acknowledges that the *Iphigeneia among the Taurians* is constantly questioning the categories of Greek and barbarian. See also Belpassi (1990), who describes a simple movement from barbarian land to Greece.

nize him. Citing images on tapestries, woven by Iphigeneia, he recounts first the quarrel of the brothers Atreus and Thyestes, which led to the eating of his children by the luckless father, and second the moment when the sun changed course in order to mark the unprecedented horror of the Atreid crimes (811–17). The final token cited is the spear with which Pelops, founder of the line, killed his father-in-law, Oinomaos. This spear was kept in Iphigeneia's maiden chambers in Argos, underlining the intimacy of her relations with the familial violence (822–26).

A familiar theory of sacrificial ritual, often identified with the work of Girard, explains it as violent action that paradoxically unites the community. Given the strict polarization of inside and out that their sacrificial practice maintains, this account seems to hold particularly well for the Taurians. For the exiled Greeks in the play, however, no community is available. The play will send them to Athens, where, it is implied, a different community will be able to manage their inheritance of violence and incorporate them as it has incorporated, on the tragic stage, so many other survivors of the destructive myths ascribed to other cities (e.g., Medea, Herakles, Oedipus at Colonus, and the Furies of the Oresteia). Ritual practice in Athens will construct an equivocal form of community for the Argives, but, as we shall see, Athenian identity will itself be questioned in the same gesture.

The idealized destination that is Athens gives added urgency to the theme of *soteria,* or salvation, which is repeatedly emphasized throughout the play. Although the date of the *Iphigeneia among the Taurians* is uncertain, most scholars agree in placing it in the mid- to late teens of the fifth century, so that it may well have fallen between the launching by Athens of the disastrous Sicilian Expedition (in 415 B.C.E.) and its final defeat (in 412 B.C.E.). The safety of Athens itself was at stake in the closing years of the war, and the histories of Thucydides suggest, in the plague speech of Perikles and in the Melian Dialogue, that the term *soteria* began to dominate the public discourse of the city even before it became the watchword of the oligarchic plotters who in 411 B.C.E. brought down the democratic government. Among Euripidean plays, the twenty-six uses of the word in the *Iphigeneia among the Taurians* are only exceeded by the *Helen*'s thirty, and there are further differences that make the insistence on the term in the *Iphigeneia among the Taurians* more prominent. Whereas in the *Helen* the rescue action is single, in the *Iphigeneia among the Taurians* Iphigeneia and Orestes not only require rescue now but have both been saved before, by Artemis at Aulis and Athena in Athens. In addition, *soteria* and its cognates are invoked to describe the destiny of the Atreid house (984, 995) and of the letter that Pylades is to deliver to Argos (757–65).

The *Iphigeneia among the Taurians* claims that Orestes has already been through one Athenian crucible of violence, community, and *soteria;* he has already experienced the *Eumenides.* The later play offers itself as an alternative anti-Aeschylean ending not only to Iphigeneia's story but also to that of Orestes. Although Orestes must now travel back to Athens with the wooden statue of Artemis, in an earlier encounter with the city he stood trial for matricide, just as the Aeschylean play claimed (961–67):

> When I came to the hill of Ares and stood trial,
> I took one seat and the other, the eldest of the Furies.
> Speaking and listening about the blood of my mother,
> Phoebus bore witness and saved me,
> And Pallas who numbered the equal votes for me with her hand.

Unlike the outcome of the Oresteian trial, however, this procedure fails. In the *Eumenides,* the Furies are enraged at the acquittal but are eventually persuaded by Athena to accept the verdict and stay in Athens as the objects of cult and the guardians of the city's prosperity.[89] In their new incarnation as "Kindly Ones," rather than as Furies, they will provide the wholesome fear that keeps a community virtuous, and thereby preside over the city's ever-increasing fame and glory. In the *Iphigeneia among the Taurians,* a very different outcome is proposed (968–72):

> Some of the Furies sitting in judgment were convinced
> And rose to take their temple by the very place of voting;
> Those who were not persuaded by the law
> Pursued me still, chasing in every direction,
> Until I came to the holy ground of Phoebus.

In the *Iphigeneia among the Taurians,* then, the *soteria* devised by the *Eumenides* has already failed. The Oresteia's vision of a community that could overcome violence by a combination of judicial process and persuasive language, and that could thereby proceed forward into history united, is here blown apart. If the *Eumenides* has failed, then the ideal construction of Athens undertaken by that drama is work that still needs to be done, and everything is still to play for.[90]

The play goes on to confirm the failure of the *Eumenides'* vision when it recounts the narrative of the succession at Delphi, in the choral song that intervenes between the deception of Thoas and the arrival of the soldier with news of the Greeks' escape (1234–82). There are a number of Greek accounts of Apollo's acquisition of the shrine available to us, of which the

---

89. Scholars disagree whether the votes in the *Eumenides* were evenly cast before or after Athena's intervention, and the lines in the *Iphigeneia among the Taurians* are not unequivocal. See Sommerstein's discussion (1989: 222–26) of opposing viewpoints.

90. Wolff (1992: 328–29) notes the failure of the Areopagos but does not argue from it. We should also note that the Areopagos in the *Iphigeneia among the Taurians* has already been founded to try Ares and is not the result of Orestes' own story, as it is in the *Eumenides.*

most important are those in the *Homeric Hymn to Pythian Apollo,* the *Eumenides,* and here in the *Iphigeneia among the Taurians.* Earliest version of the three, the *Homeric Hymn* has Apollo vanquish the female monster snake, Pytho, who guards the oracle. The *Eumenides,* as we have seen, crucially bypasses this story and claims in the words of the Pythia that Earth gave the oracle to her daughter Themis, who passed it to Phoebe, who gave it to Phoebus. What is thus stressed is that the passage from female to male ownership was accomplished willingly and not by force, and the critical consensus is that this peaceful transfer of power foreshadows what will be enacted in the rest of the play. What the *Iphigeneia among the Taurians* subsequently does, then, in its own rehearsal of the narrative, is to undo the work of the *Eumenides* and revert to the story of violent overthrow.

The play goes on to add its own idiosyncratic details. Once Apollo is on the mantic throne and prophesying, the dispossessed Earth, who had wished to bequeath the oracle to her daughter Themis, sends out prophetic dreams by night to undermine Apollo's pronouncements (1259–69). Apollo in turn complains to Zeus, who compliantly (1278–82)

> Shook his head to stop the night-time voices,
> Took away from humans the truth shown in night visions,
> Gave back his honor to Loxias;
> He sits on his throne thronged with many foreign guests
> The singer of prophecies for mortals.

Whatever exact status is assigned by this song to dreams, we can nonetheless conclude that this narrative shows the status of truth to be problematic. Since Earth, after the defeat of Pytho, returns to engage in another round, the victory of Apollo does not end the story, in the same way that neither sacrifice nor acquittal ends those of Iphigeneia and Orestes. Furthermore, this choral narrative links truth and violence again as did the *Homeric Hymn,* and as the prologue to the *Eumenides* resolutely refused to do. The truth of the oracles at Delphi is secured only by repeated struggle and by the deliberate quashing of other, equally prophetic voices.[91]

The narrative about the Delphic oracle is challenged head-on by the dream that Iphigeneia reports at the beginning of the play. She dreams that she sees her paternal house fall; only one pillar is left, and that is in the form of a living man ("from the top, bright hair flowed down, and it took on a human voice," 51–52), whom she identifies as her brother Orestes. In the dream, Iphigeneia touches the man with the water used for sacrifice at

---

91. Hence I do not find completely convincing Sourvinou-Inwood's positive interpretation of this song (1991: 231–32), in which the happy ending of the Delphic myth foreshadows unproblematically the happy ending of the play. Wolff too is sanguine about the new oracle (1992: 315).

Tauri. Since only those who are about to die are thus touched, she concludes that Orestes is dead (58). Going beyond her ritual role of priestess, she operates as prophetess as well, with results that are very nearly fatal. The dream is not prophetic of Orestes' death, as she quickly finds out when the two unrecognized Argive strangers tell her Orestes is still living. This does not mean, however, that the dream is not prophetic. It did prophesy, quite clearly for those who could read it, that Orestes would come to the Taurians; he is alive, like the last remaining pillar of the house, and since he is touched by his sister, he must be in her vicinity. If Iphigeneia had interpreted the dream correctly, as she might have done were she not disposed to mourn by the grievous conditions of her service, she would have been alert to the possibility of his arrival and might not have come so close to killing him. That the dream is in fact prophetic, despite Iphigeneia's erroneous interpretation, casts doubt on the claims by the Delphic narrative that Earth's prophetic dreams have been robbed of their power. How can these two episodes of the play be reconciled? Does Iphigeneia's dream fall in the interstices between Earth's sending of the dreams and Apollo's disabling of them?[92] If this is not a plausible conclusion, we must allow that the dream contradicts the choral ode. Even though the ode claims that all disputes have been settled, the source of truth in a post-Oresteian world is still contested.

The play's concern with interpretation comes to a head in the letter scene. Despite Iphigeneia's ritual authority, she cannot read her dream correctly, and in the letter scene she is again shown to be at a disadvantage with signs. She cannot read or write but has in her possession a letter, dictated by her to a friendly Greek who was then sacrificed, leaving the letter, like herself, in need of transportation to Greece (584–87). The letter is lying in wait for whoever can next go to Argos, and, like a tiny time bomb, it is detonated in this scene. Iphigeneia offers to release one of the Greeks on the condition that he take the letter back with him;[93] oaths to this effect exchanged between her and Pylades eventually lead the latter to the realization that if he is shipwrecked and the letter lost, he will suffer the oath's penalties through no fault of his own. Iphigeneia then supplements the vulnerable letter, not by reading it, but by reciting its contents from memory. Either Pylades and the letter will be saved so that the letter can "silently speak" (763) its message, or Pylades alone will be saved but will save the let-

92. Sourvinou-Inwood (1991: 232 and 242 n. 67) has trouble with this point; she suggests that Earth's prophecy proves fallacious in the play because Iphigeneia misunderstood her prophetic dream. I do not find this a convincing argument.

93. She is confident that she can persuade Thoas to let one of the prisoners go (742), as later (1049) she is confident that she can persuade him of the necessity for the ritual of purification.

ter in his memory. Iphigeneia's speech naming herself as Iphigeneia and describing her plight to the imaginary Orestes in Argos enables the real Orestes in Tauri to complete the recognition scene.

While there are other unsettling letter scenes in Greek drama, this is probably the most complex of all. Other tragic letters, such as those by Phaidra in the *Hippolytos* and by Agamemnon in the *Iphigeneia in Aulis,* are harbingers of death on the model of the Homeric "baneful signs" that Bellerophon is forced to take to Iobates at *Iliad* 6.168. This letter by contrast helps everyone to evade death, although it does cling to the convention whereby writing enables the dead to "speak"; Iphigeneia herself says: "She who was killed at Aulis, Iphigeneia, sends you this"; and Orestes obligingly interjects: "Where is she? Has she died and come back again?" (770–72). Other conventions that surround the Greek understanding of writing, articulated in texts such as Plato's *Phaidros,* are mercilessly disrupted. Iphigeneia's words verbally supplement the letter, instead of writing being the handmaiden of speech as Plato prescribes; the letter overcomes absence not because it is exchanged between two parties widely separated but because it is produced in a situation where the interlocutors are already face to face. The effect of the letter is inescapably comic in its release of the tension built up by the threat that the sister will unknowingly sacrifice the brother. Helpless in the face of the letter's comic power, Iphigeneia is proved to be no Klytaimestra with a dangerous relationship to language and sign systems, and the way is prepared for her to learn duplicity only in order to help rescue her brother and his friend. The fake ritual, as we have seen, can be understood to have learned from the duplicity of Artemis, but it may also draw on the contrary exemplar of the unnaturally effective letter.

The letter, with its instant and untroubled communication, offers a model of efficacious language such as the rest of the play can only dream of. The play may indeed dream of acquiring the letter's status, of immediately finding an audience and delivering an incontrovertible message, but if so it frustrates its own project at every other turn by an equal insistence on the difficulties that attend the pursuit of truth. In the play's post-Oresteian universe, the signs as well as the *soteria* are inconclusive. At the close of the play, when Athena appears in order to rescue the protagonists from their own rescue plot, her speech raises again the possibility of successful communication. When she bids Orestes listen to her instructions, the word she uses is *epistolai* (1446), which can mean "commands" but also "written letters," and she goes on to explain that even though she is in Tauri and Orestes on the sea, he can hear her because gods can be heard wherever they choose. Her "letters," then, overcome distance in the same way that Iphigeneia's miraculously did, and invite comparison with the earlier scene. The effectiveness of her communication is immediately undermined, however, by the ritual etiologies that she proceeds to deliver, which, as Wolff notes, raise once more the issue of interpretation.[94] These etiologies seem to play again with the terms set up in Tauri—with *soteria*, violence, and community—and to try to forge an Athenian identity to take the place of that abandoned with the abandonment of the Oresteia. Although the letter forges a tiny community of Greeks on the hostile Taurian shore, the issue of community at Athens, the play's ultimate destination, is harder to resolve. [95]

With the command to steal the statue of Artemis and take it to Attica, the play had begun to replace Argos, or Greece as a whole, with Athens as its destination. If Tauri is a place that resolutely keeps strangers out, Athens, especially as represented on the tragic stage, can accommodate numerous difficult characters from elsewhere. In the case of Orestes and Iphigeneia, however, this feat is undertaken only by ritual forms and is accomplished tentatively, with some hesitation. The wider vision of political and legal discourse offered by the *Eumenides* is no longer relevant, and ritual forms are apparently all that is left.[96]

As we have seen, Orestes has already traveled to Athens once before, seeking not only the trial that Apollo had promised him but also the simple hospitality owed by Greeks to Greeks. As a matricide, however, Orestes is shunned by his hosts (947–54). They require him to eat and drink in silence at a separate table, even though they are all in the same room, and they pour the "equal measure of Bakchos" into separate cups instead of sharing a common bowl. Orestes goes on to relate that he has heard the Athenians, like Iphigeneia, made of his misfortunes a rite, and that the custom still is for the people of Pallas to honor the *choes* cup (958–60). Choes, or Pitchers, is the day of the Anthesteria on which small boys are presented with their first wine cup; adult men compete in drinking but preserve the antisocial practice of silence and separate cups.

Faced with the violence of the matricide, Athens compromises its community. At first, confining him to a separate table, the city can manage Orestes by making him into the outsider who paradoxically sits inside. Then, disrupted by his presence, the Athenians partially imitate the matricide by drinking from separate bowls of wine; the "equal measure" that they drink retains their sociality but in a modified form.[97] Finally, after the depar-

---

94. Wolff 1992: 332.

95. Again I disagree with the optimistic construction of Belpassi (1990), who sees an untroubled movement from the *genos* to the city. On my reading the city has still to be constructed.

96. This is not to suggest, of course, that ritual does not play an important part in the final settlement of the *Eumenides*. What I do suggest is that in a comparison between the two plays, the *Eumenides*' legal and political solutions stand out by contrast with their absence from the *Iphigeneia among the Taurians*.

97. The measure of Bakchos here might well be assimilated to the Dionysos that Seaford (1995) constructs, who destroys noble houses in order to build on them institutions beneficial

ture of Orestes, the Athenians fully adopt the role of Orestes, each drinking separately and in silence. Only by the expedient of each Athenian pretending to be a matricide himself can the city manage Orestes' guilt. Transforming all insiders into outsiders, the Choes festival offers a thoroughly equivocal set of terms for Athenian identity to the young boys whom it introduces to the adult practice of drinking wine.[98] In the narrative of the *Iphigeneia among the Taurians,* moreover, this ritual is the only product of Orestes' stay in Athens; the play makes it clear that the court of the Areopagos is already in operation, and Athena does not make the pronouncement instituting the tie-breaking "vote of Athena" until the end of this play, while still in Tauri. Neither of the results of the Oresteia's trial are allowed to emerge from the account, in the *Iphigeneia among the Taurians,* of Orestes' experience in Athens. Again we are invited to conclude that any political version of Athens is eschewed by this play in favor of a version that is instead constructed through ritual. The ritual forms, however, bring their own problems.

In its equivocation over inside and outside, the foundation of the Choes in the play can be read as a response to the Taurian sacrifice and its definitive separation of citizens and strangers. But the play also puts this foundation into a dynamic relationship with the two other rites instituted by Athena in her closing speech. This speech introduces the record number of three etiological foundations, a rite each for Orestes and Iphigeneia and, for Athens as a whole, the institution of the "vote of Athena," which declares that a hung jury will always result in acquittal. Athena appears in salvific guise; the rescue plot, devised on the ground of ritual by Iphigeneia, is foundering and has itself to be saved by the goddess. She announces means to end the stories of Orestes and Iphigeneia by instituting rites that will incorporate them both into Athens. Both rites, however, will rework and reinvigorate the sacrificial metaphor that had begun to fade away with the purification staged by Iphigeneia. Orestes is to take the statue of Artemis to Halai, on the *eschata,* or border territory, of Attica, and there found a temple. At the festival of Artemis a sword will draw blood from the neck of a man and blood will flow, "on account of holiness and so that the goddess may have honors" (1461). In place of the full-fledged human sacrifice demanded among the Taurians, Artemis at Halai will be content with this partial and deflected form. At Brauron, however, where Iphigeneia will preside, the sacrificial metaphor becomes more threatening. Keeper of the keys at Brauron, Iphigeneia will be buried there and will receive as offerings garments left in the house by women who die in childbirth (1462–66).

---

to the polis. The only difficulty with this suggestion is that the ritual seems in fact to figure not productive solidarity among the members of the polis but their separation.

98. On the Choes as "a significant ritual in a child's maturation" (Hamilton 1992: 114) see also Ham 1999.

We have no independent corroboration for either of the rituals that Athena describes. Dedications of garments are known at Brauron, as we have seen, but it is not clear which if any of them were offered in memory of dead women. For the Tauropolia we have other kinds of evidence. In Menander *Epitrepontes* 234ff., a group of women hire a female flute-player to entertain them on the occasion of the festival, which seems also to have involved an all-night celebration among women of marriageable age. In the fourth century one Philoxenos is honored by the people of the deme of Halai for his performance as *choregos* in the Pyrrhic dances.[99] Although other Euripidean ritual etiologies can be shown to have analogues in historical cult, none of the activity thus attested for this festival bears any resemblance to the rite described in the *Iphigeneia among the Taurians*. Leaving aside the historicity of the rites, we can say that in the rhetoric of the play the representations of both these etiologies and of the Choes can be seen to concern the maturation of citizens and the reproduction of community. In the Choes the community, as we have seen, is dramatized in a troubled scene of separation, while its youngest male members are introduced to a new stage in their lives. With the etiologies in Athena's speech the scene moves from the center of the city to its marginal territories. At Brauron, with its emphasis on the maturation of young girls, it is the physical reproduction of the community that is foregrounded, but the observance directed toward Iphigeneia commemorates only its failure and its high costs. Finally at Halai, where scholars usually understand the etiology to describe a rite of maturation for young men,[100] new citizens are made only by being threatened with the treatment doled out to outsiders at Tauri. In her demands for bloodshed at Halai, and for death at Brauron, Artemis indicates that her nature remains equivocal and untamed even in Attica; although human sacrifice itself is now ruled out, versions of it in a minor key persist and cast doubt on the comforting notion that the move from Tauri to Athens is also a simple move from barbarity to civilization.[101] In the absence of the *Oresteia*'s heroic solution, Athens itself must be built again from the ground up, in its marginal spaces and in the difficult, perplexing rites that count the cost of making citizens.

Soteria remains problematic even when we have reached Athens. Orestes was received and protected by the city but made to eat in isolation, and the first act of salvation by the Areopagos was thoroughly incomplete. While the foundation of the temple at Halai may indicate "stability recovered,"[102] vio-

---

99. *REG* 47 [1934] 224.

100. See, for example, Wolff 1992: 322.

101. Wolff (1992: 329 and n. 60) makes the same point but in a different connection. Sourvinou-Inwood (1991: 231) by contrast sees "a new, superior, civilized cult."

102. Wolff 1992: 313.

lence will nonetheless be rehearsed in the drawing of blood. Finally, for Iphigeneia only a very limited form of salvation will be accomplished, and for the women who leave garments behind for her only its absence will be commemorated. Having organized the sacrifice of men, Iphigeneia is now closely associated with the deaths of women. If the beneficent duplicity of the purification ceremony first began to tame her dangerous role as female sacrificer, this move from the deaths of one sex to those of the other perhaps completes the process.[103] Having enjoyed if not ritual autonomy, at least a position of authority threatening to men she encountered, Iphigeneia is now divested of menace by another variety of ritual practice. Even after Iphigeneia's cult position has enabled the rescue plot, the play drifts toward the paradigm familiar from earlier dramas, where ritual first empowers illegitimately and subsequently tames.

Both women's ritual practice and the issue of Athenian identity are in play in the drama of the priestess, although the women, or Iphigeneia at least, do not seem to attain and celebrate Athenian identity as they arguably did in the *Erechtheus, Suppliant Women,* and *Ion.* Although her own destiny is anything but a blueprint for the normal female trajectory, Iphigeneia seems finally to be offered as a paradigm for the vulnerabilities of female lives, rather than for women's possible significance as ritual practitioners within a civic context. Yet Athenian identity appears to be as difficult of attainment as is, at Brauron, a successful female trajectory; the etiologies represent attempts to produce such identity rather than assuming it as a given, and part of their significance seems to lie in the way they refuse to offer a simple celebration of such identity and instead count the cost of achieving it.

Produced in a time of impending crisis for Athens, the *Iphigeneia among the Taurians* suggests, alongside its narrative of escape and liberation, some driving anxieties of its own. In contrast the *Helen,* produced a few years later, in 412, sets its sights simply on Greece as a place of rescue and, unless we cite the hymn to the Great Mother as an evocation of the Eleusinian dimension to the city, does not mention Athens at all. I have suggested that between the mid-420s and the mid-410s certain plays, by figuring an Athenian identity for women accessible through cult, seem to offer an alternative to the paradigmatic hostility and difficulty that seem earlier to have attended the tragic representation of women's ritual practice. Although both Athens and women's cult practice are of concern to the *Iphigeneia among the Taurians,* the drama begins to undo this comforting narrative, and the three plays that constitute, for us, the last of Athenian tragedy seem to mark a complete reversal. Although written before 406 B.C.E., the year both Sophocles and Euripides died, the *Bakchai, Iphigeneia at Aulis,* and *Oedipus at*

---

103. See Wolff 1992: 324 and 330.

Colonus were all produced posthumously, the first two in 405 and the last in 401; their new defensiveness may perhaps be related to the wake of the oligarchic coup in 411 and the sufferings of the last years of the war.

THREE LAST PLAYS

Bakchai

Both Euripides' *Bakchai* and *Iphigeneia at Aulis* suggest that ritual is hopelessly corrupted, whether women are its subjects, as in the former play, or its objects, as in the latter. Far from renegotiating relations between women and the polis, these plays operate on the premise that there is no functioning polis anymore. The *Iphigeneia in Aulis* is set in an armed camp; the *Bakchai* takes to its logical extreme the paradigm of Thebes as anti-city, because it contrives that Thebes itself is threatened with annihilation by the anti-city of women that has left its civilized space to convene on the mountain outside the gates. The play supplies the most extreme and polarized versions of women's ritual legible within the extant corpus of tragedy; although it opens with a compelling vision of ecstatic maenadism, at one with nature and offering a seductively preferable alternative to Pentheus's rigid notions of appropriate behavior, it moves precipitately to replace that vision with the brutality of Pentheus's death at the hands of the maddened women.

The *Bakchai* can be construed within the model explored in this chapter, according to which Thebes is the city that denies ritual activity to women and thereby deprives them of their main avenue of civic identification. Caught between Dionysos's insistence that Thebes worship him and Pentheus's resistance to that worship, the Theban women on Mt. Kithairon can produce only those deformed versions of ritual that eventually substitute human for animal in the mock-sacrifice of Pentheus. The women's ritual autonomy brings wholesale disaster to the city, and no new ritual is devised that will heal the violence or contain the women. What the women's cult signifies is not so much a threat to the polis as its very end.[104] I am not persuaded by Seaford's argument that the lost ending envisaged a benign polis cult erected on the fallen body of the royal house: "Civilized order is nevertheless eventually restored to the Theban polis: in the future Dionysos will be honoured, without catastrophic consequences, in the polis cult."[105] Nothing in the present ending, the restorations by scholars, or the ancient

---

104. As we have seen, the end of Troy too is figured by the deformed marriage rites and hasty funerals that the Trojan women perform in their eponymous play. Foley 1985 has an important chapter on the *Bakchai*. Foley's position is summed up on p. 258: "Euripides can find no order outside ritual and myth and rational speech, yet in the end the order provided by myth, ritual and speech remains in an uncertain relation to the reality of the contemporary world."

105. Seaford 1995: 255 and n. 96.

hypothesis suggests this possibility. While Dionysos announces in the prologue that he has come to teach the city his rites (39–40), such "learning"
might be understood as accomplished in the action of the drama rather
than as envisaging some moment subsequent to the play when city and cult
can live together in harmony. That this learning is less auspicious than
Seaford claims is perhaps suggested especially by Dionysos's insistence that
the city will learn "even if it doesn't want to" (39).[106]

The *Bakchai* is sometimes described as formally conservative and as marking a return to the theatrical practices of the period before the Euripidean
experiments of the 410s.[107] The chorus, for instance, is often said to be
closely integrated with the action in a way that is not characteristic of all late
Euripidean plays. While this general description is only partly useful, the
Bakchai does seem to regress in its vision of women's ritual. The maenadism
of the Theban women is inflicted by Dionysos as a punishment for their
refusal to believe in his divinity, and despite the beautiful descriptions of the
women's activities in the choral odes and the Messenger speeches, their
maenadism reveals itself as ultimately disastrous. A more productive version
of women's ritual may perhaps be read close to the end of the play, in the
faint echoes of wedding celebrations that help to bring Agave back to her
senses, and in the slightly clearer echoes of funeral lamentation that accompany her attempts to reassemble Pentheus's fragmented body. No new cult
is founded, but in place of the disastrous autonomy of the group we are
offered the lone figure of Agave groping towards normality with the help of
partially realized ritual forms.

As Agave has been driven away from her proper roles in oikos and polis
by Dionysos, so she is brought back to her senses—and to what is left of her
roles—by the sole remaining figure of authority in the household and city,
namely her father Kadmos. He first asks her to look up at the sky, and she
reports that she feels a change coming over her thought processes (1264–
70). She has forgotten their previous conversation about the "young lion"
that she thinks she has killed on Kithairon and whose head she thinks she
carries (1272). He next asks her "To what house did you go with wedding
songs?" (1273). While this phrase can be taken, as Agave takes it, as a para-
phrase for "Whom did you marry?" we might also suggest that it can evoke
the entire ritual occasion of the wedding, during which the bride is transferred from her natal to her marital home amid accompanying jubilation.[108]

---

106. Seaford (1995: 255 n. 96) claims that Agave refers to Theban maenads to come at
1387, when she says that "other bakchai may be concerned" (with the thyrsus and the mountain). It seems to me that this line could equally well refer to other maenads in any location.

107. See, for example, Dodds 1960: xl.

108. Segal, strangely enough, makes little of marriage ritual even in the expanded version
of *Dionysiac Poetics* (1997). On the maenad as antiwife see Seaford 1996: ad loc.

Agave is thus not only induced to remember her position as wife of Echion and mother of Pentheus but also offered a vision of normal, productive ritual to set against the distorted horrors of the Dionysiac festival. Shortly after her recognition of Pentheus's head, the text as we have it falls into disarray, but fragments from the twelfth-century play *Christus Patiens*, which are generally accepted as deriving from a text of the *Bakchai*, indicate that Agave gathers up the shattered pieces of Pentheus's body preparatory to burial.[109] Thus she is offered the proper parameters of women's ritual involvement, in weddings and funerals, in order to correct the mistaken autonomy that led her to Mt. Kithairon. This version of cult is hardly powerful enough to overcome the terrors that have preceded it, but it may be thought to offer the possibility of appropriate identifications to women whose subjected lives might otherwise drive them to maenadism. Since Agave and Kadmos have to leave in exile, however, it is not at all clear that the city can be quickly remade by the kinds of ritual practice adumbrated in the play's closing scenes.

Iphigeneia at Aulis

The *Iphigeneia at Aulis* explores the dynamics of women's subjection in its most dramatic form; Iphigeneia is offered as a sacrificial victim in order to secure a fair wind for the expedition to Troy. The play again stages the end of the polis, by eschewing a civic location and siting the sacrifice instead in the camp of the Panhellenic army. Never seen on stage, the army is represented as an anonymous and undifferentiated mass to which its commanders are in thrall, as Agamemnon acknowledges at 450. It can be roused only by the dangerous seer Kalchas and the demagogue Odysseus, who are also kept out of sight. As the city is replaced by an armed encampment and the democracy by a dangerous mob, all initiative seems to pass from the figures onstage to this brooding offstage presence that mocks the individual characters' attempts to manage the situation. Marking its departure from the heroic epic tradition, the play makes Agamemnon into a fifth-century politician who courts the people for his office, rather than receiving it as his kingly inheritance (337–45). To compound the degradation of the Atreid house Klytaimestra is given a previous marriage from which Agamemnon took her by force, having killed her husband and dashed out the brains of her baby son (1149–52). So corrupted has this social context become that what it requires for the success of its projects is a human sacrifice.[110]

Foley has shown that a wider context of normative ritual practice makes possible this outrageous act;[111] the play insists on the homologies between sacrifice and marriage so that Iphigeneia is positioned to accept the one in

109. See Dodds 1960: lv–lvi and appendix.
110. Rabinowitz (1993: 42) writes of a "cultural crisis at the heart of the play."
111. Foley 1985: 65–105.

the guise of the other.[112] Numerous similarities between the two ceremonies facilitate the identification: both bride and sacrificial victim are garlanded; Artemis both presides over the young girl's ordinary preparations for womanhood and requires the sacrifice that cuts short Iphigeneia's youth; Iphigeneia herself makes the equation explicit when she says that the sacrifice will be "children and marriage" (1399) for her. Bringing success to the Greek expedition, she also gives new significance to the trope of death as marriage and the representation of the unwedded dead as brides.

In this tactic of conflation the play does no more, of course, than reproduce Agamemnon's ruse whereby he enticed Iphigeneia to Aulis on the pretext of a marriage to Achilles (98–100). This marriage offers to become a reality when the two meet and are erotically impressed with each other, but the sexual energies thus released are diverted into the sacrifice, and the conflation between the two enables Iphigeneia not only to accept the imminent sacrifice but also actively to organize her own immolation and the other ritual activity that it entails. Whereas the Herald at 434ff. urged everyone to prepare for the wedding, she at 1470ff. takes charge of arrangements for the sacrifice. She goes on to prescribe the mourning practice of her mother and sisters, or rather its absence; she requires that they not cut their hair or wear black clothes. Despite her youth and marginal social status as unmarried girl, she exercises unwonted authority over both her wedding and her own funeral. Victim and object of the sacrificial scenario, she nonetheless lays claim to a subject position.

Insofar as the *Iphigeneia in Aulis* allows the victim to take center stage, it begs the question, How can the sacrifice speak? In other plays where young people die, they are not permitted to expand out into the entire drama as Iphigeneia does here. In the *Children of Herakles* Makaria agrees to die in order to save her siblings, but once she has made her voluntary choice, the play moves on, and she is forgotten. Similarly, Menoikeus in the *Phoenician Women*, as the last of the Earth-born, must be sacrificed in order to save Thebes. His father, Kreon, is ready to hide him away and save him, but he goes voluntarily to his death; yet once he is gone, the play makes no further mention of him. In contrast to these plays, in the *Iphigeneia in Aulis* the sacrifice marks Iphigeneia's difference not only from other Euripidean victims but also from the Iphigeneia of the *Agamemnon*, who died with a gag in her mouth (235–37).

That the position of the speaking sacrifice is an impossible one is suggested by the fact that Iphigeneia delivers two diametrically opposed speeches on the single topic of her death. When she first hears of the plan to sacrifice her she pleads with Agamemnon for her life, but after the exchange between Klytaimestra and Achilles, in which he explains how the army was ready to

---

112. See also Seaford 1987.

lynch him for his protection of Iphigeneia, she announces her readiness to die. The first speech needs little interpretation; the second has presented commentators with problems since Aristotle first complained that Iphigeneia is an "inconsistent character . . . for [she] as a suppliant is quite unlike what she is later" (*Poetics* 15.9, 1454a31).[113] What seems to happen is that Iphigeneia deploys, in order to render the sacrifice palatable, not only the ritual paradigm but also a political and an erotic discourse.[114] In her second speech embracing the sacrifice she repeats Agamemnon's political tropes almost word for word.[115] He had claimed that the army wanted to "put an end to the rape of Greek marriages" (1266) and that Greece, to whom Iphigeneia will be sacrificed, relied on him and on her to guarantee its freedom and to protect Greek marriages from forcible spoliation (1271–75). In her speech at 1368–1401 Iphigeneia plays repeatedly on the theme of Greece, claiming that she will gain the fame of a liberator (1384), and that Greece looks to her for the success of the expedition that will ensure no more kidnapping of Greek women (1378–81); she seems oblivious to Klytaimestra's charge, made in her hearing, that Agamemnon took her by force. Iphigeneia closes with the statement "It is right for Greeks to rule barbarians, and not barbarians Greeks, mother; for they are slaves, while we are free." Yet all the play's adult male characters have proclaimed their enslavement to the army or each other. Iphigeneia's repetitions of Agamemnon's tropes freight the notions of Greece and of freedom with the weight of a moral imperative that tries to establish a distance between her usage and the debased contexts in which the words have previously appeared. Iphigeneia's sacrifice must not only save the expedition but also find a way of freeing language from its corruption.

When Iphigeneia employs an erotic as well as a political discourse, she both elaborates on the repeated trope of marriage and also challenges it. Shy at first in front of the fake bridegroom Achilles (1340–42), she now speaks openly of having the eyes of all Greece trained upon her (1378) and of giving her body to Greece (1397). At 1393 she argues that Achilles should not have to oppose the Greeks and fight or die over "one woman." Whereas the "one woman" who is described as traded for the lives of men is usually Helen, here it is Iphigeneia, whose eroticized speech now threatens to identify her with her antithesis.[116] The unlovely gender calculus emerges again when Iphigeneia says that it is better for one man to live than one thousand

---

113. On the problems of the second speech see Foley 1985: 67 and n. 4.

114. These discourses may be thought to identify her less with the women in the play, Klytaimestra and the chorus, and more with the men who are determining events. See Rabinowitz 1993a: 45 and 51.

115. On Agamemnon's rhetoric see Rabinowitz 1993a: 49–50.

116. Rabinowitz (1993a: 39) argues that the play eroticizes the sacrifice, but my suggestion here is slightly different.

women (1394); this is simply an inversion of the trope that laments how thousands of men will die for the one woman Helen. In the lyrics that precede and that follow her second speech, the equation between herself and Helen is made even more explicit . Her appeal rebuffed by Agamemnon, she sings of herself as facing a *duselenan*, an "evil Helen" (1315–16). Having introduced this Homeric word,[117] she proceeds to sing of herself as *heleptolin* at 1476, and the phrase is repeated by the chorus at 1511. *Heleptolin* means "taker or destroyer of cities," but it is also an Aeschylean pun (*Agamemnon* 689) on the name of Helen. Helen and Iphigeneia together will be responsible for the sack of Troy. In order successfully to maneuver herself into the sacrificial victim's position, the pure virgin who makes the expedition possible has to identify with the adulteress who makes it necessary.[118]

In the political and erotic discourses that it attracts to itself, the sacrifice takes on some of the corruption in its environment. Whereas sacrifice may, in dramas and in cult etiologies, provide some form of healing resolution, Iphigeneia's second speech here seems simply to let the Greeks off the hook and to save them from the consequences of their own action. Although some critics have discerned positive possibilities in Iphigeneia's voluntary gesture,[119] the sacrifice is as problematic as the situation it is designed to remedy; this is indicated by the fact that the ritual action must itself be rescued, by the substitution of the deer. This substitution is, of course, questioned by Klytaimestra, who asks whether the Messenger is not telling her a fiction designed to console and thus silence her (1615–18). As the only moment in extant Greek tragedy when the veracity of a messenger speech is questioned, this passage and indeed the whole ending of the play is suspected of being spurious. Yet if it is not a Euripidean ending, it ought to be; it is compatible both with the other formal innovations of the later plays and with the specific concerns of the *Iphigeneia at Aulis*. Just as there are two opposed speeches about the sacrifice, so there are two endings; Iphigeneia both is and is not killed.

In its equivocation about the ultimate outcome of the sacrificial act, the ending pursues the theme of rewriting that dominates the drama. Conscious of itself as inheritor of a long epic and dramatic tradition, the *Iphigeneia at Aulis* plays throughout with the proposition that "the Trojan War will not take place." Imagining that there can be another end to the story, it offers a plurality of attempts to rewrite the narrative; these begin with the opening scene

117. Compare *dusparis* at *Iliad* 3.39 and 13.769.

118. The eroticism of this stance may be thought of as determined by the eroticism of the army, which is variously described as being seized by an eros or an Aphrodite (1264) that makes it passionate for war.

119. See especially Foley 1985, but also Castellani (1985: 4), who writes of an "exemplary princess" and a "true patriot."

of the play when Agamemnon frantically writes a second letter to Klytaimestra and cancels his previous deceptive command to bring Iphigeneia to the camp. Several characters try to rewrite the plot by changing their minds:[120] Agamemnon and Menelaos change from desiring the sacrifice to abhorring it, Achilles changes from a stalwart defense of Iphigeneia to acquiescence in the sacrifice, and Iphigeneia herself, as we have seen, makes one speech in favor of life and a second in favor of her own immolation.

With its persistent trope of rewriting, the play is enabled to explore its central dilemma—should the sacrifice take place and the war proceed?—from a plurality of perspectives. Iphigeneia both is and is not willing to give up her life; she both is and is not replaced on the altar at the last minute by a deer. It is almost as if the text offers us a choice of plays and puts us in the position of the other moral agents who fail so miserably throughout the drama; our choice determines the fate of Iphigeneia. To this extent, Klytaimestra's doubts about the Messenger's speech reproduce those of the reader or audience about the entire play: has Iphigeneia's heroism been rewarded, or has the political corruption of the Greek camp won out? Is the play a real consolation or a fiction designed to keep us quiet? To put the audience in the position of making this choice is also, of course, to ask whether that audience can avoid or transcend the corruption that both makes the sacrifice necessary and threatens to undermine its efficacy.

The *Bakchai* and the *Iphigeneia at Aulis* between them dramatize what are perhaps the most compelling ritual actions in the extant corpus and correspondingly abandon all notion of the polis. The *Bakchai* posits a total contradiction between its women's ritual forms and the values of the polis, while the elaboration by the *Iphigeneia at Aulis* on the woman's ritual gesture exposes the limitations of the community for which she makes it. Both plays show signs of the protracted warfare that undermined the polis ideal; neither the corruptions of the community nor the proposed remedies can be endured. Last of the extant tragedies, the *Oedipus at Colonus* takes a different approach and, in the wake of the oligarchic coup of 411 B.C.E., uses ritual figures in an endeavor to rebuild the polis. But the newly restated opposition between women and the city ensures that once again women will be excluded from the city's ritual practice and to some extent sacrificed for it.

Oedipus at Colonus

Various scholars have convincingly construed Sophocles' *Oedipus at Colonus* as a response to the oligarchic coup staged in 411.[121] Set in the deme of Colonus, site of the famous assembly that voted itself out of existence when,

120. Foley (1985: 96) points out that "in no other Euripidean play are changes of mind as pervasive as [here]."

121. Early work on this topic includes Jameson 1971 and Calder 1985; recent work includes that of Wilson (1992), who explicitly calls the play "antidemocratic"; also Edmunds

impelled by the need to attract the finances of the Persians, it dissolved the democracy (Thucydides 8.67), the play resolutely avoids the city itself in favor of a different topography. Oedipus is brought by Antigone to Colonus on the outskirts of Athens, where he is first rebuffed and then embraced by the chorus of citizens of Athens. He recognizes the sanctuary of the Furies as the place where he is destined to die, and in the course of the play he also realizes that here is the fulfilment of the oracle that promised his tomb as a benefit to some and a curse to others. The play unfolds as a series of more or less hostile encounters between Oedipus and Thebans like Kreon and Polyneikes, closing with his mysterious death offstage, which is witnessed only by his new Athenian patron, Theseus. Throughout, the play elaborates a more rustic version of Athens, distinguished by the natural features of the holy grove where the play is set, replete with living rock, nightingales, burgeoning trees, and vines (16–19). Despite this evasion, or perhaps because of it, the play attempts to construct a new Athens, in terms of ritual rather than of political figures. The sanctuary extended by Athens to Oedipus will heal the troubled saga of the Theban royal house, but in exchange the tomb of Oedipus, honored with hero cult, will protect the Athenians from assault. For the duration of the play, Oedipus remains safe in the grove dedicated to the Furies, so that the whole drama unfolds in Athenian sacred space. While repeated rituals are performed offstage where Theseus sacrifices to Poseidon, the chorus also requires that Oedipus perform a ritual to placate the Furies, and the description of this ritual is the longest and most detailed in extant tragedy.[122] Athens thus appears not with a political profile but as a cult center. Oedipus himself, rebutting Kreon, describes the city as one that knows "better than any other how to honor the gods" (1006–7)

Despite this emphasis on Athenian ritual proficiency, the Theban disease, constituted by the inability of ritual to achieve completion and success, threatens to infect Athens. Since Oedipus is too old and weak to perform the ritual prescribed by the chorus, and since he will not stir from his chosen sanctuary, Ismene goes to discharge this duty for him; her isolation then renders her vulnerable to kidnap by Kreon's forces, and we never learn whether or not she successfully completes the ritual. The Theban syndrome then spreads to the Athenians. Theseus is summoned by the chorus to help Oedipus against Kreon and has to abandon his sacrifice to Poseidon. Since he consequently orders everyone else to leave the sacrifice and ride to the rescue, the ritual is completely disrupted.[123] When later in the play peals of

1996. None of these texts is, however, particularly interested in ritual. Both Blundell 1993 and Slatkin 1986 see the play as concerned with the health of Athens in general rather than in specifically political terms.

122. Krummen (1993: 195, 198) stresses the local character of this ritual but also its function of giving confidence to the demesmen. She does not note that it may be left incomplete!

123. Blundell (1993: 290) sees this ritual as a sign of unity.

thunder herald Oedipus's imminent demise, he summons Theseus once again and thus once again disrupts a sacrifice. Even if Athens does know better than any other how to honor the gods, the play seems to question whether this privileged knowledge will survive the Theban onslaught, or whether Athens will suffer some diminution of her identity. This, of course, is the issue that commands the play's attention in multiple ways throughout its narrative.

Ismene departs to perform a rite of intercession for Oedipus, but other rituals she and Antigone are not to perform. Oedipus can escape the Theban myth by entering Athens, and Athens can gain some kind of salvation by embracing Oedipus, but in neither rescue action is there room for the Theban women. When he receives his final sign, Oedipus leads his daughters and Theseus offstage to the "steep descent, the threshold" reported by the Messenger (1590–91), and there requires the women to prepare him for death by bathing him in running water and dressing him in clean clothes (1598–99). Once they have performed these tasks, however, they learn that they are permitted no further involvement; they are not to see or hear what becomes of Oedipus, and their place at his side is to be occupied by Theseus (1640–44). As Oedipus had shed his sons in the scene with Polyneikes, so here he sheds his daughters, and thus replaces the unsatisfactory Theban oikos with the polis of the Athenians. The knowledge of the secret grave site is to be passed on by Theseus to his political heirs (1530–32).[124]

Antigone and Ismene are prevented from discharging the important female ritual task of tending their father's grave. As we have seen, the prohibition is common to the women of theatrical Thebes, but here it is not issued by that dysfunctional city; the injunction stems instead from one who is in the process of becoming a part of Athens. We might suppose that the prohibition itself would appear somehow ameliorated and rendered palatable by the Athenian context, but this does not seem to be the case. The daughters suffer acutely, and "long" (1725) to perform the characteristic Oedipal act of looking upon what is forbidden. They are completely unable to accept that they are barred from their father's grave, and the conflict between them and the chorus, and to an extent between them and Theseus, renders the last scene of the play disturbing in its vehemence. Unlike Oedipus, they find no peace. Prevented by Theseus from visiting the grave, they choose instead to return to Thebes in order to stop the slaughter that threatens their brothers. By thus reversing Oedipus's healthful trajectory from Thebes to Athens, and by continuing to identify themselves as Thebans, they seal their fate. The play appropriates the benefit to be derived from Theban Oedipus for Athens, but then rejects Thebes even

---

124. Although Fagles translates as "eldest, dearest son," Edmunds points out that the words do not necessarily denote an heir of the blood.

more decisively in the persons of the deprived daughters. It is hard to avoid the conclusion that the *Oedipus at Colonus* enacts a sacrificial paradigm, opposing women to the city and constructing the successful city on their exclusion.

Even though women's ritual practice is not of as much concern to the *Oedipus at Colonus* as it is to the *Bakchai* or *Iphigeneia at Aulis*, discernible contours link all three plays. Each has as its premise the death or debility of a community, and in each the figure of women's ritual practice is intimately bound up with the representation of that civic failure. In the *Bakchai* the two are synonymous, in the *Iphigeneia at Aulis* the central character's sacrifice represents an equivocal attempt to restore the community to health, and in the *Oedipus at Colonus* the city attains a measure of success at the price of the women's pain. The possibility of mediating between women and the city by means of ritual, which some earlier plays briefly explored, is thoroughly abandoned by the close of the century.

COMIC EXAGGERATION

If the tragedies that close the century tend to figure the city's end with rituals involving women, the comedies of the last decade take a somewhat different track. The four last comedies of Aristophanes all enact a rescue:[125] in the *Frogs,* Dionysos descends into the underworld in order to bring back the dead poet who is most qualified to save the city of Athens; in the *Women at the Thesmophoria,* Euripides has to be rescued from irate women; but in the *Lysistrata* and the *Women in Assembly,* women themselves convene in order to save the city. In the last three plays, where women's collective action is involved, their ritual practice is constantly foregrounded.

The *Lysistrata* and *Women at the Thesmophoria* were produced in the same year, 411 B.C.E. Henderson's edition argues that the *Lysistrata* was produced first, at the Lenaia festival of mid-February rather than the Dionysia of mid-April, so that the first play preceded and the second succeeded the oligarchic coup.[126] At a moment of acute debate about the nature and future of the democratic city, comedy explores two violently opposed versions of women and women's rituals. In the *Women at the Thesmophoria,* massed

125. I am here excluding from consideration the *Wealth,* which is generally considered to be a "middle" rather than an "early" comedy and so to exhibit marked generic differences from the rest of the Aristophanic oeuvre.

126. Henderson 1987. See also Sommerstein 1990. Taaffe (1993), however, argues that the *Women at the Thesmophoria,* being more "Athenian" in outlook, was produced at the Athenians-only Lenaia, while the Panhellenic *Lysistrata* was produced at the later festival that was open to all comers. In his edition of *Thesmophoriazusae* (1994), Sommerstein suggests that the play takes place before the campaign by the oligarchs and the associated coup are actually underway; but he also holds that the play is not at all political (1994: 4).

women threaten the male who intrudes into their rituals, conforming to the pattern laid down by the accounts of Battos and Aristomenes (see chapter 2); but in the *Lysistrata* the women's ability to "save the city" is figured throughout by their roles as ritual practitioners.

Lysistrata

Thoroughly fed up with war and the prolonged absence of their men, the women of Greece, led by Lysistrata, declare a sex strike in order to force their men to arrange a peace. The young wives take an oath to abstain from sex and then retire to the Acropolis, where the older women have already barricaded themselves in to prevent the men from getting access to the treasury. An Athenian official, the Magistrate, tries to confront the women but suffers ignominious defeat. A husband approaches and is teased by his wife but left unsatisfied. Eventually Spartans and Athenians alike are so reduced by lust that they do conclude a peace, under the auspices of Lysistrata, who brings on stage a naked female called Reconciliation.

K. J. Dover claims that the *Lysistrata* is a play about marriage, and it does place unusual emphasis on the delights of legitimate heterosexual union. Since the war has disrupted marriage along with all other peaceful civilized pursuits, to disrupt it further with a sex strike seems a logical response on the part of the women. The restoration of peace to the Greek world and of harmony to Athenian marriages then becomes synonymous, so that one character, sometimes identified as Lysistrata, can encourage both the warring states and the warring wedded partners (1273–78):

> You Spartans take these women, and you Athenians these.
> Let the man stand by his wife and the woman by her husband.
> Let us dance for the gods on this happy occasion
> And take care not to screw up again.

Early on in the play, when the chorus of old women pour water on the chorus of old men to put out the fires with which they menace the Acropolis, they describe their action as a nuptial bath, so that the vocabulary of marriage is distorted to another and more hostile end. Toward the close of the play, however, the male and female choruses are reconciled (1040), and the women entertain the men with a wedding feast (1189). But it is not only as married women, responsible for legitimate heirs—the "tax" that they pay to the city (589–90, 651)—that the women of the play are significant. They are also foregrounded in their roles as ritual practitioners. When Lysistrata first appears onstage, she complains that the women have not arrived at her quasi-political meeting, although they would have come quickly enough to a festival of Dionysos or Pan or the Birth-Goddesses (1–2). The first ritual possibility for women, then, is to improvise and schedule their own celebrations as they think fit, and although this seems at first to conflict with the political role that Lysistrata is offering, it is quickly demonstrated that the one can be successfully figured by the other. To a large extent the women, and the play, continue to extemporize, for the good of the city, on the theme of women's festivals.

In an influential piece Loraux has argued that the play mobilizes ritual practice to figure its adult women as young virgins, engaged only in unthreatening activities that promote the city's welfare.[127] By withdrawing to the Acropolis and identifying with Athena, the women can be seen to occupy the position of *arrhephoroi,* seceding from the oikos in order to identify instead with the city. As *arrhephoroi,* the women work for the city's good with both their sexuality and their skills at weaving, which Lysistrata draws on to explain how women will run the city better than men (565–86).[128] They will disentangle the threads of the international situation, comb out the bad citizens from Athens, and knit mother city and colonies together in friendship. The chorus of old women repeatedly articulate this paradoxical vision of the "monstrous regiment" as nonthreatening virgins. In their encounter with the forces of the Magistrate they claim, while beating up his policemen, that all they want to do is sit peacefully *(sophronos)* like a *kore,* or unmarried daughter (473). Later, when inviting everyone to a feast, they say it will be their pleasure to provide clothes and jewelry for any daughter who is serving as a *kanephoros* (1193). Although they are not claiming to be *kanephoroi* themselves, it seems that their version of female identity and of female service to the polis foregrounds the contributions of ritually active *parthenoi* as much as it does their own alarming feistiness.

The most striking identification that the chorus make between themselves and the ritual virgins is in the lines where they describe an imaginary *cursus honorum* of ritual offices for the young girls of the city (638–46). The women claim to have served successively as *arrhephoros, aletris, arktos,* and *kanephoros,* a trajectory that commentators agree is highly unlikely to have applied to any but a very few Athenian girls, and certainly not to a whole chorusful. The chorus women exaggerate their claim, but its basic premise is upheld by the play; it is as ritual practitioners that women serve the city, and they are consequently entitled to address it in that role. Establishing the claim explicitly on the grounds of the *parthenos*'s ritual service, the play proceeds by implicitly figuring the women's collective political action in the form of rituals for adult women, with special reference to the Thesmophoria and Adonia.

---

127. Loraux 1981a.

128. Weaving also continues to connote women's sexuality and deceptiveness, as it does in Homeric epic and in tragedy (e.g., Kirke's weaving of spells against Odysseus's men and Klytaimestra's web, in which she binds Agamemnon); one of the women bent on leaving the Acropolis in order to get back to marital sex says she just has to go and spread her wool out on the bed (728–34).

As Foley has shown,[129] abstinence from sex and withdrawal to the Acropolis can together be seen to figure not only the Arrhephoria but also the Thesmophoria, most important of rituals for adult women's lives. The sex strike is thus made to resonate not only with women's potentially alarming ritual autonomy but also with their vital contributions to civic welfare in the promotion of crops and provision of children. Other versions of women's ritual practice are also pressed into service; not only do the women offer nuptial baths to the old men, as we have seen, but they also prepare the Magistrate for his mock-funeral by sprinkling him with herbs and adorning him in garlands (599–607). Many commentators also suggest that the play goes so far in its ritual references as to equate Lysistrata and Myrrhine with living priestesses.[130] D. M. Lewis first made this suggestion, showing that the contemporary priestess of Athena Polias was called Lysimache, a synonym for Lysistrata, and pointing out further that the contemporary priestess of Athena Nike may well have been named Myrrhine.[131] Even if the play does indeed invoke these historical priestesses, its innovation of dramatizing and naming real women was not a tactic pursued by any later plays; yet the argument for this isolated instance may be found persuasive if we take into account the play's persistent desire to show its women as cult practitioners. Several scholars have looked to the identification with the priestess Lysimache to explain Lysistrata's aloof stance, her freedom from the weaknesses of other women, her facility with a public role, and the theatrical nonappearance of her husband or son.[132] In the case of Myrrhine, however, the identification does not work so well, since the Aristophanic Myrrhine is represented as sensual and frivolous, in no way a serious proposition like Lysistrata, and since the priestess in question would be about sixty at the time of the play.[133] Rather than pressing any strict identification between the play's women and historical priestesses, we should probably understand the women as invoking the latters' cultic authority for their own political project. In numerous ways, then, the first extant comedy to feature a female hero looks to the sphere of ritual for its paradigms.

While many commentators note both the resonance of the Thesmophoria and the oblique invocation of historical priestesses, fewer draw attention to the model provided by the Adonia.[134] Douglas MacDowell allows it

129. Foley 1982: 8.

130. E.g., Foley 1982: 8 n. 18; MacDowell 1995: 239–43.

131. Lewis 1955.

132. MacDowell (1995: 241) asks how an ordinary woman, rather than a priestess, would be able to summon the other women to a meeting and expect them to follow her lead, but this seems to me to apply too much expectation of rationality to the devices of comedy.

133. This could, of course, be a joke. Foley (1982) also notes that Lampito was the name of the mother of the contemporary king of Sparta.

134. Bowie (1993a: 181) points out that "the plot of *Lysistrata* will be inscribed within these contradictions in the male views of women and their role in society, and will clearly expose

only negative value, claiming: "The women in this play do not in fact indulge in [these] celebrations. Instead they are upholders of the traditional religion of Athens."[135] Yet the Adonia is the only ritual explicitly mentioned in the play, by the Magistrate, who compares the women's seizing of the Acropolis to this festival and goes on to complain, as we saw in chapter 3, about the disruption caused to an earlier meeting of the men's assembly by the women's celebration. Implicitly, then, the Magistrate begins with a model in which the male and female spheres should be strictly separated to prevent the contamination of political by ritual discourse, and in which women's autonomy, as enacted in their rituals, can be only destructive of the political community. The drama proceeds to deconstruct the oppositions put into play by the Magistrate, using ritual to articulate the women's commitment to their community and their work for its welfare. Lysistrata points out in her weaving metaphor that women's oikos-based skills may yet equip them to save the city, and by the same token women's public interventions by means of their rituals need not be destructive. Through ritual the play elaborates a more inclusive vision of the city than that espoused by the Magistrate in his castigation of the Adonia, in which male and female concerns cannot be hermetically sealed off from one another.

If, moreover, the Adonia may be understood as the festival of the eroticized wife, as suggested in chapter 2, then it offers an appropriate paradigm for the actions of the women of the *Lysistrata,* who temporarily deny and suspend the traditional version of marriage in order finally to uphold it. Whereas Ischomachos counsels his child-bride, in Xenophon's *Oikonomikos,* to eschew ornament and present herself always au naturel, the wives in the *Lysistrata* deliberately set out to tease and tantalize with every artifice at their disposal (148–54):

> If we sit inside all dolled up,
> Half-naked in those tunics from Amorgos,
> Smooth and hairless where it counts—
> Our men will get hard and be hot to trot,
> And we won't let them! We'll run away.
> They'll come to the table quick enough, I bet.

Like the Adonia, they confound the categories of respectable wife and licentious harlot. Their ultimate aim, however, is support of the legitimate rights only of the former.

In keeping with this essentially conservative agenda, which uses radical tactics only as a temporary ploy, the women close by leaving the stage to men. It is not even clear if Lysistrata herself speaks after 1187, when she

---

those contradictions, which are constructed between Thesmophoria and Adonia," but does not mention the Adonia again.

135. MacDowell 1995: 245.

urges Spartans and Athenians to exchange oaths of friendship, and wives and husbands to be reconciled.[136] The place of the active energetic women is taken by Reconciliation, a nude female figure whose passive body is divided up between Athenians and Spartans (1112–89). The figure of women's ritual practice disappears, to be replaced by references to the Panhellenic religion that ought to unite Sparta and Athens (1128–32), and the pugnacious choruses of old men and women give way to choruses of Athenians and Spartans in the symposiastic closing moments. While the theatrical and almost mythical strategy of the "unlikely savior" succeeds on stage, in historical Athens it is still the men who have to work out the city's *soteria*, and the imaginary action by the women is simply a sign of the extremity of the city's real plight. Although the *Lysistrata*, like some contemporary tragedies, represents women's stake in the city through their rituals, it eventually retreats from the logical consequences of its own radical premise. This gesture will be repeated in the *Women in the Assembly*.

Women at the Thesmophoria

By the time of the *Women at the Thesmophoria*, if we follow the dating of Henderson and Sommerstein, the oligarchic tendencies represented by the Magistrate had won, and the democratic constitution had been replaced by an oligarchy that soon showed itself to be violent and unscrupulous. The comic response to these events is, in part, a very different version of women's ritual practice; whereas the *Lysistrata* had envisaged women's rituals as part of a positive and regenerative process, in which women are represented as full participants in the civic community, the *Women at the Thesmophoria* reverts to the earlier view that constructs women's ritual as the ground and scene of conflict between the sexes. If the *Lysistrata*'s vision is properly "comic" in its emphasis on positive energies, the *Women at the Thesmophoria* is "tragic," and especially so when we consider that its plot rehearses the contours not only of the narrative of Battos and Aristomenes, but also that of Euripides' *Bakchai*, produced six years later.

Set during the festival of the Thesmophoria, the play supposes that the assembled women hold a quasi-political meeting on the second day of the festival, where they constitute themselves as a law court in order to try to condemn Euripides for his misogyny. Euripides hears of the plan and takes his In-Law with him to persuade Agathon, an effeminate tragedian, to go to the Thesmophoria disguised as a woman and plead for him. When Agathon declines, the In-Law is prevailed upon to go instead, and is duly depilated and dressed up. Once at the festival, he does defend Euripides but is exposed

---

136. See Henderson 1987: 206–7 and 214–15; also Taaffe 1993: 71 n. 46. Henderson (1987: 215) notes that the *Women in Assembly* also drops its heroine long before the ending of the play.

as a man and imprisoned by the women. Euripides comes to save him, and together they enact scenes from several of those Euripidean plays that stage a rescue. None of these works, however, until Euripides dresses as a woman too, specifically as an old procuress, and brings on a dancing-girl to distract the policeman guarding the In-Law so that he can make his getaway.[137]

The trope of ritual as affording women illegitimate power is played in full force when the women steal the men's cultural forms of assembly and law court during the Thesmophoria. In the wake of the coup that deprived men of democratic practice, such forms have nowhere else to go. Occupying a site close to that reserved for the meetings of the democracy, the women stage a temporary usurpation that models on a separate plane the usurpation recently enacted in Athenian politics. Since the figure of ritual has been repeatedly deployed in the theater to discuss the illegitimacy of female power, issues of legitimacy may themselves be debated with the figure of women's ritual. The women themselves, who begin the proceedings in proper form, quickly turn nasty when the In-Law tries to defend Euripides by pointing out all the dreadful things women do that he has *not* dramatized; the women threaten the In-Law physically, and he, still in disguise, desperately claims the right of *parrhesia*, or free speech (540–43). The assembled women's failure to honor this fundamental Athenian right perhaps registers the restrictions on political discourse put in place by the oligarchic coup. This persistent conflation of the women's rituals and the men's politics allows the play to mock both sexes at once.

The evocation of the Thesmophoria raises the issue of ritual secrecy and of its antithesis, exposure, both of which may be thought to resonate in the atmosphere of distrust that characterized contemporary politics. In the world of this comedy no one can keep a secret; the play's drive is to expose not only the false politics of the women but also the collusion of the men. The poet Agathon is revealed to the drama's searching gaze as he is wheeled out on stage and made to explain the principles of his art, and the In-Law's deception is eventually laid bare to the women. The main target of the play's revelatory drive, however, is the women at the Thesmophoria. Although the ritual is secret, and men are forbidden to attend, the men of the Athenian audience are enabled by the drama to see the women and their ritual. Like the In-Law or Pentheus in the *Bakchai*, they intrude, but, unlike these, they are preserved in safety by the theatrical distance between stage and audience. They are safe too in the sense that what they see does not menace their preconceptions. What happens is that the women in their rituals simply mimic the men's forms of democratic practice; they have no initiative of their own, and to that extent they cannot undermine the male polity. The

137. Discussion here is indebted to Zeitlin 1981.

In-Law models men's knowledge of women when he successfully answers questions about Thesmophoric ritual that are put to him in an endeavor to find out who has penetrated the women's spaces. To each question about procedure he simply answers "We drank" and is correct. What women do when they are alone is exactly what men think they do.

The same device is at work when the In-Law speaks up in defense of Euripides. Complaining that Euripides has now exposed on stage the secret ruses that they have for getting around their men, the women have already begun to condemn themselves out of their own mouths. The In-Law, as a "woman," continues this process by listing all the even more outrageous things that Euripides has not found out and has not dramatized. The other women's scandalized reactions prove that the In-Law is correct and that women do indeed do these things; men, then, know all there is to know about women.

The men in the play or in the audience do not, however, have it all their own way. The exposure of the women is compensated by the exposure and punishment of the In-Law, and his unwarranted intrusion into the women's ritual space is answered in advance by their sanctioned intrusion into the space of men's political gatherings. All the men in the comedy pay for their part in the plot by undergoing a process of feminization. Agathon and Kleisthenes are represented as already effeminate, of course, and the In-Law's transformation into a woman is staged in all its humiliating detail. Even Euripides has to adopt the quintessential comic tactic of cross-dressing in order finally to rescue the In-Law, who for his part has to give up acting male parts from Euripidean plays, such as those of Telephos and Palamedes, and has to embrace his new female identity fully in scenes from the *Helen* and *Andromeda* before he can escape.[138] Again, this persistent trope may be understood, in the wake of the oligarchic coup, to have a political resonance, as the men of Athens give up their democratic heritage.

The second half of the play, after the In-Law is captured and imprisoned, abandons political discourse in order to rehabilitate both the women and their festival. Singing a long song in their own defense (785–845), the women balance the In-Law's defense of Euripides, and the play then proceeds antiphonally as the scenes of Euripidean parody that stage attempts to rescue the In-Law are intercut with hymns from the women (947–1000, 1136–59). This restoration of cultic normality is accompanied by a reduction in the women's belligerence, so that a truce is finally concluded between them and Euripides. Underlining this reconciliation are the properly comic "marriages" that end the play, whereby not only do "Perseus" and "Andromeda" (played by Euripides and the In-Law respectively) find each

---

138. On this tactic see Zeitlin 1981.

other, but so do the policeman and the dancing-girl. In order to achieve its comic resolution, the play relinquishes its exclusive focus on the menacing aspects of women's ritual, and similarly retreats from political commentary, however veiled.

Women in the Assembly

The *Women in the Assembly*, produced in 392, mobilizes its women to save the city, as does the *Lysistrata,* and again figures this salvation by means of women's ritual practice. In the problematic postwar conditions at the beginning of the fourth century, however, the drama has considerable difficulty in reconstructing the city, and even women's ritual no longer has the potency that it possessed in the *Lysistrata*. Instead of remaking the city in the traditional form of marriage, guaranteed by all the rituals deployed by the *Lysistrata,* the *Women in the Assembly* looks to drastic new remedies like common ownership of property, wives, and children. Instead of drawing on the marital metaphor to exaggerate the femininity of women and the masculinity of men, as did the *Lysistrata,* the play goes one better than the *Women at the Thesmophoria* in dressing not only men as women but also women as men.[139]

The women of Athens have met at their festival of the Skira and devised a plot to take over the Assembly, disguised as men, and to push through the motion that the affairs of the city be turned over to women. While their ability to save the city is again placed under the sign of their rituals, the infiltration of the Assembly has no cultic precedent, as does Lysistrata's occupation of the Acropolis or the Thesmophoric women's of the Pnyx.[140] A dominant metaphor in the two earlier plays, the Thesmophoria is mobilized here by the women as part of the justification for their management of the city's affairs. Practicing the speech that she will give in disguise to the Assembly, Praxagora, the leader of the women, claims that women are better qualified to rule than men because they do not innovate but cling to traditional ways (221–23). They sit down to do their roasting, they carry things on their heads, they bake flat cakes, and they celebrate the Thesmophoria, just as they have always done. This list of unexceptionable accomplishments is quickly undermined by another list that claims that they also annoy husbands, keep lovers, and enjoy wine and sex as they have always done (224–28), but the reference to the Thesmophoria may nonetheless stand as a sign and guarantee of the women's potential for civic virtue. At the Assembly Praxagora makes even more telling use of the Thesmophoria, again in a comparison between men and women. As the neighbor Chremes

139. See Taaffe 1993.
140. Keuls (1985: 357) suggests that women at the historical Skira did indeed dress as men, but her evidence is not accepted by all scholars.

recounts to Blepyros, Praxagora's husband, what happened in the Assembly, he says that Praxagora (in disguise) pointed out that women never tell the secrets of the Thesmophoria, whereas men willingly betray state secrets all the time (442–44). Blepyros agrees heartily. The first part of this play thus indicts Athenian political practice and looks to women's ritual practice for the alternative of *soteria*.

If the men fail in the first half, however, the women fail in the second; they undermine their claims to the virtue of consistency, signed by the Thesmophoria, by wildly innovating in politics and sexual relations. The consequences of their new dispositions are examined in a series of unpleasant scenes that are finally abandoned for the familiar Aristophanic trope of the drunken party. The women do not offer any workable civic vision on Lysistrata's model; the only thing they can get right is to continue to look after the men. Far from using ritual to mediate a civic identity, the women transform the polis into an oikos, as Foley points out,[141] where they continue to be in charge of food and clothing. The play ends with Blepyros's exit to the customary feast, 450 lines after Praxagora's last speech. The women's ascendancy is used to point up the inadequacies of the men, who readily abandon their political duties for the infantilizing new oikos and who show considerably less enthusiasm than the women for "saving the city."

The last four "old" comedies still available to us turn to the theme of *soteria* and rescue as had the Euripidean tragedies of the 410s, and this theme is frequently figured by the invocation of women's ritual forms. Produced at a moment when the city is grappling with the crisis of internal as well as external strife, the *Women at the Thesmophoria* presses the figure of women's ritual into service in order to dramatize this threat to the polity, and the rescue must be effected from the women's ritual gathering. For the *Lysistrata* and *Women in the Assembly*, however, the women's rituals can themselves figure the possibility of rescue for the city; these comedies thus present a potentially more radical version of the ritual mediation of women's civic identity than do the tragedies discussed earlier. Despite this incipient radicalism, however, all three comedies moderate the destabilizing energies of the women's rituals, achieving reconciliation in the *Women at the Thesmophoria* and abandoning Lysistrata and Praxagora long before the end of their respective plays.

Athenian drama is not interested in representing the realities of women's lives, but certain aspects of those lives nonetheless exert a felt pressure on the dramatic form. We have seen that the ritual sphere afforded historical

141. Foley 1981a and 1982.

women a public presence, a public voice, and a measure of autonomy, and drama can consequently draw upon ritual practice to motivate the actions of its female characters. Although ritual thus leaves legible traces in drama, these traces are rarely in excess of the drama's very specific requirements. In particular, Athenian drama uses women's ritual to articulate anxieties about women's place in the community, about their relation with the city, and sometimes about the city itself. In the earliest plays that have been preserved for our inspection women's ritual practice is represented as a source of illegitimate female power, which must be neutralized by the provision of rituals organized by the polis in order to diminish women's control and autonomy. This highly polarized view of ritual as source and ground of conflict between the sexes is put in abeyance for part of the second half of the century but returns with a vengeance in the plays that close the century, like the *Bakchai* and *Women at the Thesmophoria*. In the second half of the century, tragedy begins instead to forge links between female identity and civic identity, using ritual to figure women as Athenians, and it is aided in this project by the fact that the women of Thebes had always been represented on the tragic stage as denied the ritual practice that was historical women's claim to civic status. Other plays mobilize the figure of the prophetess or priestess, allowing ritual to provide women with a legitimate power.

The prolonged Peloponnesian War put a strain on many aspects of Athenian life, and drama's representations of relations between male and female show the symptoms of this strain. Some scholars, such as Peter Rose,[142] have argued that the changing emphases on women in the plays at the end of the century register the protests of historical women, albeit in a distorted form. It has often been suggested that the radical departures of, for instance, the *Lysistrata*, are generated by the historical situation in which there are literally "no men in the city" (524), because the manpower of Athens has been depleted by the Sicilian expedition.[143] Whatever the cause, the plays of the later years of the century experiment briefly with a more inclusive version of the city, to which women belong as ritual practitioners, and where ritual is a ground of cooperation and not conflict. Such experiments are, however, quickly shut down as Athens loses first its democratic constitution and then the war. The dynamic can be tracked even between the *Lysistrata* and the *Women at the Thesmophoria;* and the three tragedies that for us end the century are unanimous in depicting the difficulties of building a city that will include women in any role other than that of sacrificial victim.

Whether or not women were actually present in the theater, Athenian

---

142. See, for instance, Rose 1992: 359 n. 64.

143. Thucydides 8.97, however, notes that Athens could equip another twenty ships after the Sicilian debacle.

drama of the fifth century was produced for a male audience. Although we can quite possibly read in drama some kind of pressure from historical women's grievances as the contrast between Athens's democratic claims and its exclusive politics became more acute,[144] the version of women's ritual practice presented is one that addresses male anxieties about the role of the democratic city and its ability to cope with "the other," signified as so often by the female. Our access to the texts of tragedy and old comedy, with their energetic discussions of women's rituals, ends in 392. The women of ancient Greece continued to participate in cult, of course, for several centuries beyond that time, but we are not able to see so clearly how their participation figured in the fantasies of husbands and fathers. If this book as a whole has shown anything, I hope it has shown that women's ritual practice in ancient Greece dramatized for historical women a far richer array of concerns, and proffered a much more engrossing range of subject positions, than the men in the theater could imagine.

144. Such contradictions are made evident in the case of the Athenian ideology of empire during the Mytilenian Debate in Thucydides book 3.

REFERENCES

Alcock, Susan E., and Robin Osborne, eds. 1994. *Placing the gods: Sanctuaries and sacred space in ancient Greece*. Oxford.

Aleshire, Sara B. 1989. *The Athenian Asklepieion: The people, their dedications, and the inventories*. Amsterdam.

———. 1994. The demos and the priests. In *Ritual, finance, politics,* edited by Robin Osborne and Simon Hornblower, 325–38. Oxford.

Alexiou, Margaret. 1974. *The ritual lament in Greek tradition*. Cambridge.

Ardener, Edwin. 1972. Belief and the problem of women. In *Interpretation of ritual,* edited by J-S. La Fontaine, 135–58. London.

Arias, P. E. 1961. *A history of Greek vase painting*. Revised by B. Shefton. New York.

Armstrong, David, and Elizabeth A. Ratchford. 1985. Iphigeneia's veil: Aeschylus *Agamemnon* 228–248. *BICS* 32: 1–12.

Arthur, Marilyn. 1977. Politics and pomegranates: An interpretation of the *Homeric Hymn to Demeter*. *Arethusa* 10.1: 7–47.

———. 1983. The dream of a world without women: Poetics and the circle of order in the *Theogony* prooemium. *Arethusa* 26: 9–116.

Atkinson, Clarissa W., Constance H. Buchanan, and Margaret R. Miles, eds. 1985. *Immaculate and powerful: The female in sacred image and social reality*. Boston.

Austin, C., ed. 1968. *Nova fragmenta Euripidea in papyri reperta*. Berlin.

Babcock, Barbara A., ed. 1978. *The reversible world: Symbolic inversion in art and society*. Ithaca, N.Y.

Bain, D. M. 1983. *Menander, 'Samia.'* Edited with translation and notes. Warminster.

Bakhtin, Mikhail. 1968. *Rabelais and his world*. Translated by Helene Iswolsky. Cambridge, Mass., and London.

Bamberger, J. 1974. The myth of matriarchy: Why men rule in primitive societies. In *Woman, culture, and society,* edited by M. Z. Rosaldo and L. Lamphere, 263–80. Stanford.

Bartky, Sandra Lee. 1990. *Femininity and domination: Studies in the phenomenology of oppression*. London.

Bassi, Karen. 1998. *Acting like men: Gender, drama, and nostalgia in ancient Greece*. Ann Arbor.

Beard, Mary. 1991. Adopting an approach II. In *Looking at Greek vases*, edited by Tom Rasmussen and Nigel Spivey, 14–37. Cambridge.

Becher, Jeanne, ed. 1990. *Women, religion, and sexuality: Studies on the impact of religious teachings on women*. Philadelphia.

Bekker, Immanuel. 1814. *Anecdota graeca*. 3 vols. Berlin.

Bell, Shannon. 1994. *Reading, writing, and rewriting the prostitute body*. Bloomington and Indianapolis.

Belpassi, L. 1990. La follia del genos: Un'analisi del "discorso mitico" nella *Ifigenia Taurica* di Euripide. *QUCC* 34: 353–67.

Bérard, Claude. 1989. The order of women. In *A city of images: Iconography and society in ancient Greece*, edited by C. Bérard et al. and translated by Deborah Lyons, 89–108. Princeton.

Berger, John. 1977. *Ways of seeing*. London.

Bergren, A. L. 1983. Language and the female in early Greek thought. *Arethusa* 16: 69–95.

Berti, Fede, ed. 1991. *Dionysos: Mito e mistero*. Ferrara.

Blok, Josine, and Peter Mason, eds. 1987. *Sexual asymmetry: Studies in ancient society*. Amsterdam.

Blundell, M. 1993. The ideal of Athens in *Oedipus at Colonus*. In *Tragedy, comedy, and the polis*, edited by A. Sommerstein, 287–306. Bari.

Blundell, Sue. 1995. *Women in ancient Greece*. London.

Blundell, Sue, and Margaret Williamson, eds. 1998. *The sacred and the feminine in ancient Greece*. London.

Boardman, John. 1975. *Athenian red figure vases: The archaic period*. London.

Boddy, Janice. 1989. *Wombs and alien spirits: Women, men, and the zar cult in northern Sudan*. Madison.

Boedeker, Deborah. 1991. Euripides' *Medea* and the vanity of *logoi*. *CP* 86: 95–112.

Boegehold, Alan L., and Adele C. Scafuro. 1994. *Athenian identity and civic ideology*. Baltimore and London.

Bookidis, Nancy. 1993. Ritual dining at Corinth. In *Greek sanctuaries: New approaches*, edited by Nanno Marinatos and Robin Hägg, 45–61. London and New York.

Bourdieu, P. 1998. *Practical reason*. Cambridge.

Bourguignon, E. 1973. *Religion, altered states of consciousness, and social change*. Columbus.

Bourke, Angela. 1993. More in anger than in sorrow: Irish women's lament poetry. In *Feminist messages: Coding in women's folk culture*, edited by Joan Newton Radner, 160–82. Urbana and Chicago.

Bowie, A. M. 1993a. *Aristophanes: Myth, ritual, comedy*. Cambridge.

———. 1993b. Religion and politics in the *Oresteia*. *CQ* 43: 10–31.

Bremen, Riet van. 1983. Women and wealth. In *Images of women in antiquity*, edited by Averil Cameron and Amelie Kuhrt, 223–42. London.

———. 1996. *The limits of participation: Women and civic life in the Greek East in the Hellenistic and Roman periods*. Amsterdam.

Bremmer, J. N. 1984. Greek maenadism reconsidered. *ZPE* 55: 267–86.

————. 1987. The old women of ancient Greece. In *Sexual asymmetry: Studies in ancient society,* edited by Josine Blok and Peter Mason, 19–216. Amsterdam.

Broneer, Oscar. 1942. The Thesmophorion in Athens. *Hesperia* 11: 265–67.

Brooten, Bernadette J. 1985. Paul's views on the nature of women and female homoeroticism. In *Immaculate and powerful: The female in sacred image and social reality,* edited by Clarissa W. Atkinson, Constance H. Buchanan, and Margaret R. Miles, 61–87. Boston.

Brown, M. E., ed. 1990. *Television and women's culture: The politics of the popular.* London.

Brulé, Pierre. 1987. *La fille d'Athènes: La religion des filles à Athènes à l'époque classique.* Paris.

Brumfield, A. C. 1981. *The Attic festivals of Demeter and their relation to the agricultural year.* Salem, N.H.

Bruneau, Philippe. 1970. *Recherches sur les cultes de Delos à l'époque héllenistique et à l'époque imperiale.* Paris.

Bryant, Christopher G. A., and David Jary. 1991. *Giddens' theory of structuration: A critical appreciation.* London and New York.

Burk, Martha, and Heidi Hartmann. 1996. Beyond the gender gap. *The Nation,* 10 June, 18–21.

Burkert, Walter. 1966. Kekropidensage und Arrhephoria. *Hermes* 94: 1–25.

————. 1970. Jason, Hypsipyle, and new fire at Lemnos: A study in myth and ritual. *CQ* 20: 1–16.

————. 1983. *Homo necans.* Translated by Peter Bing. Berkeley, Los Angeles, and London.

————. 1985. *Greek religion.* Translated by John Raffan. Cambridge, Mass.

————. 1987. *Ancient mystery cults.* Cambridge, Mass., and London.

Burn, Lucilla. 1991. Red figure and white ground of the later fifth century. In *Looking at Greek vases,* edited by Tom Rasmussen and Nigel Spivey, 118–30. Cambridge.

Burnett, A. P. 1979. Desire and memory (Sappho frag. 94). *CP* 74: 16–27.

————. 1983. *Three archaic poets: Archilochus, Alcaeus, Sappho.* Cambridge, Mass.

Bushnell, Rebecca W. 1988. *Prophesying tragedy: Sign and voice in Sophokles' Theban plays.* Ithaca, N.Y.

Butler, Judith. 1990. *Gender trouble.* New York and London.

————. 1997. *The psychic life of power: Theories in subjection.* Stanford.

Calame, Claude. 1977. *Les choeurs de jeunes filles en Grèce archaïque.* 2 vols. Rome.

————. 1996. Sappho's group: An initiation into womanhood. In *Reading Sappho: Contemporary approaches,* edited by Ellen Greene, 113–25. Berkeley and Los Angeles.

Calder, W. 1985. The political and literary sources of Sophocles' *Oedipus Coloneus.* In *Hypatia: Essays in classics, comparative literature, and philosophy presented to Hazel E. Barnes on her 70th birthday,* edited by W. Calder, Ulrich K. Goldstein, and Phyllis B. Kenevan, 1–16. Boulder.

Calder, W., Ulrich K. Goldstein, and Phyllis B. Kenevan, eds. 1985. *Hypatia: Essays in classics, comparative literature, and philosophy presented to Hazel E. Barnes on her 70th birthday.* Boulder.

Caldwell, Richard. 1974. Tragedy romanticized: The *Iphigeneia Taurica. CJ* 70: 23–40.

Callinicos, A. 1999. Social theory put to the test of politics: Pierre Bourdieu and Anthony Giddens. *New Left Review* 8236, July and August, 77–102.

Cameron, Averil, and Amelie Kuhrt, eds. 1983. *Images of women in antiquity.* London.

Campbell, D. A., ed. 1982. *Greek lyric.* 4 vols. Loeb Classical Library. London.

Caraveli, Anna. 1986. The bitter wounding: The lament as social protest in rural Greece. In *Gender and power in rural Greece,* edited by Jill Dubisch, 169–94. Princeton.

Carpenter, T. H. 1986. *Dionysian imagery in archaic Greek art.* Oxford.

——. 1997. *Dionysian imagery in fifth century Athens.* Oxford.

Carpenter, T. H., and Christopher A. Faraone, eds. 1993. *Masks of Dionysus.* Ithaca, N.Y.

Carrara, P. 1977. *Euripide: Eretteo.* Florence.

Carson, Anne. 1990. Putting her in her place: Woman, dirt, and desire. In *Before sexuality: The construction of erotic experience in the ancient Greek world,* edited by David M. Halperin, John J. Winkler, and Froma I. Zeitlin, 135–70. Princeton.

Cartledge, Paul. 1981. Spartan wives: Liberation or licence. *CQ* 31: 84–105.

Cartledge, Paul, and F. D. Harvey, eds. 1985. *Crux: Essays presented to G. E. M. de Ste Croix.* Exeter.

Casabona, Jean. 1966. *Recherches sur le vocabulaire des sacrifices en grec: Des origines à la fin de l'époque classique.* Aix-en-Provence.

Castellani, V. 1985. Warlords and women in Euripides' *Iphigenia at Aulis.* In *Drama, sex, and politics,* edited by James Redmund, 1–10. Cambridge.

Chodorow, Nancy. 1978. *The reproduction of mothering: Psychoanalysis and the sociology of gender.* Berkeley.

Clark, Gillian. 1989. *Women in the ancient world.* Oxford.

——. 2000. *Porphyry: On abstinence from killing animals.* Translated with introduction. London.

Clement, Paul. 1934. New evidence for the origin of the Iphigeneia legend. *AC* 3: 393–409.

Clinton, K. 1974. *The sacred officials of the Eleusinian Mysteries.* Philadelphia.

——. 1988. Sacrifice at the Eleusinian Mysteries. In *Early Greek cult practice,* edited by Robin Hägg, Nanno Marinatos, and G. C. Nordquist, 69–80. Stockholm.

——. 1989. The Eleusinian Mysteries: Roman initiates and benefactors, second century B.C. to A.D. 267. *ANRW* 18.2. Berlin.

——. 1992. *Myth and cult: The iconography of the Eleusinian Mysteries.* Stockholm.

——. 1993. The sanctuary of Demeter and Kore at Eleusis. In *Greek sanctuaries: New approaches,* edited by Nanno Marinatos and Robin Hägg, 110–24. London and New York.

——. 1996. The Thesmophorion in central Athens and the celebration of the Thesmophoria in Attica. In *The role of religion in the early Greek polis,* edited by R. Hägg, 111–25. Stockholm.

Cohen, David. 1989. Seclusion, separation, and the status of women in classical Athens. *G&R* 36.1: 3–15.

——. 1990. The social context of adultery at Athens. In *Nomos: Essays in Athenian law, politics, and tragedy,* edited by P. Cartledge, P. Millett, and Stephen Todd, 147–65. Cambridge.

———. 1991. *Law, sexuality, and society: The enforcement of morals in classical Athens.* Cambridge.

Cohen, Edward. 1992. *Athenian economy and society: A banking perspective.* Princeton.

Cole, Susan Guettel, ed. 1984. *Male and female in Greek cult.* Cologne.

———. 1993. Voices from beyond the grave: Dionysus and the dead. In *Masks of Dionysus,* edited by T. H. Carpenter and Christopher A. Faraone, 276–96. Ithaca, N.Y.

———. 1994. Demeter in the ancient Greek city and its countryside. In *Placing the gods: Sanctuaries and sacred space in ancient Greece,* edited by Susan E. Alcock and Robin Osborne, 199–216. Oxford.

———. 1995. Women, dogs, and flies. *The Ancient World* 26.2: 182–91.

———. 1998. Domesticating Artemis. In *The sacred and the feminine in ancient Greece,* edited by Sue Blundell and Margaret Williamson, 27–43. London.

Collard, Christopher, ed. 1974. *Euripides: Hiketides.* Groningen.

Conacher, D. 1987. *Aeschylus's Oresteia.* Toronto.

Connelly, Joan. 1996. Parthenon and *parthenoi:* A mythological interpretation of the Parthenon frieze. *AJA* 100: 53–80.

Conomis, N. C., ed. 1970. *Lykourgos: Oratio in Leocratem.* Leipzig.

———, ed. 1975. *Dinarchi Orationes.* Leipzig.

Cook, R. M. 1972. *Greek painted pottery.* London.

Cott, Nancy F. 1977. *The bonds of womanhood: Woman's "separate sphere" in New England, 1780–1835.* New Haven and London.

Croally, N. 1994. *Euripidean polemic.* Cambridge.

Crocker, J. C. 1977. My brother the parrot. In *The social use of metaphor,* edited by J. D. Sapir and J. C. Crocker, 164–92. Philadelphia.

Daux, G. 1963. La grande démarchie: Un nouveau calendrier sacrificiel d'Attique (Erchia). *BCH* 87: 603–33.

———. 1971. Sur quelques inscriptions. *REG* 84: 350–83.

———. 1983. Le calendrier de Thorikos au musée J. Paul Getty. *AC* 52: 150–74.

David, Ephraim. 1989. Laughter in Spartan society. In *Classical Sparta: Techniques behind her success,* edited by Anton Powell, 1–26. London.

Davies, J. K. 1971. *Athenian propertied families, 600–300 B.C.* Oxford.

Dean-Jones, Lesley. 1994. *Women's bodies in classical Greek science.* Oxford.

Delacoste, F., and P. Alexander. 1982. *Sex work: Writings by women in the sex industry.* Pittsburgh.

De Lauretis, Teresa. 1990. Eccentric subjects: Feminist theory and historical consciousness. *Feminist Studies* 16.1: 115–50.

Demand, Nancy. 1994. *Birth, death, and motherhood in classical Greece.* Baltimore.

De Polignac, François. 1984. La naissance de la cité grecque: Cultes, espace et société VIIIe-VIIe siècles. Paris. Translated by Janet Lloyd as *Cults, territory, and the origins of the Greek city-state.* Chicago, 1996.

Detienne, Marcel. 1977. *The gardens of Adonis: Spices in Greek mythology.* Translated by J. Lloyd. Atlantic Highlands, N.J.

———. 1989. The violence of well-born ladies. In *The cuisine of sacrifice among the*

Greeks, edited by Marcel Detienne and J-P. Vernant, 129–47. Chicago and London.

Detienne, Marcel, and J-P. Vernant. 1989. *The cuisine of sacrifice among the Greeks.* Translated by Paula Wissing. Chicago and London.

Deubner, Ludwig. 1966. *Attische Feste.* Hildesheim.

Dewald, Carolyn. 1981. Women and culture in Herodotus' *Histories.* In *Reflections of women in antiquity,* edited by Helene P. Foley, 91–126. New York, London, and Paris.

Diehl, E. 1949. *Anthologia lyrica graeca.* Vol. 2. Leipzig.

Dillon, Matthew. 2002. *Girls and women in classical Greek religion.* London.

Dilts, Mervin R. 1983. *Scholia Demosthenica.* Leipzig.

Dodds, E. R. 1960. *Euripides' "Bacchae."* Edited with introduction and commentary. Oxford.

Dontas, G. 1983. The true Aglaurion. *Hesperia* 52: 48–63.

Dougherty, Carol, and Leslie Kurke, eds. 1993. *Cultural poetics in archaic Greece.* Cambridge.

Dowden, Ken. 1989. *Death and the maiden: Girls' initiation rites in Greek mythology.* London and New York.

Dubisch, Jill, ed. 1986. *Gender and power in rural Greece.* Princeton.

Dübner, F., ed. 1969. *Scholia to Aristophanes.* Hildesheim.

DuBois, Page. 1982. *Centaurs and Amazons: Women and the pre-history of the great chain of being.* Ann Arbor.

———. 1984. Sappho and Helen. In *Women in the ancient world: The Arethusa papers,* edited by John Peradotto and J. P. Sullivan, 95–107. Albany.

———. 1988. *Sowing the body: Psychoanalysis and ancient representations of women.* Chicago.

———. 1995. *Sappho is burning.* Chicago and London.

Du Boulay, Juliet. 1986. Women: Images of their nature and destiny in rural Greece. In *Gender and power in rural Greece,* edited by Jill Dubisch, 139–68. Princeton.

Dunn, Francis. 1994. Euripides and the rites of Hera Akraia. *GRBS* 35: 103–15.

Eagleton, Terry. 1991. *Ideology: An introduction.* London.

Easterling, P. E. 1988. Women in tragic space. *BICS* 34: 15–26.

———. 1993. Tragedy and ritual. In *Theater and society in the classical world,* edited by Ruth Scodel, 7–24. Ann Arbor.

Easterling, P. E., and J. V. Muir, eds. 1985. *Greek religion and society.* Cambridge.

Edelstein, Emma J., and Ludwig Edelstein. 1945. *Asclepius: A collection and interpretation of the testimonies.* 2 vols. Baltimore.

Edmondson, Colin N. 1959. A graffito from Amyklai. *Hesperia* 28: 162–64.

Edmunds, Lowell. 1996. *Theatrical space and historical place in Sophocles' "Oedipus at Colonus."* Lanham, Md.

Edwards, M. W. 1960. Representations of maenads on archaic red-figure vases. *JHS* 80: 778–87.

Euben, J. Peter, ed. 1986. *Greek tragedy and political theory.* Berkeley.

Fantham, Elaine, Helene Peet Foley, Natalie Boymel Kampen, Sarah B. Pomeroy, and H. Alan Shapiro, eds. 1994. *Women in the classical world.* New York.

Feaver, Douglas D. 1957. Historical developments in the priesthoods of Athens. *YCS* 15: 123–58.

Fehrle, E. 1910. *Die kultische Keuschheit im Altertum*. Giessen.

Ferguson, W. S. 1938. The Salaminioi of Heptaphylai and Sounion. *Hesperia* 87: 1–74.

———. 1944. The Attic Orgeones. *HTR* 37: 61–140.

Fiske, John. 1990. Consumerism, patriarchy, and resisting pleasures. In *Television and women's culture: The politics of the popular*, edited by M. E. Brown, 134–43. London.

Foley, Helene P. 1981a. The concept of women in Athenian drama. In *Reflections of women in antiquity*, edited by Helene P. Foley, 127–68. New York, London, and Paris.

———, ed. 1981b. *Reflections of women in antiquity*. New York, London, and Paris.

———. 1982. The "female intruder" reconsidered: Women in Aristophanes' *Lysistrata* and *Eccclesiazusae*. *CP* 77: 1–21.

———. 1985. *Ritual irony*. Ithaca, N.Y.

———. 1993. The politics of tragic lamentation. In *Tragedy, comedy, and the polis*, edited by A. Sommerstein, 101–44. Bari.

———. 1994. *The Homeric Hymn to Demeter: Translation, commentary, and interpretive essays*. Princeton.

———. 1995. Tragedy and democratic ideology: The case of Sophocles *Antigone*. In *History, tragedy, theory: Dialogues on Athenian drama*, edited by B. Goff, 131–50. Austin.

———. 2001. *Female Acts in Greek Tragedy*. Princeton and Oxford.

Fontenrose, Joseph. 1978. *The Delphic oracle: Its responses and operations*. Berkeley, Los Angeles, and London.

Foucart, P. 1914. *Les Mystères d'Eleusis*. Paris.

Foucault, Michel. 1987. *The use of pleasure*. Vol. 2 of *The history of sexuality*. Translated by Robert Hurley. Harmondsworth.

Foxhall, Lin. 1989. Household, gender, and property in classical Athens. *CQ* 39.1: 22–44.

———. 1995. Women's ritual and men's work in ancient Athens. In *Women in antiquity: New assessments*, edited by Richard Hawley and Barbara Levick, 97–110. London and New York.

French, Valerie. 1987. Midwives and maternity care in the Roman world. In *Rescuing Creusa: New methodological approaches to women in antiquity*, edited by Marilyn Skinner, 69–84. Lubbock.

Friedrich, Paul. 1978. *The meaning of Aphrodite*. Chicago.

Frontisi-Ducroux, Françoise. 1991. Le masque du dieu or le dieu-masque? In *Dionysos: Mito e mistero*, edited by Fede Berti, 321–33. Ferrara.

———. 1995. *Du masque au visage*. Paris.

———. 1996. Eros, desire, and the gaze. Translated by Nancy Kline. In *Sexuality in ancient art*, edited by Natalie B. Kampen, 81–100. Cambridge.

Frontisi-Ducroux, Françoise, and J-P. Vernant. 1997. *Dans l'oeil du miroir*. Paris.

Fuss, Diana. 1989. *Essentially speaking: Feminism, nature, and difference*. New York and London.

———. 1992. Fashion and the homospectatorial gaze. *CI* 18: 713–37.

Gagarin, M. 1998. Women in Athenian courts. *Dike* 1: 39–51.

Garland, Robert. 1984. Religious authority in archaic and classical Athens. *BSA* 79: 75–123.

————. 1985. *The Greek way of death*. London.

————. 1987. *The Piraeus: From the fifth to the first century B.C.* Ithaca, N.Y.

————. 1990. *The Greek way of life: From conception to old age*. Ithaca, N.Y.

————. 1992. *Introducing new gods: The politics of Athenian religion*. London.

Garvie, A. F. 1969. *Aeschylus: Supplices*. Cambridge.

————. 1986. *Aeschylus: Choephori*. Oxford and New York.

Gasparo, Giulia Sfameni. 1985. *Soteriology and mystic aspects in the cult of Cybele and Attis*. Leiden.

Gauthier, Philippe. 1985. *Les cités grecques et leurs bienfaiteurs*. Athens.

Gentili, Bruno. 1988. *Poetry and its public in ancient Greece*. Translated by A. Thomas Cole. Baltimore.

Giddens, Anthony. 1984. *The constitution of society: Outline of the theory of structuration*. Berkeley and Los Angeles.

Giles, Linda. 1987. Possession cults on the Swahili coast: A reexamination of theories of marginality. *Africa* 57: 234–89.

Gilligan, Carol. 1982. *In a different voice: Psychological theory and women's development*. Cambridge, Mass.

Girard, René. 1977. *Violence and the sacred*. Translated by Patrick Gregory. Baltimore and London.

Gleason, Maud. 1990. The semiotics of gender: Physiognomy and self-fashioning in the second century C.E. In *Before sexuality: The construction of erotic experience in the ancient Greek world*, edited by David M. Halperin, John J. Winkler, and Froma I. Zeitlin, 389–415. Princeton.

Gluckman, M. 1954. *Rituals of rebellion*. Manchester.

Goff, Barbara. 1988. Euripides' *Ion* 1132–65: The tent. *PCPS* n.s. 34: 42–54.

————. 1990. *The noose of words*. Cambridge.

————, ed. 1995. *History, tragedy, theory: Dialogues on Athenian drama*. Austin.

Goldhill, Simon. 1986. *Language, sexuality, narrative: The "Oresteia."* Cambridge.

————. 1990. The Great Dionysia and civic ideology. In *Nothing to do with Dionysos? Athenian drama in its social context*, edited by John J. Winkler and Froma I. Zeitlin, 97–129. Princeton.

————. 1992. *Aeschylus: The Oresteia*. Cambridge.

————. 1994. Representing democracy: Women at the Great Dionysia. In *Ritual, finance, politics*, edited by Robin Osborne and Simon Hornblower, 347–70. Oxford.

Gordon, R. L., ed. 1981. *Myth, religion, and society*. Cambridge.

Gould, J. 1980. Law, custom, and myth. *JHS* 100: 38–59.

Graf, F. 1978. Die lokrischen Mädchen. *Studi Storice-Religiosi* 2: 61–79.

————. 1985. *Nordionische Kulte*. Rome.

————. 1993. Dionysian and Orphic eschatology: New texts and old questions. In *Masks of Dionysus*, edited by T. H. Carpenter and Christopher A. Faraone, 239–58. Ithaca, N.Y.

Grant, Michael. 1982. *From Alexander to Cleopatra: The Hellenistic world*. London.

Greene, Ellen, ed. 1996a. *Reading Sappho: Contemporary approaches*. Berkeley and Los Angeles.

————, ed. 1996b. *Re-reading Sappho: Reception and transmission*. Berkeley and Los Angeles.

Griffiths, Frederick T. 1981. Home before lunch: The emancipated woman in The-
ocritus. In *Reflections of women in antiquity,* edited by Helene P. Foley, 247–73. New
York, London, and Paris.

Hägg, Robin, ed. 1994. *Ancient Greek cult practice from the epigraphical evidence.* Stockholm.

———, ed. 1996. *The role of religion in the early Greek polis.* Stockholm.

Hägg, Robin, Nanno Marinatos, and G. C. Nordquist, eds. 1988. *Early Greek cult practice.* Stockholm.

Hall, Edith. 1989. *Inventing the barbarian: Greek self-definition through tragedy.* Oxford.

Hallett, Judith. 1996. Sappho and her social context: Sense and sensuality. In *Reading Sappho: Contemporary approaches,* edited by Ellen Greene, 125–42. Berkeley
and Los Angeles.

Halperin, David M., John J. Winkler, and Froma I. Zeitlin, eds. 1990. *Before sexuality:
The construction of erotic experience in the ancient Greek world.* Princeton.

Ham, G. 1999. The Choes and Anthesteria reconsidered: Male maturation rites and
the Peloponnesian Wars. In *Rites of passage in ancient Greece: Literature, religion, society,* edited by Mark Padilla, 201–20. Bucknell Review 43.1. Lewisburg.

Hamilton, Richard. 1992. *Choes and Anthesteria: Athenian iconography and ritual.* Ann
Arbor.

Hanson, Ann Ellis. 1990. The medical writers' woman. In *Before sexuality: The construction of erotic experience in the ancient Greek world,* edited by David M. Halperin,
John J. Winkler, and Froma I. Zeitlin, 309–38. Princeton.

Harrison, E. 1996. The web of history: A conservative reading of the Parthenon
frieze. In *Worshipping Athena: Panathenaia and Parthenon,* edited by Jenifer Neils,
198–214. Madison.

Hatzopoulos, M. 1994. *Cultes et rites de passage en Macedoine.* Athens.

Havelock, Christine. 1981. Mourners on Greek vases: Remarks on the social history
of women. In *The Greek vase,* edited by Stephen L. Hyatt, 103–18. New York.

Hawley, Richard, and Barbara Levick, eds. 1995. *Women in antiquity: New assessments.*
London and New York.

Hedreen, G. 1994. Silens, nymphs, and maenads. *JHS* 114: 47–69.

Helly, Bruno. 1973. *Gonnoi.* 2 vols. Amsterdam.

Henderson, J. 1987. *Aristophanes: Lysistrata.* Oxford and New York.

———. 1991. Women and the Athenian dramatic festivals. *TAPA* 121: 133–47.

Henrichs, Albert. 1969. Die Maenaden von Milet. ZPE 4: 223–41.

———. 1978. Greek maenadism from Olympias to Messalina. *HSCP* 82: 121–60.

———. 1982. Changing Dionysiac identities. In *Self-definition in the Graeco-Roman
world,* edited by B. F. Meyer and E. P. Sanders, 137–60. London and Philadelphia.

———. 1984. Male intruders among the maenads: The so-called male celebrant. In
Mnemai: Classical studies in memory of Karl K. Hulley, edited by H. V. Evjen, 69–92.
Chico, Calif.

Heyob, Sharon Kelly. 1975. *The cult of Isis among women in the Graeco-Roman world.* Leiden.

Hoch-Smith, Judith, and Anita Spring, eds. 1978. *Women in ritual and symbolic roles.*
New York and London.

Hodkinson, Stephen. 1989. Inheritance, marriage, and demography: Perspectives upon the success and decline of classical Sparta. In *Classical Sparta: Techniques behind her success,* edited by Anton Powell, 79–121. London.

Holden, Pat, ed. 1983. *Women's religious experience: Cross-cultural perspectives.* London and Canberra.

Holst-Warhaft, Gail. 1992. *Dangerous voices: Women's laments and Greek literature.* London and New York.

Homans, Margaret. 1987. Feminist criticism and theory: The ghost of Creusa. *Yale Journal of Criticism* 1: 153–82.

hooks, bell. 1984. *Feminist theory: From margins to center.* Boston.

Hughes, Dennis D. 1991. *Human sacrifice in ancient Greece.* London and New York.

Humphreys, Sally. 1983. *The family, women, and death: Comparative studies.* London.

Isler-Kerenyi, Cornelia. 1991. Dionysos; dio delle donne? Iconografia dionisiaca II. In *Dionysos: Mito e mistero,* edited by Fede Berti, 293–308. Ferrara.

Jackson, E. 1988. The argument of *Septem contra Thebas. Phoenix* 42: 287–303.

Jameson, M. 1971. Sophocles and the Four Hundred. *Historia* 20: 541–68.

Jenkyns, Richard. 1982. *Three classical poets.* Cambridge, Mass.

Johnston, S. 1995. Defining the dreadful: Remarks on the Greek child-killing demon. In *Ancient magic and ritual,* edited by M. Meyer and P. Mirecki, 361–87. Leiden.

———. 1997. Corinthian Medea and the cult of Hera Akraia. In *Medea: Essays on Medea in myth, literature, philosophy, and art,* edited by James J. Clauss and Sarah Iles Johnston, 44–70. Princeton.

Johnston, S., and Timothy McNiven. 1996. Dionysos and the underworld in Toledo. *Museum Helveticum* 53: 25–36.

Jordan, B. 1979. *Servants of the gods.* Hypomnemata 55. Göttingen.

Just, Roger. 1989. *Women in Athenian law and life.* London and New York.

Kahil, Lilly. 1965. Autour de l'Artemis attique. *Antike Kunst* 8: 20–33.

———. 1977. L'Artemis de Brauron: Rites et mystères. *Antike Kunst* 20: 80–98.

———. 1983. Mythological repertoire at Brauron. In *Ancient Greek art and iconography,* edited by W. G. Moon, 231–44. Madison.

Kampen, Natalie Boymel, ed. 1996. *Sexuality in ancient art.* Cambridge.

Kaplan, E. Ann. 1983. *Women and film: Both sides of the camera.* London and New York.

Kearns, Emily. 1985. Religious structures after Cleisthenes. In *Crux: Essays presented to G. E. M. de Ste Croix,* edited by P. A. Cartledge and F. D. Harvey, 189–207. Exeter.

———. 1990. Saving the city. In *The Greek city from Homer to Alexander,* edited by Oswyn Murray and Simon Price, 323–46. Oxford.

Kehoe, Alice B., and Dody H. Giletti. 1981. Women's preponderance in possession cults: The calcium-deficiency hypothesis expanded. *American Anthropologist* 83: 549–61.

Keirn, Susan Middleton. 1978. Convivial sisterhood: Spirit mediumship and client-core network among black South African women. In *Women in ritual and symbolic roles,* edited by Judith Hoch-Smith and Anita Spring, 191–206. New York and London.

Kelly, Joan. 1976. The social relations of the sexes: Methodological implications of women's history. *Signs* 1: 809–23.

———. 1986. *Women, history, and theory.* Chicago and London.

Kennedy, Robinette. 1986. Women's friendships on Crete. In *Gender and power in rural Greece,* edited by Jill Dubisch, 121–38. Princeton.

Keuls, Eva. 1985. *The reign of the phallus.* New York.

King, Deborah K. 1988. Multiple jeopardy, multiple consciousness: The context of black feminist ideology. *Signs* 14: 42–72.

Korshak, Yvonne. 1987. *Frontal faces in Attic vase painting of the archaic period.* Chicago.

Kraemer, Ross. 1979. Ecstasy and possession: The attraction of women to the cult of Dionysus. *HTR* 72: 59–65.

———. 1988. *Maenads, martyrs, matrons, monastics: A sourcebook on women's religions in the Greco-Roman world.* Philadelphia.

———. 1992. *Her share of the blessings.* New York.

Krummen, E. 1993. Athens and Attica: Polis and countryside in Greek tragedy. In *Tragedy, comedy, and the polis,* edited by A. Sommerstein, 191–217. Bari.

Kuenen-Janssens, L-J. Th. 1941. Some notes on the competence of the Athenian woman to conduct a transaction. *Mnemosyne* 9: 199–214.

Kunstler, Barton. 1987. Family dynamics and female power in ancient Sparta. In *Rescuing Creusa: New methodological approaches to women in antiquity,* edited by Marilyn Skinner, 31–48. Lubbock.

Kurtz, Donna C. 1975. *Athenian white lekythoi.* Oxford.

La Fontaine, J-S., ed. 1972. *Interpretation of ritual.* London.

Lambek, Michael. 1981. *Human spirits: A cultural account of trance in Mayotte.* Cambridge.

Lane, Warren J., and Ann M. Lane. 1986. The politics of *Antigone.* In *Greek tragedy and political theory,* edited by J. Peter Euben, 162–82. Berkeley.

Lardinois, André. 1994. Subject and circumstance in Sappho's poetry. *TAPA* 124: 57–84.

———. 1996. Who sang Sappho's songs? In *Reading Sappho: Contemporary approaches,* edited by Ellen Greene, 150–72. Berkeley and Los Angeles.

Larson, Jennifer. 1995a. The Corycian nymphs and the bee maidens of the *Homeric Hymn to Hermes. GRBS* 36: 341–57.

———. 1995b. *Greek heroine cults.* Madison.

Lasserre, François. 1989. *Sappho: Une autre lecture.* Padova.

Lavelle, Brian M. 1986. The nature of Hipparchus' insult to Harmodius. *AJP* 107: 318–31.

Lawler, Lilian B. 1927. The maenads. *Memoirs of the American Academy in Rome* 6: 69–112.

Lazzarini, M. 1976. *Le formule delle dediche votive nella Grecia arcaica.* Rome.

Lebeck, A. 1971. *The Oresteia.* Washington and Cambridge, Mass.

Lefkowitz, Mary, and Maureen Fant. 1992. *Women's life in Greece and Rome.* Baltimore.

Leitao, David. 1995. The perils of Leukippos: Initiatory transvestism and male gender ideology in the Ekdusia at Phaistos. *CA* 41: 130–64.

Lerner, Gerda. 1986. *The creation of patriarchy.* New York and Oxford.

Leslie, Julia. 1983. Essence and existence: Women and religion in ancient Indian texts. In *Women's religious experience: Cross-cultural perspectives,* edited by Pat Holden, 89–122. London and Canberra.

Lévi-Strauss, Claude. 1967. The structural study of myth. In *structural anthropology,* translated by Claire Jacobson and B. G. Schoepf, XXX. Garden City.

Lewis, D. M. 1955. Notes on Athenian inscriptions. *BSA* 50: 1–12.

Lewis, I. M. 1971. *Ecstatic religion: An anthropological study of spirit possession and shamanism.* Harmondsworth.

Lincoln, Bruce. 1991. *Emerging from the chrysalis: Studies in rituals of women's initiation.* Cambridge, Mass., and London.

Lissarrague, F. 1990a. *L'autre guerrier.* Paris.

———. 1990b. Why satyrs are good to represent. In *Nothing to do with Dionysos? Athenian drama in its social context,* edited by John J. Winkler and Froma I. Zeitlin, 228–36. Princeton.

———. 1991. Un peintre de Dionysos: Le peintre de Kleophrades. In *Dionysos: Mito e mistero,* edited by Fede Berti, 257–76. Ferrara.

———. 1993. On the wildness of satyrs. In *Masks of Dionysus,* edited by T. H. Carpenter and Christopher A. Faraone, 201–20. Ithaca, N.Y.

Lloyd, Geoffrey. 1987. *The revolutions of wisdom.* Berkeley and London.

Lonsdale, Stephen. 1993. *Dance and ritual play.* Baltimore and London.

Loraux, Nicole. 1978. Sur la race des femmes et quelques-unes de ses tribus. *Arethusa* 11: 43–71.

———. 1981a. L'acropole comique. In *Les enfants d'Athena,* by Nicole Loraux, 157–96. Paris.

———. 1981b. *Les enfants d'Athena.* Paris.

———. 1986. *The invention of Athens: The funeral oration in the classical city.* Translated by Alan Sheridan. Cambridge, Mass.

———. 1990. Kreousa the autochthon: A study of Euripides' *Ion.* In *Nothing to do with Dionysos? Athenian drama in its social context,* edited by John J. Winkler and Froma I. Zeitlin, 168–206. Princeton.

Lowe, N. J. 1998. Thesmophoria and Haloa: Myth, physics, and mysteries. In *The sacred and the feminine in ancient Greece,* edited by Sue Blundell and Margaret Williamson, 149–73. London.

MacDowell, Douglas. 1995. *Aristophanes and Athens.* Oxford.

Marinatos, Nanno. 1996. Cult by the seashore: What happened at Amnisos? In *The role of religion in the early Greek polis,* edited by Robin Hägg, 135–39. Stockholm.

Marinatos, Nanno, and Robin Hägg. 1993. *Greek sanctuaries: New approaches.* London and New York.

Mattingly, H. 1982. The Athena Nike temple reconsidered. *AJA* 86.3: 381–85.

Maurizio, Lisa. 1995. Anthropology and spirit possession. *JHS* 115: 69–87.

McClees, H. 1920. *A study of women in Attic inscriptions.* New York.

McClure, Laura. 1999. *Spoken like a woman: Speech and gender in Athenian drama.* Princeton.

McDermott, Emily A. 1989. *Euripides' "Medea": The incarnation of disorder.* University Park, Pa.

McEvilley, Thomas. 1972. Sappho, fragment two. *Phoenix* 26: 323–33.

McLachlan, Bonnie. 1992. Sacred prostitution and Aphrodite. *Studies in Religion* 21: 145–62.

McNally, Sheila. 1978. The maenad in early Greek art. *Arethusa* 11: 107–41.

Meier, Christian. 1993. *The political art of Greek tragedy.* Translated by Andrew Webber. Cambridge.

Meiggs, Russell, and David Lewis. 1969. *A selection of Greek historical inscriptions.* Oxford.

Meiksins Wood, Ellen. 1988. *Peasant citizen and slave: The foundations of Athenian democracy.* London and New York.

Meineke, A. 1958. *Ethnica: Stephani Byzantii ethnicorum quae superstunt.* Graz.

Meyer, Marvin M. 1987. *The ancient mysteries: A sourcebook.* San Francisco.

Michelini, Ann. 1991. The maze of the *logos:* Euripides' *Suppliants. Ramus* 20.1: 16–36.

Migeotte, Leopold. 1992. *Les souscriptions publiques dans les cités grecques.* Geneva.

Mikalson, Jon D. 1975. *The sacred and civil calendar of the Athenian year.* Princeton.

———. 1983. *Athenian popular religion.* Chapel Hill and London.

———. 1998. *Religion in Hellenistic Athens.* Berkeley and Los Angeles.

Miles, Margaret. 1985. Introduction to *Immaculate and powerful: The female in sacred image and social reality,* edited by Clarissa W. Atkinson, Constance H. Buchanan, and Margaret R. Miles. Boston.

Miller M. L. 1992. The parasol: An oriental status-symbol in late archaic and classical Athens. *JHS* 112: 91–105.

Modleski, Tania. 1991. *Feminism without women: Culture and criticism in a "postfeminist" age.* New York.

Mook, Margaret S. 1996. Review of *Birth, death, and motherhood in classical Greece,* by Nancy Demand. *Women's Classical Caucus Newsletter* 24 (Spring 1996): 31–36.

Mora, Fabio. 1990. *Prosopografia Isiaca.* 2 vols. Leiden and New York.

Moraga, Cherrie, and Gloria Anzaldua. 1983. *This bridge called my back: Writings by radical women of color.* New York.

Morgan, C. 1990. *Athletes and oracles: The transformation of Olympia and Delphi in the eighth century B.C.* Cambridge.

———. 1993. The origins of pan-Hellenism. In *Greek sanctuaries: New approaches,* edited by Nanno Marinatos and Robin Hägg, 18–44. London and New York.

Morris, Ian. 1993. Poetics of power: The interpretation of ritual action in archaic Greece. In *Cultural poetics in archaic Greece,* edited by Carol Dougherty and Leslie Kurke, 15–45. Cambridge.

———. 1994. Everyman's grave. In *Athenian identity and civic ideology,* edited by Alan L. Boegehold and Adele C. Scafuro, 67–101. Baltimore and London.

Mulvey, Laura. 1989 (1975). Visual pleasure and narrative cinema. In *Visual and Other Pleasures,* by Laura Mulvey, 14–28. Bloomington and Indianapolis.

Murnaghan, Sheila. 1986. *Antigone* 904–20 and the institution of marriage. *AJP* 107: 192–207.

———. 1988. How a woman can be more like a man: The dialogue between Ischomachos and his wife in Xenophon's *Oeconomicus. Helios* 15: 9–22.

Murray, Oswyn, and Simon Price, eds. 1990. *The Greek city from Homer to Alexander.* Oxford.

Myerhoff, Barbara. 1978. Bobbes and Zeydes: Old and new roles for elderly Jews. In *Women in ritual and symbolic roles,* edited by Judith Hoch-Smith and Anita Spring, 207–40. New York and London.

Myerowitz, Molly. 1992. The domestication of desire: Ovid's *parva tabella* and the theater of love. In *Pornography and representation in Greece and Rome,* edited by Amy Richlin, 131–57. New York and Oxford.

Mylonas, George E. 1961. *Eleusis and the Eleusinian Mysteries.* Princeton.

Nagy, Gregory. 1990. *Greek mythology and poetics.* Ithaca, N.Y.

Narayanan, Vasudha. 1990. Hindu perceptions of auspiciousness and sexuality. In *Women, religion, and sexuality: Studies on the impact of religious teachings on women,* edited by Jeanne Becher, 64–92. Philadelphia.

Neils, Jenifer, ed. 1996. *Worshipping Athena: Panathenaia and Parthenon.* Madison.

Nemeth, G. 1994. Regulations concerning everyday life in a Greek temenos. In *Ancient Greek cult practice from the epigraphical evidence,* edited by Robin Hägg, 59–64. Stockholm.

Neuburg, Matt. 1990. How like a woman: Antigone's inconsistency. *CQ* 40: 54–76.

Nilsson, M. P. 1961. *Greek folk religion.* 1940. Reprint, New York.

Nisetich, Frank J. 1980. *Pindar's victory songs.* Baltimore and London.

Nixon, Lucia. 1995. The cults of Demeter and Kore. In *Women in antiquity: New assessments,* edited by Richard Hawley and Barbara Levick, 75–96. London and New York.

Oakley, John H., and Rebecca H. Sinos. 1993. *The wedding in ancient Athens.* Madison and London.

O'Brien, Joan V. 1993. *The transformation of Hera.* Lanham, Md.

Olender, Maurice. 1990. Aspects of Baubo: Ancient texts and contexts. In *Before sexuality: The construction of erotic experience in the ancient Greek world,* edited by David M. Halperin, John J. Winkler, and Froma I. Zeitlin, 83–114. Princeton.

Ormand, K. 1999. *Exchange and the maiden.* Austin.

Ortner, Sherry. 1974. Is female to male as nature is to culture? In *Woman, culture, and society,* edited by M. Z. Rosaldo and L. Lamphere. Stanford, Calif.

Osborne, Robin. 1985. *Demos: The discovery of classical Attika.* Cambridge.

———. 1987. *Classical landscape with figures: The ancient Greek city and its countryside.* London.

———. 1993. Women and sacrifice in classical Greece. *CQ* 43: 392–405.

———. 1994. Archaeology, the Salaminioi, and the politics of sacred space in archaic Attica. In *Placing the gods: Sanctuaries and sacred space in ancient Greece,* edited by Susan E. Alcock and Robin Osborne, 143–60. Oxford.

———. 1996. Desiring women on Athenian pottery. In *Sexuality in ancient art,* edited by Natalie Boymel Kampen, 65–80. Cambridge.

———. 1997. The ecstasy and the tragedy: Varieties of religious experience in art, drama, and society. In *Greek tragedy and the historian,* edited by Christopher Pelling, 187–212. Oxford.

Osborne, Robin, and Simon Hornblower, eds. 1994. *Ritual, finance, politics.* Oxford.

Oudemans, T., and André Lardinois. 1987. *Tragic ambiguity: Anthropology, philosophy, and Sophocles' "Antigone."* Leiden.

Padel, Ruth. 1983. Women: Model for possession by Greek daemons. In *Images of women in antiquity,* edited by Averil Cameron and Amelie Kuhrt, 3–19. London.

———. 1992. *In and out of the mind: Greek images of the tragic self.* Princeton.

Padgug, R. 1972. Eleusis and the union of Attika. *GRBS* 13: 135–50.

Page, D. L. 1951. *The Partheneion.* Oxford.

Paige, Karen M. E., and Jeffery M. Paige. 1981. *The politics of reproductive ritual.* Berkeley, Los Angeles, and London.

Palaiokrassa, L. 1989. Neue Befunde aus dem Heiligtum der Artemis Munichia. AM 104: 1–40.

Parke, H. W. 1939. *History of the Delphic oracle.* Oxford.

———. 1977. *Festivals of the Athenians.* London.

Parke, H. W., and D. E. W. Wormell. 1956. *The Delphic oracle.* 2 vols. Oxford.

Parker, Holt. 1993. Sappho schoolmistress. *TAPA* 123: 309–51. Also reprinted in *Rereading Sappho: Reception and transmission,* ed. Ellen Greene (Berkeley and Los Angeles, 1996).

Parker, Robert. 1983. *Miasma: Pollution and purification in early Greek religion.* Oxford.

———. 1985. Greek states and Greek oracles. In *Crux: Essays presented to G. E. M. de Ste Croix,* edited by Paul Cartledge and F. D. Harvey, 298–326. Exeter.

———. 1989. Spartan religion. In *Classical Sparta: Techniques behind her success,* edited by Anton Powell, 142–72. London.

———. 1996. *Athenian religion: A history.* Oxford.

Patterson, Cynthia. 1987. *Hai Attikai:* The other Athenians. In *Rescuing Creusa: New methodological approaches to women in antiquity,* edited by Marilyn Skinner, 49–68. Lubbock.

———. 1994. The case against Neaira and the public ideology of the Athenian family. In *Athenian identity and civic ideology,* edited by Alan L. Boegehold and Adele C. Scafuro, 199–216. Baltimore and London.

Peirce, S. 1984. Representation of animal sacrifice in Attic vase-painting 580–530 B.C. Ph.D. diss., Bryn Mawr College.

Pelling, Christopher, ed. 1997. *Greek tragedy and the historian.* Oxford.

Perlman, Paula. 1983. Plato Laws 833C–834D and the bears of Brauron. *GRBS* 20: 115–30.

———. 1989. Acting the she-bear for Artemis. *Arethusa* 22: 111–34.

———. 1995. *Theorodokountes en tais polesin:* Panhellenic *epangelia* and political status. In *Sources for the ancient Greek city-state,* edited by M. C. Hansen, 113–64. Copenhagen.

Pickard-Cambridge, Arthur. 1968. *Dramatic festivals of Athens.* 2d ed. Revised by John Gould and D. M. Lewis. Reprinted in 1991, Oxford.

Pleket, H. W. 1969. *Epigraphica.* Vol. 2 of *Texts on the social history of the Greek world.* Leiden.

Pomeroy, Sarah. 1975. *Goddesses, whores, wives, and slaves.* New York.

———. 1976. A classical scholar's perspective on matriarchy. In *Liberating women's history: Theoretical and critical essays,* edited by Berenice A. Carroll. Urbana and Chicago.

———. 1984. *Women in Hellenistic Egypt.* New York.

———, ed. 1991. *Women's history and ancient history.* Chapel Hill.

Powell, Anton, ed. 1989. *Classical Sparta: Techniques behind her success.* London.

Price, Simon. 1984. *Rituals and power: The Roman imperial cult in Asia Minor.* Cambridge.

Pucci, Pietro. 1980. *The violence of pity in Euripides' "Medea."* Cornell Studies in Classical Philology 41. Ithaca, N.Y., and London.

Rabe, H. 1906. *Scholia in Lucianum.* Leipzig.

Rabinowitz, Nancy. 1987. Female speech and female sexuality: Euripides' *Hippolytos* as model. In *Rescuing Creusa: New methodological approaches to women in antiquity,* edited by Marilyn Skinner, 127–40. Lubbock.

———. 1993a. *Anxiety veiled: Euripides and the traffic in women.* Ithaca, N.Y.

———. 1993b. Introduction to *Feminist theory and the classics,* edited by Nancy Rabinowitz and Amy Richlin, 1–22. New York and London.

Rabinowitz, Nancy, and Amy Richlin, eds. 1993. *Feminist theory and the classics.* New York and London.

Rabuzzi, Kathryn Allen. 1982. *The sacred and the feminine: Toward a theology of housework.* New York.

Radner, Joan Newton, ed. 1993. *Feminist messages: Coding in women's folk culture.* Urbana and Chicago.

Radway, Janice A. 1984. *Reading the romance: Women, patriarchy, and popular literature.* Chapel Hill.

Ramsay, William. 1895. *Cities and bishoprics of Phrygia.* Vol. 1. Oxford.

Rasmussen, Tom, and Nigel Spivey, eds. 1991. *Looking at Greek vases.* Cambridge.

Raubitschek, Anthony, and Lilian Jeffery. 1949. *Dedications from the Athenian Akropolis: A catalogue of the inscriptions of the sixth and fifth centuries B.C.* Cambridge, Mass.

Redfield, James. 1978. The women of Sparta. *CJ* 73: 146–61.

———. 1982. Notes on the Greek wedding. *Arethusa* 15: 181–201.

Reed, Joseph. 1995. The sexuality of Adonis. *CA* 14:2: 317–48.

Reeder, Ellen. 1995. *Pandora: Women in classical Greece.* Baltimore.

Rehm, R. 1994. *Marriage to death.* Princeton.

Reilly, Joan. 1989. Many brides: "Mistress and maid" on Athenian lekythoi. *Hesperia* 58: 411–44.

Reinach, Théodore. 1899. Un temple élevé par les femmes de Tanagra. *REG* 12: 53–115.

Richardson, Rufus B. 1891. Votive inscription from Plataia. *AJA* 7: 406–21.

Richlin, Amy, ed. 1992. *Pornography and representation in Greece and Rome.* New York and Oxford.

———. 1993. The ethnographer's dilemma and the dream of a lost golden age. In *Feminist theory and the classics,* edited by Nancy Rabinowitz and Amy Richlin, 272–304. New York and London.

Richter, G. 1946. *Attic red-figured vases: A survey.* New Haven.

Riddle, John M. 1992. *Contraception and abortion from the ancient world to the Renaissance.* New Haven.

Ridgway, Brunilde S. 1987. Ancient Greek women and art: The material evidence. *AJA* 91: 399–409.

Robert, Louis. 1937. *Etudes anatoliennes: Recherches sur les inscriptions grecques de l'Asie Mineure.* Paris.

Robertson, Noel. 1983a. Greek ritual begging in aid of women's fertility and childbirth. *TAPA* 113: 143–71.

———. 1983b. The riddle of the Arrhephoria at Athens. *HSCP* 87: 241–88.

———. 1988. Melanthus, Codrus, Neleus, Caucoli: Ritual myth as Athenian history. *GRBS* 29.3: 201–62.

———. 1995. The magic properties of female age-groups in Greek ritual. *The Ancient World* 26.2: 193–203.

Rolley, Claude. 1965. Le sanctuaire des dieux patrooi et le thesmophorion de Thasos. *BCH* 85: 441–71.

Romano, I. B. 1988. Early Greek cult images and cult practices. In *Early Greek cult practice*, edited by Robin Hägg, Nanno Marinatos, and G. C. Nordquist, 127–34. Stockholm.

Rosaldo, M. Z. 1980. The use and abuse of anthropology: Reflections on feminism and cross-cultural understanding. *Signs* 5: 389–417.

Rosaldo, M. Z., and L. Lamphere, eds. 1974. *Woman, culture, and society*. Stanford.

Rose, Peter. 1992. *Sons of the gods, children of earth: Ideology and literary form in ancient Greece*. Ithaca, N.Y.

———. 1993. The case for not ignoring Marx in the study of women. In *Feminist theory and the classics*, edited by Nancy Rabinowitz and Amy Richlin, 211–37. New York and London.

Rosenbloom, David. 1995. Myth, history, and hegemony in Aeschylus. In *History, tragedy, theory: Dialogues on Athenian drama*, edited by Barbara Goff, 91–130. Austin.

Rouse, W. H. D. 1975. *Greek votive offerings*. 1902. Reprint, New York.

Rushton, Lucy. 1983. Doves and magpies: Village women in the Greek Orthodox Church. In *Women's religious experience: Cross-cultural perspectives*, edited by Pat Holden, 57–70. London and Canberra.

Rusten, Jeffrey. 1993. *Theophrastus: Characters*. Cambridge, Mass.

Salmon, J. 1984. *Wealthy Corinth: A history of the city to 338 B.C.* Oxford.

Sansone, D. 1985. Theonoe and Theoclymenus. *SO* 60: 17–36.

Scafuro, Adele. 1994a. Introduction to *Athenian identity and civic ideology*, edited by Alan L. Boegehold and Adele C. Scafuro. Baltimore and London.

———. 1994b. Witnessing and false witnessing. In *Athenian identity and civic ideology*, edited by Alan L. Boegehold and Adele C. Scafuro, 156–98. Baltimore and London.

Scarborough, J. 1991. The pharmacology of sacred plants, herbs, and roots. In *Magika hiera: Ancient magic and religion*, edited by C. Faraone and D. Obbink, 138–74. New York.

Schaps, David. 1977. The women least mentioned: Etiquette and women's names. *CQ* 27: 323–30.

———. 1979. *Economic rights of women in ancient Greece*. Edinburgh.

Schlesier, R. 1993. Mixtures of masks: Maenads as tragic models. In *Masks of Dionysus*, edited by T. H. Carpenter and Christopher A. Faraone, 89–114. Ithaca, N.Y.

Schmitt-Pantel, P. 1977. Athéna Apatouria et la ceinture: Aspects féminines des Apatouria à Athènes. *Annales ESC* 32.6: 1059–73.

Seaford, R. 1987. The tragic wedding. *JHS* 107: 106–30.

———. 1993. Dionysus as destroyer of the household: Homer, tragedy, and the polis. In *Masks of Dionysus*, edited by T. H. Carpenter and Christopher A. Faraone, 115–46. Ithaca, N.Y.

———. 1995. *Reciprocity and ritual*. Oxford.

———. 1996. *Euripides: Bacchae*. Warminster.

Sealey, R. 1990. *Women and law in classical Greece*. Chapel Hill.

Segal, C. 1971. The two worlds of Euripides' *Helen*. *TAPA* 102: 553–614.

————. 1995. Lament and closure in *Antigone*. In *Sophocles' tragic world: Divinity, nature, society*, by C. Segal, 119–37. Cambridge, Mass., and London.

————. 1997. *Dionysiac Poetics*. Expanded ed. Princeton.

Sered, Susan Starr. 1994. *Priestess, mother, sacred sister: Religions dominated by women*. New York and Oxford.

Shapiro, H. 1991. The iconography of mourning in Athenian art. *AJA* 95: 629–56.

Sherwin-White, Susan. 1978. *Ancient Cos*. Hypomnemata 51. Göttingen.

Simms, Ronda. 1998. Mourning and community at the Athenian Adonia. *Classical Journal* 93: 121–41.

Simon, Erika. 1983. *Festivals of Attica: An archaeological commentary*. Madison.

Sinos, Rebecca H. 1993. Divine selection. In *Cultural poetics in archaic Greece*, edited by Carol Dougherty and Leslie Kurke, 73–91. Cambridge.

Sissa, Giulia. 1990. *Greek virginity*. Translated by Arthur Goldhammer. Cambridge, Mass., and London.

Skinner, Marilyn, ed. 1987. *Rescuing Creusa: New methodological approaches to women in antiquity*. Helios 13.2. Lubbock.

————. 1989. Sapphic Nossis. *Arethusa* 22 (1989) 5–18.

————. 1991. Nossis Thelyglossos: The private text and the public book. In *Women's history and ancient history*, edited by Sarah Pomeroy, 20–47. Chapel Hill.

————. 1996. Why is Sappho a woman? Women and language in archaic Greece. In *Reading Sappho: Contemporary approaches*, edited by Ellen Greene, 175–92. Berkeley and Los Angeles.

Slatkin, L. 1986. *Oedipus at Colonus*: Exile and integration. In *Greek tragedy and political theory*, edited by J. Peter Euben, 210–21. Berkeley.

Smith, Barbara, Gloria T. Hull, and Patricia Bell Scott, eds. 1982. *All the women are white, all the blacks are men, but some of us are brave: Black women's studies*. New York.

Snyder, Jane. 1989. *Women and the lyre: Women writers in classical Greece and Rome*. Bristol.

————. 1991. Public occasion and private passion in the lyrics of Sappho of Lesbos. In *Women's history and ancient history*, edited by Sarah Pomeroy, 1–19. Chapel Hill.

Sommerstein, A. 1989. *Aeschylus: Eumenides*. Cambridge.

————. 1990. *Aristophanes: Lysistrata*. Warminster.

————, ed. 1993. *Tragedy, comedy, and the polis*. Bari.

————, ed. 1994. *Aristophanes: Thesmophoriazusae*. Warminster.

————. 1996. *Aeschylean tragedy*. Bari.

Sourvinou-Inwood, C. 1974. The votum of 477/6 B.C. and the foundation legend of Locri Epizephyrii. *CQ* 24: 186–98.

————. 1988a. Priestess in the text. *G & R* 35.1: 29–30.

————. 1988b. *Studies in girls' transitions: Aspects of the arkteia and age representation in Attic iconography*. Athens.

————. 1990. What is polis religion? In *The Greek city from Homer to Alexander*, edited by Oswyn Murray and Simon Price, 295–322. Oxford.

————. 1991. *"Reading" Greek culture: Texts and images, rituals and myths*. Oxford.

————. 1995. Male and female, past and present, ancient and modern. In *Pandora: Women in classical Greece*, by Ellen Reeder, 111–22. Baltimore.

Spaeth, Barbette Stanley. 1991. Athenians and Eleusinians in the west pediment of the Parthenon. *Hesperia* 60.3: 331–62.

Spring, Anita. 1978. Epidemiology of spirit possession among the Luvale of Zambia. In *Women in ritual and symbolic roles,* edited by Judith Hoch-Smith and Anita Spring, 165–90. New York and London.

Stears, Karen. 1998. Death becomes her: Gender and Athenian death ritual. In *The sacred and the feminine in ancient Greece,* edited by Sue Blundell and Margaret Williamson, 113–27. London.

Ste-Croix, G. E. M. de. 1981. *Class struggle in the ancient world.* London.

Stehle, Eva. 1990. Sappho's gaze: Fantasies of a goddess and young man. *Differences* 2.1: 88–125.

———. 1997. *Performance and gender in ancient Greece.* Princeton.

Stehle, Eva, and Amy Day. 1996. Women looking at women: Women's ritual and temple sculpture. In *Sexuality in ancient art,* edited by Natalie Boymel Kampen, 101–16. Cambridge.

Stewart, Andrew. 1996. Reflections. In *Sexuality in ancient art,* edited by Natalie Boymel Kampen, 136–54. Cambridge.

Stockton, David. 1990. *The classical Athenian democracy.* Oxford.

Stone, Merlin. 1976. *When God was a woman.* San Diego.

Sutton, Robert. 1992. Pornography and persuasion on Attic pottery. In *Pornography and representation in Greece and Rome,* edited by Amy Richlin, 3–35. New York and Oxford.

Taaffe, Lauren K. 1993. *Aristophanes and women.* London and New York.

Tapper, Nancy. 1983. Gender and religion in a Turkish town. In *Women's religious experience: Cross-cultural perspectives,* edited by Pat Holden, 71–88. London and Canberra.

Tarn, William, and G. T. Griffith. 1952. *Hellenistic civilisation.* 3d ed. London.

Thesleff, H. 1965. *The Pythagorean texts of the Hellenistic period.* Abo.

Thompson, Catherine. 1983. Women fertility and the worship of the gods in a Hindu village. In *Women's religious experience: Cross-cultural perspectives,* edited by Pat Holden, 113–31. London and Canberra.

Thompson, Homer. 1936. Pnyx and Thesmophorion. *Hesperia* 5: 151–201.

———. 1978. Some hero shrines in early Athens. In *Athens comes of age: From Solon to Salamis,* edited by W. A. P. Childs, 96–105. Princeton.

Tod, Marcus N. 1985. *Greek historical inscriptions.* Vols. 1 and 2. 1946–48, Oxford. Reprint, Chicago.

Turner J. A. 1983. *Hiereiai: Acquisition of feminine priesthoods in ancient Greece.* Ann Arbor.

Turner, Victor. 1967. *The ritual process: Structure and anti-structure.* Chicago.

Tyrrell, W. Blake, and Larry J. Bennett. 1998. *Recapturing Sophocles' "Antigone."* Lanham, Md.

Van Gennep, A. 1960. *The rites of passage.* Chicago.

Van Straten, F. 1981. Gifts for the gods. In *Faith, hope, and worship: Aspects of religious mentality in the ancient world,* edited by H. S. Versnel, 65–151. Leiden.

Vellacott, Philip. 1975. *Ironic drama: A study of Euripides' method and meaning.* London and New York.

Vermaseren, M. J. 1977. *Cybele and Attis: The myth and the cult.* London.

Vernant, J-P. 1980. *Myth and society in ancient Greece.* Translated by Janet Lloyd. London.

Versnel, H. S., ed. 1981a. *Faith, hope, and worship: Aspects of religious mentality in the ancient world.* Leiden.

———. 1981b. Religious mentality in ancient prayer. In *Faith, hope, and worship: Aspects of religious mentality in the ancient world,* edited by H. S. Versnel, 1–64. Leiden.

———. 1990. *Ter unus.* Leiden.

Vicinus, Martha. 1986. Male space and women's bodies: The English suffragette movement. In *Women in culture and politics: A century of change,* edited by Judith Friedlander et al., 209–22. Bloomington.

Vidal-Naquet, P. 1981. The black hunter and the origins of the Athenian *ephebeia.* In *Myth, religion, and society,* edited by R. L. Gordon, 147–62. Cambridge.

———. 1986. *The black hunter: Forms of thought and forms of society in the Greek world.* Translated by Andrew Szegedy-Maszak. Baltimore and London.

Voigt, Eva-Maria. 1971. *Sappho et Alcaeus fragmenta.* Amsterdam.

Walbank, F. 1992. *The Hellenistic world.* London.

Walker, Susan. 1983. Women and housing in classical Greece: The archaeological evidence. In *Images of women in antiquity,* edited by Averil Cameron and Amelie Kuhrt, 81–91. London.

Walter, Elizabeth J. 1988. *Attic grave reliefs that represent women in the dress of Isis.* Princeton.

Walz, Christian. 1833. *Rhetores graeci.* 9 vols. Stuttgart and London.

Wasowicz, A. 1988. Mirror or distaff? In *Mélanges Pierre Leveque,* edited by M. M. Mactoux and E. Geny, 2.413–38. Paris.

Webster T. B. L. 1972. *Potter and patron in classical Athens.* London.

Weill, Nicole. 1966. *Adôniazousai* ou les femmes sur le toit. *BCH* 90: 664–98.

Whitehead, David. 1990. *How to survive under siege: Aineias the Tactician.* Oxford and New York.

Willetts, R. F. 1965. *Ancient Crete: A social history from early times until the Roman occupation.* London and Toronto.

———. 1967. *The law code of Gortyn.* Edited with introduction, translation, and commentary. Berlin.

Williams, Dyfri. 1983. Women on Athenian vases: Problems of interpretation. In *Images of women in antiquity,* edited by Averil Cameron and Amelie Kuhrt, 92–106. London.

Williamson, Margaret. 1995. *Sappho's immortal daughters.* Cambridge, Mass., and London.

Wilson, J. 1992. *The hero and the city.* Ann Arbor.

Wilson, Lyn Hatherly. 1996. *Sappho's sweetbitter songs: Configurations of female and male in ancient Greek lyric.* London and New York.

Winkler, John J. 1981. Gardens of nymphs: Public and private in Sappho's lyrics. In *Reflections of women in antiquity,* edited by Helene P. Foley, 63–89. New York, London, and Paris.

———. 1990a. *Constraints of desire: The anthropology of sex and gender in ancient Greece.* New York.

———. 1990b. Laying down the law: The oversight of men's sexual behavior in classical Athens. In *Before sexuality: The construction of erotic experience in the ancient Greek world*, edited by David M. Halperin, John J. Winkler, and Froma I. Zeitlin, 171–210. Princeton.

Winkler, John J., and Froma I. Zeitlin, eds. 1990. *Nothing to do with Dionysos? Athenian drama in its social context*. Princeton.

Wolff, Christian. 1992. Euripides' *Iphigeneia among the Taurians:* Aetiology, ritual, and myth. *CA* 11: 308–34.

Zanker, Paul. 1993. The Hellenistic grave stelai from Smyrna: Identity and self-image in the polis. In *Images and ideologies: Self-definition in the Hellenistic world*, edited by Anthony Bulloch et al., 212–30. Berkeley, Los Angeles, and London.

Zeitlin, F. 1965. The motif of the corrupted sacrifice in Aeschylus' *Oresteia*. *TAPA* 96: 463–505.

———. 1970. The Argive festival of Hera and Euripides' *Electra*. *TAPA* 101: 645–69.

———. 1978. The dynamics of misogyny in the *Oresteia*. *Arethusa* 11: 149–84.

———. 1981. Travesties of gender and genre in Aristophanes' *Thesmophoriazousai*. *CI* 8:2: 301–27.

———. 1982a. Cultic models of the female: Rites of Dionysus and Demeter. *Arethusa* 15: 129–57.

———. 1982b. *Under the sign of the shield*. Rome.

———. 1988. La politique d'éros: Féminin et masculin dans les *Suppliants* d'Eschyle. *Métis* 3: 231–59.

———. 1989. Mysteries of identity and designs of the self in Euripides' *Ion*. *PCPS* 35: 144–97.

———. 1990a. Patterns of gender in Aeschylean drama: *Seven Against Thebes* and the Danaid trilogy. In *The cabinet of the Muses: Essays in classical and comparative literature in honor of Thomas G. Rosenmeyer*, edited by M. Griffith and D. J. Mastronarde, 103–15. Atlanta.

———. 1990b. Playing the other: Theater, theatricality, and the feminine in Greek drama. In *Nothing to do with Dionysos? Athenian drama in its social context*, edited by John J. Winkler and Froma I. Zeitlin, 63–96. Princeton.

———. 1990c. Thebes: Theater of self and society in Athenian drama. In *Nothing to do with Dionysos? Athenian drama in its social context*, edited by John J. Winkler and Froma I. Zeitlin, 130–67. Princeton.

———. 1992. The politics of eros in the Danaid trilogy of Aeschylus. In *Innovations of antiquity*, edited by Ralph Hexter and Daniel Selden, 203–52. New York and London.

———. 1996. *Playing the other: Gender and society in classical Greek literature*. Chicago and London.

Zuntz, G. 1955. *The political plays of Euripides*. Manchester.